LIVES AND TIMES
A WORLD HISTORY READER
VOLUME I

EDITED BY

JAMES P. HOLOKA
EASTERN MICHIGAN UNIVERSITY

JIU-HWA L. UPSHUR
EASTERN MICHIGAN UNIVERSITY

WEST PUBLISHING COMPANY
MINNEAPOLIS/ST. PAUL   NEW YORK   LOS ANGELES   SAN FRANCISCO

WEST'S COMMITMENT TO THE ENVIRONMENT

In 1906, West Publishing Company began recycling materials left over from the production of books. This began a tradition of efficient and responsible use of resources. Today, up to 95% of our legal books and 70% of our college texts and school texts are printed on recycled, acid-free stock. West also recycles nearly 22 million pounds of scrap paper annually—the equivalent of 181,717 trees. Since the 1960s, West has devised ways to capture and recycle waste inks, solvents, oils, and vapors created in the printing process. We also recycle plastics of all kinds, wood, glass, corrugated cardboard, and batteries, and have eliminated the use of Styrofoam book packaging. We at West are proud of the longevity and the scope of our commitment to the environment.

Production, Prepress, Printing and Binding by West Publishing Company.

Artwork by Christian Holoka.

 TEXT IS PRINTED ON 10% POST CONSUMER RECYCLED PAPER    PRINTED WITH SOY INK™

COPYRIGHT © 1995 by WEST PUBLISHING CO.
610 Opperman Drive
P.O. Box 64526
St. Paul, MN 55164–0526

ISBN 0–314–04579–1

CONTENTS

PREFACE

Lives and Times is intended to introduce undergraduate history students to original source materials that are both intrinsically interesting and useful for the development of a deeper understanding of history. In considering the vast array of available sources, we decided wherever possible to select autobiographical and biographical accounts, in the latter case, preferring items written by authors contemporary with their subjects rather than works by modern scholars. Such accounts tell us what the people thought about themselves, the world they lived in, and the problems they faced living together.

Biographies and autobiographies have always held a special attraction for students of history. Our discipline is multi-faceted. To gain a detailed knowledge of any era or person, the historian must consult various types of sources of information, including statistical data, legal documents, government files, and diaries and personal letters, among others. No single collection of readings on world history can embrace all these types sources; nor can beginning history students be expected to deal with some of the more complex documents. We have chosen to limit ourselves primarily to biographical and autobiographical sources because of their human interest and the light they shed on their subjects' motivations, emotions, ambitions, and conflicts. Moreover, the study of people of different eras and cultures lends immediacy to history and bridges the gap between centuries and continents through our common humanity. When suitable contemporary biographical or autobiographical information was lacking, we have drawn on other sources such as poetry, inscriptions, archaeological reports, and newspaper accounts to help form an accurate picture of life in other eras.

The selections in this anthology tell the stories of people from the earliest times to the present around the world; they reflect a wide range of perspectives and experiences, featuring men, women, and children from many different walks of life and social classes. Kings, queens, generals, statesmen and government leaders, great religious leaders and philosophers are represented because their lives and deeds shaped history. Accounts of major battles and political affairs are featured for the same reason. However, we have sought to put the spotlight on individuals from many other walks of life, including explorers, inventors, scientists, recluses, merchants, farmers, factory workers, priests, nuns, and even slaves. Throughout, we have aimed to lead readers to a wider, global view of history by exploring the lives and thoughts of ordinary and extraordinary men and women, with all their human idiosyncrasies, strengths, and frailties.

Although we have relied mostly on sources originally written in English or already translated into English, we have also translated from a number Greek, Latin, French, and Chinese sources. We hope the result is a truly ecumenical collection that illuminates the lives and times of many people from antiquity to the present.

The readings in the two volumes of *Lives and Times* are grouped in eleven sections, by chronology and subject matter. A short essay introduces each section and explains the mutual relationship of the readings grouped therein.

This anthology is not intended for use in association with any one textbook; rather, it is designed to accompany any textbook in a variety of courses. Instructors may choose from the anthology to suit their own purposes. Each reading is equipped with an introduction providing essential background. Introductions are followed by questions meant to assist the reader in identifying important points in the selection.

For their encouragement in our endeavor and for specific suggestions, we are thankful to many colleagues, especially professors George Cassar, Richard Goff, Michael Homel, and Janice Terry, and to Mr. Charles Zwinak. We are grateful also to Professor Kuei-sheng Chang of the Geography Department of the University of Washington for graciously letting us use a chapter of his Ph.D. dissertation on the Ming Chinese explorer Cheng Ho (Reading 6.12), to Mrs. Helen Hsiung (Mao Yen-wen) for allowing us to translate a passage from her privately published memoirs, *Wan Shih* (Reading 11.10), to Professor Benjamin Stolz of the Department of Slavic Languages and Literature of the University of Michigan for his kind permission to quote from his translation of Konstantin Mihailovic's *Memoirs of a Janissary* (Reading 6.6), and to Professor Paul Kahn for permitting us to excerpt from his translation of *The Secret History of the Mongols* (Reading 6.1). A number of public institutions in several countries allowed us to quote from their publications without fee. We are indebted to the University of Michigan's Harlan Hatcher Library for privileges and the guidance of its staff. We are much beholden to Ms. Nancy Snyder, head secretary of the Department of History, Eastern Michigan University, for her administrative assistance. Mr. Daniel Sprung of the Eastman Kodak Company in Rochester, New York was instrumental to our production of camera-ready pages. At West Educational Publishing, Mr. Clark Baxter, Ms. Patricia MacDonald, and their staff were consistently helpful and supportive. Finally, we thank Christian Holoka for the extraordinary talent and efficiency he brought to the creation of the art that graces our collection.

                                                                                                          J.P.H.
                                                                                                          J-H.L.U.

SECTION 1

THE FORMATIVE AGE OF EARLY CIVILIZATIONS

Over a million years ago the first hominids ev[...]d erect, freeing their hands for other tasks. Paleo-archaeologists [...] skeleton of the first hominid "Lucy." Ancestors of modern human[...] into *homo sapiens*; they spread across many continents, hunting a[...] [ab]out 9000 years ago early humans began to develop permanent se[...] plants and animals. This momentous event, called the agricultural [...] West Asia, and then rapidly spread through north Africa, Europe, a[...] [contine]nt.

Around 3000 B.C.E. human beings in We[...] and smelted ore to make metals; they also developed complex po[...] advances began the historic era. Major civilizations developed acr[...] [Afri]ca, and southeastern Europe. Somewhat later, although scholars [...] origins, advanced preliterate civilizations also began to develo[...] Western Hemisphere. This section explores the first great cultures of Egypt, Mesopotamia, Greece, India, China, and South and Central America. Its sources vary from traditional, oral accounts of semi-legendary heroes, later written down, to recently discovered and deciphered ancient documents. Accounts of archaeological finds of sites of cities, graves, and artifacts corroborate many ancient accounts and add much invaluable new information.

These sources of information enable us to reconstruct many aspects of ancient life, including warfare, government, commerce, manufacturing, religious practices, career choices, gender roles for men and women, and social mobility. The readings exhibit common human values and aspirations, but also great differences among cultures. Thus, despite the millennia that divide the men and women of ancient times from present-day people, such issues as careers, family, and material well being, and moral values like loyalty, bravery, and faithfulness, as well as shortcomings like pride and greed prove to be common and universal. All these elements in the sources gathered in this section show how advanced and "modern" many societies were thousands of years ago.

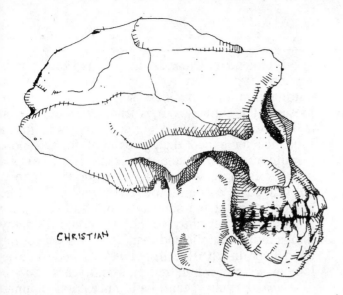

► Hominid Skull

INTRODUCING LUCY--A VERY EARLY ANCESTOR

Ever since Charles Darwin's pioneering work in the field of human evolution, archaeologists and anthropologists have been expanding our knowledge of the origins of mankind. They have identified the family of *Hominidae*, which includes both *homo sapiens* (human beings) and our extinct ancestors.

Several distinct physical characteristics evolved gradually in prehuman hominids, beginning about five million years ago. They include bipedalism or walking on two legs; a large-capacity braincase (between 1300 and 1500 cc.); and a relatively small jaw and teeth. The earliest human ancestors with these characteristics belonged to the genus *Australopithecus*, which many scientists believe evolved into the genus *Homo*. For this reason, Australopithecine fossils hold special interest.

Parts of east and south Africa are particularly rich in fossils. Paleoanthropologists Richard and Mary Leakey have made important discoveries of humanoid ancestors in the Olduvai Gorge in Tanzania and Kenya in eastern Africa. Their popular writings have acquainted many readers with their crucial findings.

In 1974, another paleoanthropologist, Dr. Donald C. Johanson, made a stunning discovery at Hadar in the Rift Valley in Ethiopia: the earliest and most complete set of skeletal remains of an erect-walking human ancestor. His exciting description of his find and its significance for our understanding of human evolution is quoted below.

QUESTIONS:

1) How do anthropologists discriminate between human and non-human ancestors of Homo Sapiens?

2) What is so distinctive about Lucy as a fossil find?

3) What sorts of deductions does Donald Johanson make in examining the evidence of the remains of Lucy?

"Lucy?"

That is the question I always get from somebody who sees the fossil for the first time. I have to explain: "Yes, she was a female. And that Beatles song. We were sky-high, you must remember, from finding her."

Then comes the next question: "How did you know she was a female?"

"From her pelvis. We had one complete pelvic bone and her sacrum. Since the pelvic opening in hominids has to be proportionately larger in females than in males to allow for the birth of large-brained infants, you can tell a female."

And the next: "She was a hominid?"

"Oh, yes. She walked erect. She walked as well as you do."

"Hominids all walked erect?"

"Yes."

"Just exactly what is a hominid?"

This usually ends the questions, because that one has no simple answer. Science has had to leave the definition rather flexible because we do not yet know exactly when hominids first appeared. However, it is safe to say that a hominid is an erect-walking primate. That is, it is either an extinct ancestor to man ["man" refers to both males and females of the genus *Homo*], a collateral relative to man, or a true man. All human beings are hominids, but not all hominids are human beings.

We can picture human evolution as starting with a primitive apelike type that gradually, over a long period of time, began to be less and less apelike and more manlike. There was no abrupt crossover from ape to human, but probably a rather fuzzy time of in-between types that would be difficult to classify either way. We have no fossils yet that tell us what went on during the in-between time. Therefore, the handiest way of separating the newest types from their ape ancestors is to lump together all those that stood up on their hind legs. That group of men and near-men is called hominids.

I am a hominid. I am a human being. I belong to the genus *Homo* and to the species *sapiens*: thinking man. Perhaps I should say wise or knowing man--a man who is smart enough to recognize that he is a man. There have been other species of *Homo* who were not so smart, ancestors now extinct. *Homo sapiens* began to emerge a hundred thousand--perhaps two or three hundred thousand --years ago, depending on how one regards Neanderthal Man. He was another *Homo*. Some think he was the same species as ourselves. Others think he was an ancestor. There are a few who consider him a kind of cousin. That matter is unsettled because many of the best Neanderthal fossils were collected in Europe before anybody knew how to excavate sites properly or get good dates. Consequently, we do not have exact ages for most of the Neanderthal fossils in collections.

I consider Neanderthal conspecific with *sapiens*, with myself. One hears talk about putting him in a business suit and turning him loose in the subway. It is true; one could do it and he would never be noticed. He was just a little heavier-boned than people of today, more primitive in a few facial features. But he was a man. His brain was as big as a modern man's, but shaped in a slightly different way. Could he make change at the subway booth and recognize a token? He certainly could. He could do many things more complicated than that. He was doing them over much of Europe, Africa and Asia as long as sixty or a hundred thousand years ago.

Neanderthal Man had ancestors, human ones. Before him in time was a less advanced type: *Homo erectus*. Put him on the subway and people would probably move to the other end of the car. Before *Homo habilis* the human line may run out entirely. The next stop in the past, back of *Homo habilis*, might be something like Lucy.

All of the above are hominids. They are all erect walkers. Some were human, even though they were of exceedingly primitive types. Others were not human. Lucy was not. No matter what kind of clothes we put on Lucy, she would not look like a human being. She was too far back, out of the human range entirely. That is what happens going back along an evolutionary line. If one goes back far enough, one finds oneself dealing with a different kind of creature. On the hominid line the earliest ones are too primitive to be called humans. They must be given another name. Lucy is in that category.

For five years I kept Lucy in a safe in my office in the Cleveland Museum of Natural History. I had filled a wide shallow box with yellow foam padding, and had cut depressions in the foam so that each of her bones fitted into its own tailor-made nest. *Everybody* who came to the Museum--it seemed to me--wanted to see Lucy. What surprised people most was her small size.

Her head, on the evidence of the bits of her skull that had been recovered, was not much larger than a softball. Lucy herself stood only three and one-half feet tall, although she was fully grown. That could be deduced from her wisdom teeth, which were fully erupted and had been exposed to several years of wear. My best guess was that she was between twenty-five and thirty years old when she died. She had already begun to show the onset of arthritis or some other bone ailment, on the evidence of deformation of her vertebrae. If she had lived much longer, it probably would have begun to bother her.

Her surprisingly good condition--her completeness--came from the fact that she had died quietly. There were no tooth marks on her bones. They had not been crunched and splintered, as they would have been if she had been killed by a lion or a saber-toothed cat. Her head had not been carried off in one direct and her legs in another, as hyenas might have done with her. She simply settled down in one piece right where she was, in the sand of a long-vanished lake edge or stream--and died. Whether from illness or accidental drowning, it was impossible to say. The important thing was that she had not been found by a predator just after death and eaten. Her carcass had remained inviolate, slowly covered by sand or mud, buried deeper and deeper, the sand hardening into rock under the weight of subsequent depositions. She had lain silently in her adamantine grave for millennium after millennium until the rains at Hadar had brought her to light again.

That was where I was unbelievably lucky. If I had not followed a hunch that morning with Tom Gray, Lucy might never have been found. Why the other people who looked there did not see her, I do not know. Perhaps they were looking in another direction. Perhaps the light was different. Sometimes one person sees things that another misses, even though he may be looking directly at them. If I had not gone to Locality 162 that morning, nobody might have bothered to go back for a year, maybe five years. Hadar is a big place, and there is a tremendous amount to do. If I had waited another few years, the next rains might have washed many of her bones down the gully. They would have been lost, or at least badly scattered; it would not have been possible to establish that they belonged together. What was utterly fantastic was that she had come to the surface so recently, probably in the last year or two. Five years earlier, she still would have been buried. Five years later, she would have been gone. As it was, the front of her skull was already gone, washed away somewhere. We never did find it.

Consequently, the one thing we really cannot measure accurately is the size of her brain.

Lucy always managed to look interesting in her little yellow nest--but to a nonprofessional, not overly impressive. There were other bones all around her in the Cleveland Museum. She was dwarfed by them, by drawer after drawer of fossils, hundreds of them from Hadar alone. There were casts of hominid specimens from East Africa, from South Africa and Asia. There were antelope and pig skulls, extinct rodents, rabbits and monkeys, as well as apes. There was one of the largest collections of gorilla skulls in the world. In that stupefying array of bones, I kept being asked, What was so special about Lucy? Why had she, as another member of the expedition put it, "blown us out of our little anthropological minds for months"?

"Three things," I always answered. "First: what she is--or isn't. She is different from anything that has been discovered and named before. She doesn't fit anywhere. She is just a very old, very primitive, very small hominid. Somehow we are going to have to fit her in, find a name for her.

"Second," I would say, "is her completeness. Until Lucy was found, there just weren't any very old skeletons. The oldest was one of those Neanderthalers I spoke of a little while ago. It is about seventy-five thousand years old. Yes, there *are* older hominid fossils, but they are all fragments. Everything that has been reconstructed from them has had to be done by matching up those little pieces--a tooth here, a bit of jaw there, maybe a complete skull from somewhere else, plus a leg bone from some other place. The fitting together has been done by scientists who know those bones as well as I know my own hand. And yet, when you consider that such a reconstruction may consist of pieces from a couple of dozen individuals who may have lived hundreds of miles apart and may have been separated from each other by a hundred thousand years in time--well, when you look at the complete individual you've just put together you have to say to yourself, 'Just how real is he?' With Lucy you know. It's all there. You don't have to guess. You don't have to imagine an arm bone you haven't got. You *see* it. You see it for the first time from something older than a Neanderthaler."

"How much older?"

"That's point number three. The Neanderthaler is seventy-five thousand years old. Lucy is approximately 3.5 million years old. She is the oldest, most complete, best-preserved skeleton of any erect-walking human ancestor that has ever been found."

That is the significance of Lucy: her completeness and her great age. They make her unique in the history of hominid fossil collecting.

Johanson, Donald C., and A. Edey Maitland. *Lucy: The Beginnings of Mankind*. New York: Simon and Schuster, 1981. Pp. 18-24.

KING SENNACHERIB OF ASSYRIA BOASTS OF BATTLES AND BUILDINGS

▶ **Assyrian God**

Assyria was located in the northern part of ancient Mesopotamia (roughly present-day Iraq); the Assyrian civilization began in the third millennium B.C.E. For many hundreds of years, Assyrians, Sumerians, Babylonians, and others vied for power in the region and rose and fell in succession. Beginning about 900 B.C.E., Assyria experienced tremendous political and cultural advances, and made extensive conquests until it became the pre-eminent power in the Near East. Kings Adadnirari (r. 911-891) and Ashurnasirpal II (r. 883-859) strengthened the army, built a magnificent new capital at Calah, and established a stable administration to manage a growing empire.

The pace of Assyrian expansion quickened with the accession of King Tiglath-Pileser I (r. 744-727 B.C.E.). He conquered Syria and marched his armies west to the shores of the Mediterranean. Sargon II (r. 721-705) defeated the Chaldeans, the ruling dynasty in neighboring Babylonia, and the Hebrew kingdom of Israel, breaking up its tribes and exiling its leaders. He also intimidated the Greeks on the island of Cyprus into paying tribute. Because the task of controlling such an extensive realm proved too demanding, the Assyrian empire was relatively short-lived, lasting about a century and a half, till its fall in 612. In that time, the Assyrians' fearsome military machine, the first in history to make significant use of iron weapons, gained a deserved reputation for mobility, discipline, and brutality.

The Assyrian empire prospered under King Sennacherib (r. 704-681 B.C.E.), a typically ruthless and energetic leader. He moved the capital to Nineveh on the Tigris River, drafting thousands of slaves laborers to erect its great buildings, massive walls, and fortifications. His successors Esarhaddon (r. 680-669) and Ashurbanipal (r. 668-ca. 633) extended Assyrian control to Egypt, in North Africa, making the largest empire the world had yet seen.

In the first passage below, Sennacherib boasts delightedly and graphically of his military successes against rebellious Babylonians and Elamites. In the second and third passages, he describes the splendor of his capital Nineveh and beseeches his god, Assur, to guarantee the durability of the monuments he built to glorify himself.

QUESTIONS:

1) Consider the way Sennacherib describes his victories and draw conclusions about the purpose of such an inscription.

2) How do the gods of the Assyrians seem to figure in Sennacherib's view of the world and of his own accomplishments.

3) What is the point of the architectural marvels that Sennacherib commissioned?

Sennacherib, the great king, the mighty king, king of the universe, king of Assyria, king of the four quarters [of the earth]; the wise ruler [shepherd], favorite of the great gods, guardian of the right, lover of justice; who lends support, who comes to the aid of the needy, who turns [his thoughts] to pious deeds; perfect hero, mighty man; first among all princes, the flame that consumes the insubmissive, who strikes the wicked with the thunderbolt; the god Assur, the great mountain, has intrusted to me an unrivaled kingship, and, above all those who dwell in palaces, has made powerful my weapons; from the upper sea of the setting sun to the lower sea of the rising sun, all humankind [the black-headed race] he has brought in submission at my feet and mighty kings feared my warfare--leaving their abodes and flying alone, like the *sudinnu*, the bird of the cave to [some] inaccessible place....

As for me,--to Assur, Sin, Shamash, Bêl, Nabû, Nergal, Ishtar of Nineveh, Ishtar of Arbela, the gods in whom I trust, I prayed for victory over the mighty foe. They speedily gave ear to my prayers and came to my aid. Like a lion I raged. I put on [my] coat of mail. [My] helmet, emblem of victory [in battle], I placed upon my head. My great battle chariot, which brings low the foe, I hurriedly mounted in the anger of my heart. The mighty bow which Assur had given me, I seized in my hands; the javelin, piercing to the life, I grasped. Against all the hosts of wicked enemies, I raised my voice, rumbling like a storm. Like Adad I roared.

At the word of Assur, the great lord, my lord, on flank and front I pressed upon the enemy like the onset of a raging storm. With the weapons of Assur, my lord, and the terrible onset of my attack, I stopped their advance, I succeeded in surrounding them [or turning them back], I decimated the enemy host with arrow and spear. All of their bodies I bored through like a sieve. Humbanundasha, the field-marshal of the king of Elam, a trustworthy man, commander of his armies, his chief support, together with his nobles, who wear the golden girdle dagger and whose hands [wrists] are encircled with heavy ... rings of shining gold,--like fat steers who have hobbles put on them,--speedily I cut them down

and established their defeat. I cut their throats like lambs. I cut off their precious lives [as one cuts] a string. Like the many waters of a storm, I made [the contents of] their gullets and entrails run down upon the wide earth. My prancing steeds harnessed for my riding, plunged into the streams of their blood as [into] a river. The wheels of my war chariot, which brings low the wicked and the evil, were bespattered with blood and filth. With the bodies of their warriors I filled the plain, like grass. [Their] testicles I cut off, and tore out their privates like the seeds of cucumbers of *Simânu* [June]. Their hands I cut off. The heavy rings of brightest gold [and] silver which [they had] on their wrists I took away. With sharp swords I pierced their belts and seized the girdle daggers of gold and silver which [they carried] on their persons. The rest of his nobles, together with Nabûshum-ishkun, son of Merodach-baladan, who had taken fright at ... my onslaught and had gone over to their side, [these] my hands seized in the midst of the battle. The chariots and their horses, whose riders had been slain at the beginning of the terrible onslaught, and who had been left to themselves, kept running back and forth ... for a distance of two bêru [double hours],--I put an end to their [the riders'] fighting. That Umman-menanu, king of Elam, together with the king of Babylon [and] the princes of Chaldea, who had gone over to his side, the terror of my battle overpowered them ... like a bull. They abandoned their tents and to save their lives they trampled the bodies of their [fallen] soldiers, they fled like young pigeons that are pursued. They were beside themselves ... they held back their urine, but let their dung go in their chariots. In pursuit of them I dispatched my chariots and horses after them. Those among them who had escaped, who had fled for their lives, wherever they [my charioteers] met them, they cut them down with the sword....

* * * * *

That I might accomplish the construction of my palace, and bring to an end the work of my hands, at that time, Assur and Ishtar, who love my priesthood, and have called me by name, showed me how to bring out the mighty cedar logs which had grown large in the days gone by, and had become enormously tall as they stood concealed in the mountains of Sirara. Alabaster which in the days of the kings, my fathers, was precious enough for [inlaying] the hilt of a sword, they disclosed to me in the darkness of Mount Ammanana [on the Syria-Lebanon border]. And breccia for all kinds of great jars, such as had never been seen before, in ... the city of Kapridargilâ, which is on the border of Til-Barsip, disclosed itself. Near Nineveh, in the land of Balatai, by decree of the god, white limestone was found ... in abundance; and bull-colossi and sculptured statues of alabaster, which were carved out of one stone, of enormous proportions, towering high upon their own bases; alabaster cow-colossi, whose appearance was splendid, whose bodies shown like the bright day; great slabs of breccia I fashioned and cut free on both sides, in their mountain, and had them dragged to Nineveh for the construction of my palace. The bull and cow-colossi of white limestone, with Ninkurra's help, I had fashioned ..., in the land of Balatai, and made complete as to their members.

In times past, when the kings, my fathers, fashioned a bronze image in the likeness of their members, to set up in their temples, the labor on them exhausted every workman; in their ignorance and lack of knowledge, they drank oil, and wore sheepskins to carry on the work they wanted to do in the midst of their mountains. But I, Sennacherib, first among all princes, wise in all craftsmanship,--great pillars of bronze, colossal lions, open at the knees, which no king before my time had fashioned, through the clever understanding which the noble Nin-igi-kig had given me, [and] in my own wisdom, I pondered deeply the matter of carrying out that task. Following the advice of my head ... and the prompting of my heart, I fashioned a work of bronze and cunningly wrought it. Over great posts and crossbars of wood, 12 fierce lion-colossi together with 12 mighty bull-colossi, complete in form, 22 cow-colossi, clothed with exuberant strength and with abundance and splendor heaped upon them,--at the command of the god, I built a form of clay and poured bronze into it, as in making half-shekel pieces, and finished their construction.

Bull-colossi, made of bronze, two of which were coated with enamel, bull-colossi of alabaster, together with cow-colossi of white limestone, I placed at the thresholds of my palaces. High pillars of bronze, together with tall pillars of cedar, the product of Mount Amanus, I inclosed in a sheathing of bronze and lead, placed them upon lion-colossi, and set them up as posts to support their doorways. Upon the alabaster cow-colossi, as well as the cow-colossi made of bronze, which were coated with enamel and the cow-colossi made of ..., whose forms were brilliant, I placed pillars of ebony, cypress, cedar, *dupranu*-wood, spruce and *sindu*-wood, with inlay of *pasalli* and silver, and set them up as columns in the rooms of my royal abode. Slabs of breccia and alabaster, and great slabs of limestone, I placed around their walls; I made them wonderful to behold.

* * * * *

May any future prince whose name Assur shall call for the rulership ... of land and people, in whose reign that temple shall fall to ruins, restore its ruins; may he look upon my memorial stele, anoint it with oil, offer sacrifices, and restore it to its place. And Assur will hear his prayers. But the destroyer of my stele, who ignores my word, who does that which is not good for .... And their offspring,--may Assur, king of the gods, and the great gods, of heaven and earth, curse him with an evil curse which cannot be removed, may they overthrow his kingdom, deprive him of life, and destroy his name, his seed, his kith and his kin, in every land.

Luckenbill, Daniel D. *Ancient Records of Assyria and Babylonia*. Chicago: Univ. of Chicago Press, 1927. Vol. 2. Pp. 115-116, 126-128, 168-169, 186.

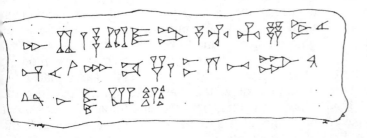

LETTER-WRITING IN ANCIENT MESOPOTAMIA

▶ **Cuneiform Writing**

A very important aspect of civilized life is writing. Writing first appeared about five or six thousand years ago in the great city-based civilizations of Mesopotamia, a fertile alluvial plain in that part of the Fertile Crescent embraced by the Tigris and Euphrates rivers. The Mesopotamians wrote by impressing cuneiform (wedge-shaped) marks in clay tablets, which when dried or baked are nearly indestructible.

Archaeologists have found thousands of cuneiform-inscribed clay tablets from nearly all periods of Mesopotamian civilization (c. 3000-c. 600 B.C.E.). Shedding valuable light on the Sumerian, Babylonian, and Assyrian cultures, these tablets record business transactions, inventories of supplies, production and taxation figures, wage payments, and mathematical calculations. In addition, many surviving public and private letters inform us about the concerns, hopes, and grievances of men and women who lived thousands of years ago.

The following reading describes the mechanics of letter-writing in ancient Mesopotamia: the writing system, the materials used, and the methods of conveying letters. It also includes quotations from some Babylonian and Assyrian letters.

QUESTIONS:

1) What seem to be the advantages and disadvantages of the mechanics of cuneiform system of writing in ancient Mesopotamia?

2) What sort of light do the personal letters that have survived from Mesopotamia shed on daily lives and attitudes?

3) Is there a distinct tone about the letters written to the king? Is this tone like that used today when one is writing to government or other high officials?

While in Egypt the letter was usually written upon papyrus, in Western Asia the ordinary writing material was clay. Babylonia had been the nurse and mother of its culture, and the writing material of Babylonia was clay. Originally pictorial hieroglyphics had been drawn upon the clay, but just as in Egypt the hieratic or running-hand of the scribe developed out of the primitive pictographs, so too in Babylonia the pictures degenerated into cuneiform characters which corresponded with the hieratic characters of the Egyptian script. What we call cuneiform is essentially a cursive hand....

The acquisition of the cuneiform system of writing was a task of labor and difficulty which demanded years of patient application. A vast number of characters had to be learned by heart. They were conventional signs, often differing but slightly from one another, with nothing about them that could assist the memory; moreover, their forms varied in different styles of writing, as much as Latin, Gothic, and cursive forms of type differ among ourselves, and all these the pupil was expected to know. Every character had more then one phonetic value; many of them, indeed, had several, while they could also be used ideographically to express objects and ideas....

The children, however, must have been well taught. This is clear from the remarkably good spelling which we find in the private letters; it is seldom that words are misspelt. The language may be conversational, or even dialectic, but the words are written correctly. The school-books that have survived bear testimony to the attention that had been given to improving the educational system. Every means was adopted for lessening the labor of the student and imprinting the lesson upon his mind.... Dictionaries had been compiled of Sumerian words and expressions, as well as lists of Semitic synonyms.... There were reading-books filled with extracts from the standard literature of the country....

While the clay was still soft, the cuneiform or "wedge-shaped" characters were engraved upon it by means of a stylus. They had originally been pictorial, but when the use of clay was adopted the pictures necessarily degenerated into groups of wedge-like lines, every curve becoming an angle formed by the junction of two lines. As time went on, the characters were more and more simplified, the number of wedges of which they consisted being reduced and only so many left as served to distinguish one sign from another....

As for books, so also for letters the clay tablet was employed. It may seem to us indeed a somewhat cumbrous mode of sending a letter; but it had the advantage of being solid and less likely to be injured or destroyed than other writing materials. The characters upon it could not be obliterated by a shower of rain, and there was no danger of its being torn. Moreover, it must be remembered that the tablet was usually of small size. The cuneiform system of writing allows a large number of words to be compressed into a small space, and the writing is generally so

minute as to try the eyes of the modern decipherer....

That the clay tablet should ever have been used for epistolary purposes seems strange to us who are accustomed to paper and envelopes. But it occupied no more space than many modern official letters, and was lighter to carry than most of the packages that pass through the parcel-post. Now and then it was enveloped in an outer covering of clay, on which the address and the chief contents of it were noted; but the public were usually prevented from knowing what it contained in another way. Before it was handed over to the messenger or postman it was "sealed," ... deposited in some receptacle, perhaps of leather or linen, which was then tied up and sealed. In fact, Babylonian and Assyrian letters were treated much as ours are when they are put into a post-bag to which the seals of the post-office are attached. There were excellent roads all over Western Asia, with post-stations at intervals where relays of horses could be procured. Along these all letters to or from the King and the government were carried by royal messengers. It is probable that the letters of private individuals were also carried by the same hands....

Some of the letters ... go back to the early days of the Babylonian monarchy. Many of them are dated in the reign of Khammurabi [Hammurabi, r. 1792-1750 B.C.E.], or Amraphel, among them being several that were written by the King himself. That we should possess the autograph letters of a contemporary of Abraham is one of the romances of historical science, for it must be remembered that the letters are not copies, but the original documents themselves....

Long before the age of Khammurabi a royal post had been established in Babylon for the conveyance of letters. Fragments of clay had been found at Tello, bearing the impressions of seals belonging to the officials of Sargon of Akkad and his successor, and addressed to the viceroy of Lagas, to King Naram-Sin and other personages. They were, in fact, the envelopes of letters and despatches which passed between Lagas and Agadê, or Akkad, the capital of the dynasty. Sometimes, however, the clay fragment has the form of a ball, and must have been attached by a string to the missive like the seals of mediaeval deeds. In either case the seal of the functionary from whom the missive came was imprinted upon it as well as the address of the person for whom it was intended. Thousands of letters seem to have passed to and fro in this manner, making it clear that the postal service of Babylonia was already well organized in the time of Sargon and Naram-Sin. The Tel-el-Amarna letters show that in the fifteenth century before our era a similar postal service was established throughout the Eastern world, from the banks of the Euphrates to those of the Nile. To what an antiquity it reached back it is … impossible to say.

At all events, when Khammurabi was King, letters were frequent and common among the educated classes of the population. Most of those which have been preserved are from private individuals to one another, and consequently, though they tell s nothing about the political events of the time, they illustrate the social life of the period and prove how like it was to our own. One of them, for instance, describes the writer's journey to Elam and Arrapakhitis, while another relates to a ferry-boat and the boat-house in which it was kept. The boat-house, we are told, have fallen into decay in the reign of Khammurabi, and was sadly in want of repair, while the chief duty of the writer, who seems to have been the captain of the boat, was to convey the merchants who brought various commodities to Babylon. If the merchant, the letter states, was furnished with a royal passport, "we carried him across" the river; if he had no passport, he was not allowed to go to Babylon. Among other purposes for which the vessel had been used was the conveyance of lead, and it was capable of taking as much as ten talents [c. 600 pounds] of the metal. We further gather from the letter that it was the custom to employ Bedâwin [Bedouin, nomadic Arabs] as messengers.

Among the early Babylonian documents found at Sippara … are two private letters of the same age and similar character. The first is as follows: "To my father, thus says Zimri-eram: May the Sun-god and Merodach grant thee everlasting life! May your health be good! I write to ask you how you are; send me back news of your health. I am at present at Dur-Sin on the canal of Bit-Sikir. In the place where I am living there is nothing to be had for food. So

I am sealing up and sending you three-quarters of a silver shekel. In return for the money, send some good fish and other provisions for me to eat." The second letter was despatched from Babylon, and runs thus: "To the lady Kasbeya thus says Gimil-Merodach: May the Sun-god and Merodach for my sake grant thee everlasting life! I am writing to enquire after your health; please send me news of it. I am living at Babylon, but have not seen you, which troubles me greatly. Send me news of your coming to me, so that I may be happy. Come in the month of Marchesvan (October). May you live for ever for my sake!"

It is plain that the writer was in love with his correspondent, and had grown impatient to see her again. Both belonged to what we should call the professional classes, and nothing can better illustrate how like in the matter of correspondence the age of Abraham was to our own. The old Babylonian's letter might easily have been written to-day, apart from the references to Merodach and the Sun-god. It must be noticed, moreover, that the lady to whom the letter is addressed is expected to reply to it. It is taken for granted that the ladies of Babylon could read and write as well as the men…. Even among the Tel-el-Amarna [letters] we find one or two from a lady who seems to have taken an active part in the politics of the day. "To the king my lord," she writes in one of them, "my gods, my Sun-god, thus says Nin, thy handmaid, the dust of thy feet. At the feet of the king my lord, my gods, my Sun-god, seven times seven I prostrate myself. Let the king my lord wrest his country from the hand of the Bedâwin, in order that they may not rob it. The city of Zaphon has been captured. This is for the information of the king my lord."

The letters of Tel-el-Amarna bridge over the gulf that separates the early Babylonia of Khammurabi from the later Assyria of Tiglath-pileser III and his successors. The inner life of the intervening period is still known to us but imperfectly…. We have to descend to the days of the second Assyrian empire before we find again a collection of letters.

These are the letters addressed to the Assyrian government, or more generally to the King …. Many of them are despatches from generals in the field or from the governors of frontier towns who write to inform the Assyrian government of the movements of the enemy or of the political events in their own neighborhood....

Some [are] of a more private character. Here, for instance, is one which reminds us that human nature is much the same in all ages of the world: "To the king my lord, thy servant, Saul-miti-yuballidh: Salutation to the king my lord; may Nebo and Merodach for ever and ever be gracious to the king my lord. Bau-gamilat, the handmaid of the king, is constantly ill; she cannot eat a morsel of food; let the king send orders that some physician may go and see her." In another letter the writer expresses his gratitude to the King for his kindness in sending him his own doctor, who had cured him of a serious disease. "May Istar of Erech," he says, "and Nana (of Bit-Ana) grant long life to the king my lord, for he sent Basa the physician of the king my lord to save my life and he has cured me; therefore may the great gods of heaven and earth be gracious to the king my lord, and may they establish the throne of the king my lord in heaven for ever; since I was dead, and the king has restored me to life."

The astronomers also sent letters to [the king] on the results of their observations. Among the letters ... is an interesting one--unfortunately defaced and imperfect--which was sent to Nineveh from one of the observatories in Babylonia.... The writer, Abil-Istar, says: "As for the eclipse of the moon about which the king my lord has written to me, a watch was kept for it in the cities of Akkad, Borsippa, and Nippur. We observed it ourselves in the city of Akkad.... And whereas the king my lord ordered me to observe also the eclipse of the sun, I watched to see whether it took place or not, and what passed before my eyes I now report to the king my lord. It was an eclipse of the moon that took place.... It was total over Syria and the shadow fell on the land of the Amorites, the land of the Hittites, and in part on the land of the Chaldees." We gather from this letter that there were no less than three observatories in Northern Babylonia: One at Akkad, near Sippara; one at Nippur, now Niffer; and one at Borsippa, within sight of Babylon. As Borsippa possessed a university, it was natural that one of the three observatories should be established there....

Letters ... were written to the King by all sorts of people, and upon all sorts of business. Thus we find Assur-bani, the captain of a river-barge, writing about the conveyance of some of those figures of colossal bulls which adorned the entrance to the palace of Sennacherib. The letter is short and to the point: "To the king my lord, thy servant Assur-bani: Salutation to the king my lord. Assur-mukin has ordered me to transport in boats the colossal bulls and cherubim of stone. The boats are not strong enough and are not ready. But if a present be kindly made to us, we will see that they are got ready and ascend the river." The unblushing way in which *bakshish* [tip or gratuity] is here demanded shows that in this respect, at all events, the East has changed but little.

Of quite a different character is a letter about some wine that was sent to the royal cellars. The writer says in it: "As for the wine about which the king my lord has written to me, there are two homers [c. 120 liters] of it for keeping, as well as plenty of the best oil."...

A good deal of the correspondence relates to the importation of horses from Eastern Asia Minor for the stables of the Assyrian King...: "To the king my lord, thy servant Nebo-sum-iddin: Salutation to the king my lord; for ever and ever may Nebo and Merodach be gracious to the king my lord. Thirteen horses from the land of Kusa, 3 foals from the land of Kusa--in all 16 draught-horses; 14 stallions; altogether 30 horses and 9 mules--in all 39 from the city of Qornê .... In all 54 horses from Kusa and 104 stallions, making 148 horses and 30 mules--altogether 177 have been imported. (Dated) the second day of Sivan."... The writer ... goes on to say: "What are the orders of the king about the horses which have arrived this very day before the king? Shall they be stabled in the garden-palace, or shall they be put out to grass? Let the king my lord send word whether they shall be put out to grass or whether they are to be stabled?"

Sayce, Archibald H. *Babylonians and Assyrians: Life and Customs*. New York: Scribner's, 1899. Pp. 49-51, 209-210, 212-223, 227-228.

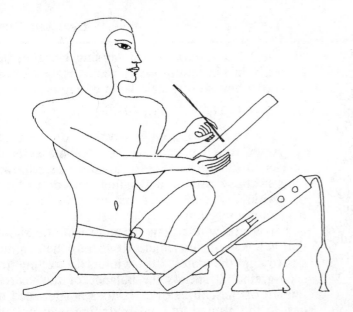

► Egyptian Scribe at Work

READING 1.4

"IF YOU HAVE ANY SENSE, BE A SCRIBE!" CHOOSING A CAREER IN NEW KINGDOM EGYPT

Surviving documents from ancient Egypt attest to the existence of an educational system designed to prepare young boys to become professional scribes. Since the government needed trained scribes to run its business, it took an interest in the preparation of young men for their careers. Senior officials of the civil and military administration frequently instructed students who aspired to become scribes, clerks, paymasters, record keepers, and secretaries. The curriculum consisted of reading and writing, copying and memorization of texts, and the taking of dictation; students were expected to acquire an adequate vocabulary and to master the niceties of spelling, grammar, syntax, and composition. This involved long hours of drill and the completion of endless exercises.

Like young people in other places and eras, ancient Egyptian students were sometimes tempted to neglect their studies in favor of more immediately enjoyable activities. To counteract such temptation, the masters set their apprentices to copy passages that focused on the need for discipline, the honors and attractions of the scribe's profession, and the debt of gratitude dutiful students owed their teachers. The passage that follows is from such an assignment. The document, known as the *Papyrus Lansing*, dates to the twentieth dynasty of New Kingdom Egypt (c. 1200-1090 B.C.E.), and is now in the British Museum. It stresses the professional and personal advantages of the educated man in contrast to untutored fellow citizens who were mere peasants and soldiers. The moral is clear: "All occupations are bad except that of scribe."

QUESTIONS:

1) What are the signs of good academic aptitude and achievement, in the view of the author?

2) Why is the author so insistent that the scribe's profession is preferable to all others? What does he identify as the disadvantages of various other occupations?

3) Does the devotion of pupil to teacher seem plausible? Or would you surmise that it represents wishful thinking on the author's part?

---

1. Title

[Beginning of the instruction in letter-writing made by the royal scribe and chief overseer of the cattle of Amen-Re, King of Gods, Nebmare-nakht] for his apprentice, the scribe Wenemdiamun.

15

2. Praise of the scribe's profession

[The royal scribe] and chief overseer of the cattle of Amen-[Re, King of Gods, Nebmare-nakht speaks to the scribe Wenemdiamun]. [Apply yourself to this] noble profession. "Follower of Thoth" is the good name of him who exercises it.... He makes friends with those greater than he. Joyful.... Write with your hand, read with your mouth. Act according to my words. ... my heart is not disgusted.... ... to my instructing you. You will find it useful. ... [with bread and] beer. You will be advanced by your superiors. You will be sent on a mission .... Love writing, shun dancing; then you become a worthy official. Do not long for the marsh thicket. Turn your back on throw stick and chase. By day write with your fingers; recite by night. Befriend the scroll, the palette. It pleases more than wine. Writing for him who knows it is better than all other professions. It pleases more than bread and beer, more than clothing and ointment. It is worth more than an inheritance in Egypt, than a tomb in the west.

3. Advice to the unwilling pupil

Young fellow, how conceited you are! You do not listen when I speak. Your heart is denser than a great obelisk, a hundred cubits high, ten cubits thick. When it is finished and ready for loading, many work gangs draw it. It hears the words of men; it is loaded on a barge. Departing from Yebu it is conveyed, until it comes to rest on its place in Thebes.

So also a cow is brought this year, and it plows the following year. It learns to listen to the herdsman; it only lacks words. Horses brought it from the field, they forget their mothers. Yoked they go up and down on all his majesty's errands. They become like those that bore them, that stand in the stable. They do their utmost for fear of a beating.

But though I beat you with every kind of stick, you do not listen. If I knew another way of doing it, I would do it for you, that you might listen. You are a person fit for writing, though you have not yet known a woman. Your heart discerns, your fingers are skilled, your mouth is apt for reciting.

Writing is more enjoyable than enjoying a basket of ... and beans; more enjoyable than a mother's giving birth, when her heart knows no

distaste. She is constant in nursing her son; her breast is in his mouth every day. Happy is the heart [of] him who writes; he is young each day.

4. The idle scribe is worthless

The royal scribe and chief overseer of the cattle of Amen-Re, King of Gods, Nebmare-nakht, speaks to the scribe Wenemdiamun, as follows. You are busy coming and going, and don't think of writing. You resist listening to me; you neglect my teachings.

You are worse than the goose of the shore, that is busy with mischief. It spends the summer destroying the dates, the winter destroying the seed-grain. It spends the balance of the year in pursuit of the cultivators. It does not let seed be cast to the ground without snatching it in its fall. One cannot catch it by snaring. One does not offer it in the temple. The evil, sharpeyed bird that does no work!

You are worse than the desert antelope that lives by running. It spends no day in plowing. Never at all does it tread on the threshing-floor. It lives on the oxen's labor, without entering among them. But though I spend the day telling you "Write," it seems like a plague to you. Writing is very pleasant!...

5. All occupations are bad except that of scribe

See for yourself with your own eye. The occupations lie before you.

The washerman's day is going up, going down. All his limbs are weak, [from] whitening his neighbor's clothes every day, from washing linen.

The maker of pots is smeared with soil, like one whose relations have died. His hands, his feet are all full of clay; he is like one who lives in the bog.

The cobbler mingles with vats. His odor is penetrating. His hands are red with madder [dye], like one who is smeared with blood. He looks behind him for the kite, like one whose flesh is exposed.

The watchman prepares garlands and polishes vase-stands. He spends a night of toil just as one on whom the sun shines.

The merchants travel downstream and upstream. They are as busy as can be, carrying goods from one town to another. They supply him who has wants. But the tax collectors carry off the gold, that most precious of metals.

The ships' crews from every house (of commerce), they receive their loads. They depart from Egypt for Syria, and each man's god is with him. [But] not one of them says: "We shall see Egypt again!"

The carpenter who is in the shipyard carries the timber and stacks it. If he gives today the output of yesterday, woe to his limbs! The shipwright stands behind him to tell him evil things.

His outworker who is in the fields, his is the toughest of all jobs. He spends the day loaded with his tools, tied to his tool-box. When he returns home at night, he is loaded with the tool-box and the timbers, his drinking mug, and his whetstones.

The scribe, he alone, records the output of all of them. Take note of it!

6. The misfortunes of the peasant

Let me also expound to you the situation of the peasant, that other tough occupation. [Comes] the inundation and soaks him ..., he attends to his equipment. By day he cuts his farming tools; by night he twists rope. Even his midday hour he spends on farm labor. He equips himself to go to the field as if he were a warrior. The dried field lies before him; he goes out to get his team. When he has been after the herdsman for many days, he gets his team and comes back with it. He makes for it a place in the field. Comes dawn, he goes to make a start and does not find it in its place. He spends three days searching for it; he finds it in the bog. He finds no hides on them; the jackals have chewed them. He comes out, his garment in his hand, to beg for himself a team.

When he reaches his field he finds [it broken up]. He spends time cultivating, and the snake is after him. It finishes off the seed as it is cast to the ground. He does not see a green blade. He does three plowings with borrowed grain. His wife has gone down to the merchants and found nothing for [barter]. Now the scribe lands on the shore. He surveys the harvest. Attendants are behind him with staffs, Nubians with clubs. One say [to him]: "Give grain." "There is none." He is beaten savagely. He is bound, thrown in the well, submerged head down. His wife is bound

in his presence. His children are in fetters. His neighbors abandon them and flee. When it's over, there's no grain.

If you have any sense, be a scribe. If you have learned about the peasant, you will not be able to be one. Take note of it!

7. Be a scribe

The scribe of the army and commander of the cattle of the house of Amun, Nebmare-nakht, speaks to the scribe Wenemdiamun, as follows. Be a scribe! Your body will be sleek; your hand will be soft. You will not flicker like a flame, like one whose body is feeble. For there is not the bone of a man in you. You are tall and thin. If you lifted a load to carry it, you would stagger, your legs would tremble. You are lacking in strength; you are weak in all your limbs; you are poor in body.

Set your sight on being a scribe; a fine profession that suits you. You call for one; a thousand answer you. You stride freely on the road. You will not be like a hired ox. You are in front of others.

I spend the day instructing you. You do not listen! Your heart is like an [empty] room. My teachings are not in it. Take their [meaning] to yourself.

The marsh thicket is before you each day, as a nestling is after its mother. You follow the path of pleasure; you make friends with revellers. You have made your home in the brewery, as one who thirsts for beer. You sit in the parlor with an idler. You hold the writings in contempt. You visit the whore. Do not do these things! What are they for? They are of no use. Take note of it!

8. The scribe does not suffer like the soldier

Furthermore. Look, I instruct you to make you sound; to make you hold the palette freely. To make you become one whom the king trusts; to make you gain entrance to treasury and granary. To make you receive the ship-load at the gate of the granary. To make you issue the offerings on feast days. You are dressed in fine clothes; you own horses. Your boat is on the river; you are supplied with attendants. You stride about inspecting. A mansion is built in your town. You have a powerful office, given you by the king. Male and female slaves are about you.

Those who are in the fields grasp your hand, on plots that you have made. Look, I make you into a staff of life! Put the writings in your heart, and you will be protected from all kinds of toil. You will become a worthy official.

Do you not recall the [fate of] the unskilled man? His name is not known. He is ever burdened [like an ass carrying] in front of the scribe who knows what he is about.

Come, [let me tell] you of the woes of the soldier, and how many are his superiors: the general, the troop-commander, the officer who leads, the standard-bearer, the lieutenant, the scribe, the commander of fifty, and the garrison-captain. They go in and out of the halls of the palace, saying: "Get laborers!" He is awakened at any hour. One is after him as [after] a donkey. He toils until the Aten [solar disk] settles in his darkness of night. He is hungry, his belly hurts; he is dead while yet alive. When he receives the grain ration, having been released from duty, it is not good for grinding.

He is called up for Syria. He may not rest. There are no clothes, no sandals. The weapons of war are assembled at the fortress of Sile. His march is uphill through mountains. He drinks water every third day; it is smelly and tastes of salt. His body is ravaged by illness. The enemy comes, surrounds him with missiles, and life recedes from him. He is told: "Quick, forward, valiant soldier! Win for yourself a good name!" He does not know what he is about. His body is weak, his legs fail him. When victory is won, the captives are handed over to his majesty, to be taken to Egypt. The foreign woman faints on the march; she hangs herself [on] the soldier's neck. His knapsack drops, another grabs it while he is burdened with the woman. His wife and children are in the village; he dies and does

not reach it. If he comes out alive, he is worn out from marching. Be he at large, be he detained, the soldier suffers. If he leaps and joins the deserters, all his people are imprisoned. He dies on the edge of the desert, and there is none to perpetuate his name. He suffers in death as in life. A big sack is brought for him; he does not know his resting place.

Be a scribe, and be spared from soldiering! You call and one says: "Here I am." You are safe from torments. Every man seeks to raise himself up. Take note of it!

9. The pupil wishes to build a mansion for his teacher

Furthermore. [To] the royal scribe] and chief overseer of the cattle of Amen-Re, King of Gods, Nebmare-nakht. The scribe Wenemdiamun greets his lord: In life, prosperity, and health! This letter is to inform my lord. I grew into a youth at your side. You beat my back; your teaching entered my ear. I am like a pawing horse. Sleep does not enter my body by day; nor is it upon me at night. [For I say]: I will serve my lord just as a slave serves his master.

I shall build a new mansion for you [on] the ground of your town, with trees [planted] on all its sides. There are stables within it. Its barns are full of barley and emmer [grain], wheat, cumin, dates, ... beans, lentils, coriander, peas, seed-grain, ... flax, herbs, reeds, rushes, ... dung for the winter, alfa grass, reeds, ... grass, produced by the basketful. Your herds abound in draft animals, your cows are pregnant. I will make for you five aruras of cucumber beds to the south.

Lichtheim, Miriam, comp. *Ancient Egyptian Literature: A Book of Readings, II: The New Kingdom.* Berkeley: Univ. of California Press, 1976. Pp. 168-173.

TUTANKHAMEN AND HOWARD CARTER

▶ **Tutankhamen**

Ancient Egypt was ruled by the pharaoh, a god-king. The pharaoh wielded extensive powers because service to him was a religious as well as a civic duty. Egyptian religion was polytheistic; most divinities were associated with the agrarian rhythms of fertility and germination, death and regeneration.

The gods were generally anthropomorphic (having human shapes and personalities), but could also have the form of beasts, or could combine human and animal form. The pharaoh exercised his powers through a rigid hierarchy of royal agents, nobles, and local officials. He financed a complex government, extensive public works projects, and elaborate tombs for himself and his family by exploiting his subjects' labor and the tremendous agricultural surplus produced the peasants who farmed the land irrigated by the annual flooding of the Nile River. Peasants worked on government projects during seasons when the Nile's waters were too high for farm work and when transport by water was easiest.

According to an Egyptian myth, the dying god Osiris was slain by the evil Set but reborn through the efforts of his sister/wife Isis. Osiris was the father of Horus, and Horus was embodied by the king. Since the well-being of the state and of the whole universe was directly linked to the well-being of the king, he was honored in this life and--through elaborate funeral rites--given a proper send-off to the next life as well. This accounts for the practice of mummification of the body after death, and the fantastic expenditure of time and resources on memorials, temples, and tombs.

The pyramids at Giza near Cairo are the most famous examples of Egyptian pharaonic tombs. Many others have been found in the Valley of the Kings, near Luxor in Upper Egypt. The desert climate of Egypt helped preserve the tombs' magnificent sculptures, paintings, and hieroglyphic inscriptions. Beginning already in ancient times, however, tomb robbers have emptied most tombs of their treasures.

The most famous tomb in the Valley of the Kings is that of Tutankhamen (r. 1343-1325 B.C.E.), or King Tut, an insignificant boy-pharaoh who died at age eighteen. The discovery of his well-preserved and richly furnished unplundered tomb in 1922 made Tutankhamen a household name more than three thousand years after his death. The British archaeologist Howard Carter describes here how he and Egyptologist George Herbert, the Earl of Carnarvon, entered Tutankhamen's tomb. It remains one of the most sensational and celebrated archaeological finds of this century.

QUESTIONS:

1) What feelings did Howard Carter experience during his opening of the tomb of Tutankhamen? How might his description of those feelings contribute to the myth of a "curse of the mummy"?

2) What religious attitudes seem to underlie the furnishings of the tomb?

3) What do the decorations of the tomb imply about Egyptian notions of an afterlife?

By the middle of February [1922] our work in the Antechamber was finished.... We were ready at last to penetrate the mystery of the sealed door.

Friday, the 17th, was the day appointed, and at two o'clock those who were to be privileged to witness the ceremony met by appointment above the tomb.... By a quarter past two the whole company had assembled, so we removed our coats and filed down the sloping passage into the tomb.

In the Antechamber everything was prepared and ready, and to those who had not visited it since the original opening of the tomb it must have presented a strange sight. We had screened the statues with boarding to protect them from possible damage, and between them we had erected a small platform, just high enough to enable us to reach the upper part of the doorway, having determined, as the safest plan, to work from the top downwards. A short distance back from the platform there was a barrier, and beyond, knowing that there might be hours of work ahead of us, we had provided chairs for the visitors. On either side standards had been set up for our lamps, their light shining full upon the doorway.... There before us lay the sealed door, and with its opening we were to blot out the centuries and stand in the presence of a king who reigned three thousand years ago. My own feelings as I mounted the platform were a strange mixture, and it was with a trembling hand that I struck the first blow.

My first care was to locate the wooden lintel above the door: then very carefully I chipped away the plaster and picked out the small stones which formed the uppermost layer of the filling. The temptation to stop and peer inside at every moment was irresistible, and when, after about ten minutes' work, I had made a hole large enough to enable me to do so, I inserted an electric torch. An astonishing sight its light revealed, for there, within a yard of the doorway, stretching as far as one could see and blocking the entrance to the chamber, stood what to all appearance was a solid wall of gold. For the moment there was no clue as to its meaning, so as quickly as I dared I set to work to widen the hole. This had now become an operation of considerable difficulty, for the stones of the masonry were not accurately squared blocks built regularly upon one another, but rough slabs of varying size, some so heavy that it took all one's strength to lift them: many of them, too, as the weight above was removed, were left so precariously balanced that the least false movement would have sent them sliding inwards to crash upon the contents of the chamber below. We were also endeavouring to preserve the seal-impressions upon the thick mortar of the outer face, and this added considerably to the difficulty of handling the stones. Mace and Callender were helping me by this time, and each stone was cleared on a regular system. With a crowbar I gently eased it up, Mace holding it to prevent it falling forwards; then he and I lifted it out and passed it back to Callender, who transferred it on to one of the foremen, and so, by a chain of workmen, up the passage and out of the tomb altogether.

With the removal of a very few stones the mystery of the golden wall was solved. We were at the entrance of the actual burial-chamber of the king, and that which barred our way was the side of an immense gilt shrine built to cover and protect the sarcophagus. It was visible now from the Antechamber by the light of the standard lamps, and as stone after stone was removed, and its gilded surface came gradually into view, we could, as though by electric current, feel the tingle of excitement which thrilled the spectators behind the barrier.... We who were doing the work were probably less excited, for our whole energies were taken up with the task in hand--that of removing the blocking without an accident. The fall of a single stone might have done irreparable damage to the delicate surface of the shrine, so, directly the whole was large enough, we made an additional protection for it by inserting a mattress on the inner side of the door-blocking, suspending it from the wooden lintel of the doorway. Two hours of hard work it took us to clear away the blocking ... and at one point, when near the bottom, we had to delay operations for a space while we collected the scattered beads from a necklace brought by the plunderers from the chamber within and dropped on the threshold. This last was a terrible trial to our patience, for it was a slow business, and we were all of us excited to see what might be within; but finally it was done, the last stones were removed, and the way to the innermost chamber lay open before us.

In clearing away the blocking of the doorway we had discovered that the level of the inner chamber was about four feet lower than that of the Antechamber, and this, combined with the fact that there was but a narrow space between door and shrine, made an entrance by no means easy to effect. Fortunately, there were no smaller antiquities at this end of the chamber, so I lowered myself down, and then, taking one of the portable lights, I edged cautiously to the corner of the shrine and looked beyond it. At the corner two beautiful alabaster vases blocked the way, but I could see that if these were removed we should have a clear path to the other end of the chamber; so, carefully marking the spot on which they stood, I picked them up --with the exception of the king's wishing-cup they were of finer quality and more graceful shape than any we had yet found--and passed them back to the Antechamber. Lord Carnarvon and M. Lacau now joined me, and, picking our way along the narrow passage between shrine and wall, paying out the wire of our light behind us, we investigated further.

It was, beyond any question, the sepulchral chamber in which we stood, for there, towering above us, was one of the great gilt shrines beneath which kings were laid. So enormous was this structure (17 feet by 11 feet, and 9 feet high, we found afterwards) that it filled within a little the entire area of the chamber, a space of some two feet only separating it from the walls on all four sides, while its roof, with cornice top and torus moulding, reached almost to the ceiling. From top to bottom it was overlaid with gold, and upon its sides there were inlaid panels of brilliant blue faience, in which were represented, repeated over and over, the magic symbols which would ensure its strength and safety. Around the shrine, resting on the ground, there were a number of funerary emblems, and, at the north end, the seven magic oars the king would need to ferry himself across the waters of the underworld. The walls of the chamber, unlike those of the Antechamber, were decorated with brightly painted scenes and inscriptions, brilliant in their colours, but evidently somewhat hastily executed.

These last details we must have noticed subsequently, for at the time our one thought was of the shrine and of its safety. Had the thieves penetrated within it and disturbed the royal burial? Here, on the eastern end, were the great folding doors, closed and bolted, but not sealed, that would answer the question for us. Eagerly we drew the bolts, swung back the doors, and there within was a second shrine with similar bolted doors, and upon the bolts a seal, intact. This seal we determined not to break, for our doubts were resolved, and we could not penetrate further without risk of serious damage to the monument. I think at the moment we did not even want to break the seal, for a feeling of intrusion had descended heavily upon us with the opening of the doors, heightened, probably, by the almost painful impressiveness of a linen pall, decorated with golden rosettes, which dropped above the inner shrine. We felt that we were in the presence of the dead King and must do him reverence, and in imagination could see the doors of the successive shrines open one after the other till the innermost disclosed the King himself. Carefully, and as silently as possible, we re-closed the great swing doors, and passed on to the farther end of the chamber.

Here a surprise awaited us, for a low door, eastwards from the sepulchral chamber, gave entrance to yet another chamber, smaller than the outer ones and not so lofty. This doorway, unlike the others, had not been closed and sealed. We were able, from where we stood, to get a clear view of the whole of the contents, and a single glance sufficed to tell us that here, within this little chamber, lay the greatest treasures of the tomb. Facing the doorway, on the farther side, stood the most beautiful monument that I have ever seen--so lovely that it made one gasp with wonder and admiration. The central portion of it consisted of a large shrine-shaped chest, completely overlaid with gold, and surmounted by a cornice of sacred cobras. Surrounding this, free-standing, were statues of the four tutelary goddesses of the dead--gracious figures with outstretched protective arms, so natural and lifelike in their pose, so pitiful and compassionate the expression upon their faces, that one felt it almost sacrilege to look at them. One guarded the shrine on each of its four sides, but whereas the figures at front and back kept their gaze firmly fixed upon their charge, an additional note of touching realism was imparted by the other two, for their heads were turned sideways, looking over their shoulders towards the entrance, as though to watch against surprise. There is a simple grandeur about this monument that made an irresistible appeal to the imagination, and I am not ashamed to confess that it brought a lump to my throat. It is undoubtedly the Canopic chest and contains the jars which play such an important part in the ritual of mummification.

There were a number of other wonderful things in the chamber, but we found it hard to take them in at the time, so inevitably were one's eyes drawn back again and again to the lovely little goddess figures. Immediately in front of the entrance lay the figure of the jackal god Anubis, upon his shrine, swathed in linen cloth, and resting upon a portable sled, and behind this the head of a bull upon a stand--emblems, these, of the underworld. In the south side of the chamber lay an endless number of black shrines and chests, all closed and sealed save one, whose open doors revealed statues of Tut·ankh·Amen standing upon black leopards. On the farther wall were more shrine-shaped boxes and miniature coffins of gilded wood, these last undoubtedly containing funerary statuettes of the king. In the centre of the room, left of the Anubis and the bull, there was a row of magnificent caskets of ivory and wood, decorated and inlaid with gold and blue faience, one, whose lid we raised, containing a gorgeous ostrich-feather fan with ivory handle, fresh and strong to all appearance as when it left the maker's hand.

There were also, distributed in different quarters of the chamber, a number of model boats with sails and rigging all complete, and, at the north side, yet another chariot.

Such, from a hurried survey, were the contents of this innermost chamber. We looked anxiously for evidence of plundering but on the surface there was none. Unquestionably the thieves must have entered, but they cannot have done more than open two or three of the caskets. Most of the boxes, as has been said, have still their seals intact, and the whole contents of the chamber, in fortunate contrast to those of the Antechamber and the Annexe, still remain in position exactly as they were placed at the time of burial.

How much time we occupied in this first survey of the wonders of the tomb I cannot say, but it must have seemed endless to those anxiously waiting in the Antechamber. Not more than three at a time could be admitted with safety, so, when Lord Carnarvon and M. Lacau came out, the others came in pairs .... It was curious, as we stood in the Antechamber, to watch their faces as, one by one, they emerged from the door. Each had a dazed, bewildered look in his eyes, and each in turn, as he came out, threw up his hands before him, an unconscious gesture of impotence to describe in words the wonders that he had seen. They were indeed indescribable, and the emotions they had aroused in our minds were of too intimate a nature to communicate, even though we had the words at our command. It was an experience which, I am sure, none of us who were present is ever likely to forget, for in imagination--and not wholly in imagination either --we had been present at the funeral ceremonies of a king long dead and almost forgotten. At a quarter past two we had filed down into the tomb, and when, three hours later, hot, dusty, and dishevelled, we came out once more into the light of day, the very Valley seemed to have changed for us and taken on a more personal aspect. We had been given the Freedom.

Carter, Howard, and A.C. Mace. *The Tomb of Tut·ankh·Amen, Discovered by the Late Earl of Carnarvon and Howard Carter*. London: Cassell, 1923. Pp. 178-186.

THE PALACES OF GREEK HEROES, AS SEEN IN HOMER AND MODERN ARCHAEOLOGY

▶ Linear B Tablet

Until the advent of scientific archaeology in the second half of the nineteenth century, historians began their descriptions of ancient Greek civilization with the archaic period beginning around 800 BCE. Before that lay a long "Dark Age" and the mythic heroic era of epic poetry and folklore. There was no way to verify whether the Trojan War of Homer's poetry or the "Dorian Invasion" shortly after it were fictional sagas of a heroic age or actual events. Then, in the 1870s, Heinrich Schliemann, a wealthy German merchant and amateur Homeric scholar, fulfilled a lifelong dream by excavating the remains of ancient cultures in northwest Turkey at the site of Troy and in Greece at Mycenae, the home of king Agamemnon in Homer's epic. By 1900, the English archaeologist Sir Arthur Evans was making equally momentous finds on the island of Crete, and in the succeeding decades other investigators found significant Mycenaean settlements at Pylos and elsewhere on mainland Greece. All the new revelations gave stunning evidence of an advanced civilization in the ancient Aegean region long before the period at which standard history texts began their story.

The burning question was whether any of the archaeological remains were those of a *Greek* culture and specifically of the people whose heroes are depicted in the *Iliad* and *Odyssey*. (See the first passage below, from Homer's account of Odysseus's son Telemakhos's visit to the palace of Menelaos and Helen.) If not, had the Greeks immigrated to the area only later as part of the so-called Dorian Invasion that submerged the Mycenaean civilization? The discovery and decipherment of Bronze Age written records provided the answer to these questions.

Although alphabetic writing came to Greece only some two or three centuries after the end of Bronze Age, the discovery of several hundred inscribed clay tablets proved that the culture was not entirely illiterate. But was the language transcribed on the tablets Greek? Debate over this question raged for half a century, but the script known as Linear B defied attempts at decipherment. Finally, in 1952, a brilliant young British architect, Michael Ventris, encouraged by the Cambridge classicist John Chadwick, succeeded in "cracking the code" and demonstrating that the tablets from Mycenae and Pylos and Knossos were in fact the records of Greek speakers.

The second passage below is from Chadwick's account of how an experience in Ventris's boyhood ultimately led to this crucial breakthrough in the study of ancient Greek history. Although Ventris himself died in an auto accident in 1956 at age 34, his pioneering work has enabled others to rewrite history, by including the Bronze Age civilization among the achievements of the Greek people.

Even before Ventris deciphered Linear B, it was clear that the tablets contained business or government records and not literary works. The deciphered records nonetheless surprised scholars by the extent of their detail; they have given us invaluable new insights into the economic and social structure of the impressive palace-centered Mycenaean civilization that Schliemann discovered nearly a century earlier. The final passage below is translated from the tablets. It reveals a society in which people's lives were closely monitored by officials in the great palaces.

QUESTIONS:

1) What is it about the palace of Menelaus that makes such an impression on the youthful Telemakhos in the passage from the *Odyssey*?

2) What was it about the problem of Linear B that appealed so strongly to the young Michael Ventris?

3) What are the implications of the Linear B records regarding the palace bureaucracy that produced them?

The Palace of Menelaos and Helen.

These marveled/ as they admired the palace of the king whom Zeus loved,/ for as the shining of the sun or the moon was the shining/ all through this high-roofed house of glorious Menelaos./ When with their eyes they had had their pleasure in admiration,/ they stepped into the bathtubs smooth-polished and bathed there./ Then when the maids had bathed them and anointed them with oil,/ and put cloaks of thick fleece and tunics upon them, they went/ and sat on chairs beside Menelaos the son of Atreus./ A maidservant brought water for them and poured it from a splendid/ and golden pitcher, holding it above a silver basin/ for them to wash, and she pulled a polished table before them./ A grave housekeeper brought in the bread and served it to them,/ adding many good things to it, generous with her provisions,/ while a carver lifted platters of all kinds of meat and set them/ in front of them, and placed beside them the golden goblets./ Then in greeting fair-haired Menelaos said to them:/ "Help yourselves to the food and welcome, and then afterward,/ when you have tasted dinner, we shall ask you who among/ men you are, for the stock of your parents can be no lost one,/ but you are of the race of men who are kings, whom Zeus sustains,/ who bear scepters; no mean men could have sons such as you are."/ So he spoke, and taking in his hands the fat beef loin/ which had been given as his choice portion, he set it before/   them./ But when they had put away their desire for eating and drinking,/ then Telemakhos talked to the son of Nestor, leaning/ his head close to his, so that none of the others might hear him:/ "Son of Nestor, you who

delight my heart, only look at/ the gleaming of the bronze all through these echoing mansions,/ and the gleaming of gold and amber, of silver and ivory./ The court of Zeus on Olympos must be like this on the inside,/ such abundance of everything. Wonder takes me as I look on it."

Michael Ventris.

The urge to discover secrets is deeply ingrained in human nature; even the least curious mind is roused by the promise of sharing knowledge withheld from others. Some are fortunate enough to find a job which consists in the solution of mysteries, whether it be the physicist who tracks down a hitherto unknown nuclear particle or the policeman who detects a criminal. But most of us are driven to sublimate this urge by the solving of artificial puzzles devised for our entertainment. Detective stories or crossword puzzles cater for the majority; the solution of secret codes may be the hobby of a few. This is the story of the solving of a genuine mystery which had baffled experts for half a century.

In 1936 a fourteen-year-old schoolboy was among a party who visited Burlington House in London to see an exhibition organized to mark the fiftieth anniversary of the British School of Archaeology at Athens. They heard a lecture by the grand old man of Greek archaeology, Sir Arthur Evans; he told them of his discovery of a long forgotten civilization in the Greek island of Crete, and of the mysterious writing used by this fabulous people of prehistory. In that hour a seed was planted that was dramatically to bear fruit sixteen years later; for this boy was already keenly interested in ancient scripts and languages.

At the age of seven he had bought and studied a German book on the Egyptian hieroglyphs. He vowed then and there to take up the challenge of the undeciphered Cretan writing; he began to read books on it, he even started a correspondence with the experts. And in the fullness of time he succeeded where they had failed. His name was Michael Ventris.

The Linear B Tablets.

These palace archives are the records of a comprehensive and pervasive bureaucracy, administering for hundreds of years a most elaborately organized society. We did not, and could not, know that it ever existed; for suddenly the whole complex system disappeared from the earth, soon to be forgotten, never to be revived. The total extinction of a system so long enduring, so elaborately constructed, and so rigidly administered, bears eloquent testimony to the depth and darkness of the flood which submerged Hellas when the Dorian peoples settled in the realms of Agamemnon and Menelaos and Nestor.

Observe now these bureaucrats, how wide their scope and how insatiable their thirst for information. They probe into the affairs of people in every gradation of society, from the highest officers of state down to the slave of a manual worker. They have the power to demand, and the duty to record, infinite detail about men and women and children, industrial manufactures and materials, agricultural produce and livestock, all kinds of holdings of all kinds of land, the administration of religious ritual, movements of troops and the manning of ships. There is endless counting and classifying, measuring and weighing, assessing and collecting and distributing. It is as if everything done by everybody was open to official inquiry and subject to official orders. We possess a part only of the archives for a single year at Pylos: they record thousands of transactions in hundreds of places.

Here, for example, are eighteen places, each obliged to make contributions of six commodities, and relative assessments are fixed for each of the places and for each of the commodities within the schedule. Here again is a distribution of bronze, enough to make half a million arrowheads or 2,300 swords, allocated to a large number of places, with a note to say how many smiths in each place are active, how many inactive, and what is the allocation to each. In Crete we count sheep up to 25,051; and again up to 19,000.

But more astonishing and significant is the omniscience, the insatiable thirst for intimate detail. Sheep may be counted up to a glittering total of twenty-five thousand: but there is still a purpose to be served by recording the fact that *one* animal was contributed by Komawens and another by Etewano. Restless officialdom notes the presence in Pesero's house of one woman and two children; the employment of two nurses, one girl, and one boy, in a Cretan village; the fattening of an insignificant number of hogs in nine places; the existence somewhere of a single pair of brassbound chariot wheels labelled "useless,"--these things and hundreds more of the same type were duly recorded in the palaces of Pylos and Cnossos. A glance at these documents enables you at once to answer such questions as these: How many slaves has Korudallos, and what are they doing? How many sons did the weaving women from Tinwato bear to the rowing-men at Apunewe? Who is watching over the cattle of Thalamatas? What are the wheat and fig rations for thirty-seven female bath attendants and twenty-eight children at Pylos? What is the acreage of Alektruon's estate, and how much ought he to pay (1) in annual tax, (2) to Poseidon, (3) to Diwieus? How much linen is to be expected from Rhion; what deduction must be made by reason of the exemption of what class of craftsmen? In a given room or other space, how many pans, cauldrons, lamps, hammers, brushes, and fire tongs are to be found? To whom, in what amounts, and for what purpose, did Akosota issue coriander, cyperus, fruits, wine, honey, and what else? How much is due from Dunios to the palace?--Answer: 2,200 litres of barley, 526 of olives, 468 of wine; 15 rams, 8 yearlings, 1 ewe, 13 he-goats, 12 pigs, 1 fat hog, 1 cow, and 2 bulls. What are the personal names of two oxen belonging to Tazaro?--Answer: Glossy and Blackie.

I do not say that these are questions which anyone was likely to ask: the point is that these-- and hundreds if not thousands like them--can all be *answered* from the records. They serve to illustrate the omniscience of the bureaucracy. One would suppose that not a seed could be sown, not a gram of bronze worked, not a cloth woven, not a goat reared or a hog fattened, without the filling of a form in the royal palace; such is the impression made by only part of the files for a single year.

What was the purpose of this annual amassing of infinite detail about so many activities in so many places? Some of the Tablets are simply inventories,--descriptions of furniture and equipment of various kinds, presumably in use at the Palace or in store near by. But the great majority are records of assessments, deliveries, and distributions,--distributions both of materials for production and of commodities so produced. And now we must ask, what is the political background necessarily implied by this wonderfully elaborate and centralized administrative system?

One thing is surely manifest: that whoever controlled this secretariat must to some extent have authorized and controlled the transactions which it records. These archives were not compiled without the exercise of extensive powers, especially the power to extract information about all kinds of activities from all classes in the kingdom. And presumably the source of that power is the same as that which authorized the actions consequent upon the information thus collected,--the fixing of assessments, the exacting of dues, the allocation of rations. From the fact that the archives were found *in the palaces* we naturally infer that the supreme central authority was that of the king himself; though we do not know whether his power was absolute or limited (whether by a council of state or some other body).

Lattimore, Richmond, trans. *The Odyssey of Homer*. New York: Harper & Row, 1965. Pp. 66-67. [Book 4, lines 43-75.] Chadwick, John. *The Decipherment of Linear B*. 2nd ed. Cambridge: Cambridge Univ. Press, 1967. P. 1. Page, Denys. *History and the Homeric Iliad*. Berkeley: Univ. of California Press, 1959. Pp. 180-182.

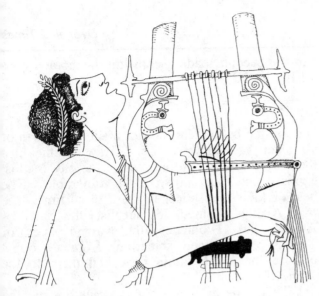

Greek Singer of Tales

THE TROJAN WAR AND THE PRIDE OF HEROES

Homer's epic poem, the *Iliad*, composed around 725 B.C.E., tells part of the story of the Trojan War. Although Homer's tale is based mostly on myth, archaeological finds tell us that a war between Greeks and Trojans likely did take place around 1225 B.C.E. Since alphabetic writing was not known in Greece till c. 800 B.C.E., the story of the war was handed down for centuries in a long tradition of oral poetry. Naturally, generations of poet-singers altered the details of the story, added characters, and greatly embellished various exploits to suit their narrative purposes.

Although there is little historical fact in Homer's epic, it nevertheless provides important insights into the values and the ethics of the ancient Greeks. In depicting the actions and motives of his heroes, Homer presents a warrior's code of behavior that may reflect the late Bronze Age setting of his epic.

The Mycenaean Greeks (c. 1500-1100 B.C.E.) were a warlike people; this is obvious from archaeological finds, which are replete with heavily fortified citadels and many examples of bronze weapons and armor, chariots, and depictions of warfare. Mycenaean civilization collapsed under a variety of pressures beginning around 1200 B.C.E., including invasion of the Balkan Peninsula by newcomers called Dorian Greeks. Historians speculate that military overextension, including the Trojan War and earlier campaigns to gain control of Crete weakened and exhausted the Mycenaean Greeks and contributed to their fall before the Dorian invaders. If there is some truth in the sagas about Troy--the long siege and the ultimate fall of the city, according to Homer, through the stratagem of the wooden horse, this campaign may have been one of the last Mycenaean military triumphs. A so-called Dark Age followed the collapse of Mycenaean civilization.

The first below is from Book 6 of the *Iliad*. It is a conversation between the greatest of Trojan warrior, Hektor, and his wife Andromakhe. She is fearful for her own future and that of their infant son. Hektor's reply reveals the responsibility he feels to behave in a heroic fashion. The second passage is from *Iliad* 9. Here Akhilleus, the greatest Akhaian (Greek) warrior, refuses to fight because King Agamemnon, the commander-in-chief of the Greek forces, has dishonored him by taking away his most valued war-prize, a girl named Briseis. Though Agamemnon tries to mollify him by a generous offer of compensation, Akhilleus remains angry and denounces his leader. Both passages well illustrate the heroes' exalted sense of self-worth as well as the notions of honor and shame that motivate them.

QUESTIONS:

1) How are Hektor's actions and decisions affected by what he imagines others will think and say about him?

2) If you were Andromakhe, how would you feel about this conversation with Hektor?

3) How does the attitude expressed by Akhilleus in the second reading constitute a threat to the Trojan expedition of the Greeks and to the heroic way of life itself?

Hektor hurried … along the well-paved streets. When he arrived at the gates of the great town, the Skaian Gates, through which he used to go forth to the plain, he encountered his richly dowered wife hastening to meet him. This was Andromakhe, the daughter of magnanimous Eëtion, who lived in the city of Thebe in shade of woody Mt. Plakos and was ruler to the Kilikian men. His daughter was given to bronze-helmed Hektor.

Andromakhe met him at the Gates together with a handmaid who carried a happy babe clutched to her bosom. This was the beloved scion of Hektor, bright like a shining star. Hektor used to call him Skamandrios, but everyone else knew him as Astyanax [city-lord], for Hektor alone was saving the city. And the great man smiled in silence as he gazed at his son, but Andromakhe stood close by him, took his hand, and spoke through her tears, calling on his name: "Hektor, my love, your might will be the death of you, and you pity neither the babe your child nor luckless me, soon to be bereft of you. For soon the Akhaians, charging at you, will surround and kill you. Better it would be for me to be swallowed by the earth when you are gone--there will be no solace but only grief for me when you have met your fate. There is no father or queenly mother left for me, since shining Akhilleus killed Eëtion my father while sacking the Kilikians' well-built city, towering Thebe. He killed my father, but did not despoil him. He esteemed the dead man in his heart and burned the corpse with the splendid armor and raised him a monument. The mountain-nymphs, daughters of aegis-bearing Zeus, planted elm trees all round it. My home held seven brothers, too, but swift-foot Akhilleus sent them all to Hades' House of Death on the very same day, as they tended their sheep and oxen. My mother, who reigned there under woody Plakos, Akhilleus brought here with all her belongings and then released her for a countless ransom; but Artemis of the arrows struck her down in her father's palace. So you see, beloved Hektor, you are both father, mother, and brother to me, besides my thriving husband. Pity me and stay here on the battlement; do not make an orphan of your son, a widow of me. Draw up the host there by the wild fig-tree, where the city is most exposed and the rampart most vulnerable. The best of their men attacked there three times--the two Aiantes, famed Idomeneus, the sons of Atreus, and [Diomedes] the warrior scion of Tydeus. They knew something from a prophet or else the spirit within provoked them to the assault."

Then in answer mighty Hektor of the glinting helmet spoke forth: "All these things trouble me, too, woman, but I would suffer burning shame before the Trojan men and the Trojan women with their flowing robes, if I were basely to shirk my part in the fighting. The spirit within me will not permit it. I have learned always to fight in the forefront of the Trojans, winning much glory for my father and myself. For I know very well with my heart and soul that a day will come when holy Troy, and [King] Priam, and the people of Priam the spearman will die. But the future sufferings of the Trojans, of King Priam and [his wife] Hekabe, of my brothers who will fall at the hands of warriors who detest them--none of this disturbs me so much as the thought that one day some bronze-clad Akhaian will lead you off weeping, stripped of your freedom. In Argos you will endure the iron necessity to labor for another, working his loom, fetching his water. Someone seeing you weep will say: 'That was Hektor's wife; he was best of the horse-breaking Trojan warriors in the time of the war at Troy.' So they will speak of you and you will grieve afresh at the memory of the husband who could keep off the day of your captivity. But may the earth lie deep over me before I ever hear your cries as you are carried off into slavery."

When he had spoken thus, Hektor reached out to his baby son, but he shrieked and hid in the bosom of his fair-girt nurse, scared at the sight of his father in his bronze arms and with the horse-hair crest looming on his helmet. His dear father and mother laughed out loud and Hektor quickly removed his helmet and laid it glittering on the ground. Taking his son, he dandled him in the air and kissed him, saying a prayer to Zeus and the other gods: "Zeus and all you other gods, let this boy, my son, be like me, foremost among the Trojans, strong like me and a ruler like me of Troy. May men say of him one day, 'He is much better than his father,' when he returns from battle. Let him kill his foe and bring back bloody spoils to warm his mother's heart."

With these words, he handed back the boy to his cherished wife, who took him to her perfumed bosom and smiled through her tears. Her husband in pity for her caressed her face and spoke thus to her: "My darling wife, do not grieve so for me. No one will cast me down to Hades before my time has come. What is fated to be will be, for the courageous and the cowardly alike. Return now to our home and see to your weaving and bid the handmaids do their work, too. Warfare is a concern for the men of Troy, and for me above all the others."

* * * * *

"Agamemnon, son of Atreus, will not persuade me, nor will the other Danaans, since I got no thanks for fighting constantly against your foes. The day of one's destiny awaits both he who hangs back and he who fights in earnest. Good man or bad--it matters not. One dies all the same, whether one achieves much or nothing whatever. I've gained nothing now, despite enduring pains in my spirit in forever staking my life on the chances of battle. Just as the mother bird suffers long and hard herself to bring back bits of food to her wingless young, so too I lay awake many sleepless nights and lived through many bloody days of battle, contending for the women of these men. I have sacked twelve cities of men from my ships and eleven more by land throughout Troy land. From all these we seized booty, plentiful and worthy, which we brought back to Agamemnon. And he, sitting beside the swift ships, received it all, doling out a little while keeping much for himself. Now all the other leaders and princes keep fast the prizes he awarded; only I of the Akhaians am deprived of my woman, the apple of my eye. Well, let him sleep by her side and take pleasure of her. But why then should the Argives fight the Trojans? Why did the son of Atreus lead the assembled host here to begin with? Was it not for the sake of fair-haired Helen? Out of all mortal men, do the sons of Atreus alone love their women? No, any man worth his salt cares for and cherishes his own woman, as I did love from mine own heart my woman [Briseis], won by the strength of my spear. Now, having reclaimed my prize and cheated me, let him test me no more; I'm wise to him. Let him consult you and the others, Odysseus, about ways to keep off the devouring flames from his ships. In my absence already, he has had to build a wall round the vessels, and a ditch, broad and deep, with sharpened stakes in it. Despite that, he cannot restrain Hektor the killer of men. Yet, when I was fighting alongside the Akhaians, Hektor never sallied forth beyond the protecting wall, but came out only as far as the Skaian Gates and the oak tree nearby. There I faced him man against man and he scarcely avoided death. Now I no longer choose to face brilliant Hektor. Tomorrow, I will make sacrificial offerings to Zeus and all the immortals and then load my ships and launch them onto the salt sea. Then you will see, if you care to, my vessels sailing at first light on the fishing-abounding Hellespont, my men earnestly plying the oars. If earth-shaking Poseidon is willing, a favorable passage will bring us to fertile Phthia on the third day out. There are all my possessions, left behind when I joined this ill-fated expedition. And I will be bringing from here still more gold, and bronze, and iron, and fine-girdled women, all allotted to me. But mighty Agamemnon the son of Atreus has withdrawn [Briseis] my prize of honor, scorning me. Go and tell him what I have said for all to hear, so that the other Akhaians may turn on him in their anger if this shameless leader tries yet another time to cheat one of them. The lowly dog had not the courage to look me in the eye. I will make no plans with him, take no action with him. He betrayed me and wronged me; he will not dupe me with his words again. But enough-- let him go to hell, since Zeus the counselor has robbed his brains. I despise his offered gifts and give not a damn what he thinks. Even if he offered ten or twenty times the wealth, even all he owns, even if he had [the wealth of Egypt] .... not even if he offered gifts as countless as sand, not even so will he change my resolve till he has made good the wrongs and the disdain that grieve my heart. As for marrying the daughter of Agamemnon son of Atreus--No! Not even if she rivaled golden Aphrodite in beauty or bright-eyed Athena in handiworks. Let him find some other, more suitable and lordly Akhaian to bestow his daughter on. For if the gods favor me and I return home alive, my father [Peleus] will choose a wife for me. And many Akhaian women in Hellas and Phthia, the daughters of eminent men who rule over cities, would be my beloved wife for the asking. My heart leads me to take a woman to wife there in Phthia, as delights me, and there enjoy with her the wealth won by elderly Peleus. My life is worth more than all the riches held in well-founded Troy in the peaceful days gone by, before the sons of the Akhaians came. Worth more, too, than the wealth within the threshold of the Archer, Phoibos Apollo's temple at rocky Pytho [Delphi]. Men may plunder oxen and fat sheep or tripods or tawny horses, but once he has lost his life, it cannot be captured or plundered after it has departed through the barrier of his teeth. My mother, Thetis, the silver-foot goddess warns that I bear two types of fate toward my final hour. If I remain and fight here at Troy, I shall never see home again, but shall win unending renown; on the other hand, if I return to my beloved fatherland now, I lose that renown, but gain a long life and a death that comes not too soon. I would advise all of you, too, to sail back homeward; you will not make an end of the steep city of Troy, for wide-browed Zeus has held his strong hand over it and emboldened its people."

Monro, David B., and Thomas W. Allen, eds. *Homeri Opera*. Vol. 1: *Iliadis libros I-XII continens*. 3rd ed. Oxford: Clarendon Press, 1920. Pp. 132-135, 184-188. Translation by James P. Holoka.

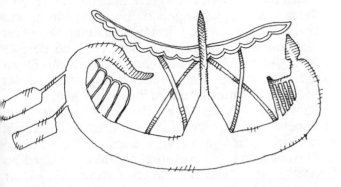

THE PHOENICIANS: COMMERCIAL AND CULTURAL CATALYSTS OF THE ANCIENT MEDITERRANEAN

▶ **Phoenician Ship**

The Phoenicians were a Semitic people whose homeland was roughly coextensive with present-day Lebanon. They were sandwiched between the great powers of Anatolia, Mesopotamia, and Egypt. They functioned as a kind of catalytic agent in the ancient world, because they sent forth from their small base the best seafarers of the ancient Mediterranean world. Their trade routes crisscrossed the Mediterranean and opened its farther reaches to crucial commercial contacts. Phoenician sailors became middlemen for business transactions of all sorts. However, the most important commodity they transshipped was an intellectual one--literacy. For the Phoenicians were the first people to put an alphabetic writing system into common use. Simpler and more easily adapted to various languages than hieroglyphic or pictographic writing, it was adopted by the Greeks around 850 B.C.E. and subsequently by the Romans and many other cultures up to the present day.

The discussion in this segment concentrates on the period approximately 1000 to 700 B.C.E., although Phoenician influence persisted long afterward. The city of Carthage, in present-day Tunisia, was a Phoenician foundation that contested Rome for dominance in the western Mediterranean in the third century B.C.E.

The following passage is an account of Phoenician achievements by a specialist in the history of ancient seafaring.

QUESTIONS:

1) How do the Phoenicians fit the description of "middlemen"?
2) How was Phoenician colonization in the Mediterranean carried out over time? Did the process resemble or differ from other colonial enterprises in history?
3) How did other people in the Mediterranean seem to view the Phoenicians?

There was a time when [European] sailors, leaving behind the seas they knew, turned their prows toward the west, into uncharted waters, and stumbled upon a new world. The effect was electrifying. Nations rushed men to explore and colonize the new territories, freighters to trade with them, and warships to settle disputes. History in a way was only repeating itself when the Portuguese opened up Africa, and the Spanish, America. The first great age of western discovery and colonization took place almost two and a half millennia earlier, and the principal roles were played by the Greeks and the Phoenicians.

The years around 1200 B.C. mark a critical period in the history of the eastern Mediterranean. This was when huge migrations of aggressive peoples, such as those thrown back by Ramses III at the doors of Egypt ..., descended upon the area and snuffed out much of the thriving civilization that was there. On the seas, lawlessness prevailed: rovers [and] ... pirate bands ... prowled unchecked and all but banished trade from the water. Over the Greek world a dark age descended .... From 900 B.C. on things slowly got better, and ultimately a new civilization began to emerge--that of the Greeks familiar to us from written history.

Conditions on the sea started to improve even earlier, about 1000 B.C., and merchants were once again willing to send goods to destinations overseas. Here was an opening for some enterprising maritime people, and there happened to be one such available to seize it--the inhabitants of that part of the coast of the Levant where the great ports of Byblos, Tyre, and Sidon lay. They had been keen and active traders as far back as the days when they sold boatloads of Lebanese cedar to Snefru of Egypt. Now their descendants, the Phoenicians--to give them the name they bear in history from this point on-- become major figures in the burgeoning trade of the eastern Mediterranean. Their geographical location was ideal. From Tyre and Sidon routes led into the hinterland and beyond, connecting eventually with India, and over them caravans brought to Phoenician warehouses the luxury products of the east. Just to the south lay Egypt, which had connections with Arabia and Somalia, the prime source of frankincense and myrrh. No other nation was as well located to serve as middleman in the distribution of wares from all these quarters.

It is hard to tell much in detail about the Phoenicians. Even their name is a puzzle. They called themselves Sidonians, from the city that was their chief center until Tyre outstripped it about the beginning of the first millennium B.C., and their land Canaan. It was the Greeks who named them *Phoinikes*, which some linguists think comes from a root meaning "sea" but which

most connect with the Greek adjective *phoinos*, "dark red." The Phoenicians made a specialty of dyeing textiles, using certain species of a sea snail, Murex, which has a glandular secretion that produces various shades of red and purple. (There are actual hills outside Tyre and Sidon today, made up from bottom to top of the shells of these creatures discarded by the ancient dye factories.) To their Greek customers the Phoenicians may have seemed principally textile traders, "red(-garment)" men. They were businessmen first and foremost, they produced no poets or historians to chronicle their accomplishments for posterity--and their business ledgers have gone the way of all such objects. Moreover, being more interested in profit than publicity, they kept their trade secrets to themselves. The story is told that once, when a Phoenician merchant was being tailed by a foreign skipper out to discover the source of certain trade items, he deliberately ran his ship on the rocks to thwart such snooping. To honor this heroic sacrifice on behalf of the national income, the government rewarded him not with anything trivial like a statue or monument but with reimbursement in toto for all loss sustained....

The Phoenicians were involved in some celebrated business deals. When King Solomon [of Israel] was about to proceed with the building of his famous temple about 970 B.C. and needed timber, he naturally turned to Phoenician with its well-known Lebanese cedar and negotiated a contract. He wrote to Hiram, who was king of the great export center of Tyre at the time:

Now therefore command thou that they hew me cedar trees out of Lebanon; and my servants shall be with thy servants: and unto thee will I give hire for thy servants according to all that thou shalt appoint: for thou knowest that there is not among us any that can skill to hew timber like unto the Sidonians....

And Hiram sent to Solomon, saying, I have considered the things which thou sentest to me for: and I will do all thy desire concerning timber of cedar, and concerning timber of fir.

My servants shall bring them down from Lebanon unto the sea: and I will convey them by sea in floats unto the place that thou shalt appoint me, and will cause them to be discharged there, and thou shalt receive them: and thou shalt accomplish my desire, in giving food for my household.

So Hiram gave Solomon cedar trees and fir trees according to all his desire. And Solomon gave Hiram twenty thousand measures of wheat for food to his household, and twenty measures of pure oil: thus gave Solomon to Hiram year by year.

In the days before money was invented, a buyer had the choice of paying in uncoined precious metal, or of bartering. It was because Solomon had no access to gold--he had to exchange Palestinian wheat and oil for his timber--that he entered into his next business operation with the Phoenicians.

For centuries the inhabitants of the northern end of the Persian Gulf had been trading with India and Arabia and Africa). The products involved were for the most part luxuries: ivory, silks, and spices from India; ivory and incense from Africa; incense and perfumes from Arabia. The profits were correspondingly large. Solomon, though he controlled a port on the appropriate waters in Ezion Geber at the southern end of the Negev, ruled a nation that had no merchant marine or, for that matter, no experience with the sea at all, and was consequently in the exasperating position of seeing all this lucrative trade bypass him. What arrived at the Persian Gulf was transported for Mediterranean distribution by caravan to the Phoenician ports, especially Tyre; what came to Egypt was floated downriver to the mouth of the Nile and carried from there in Phoenician bottoms. Even the Phoenicians, though so much of the trade passed through their hands, were not satisfied: they had to share the profits with caravaneers in the one case or Egyptian middlemen in the other. So when Solomon conceived the idea of building a fleet of his own which, working out of Ezion Geber, could trade with India--for that is most probably what Ophir, the place-name he uses, refers to--and of manning it with Phoenician sailors, Hiram didn't have to be asked twice:

And king Solomon made a navy of ships in Ezion-geber, which is beside Eloth, on the shore of the Red sea, in the land of Edom.

And Hiram sent in the navy his servants, shipmen that had knowledge of the sea, with the servants of Solomon.

And they came to Ophir, and fetched from thence gold, four hundred and twenty talents, and brought it to king Solomon.

From Egypt in the south to Asia Minor in the north and westward to Cyprus, Rhodes, and Crete, Phoenicians had the trade routes more or less to themselves for the centuries between ca. 1000 and 800 B.C. It must have been some time during this period--the date cannot be fixed exactly--that they passed along to the Greeks one of the greatest gifts that the East was to give to the West. The Phoenicians, unlike their neighbors who wrote in complicated hieroglyphs or cuneiform, used an alphabetic system of writing that a Semitic people had invented, probably centuries earlier. In the course of trading operations, most likely in the lower Aegean area, some of their merchants brought it to the attention of the Greeks, who immediately recognized its superlative convenience and swiftly adapted it for writing their language. Subsequently they in turn gave it to the Romans, who passed it on to the Western world. In this transfer the Phoenicians were not creators but middlemen. Their next great contribution was one that they conceived and carried out completely by themselves.

Even in the great days of Minoan and Mycenaean expansion, the western limit of the ancient world had been Sicily and Sardinia. Beyond this lay uncharted seas and terra incognita [unknown lands]. Not long after the turbulent conditions that prevailed in the Mediterranean between 1200 and 1000 B.C. had calmed down, daring Phoenician sailors headed their prows into the waters beyond. Within a short time they had put the stamp of success on their venture by planting the outposts of Utica and Carthage in North Africa, not far from where Tunis is today. Phoenicians rarely did anything for mere curiosity or adventure; it must have been maritime commerce that was the attraction. Their merchants are next reported sailing even beyond Gibraltar into the Atlantic to trade with Tartessus, as the coast of Spain beyond the strait was called. Here the natives mined silver locally, but, even more important, here tin was to be had, a metal that was much in demand for two reasons: there were no deposits easily available in the Mediterranean area, and it was of vital importance because, fused with copper, it forms bronze. The tin to be bought at Tartessus came from regions farther north, so far out of the ken of the ancient mariner that he long knew them only vaguely as the "Tin Isles"; the best guess is that the source was Cornwall in England. Around 800 B.C. or so the Phoenicians set themselves up permanently in the far west by establishing on a fine harbor beyond the strait the key center of Gadir, or Cadiz, as we call it now.

The first great line of travel the Phoenicians laid down was from Tyre to Utica and Carthage. Climate and current dictated the next step. The western Mediterranean is swept by northwest winds during the summer months, which made up the ancient mariner's chief period of activity. To sail westward along the North African coast from Utica or Carthage was to risk a lee shore and buck a hostile current in the bargain. By working to the north at the outset, and following a general southwesterly slant from there to the strait and using the African shore only for the homeward leg, Phoenician skippers were assured of favorable wind and current for the round-trip. And so the Phoenicians planted way stations at strategic points: on Sardinia for that first leg northward, on Ibiza [in the Balearic Islands, near Majorca] and the Spanish Mediterranean coast for the long slant to the strait, and in the neighborhood of Algiers or Oran for the homeward lap. No details about any part of this striking achievement are known. The Phoenicians wanted no competitors, and they not only were tight-lipped about what they were doing but even surrounded their activities with an effective smoke screen of sailors' yarns no

doubt filled with hair-raising details of shipwrecks and sea monsters.

It was the colony of Carthage that was destined to become the greatest Phoenician center in the western Mediterranean. According to legend, its founding took place under the leadership of Queen Dido. It carried out a program of colonization of its own, sending out expeditions to explore and occupy new sites and to convert former way stations into full-sized communities. By 700 B.C., Carthaginians had moved into Sardinia, had founded several colonies in Sicily, including Palermo with its fine natural harbor, and had planted Malaga plus a few other towns on the Mediterranean coast of Spain. Their ships even traversed the Strait of Gibraltar to sail down the African coast and establish there a pair of colonies, one as far south as Mogador due west of Marrakesh. This took care of the new territory to the west, but there was still the link to the homeland far to the east to think about. So Carthage occupied Pantelleria and Malta, which, combined with Phoenician settlements that had long been established on Crete and Rhodes and Cyprus, gave it a set of convenient stepping-stones back to the home port of Tyre.

Carthage's work was now complete. The west was fully open--but to Phoenicians alone. Through a wide-flung network of stations, the trade in tin from the Atlantic coast and in silver and lead and iron from Spain was firmly in her hands. She became one of the foremost powers of the ancient world. But over three centuries had now passed since the Phoenicians had discovered this new world, and during this time another energetic maritime people [the Greeks] had embarked upon a career of colonization.

Casson, Lionel. *The Ancient Mariners: Seafarers and Sea Fighters of the Mediterranean in Ancient Times.* 2nd ed. Princeton: Princeton Univ. Press, 1991. Pp. 61-62, 63-66.

► **Indus Bronze Figurine**

DISCOVERING ANCIENT INDIA

Archaeological excavations begun in 1921 in the Indus River valley unveiled an advanced ancient civilization of great wealth and sophistication that lasted approximately between 3000-1500 B.C.E. Mohenjo-daro and Harappa, two major cities of the Indus civilization, are located four hundred miles apart, though other sites span over nine hundred miles along the Indus River and its tributaries.

Sir John Marshall, pioneer of Indian archaeology who headed the team that excavated Mohenjo-daro, created a sensation among ancient historians and archaeologists when he announced his findings in 1924. Marshall's team continued to uncover the site at Mohenjo-Daro until 1927 and compiled its findings in the three-volume *Mohenjo-Daro and the Indus Civilization*. As Arthur Keith, reviewer of Marshall's book said in 1931,

> Henceforth there are to be two Mesopotamias of ancient date. The one which lies along the lower reaches of the Euphrates and Tigris has long been known as the cradle of civilization; but that there existed an equally extensive and equally elaborate civilization on the banks of the lower Indus and of its twin river the Mihran is a new discovery.

Since the 1920s Indologists have uncovered many other sites along the Indus river and beyond. Their findings have fleshed out the information that Marshall and his colleagues first proclaimed to the world, but have not diminished the importance of their spectacular initial finds.

This reading is taken from Sir John Marshall's account of the discoveries made under his direction. Marshall not only vividly describes the ancient ruins that have lain buried for thousands of years, his comparisons of Mohenjo-daro with modern English cities show how "modern" and advanced urban life in India was four thousand years ago.

QUESTIONS:

1) In what ways does Mohenjo-daro resemble a modern city?
2) Why do we still call the Indus civilization pre-historic?
3) Give examples of a high standard of living of the Indus people.

The story of the excavation of Mohenjo-daro may quickly be told. The site had long been known to district officials in Sind, and had been visited more than once by local archaeological officers, but it was not until 1922, when Mr. R.D. Banerji started to dig there, that the prehistoric character of its remains was revealed. This was not greatly to be wondered at; for the only structures then visible were the Buddhist Stupa and Monastery at the north-west corner of the site, and these were built exclusively of brick taken from the older ruins, so that it was not unnatural to infer that the rest of the site was referable to ... the early centuries of the Christian era. Indeed, when Mr. Banerji himself set about his excavations here, he had no idea of finding anything prehistoric. His primary object was to lay bare the Buddhist remains, and it was while engaged on this task that he came by chance on several seals which he recognized at once as belonging to the same class as the remarkable seals inscribed with legends in an undecipherable script which had long been known to us from the ruins of Harappa in the Panjab. As it happened, the excavations of Harappa itself had at my instance been taken up in the year previous by Rai Bahadur Daya Ram Sahni, and enough had already been brought to light to demonstrate conclusively that its remains, including the inscribed seals, were referable to the Chalcolithic Age. Thus Mr. Banerji's find came at a singularly opportune moment, when we are especially eager to locate other sites of the same early age as Harappa....

[Marshall describes the full extent of Mohenjo-daro revealed after years of digging.] Anyone walking for the first time through Mohenjo-daro might fancy himself surrounded by the ruins of some present-day working town of Lancashire. That is the impression produced by the wide expanse of bare red brick structures, devoid of any semblance of ornament, and bearing in every feature the mark of stark utilitarianism. And the illusion is helped out, or perhaps rather the comparison is prompted by the fact that the bricks themselves of which these buildings are composed are much of a size with modern English bricks, but differ conspicuously from any used during the historic period in India. The workaday appearance of the buildings and signal absence of decoration is the more remarkable, because Indian architecture is notorious for the rich exuberance of its ornament, and the art of brick carving itself was developed to a wonderful pitch as far back even as the Gupta Age. It may be, of course, that originally there was ornament in plenty but that it was confined to the woodwork only, and has,

therefore, inevitably perished.... We know moreover, from the evidence of the fires whic consumed many of the Mohenjo-daro buildings that wood must have been freely used in thei superstructures, and we cannot, therefore, ignor the likelihood that they were just as effectivel decorated as the early rock-cut temples.... Fo the present, however, we must take the Indu buildings as we find them, and not assume th existence of ornament of which there is now n visible proof.

If, however, these buildings were destitute o embellishment, they more than atone for thei plainness by the excellence of thei construction.... Crude brick was well known t the builders of Mohenjo-daro, but was neve used, as it was in Mesopotamia and Egypt, in th exposed parts of buildings. It was reserved fo foundations or for the packing of terraces and th like, where it could not be affected by th elements. Walls above ground--both exterior an interior--were built of burnt brick laid in mud o in mud and gypsum mortar combined.... Th remarkable massiveness which distinguishe many of the walls was proportional to thei height and the weight they had to support, but i part also it was necessitated by the constan danger of floods....

Floors were made of brick either flat or o edge, the latter method being almost invariable i the case of bathrooms and common wherever th flooring was exposed or subjected to excessive wear and tear.

Ground-floor chambers, which alone have survived at Mohenjo-daro, received their ligh and air generally through doorways, bu occasionally through interior windows as well.... Windows in the outer walls were rare and sometimes took the form of mere slits, but there may have been other windows higher up which have been destroyed. It is probable that both doorways and windows were generally spanned by flat wooden lintels, but corbelled arches were also used for these as well as for other purposes, such as covering of drains. The true arch does not appear to have been known. Stairways leading to the upper storeys are universal, the treads generally, though not always, being steep and narrow.

Most buildings of any size had wells of their own--admirably built of burnt brick and usually circular in plan, but in one or two instances, oval. Wells for public use are sometimes provided in private houses with an entrance to the well-chamber direct from the street. With the exception of three somewhat doubtful examples, there are no fireplaces at Mohenjo-daro.

Two specially characteristic features of these buildings are their bathrooms and drains. The former are invariably well paved and usually connected with the street drainage system. In private houses they appear to have been located on the upper as well as on the ground floor. Horizontal drains are ordinarily constructed of brick; vertical ones, which were provided for the upper storeys, of terra-cotta pipes with closely fitting spigot and faucet joints, either protected by brickwork or let into the thickness of the walls. Rubbish chutes or flues descending from the upper storeys were also constructed in the thickness of the walls and were sometimes provided on the outside with a bin which could be cleared by scavengers from the street. Besides these private dustbins, public ones were provided at convenient spots at the sides of the streets, and street drains were constructed with as much care as private ones. Indeed, there are unmistakable signs on every hand that the question of conservancy was one of prime concern to the civic authorities, and, seeing how much attention was given to the matter of drainage, it is not a little surprising to find that the street drains merely discharged into soak-pits in the open thoroughfares, and that no attempt was made to carry them outside the limits of the town.

Roofs, as a rule, were probably flat and were carried, like the ceilings below them, on stout timbers covered with planking and beaten earth, with a protective course of brick, matting, or other material between....

The buildings thus far exhumed at Mohenjo-daro fall into three main classes, viz. (1) Dwelling houses; (2) Buildings whose purpose has not yet been determined; (3) Public baths which may have had either a religious or secular character....

The Great Bath, which I have reserved to the last, was part of what appears to have been a vast hydropathic establishment and most imposing of all the remains unearthed at Mohenjo-daro. Its plan is simple: in the centre, an open quadrangle with verandahs on its four sides, and at the back of three of the verandahs various galleries and rooms.... In the midst of the open quadrangle is a large swimming-bath, some 39 feet long by 23 feet broad and sunk about 8 feet below the paving of the court, with a flight of steps at either end, and at the foot of each a low platform for the convenience of bathers, who might otherwise have found the water too deep. The bath was filled from the well in Chamber 16 and possibly from other wells besides, and the waste water was carried off through a covered drain near the S.W. corner, the corbelled roof of which is some 6 ft. 6 in. in height....

That the Great Bath had at least one upper storey is evident from the stairway ascending to the latter in Room 19, as well as from the drains descending from it; but what sort of elevation it had can only be conjectured....

It remains to be said that for careful and massive construction the Great Bath could hardly have been improved upon. From N. to S. its overall measurement is 180 feet; from E. to W. 108 feet.... In the construction of the swimming-bath in the middle of the quadrangle, every possible precaution was taken to make its walls watertight and prevent any settlement of the foundations....

In a city as cosmopolitan as Mohenjo-daro, with elements in its population drawn from at least four different races, the dress of the people was probably as varied as their personal appearance, but unfortunately our evidence on the subject is at present very scanty....

As to the head and head-dress, the men wore short beards and whiskers, with the upper lip sometimes shaven, as in Sumer, sometimes not. Their hair was taken back from the forehead and either cut short behind ... or coiled in a knot or chignon at the back of the head, with a fillet to support it....

The one and only head that we possess belonging to what appears to be a female statue exhibits the hair falling loose behind. The bronze dancing-girl, on the other hand, has it coiled in a heavy mass which starts from above the left ear and falls over the right shoulder....

Ornaments were freely worn by all classes alike; necklaces, fillets, armlets, and finger-rings by both men and women, girdles, ear-rings, and anklets by women alone....

Weapons of war or of the chase comprised axes, spears, daggers, bows and arrows, maces, slings, and possibly--though not probably--catapults.... They are weapons of offence only. Of shields, helmets, graves, or other defensive armour, there is no trace, nor has the sword, which was to become one of the characteristic weapons of the later Copper Age in the Jumna-Ganges valley, yet to make its appearance....

Just as copper and bronze had already superseded stone for weapons of war and the chase, so, too, they had superseded stone for ordinary household implements and utensils. Indeed, it is true to say that the only utensil now in daily use that was really characteristic of the stone culture was the flake knife of chert, provided no doubt with a handle and used for cutting up food, just as the obsidian flake was used in the Nearer East....

Vessels of copper and bronze were relatively rare, of silver still rarer; and faience was used only for small ornamental vases intended for cosmetics and the like. Of ordinary domestic vessels 99 per cent were earthernware. These exhibit a great variety of shapes....

Most of the Indus pottery was wheel-made, well fired and plain, but painted ware was by no means uncommon. As a rule, the designs were executed in black on a dark red slip, and consisted ordinarily of foliate and geometrical devices.... Animal motifs are very rare, and the few pieces on which they do occur were probably imports from Baluchistan....

Besides this red-and-black ware, which is peculiar to the Indus culture, the pottery of Mohenjo-daro comprised a few specimens of three other decorated wares, viz. "incised," "polychrome," and "glazed."

Two of these are very interesting, the polychrome by reason of the rare stylishness of its colouring--vermilion and black on a ground of cream--and because it is quite different from the polychrome wares of Baluchistan or Mesopotamia; the glaze ware because it is not only the earliest example of its kind known to us in the ancient world, but a singularly fine fabric into the bargain, with the appearance almost of an opaque cream-coloured glass with purplish black markings....

For toys the children had rattles, whistles, and clay models of men and women, animals, birds, carts, and household articles.... Some of the animals had movable heads; whistles might take the form of birds; birds might be mounted on wheels and oxen might be yoked to toy carts. These little toy carts are particularly interesting as being among the earliest representations of wheeled vehicles known to us, approximately contemporary, that is to say, with the chariot depicted on a stone slab at Ur (c. 3200 B.C., according to Mr. Woolley).... The toy carts from Mohenjo-daro are all of terra-cotta and of the most part of the type ... where they are compared with the modern farm carts of Sind.... No doubt many other children's toys were made of less durable materials than terra-cotta, and have perished in the course of the ages.

For games they had marbles and dice. The former are of agate, onyx, slate, and other hard stones, sometimes very beautifully made. The dice are usually cubes like our modern European dice, not oblong like modern Indian ones, and they differ from the latter also in the disposition of their numbers....

Marshall, Sir John, ed. *Mohenjo-daro and the Indus Civilization* .... Vol. 1. Delhi: Indological Book House, 1973. Pp. 10-11, 15-17, 24-25, 33-34, 37-39.

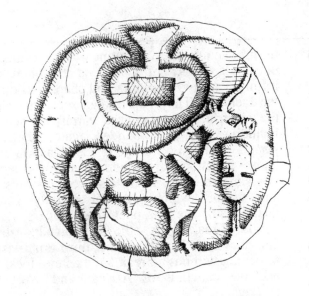

READING 1.10

LOTHAL: INDUSTRIAL CENTER AND PORT OF THE INDUS EMPIRE

Ever since Sir John Marshall's pioneering work on the Indus civilization in the 1920s, archaeologists have continued to uncover and evaluate finds throughout the northwestern portion of the Indian subcontinent. After the partition of India in 1947, Pakistani archaeologists have uncovered more sites along the Indus and its tributaries while their Indian counterparts have added 700 sites south and east of the Indus valley. These findings show that the geographical boundaries of this civilization stretched far beyond the Indus River valley, from Iran on the west, to Turkmenia and Kashmir in the north, to the Godavari Valley in the south, and Delhi in the east. Since this Bronze Age civilization spans regions much beyond the Indus valley, some Indologists now call it the Harappan civilization, after Harappa, discovered in 1921. But because of striking similarities throughout the culture, other archaeologists also call it the Indus Empire.

The Indian finds have shed new light on the maritime activities of the Harappan peoples, their contributions to the sciences and technology, and the international trade between ancient India and western Asia. Among the over two hundred Harappan sites uncovered near the coast of present-day Gujrat in western India, Lothal discovered by S.R. Rao in 1954 is the most important. The name means "mound of the dead" in the modern local language, exactly the same meaning for Mohenjo-daro in the present-day language of its region. This is because each city center was on an elevated mound.

The Indus Empire was primarily a commercial one, dedicated to the unimpeded flow of industrial and agricultural products, and the regulation of trade. It was not a warrior empire, and maintained peace and order because they enabled trade to prosper. It also tolerated diversity in religious practices.

The following reading from S.R. Rao's *Dawn and Devolution of the Indus Civilization* concentrates on metallurgy and other technologies of the Harappan civilization, as well as on Lothal, its industries and role as a maritime port in ancient international trade.

QUESTIONS:

1) How do the findings at Lothal prove that trade was important to the Indus people?
2) What purpose did Lothal serve and why was it important?
3) How do we know that there were industries at Lothat? What were they?

One of the factors contributing to the urbanization of Harappan settlements was the abundant supply of metals, especially copper. Every Harappan site, big or small ... used copper and bronze tools and ornaments. They were not manufactured in small towns and villages. Only industrial cities of Harappa, Mohenjo-daro, Lothal and perhaps Rehman Dheri obtained copper or copper alloy in the form of ingots, remelted them in the furnaces and produced agricultural implements, craftsmen's tools, and personal ornaments. The ancient copper workings at Dariba ... in Rajasthan where even now copper is mined seems to have met, to a large extent, the requirement of the Harappans....

The Harappans equipped themselves with a large variety of tools and weapons of copper. A few were in bronze. They were as much fond of copper and bronze ornaments as they were of necklaces of gemstones and gems. Owing to scarcity of tin, bronze objects were limited in numbers....

Alloying for increasing the hardness of copper was known to the Harappans. They also understood that adding more than 12% of tin with copper makes the artifact brittle.... Harappan technology sometimes shows extreme contrasts. The most sophisticated technique of casting *cire perdue* [lost wax] was adopted for casting figures such as the dancing girl of Mohenjo-daro, the chariot of Daimabad and the dog and bird of Lothal.... Among the advanced tools types invented by the Lothal smiths, particular mention must be made of the incurved saw and the twisted drill, which were unknown in Mesopotamia. It must however be admitted that the flat celts without a splay and axes without a shaft-hole produced in the Indus Valley were primitive compared to the splayed celt and shaft-hole axes of Mesopotamia....

Another major Harappan industry which catered to international and domestic market is bead-making.

The beads were a prized cargo carried in leather bags in the poop of the ships to distant countries, among which Bahrain, Failaka, Mesopotamian cities and perhaps Oman and Socotaro may be mentioned. A reference to the care taken in carrying beads of gemstones safely in the Dilmun [Mesopotamian texts called the Indus civilization Dilmun] boats is made in the clay tablets of Ur. Lothal and Chanhu-daro were two great centres of bead-making in the Indus Empire and perhaps Mohenjo-daro had a share in

its production and marketing. The refined taste of the lapidaries of Lothal is exhibited in the infinite variety of colours and shapes produced in the factory. They had a keen sense of selecting the materials from a large variety of semigem including carnelian, banded agate, chalcedony, jasper, opal, onyx, chrysoprase, plasma, crystal lapis lazuli, sard and amazon stone... Afghanistan is the nearest source for lapis lazuli and turqois which were used only in small quantities by the Harappan bead-makers....

Bead-making is still a living industry [in Gujrat] which has flourished during the last four millennia without a break and has met local needs and the demands of African and West Asian markets....

Drilling was done by the Harappan bead-makers by means of two flanged drills of bronze placed pointed towards the centre at either end of the bead. Bronze drills used for the purpose have been recovered at Lothal. The last stage of manufacture of beads at Lothal was to cook the polished bead once again to get the necessary glow as is being done even now at Cambay.

The Bead Factory where beads of carnelian and agate were produced on mass scale by a number of lapidaries who worked and lived under a single roof has been laid bare in Block F of the Lower Town [in Lothal]. It consists of a working platform in an open courtyard with eleven rooms built around it for the workers to live in. At the entrance there is a guard room also. Two large jars containing more than 600 beads in various stages of manufacture were found *in situ* on the platform. A kiln was built close to the Bead Factory for heating the raw material as well as finished beads. Gold pendants and beads reveal the skill of the goldsmith. Micro gold beads of Lothal are a unique product of the jeweller, and a necklace of such beads is a rare find. Lothal is unmatched for the variety of shapes of beads and materials used for the purpose.... Among the rare types the double-eyed beads of agate, gold-capped beads of jasper and etched beads of carnelian are noteworthy. The beadmakers of Lothal had a sound knowledge of the chemical process involved in etching, which they did by using an alkali.... It is interesting to find that even now the Bharwar women of Gujarat wear ornaments similar to Harappan necklaces, ear pendants and rings.

Harappan sites have yielded thousands of micro-beads of steatite with an aperture ranging from 3000 to 75 microns. It is found that as many as 300 beads weigh just 1 gram. Invariably such microbeads were preserved in small pots.... It is generally believed that the steatite paste was rolled on a thin thread and the tube so formed was burnt along with the thread and then cut into small beads of required size to produce microbeads....

Kathiawad coast yields a fine variety of conch shell which was cut with a wire-saw or toothed saw of bronze to produce bangles, beads, gamesmen, ladles, inlays, weights, engravers and compass. At Mohenjo-daro a graduated scale made of shell has been found.

[Ivory-working] was an important industry so much so that ivory-workers occupied the Acropolis after the Ruler left Lothal. Ivory rods with rounded ends, lathe-turned and carved inlays and terracotta chessmen with ivory handles are found at Lothal. At Mohenjo-daro ivory combs were produced for export to Syria and elsewhere.... A small block sawn off a large tusk of the elephant was recovered from the ivory worker's shop at Lothal....

The stamp seals of Harappa, Mohenjo-daro, Lothal ... and other sites carved in intaglio with beautiful animal figures are masterpieces of art noted for realism. The calligraphy of the short inscriptions on the seals is known for the symmetry of the signs engraved. From the minute muscular details and the moods of the animals, both domesticated and wild, shown on the seals, it is obvious that the seal-engravers had studied them at close quarters. The realistic rendering of the elephant, tiger, rhinoceros, water buffalo, bull and goat in various moods is remarkable for the age. The Harappans maintained their individuality both in the shape of the seals and in the script adopted for communicating their ideas. More than 3000 Indus seals and sealings have been found throughout the Indus Empire. But their concentration and use was mostly in industrial and commercial centres like Mohenjo-daro, Harappa, Lothal.... Being the major port of the Indus Empire, Lothal sealed the outgoing cargo in the warehouse....

The purpose of producing seals was mainly commercial as attested to by 71 terracotta sealings from Lothal. They bear impressions of the seal on the face and that of the packing material such as cloth, reeds and cords on the back. Obviously seals must have been used for sealing cargo wrapped in cloth or bamboo mats and secured by cords. These impressions reveal the whole process of sealing. After wrapping the packages with vegetable mats, reeds or textiles they were secured by tying cords around them. Labels of wet clay covering the knots were impressed with seals in order to authenticate the contents and secure them against pilfering. Thereafter wet clay on the margin of seal-impressions was pressed with finger. Perhaps the finger impression was a further authentication of the genuineness of the contents and the source which could be verified by the recipient....

Although the purpose of the seals was commercial, it is now possible to postulate on the basis of the motifs and inscriptions that they had a religious context. The owner of the seal got engraved the figure of a mythical or real animal which symbolised the deity he venerated, for instance, unicorn, bull, goat, elephant, buffalo and even tiger and rhinoceros.... A few terracotta sealings from Harappa bear the motif of the fire-altar, or tree alone. The bull and unicorn motifs are seen below an inscription on one surface of a Lothal sealing, and on the other, there is an inscription. Such sealings seem to have served as tokens or prayer tablets or identity cards of the person carrying them. A similar use can be attributed to the tiny seals of Harappa and Mohenjo-daro....

The seal-cutters used agate, steatite, terracotta and rarely ivory and conch shell. The whole process of sawing blocks of steatite to required size, cutting a button on the back, engraving the motif and script, and smoothening and perforating the button can be followed at Lothal and Mohenjo-daro from the unfinished seals.

The sudden disappearance of seals except for the few in the late levels of Mohenjo-daro and Lothal ... should be attributed not only to the stoppage of long-distance trade but also to the declining economic condition. This does not imply that the Late Harappans became suddenly

illiterate.   Survival of writing is attested to on a
few Late Harappan seals and pottery.

Rao, S.R. *Dawn and Devolution of the Indus Civilization*.
New Delhi: Aditya Prakashan, 1991. Pp. 171-173, 181-
183, 185-186, 193-195.

ARYAN SOCIETY FROM THE RIG VEDA

The thousand years between approximately 1500 and 500 B.C.E. is called the Vedic age in Indian history. The period is further divided into the Rig Vedic age and the late Vedic age; the former, between around 1500 to 1000, is named after the *Rig Veda,* a collection of over a thousand hymns and prayers.

The *Rig Veda* is the earliest textual source for the history and culture of India. Although primarily concerned with religion, the hymns also supply information on the manners, morals, and values of the Aryans who invaded and settled northwestern India. Dr. P. Basu's *Indo-Aryan Polity,* from which this reading is taken, draws primarily from the Vedas.

QUESTIONS:

1) What are the names and functions of the three Aryan castes?
2) Who are the *dasyus* and how do they differ from the Aryans?
3) How did most Indians make their living during the Vedic age?

The caste system in India is clearly recognized in the period of the Atharva Veda [composed c. 1000 B.C.E.].... The Rig Veda, of course, recognizes the Aryans as distinguished from the Dasyus, the non-Aryans, but further than this it is not possible to assert with regard to the caste system in the Rig Veda....

The word Kshatriya ... occurs in many passages of the Rig Veda, its usual meaning being royal or of divine authority. As a class the Kshatriyas are recognized as warriors. In one passage Agni is said to possess the Kshatriya quality of strength. Another use of the word clearly recognizes the military order....

In all the above passages the Kshatriyas are spoken of as the rulers, they being powerful and, as warriors, wielding *kshtra* or dominion....

The professional priesthood is seen practically from the very beginning of the Rig Vedic period. Its position is entirely separate from that of monarchy.... [This] fact is clear from the subsequent history of the race during which, in spite of the predominant influences of the priests, there was no attempt on their part to become king.... The Brahmanas ... are called the progenitors and presenters of Soma [a hallucinigent drink and the god of that drink], which gives a glimpse of their function at the sacrifice. Perhaps they are also called observers of truth and they are invoked for protection. So that this class of men are looked upon as superior order of beings capable of some of the godly functions, perhaps supposed to have acquired by their professional contact with the deity. The Brahmanas, in their performance of sacrificial rites, had to chant *mantras* [prayers], sometimes throughout the night ... or throughout the year ... perhaps during the sacrificial session.... They also practised penance throughout the year, being observant of their vows.... They are called learned because they possess the investigated Brahma consisting of knowledge, or divine lore, and thought and wisdom....

The the Vaisya, and the Sudra as different castes appear ... in the last Mandala of the Rig Veda.

The third class was the agricultural people, practically the whole population being included under this. Of course, there are passages in the Rig Veda where it is doubtful what exactly is the idea conveyed by the word *vis* [from which the word *vaisya* derives]. The most consistent meaning can be gathered only by interpreting it as settlement or dwelling.... The word has again been used in connection with the Arya people [as opposed to *jana*, meaning all people, which would include the Dasas].....

Dasa is used for the non-Aryans, as also *dasyu*. But *dasa* equally refers to slaves who were under the control of the Aryans. The fact perhaps is that some of the conquered people were slain, others not exactly conquered were allowed to live independently, while the prisoners of war who escaped death were converted into slaves. In one passage the deity is asked to give, among other things, troops of *dasas*. This would not be a boon but a curse if it is interpreted to mean free non-Aryans, hostile to the Aryans.... The possession of slaves is compared to that of numerous cattle, they being liable to be given away for the enjoyment of the donee....

A series of questions naturally arises as to [the *dasa*'s] historic position, the principal points of their differences from the Aryans, their organization and mode of life, their wealth, and their civilization.

These aborigines have been repeatedly referred to in the Rig Veda either as the *dasyu* or *dasa* ... as contrasted with the Aryas [Aryans]. Indra ... attacks and slays with his thunderbolt the *dasyus* and the *simyus*. That the *dasyus* and

the *simyus* were not Aryans is certain, but the doubt remains whether *dasyus* and *simyus* refer to different classes among the aborigines. This cannot, at this distant date, be ascertained. The next passage on the point speaks of the thunderbolt armed with which Indra goes on destroying the cities of the *dasyus*....

The main difference between the *dasyu* and the Aryans must have been one of religion. In the early stages of a nation's growth, particularly of the Aryans, the religious notions pervade their whole being. Gods being thrust into every successful act as its cause, and the belief being universal that the performance of religious rites according to certain fixed unalterable rules only would please the gods, the natural consequence is that the race continually fights against aliens even when there may not be any necessity for it. Caution is required that the rites, etc., are not contaminated by even an unconscious admixture of barbarian customs.... In the Rig Veda the non-Aryans are repeatedly spoken of in derogation as to their religious rites, which differed from the Aryans.... The *daysu* has been described ... as impious, perhaps meaning without devotion. A severe verse occurs in the Rig Veda in which the *dasyu* is called without sacrifice, and other uncharitable names, and the main cause of offence on the part of the *dasyu* seems to be that he does not perform sacrifices after the Aryan method....

The non-Aryans possessed cities or forts [purah].... Indra is said to have gone on destroying the *dasi purah*. The combined effort of Indra and Agni is the subject of another verse which goes to overthrow ninety strongholds ruled over by the *dasas*....

Another distinguishing feature of the non-Aryans seems to be their black skin. Indra punishes the aggressors by tearing off the black skin. This seems to refer to flaying alive....

[The] references to [the *dasyus'*] wealth ... though few in number, are scattered throughout the whole of the Rig Veda. Mention of their wealth is made when the deity is asked to slay every one of them and bestow upon the worshippers the wealth belonging to them, so that here the amount of the wealth, whatever it might consist of, is coveted by the Aryas.... In another passage, the deity is said to have carried off the wealth of one of the aboriginal chiefs, after demolishing his cities. Again, Indra is asked to cut off the foe as an old pruner cuts off the protruding branch of a creeper and humble the *dasa* so that the worshippers may divide his accumulated treasure....

In later Samhitas and particularly in the Brahmanas [appendices of the Rig Veda], we find reference to some classes, called the outcastes, who could not be touched or with whom it would be derogatory to eat together....

Turning to the settlement of the families on land, we find that the Vedic Aryans lived in villages. Whether these villages were close to one another or were scattered far and wide, and, if so, whether there were roads to connect them, cannot be ascertained from the Rig Veda. But the universal practice of certain religious rites and the substantial unity in the development of Vedic life point to the probability that they used to be either close to one another or had means to go from one place to another.... [As Aryans settled in India] They might have gone along the five rivers of the Punjab, and there is evidence to support that they reached Sind and knew the ocean.... There is additional ground to suppose in the case of Vedic Aryans that they did not go to the interior. The non-Aryans were a powerful race, and the frequent hymns of victories and prayers for protection from the Asuras and Dasyus clearly prove that they were harassed by the latter.... Later on, of course, with the pressure of population, they had to move to the east and south-east.... All this expansion must have been towards the end of the Rig Veda period....

The existence of villages is seen beyond all doubt even in the Rig Vedic period. The resplendent Agni is invoked as the protector of the people in villages. The mighty Rudra is propitiated in another skola [verse] in order that all things in the village may be well nourished and exempt from disease.... Cattle are spoken of as hastening to the village....

The question can pertinently be raised ... whether the Aryans at this stage lived a pastoral or an agricultural life. The answer to this can, it seems, be given more or less definitely. They were settling down to a life of agriculture and indeed agriculture developed very highly. But at the same time pasturage was undertaken universally....

Of all the animals the cow was undoubtedly the most important, as we would naturally expect from a people who are yet primarily pastoral. *Go*, denoting cow, is repeatedly mentioned in the Rig Veda as requiring the special protection of the gods; this shows the important functions performed by this animal in the economy of the primitive life.... The proverbial motherly instincts [of cows] are perceived and recognized in [one] hymn where cows in their stalls long for their calves. The Maruts shower abundant food upon the worshippers as a milch cow gives milk to her calf.... Another prayer to the Aswins gives cows the position next to the worshippers, thus showing the great solicitude for cattle. They are recognized as such because cows are a means of nourishment. So, they pray that these may not stray from the house of the worshippers nor may they be separated from their calves.... Finally, we come across a whole hymn of which the subject is cow ... where cows are said to bring good fortune, showing that wealth primarily consisted of cattle.... They lie down in the stalls and are pleased with the treatment of men, i.e., they are very well cared for. They are also spoken of as prolific. Protection is asked against their loss, and against any hostile weapon falling upon them.... Protection is also sought for them against the dust-churning war horse coming in their midst. Thus protected, the cows of a sacrificer, pleasing the deity, wander about at large without fear.... Finally, Indra is asked to look after the nourishment of the cows and the vigour of the bull, since the invigoration of the deity (with milk and butter) depends upon them, milk and butter being dependent upon the cows bearing calves.

Agriculture must have been universal in the period of the Rig Veda.... There is almost a continuous reference to fields and cognate matters in the whole of the Rig Veda, showing the importance of agriculture.... The fields were not held in communal ownership but each householder had his separate share which belonged to him definitely. This is proved, among others, by the three prayers of Apala, daughter of Atri. When Indra, pleased with her, consented to grant her three boons, she asked him to cause three places to grow, viz., her father's bald head, his barren field, and her body.... This fact of individual ownership is further confirmed by references to the winning of lands....

From the available materials in the Rig Veda it is difficult to find out the grains that were produced by agriculture.... But one fact stands out as certain, that is, that the people of the time produced many kinds of grain. This is proved by the various names used. Probably it was an age during which they had just learnt the cultivation or use of some new products, but which, being recent, were not as yet given any special name.

Basu, Praphullachandra. *Indo-Aryan Polity, Being a Study of the Economic and Political Condition of India as Depicted in the Rig Veda*. London: King and Son, 1925. Pp. 32-43, 45-53, 81-82, 90.

CHINA'S LEGENDARY IDEAL RULERS

The Chinese traditionally believed that their history began around five thousand years ago when several semi-divine culture heroes invented agriculture, animal husbandry, and the other arts of civilization. These legendary heroes were followed by three emperors of exceptional ability and wisdom: Yao, Shun, and Yu, who ruled around 2200 B.C.E. Yu founded the first dynasty, the Hsia.

The *Shu Ching* or *Book of History* contains accounts of the virtuous lives and great deeds of the Three Emperors. This and other canonical books (*Book of Change*, *Book of Poetry*, and *Book of Rites*) were reputedly edited by Confucius, who also wrote short introductions to explain each work. Although archaeological digs this century have revealed much information about early Chinese civilization, they have not authenticated the lives and reigns of the Three Emperors. Historians and philologists date the *Book of History* to the middle and late Chou dynasty (c. 1122-256 B.C.E.). Thus while writings pertaining to the Chou dynasty are generally authentic, accounts of earlier eras are likely based on unreliable oral traditions.

Although accounts of early sage rulers in the *Book of History* are unreliable as history, they do teach us about Chinese ideals. This reading is taken from the "Canon of Yao," "the Canon of Shun," and the "Tribute of Yu" in the *Book of History*. They tell why each was revered as a model ruler: for his wisdom, humility, personal virtue, and public spirit. Each moreover unselfishly set aside his son as heir to seek the best qualified successor. Before becoming ruler, Yu spent years channeling the major rivers of north China to eliminate chronic, devastating flooding. He also surveyed the land and assessed taxes equitably according to the productivity of the soil. His accomplishments earned him the title of Yu the Great. After Yu's death, a grateful people refused to honor his choice as successor and instead set his son on the throne. Thus, according to legend, began China's first hereditary dynasty, the Hsia, c. 2205-1766 B.C.E.

QUESTIONS:

1) What virtues did each Yao and Shun show that made them sages?
2) In the idealized Chinese political order, how did one become ruler?
3) How did Shun show filial piety toward his parents and how did that prepare him to be a good ruler?

Examining into antiquity, we find that the emperor Yao was called Fang-hsun. He was reverential, intelligent, accomplished, and thoughtful,--naturally and without effort. He was sincerely courteous, and capable of all complaisance. The display of these qualities reached into the four extremities of the empire, and extended from earth to heaven. He was able to make the able and virtuous distinguished, he thence proceeded to the love of the nine classes of his kindred, who all became harmonious. He also regulated and polished the people of his domain, who all became brightly intelligent. Finally, he united and harmonized the myriad states of the empire.... The result was universal accord.

[As he grew old] The emperor said, "Who will search out for me a man according to the times, whom I may raise and employ?" Fang-ts'e said, "There is your heir-son Chu, who is highly intelligent." The emperor said, "Alas! he is insincere and quarrelsome." ... Hwan-tow said, "Oh! there is the minister of Works, whose merits have just been displayed in various ways." The emperor said, "Alas! when unemployed, he can talk; but when employed, his actions turn out differently. He is respectful only in appearance, See! the floods assail the heavens." ...
The emperor said, "Point out some one among the illustrious, or set forth one from among the poor and mean." All in the court said to the emperor, "There is an unmarried man among the lower people, called Shun of Yu." The emperor said, "Yes, I have heard of him. What is his character?" His Eminence said, "He is the son of a blind man. His father was obstinately unprincipled; his step-mother was insincere; his half brother Hsiang was arrogant. He has been able, however, by his filial piety to live in harmony with them, and to lead them gradually to self-government, so that they no longer proceed to great wickedness." The emperor said, "I will try him! I will wive him, and then see his behaviour with my two daughters." On this he gave orders, and sent down his two daughters to the north of the Kwei, to be wives in the family of Yu....

[Being tried with state responsibilities] Shun carefully set forth the beauty of the five cardinal duties; and they came to be universally observed. Being appointed to be General Regulator, the affairs of each department were arranged in their proper seasons. Having to receive the princes from the four quarters of the empire, they all were docilely submissive. Being sent to the great plains at the foot of the mountains, amid violent wind, thunder, and rain, he did not go astray.

The emperor said, "Come, you Shun. I have consulted you on all affairs, and examined your words, and found that your words can be carried into practice.... Do you ascend the imperial throne." Shun wished to decline in favour of some one more virtuous, and not to consent to be successor. On the first day, of the first month however, he received Yao's retirement from the imperial duties in the temple of the Accomplished Ancestor....

Shun instituted the division of the empire into twelve provinces, raising the altars upon twelve hills in them. He likewise deepened the rivers.

He gave delineation of the statutory punishments, enacting banishment as a mitigation of the five great inflictions; with the whip to be employed in the magistrates' courts, the stick to be employed in schools, and money to be received for redeemable crimes. Inadvertent offences and those which might be caused by misfortune were to be pardoned, but those who offended presumptuously or repeatedly were to be punished with death. "Let me be reverent...." He said, "Let compassion rule in punishment."

[Great floods inundated the land causing widespread devastation. Yu was given the task of easing the floods.] Yu divided the land. Following the course of the hills, he hewed down the woods. He determined the high hills and great rivers.... [After twelve arduous years] throughout the nine provinces ... order was effected:--the grounds along the waters were everywhere made habitable; the hills were cleared of their superfluous wood and sacrificed to; the sources of the streams were cleared; the marshes were well banked; access to the capital was secured for all within the four seas.

A great order was effected in the six magazines of material wealth; the different parts of the country were subjected to an exact comparison, so that contributions of revenue could be carefully adjusted according to their resources. The fields were all classified with reference to the three characters of the soil; and the revenues for the Middle region were established....

Shun said, "... is there any one who can vigorously display his merits, and give wide development to the undertakings of the emperor, whom I may make General Regulator, to aid me in all affairs, and manage each department according to its nature?" All in the court said, "There is baron Yu, the superintendent of Works." The emperor said, "Yes! Yu, you have regulated the water and the land. In this office exert yourself." Yu did obeisance with his head to the ground, and wished to decline in favour of the minister of Agriculture...." The emperor said, "Yes; but do you go, and undertake the duties." ...

Every three years there was an examination of merits, and after three examinations the underserving were degraded, and the deserving promoted. By this arrangement the duties of all the departments were fully discharged....

[Like Yao, Shun too began a search for the best qualified man to succeed him.] The emperor said, "Come, you, Yu. I have occupied the imperial throne for thirty and three years. I am between ninety and a hundred years old, and the laborious duties weary me. Do you, eschewing all indolence, take the leadership of my people." Yu said, "My virtue is not equal to the position; the people will not repose in me...." [He then recommended others.]

The emperor said, "Come Yu. The inundating waters filled me with dread, when you realized all that you represented, and accomplished your task,--thus showing your superiority to other men. Full of toilsome earnestness in the service of the State, and sparing in your expenditure on your family; and this without being full of yourself or elated; you again show your superiority to other men. Without any prideful presumption, there is no one in the empire to contest with you the palm of ability; without any boasting, there is no one in the empire to contest with you the claim of merit. I see how great is your virtue, how admirable your vast achievements. The determinate appointment of Heaven rests on your person; you must eventually ascend the throne of the great sovereign. The mind of man is restless,--prone to err; its affinity for the right way is small. Be discriminating, be undivided, that you may sincerely hold fast the Mean. Do not listen to unsubstantiated words; do not follow undeliberated plans. Of all who are to be loved, is not the sovereign the chief? Of all who are to be feared, are not the people the chief? If the multitude were without the sovereign, whom should they sustain aloft? If the sovereign had not the multitude, there would be none to guard the country for him. Be reverent. Carefully demean yourself on the throne which you will occupy, respectfully cultivating the virtues which are to be desired in you. If within the four seas there be distress and poverty, your Heaven-conferred revenues will come to a perpetual end. It is the mouth which sends forth what is good, and gives rise to war. My words I will not repeat."

Legge, James, ed. and trans. *The Chinese Classics*. Vol. 3: *The Shoo King*. Rpt. Hong Kong: Hong Kong Univ. Press, 1960. Pp. 15, 17, 23-24, 26-27, 29, 31-32, 38-39, 42-43, 50-51, 57, 60-63, 92, 141.

FROM DRAGON BONES TO A QUEEN'S TOMB

▶ Animal Mask, from Shang Bronze Vessel

Although traditional Chinese historical accounts accepted the Shang dynasty as historic (c. 1760-1122 B.C.E.) they were unsupported by either documentary or archaeological evidence. Since the sixth century there were accounts of sporadic discoveries of inscribed bones from around Yinshu ("Waste of Yin", reputedly the last capital of the Shang dynasty) by peasants digging graves, but no scholarly investigations followed. Since about the tenth century, connoisseurs have collected bronze vessels reportedly from Shang graves. The high price such antique pieces fetched led to the looting of ancient tombs, and also to the faking of antiquities; again there were no systematic investigation of reputed Shang sites.

The "discovery" and scientific study of inscribed oracle bones from the Shang dynasty at the end of the nineteenth century has revolutionized our knowledge of ancient China and led to the development of scientific archaeology of early China. The first selection below tells how it happened.

Scientific excavations of the last Shang capital began at Anyang in 1928 and continued until the Japanese invasion of China in 1937. They were resumed in the 1950s and have continued sporadically since.

According to tradition the last twelve kings of the Shang ruled from Yin (Anyang) for 273 years. Tens of thousands of oracle bones have been found at sites around Anyang; they give abundant contemporary written information of the late Shang. Presumably Shang people also wrote on silk and bamboo or wood but they have perished. Some bronze ritual vessels also have writing cast into them, but they are short and contain only the owners' names and the uses of the vessels.

Only the king was permitted to consult his ancestors and gods through oracles cast by priests. Each oracle contained a question, or was a report of some event. The question was inscribed on the prepared tortoise shell or scapula bone of an ox; a heated metal rod was inserted into a previously drilled indentation in the shell; the answer lay in the shape of the crack caused by the heat. The diviner noted down the answer, and often later added the outcome. The used oracles bones were stored.

Study of the oracle bones has yielded much information about the Shang, says David Keightley, an expert on Shang inscriptions, "because the topics covered by the divinations are numerous and varied. [They are] concerned with the content, nature, and timing of religious sacrifices ... weather, agriculture, hunting, warfare, travel plans, selection of personnel, sickness, dreams, childbearing, and so on. Many of these are subjects that we would regard as falling within the secular province of the meteorologist, farmer, hunter, doctor, psychoanalyst, obstetrician, and so on, but the presence of these topics on the bones indicates that for the Shang ruler they had their supernatural dimensions. It seems that virtually all political questions were religious questions too, and therefore legitimate topics ... for divination.... [Oracle inscriptions are important also] because it is the king who, either directly or by proxy, divined.... The king was a theocrat who presumably ruled in part by virtue of his extraordinary ability to communicate with the ultrahuman powers. The bone records, therefore, are not simply a discarded priestly archive. They are religious-political records of decision making, incantation, reassurance, and communication at the highest level of theocratic government. If a topic does appear in the bones, we are justified in thinking that it was a topic of central concern to the Shang kings and--since there are likely to have been few atheists in a Bronze Age theocracy--to Shang state as a whole.... The oracle-bone inscriptions, in short, are "hard" documents in the best historiographical sense" [David N. Keightley, *Sources of Shang History The Oracle-Bone Inscriptions of Bronze Age China* (Berkeley: Univ. of California Press, 1978), pp. 136, 153].

Two categories of people often mentioned in the oracle inscriptions are the *tzu* or royal princes and the *fu* or royal consorts. Generally the fu are not mentioned by name, and most questions about them concern childbearing and their participation at ritual ceremonies. However at least one hundred and seventy inscriptions bear the name of Fu Hao, an important consort of King Wu Ting, fourth king to rule at Yin, and she is mentioned in many contexts in addition to her childbearing such as the estates and the walled towns she ruled, military expeditions she led, and her presiding at sacrifices on the king's behalf. They tell us she died before the king and was given a posthumous title.

In 1975 a group of hitherto undisturbed tombs were discovered in a corner of the royal cemetery. The largest and most elaborate (although small compared with some of the looted tombs discovered earlier) belonged to Fu Hao. Part of the archaeological report on the excavation of Lady Fu's tomb is quoted in the second selection.

A great quantity of data is now available on the Shang culled from several decades of archaeological investigation around Anyang and sites all over China. Kwang-chih Chang, a leading authority on ancient China, gives an account of some aspects of Shang life, quoted in the third selection.

QUESTIONS:

1) What are oracle bones and why are they important?
2) Who was Fu Hao and what do we learn from her tomb?
3) Why were farming and hunting both important to the Shang?

Formerly, long before this year [1899], in the farming land on the bank of the Huan River, north of the village of Hsiao-t'un, located in the Anyang district of Honan Province, oracle bones (*chia ku*) were frequently found. The villagers treated them as things of medical value, so collected them and sold them to drugstores; they were generally known as dragon bones (*lung ku*).

Li Ch'eng, a barber and a native of the village, made a business of dealing in dragon bones; he is now dead. The so-called dragon bones, are, in fact, largely oracle bones; and according to the folklore prevailing in Hsiao-t'un village, the majority of these bones bear inscriptions. The villagers sold them either retail or wholesale. In retail dealings, the dragon bones were first ground into a powder known by its native name as "knife point medicine" (*tao chien yo*), which Chinese medical practitioners

considered effective in healing cuts and surgical wounds. The buyers in the wholesale market were usually managers of Chinese drugstores. The price charged was six cash per catty [according to the money system then in use in China, one thousand cash made up a tael or about one and a third ounces of silver; a catty was equivalent to about one and a third pound in weight]. The inscribed pieces at that time had no market value, and were considered worthless; so it was the usual practice among the sellers to polish off those inscriptions, before the dragon bones were brought to the market....

In this year, Liu T'ieh-yun of Tan-t'u was visiting in the capital [Peking] as a house guest of Wang I-yung. the host of Liu T'ieh-yun was attacked by malarial fever. The doctor's prescriptions included an ingredient of decayed tortoise shell purchased at the drugstore Ta-jen-t'ang [name of the store] in Ts'ai-shih-k'ou [street name]. On the tortoise shells Liu Tieh-yun saw seal characters (*chuan wen*), which he picked out and showed to his host; both of them were somewhat astonished at this discovery. Wang, a student of bronze inscriptions, immediately realized that these tortoise shells must be ancient. He went to the drugstore, to inquire about the source of supply of these ingredients. The manager told him that they came form T'ang-yin and Anyang of Honan province. They were sold at a very low price.... Liu T'ieh-yun went to the drugstores in the city and purchased them all.

* * * * *

In July, 1976, the Institute of Archaeology of the Chinese Social Sciences Academy excavated a tomb to the northwest of Hsiao-t'un in Anyang of the late Shang period (numbered as M5). That tomb was well preserved, and contained a rich array of burial goods. It is noteworthy that a large number of bronze vessels from the tomb were inscribed with the two characters "Fu Hao." That the tomb contains many pieces inscribed with the characters "Fu Hao," and other associated inscribed bronze pieces makes clear that Fu Hao was the owner of M5 tomb....

A wood coffin [had originally been] placed inside a wood-lined chamber, but since the chamber is under the water table, and because both wood lining of the chamber and coffin have rotted ... it is only possible to give some general information about the inner grave itself....

Judging from traces of red and black lacquer and the patterns they formed ... and from the traces of coarse linen like fabric and fine silken type fabric patterns, it is possible to surmise that the woodwork of the chamber, the coffin and its contents were of high quality.

No traces of human skeleton were found inside what remained of the coffin. Thus it is not possible to determine the person buried therein....

At least sixteen humans [sacrificial victims] were [also] buried in the tomb.... It has been determined that four were males, one a youth; two were females; two were children; the sex of the remaining eight cannot be determined. At least one of the sacrificial victims had been killed previous to burial, perhaps by being cut in two at the waist.

There were also six dogs buried in the grave....

More than one thousand six hundred objects were buried in the grave, in addition to almost seven thousand pieces of cowrie shells [used as large denomination money]. Of the one thousand six hundred plus buried objects, there were more than four hundred and forty bronze pieces, over five hundred and ninety jade items, over five hundred and sixty bone objects; in addition there were over seventy stone objects, several of each ivory carvings, pottery objects, more than ten shell objects, two made from sea shells and one from a large sea shell.

After preliminary study of the burial items, and the deciphering of the inscriptions on the bronze vessels, it would seem that most of them had been the accumulated possessions of the owner of the grave; and that a minority of the pieces had been made expressly as sacrificial items for the person buried. Their sources likely were: (1) objects made for the owner during her lifetime, for example the bronze vessels marked with the characters "Fu Hao"; (2) ornaments and "toys" that had belonged to the grave owner during her lifetime, for example the large quantities of carved jade and bone ornaments and pendants, and jade objects of art; (3) tribute gifts from other nations...; (4) sacrificial bronze vessels ordered by members of the royal family for the grave owner and inscribed with [her ancestral temple name] "Shih Mu Hsing"; (5) sacrificial bronze vessels ordered by nobles for the grave owners...; (6) small numbers of [other] items expressly made for inclusion in the grave; and (7) objects obtained through "exchanges" such as those made from sea shells.

* * * * *

The wild animals, especially wild boar, elephant, sika deer, and water deer, were dwellers of the forests and marshes near and to the east of Anyang, and some of them as well as other mammals such as the mountain goat and the antelope may have come from the T'ai-hang Mountains to the west. Many of these animals undoubtedly provided meat, skin, horn, and bone for the Shang, but hunting of them was also a major royal sport.

To what extent wild animals were depended upon for food by the Shang is a debatable point. Insofar as the hunting records in the oracle bone inscriptions are concerned, hunting was more a sport than a subsistence activity, but the game that was hunted was presumably to be consumed. From hunting records, at least one thing was quite certain: the forests were densely inhabited. One such record, dated to King Wu Ting's reign, lists the following game:

Divined on the day Wu-wu
Ku made the inquiry:
We are going to chase at "Ch'iu"; any capture?
Hunting on this day, (we) actually capture:
Tigers, one;
Deer, forty;
Foxes, one hundred and sixty-four;
Hornless deer, one hundred and fifty-nine;
and so forth.

Hunts thus described were numerous....

Domesticated and tamed animals were probably of much greater importance as sources of meat, skin, antler, and bones, and some of these were also of ritual significance. These include dog, cattle, water buffalo, sheep, horse, pig, and, in all probability, the elaphure [a kind of deer].... The elaphure was not domesticated in the same sense as the others, but elaphure herds are sometimes thought to have been fenced in to assure a steady supply, as a supplement to hunted animals. The water buffalo, on the other hand, was a fully domesticated animal and a major source of shoulder blades for the diviners.

Dogs, cattle, sheep, horses, pigs, and chickens were used for ritual purposes and found in burials. On these, all but the horse were identified also in garbage heaps and were, thus, consumed. The horse, however, was probably used exclusively to pull the chariots. It was probably not raised locally and had to be imported. Oracle records mentioned the "entry" of horses ....

There is no evidence that land was privately owned during any of the Shang period. On the contrary, in Shang divinations farming fields on the northwestern border that were reportedly being attacked by an alien state were referred to as ... "My fields" or "our fields" [that is, the king's]....

New land was cleared and opened for farming on the order of the king.... [Trees were barked] to kill them and ready them for burning the following year. [Barking was used] ... because of the lacking of effective (e.g. metal) tree-felling implements.... Shang implements that are attributable to uses in agriculture were probably manufactured of wood, stone, bone, and shell for the most part. Despite occasional claims to the contrary, bronze was not an oft-used material for implements....

The fact that with the aid of such primitive tools (wooden *lie* [plow or digging stick], stone and shell sickles, and stone axes and spades) the Shang were able to produce enough food to build a great civilization is sufficient grounds for speculating that it was at the level of labor that the Shang agriculture received its greatest energy input, and the oracle bone records clearly bear this out....

Lineage groups (*tsu*) appear to have been occupational units engaging in the production of various industrial goods and in specialized services.... The names of these *tsu* are often occupation-related: T'ao (pottery); Shih (flag); Ch'i (cooking-pot); Ch'ang shuo and Wei shuo (wine vessels); So (cordage); Fan (horse plume); Fan (fence).

[Among manufacturing bronze was the most important] ... two major bronze workshops have been located in the An-yang areas.... At the latter site, remains of a ground house, approximately 8 by 4 meters and built on rammed earth foundations and with rammed earth walls, were found associated with clay molds and crucible fragments. Since both ground houses and rammed earth architecture were often associated with people of higher status, one is tempted to infer that bronze smiths, or at least the higher-status ones among them enjoyed perquisites reserved for the upper class.

Most if not all of the court officials, including the king's consorts and princes, appear to have been granted title to land with income from harvests and walled towns for their *tsu* people. ...The lords whose land was within the outer limits of the capital were able to serve on the royal court as fulltime officials, but the lords whose land was outside the capital's limits-- sometimes quite far away--presumably moved between their court jobs and their own towns under some kind of arrangement....

Each of the lords represented his *tsu*, his walled town, and his land of whatever size, with the man himself, his *tsu*, and the town all known by the same name....

Li, Chi. *Anyang*. Seattle: Univ. of Washington Press, 1977. P. 8 [from an account by Tung Tso-ping, the first and foremost scholar on oracle bone inscriptions]. *Kaogu Xuebao*. 1977. No. 2. Peking: Institute of Archaeology, Chinese Academy of Social Sciences. Pp. 1, 59-60, 62. Translation by Jiu-Hwa Lo Upshur. Chang, Kwang-chih. *Shang Civilization*. New Haven: Yale University Press, 1980. Pp. 142-143, 193, 223, 225, 230-231, 233.

Woman's Work

THE RISE OF THE CHOU DYNASTY AND LIFE AROUND 1000 B.C.E.

The house of Chou originated in the Plain of Chou in the Wei River valley in north China. The Chou people shared the same cultural roots as the Shang further east, but were considered rude country cousins by the more advanced Shang people. The Shang kings gave the Chou leader the title of Chief of the West because he held at bay the barbarians who lived further west.

As the Shang dynasty weakened in the twelfth century B.C.E., the Chou rose to challenge it under an able ruler called King Wen (the Accomplished or Cultured) who began to build an alliance to undermine the Shang. Wen was succeeded by his son King Wu (the Martial) who led a campaign that toppled the Shang monarchy c. 1122 B.C.E.; the last Shang king was killed in a fire that consumed his palace in Anyang. Wu, however, died before he could consolidate the Chou dynasty, leaving his son, still a child, on the throne. The boy's uncle and regent, the Duke of Chou, finished the campaigns that solidified Chou power, established the institutions and statutes that made the Chou the longest dynasty in Chinese history (1122-256 B.C.E.), and instructed his nephew in the duties of kingship. His tasks finished, and his nephew now an adult, the Duke of Chou ended his regency and retired. Their characters and actions have made Kings Wen and Wu and the Duke of Chou paragons of virtue and statesmanship to later Chinese rulers.

The *Shih Ching* (*Book of Poetry*), one of the revered classics, is a collection of ancient verse concerning many subjects. The first three poems cited below deal with the qualities of Kings Wen and Wu and the Duke of Chou that made them the universally admired rulers, and won for them the mandate of heaven, or heaven's permission to rule. They also warn future Chou kings to rule wisely in order to deserve the continuation of heaven's mandate. Because surviving ancient texts are mainly concerned with government, politics, war, and the lives and doings of the high and mighty, the verses in the *Shih Ching* dealing with the lives of ordinary men and women are especially precious. The last selection deals with the life cycle of ordinary people.

QUESTIONS:

1) What qualities made King Wen and the Duke of Chou great men?
2) Describe the role and power of heaven in Chinese politics.
3) What did men and women do respectively in the countryside?

KING WEN

The royal Wen now rests on high,
Enshrined in brightness of the sky.
Chou as a state had long been known,
And Heaven's decree at last was shown.
Its lords had borne a glorious name;
God kinged them when the season came.
King Wen ruled well when earth he trod;
Now moves his spirit near to God.

A strong-willed, earnest king was Wen,
And still his fame rolls widening on.
The gifts that God bestowed on Chou
Belong to Wen's descendants now.
Heaven blesses still with gifts divine
The hundred scions of his line;
And all the officers of Chou
From age to age more lustrous grow.

More lustrous still from age to age,
All reverent plans their zeal engage;
And brilliant statesmen owe their birth
To this much-favored spot on earth.
They spring like products of the land,--
The men by whom the realm doth stand.
Such aid their numerous bands supply,
That Wen rests tranquilly on high.

Deep were Wen's thoughts, sustained his ways;
His reverence lit its trembling rays.
Resistless came great Heaven's decree;
The sons of Shang must bend the knee;--
The sons of Shang, each one a king,
In numbers beyond numbering.
Yet as God spoke, so must it be:--
The sons of Shang all bent the knee.

Now each to Chou his homage pays,--
So dark and changing are Heaven's ways.
When we pour our libations here,
The officers of Shang appear,
Quick and alert to give their aid;--
Such is the service by them paid,
While still, they do not cast aside
The cap and broidered ax,--their pride.
Ye servants of our line of kings,
Remember him from whom it springs.

Remember him from whom it springs;--
Let this give to your virtue wings.

Seek harmony with Heaven's great mind;--
So shall you surest blessing find.
Ere Shang had lost the nation's heart,
Its monarchs all with God had part
In sacrifice. From them you see
'Tis hard to keep high Heaven's decree.

'Tis hard to keep high Heaven's decree!
O sin not, or you cease to be.
To add true luster to your name,
See Shang expire in Heaven's dread flame.
For Heaven's high dealings are profound,
And far transcend all sense and sound.
From Wen your pattern you must draw,
And all the states will own your law.

TA MING (GRAND APPOINTMENT)

Heaven thus its grand appointment made,
And Wen to all the land displayed,
While still he ruled in Feng.
Hsin's eldest daughter was the wife,
Whom Heaven prepared to bless his life.
And take his virtuous mother's place.
And Heaven soon gave them further grace;
'Twas from King Wu spring.
Heaven kept and helped the child, until
Its summons to him came.
Then Wu marched forth to do its will,
Smote Yin [Shang], and won his fame.

Countless as forest leaves, Yin's hosts,
Collected from its utmost coasts,
Were marshaled in Mu's famous plain,
To meet King Wu;--but all in vain.
Chou to the crisis rose.
Wu viewed their multitude with fear,
But Shang-fu's words soon gave him cheer:--
"With you is God; your doubts dispel.
With Him as helper, we shall quell
The pride of all our foes."

Vast was the plain. Each sandal car,
That brightly shone amidst the war,
Dashed rapidly along.
Each team of steeds, black-maned and bay.
Against all obstacles made way.
Like mighty eagle on the wing,
Shang-fu was ever near the king.
Whose heart was thus made strong.

At the first charge Yin's troops gave way,
And took to shameful flight.
That morn a long and brilliant day
Displaced the previous night.

P'O FU (BROKEN AX)

We splintered our axes, and brought
Our hatchets all the same plight.
But the duke of Chou meant, when eastward he went,
What was wrong in those, four states to right.
Oh! the pity was great
Which he felt for their state!

Our axes and chisels we broke
To pieces, and splintered and rent.
But the duke of Chou meant, when eastward he went,
The four states all reformed to present.
Oh! the pity was good
That on them he bestowed!

Our axes we broke, and our clubs
To fragments were splintered and split.
But the duke of Chou meant, when eastward he went,
The four states in close union to knit.
Oh! the pity was rare
That he showed for them there!

CH'I YUEH (SEVENTH MONTH)

The seventh month sees the *Ho* [Mars?] go down the sky,
And in the ninth, the stores warm clothes supply.
Our first month's days, the wind blows cold and shrill;
Our second's days, wind hushed, the air is chill.
But for those clothes, and garments made of hair,
At year's end, how badly all would fare!
Our third month's days, their plows in hand they take,
And all the fourth the fields their home they make.
I wish my wife and children take my way,
And to the southern acres food convey
For those who toil. Appears the inspector then,
Surveys the fields, and cheers the working men,

The seventh month sees the *Ho* go down the sky,
And in the ninth, the stores warm clothes supply.
The warmth begins when come the days of spring,
And then their notes we hear the orioles sing.
See the young women, with their baskets high,
About the mulberry trees their labors ply!

The softest leaves, along the pathes, they seek,
To feed their silkworms, newly hatched and weak.
For such, as longer grow the days of spring,
In crowds they haste white southernwood to bring.
'Mongst them are some who grieve with wounded heart;--
To wed young lords, from parents soon they part!

The seventh month sees the *Ho* go down westward go;
The eighth, the reeds and sedges thickly grow.
The months the silkworms' eggs are hatched, they break
The mulberry branches, thus their leaves to take;
And where those branches stretch out far and high,
Hatchets and axes on them boldly ply,
While young trees only their leaves supply.
In the seventh month, the shrike's notes shrilly sound,
And on the eighth, twisting the hemp they're found.
Their woven fabrics, dark or yellow dyed,
Are valued highly over a circle wide.
Our brilliant red, the triumph of our art,
For young lords' lower robes is set apart.

In the fourth month, the snakeroot bursts the ear;
The shrill cicadas in the fifth we hear.
When comes the eighth, the ripened grain they crop,
And in the tenth the leaves begin to drop.
In our first month for badgers quest they make;
The wildcat also and the fox they take:--
These last furs for young lords to supply.
Our second month, there comes the hunting high,
When great and small attend our ruler's car,
And practice all the exercise of war.
The hunters hit the younger boars they find;
Those three years old are to the prince assigned.

The locust in the fifth month beats its thighs;
And in the sixth, its wings the spinner plies.
The next, we find the crickets in the field;
Under our eaves, the eighth, they lie concealed;
The ninth, they come and near our doorways keep;
The tenth, beneath our beds they slyly creep.
The rats we smoke out; chinks we fill up tight;--
And close each opening on the north for light,
And plaster wicker doors; then each one says,
"O wife and children, this year's toiling days
Are over, and soon another year will come;
Enter and dwell in this our cozy home."

For food the sixth month, plums and vines they spoil;
The seventh, the beans and sunflower seeds they boil;
The eighth, they strike the jujube dates all down;
The tenth, they reap the paddy full grown,

And with the grain make spirits against the spring,
Which to the bushy eyebrows comfort bring.
In the seventh month, their food the melons make;
And in the eighth, the bottle gourds they take.
The ninth, in soups hempseed they largely use,
Nor *Sonchus* leaves do they for these refuse.
The *ailanthus* foul, for other use not good,
They fell, and then for fuel burn the wood:--
'Tis thus the laborer is supplied with food.

In the ninth month, the yards, now stript and bare,
They for the produce of the fields prepare.
The tenth month sees the carrying all complete,--
Of early millets and the late, the wheat,
The hemp, the pulse,--whatever grain we eat.
This labor done, the husbandmen all say,
"Our harvest here is well secured. Away
To town, and see what for our houses there
We need to do, to put them in repair!
The reeds we'll gather while we have the light,
And firmly twist them into ropes at night.
Up on the roofs we'll haste with these in hand:--
Soon will the fields our time again demand."

Our second month, they, with harmonious blows,
Hew out the ice,--housed ere our third month close.
The following month, and in the early dawn,
They open the doors;--forth now may ice be drawn;
A lamb being offered, after rites of old,
With scallions flanked, to him who rules the cold.
In the ninth month, the cold begins, with frost;
The tenth their cornyards swept and clean they boast.
Good spirits, in two vessels kept, they take,
To help their joy, and this proposal make:--
"We'll kill both lambs and sheep," they joyous say,
"And to the ruler's quickly take our way.
We'll mount his hall; the massive cup we'll raise,
Wish him long life, the life of endless days."

Legge, James, trans. *Shih Ching* (*The Book of Poetry*). Rpt.
New York: Paragon, 1967. Pp. 168-173, 178-179, 331-
334, 336-338.

WARS AND SOCIAL MOBILITY DURING THE LATE CHOU

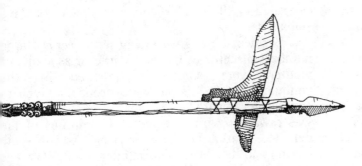

▶ **Iron Spear/Battle-ax**

The founders of the Chou Dynasty (1122-256 B.C.E.) established feudalism to regulate government and society. Under feudalism sons inherited their fathers' political positions and social status. Serfs cultivated the soil for their lords and were transferred with the land with every new enfeoffment (granting of a feudal domain). Artisans and merchants, who enjoyed a higher status than serfs, lived in or near walled towns.

This rigid social order broke down during the Eastern Chou era (770-256 B.C.E.). The endemic wars of these centuries destroyed the old order, as the hundreds of feudal states and their ruling clans at the beginning of the period were reduced to one. In a violent and unstable era, inherited status began to mean less, and ability more. Increasingly the states emancipated their serfs because free men fought harder and worked more diligently than serfs. Merchants too rose in social status because trade created wealth. Knights lost their prerogative as the fighting elite because innovations in warfare favored common soldiers.

Sociologists use abundant demographic data to study social mobility in modern societies. Hsu Cho-yun's excellent book *Ancient China in Transition* analyzes ancient texts and archaeological finds for evidence about social mobility in the Eastern Chou. These pages from his book show how wars affected both upward and downward mobility during the Eastern Chou Dynasty.

QUESTIONS:

1) How did the outcome of a war affect the social status of people involved?
2) Why did cavalry and infantry replace chariot fighting during this period?
3) What was life for a soldier like and why was it an attractive life for some men?

The Ch'un Ch'iu [722-481 B.C.E.] and Chan Kuo [403-221 B.C.E.] periods differ in many ways, but they share one point of similarity: a high frequency of wars. These periods were two stages of an epoch of transition from feudalism to a unified empire. In the Ch'un Ch'iu period the old order broke down; in the Chan Kuo period a new order began to emerge. The people living in the interval between the breakdown of the old and the establishment of the new were bewildered by the lack of standards for settling disputes and for maintaining harmonious relationships. Continuous struggle was the only proven means of survival, and was therefore held to be justified. Group fought with group, and state assaulted state; the war drums echoed for five centuries. It is not that the people of this time were unusually militant, but that they lived in a period of instability.

After centuries of bloody strife, only a handful of states, and finally just one, survived; all the others had been exterminated. Most of the old institutions having been uprooted, many members of the erstwhile upper classes were relegated to lower positions in the social scale.... A sharp increase in social mobility accompanied the profound changes in social stratification....

What became of the aristocrats of the subjugated states? In general, the extant records give no answer, although some bits of information have been more or less accidentally included. In Ch'un Ch'iu times a defeated ruler usually did not know whether his conqueror would spare his life; a coffin was carried by the vanquished ruler in making his surrender to the victor.... Unfortunate rulers were sometimes put to death as sacrificial victims....

The ritual for surrendering prisoners after a state's defeat is recorded in the *Tso Chuan* [China's oldest book of narrative history for 722 to 468 B.C.E.] in some detail. In 548 B.C. Cheng occupied the capital of Ch'en. The Ch'en ruler came to surrender holding the sacred tablet of the Ch'en earth deity, and ordered that men be separated from women and the two groups be bound to await the conquerors. One Cheng commander grasped the end of the line that fettered the Ch'en captives, and another Cheng officer counted them. In this case the Ch'en people were treated mercifully and none were deported to Cheng, although on other occasions captives were presented to the royal house of Chou or to other states in order to proclaim a victory....

The *Cho Chuan* records several other instances of the presentation of captives after a victory. In 706 B.C. the heir apparent of Cheng led an army to aid Ch'i in repelling an invasion by barbarians. The barbarians were soundly defeated, and the Cheng commander presented two captive generals and three hundred warriors to the ruler of Ch'i. In 655 B.C., after Chin conquered Kuo and Yu, the duke of Yu and his minister Ching Po were presented to Ch'in as part of the dowry of a Chin princess married to the duke of Ch'in. This is a clear example of the

degradation of a ruler and a minister to slave status....

Besides those given away as presents, large numbers of captives taken in battle or as spoils of victory were sometimes retained by the conquering state. Some were probably given to generals as rewards. In 594 B.C. a Chin general was rewarded with one thousand families of the defeated barbarians for having added new territory to the state. The small state of Wey was defeated in 500 B.C. by troops commanded by a powerful Chin minister who later appropriated for himself five hundred Wey families allegedly given as tribute to Chin. He resettled them on his estates and kept them as his own serfs....

It is safe to assume that many captives lost all prior social status and lived out their lives in strange lands, in a degraded states, and without hope of repatriation. It follows that every defeat or conquest of a state caused the social degradation of some former citizens of the defeated state; a downward social mobility took place. The number of people who thus lost status is not even approximately known, but since several hundred battles took place and one-hundred-odd states were extinguished during the Ch'un Ch'iu period, the number must have been quite large....

If war spelled disaster to the defeated nobility of the weaker states, it spelled opportunity to an emerging class of career military men, both warriors and tacticians, many of them from classes not previously eligible for service. Both the negative and positive social effects of war became more apparent as the Chan Kuo period progressed.

During and before the Ch'un Ch'iu period, fighting was the profession of the aristocracy alone. Driving a war chariot, a light, bouncing vehicle drawn by four galloping horses, required a long training period, as did accurate bow shooting from a lurching chariot. Driving and archery were listed among the six arts that were supposed to constitute the basic knowledge of a nobleman. Thus the military profession was limited to those familiar with these special techniques. Commoners served in battle only as auxiliary foot soldiers supposedly accompanying the chariots; they must have had difficulty in keeping up with vehicles drawn by four energetic horses. All accounts of early Ch'un Ch'iu wars describe only the charges of war chariots; until 570 B.C. we do not hear of the use of infantry as the only force on the battlefield.

The art of battle became so refined that even in fiercest combat chivalrous manners were required of the nobility. Strict procedures for driver and aide were followed in the delivery of challenges. Upon encountering an enemy of superior rank, a warrior had to take care not to offend him, especially if his foe happened to be a ruler. Polite words were exchanged even between a pursued charioteer and his pursuer. Courtesy in battle was the mark of a gentleman; a Chin warrior once took the trouble to shoot a deer and present it to his foe. A Chu general, challenging the Chin ruler in 632 B.C., said, with more than a mere turn of a phrase, "Will Your Excellency permit our knights and yours to play a game?" For these aristocrats, a war was also a game....

Toward the end of the Ch'un Ch'iu period, the role of infantry gradually became more significant. Wu and Yueh, the two giant states of the south, favored the use of foot soldiers, since the many lakes, rivers, and swamps of their territory limited the use of chariots. The king of Wu brought 10,000 foot soldiers with him on his trip north to the meeting of Huang-ch'ih in 482 B.C. In the battle between Ch'i and Lu in 484 B.C., the Lu army consisted of 7,000 armored soldiers....

The reasons for replacing chariots by infantry are not clear, although two causes may be suggested. The first is that chariots were quite expensive; the second, that they were inefficient. They were counted as units of wealth; a state would be said to possess about a thousand chariots while a noble family might own a hundred. A favorite of the chancellor of Ch'u was once envied for being rich enough to own horses for several chariots. Thus the expansion of an army consisting mostly of chariots could be prohibitively expensive to a state. A solution to the cost problem was the increase of foot soldier units in an army, which lessened the importance of the war chariots. The usual description of the military strength of a Chan Kuo state was "one thousand chariots, ten thousands of cavalry, and several hundred thousand armored soldiers." The number of chariots remained about the same as in

the Ch'un Ch'iu period, while other units of the army were greatly augmented or newly added.

Cavalry first made its appearance in China during the Chan Kuo period. The northern states apparently adopted the idea of cavalry warfare from nomadic tribes. King Wu-ling of Chao adopted the dress of the nomads as well as their horse tactics. Cavalry was probably a good substitute for war chariots, especially when high speed was required, as in charging and flanking movements....

The second reason for the replacement of chariots by infantry concerns the innate disadvantages of chariot warfare. As early as the beginning of the Ch'un Ch'iu period, a Cheng general, in a campaign of 714 B.C. against the barbarian Jung, worried over the danger of a raid on his chariots by the light infantry of the enemy. In swampy areas chariots were very easily trapped; Duke Hui of Chin was captured by Ch'in troops when his chariot stuck fast in the mud. Chariots were also of little use in mountainous terrain with poor roads or no roads at all....

The aristocratic warfare of chariots and archery finally gave way to infantry tactics using masses of foot soldiers advancing on foot with spears or swords in hand. Such tactics required less individual skill but many more soldiers; hence the Chan Kuo army differed radically from its Ch'un Ch'iu counterpart. Chivalry and gentlemanly conduct disappeared from combat; masses of tough foot soldiers mostly hardworking peasants inured to hardship and toil, replaced the gallant, chariot-riding nobleman....

Using the common people as a source of manpower, Han and Wei, the smallest states, each maintained an army of about 300,000 men, while Ch'in and Ch'u, the largest states, were able to support armies of about 1,000,000 men; these were mostly seasonal armies of peasant draftees. A large city such as Lin-tzu could have provided 210,000 men for military service from a population of 70,000 families.

Although we know very little about the common soldier and his deeds, it seems probable that many simple peasants found army life attractive and became career military men. This transformation is itself a type of large-scale social mobility when it involves great numbers of people. Changes of this kind have occurred frequently through history; but they are particularly important in a period such as the Chan Kuo, in which many wars are fought by great masses of common people....

We must also consider the upgrading of [people] who distinguished themselves in warfare. During periods of strife, a ruler is usually anxious to retain the services of those who have demonstrated skill in war and generous in rewarding them for further victories. In the Chan Kuo period, two types of military personnel were particularly needed: the fierce warrior and the cunning tactician.

The class of professional warriors had already emerged in the late Ch'un Ch'iu period, even while chivalry still survived among the aristocracy. In 552 B.C. the duke of Ch'i set up a system of conferring honorific titles on the valorous in battle and considered two of his fiercest warriors as candidates for the honor....

During the Chan Kuo period, even common soldiers had to maintain their physical strength. A Wei soldier had to be strong enough to carry armor, to pull a heavy crossbow, and to march 100 *li* [33 miles] in half a day carrying a full set of armor, weapons, and supplies. Those who met this standard were exempted from taxation and labor services. In the army of Ch'i, skill at boxing was much encouraged, and rewards were given for the killing of even one enemy in combat.

Able strategists and tacticians were also much in demand in Chan Kuo times. Sometimes both diplomatic talent and military ability were possessed by one person, as for example by Chang I and Kung-sun Yen. Both were clever in winning allies for their states and in isolating their enemies, and both were competent generals in the field.... A professional tactician known as Sun Tzu [author of *The Art of War*, a famous book on military tactics which is still studied in military academies the world over] or Sun Pin (Sun the Cripple) was so celebrated that he almost became a legend....

The way upward in the military hierarchy had already opened by the end of the Ch'un Ch'iu period; meritorious accomplishments on the battlefield were to be duly rewarded.... In 493 B.C. a war broke out between Cheng and Chin. The Chin commander announced that persons who performed well in battle were to be rewarded according to their status. Officials were to be enfeoffed; *shih* [knights] were to be given 100,000 *mou* [14,000 acres] of land; commoners, artisans, and merchants were to be given official positions; and slaves or serfs were to be freed. Thus there is no doubt that many people rose in social status at this time.

Cho-yun, Hsu. *Ancient China in Transition: An Analysis of Social Mobility, 722-222 B.C.* Stanford: Stanford Univ. Press, 1965. Pp. 53, 59, 61-2, 68-73.

DEDUCING CONDITIONS OF LIFE IN THE OLDEST CIVILIZATION OF THE AMERICAS

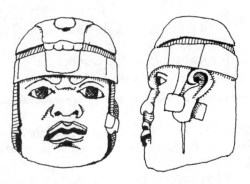

▶ **Olmec Colossal Head**

The Olmec built earliest civilization in the Western Hemisphere, in Mesoamerica c. 1200 B.C.E. In contrast to the earlier, temperate-zone, river-based civilizations of Egypt, Mesopotamia, China, and India, the Olmec culture arose in a tropical jungle region where annual rainfall exceeds 120 inches. The Olmec developed a strong agricultural base and carved cities out of the jungles. Conical pyramids built on platforms made of rammed earth dominated their cities. San Lorenzo is the oldest Olmec city; it thrived from 1200 to 900 B.C.E. Another city, La Venta was dominant from 800 to 400 B.C.E. An inscribed stone tablet, found at a late Olmec site, Tres Zapotes, and dating to 31 B.C.E., is the oldest datable writing in the Western Hemisphere.

The Olmec prized two commodities they did not have locally: obsidian (volcanic glass) and jadeite. Obsidian made good cutting tools. The Olmec also valued jadeite to make for decorative and ritual items. The Olmec bartered and fought these commodities.

The Olmec civilization was responsible for advances in both ideas and technology. The Olmec invented and transmitted a number system used almost universally later in Mesoamerica. The highly complex Olmec calendar, which applied this number system, also became prevalent throughout Mesoamerica. The Olmec also invented a crude writing system, using glyphs similar to those used later in Mesoamerica, but so few specimens survive that archaeologists have made little progress deciphering them.

Like the practitioners of later Mesoamerican religions, whose deities were part human and part animal, the Olmec worshipped a werejaguar, an animal that sported feathers for eyebrows and a forked tongue, as well as human characteristics. This jaguar-god, who was an earth spirit, was often covered in jade. The Olmec practiced human sacrifice at their temples and made offerings of jadeite and other valuables.

The cause of Olmec decline is not clear, although there are tantalizing hints. Both the San Lorenzo and La Venta sites came to sudden ends. In both cities, major monuments, especially the great basalt heads, were deliberately defaced and then carefully buried. This may have signified a ritual "killing" of the gods for having failed the people during some disaster. It is also possible that invaders took the towns and disposed of the conquered peoples' gods.

In the following passage, anthropologist Michael D. Coe offers a reconstruction of aspects of Olmec economy and society. He describes how the modern anthropological study of the current inhabitants of the Olmec regions of Central America can shed light on a vanished ancient civilization.

QUESTIONS:

1) What two goals did Michael Coe set himself in studying the present-day societies of the regions inhabited by the Olmec in the remote past? Did he reach those goals?
2) What deductions is Coe able to make about the religious beliefs of the Olmec?
3) What deductions is Coe able to make about the political system of the Olmec?

One of the principal goals of prehistory is the reconstruction of past cultures and civilizations, not only their ways of making a living, but also their society, politics, thought, and religion. By following only one line of evidence, and proceeding full speed ahead without a general knowledge of the anthropology of civilizations, the archaeologist cannot hope to put back together the fragments that he has been left into a meaningful picture. Faulty reconstructions of this sort have been the butt of many cartoons....

One obvious way of studying ancient ecology is by looking at the peoples today who are living in the same area as the earlier population, provided, of course, that the environment has not changed radically and that the modern people are living on roughly the same economic level. It would do little good, for instance, to examine the modern suburbanites of Connecticut for clues as to how the Algonquian Indians of the same area once lived. Luckily for the archaeologist, many parts of the world in which he works and digs have been only lightly touched by the Industrial Revolution, and major climatic changes have not taken place since the demise of the cultures he wants to reconstruct.

And luckily for us, the tropical lowlands of southern Mexico, where the Olmec civilization arose, is such a region, not very much altered by the Machine Age. Side by side with our archaeological work at San Lorenzo Tenochtitlán, we have been studying the local peasantry in the zone, prying into their kitchens, asking questions about farming, accompanying them on fishing expeditions, and diplomatically uncovering their social and political lives. We have two goals here. One is to discover, given native systems of agriculture and subsistence, the ultimate limit to the population which once lived in the environs of San Lorenzo Tenochtitlán: if this ultimate "carrying capacity" is substantially below that required to support the building, monument-hauling, and other public activities of these sites,

then the area which supported them must have been very large, indeed, reaching well outside the zone.

The second goal is to understand not just the limits imposed upon the ancient and modern inhabitants by their wet, tropical surroundings, but also the very complex ways in which they adapt to that environment--and, of considerable importance, the ways in which that environment has been changed by them.

Ten or twenty years ago [i.e. before 1958] these ambitious goals would have been impractical. To get quantified data of this sort, one has to map soils, vegetation types, and land-use patterns. This task has been made immeasurably easier and quicker by aerial photography, which can carry out in an hour what it would have taken teams of scientists and surveyors months to accomplish on foot. Working for our project, a Mexican company specializing in photogrammetric mapping has flown over our sample area of some thirty square miles and has produced highly detailed photographs (on which even individual corn plants in native fields can be counted) and fine-scale maps from these. From such maps and from extensive field studies they have broken down the area into types of soils (some of which are unusable savanna lands), forest and grassland formations, and potential land use.

All this would mean little if these maps were not tied in with our own ethnological investigations, often conducted on week ends or by talking to our workmen while digging was in progress. We asked all sorts of questions, particularly how much corn, beans, and other crops are produced by a specified kind of soil, how much of this soil type must be left fallow, and for how long, and consumption figures per household and per person. Once these figures are coordinated with our photogrammetric maps, we can arrive at conclusions about maximum possible populations today, and by extrapolation, about populations three thousand years ago.

Our local farmers practice "shifting" or slash-and-burn cultivation, like many of the tropical peoples of the world. A patch or forest or bush is selected and felled with ax and machete during the dry season. Just before the great rains come (at the end of May or in early June), it is burned, and towering smoke columns darken the sky. Planting takes place after the first downpour, the corn seeds being dropped in holes made through the ashes with a simple digging stick. After one or more harvests, the plot (called *milpa*, a term used over much of Mesoamerica) is abandoned and allowed to revert to bush, that is, it lies fallow and gradually recovers its lost fertility. "Shifting" cultivation, because it demands a large fallow area, is thought by many scholars to be a poor base for the development of high cultures, compared with the more intensive and occasionally irrigated kinds of cultivation in use in more temperate or drier regions. The fact remains, however, that it supported the great Maya civilization of the Classic stage and probably provided the subsistence base of the Olmec, too. The question to ask is: How?

Local agriculture in the San Lorenzo Tenochtitlán area is no simple matter. It is very much more complex and productive than one would think at first glance. Once a year during the rainy season (from May until November) the rivers rise, swelled by tremendous thunder-showers accompanied by savage lightning. All land lying below the 75-foot altitude line is inundated, and great sheets of water abounding in fish cover the low-lying savannas. The result is that the highly acid savanna soils are so heavy with clay and so poor in nutrients that they cannot be farmed at any time of the year. Above the high-water mark, in the hillier zone, soils are good and can be cultivated throughout the year, with two major harvests. The really prime land, however, is, like the savannas, the gift of the floods: the natural levees along the rivers that are covered with a deep layer of rich silt after the waters recede. Although only a dry-season crop can be brought in, the corn yield is fantastic, as high as 3,200 pounds per acre as compared with 1,780 pounds for the hillier lands.

The lucky individual who has access to the levee lands need only cultivate three-quarters of an acre during only part of the year to support himself and his family, while the "upland" farmer, denied these soils, has to work at least an acre over the entire year. Small wonder, then, that while the uplands of the area belong to an *ejido* (a communal landholding unit), the lands along the river are all in private hands. In fact, it is possession of the latter which provides the local political and economic leaders with much of their power. We think that they must have given a similar power base to the Olmec leaders of 1000 B.C.

With all this data virtually at our fingertips, we can make some sort of estimate of the human carrying capacity of the zone. Subtracting the agriculturally unusable portion of the area, and allowing for the present average fallow period of eight to ten years, then our present thinking is that the upper limit of population must be about five thousand people. What this means for the reconstruction of Olmec politics we shall see.

Ninety percent of what the modern villagers eat is corn, mainly prepared as tortillas. Fishing, hunting, and turtle-collecting provide important supplements to this dull diet, and they are carried out with the unsporting thoroughness that is typical of people who are looking for food rather than pleasure. Every week end dozens of hunters ride out to San Lorenzo with their dogs, returning to Tenochtitlán in the afternoon with white-tailed deer, the brown brocker (a diminutive and delicious tropical forest deer), and collared peccary, three creatures that also appear in the cuisine of the ancient Olmec.

Fishing goes on all year, although the kinds of fish and ways of catching them change from season to season. The small ponds and oxbows that have been left out on the savannas by former meanderings of the river system teem with fish: in former times a poison extracted from a forest vine was used to kill them in quantities. In June and July, when the great floods come, huge tarpon and gar swim out across the savannas, pursued by the villagers in canoes brandishing harpoons and pronged spears. Toward the latter part of the rainy season, when the rivers are still high and turbid, the prime target is the snook, or robalo, a keen-eyed fish that must be netted at night from canoes, since it can see the net coming during the daylight. The robalo, which can reach great size, is the favored eating fish around San Lorenzo Tenochtitlán. It was so in the past, as well, for many of its bones have been identified ... in Olmec debris from the San Lorenzo area.

So much for our studies of native subsistence patterns. What do they mean for the reconstruction of Olmec society and politics? Apparently, the support area for each Olmec center must have been very much larger than the thirty square miles we have taken as our base for San Lorenzo. There is additional information for La Venta that bears upon the subject. The island of La Venta, for instance, could only support some forty-five to fifty households under native conditions, even if all its land was available for farming, which it most certainly was not. A tract of land away from the swamps surrounding the island has been calculated as being able to contain a maximum population of sixteen thousand, but this figure is far too high, as the exact area of poor or unusable soils has not been taken into account.

It is too early to precisely define the actual territory subordinate to each Olmec center. But the man power called upon to support its activities, many of which seem to us extraordinarily wasteful, must have been truly formidable. Consider the size and weight of the monuments from San Lorenzo and La Venta. It took seventeen men to lift and transport the half-ton Monument 17 at San Lorenzo a mere two miles to the schoolhouse in Tenochtitlán. How many would it have required to drag the forty-ton Monument 14 from its quarrying place in the Tuxtla Mountains to a raft on a navigable stream, thence by waterways to the base of the San Lorenzo plateau, and from there up to the surface of the site? My guess is that at least two thousand able-bodied men would have been involved in the operation, representing the effective labor of a population of eight to ten thousand persons. There are now sixty of these monuments known for San Lorenzo Tenochtitlán (and chances are that hundreds more remain still to be discovered), which is about the same number as at La Venta, and more than twenty at Laguna de los Cerros, to mention only the most important Olmec centers.

Add to this the several thousand tons o imported serpentine blocks found at La Venta the basalt columns at the same site, and the thirty tons of drain stones at San Lorenzo. Then consider the work involved in building the top twenty-five feet of the San Lorenzo plateau and its ridges (with hundreds of thousands of tons of artificial fill) and the ceremonial center of La Venta (with its specially selected clays). The only possible conclusion is that the political power of each center was exerted many dozens of miles away from it, and that the force and authority of the Olmec were felt far beyond the heartland itself. Three thousand years ago, there just could not have been enough able-bodied men in the immediate area to have carried out all the physical labor required.

It has often been claimed that the Olmec civilization must have been a theocracy, defined as a government directed by priests, based on the analogy of the supposedly theocratic Maya. But this analogy will not work, since we can now interpret the historical part of some Classic Maya inscriptions. These speak to us of secular, rather than religious, leadership, with power in the hands of a hereditary lineage or dynasty. This conforms with what we know about all other Mesoamerican societies for which we have evidence. In these, the priesthood, while admittedly important, played second fiddle to the civil rulers.

The testimony of archaeology is that the Olmec were also ruled by great civil lords, members of royal lineages. As one line of evidence, let us take the so-called altars, those that show a figure seated cross-legged in a niche. Here there are only two themes: the person, an adult male in all cases, is holding a werejaguar baby in his arms, or else he is grasping a rope that is connected to two bound captives on the sides. These are surely the same scenes of lineage (or descent) and personal conquest that have recently been identified on the Maya monuments, and they are intended to glorify the ruler to his subjects. The Colossal Heads are a case in point: enormous sculptures that so obviously depict tough warrior dynasts rather than priests. There is some suspicion that beside playing the dual role of king and soldier, the ruler was also an outstanding athlete (like Henry VIII and other European kings). From clay figurines found at San Lorenzo we know that the sacred ball game was played by the Olmec, and details both of posture and costume imply that many monuments celebrate prowess on the playing fields....

The Olmec had probably established a far-flung trading network reaching to the state of Guerrero in the west and to El Salvador in the southeast. The purpose of such conquests was perhaps to guarantee the export of jade and serpentine from their natural sources to great centers, and jade-hungry kings, in the Olmec heartland. Much, much later the Aztec conducted a similar kind of trade. This was in the hands of a hereditary mercantile group, called the *pochteca*, and was specifically designed to bring otherwise unobtainable luxury items to the Aztec royal palace. The pochteca traders operated exclusively in foreign territory, usually traveling disguised but well-armed over vast distances to obtain these items in special "ports of trade," looking for products like quetzal feathers, amber, jade, and gold. They were also *agents provocateurs*, an attack on them bringing quick retribution from the Aztec ruler in the form of bloody conquest. In fact, this was typically the way in which foreign countries were subjugated as tribute-producing provinces within the Aztec empire.

If the Aztec pattern can be projected back to the Olmec past, then the initial contacts might have been made by the pochteca under royal protection, with conquest and organization into the Olmec state falling shortly thereafter. Accepting all this as probable, then there must have been an Olmec empire ..., the first of four that held sway over much of Mexico for fifteen centuries: Olmec, Teotihuacán, Toltec, and Aztec. It was typical of the later empires to have been governed from not just one, but two and sometimes three capitals. In the case of the Olmec, these might have been San Lorenzo, La Venta, and Laguna de los Cerros, with one and then the other in turn gaining ascendancy over the others.

Coe, Michael D. *America's First Civilization*. New York: American Heritage, 1968. Pp. 105-107, 109-111.

SECTION 2

THE DEVELOPMENT OF GREAT RELIGIONS AND PHILOSOPHIES

Although archaeological evidence shows that all early humans believed in the supernatural, most early religions lacked complex theologies or consistent moral teachings. In time most societies' material advances were paralleled by intellectual strides in the arts, sciences, religions, and philosophies. As a result religious beliefs gained in refinement and sophistication and philosophical systems developed that addressed moral questions and guided behavior.

This section examines the development of early religious and philosophical beliefs. The evidence range from songs and hymns about early Aryan god-heroes to the moral teachings of the *Upanishads*, and the breakaway faiths of Buddhism and Jainism. Other readings illustrate the emergence in China of the two very incompatible philosophies of Confucianism and Taoism, and portray the teachings of the three great monotheistic faiths that originated in West Asia: Judaism, Christianity, and Islam.

These readings demonstrate the common human quest for moral codes to shape and guide conduct, for explanations of the supernatural and the inexplicable, and for consolation in the face of dire need. They also show the different answers people found to their needs, and the varied approaches to human problems in different societies, for example, the development of life negating thoughts in India, the generally socially positive philosophies in China, and a monotheistic, all-powerful and omniscient deity in West Asia.

The selections gathered in this section reveal the ancient roots and the enduring cultural influences of major religions and philosophies that affect the lives of billions of people right up to the present.

READING 2.1

THE RIG VEDA: SACRED LITERATURE OF THE ARYANS

▶ Indra

Around 1500 B.C.E. Aryans or Indo-Europeans from the Eurasian heartland invaded India through present-day Afghanistan and destroyed the Indus Valley civilization. The Aryan farmers and pastoralists had no use for the cities of the Indus people and abandoned them after the conquest. Archaeology has yielded little of the civilization of the Aryans during the next thousand years; thus scholars must rely on the religious literature of this era.

The millennium c. 1500-500 B.C.E. is called the Vedic Age, from the sacred literature or Vedas of the Aryans. Aryans spoke dialects of a language of the Indo-European family, from which almost all European languages also stem. Their priests, called Brahmans, composed songs and hymns to the deities in a literary language called *Sanskrit*, which means "pure, perfect, sacred." Shortly after 1000 B.C.E., a Semitic type of written script, akin to Phoenician, was adopted by the Aryans; called the Brahmi script, it is the ancestor of all later Indian alphabets.

The most sacred book in Vedic and later Hindu religion is the *Rig Veda*, a collection of 1028 songs and hymns. Much of the *Rig Veda* is imperfectly understood because the true meaning of many words has been lost. It is, however, clear that most of the deities (*devas* in Sanskrit, compare *deus*, "god" in Latin) are male and associated with nature--sky, sun, fire, storm, and water. There are few goddesses in the *Rig Veda* and they are unimportant. Personified, natural forces became gods. Thus Agni was fire and the fire god, Indra was sky and the thunder god, Soma was a hemp-like hallucinogenic plant and the god of a drink made with its juice, and the Maruts were storm gods. Indra in particular was associated with drinking, feasting, and fighting, all admired manly qualities.

Agni was a very important early god, because he was everywhere. He consumed sacrifices humans offered, and his sacred flame lifted them to the sky. He was also god of the home and the hearth and an intermediary between humans and other deities. Indra was often associated with Agni, and with the Maruts, with whom he rode in shining chariots across the sky and into battle. Hymns of Indra flanked by the Maruts, singing martial songs as they sallied off to war across the sky, are perhaps glorified versions of Aryan warriors charging into battle beside their chief. Indra was also the heroic dragon slayer and destroyer of forts (possibly the walled towns of the Indus civilization), and the bringer of rain and life-giving water.

The following selections from the *Rig Veda* celebrate Agni, Indra, and the Maruts. These gods are human in figure and motive. The "Hymn to Indra and the Maruts" show that misunderstanding sometimes marred their relations. While Indra was sometimes contemptuous of the Maruts, he also recognized their power and valued their friendship. The dialogue form of the hymn indicates that it was recited by two parties during a ritual that honored the Maruts; one priest represented Indra, while others represented the Maruts. Their devotees appeal to them for favors, booty, conquests, and success. Moral and ethical values do not seem pertinent. The Dasyu are the natives and the Bharata are the Aryans.

QUESTIONS:

1) What did the hymn to Agni ask from him?
2) How would you describe Indra from the hymns to him?
3) What was the relationship between Indra and the Maruts?

Hymns to Agni:

Thee, Agni, the treasure-lord of treasures, I gladden at the sacrifices, O king! May we, striving for gain, conquer gain through thee; may we overcome the hostilities of mortals.

Agni, the bearer of oblations, our ever-young father, is mighty, brilliant, beautiful to behold among us. Shine (on us) food with a good household. Turn all glory towards us.

Establish Agni as the Hotri, the sage of the clans, the lord of human clans, the bright purifier, whose back is covered with ghee [clarified butter], the omniscient. May he obtain the best goods (for us) among the gods.

Enjoy thyself, O Agni, joined with Ida, uniting thyself with the rays of the sun. Enjoy our fuel, O Gatavedas, and bring the gods hither that they may eat our offerings.

Welcome, as our household-god and the guest in our dwelling, come to this our sacrifice as the knowing one. Dispelling, O Agni, all (hostile) attempts, bring to us the possessions of those who are at enmity with us.

Drive away the Dasyu with thy weapon, creating strength for thy own body. When thou bringest the gods across (to us), O son of strength, then, O manliest Agni, protect us in (our striving for) gain.

May we worship thee, O Agni, with hymns, with offerings, O purifier with glorious light. Stir for us wealth with all goods; bestow on us all riches!

* * * * *

The guardian of people, the watchful one, Agni, the highly dextrous, has been born, for the sake of new welfare. With ghrita on his face with his mighty, heaven-touching (light) he, the bright one, brilliantly shines for the Bharatas.

Agni, the beacon of sacrifice, the first Purohita men have kindled in the threefold abodes. (Driving) on the same chariot with Indra and with the gods, he, the highly wise Hotri, has sat down on the Barhis for sacrificing.

* * * * *

Agni, bring hither, through the power of thy splendour, powerful wealth which may manifestly prevail over all tribes in the (contests for) booty.

O powerful Agni! Bring hither that wealth powerful in battles. For thou art the true, wonderful giver of booty rich in cows.

For all men who have spread out the sacrificial grass, unanimously ask thee, the beloved Hotri in the seats (of sacrifice), for many boons.

For he who dwells among all tribes, has invested himself with power against assault. Agni! In these dwelling-places shine to us richly, O bright one, shine brilliantly, O purifier!

* * * * *

Hymns to Indra:

May our priests praise Indra! O, enemies, go away from this place, and also from another place! Our priests (may praise Indra), they who are always performing worship for Indra.

O destroyer of enemies! may the enemy call us possessed of wealth; how much more, friendly people! May we be in the happiness of Indra!

* * * * *

To the Maruts and Indra: The Dialogue.

The Maruts speak:

From whence, O Indra, dost thou come alone, thou who art mighty? O lord of men, what has thus happened to thee? Thou greetest (us) when thou comest together with (us), the bright (Maruts). Tell us then, thou with thy bay horses, what thou hast against us!

Indra speaks:

The sacred Songs are mine, (mine are) the prayers; sweet are the libations! My strength rises, my thunderbolt is hurled forth. They call for me, the hymns yearn for me. Here are my horses, they carry me hither.

The Maruts speak:

From thence, in company with our strong friends, having adorned our bodies, we now harness our fallow deer with all our might;--for, Indra, according to custom, thou hast come to be with us.

Indra speaks:

Where, O Maruts, was that custom with you, when you left me alone in the killing of Ahi? I indeed am terrible, powerful, strong,--I escaped from the blows of every enemy.

The Maruts speak:

Thou hast achieved much with us as companions. With equal valour, O hero! let us achieve then many things, O thou most powerful, O Indra! whatever we, O Maruts, wish with our mind.

Indra speaks:

I slew Vritra, O Maruts, with (Indra's) might, having grown powerful through my own vigour; I, who hold the thunderbolt in my arms, have made these all-brilliant waters to flow freely for man.

The Maruts speak:

Nothing, O mighty lord, is strong before thee: no one is known among the gods like unto thee. No one who is now born comes near, no one who has been born. Do what thou wilt do, thou who art grown so strong.

Indra speaks:

Almighty strength be mine alone, whatever I may do, daring in my heart; for I indeed, O Maruts, am known as terrible: of all that I threw down, I, Indra, am the lord.

O Maruts, now your praise has pleased me, the glorious hymn which you have made for me, ye men!--for me, for Indra, for the joyful here, as friends for a friend, for your own sake and by your own efforts.

Truly, there they are, shining towards me, bringing blameless glory, bringing food. O Maruts, wherever I have looked for you, you have appeared to me in bright splendour: appear to me also now!

Oldenberg, Hermann, trans. *Vedic Hymns*. Part II: *Hymns to Agni (Mandalas I-V)*. Rpt. Delhi: M. Banarsidass, 1967. Pp. 375, 391, 414. Müller, F. Max, trans. *Vedic Hymns*. Part I: *Hymns to the Maruts, Rudra, Vayu, and Vata*. Delhi: M. Banarsidass, 1967. Pp. xxxix, 179-181.

HINDU LESSONS ON SPIRITUAL UNDERSTANDING

▶ **Shiva as Teacher**

Early Aryan religious beliefs seemed to indicate that the dead went forever to either the "World of the Fathers" or to the "House of Clay." After settling down in the Indus and Ganges valleys in north India, the Aryans also absorbed the religious ideas and practices of natives. By the late Vedic Age (after 1000 B.C.E.) Indians believed in the transmigration of souls, or the perpetual reincarnation of souls into new bodies, determined by *karma* (action or deed). These beliefs, and the social and economic changes caused by a settled society and expanding economy, generated profound pessimism and uncertainty among Indians.

Dissatisfaction led to still newer religious ideas in the late Vedic Age. Two new and heterodox religions, Buddhism and Jainism, emerged as a result of the teachings of two sages, Gautama Buddha and Mahavira. Other sages' ideas were embodied in the *Upanishads*, a collection of one hundred and eight spiritual discourses written by scholars between c. 800-500 B.C.E. They were accepted as orthodox and as the last component part of Vedic literature. The philosophy expressed in the *Upanishads* is the most profound expression of Hinduism (the religion that emerged from Vedism); its monistic theology, mysticism, and idealization of an impersonal immortality became the highest aspiration of Hindus.

The title *Upanishads* derives from the Sanskrit *upa* meaning "near," and *shad* which means "to sit." Together, Upanishad means 'sitting near;' they are the wisdom sages taught to pupils who sat near to them. Since they were the works of many people over several hundred years, the *Upanishads* do not expound a consistent philosophy.

However the *Upanishads* do consistently seek answers to the mystery of an unintelligible world. They teach that reliance on the intellect alone will not suffice, and that worship and good works by themselves will not lead to spiritual wisdom. The person seeking wisdom must shed subjectivity and ego, through meditation, introspection, and the guidance of sages. Only then can one gain understanding through the merging of the individual ego or self (*atman*) with the universal soul or truth (*brahman*). God or the ultimate is in all things. When we realize this then the atman and brahman (the subjective and objective) become one, so that wisdom and peace, and *moksha* (release from the burden of rebirth) are achieved.

Many of the *Upanishads* are dialogues of sages struggling to explain complex and esoteric ideas to their pupils. The passage quoted below is from one of the best known, the *Khandogya-Upanishad*.

QUESTIONS:

1) How is the word "True" explained?
2) How does the "Self" relate to the "True"?
3) What sort of knowledge is the son seeking from the father?

"As the bees. my son, make honey by collecting the juices of distant trees, and reduce the juice into one form,

"And as these juices have no discrimination, so that they might say, I am the juice of this tree, or that, in the same manner, my son, all these creatures, when they have become merged in the True (either in deep sleep or in death), know not that they are merged in the True.

"Whatever these creatures are here, whether a lion, or a wolf, or a boar, or a worm, or a midge, or a gnat, or a musquito, that they become again and again.

"Now that which is that subtle essence, in it all that exists has its self. It is the True. it is the Self, and thou, O Sevtaketu, art it."

"Please, Sir, inform me still more," said the son.

"Be it so, my child," the father replied.

"These rivers, my son, run, the eastern (like the Ganga) toward the east, the western (like the Sindhu) toward the west. They go from sea to sea (i.e. the clouds lift up the water from the sea to the sky, and send it back as rain to the sea). They become indeed sea. And as those rivers, when they are in the sea, do not know, I am this or that river.

"In the same manner, my son, all these creatures, when they have come back from the True, know not that they have come back from the True. Whatever these creatures are here, whether a lion, or a wolf, or a boar, or a worm, or a midge, or a gnat, or a musquito, they become again and again.

"That which is that subtle essence, in it all that exists has its self. It is the True. It is the Self, and thou, O Svetaketu, art it."

"Please, Sir, inform me still more," said the son.

"Be it so, my child," the father replied.

"If someone were to strike at the root of this large tree here, it would bleed, but live. If he were to strike at its stem, it would bleed, but live. If he were to strike at its top, it would bleed, but live. Pervaded by the living Self that tree stands firm, drinking in its nourishment and rejoicing;

"But if the life of the living Self leaves one of its branches, that branch withers; if it leaves a second, that branch withers; if it leaves a third, that branch withers. If it leaves the whole tree, the whole tree withers. In exactly the same manner, my son, know this." Thus he spoke:

"This (body) indeed withers and dies when the living Self has left it; the living Self dies not.

"That which is that subtle essence, in it all that exists has its self. It is the True. It is the Self, and thou, Svetaketu, art it."

"Please, Sir, inform me still more," said the son.

"Be it so, my child," the father replied.

"Fetch me from thence a fruit of the Nyagrodha tree."

"Here is one, Sir."

"Break it."

"It is broken, Sir."

"What do you see there?"

"These seeds, almost infinitesimal."

"Break one of them."

"It is broken, Sir."

"What do you see there?"

"Not anything, Sir."

The father said: "My son, that subtle essence which you do not perceive there, of that very essence this great Nyagrodha tree exists.

"Believe it, my son. That which is the subtle essence, in it all that exists has its self. It is the True. It is the Self, and thou, O Svetaketu, art it."

"Please Sir, inform me still more," said the son.

"Be it so, my child," the father replied.

"Place this salt in water, and then wait on me in the morning."

The son did as he was commanded.

The father said to him: "Bring me the salt, which you placed in the water last night."

The son having looked for it, found it not, for, of course, it was melted.

The father said: "Take it from the surface of the water, How is it?"

The son replied: "It is salt."

"Taste it from the middle. How is it?"

The son replied: "It is salt."

"Taste it from the bottom. How is it?"

The son replied: "It is salt."

The father said: "Throw it away and then wait on me."

He did so; but the salt exists for ever.

Then the father said: "Here also, in this body, forsooth, you do not perceive the True, my son; but there indeed it is.

"That which is the subtile essence, in it all that exists has its self. It is the True. It is the Self, and thou, O Svetaketu, art it."

Müller, F. Max, trans. *The Upanishads*. Part I. Rpt. Delhi: M. Banarsidass, 1967. Pp. 101-105.

READING 2.3

GAUTAMA BUDDHA'S LIFE AND MESSAGE

▶ **The Buddha**

It is very difficult to reconstruct the life of Gautama Buddha, founder of Buddhism, from the welter of ancient Buddhist texts. However the exact facts about Gautama Buddha's life, his enlightenment, work, and death are less important than the Buddhists' beliefs about them and the lessons drawn from them.

Around 566 B.C.E., a son was born to the ruler of a small north Indian kingdom of the Sakyas, near to present day Nepal. His name was Siddhartha, his clan name was Gautama; later, because he founded a religion called Buddhism (the religion of enlightenment), he came to be called the Buddha ("the enlightened one") or Sakyamuni ("wise man of the Sakyas").

Despite a luxurious life as a prince, Gautama felt spiritually unfulfilled, and around age thirty left his father, wife, and son to seek spiritual enlightenment with a group of ascetics. When self-inflicted torture nearly killed him without bringing wisdom, Gautama changed to a middle path life of meditation. He attained enlightenment or nirvana six years after leaving home, and spent the remaindner of his long life teaching his faith to an ever widening circle of devotees. Gautama died at around eighty years c. 486 B.C.E.

Whether Gautama intended to start a new religion or to reinterpret Brahmanism is still debated. Buddhists, like adherents of Brahmanism and Jainism, believed in the reincarnation of the soul after death, as determined by *karma*, or deeds. All three religions believed existence was filled with pain and misery, and that joy came through release from the round of rebirths, called *nirvana*. Gautama rejected the leadership of brahman priests and taught an attainable moral system to his disciples. Buddhism spread quickly over India during the next centuries.

This reading is taken from ancient Buddhist canons, translated from the Pali, a vernacular language of north India in Gautama's time. It explains why he chose to leave home, and includes parts of his crucial sermon and another sermon which defined early Buddhist beliefs.

QUESTIONS:

1) Why did Gautama abandon extreme asceticism for the middle way?
2) What are the Four Noble Truths?
3) What is the goal of Budhists, and how did Gautama teach them to attain it?

[At twenty-nine, married to his beautiful cousin who had born him a son, Gautama was suddenly shocked by the reality of life. He said:] Then, O monks, did I, endowed with such majesty and such excessive delicacy, think thus, "an ignorant, ordinary person, who is himself subject to old age, not beyond the sphere of old age, on seeing an old man is troubled, ashamed, and disgusted, extending the thought to himself. I too am subject to old age, not beyond the sphere of old age, and should I, who am subject to old age, not beyond the sphere of old age, on seeing an old man be troubled, ashamed, and disgusted?" This seemed to me not fitting. As I thus reflected on it, all the elation in youth utterly disappeared.... [The same is repeated of sickness and death, and] the elation in life utterly disappeared.

[Gautama left his home and family to seek wisdom and spiritual liberation. He joined a group of like minded ascetics, meditated and practised austerities to attain knowledge and enlightenment.] Then I thought, what if I now set my teeth, press my tongue to my palate, and restrain, crush, and burn out my mind with my mind.... I undertook resolute effort, unconfused mindfulness was set up, but my body was unquiet and uncalmed, even through the painful striving that overwhelmed me. Nevertheless such painful feeling as arose did not overpower my mind.

Then I thought, what if I now practise trance without breathing. So I restrained breathing in and out from mouth, nose, and ears. And as I did so violent winds disturbed my head. Just as if a strong man were to crush one's head with the point of a sword, even so did violent winds disturb my mind....

Then I thought, what if I were to take food only in small amounts, as much as my hollowed palm would hold, juice of beans, vetches, chickpeas, or pulse [similar to peas]. My body became extremely lean.... The bones of my spine when bent and straightened were like a row of spindles through the little food. As the beams of an old shed stick out, so did my ribs stick out through the little food. And as in a deep well the deep low-lying sparkling of the water is seen, so in my eye-sockets was seen the deep low-lying sparkling of my eyes through the little food. And as a bitter gourd cut off raw is cracked and withered through wind and sun, so was the skin of my head withered through the little food. When I thought I would touch the skin of my stomach, I actually took hold of my spine, and when I thought I would touch my spine, I took hold of the skin of my stomach, so much did the

skin of my stomach cling to my spine through the little food. When I thought I would ease myself I thereupon fell prone through the little food. To relieve my body I stroked my limbs with my hand, and as I did so the decayed hairs fell from my body through the little food.

Some human beings seeing me then said "the ascetic Gotama is black." Some said, "no black is the ascetic Gotama, he is brown." Others said "not black is the ascetic Gotama, nor brown, his skin is that of a mangura-fish [sheat fish]," so much had the pure clean colour of my skin been destroyed by the little food.

Then I thought, those ascetics and brahmins in the past, who have suffered sudden, sharp keen, severe pains, at the most have not suffered more than this.... But by this severe mortification I do not attain superhuman truly noble knowledge and insight. Perhaps there is another way to enlightenment. Then I thought, now I realize that when my father the Sakyan was working, I was seated under the cool shade of a rose-apple tree, and without sensual desires, without evil ideas, I attained an abode in the first trance of joy and pleasure arising from seclusion, and combined with reasoning and investigation. Perhaps this is the way to enlightenment. Then arose in conformity with mindfulness the consciousness that this was the way to enlightenment. Then I thought, why should I fear the happy state that is without sensual desires and without evil ideas. And I thought, I do not fear that happy state which is without sensual desires and without evil ideas.

Then I thought, it is not easy to gain that happy state while my body is so very lean. What if I now take solid food, rice and sour milk.... But when I took solid food, rice and sour milk, then the five monks [who had been his companions] left me in disgust, saying, "the ascetic Gotama lives in abundance, he has given up striving, and has turned to a life of abundance."...

[After attaining enlightenment Gautama, now a buddha preached the first sermon to his former comapnions.]

"The First Sermon" or "The Sermon of Turning the Wheel of the Doctrine"

These two extremes, O monks, are not to be practised by one who has gone forth from the world. What are the two? That conjoined with the passion, low, vulgar, common, ignoble, and useless, and that conjoined with self-torture, painful, ignoble, and useless. Avoiding these two extremes the Tathagata has gained the knowledge of the Middle Way, which gives sight and knowledge, and tends to calm, to insight, enlightenment, Nirvana.

What, O monks, is the Middle Way, which gives sight...? It is the Noble Eightfold Path, namely, right views, right intention, right speech, right action, right livelihood, right effort, right mindfulness, right concentration. This, O monks, is the Middle Way....

(1) Now this, O monks, is the noble truth of pain: birth is painful, old age is painful, sickness is painful, death is painful, sorrow, lamentation, dejection, and despair are painful. Contact with unpleasant things is painful, not getting what one wishes is painful. In short the five khandhas of grasping are painful.

(2) Now this, O monks, is the noble truth of the cause of pain: that craving, which leads to rebirth, combined with pleasure and lust, finding pleasure here and there, namely the craving for passion, the craving for existence, the craving for non-existence.

(3) Now this, O monks, is the noble truth of the cessation of pain: the cessation without a reminder of that craving, abandonment, forsaking, release, non-attachment.

(4) Now this, O monks, is the noble truth of the way that leads to the cessation of pain: this is the noble Eightfold Path, namely, right view, right intention, right speech, right action, right livelihood, right ieffort, right mindfulness, right concentration. 'This is the noble truth of pain.' Thus, O monks, among doctrines unheard before, in me sight and knowledge arose, wisdom, knowledge, light arose. 'This noble truth of pain must be comprehended.' Thus, O monks, among doctrines unheard before, by me was this truth comprehended. And thus, O monks, among doctrines unheard before, in me sight and knowledge arose.
(Repeated in the same words for the other truths, except that the second the cause of pain, is to be abandoned, the third, the cessation of pain, is to be realised, and the fourth, the noble Eightfold Path, is to be practised.)

As long as in these noble truths my threefold knowledge and insight duly with its twelve divisions was not well purified, even so long, O monk, in the world with its gods, Mara, Brahma, with ascetics, brahmins, gods and men, I had not attained the highest complete enlightenment. Thus I knew.

But when in these noble truths my threefold knowledge and insight duly with its twelve divisions was well purified, then O monks, in the world ... I had attained the highest complete enlightenment. Thus I knew, knowledge arose in me, insight arose that the release of my mind is unshakable; this is my last existence; now there is no rebirth.

"The Sermon on the Marks of Non-Soul"

The body, monks, is soulless. If the body, monks, were the soul, this body would not be subject to sickness, and it would be possible in the case of the body to say, 'let my body be thus, let my body not be thus.' Now because the body is soulless, monks, therefore the body is subject to sickness, and it is not possible in the case of the body to say, 'let my body be thus, let my body not be thus.'

Feeling is soulless ... perception is soulless ... the aggregates are soulless....

Consciousness is soulless....

What think you, monks, is the body permanent or impermanent?

Impermanent, Lord

But is the impermanent painful or pleasant?

Painful, Lord.

But is it fitting to consider what is impermanent, painful, and subject to change as, 'this is mine, this am I, this is my soul?'

No indeed, Lord....

Thus perceiving, monks, the learned noble disciple feels loathing for the body, for feeling, for perception, for the aggregate, for consciousness. Feeling disgust he becomes free from passion, through freedom from passion he is emancipated, and in the emancipated one arises the knowledge of his emancipation. He understands that destroyed is rebirth, the religious life has been led, done is what was to be done, there is nought [for him] beyond this world.

Thus said the Lord. The five monks rejoiced at the utterance of the Lord, and when this exposition was uttered, the hearts of five monks not clinging to [existence] were emancipated from the asavas [sensual desires and ignorance].

Thomas, Edward J. *The Life of Buddha as Legend and History*, London: Kegan Paul et al., 1931. Pp. 51, 64-66, 87-89.

READING 2.4

THE TIMES AND LIFE OF MAHAVIRA

▶ **Mahavira's Birth in Jain Manuscript Illustration**

The sixth century B.C.E. was one of profound changes in India. The conquering Indo-Aryans had by then subdued all northern India and settled into territorial states. The caste system had solidified into four major divisions of people. The two dominant groups, the brahmans or religious teachers and priests and the kshatriyas or political leaders, contended for primacy. Economic advances and improved agricultural techniques fostered the growth of towns and cities; trade and crafts flourished.

Paradoxically material prosperity co-existed with spiritual despair due to the inadequacies of the traditional Vedic religion. Dissidents challenged the religious supremacy of the brahmans, their rituals, and the *Vedas*. Two new religions, Jainism and Buddhism, both founded by kshatriyas, emerged from the intellectual turmoil,

Vardhamana, better known as Mahavira (great hero), founded Jainism. Born c. 540 B.C.E., the son of a minor ruler in northern India, he left home at age thirty to pursue an austere life in quest of spiritual wisdom and freedom from the painful round of rebirths. Mahavira attained nirvana or spiritual liberation and bliss after twelve years, became *jina* or conqueror, and founded the religion called Jainism. Mahavira taught for the remainder of his life, gaining many followers. He died c. 468.

Long after Mahavira's death his followers wrote down his teaching from oral traditions; it became the canon of Jainism. Different sects of Jains followed variant forms of the canon. Since no literary works contemporary with Mahavira have survived, it is extremely difficult to reconstruct a reliable chronology of his life and to separate legend from fact. This reading is from a recent scholarly book, *Lord Mahavira and His Times*, commemorating the two thousand and five hundredth anniversary of his death. It draws on a rich array of later literary sources of the Jain, Buddhist, and Brahmanic traditions, and on recent archaeological excavations. The first part explains the economic and social conditions during the sixth century B.C.E., the second part is a brief summary of Mahavira's spiritual quest.

QUESTIONS:

1) How did most Indian people live around the sixth century B.C.E.?
2) What is the ultimate goal of Jainism and how can it be realized?
3) How did Mahavira attain spiritual enlightenment?

The four *Varnas*, Brahmanas, Kshatriyas, Vaisyas and Sudras, which were formed more or less on birth during the later Vedic period, became gradually rigid and fixed. The influence of the Brahmanas greatly diminished both in the intellectual and political field and their place was taken by the Kshatriyas who began to consider themselves superior to other classes on account of the great importance they attached to their great purity of blood.... This period also witnessed the deterioration in the position of the Sudras, with the result that a number of religious leaders raised their voice for their uplift....

Both literary and archaeological sources reveal that rice, wheat, and pulse were the main cereals which people consumed. Rice, no doubt, was known in the preceding age too, but wheat and pulse were added to the dietary system of this period.... Cooked rice was called *Bhatta* or *Bhakta*.... It was ordinarily eaten with pulses and vegetables....

Milk and milk-products like curd, butter, and ghee [clarified butter] were largely eaten. Vegetables like pumpkins, gourds, and cucumbers and fruits like mango and jamboo were included in the diet of the people.

That during this period a large number of people were nonvegetarian is proved by the discovery of bones at different archaeological sites. They seem to have been very fond of meat and fish. There were butchers who earned their livelihood by killing various animals in the slaughter-houses and by supplying their meat to the people. The flesh of goats, pig, sheep, and deer was much used. In certain sections of society and on special occasions, cows and oxen were also slaughtered, but the tendency to revere the cow and to spare the useful bull was gaining ground. The *Jataka* stories [Buddhist tales of Gautama's previous incarnations] mention pigeons, geese, herons, peacocks, crows, and cocks as eatables. A large number of people cherished fish diet. Meat and fish were carried in carts to the towns and cities where they were sold in the open market....

Drinking [of alcohol] was fairly common.... The Jaina and Buddhist sources inform us that the festive occasions were marked by feasting, drinking, and merry-making. There used to be a festival known as drinking festival which was marked by unrestricted drinking, feasting and dancing, leading finally to brawls in which the people broke their heads, feet, and hands.

Liquor was manufactured or consumed on a large scale. Taverns where various kinds of wine were sold were common. From the *Jataka* stories we know that there were crowded taverns where liquor was kept filled in jars and sold. The owners of the taverns kept apprentices who helped them in their business.... Some people used to go to these taverns for drinking with their wives....

People amused themselves by participating in festival gatherings which formed a regular feature of social life ... special gatherings where crowds of men, women and children gathered together and witnessed various kinds of shows and performances, such as dancing and music, combats of elephants, horses and rams, bouts with quarter-staff and wrestling....

Though the festive assemblies at this time were mostly secular, some of them were no doubt religious in nature. The centres of these festivals were the cities and towns where people gathered from the neighbouring villages to enjoy themselves.... Generally they were organized by the kings themselves who went on elephants round the city in solemn processions.... On the occasion of some festivals, people were given holidays. Some festivals lasted for seven days while some continued for a month....

Some household ceremonies too were celebrated with great rejoicing ... [for example] before wedding when betel leaves etc. were served ... the wedding ceremony ... the time of the bride entering the bridegroom's house ... [and] when she returned to her father's house....

The gatherings of religious preachers and learned philosophers certainly soothed their hearts and quenched their mental thirst. Besides, dramatic performances were also quite popular, and they might have been an important source of recreation. Painting and embroidery, apart from proving sources of income, must also have charmed the people. The manufacture of clay figurines of both human and animal forms was an object of amusement for children. The performances of jugglers and snake-charmers gave them special delight....

The period ... was epoch-making in economic history because of the numerous important changes that occurred in it. States well organized came into existence for the first time, leading to the establishment of peace and order. As a result, this period witnessed an allround development of agriculture, industry and trade.

The increased use of iron for different purposes resulted in the surplus of wealth and prosperity. Many new arts and crafts came into existence and they became localised and hereditary.... Population increased by leaps and bounds on account of better means of subsistence and living conditions.

Rural economy had its centre in the *grama* or village, a collection of houses and families numbering from 30 to 1000. It was closed by a wall or stockade provided with gates. Beyond this enclosure lay the arable land of the village ... which was protected by fences and field watchmen against pests like birds and beasts. This land was divided into separate holdings cut off from one another by ditches dug for co-operative irrigation. Usually these holdings were small enough to be cultivated by their owners and families....

Several industrial villages, exclusively inhabited by men of the same craft, came into existence during this period. Such villages were those of carpenters, smiths, weavers, and so on.... The number of such villages, however, was small. Most of the villages had the mixed population of persons of different castes, occupations and trade, following their own professions....

The most remarkable feature of the economic life during this period was that trade and industries were organized for the first time into guilds known as *Srenis*. These *Srenis* were the corporations of the people belonging to the same or different castes but following the same trade and industry....

There were also merchant-guilds under the chiefs called *Setthis*. Because of their wealth, they got special status in society. They visited the royal court as representatives of the business community....

These guilds were gradually converted into hereditary castes on the basis of occupation. In ordinary times, the sons pursued their paternal occupations. Besides, these guilds became localized in particular areas. They gave impetus to specialization and efficiency of labour....

The guilds were autonomous bodies having their own laws. The corporate existence of the guilds was recognized by the state. Guilds exercised considerable control over the members. Probably the settlement of disputes among its members and the solution of the problems of trade and business fell under the jurisdiction of the guild....

A guild worked for the welfare of its members, and it had a right to approach the king and demand justice. A painter was ordered to be executed by prince Malladinna; the guild of the painters visited the king, explained the matter, and requested him to quash the sentence passed against the member of the union. The king was pleased to commute the sentence into banishment....

* * * * *

Mahavira renounced the world at the age of thirty. It seems that he joined the order of Parsva [an earlier sage whose followers took four vows, not to injure life, not to steal, to own no property, and to be truthful] of which his parents were lay members.... For a year and a month since he renounced the world Mahavira did not discard his clothes. Thereafter, he gave up his garments and became naked. Even when he used his robe, he used it only in winter.... Out of all the eight months of summer and winter taken together, Mahavira spent only a single night in villages and only five nights in towns. He was indifferent alike to the smell of ordure and of sandal [wood], to straw and jewels, dirt and gold, and pleasure and pain. He was attached neither to this world nor to the world beyond. He desired neither life nor death. He arrived at the other shore of the *Samsara* [rebirth], and exerted himself for the suppression of the defilement of *Karma* [deed or action]....

During the thirteenth year, in the second month of summer, in the fourth fortnight ... in a squatting position with joined heels exposing himself to the heat of the Sun, with the knees high and the head low, in deep meditation, in the midst of abstract meditation, he reached *Nirvana*....

[Mahavira] was responsible for the codification of an unsystematic mass of beliefs inhering the earlier religion of his predecessor into a set of rigid rules of conduct for monks and laymen.... The ultimate object of Jainism is *Nirvana* which consists in the attainment of peace and infinite bliss. *Nirvana* is just another name for *Moksa* or liberation, *Mukti* or deliverance, salvation or beatitude....

Right Faith, Right Knowledge, and Right Conduct are the three essential points in Mahavira's teachings which led to perfection by the destruction of *Karmans*. Without Right Faith, there is no Right Knowledge; without Right Knowledge there is no Virtuous Conduct; without virtue, there is no deliverance and without deliverance (*Moksha*), there is no perfection.... While Parsva taught only four vows for the realization of absolute happiness, Mahavira taught five in all, making chastity a separate vow altogether.

Mahavira was one of the great religious teachers of mankind. He recognized the need for the perfection of self and prescribed certain practical rules of conduct for the attainment of this aim. He did not preach to others what he did not practise himself. For the realization of such an aim, he believed in the blissfulness of the entire being. This happy state, he said cannot be bought by the wealth, pomp, and power of the world but can certainly be realized throug patience, forbearance, self-denial, forgiveness humanity, compassion, suffering and sacrifice For this purpose, he inculcated the doctrine o *Ahimsa* or non-violence in thought, word, an action. Those who came under the influence o his personality, gave up the eating of meat an fish and took to vegetarian diet. This princip was at the back of many philanthropic an humanitarian deeds and institutions which h encouraged.

For Mahavira distinctions of caste, creed o sex did not matter. According to him, salvatio is the birthright of everyone, and it is assured i one follows the prescribed rules of conduct. Hi doctrine of Karma (action) made the individua conscious of his responsibility for all actions. I also awakened the consciousness that salvatio was not a gift or favour but an attainment withi the reach of human beings.

Jain, Kailash Chand. *Lord Mahavira and his Times*. Delh M. Banarsidass, 1974. Pp. 44, 56, 88-89, 91-93, 98 237, 264-266. 270-271, 274-276, 278, 305-306.

► Confucius Discoursing with Students

READING 2.5

CONFUCIUS AS HIS STUDENTS KNEW HIM

Confucius is the Latinized form of K'ung Fu-tzu, or Master K'ung, who lived between 551-479 B.C.E. Named Ch'iu, his father was already seventy when the boy was born and died when he was three. Although of the *shih* or knightly class he was raised under humble circumstances by his mother, but nevertheless had a good education. His hobbies were archery and music.

Confucius lived during an uncertain age because the Chou government had lost effective power and many contending feudal states were striving to fill the political vacuum. The instability and failings of the age prompted thoughtful men to formulate philosophies that would either reform government and society or offer refuge and escape from an evil world. Hence the centuries between 600-300 B.C.E. is known as the Hundred Schools of Philosophy era. Confucius was a philosopher who tried to make the world a better place. He traveled from state to state teaching high moral values and seeking a ruler who would give his ideas a chance. Disappointed that he could not implement his ideals through political action Confucius settled down to teaching; posterity would remember him as China's greatest teacher and his teaching as one of the world's great moral forces.

Men flocked to his school but he only accepted those with high principles. He reputedly had three thousand students, of whom seventy-two were counted as disciples. Like Socrates his primary goal was to inculcate moral principles and form character. He did not regard himself as an originator, rather as transmitter of ancient traditions. Among the ancients, he particularly admired the founders of the Chou dynasty, above all the Duke of Chou. Beyond them he admired the wise rulers of remote antiquity, Yao, Shun and Yu the Great, who set the ideals of civilized society and good government. Confucius believed that history is a most worthy subject for study because it is only through knowing the lessons of the past that people can have positive role models and also avoid repetition of mistakes.

Confucius' disciples continued to teach his philosophy after his death, they also debated with men who expounded other ideas. Some three hundred and fifty years after his death Confucianism became China's official ideology. In the following centuries legends developed around its founder, elevating him from a moral teacher to a wise man and a prophet.

What then was K'ung Ch'iu really like and what did he teach and believe in? The best source concerning Confucius is the *Lun Yu* or *Analects* (Selected Sayings), passages from which are quoted below.

QUESTIONS:

1) What was good government to Confucius?
2) Why did Confucius think education and the study of history were important?
3) What sort of man was Confucius and what were his concerns?

91

On Government:

The Master said, A country of a thousand war-chariots cannot be administered unless the ruler attends strictly to business, punctually observes his promises, is economical in expenditure, shows affection towards his subjects in general, and uses the labour of the peasantry only at the proper times of year. (Book I, 5)

The Master said, He who rules by moral force is like the pole-star, which remains in its place while all the lesser stars do homage to it. (II, 1)

The Master said, Govern the people by regulation, keep order among them by chastisement, and they will flee from you, and lose all self-respect. Govern them by moral force, keep order among them by ritual and they will keep their self-respect and come to you of their own accord. (II, 3)

Chi K'ang-tzu [ruler of Confucius' native state of Lu] asked whether there were any form of encouragement by which he could induce the common people to be respectful and loyal. The Master said, Approach them with dignity, and they will respect you. Show piety towards your parents and kindness toward your children, and they will be loyal to you. Promote those who are worthy, train those who are incompetent; that is the best form of encouragement. (II, 20)

Tzu-kung asked about government. The master said, sufficient food, sufficient weapons, and the confidence of the common people. Tzu-kung said, Suppose you had no choice but to dispense with one of these three, which would you forgo? The Master said, Weapons. Tsu-kung said, Suppose you were forced to dispense with one of the two that were left, which would you forgo? The Master said. Food. For from of old death has been the lot of all men; but a people that no longer trusts its rulers is lost indeed. (XII, 7)

On Proper Conduct and Behavior:

The Master said, A young man's duty is to behave well to his parents at home and to his elders abroad, to be cautious in giving promises and punctual in keeping them, to have kindly feelings towards everyone, but seek the intimacy of the Good. If, when all that is done, he has any energy to spare, then let him study the polite arts. (I, 6)

The Master said, in serving his father and mother a man may gently remonstrate with them. But if he sees that he has failed to change their opinion, he should resume an attitude of deference and not thwart them; may feel discouraged, but not resentful. (IV, 18)

The Master said, While father and mother are alive, a good son does not wander far afield; or id he does so, goes only where he has said he was going. (IV, 19)

The Master said, if a gentleman is frivolous, he will lose the respect of his inferiors and lack firm ground upon which to build up his education. First and foremost he must learn to be faithful to his superiors, to keep promises, to refuse the friendship of all who are not like him. And if he finds he has made a mistake, then he must not be afraid of admitting the fact and amending his ways. (I, 8)

On Learning and Teaching:

The Master said, At fifteen I set my heart upon learning. At thirty, I had planted my feet firm upon the ground. At forty, I no longer suffered from perplexities. At fifty, I knew what were the biddings of Heaven. At sixty, I heard them with docile ear. At seventy, I could follow the dictates of my own heart; for what I desired no longer overstepped the boundaries of right. (II, 4)

The Master said, From the very poorest upwards--beginning even with the man who could bring no better present than a bundle of dried flesh--none has ever come to me without receiving instruction. (VII, 7)

The Master said, Only one who bursts with eagerness do I instruct; only one who bubbles with excitement, do I enlighten. If I hold up one corner and a man cannot come back to me with the other three, I do not continue the lesson. (VII, 8)

The Master took four subjects for his teaching: culture, conduct of affairs, loyalty to superiors and the keeping of promises. (VII, 24)

The Master said, Learn as if you were following someone whom you could not catch up, as though it were someone you were frightened of losing (VIII, 17)

His Admiration for Past Sage Rulers:

The Master said, Sublime were Shun and Yu! All that is under Heaven was theirs, yet they remained aloof from it. (VIII, 18)

The Master said, Greatest, as lord and ruler, was Yao, Sublime, indeed, was he. "There is no greatness like the greatness of Heaven," yet Yao could copy it. So boundless was it that the people could find no name for it; yet sublime were his achievements, dazzling the insignia of his culture! (VIII, 19)

The Master said, In Yu I can find no semblance of a flaw. Abstemious in his own food and drink, he displayed the utmost devotion in his offerings to spirits and divinities. Content with the plainest clothes for common wear, he saw to it that his sacrificial apron and ceremonial head-dress were of the utmost magnificence. His place of habitation was of the humblest, and all his energy went into draining and ditching. In him I can find no semblance of a flaw. (VIII, 21)

On the Superior Man:

The Master said, (the good man) does not grieve that other people do not recognize his merits. His only anxiety is lest he should fail to recognize theirs. (I, 16)

Tzu-kung asked about the true gentleman. The Master said, He does not preach what he practises till he has practised what he preaches. (II, 13)

The Master said, A gentleman can see a question from all sides without bias. The small man is biased and can see a question only from one side. (II, 14)

Wealth and rank are what every man desires; but if they can only be retained to the detriment of the Way he professes, he must relinquish them. Poverty and obscurity are what every man detests; but if they can only be avoided to the detriment of the Way he professes, he must accept them. The gentleman who ever parts company with Goodness does not fulfill that name. Never for a moment does a gentleman quit the way of Goodness.... (IV, 5)

The Master said, A gentleman takes as much trouble to discover what is right as lesser men take to discover what will pay. (IV, 16)

What Kind of Man Was Confucius?

The Master said, I have "transmitted what was taught to me without making up anything of my own." I have been faithful to and loved the Ancients. In these respects, I make bold to think, not even our old P'eng [an old man of the past who was famous as transmitter of traditions.] can have excelled me. The Master said, I have listened in silence and noted what was said, I have never grown tired of learning nor wearied of teaching others what I have learnt. These at least are merits which I can confidently claim. The Master said, The thought that "I have left my moral power untended, my learning unperfected, that I have heard of righteous men, but been unable to go to them; have heard of evil men, but been unable to reform them,"--it is these thoughts that disquiet me. (VII, 1, 2, 3)

In his leisure hours the master's manner was very free-and-easy, and his expression alert and cheerful. (VII, 4)

If at a meal the Master found himself seated next to someone who was in mourning, he did not eat his fill. When he had wailed at a funeral, during the rest of the day he did not sing. (VII, 9)

The Master said, Give me a few more years, so that I may have spent a whole fifty in study, and I believe that after all I should be fairly free from error. (VII, 16)

The Duke of She asked Tsu-lu [a disciple] about Master K'ung. Tsu-lu did not reply. The Master said, Why did you not say "This is the character of the man: so intent upon enlightening the eager that he forgets his hunger, and so happy in doing so, that he forgets the bitterness of his lot and does not realize that old age is at hand. That is what he is." (VII, 18)

The Master said, I for my part am not one of those who have innate knowledge. I am simply one who loves the past and who is diligent in investigating it. (VII, 19)

The Master said, Even when walking in a party of no more than three I can always be certain of learning from those I am with. There will be good qualities that I can select for imitation and bad ones that will teach me what requires correction in myself. (VII, 21)

The Master fished with a line but not with a net; when fowling he did not aim at a roosting bird. (VII, 26)

When in the Master's presence anyone sang a song that he liked, he did not join in at once, but asked for it to be repeated and then joined in. (VII, 31)

The Master's manner was affable yet firm, commanding but not harsh, polite but easy. (VII, 37)

There were four things that the Master wholly eschewed: he took nothing for granted, he was never over-positive, never obstinate, never egotistic. (IX, 4)

The Grand Minister (of Wu?) asked Tsu-kung [a disciple] saying, is your Master a Divine Sage? If so, how comes it that he has many practical accomplishments? [Gentlemen do not stoop to practical accomplishments; much less the Sage--Waley] Tzu-kung said, Heaven certainly intended him to become a Sage; it is also true that he has many accomplishments.

When the Master heard of it he said, The Grand Minister is quite right about me. When was young I was in humble circumstances; that is why I have many practical accomplishments....

Lao says that the Master said, It is because have not been given a chance that I have become so handy. (IX, 6)

The Master said, Do I regard myself as a possessor of wisdom? Far from it. But if even a simple peasant comes in all sincerity and asks me a question, I am ready to thrash the matter out with all its pros and cons, to the very end. (IX, 7)

Tzu-lu asked how one would serve ghosts and spirits. The Master said, Till you have learn to serve men, how can you serve ghosts? Tzu-lu then ventured upon a question about the dead. The Master said, Till you know about the living how are you to know about the dead? (XI, 11)

Waley, Arthur, ed. and trans. *The Analects of Confucius* New York: Random House, 1938. Pp. 84-85, 87-88, 90 92, 102-103, 105-106, 123-124, 126-128, 130-131 136-137, 139-140, 155, 164.

► Taoist Sage

CHUANG TZU AND THE WISDOM OF TAOISM

Next to Confucianism Taoism has been the most influential Chinese philosophy during the past two thousand plus years. It developed during the Hundred Schools of Philosophy era of the later Chou dynasty in response to the political chaos and social disintegration that then plagued the Chinese world. Unlike Confucianism which emphasized duty and social action to improve society, Taoism stressed the mystical, quietist side of the Chinese mind, and sought to console men and women in a suffering world by teaching them non-action and the joy of inner contentment by rising above the troubles and turmoil that surround them. Thus Taoism complemented Confucianism and together they answered the need of both individuals and society. For this reason, although Confucianism became China's official philosophy after c. 100 B.C.E., Taoist books such as the *Chuang Tzu* continued to be read and enjoyed by the educated.

Chuang Chou, better known as Chuang Tzu or Master Chuang, lived circa 369-286 B.C.E. He is the second great figure of early Taoism, and unlike Lao Tzu, the mythical founder of Taoism, actually lived and compiled a book that bears his name. However little is actually known of the life of Chuang Tzu, except that he was a minor official but gave up public service to live the life of a recluse.

The *Chuang Tzu* is one of the most witty and original works in Chinese literature. It is full of parables and allegory, and contains long conversations in which human talk pure nonsense while animals expound profound philosophy, and amusing anecdotes that involve actual historical persons who often appear ridiculous.

Chuang Tzu's central theme is the eternal and universal *tao* or way. Humans can only achieve happiness and peace by understanding the tao. They must realize that they are not the measure of all things. Only then can humans be liberated from the confines of their own limited minds and their partial view of things. Only then can they enjoy spiritual freedom and a happiness that is beyond change and a life that is beyond life and death. Indeed Chuang Tzu did not fear death, rather he thought of death as a natural follow up to life, as the excerpt on the death of his wife explained. Chuang Tzu also scorned worldly success and achievements, and encouraged individuals to seek their own fulfillment in their own ways. Although some condemn Chuang Tzu's Taoist philosophy as anti-social and selfish, it is nevertheless profound and has been thought provoking for generations of thinking people.

The following quotations from the *Chuang Tzu* show first his general philosophy; in the second passage he used an anecdote, a conversation between a prince and a butcher to illustrate his views; in the third part, selections based on his personal life and conversations further illuminate his ideas.

QUESTIONS:

1) What was Chuang Tzu's attitude toward life and death?
2) Define the word "tao" and give illustrations of its meaning.
3) What is the pure man of Taoism like, why is he happy?

The pure man of old knew neither to love life nor to hate death. He did not rejoice in birth, nor did he resist death. Without any concern he came and without any concern he went, that was all. He did not forget his beginning nor seek his end. He accepted [his body] with pleasure, and forgetting [life and death], he returned to [the natural state]. He did not violate Tao with his mind, and he did not assist Nature with man. This is what is meant by a pure man.

Such being the pure man, his mind is perfectly at ease. His demeanor is natural. His forehead is broad. His is as cold as autumn but as warm as spring. His pleasure and anger are as natural as the four seasons. He is in accord with all things, and no one knows the limit thereof. Therefore the sage, in employing an army, can destroy a country without losing the affection of the people. His benefits may be extended to ten thousand generations without any [partial] love for any man.

Therefore he who takes special delight in understanding things is not a sage. He who shows [special] affection [to anyone] is not a man of humanity (*jen*, love). He who calculates opportunity is not a worthy person. He who seeks fame and thus loses his own nature is not learned. And he who loses his own nature and thus misses the true way is not one who can have others do things for him....

The pure man of old was righteous but impartial, and humble but not subservient. He was naturally independent but not obstinate. His humility was manifest but not displayed. Smiling, he seemed to be happy. He acted as if he had to. His countenance improved further and further in richness, and his virtue rested more and more in the [highest good]. His efforts seemed to be those of the common people, but his loftiness could not be restrained. Deep and profound, he seemed to be like a closed door [unfathomable]. Without any attachment, he seemed to have forgotten what he said....

Life and death are due to fate (*ming*, destiny) and their constant succession like day and night is due to Nature, beyond the interference of man. They are necessary character of things. There are those who regard Heaven as their father and love it with their whole person. How much more should they love what is more outstanding than Heaven [that is, self-transformation itself]? There are those who regard the ruler as superior to themselves and would sacrifice their lives for him. How much more should they sacrifice for what is more real than the ruler (Nature)?....

The universe gives me my body so I may be carried, my life so I may toil, my old age so I may repose, and my death so I may rest. To regard life as good is the way to regard death as good. A boat may be hidden in a creek or a mountain in a lake. These may be said to be safe enough. But at midnight a strong man may come and carry it away on his back. An ignorant person does not know that even when the hiding of things, large or small, is perfectly well done, still something will escape you. But if the universe is hidden in the universe itself, then there can be no escape from it. This is the great truth of things in general. We possess our body by chance and we are already pleased with it. If our physical bodies went through ten thousand transformations without end, how incomparable would this joy be! Therefore the sage roams freely in the realm in which nothing can escape but all endures. Those who regard dying a premature death, getting old, and the beginning and end of life as equally good are followed by others. How much more is that to which all things belong and on which the whole process of transformation depends (that is, Tao)?

Tao has reality and evidence but no action or physical form. It may be transmitted but cannot be received. It may be obtained but cannot be seen. It is based in itself, rooted in itself. Before heaven and earth came into being, Tao existed by itself from all time. It gave spirits and rulers their spiritual powers. It created heaven and earth. It is above the zenith but it is not high. It is beneath the nadir but it is not low. It is prior to heaven and earth but it is not old. It is more ancient than the highest antiquity but is not regarded as long ago....

* * * * *

There is a limit to our life, but there is n o limit to knowledge. To pursue what is unlimited with what is limited is a perilous thing. When, knowing this, we still seek to increase our knowledge, we are simply placing ourselves in peril. Shrink from fame when you do good; shrink from punishment when you do evil; pursue always the middle course. These are ways to preserve our body, to maintain our life, to support our parents, and to complete our term of years.

Prince Weh-hui's cook was cutting up a bullock. Every touch of his hand, every shift of his shoulder, every tread of his foot, every thrust of his knee, every sound of the rending flesh, and every note of the movement of the chopper was in perfect harmony--rhythmical like the dance of "The mulberry Grove," blended like the chords of the "Ching-shou" movement.

"Ah, admirable," said the prince, "that your skill should be so perfect!"

The cook laid down his chopper and replied: "What your servant loves is the Tao, which I have applied to the skill of carving. When I first began to cut up bullocks, what I saw was simply whole bullocks. After three years' practice, I saw no more bullocks as wholes. Now, I work with my mind, and not with my eyes. The functions of my senses stop; my spirit dominates. Following the natural markings, my chopper slips through the great cavities, slides through the great cleavages, taking advantage of the structure that is already there. My skill is now such that any chopper never touches even the smallest tendon or ligament, let alone the great bones. A good cook changes his chopper once a year, because he cuts. An ordinary cook changes his chopper once a month, because he hacks. Now my chopper has been in use for nineteen years; it has cut up several thousand bullocks; yet its edge is as sharp as if it just came from the whetstone. At the joints there are always interstices, and the edge of the chopper is without thickness. If we insert that which is without thickness into an interstice, then we may ply the chopper as we wish and there will be plenty of room. That is why after nineteen years the edge of my chopper is still as sharp as if it just came from the whetstone. Nevertheless, when I come to complicated joints, and see that there will be some difficulty, I proceed slowly. Then by a very gentle movement of my chopper, the part is quickly separated, and yields like earth crumbling to the ground. Then I stand up straight with the chopper in my hand, and look all round, and feel a sense of triumph and satisfaction. Finally I wipe my chopper and put it in its sheath."

"Excellent," said the prince, I have heard the words of this cook, and learned the way of cultivating life."

* * * * *

Once Chuang Tzu was fishing in the P'u River when the King of Ch'u sent two of his ministers to announce that he wished to entrust to Chuang Tzu the care of h`is entire domain.

Chuang Tzu held his fishing pole and, without turning his head, said: "I have heard that Ch'u possesses a sacred tortoise which has been dead for three thousand years and which the king keeps wrapped up in a box and stored in his ancestral temple. Is the tortoise better off dead and with its bones venerated, or would it be better of alive with its tail dragging in the mud?"

"It would be better off alive and dragging its tail in the mud," the two ministers replied.

"Then go away!" said Chuang Tzu, "and I will drag my tail in the mud!"....

Chuang Tzu's wife died and Hui Tzu went to offer his condolence. He found Chuang Tzu squatting on the ground and singing, beating on an earthen bowl. He said, "Someone has lived with you raised children for you and now she has aged and died. Is it not enough that you should not shed any tear? But now you sing and beat the bowl. Is this not too much?"

"No," replied Chuang Tzu. "When she died, how could I help being affected? But as I think the matter over, I realize that originally she had no life; and not only no life, she had no form; not only no form, she had no material force (ch'i). In the limbo of existence and non-existence, there was transformation and the material force was evolved. The material force was transformed to be form, form was transformed to become life, and now birth has transformed to become death. This is like the rotation of the four seasons, spring, summer, fall, and winter. Now she lies asleep in the great house (the universe). For me to go about weeping and wailing would be to show my ignorance of destiny. Therefore I desist."....

Chuang Tzu and Hui Tzu were taking a leisurely walk along the Hao River. Chuang Tzu said, "The white fish are swimming at ease. This is the happiness of the fish."

"You are not fish," said Hui Tzu. "How do you know its happiness?"

"You are not I," said Chuang Tzu. "How do you know that I do not know the happiness of the fish?"

Hui Tzu said, "Of course I do not know, since I am not you. But you are not the fish, and it is perfectly clear that you do not know the happiness of the fish."

"Let us get at the bottom of the matter," said Chuang Tzu. "When you asked how I knew the happiness of the fish, you already knew that I knew the happiness of the fish, but asked how. I knew it along the river."

Chan, Wing-tsit, trans. *A Source Book in Chinese Philosophy*. Princeton: Princeton Univ. Press, 1963. Pp. 192-194, 209-210. de Bary, William T., Wing-tsit Chan and Burton Watson, eds. *Sources of Chinese Tradition*. New York: Columbia Univ. Press, 1960. Pp. 75-76, 79.

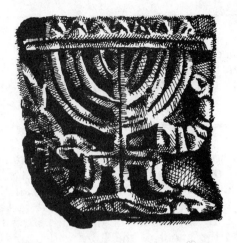

READING 2.7

ABRAHAM AND DAVID-- CULTURE HEROES OF ANCIENT ISRAEL

▶ **Marble Relief of a Menorah**

The earliest civilizations, great empires, and ancient religions rose and fell in the land between the Tigris-Euphrates valleys in present-day Iraq and the Nile valley in Egypt. Beginning about 2000 B.C.E. there emerged a people called the Hebrews. Small in number and never the lords of a large empire, the Hebrews nevertheless had a great and enduring impact on the world. Their monotheistic religion, which survives as Judaism, set them apart from the prevailing polytheistic religions of antiquity. Another concept that distinguished the Hebrews from their neighbors was that of a covenant with God: in exchange for complete faithfulness to God and obedience to his commands, he would make the Hebrews his Chosen People and reward them with a Promised Land, Canaan (Palestine). Judaism began with such a covenant between God or El (later called Yahweh) and Abraham, a Hebrew patriarch.

The book of Genesis records the beginnings of the ancient Hebrews or Israelites (descendants of Israel or Jacob, a grandson of Abraham), their covenant with God, and their settlement in Canaan. They called their land Bet Israel or the Homeland of Israel.

Around 1200 B.C.E., another people, the Philistines, invaded and settled in the same general region as the Israelites. The Philistines possessed iron weapons and tools and this gave them a military advantage over the Israelites.

The Israelites responded to the Philistine threat by forging a nation; they selected generals to be their kings. The first king was Saul (1025-1004). He failed to consolidate fully the various tribes and died in battle against the Philistines. His successor, King David (1004-965), gained victory over the Philistines on the battlefield and ended their threat by restricting them to the area of five towns in the southwest part of the region, along the Mediterranean coast.

After consolidation his conquests, King David established a capital city at Jerusalem, which became the political, military, and religious center of his realm. Through strong ties with Phoenicia, he gave Israel access to the ports of Tyre and Sidon, through which olive oil and grain could be traded for cedar, copper, and various luxury materials. David is remembered as the ideal king of Israel because of his political and military successes and the cultural flowering under his rule.

The first selection below is from the book of *Genesis* and recounts the covenant between Abraham and God. The Hebrew patriarch was willing to do anything his God commanded to win prosperity for his people and their posterity. The second passage is from the first Book of *Samuel*. It recounts the famous exploit of the future king David in the struggle against the Philistines for supremacy in Palestine.

QUESTIONS:

1) What is the moral of the story of Abraham and Isaac?
2) What are the key elements in the covenant between the Lord and Abraham?
3) Given that the story of David and Goliath is told from the Hebrew point of view, what aspect of the tale are highlighted?

And it came to pass after these things, that God did tempt Abraham, and said unto him, "Abraham"; and he said, "Behold, here I am." And he said, "Take now your son, your only son Isaac, whom you love, and get you into the land of Moriah; and offer him there for a burnt offering upon one of the mountains which I will tell you of."

And Abraham rose up early in the morning, and saddled his ass, and took two of his young men with him, and Isaac his son, and clave the wood for the burnt offering, and rose up, and went unto the place of which God had told him. Then on the third day Abraham lifted up his eyes, and saw the place afar off. And Abraham said unto his young men, "Abide you here with the ass; and I and the lad will go yonder and worship, and come again to you."

And Abraham took the wood of the burnt offering, and laid it upon Isaac his son; and he took the fire in his hand, and a knife; and they went both of them together. And Isaac spoke unto Abraham his father, and said, "My father"; and he said, "Here am I, my son." And he said, "Behold the fire and the wood: but where is the lamb for a burnt offering?" And Abraham said, "My son, God will provide himself a lamb for a burnt offering"; so they went both of them together.

And they came to the place which God had told him of; and Abraham built an altar there, and laid the wood in order, and bound Isaac his son, and laid him on the altar upon the wood. And Abraham stretched forth his hand, and took the knife to slay his son. And the angel of the Lord called unto him out of heaven, and said, "Abraham, Abraham"; and he said, "Here am I." And he said, "Lay not your hand upon the lad, neither do you any thing unto him: for now I know that you fear God, seeing you have not withheld your son, your only son from me." And Abraham lifted up his eyes, and looked, and behold behind him a ram caught in a thicket by

his horns: and Abraham went and took the ram and offered him up for a burnt offering in the stead of his son. And Abraham called the name of that place Jehovahjireh: as it is said to this day, In the mount of the Lord it shall be seen. And the angel of the Lord called unto Abraham out of heaven the second time, and said, "By myself have I sworn, says the Lord, for because you have done this thing, and have not withheld your son, your only son: That in blessing I will bless you, and in multiplying I will multiply your seed as the stars of the heaven, and as the sand which is upon the sea shore; and your seed shall possess the gate of his enemies; And in your seed shall all the nations of the earth be blessed; because you have obeyed my voice." So Abraham returned unto his young men, and they rose up and went together to Beersheba; and Abraham dwelt at Beersheba.

* * * * *

Now the Philistines gathered together their armies to battle, and were gathered together at Shochoh, which belongs to Judah, and pitched between Shochoh and Azekah, in Ephesdammim. And Saul and the men of Israel were gathered together, and pitched by the valley of Elah, and set the battle in array against the Philistines. And the Philistines stood on a mountain on the one side, and Israel stood on a mountain on the other side: and there was a valley between them.

And there went out a champion out of the camp of the Philistines, named Goliath, of Gath, whose height was six cubits and a span. And he had a helmet of brass upon his head, and he was armed with a coat of mail; and the weight of the coat was five thousand shekels of brass. And he had greaves of brass upon his legs, and a target of brass between his shoulders. And the staff of his spear was like a weaver's beam; and his spear's head weighed six hundred shekels of iron: and one bearing a shield went before him. And he stood and cried unto the armies of Israel, and said unto them, "Why are you come out to set your battle in array? am not I a Philistine, and you servants to Saul? choose you a man for you, and let him come down to me. If he be able to fight with me, and to kill me, then will we be your servants: but if I prevail against him, and kill him, then shall you be our servants, and serve us." And the Philistine said, "I defy the armies of Israel this day; give me a man, that we may fight together."

When Saul and all Israel heard those words of the Philistine, they were dismayed, and greatly afraid. Now David was the son of that Ephrathite of Bethlehemjudah, whose name was Jesse; and he had eight sons: and the man went among men for an old man in the days of Saul. And the three eldest sons of Jesse went and followed Saul to the battle: and the names of his three sons that went to the battle were Eliab the firstborn, and next unto him Abinadab, and the third Shammah. And David was the youngest: and the three eldest followed Saul. But David went and returned from Saul to feed his father's sheep at Bethlehem. And the Philistine drew near morning and evening, and presented himself forty days.

And Jesse said unto David his son, "Take now for your brethren an ephah of this parched corn, and these ten loaves, and run to the camp to your brethren; And carry these ten cheeses unto the captain of their thousand, and look how your brethren fare, and take their pledge."

Now Saul, and they, and all the men of Israel, were in the valley of Elah, fighting with the Philistines. And David rose up early in the morning, and left the sheep with a keeper, and took, and went, as Jesse had commanded him; and he came to the trench, as the host was going forth to the fight, and shouted for the battle. For Israel and the Philistines had put the battle in array, army against army. And David left his carriage in the hand of the keeper of the carriage, and ran into the army, and came and saluted his brethren. And as he talked with them, behold, there came up the champion, the Philistine of Gath, Goliath by name, out of the armies of the Philistines, and spoke according to the same words: and David heard them. And all the men of Israel, when they saw the man, fled from him, and were sore afraid.

And the men of Israel said, "Have you seen this man that is come up? surely to defy Israel is he come up: and it shall be, that the man who kills him, the king will enrich him with great riches, and will give him his daughter, and make his father's house free in Israel." And David spoke to the men that stood by him, saying, "What shall be done to the man that kills this Philistine, and takes away the reproach from Israel? for who is this uncircumcised Philistine, that he should defy the armies of the living God?" And the people answered him after this manner, saying, "So shall it be done to the man that kills him." And Eliab his eldest brother heard when he spoke unto the men; and Eliab's anger was kindled against David, and he said, "Why came you down hither? and with whom have you left those few sheep in the wilderness? I know your pride, and the naughtiness of your heart; for you are come down that you might see the battle." And David said, "What have I now done? Is there not a cause?"

And he turned from him toward another, and spoke after the same manner: and the people answered him again after the former manner. And when the words were heard which David spoke, they rehearsed them before Saul: and he sent for him. And David said to Saul, "Let no man's heart fail because of him; your servant will go and fight with this Philistine." And Saul said to David, "you are not able to go against this Philistine to fight with him: for you are but a youth, and he a man of war from his youth." And David said unto Saul, "your servant kept his father's sheep, and there came a lion, and a bear, and took a lamb out of the flock: And I went out after him, and smote him, and delivered it out of his mouth: and when he arose against me, I caught him by his beard, and smote him, and slew him. Your servant slew both the lion and the bear: and this uncircumcised Philistine shall be as one of them, seeing he has defied the armies of the living God."

David said moreover, "The Lord that delivered me out of the paw of the lion, and out of the paw of the bear, he will deliver me out of the hand of this Philistine." And Saul said unto David, "Go, and the Lord be with you." And Saul armed David with his armour, and he put an helmet of brass upon his head; also he armed him with a coat of mail. And David girded his sword upon his armour, and he assayed to go; for he had not proved it. And David said unto Saul, "I cannot go with these; for I have not proved them." And David put them off him. And he took his staff in his hand, and chose him five smooth stones out of the brook, and put them in a shepherd's bag which he had, even in a scrip; and his sling was in his hand: and he drew near to the Philistine.

And the Philistine came on and drew near unto David; and the man that bare the shield went before him. And when the Philistine looked about, and saw David, he disdained him: for he was but a youth, and ruddy, and of a fair countenance. And the Philistine said unto David, "Am I a dog, that you come to me with staves?" And the Philistine cursed David by his gods. And the Philistine said to David, "Come to me, and I will give your flesh unto the fowls of the air, and to the beasts of the field." Then said David to the Philistine, "you come to me with a sword, and with a spear, and with a shield: but I come to you in the name of the Lord of hosts, the God of the armies of Israel, whom you have defied. This day will the Lord deliver you into mine hand; and I will smite you, and take your head from you; and I will give the carcases of the host of the Philistines this day unto the fowls of the air, and to the wild beasts of the earth; that all the earth may know that there is a God in Israel. And all this assembly shall know that the Lord saves not with sword and spear: for the battle is the Lord's, and he will give you into our hands."

And it came to pass, when the Philistine arose, and came and drew near to meet David, that David hastened, and ran toward the army to meet the Philistine. And David put his hand in his bag, and took thence a stone, and slang it, and smote the Philistine in his forehead, that the stone sunk into his forehead; and he fell upon his face to the earth.

So David prevailed over the Philistine with a sling and with a stone, and smote the Philistine, and slew him; but there was no sword in the hand of David. Therefore David ran, and stood upon the Philistine, and took his sword, and drew it out of the sheath thereof, and slew him, and cut off his head therewith. And when the Philistines saw their champion was dead, they fled. And the men of Israel and of Judah arose, and shouted, and pursued the Philistines, until you come to the valley, and to the gates of Ekron. And the wounded of the Philistines fell down by the way to Shaaraim, even unto Gath, and unto Ekron. And the children of Israel returned from chasing after the Philistines, and they spoiled their tents.

And David took the head of the Philistine, and brought it to Jerusalem; but he put his armour in his tent. And when Saul saw David go forth against the Philistine, he said unto Abner, the captain of the host, "Abner, whose son is this youth?" And Abner said, "As your soul lives, O king, I cannot tell." And the king said, "Inquire you whose son the stripling is." And as David returned from the slaughter of the Philistine, Abner took him, and brought him before Saul with the head of the Philistine in his hand. And Saul said to him, "Whose son are you, you young man?" And David answered, "I am the son of your servant Jesse the Bethlehemite."

Genesis. Chap. 22. *1 Samuel*. Chap. 17. From the *King James Version of the Holy Bible*, with slight modifications.

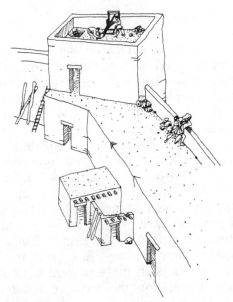

MASADA: THE LAST STAND OF JEWISH REBELS AGAINST ROME

▶ **Fortifications at Masada**

History has generally been written by the victors. This is quite true of ancient Roman history. Thus, in general we do not learn of the feelings and attitudes of those who fell under Roman dominance. In the case of the Jews, however, there is a partial exception to this rule: a Jewish aristocratic priest named Flavius Josephus wrote a history of the Jewish Revolt of 66-73 C.E. Josephus was a staunch defender of Jewish culture and religion, but he felt that the nationalistic fervor of his compatriots was futile. He served as a commander during the revolt, was captured early on, and remained with the Roman general (later emperor) Titus till the fall of Jerusalem in 70. Then he immigrated to Rome and was granted Roman citizenship and a pension. A Greek translation of his *Bellum Judaicum* (*Jewish War*), originally written in Aramaic, is extant.

Although Josephus's political outlook is distinctly pro-Roman, his history of the revolt contains a very sympathetic and moving description of the desperate final act of the ill-fated Jewish rebellion. In 73 a group of fanatic nationalist terrorists, called Sicarii ("Knife-men") by the Romans, remained entrenched near the Dead Sea at Masada, an almost impregnable fortress that they had seized from its Roman garrison seven years earlier. After a siege of six months, a force of 7,000 Roman legionaries and auxiliaries commanded by Flavius Silva finally took the fortress. Jewish resistance ended with its fall. The desperate courage of Masada's defenders, particularly their determination to die as free people, gave the conflict a special poignancy. Josephus records at length two very memorable speeches in which the rebel leader, Eleazar, successfully spurs his people to a courageous and shocking refusal to submit.

In the passages that follow, Josephus describes the fortifications at Masada and the Roman siege techniques; he quotes the speeches of Eleazar (presumably reconstructed from the account of a surviving eyewitness), and records the fate of the rebels and the Romans' stunned reaction to it.

QUESTIONS:

1) Why were the Romans so intent on taking this last Jewish stronghold?
2) What made Masada so strong a position to hold up in?
3) What seems to be the moral of the story of the defenders of Masada as Josephus tells it?

The Roman commander [Flavius Silva] led his army against Eleazar and the Sicarii who were holed up at Masada. He immediately secured control of the surrounding region, set up guard posts at suitable points, and encircled the whole site with a well-guarded wall, so that none of the besieged could flee. He himself chose to encamp at a location most suitable for conducting the siege, but less convenient in regard to provisioning: this was where the boulders of the fortress lay nearest to the outcropping mountainside. The result was much toil for the Jews assigned to bring up all the camp's supplies, including even water, since there was no spring in the vicinity. With these preparatory measures taken, Silva then turned his full attention to the siege. This required considerable technical skill and effort because of the strength of the enemy position, whose disposition was as follows:

[Masada is] an immense rocky plateau: it has a large perimeter and is lofty in elevation on all side, where there are very precipitous drops down to its distant base. The place is inaccessible to all living things, except along two very treacherous paths: one rises from Lake Asphaltitis [the Dead Sea] on the east, the other, easier, path ascends on the west side. The path on the lake side is called "The Snake," because of its narrow and coiling route; it winds around protruding rocks, doubles back on itself, and then sometimes runs for a straight stretch. Anyone climbing by this approach must place one foot carefully ahead of the other and face death at every turn, for in each direction the prospect of a tremendous cliff would frighten even the bravest climber. After traveling about thirty stades [c. 3.5 miles], one reaches the summit, which has the form not of a peak but rather of a large flat expanse. Here the high priest Jonathan [Jonathan the Hasmonean, brother of Judas Maccabaeus, and high priest 152-143 B.C.E.] was first to build a fortress and name the place Masada. Herod [the Great, king of Judaea 40-4 B.C.E.] later made elaborate improvements in the site: he encompassed the whole summit (a three-quarter-mile perimeter) by a white stone wall eighteen feet high and twelve feet thick. The wall was strengthened by thirty-seven towers each seventy-five feet high; these towers were linked by a continuous succession of rooms along the inside of the wall. The king kept clear the central part of the summit for cultivation, since it contained very fertile soil. Thus any lack of food supplies from outside could be made good for those who had taken refuge at Masada. Herod also

constructed a palace on the west face below th summit wall and extending toward the north This was massive, with ninety-foot towers a each corner. The interior, with its chambers porticoes, and baths, was luxurious. Monolithi columns supported the structure, and walls an floors throughout were covered with multi colored tiles. Furthermore, wherever there wer dwellings--on the summit and at the palace--h cut large water-holding cisterns into the rock, s that there should be as plentiful a supply as i there were springs. An underground passage le from the palace to the summit; this was entirel hidden from view. But even the two above ground paths to the top were scarcely usable b an enemy, for the east approach is virtuall impassable, as we have said, and on th narrowest point of the western approach, about third of a mile from the top, Herod placed a larg tower. There was no way around the tower an it was very hard to capture; even for friendl travelers, it was difficult to pass through. S formidably had both man and nature prepare Masada against an enemy's assault.

Even more amazing were the magnificenc and extent of the materials stored in the fortress There was sufficient grain to last for years, a well as abundant provisions of wine and [olive oil, pulse, and dates. After they ha treacherously seized control of the place, Eleaza and the Sicarii found all these stores in as goo condition as more recent supplies, even thoug they were nearly 100 years old when the fortres was captured by the Romans, who found th remaining foodstuffs quite unspoiled. The caus of this phenomenon was likely the atmosphere o the fortress, which at such a height is altogethe free from pollutants and corrupting elements The Romans also found weaponry of all kinds i great quantities, enough to equip 10,000 men there were also caches of unworked iron, bronze and lead. Herod is said to have prepared th fortress-refuge in fear of two threats: first, from the Jewish people themselves, who might depose him and restore the previous dynasty; second and more serious and immediate, from the Egyptian queen, Cleopatra, who quite openly sought the throne of Judaea and was always begging [Mark] Antony to kill Herod to this end. It is surprising that Antony did not in fac accommodate Cleopatra, since he was so infatuated with her. Such were the perceived threats that motivated Herod to fortify Masada, which was destined to be the last obstacle to the Romans in their war against the Jews.

As we have said, Flavius Silva, when he had completed the encirclement of the site and ensured there could be no escaping, proceeded to the siege operations themselves. He found only one place that could support siege platforms; this was just below the tower guarding the ascent by the western path. Here there was a large rocky projection called the "White Cliff," some 450 feet below the summit. Silva took possession of the spot and ordered his men to build an earthwork on it. The troops, working enthusiastically, built a solid embankment 300 feet high. Since this still seemed insufficient to support the siege machines, Silva had a massive platform built of fitted stone blocks, seventy-five feet in both width and height. The siege engines themselves were like those Vespasian and Titus had used. In addition, Silva had a ninety-foot tower built and covered with iron plates. From this, the Romans, by firing sharp-point throwers and stone-throwers, could easily repel defenders and keep them back from the ramparts. At the same time, Silva had a huge battering ram brought up and gave orders for it to be used incessantly; eventually, though with difficulty, part of the wall was breached and then brought down. But the Sicarii had quickly constructed another wall within the circuit of the old one. This one was less vulnerable to ramming, because it was made to be resilient and to absorb the force of the ram's blows, in the following way: large beams were laid lengthwise and fastened together at their ends in two parallel courses, the space between being filled with earth. To prevent the earth from dispersing as the wall rose, wooden cross members were used to clamp to together the long beams. Thus, the Romans saw what looked to be a conventional wall; but in fact the ram's blows were deadened by the resilient material of the structure, which settled and became stronger with each impact. Silva decided it might be better to attack this sort of wall with fire and ordered his men to throw torches onto it. Since it was wooden and hollow, the wall quickly caught fire and flames blazed up. At first, a northerly wind drove the flames in the face of the Romans, causing them to fear that their siege machinery might catch fire. However, as if by divine will, the wind veered to the opposite direction and sped up the incineration of the wall. The Romans, heartened by this divine aid, returned exulting to their camp, resolved to attack the enemy the next morning. All that night, they kept watch with special vigilance lest anyone escape.

Eleazar, however, had no intention of fleeing or of allowing anyone else to flee. The wall was convulsed in flames, and he could think of no means of resistance or evasion. As he imagined the atrocities that the Romans would inflict on the rebels and even their women and children, he decided death would be a better fate for them all. With this resolve, he called an assembly of his most fearless companions and recommended his proposal with these words:

[from Eleazar's first speech]:

Long ago, my good men, we resolved to serve neither the Romans nor any other but God, who alone is man's true and rightful master. The time has come to back those words with action. In the past, we refused to accept slavery even when no danger was involved. Let us not in this catastrophe disgrace ourselves by accepting it along with the extreme punishments that the Romans shall mete out if we are taken alive. We were the first to revolt and are the last to keep up armed resistance. I think that God has given us a chance to die honorably and as free men, something others, who have met unexpected fates, have not been granted. Once day breaks, we will surely be taken captive, but we are free to choose a noble death together with our loved ones. Our enemies cannot prevent this, much as they would like to, just as we can no longer expect to defeat them in battle....

[From Eleazar's second speech]:

What has become of that great city, the metropolis of the Jewish people, with its protective walls and forts and towers, bursting with war materials and thousands of defenders? the city we thought God had founded? It has been destroyed root and branch, and now the only sign of its existence is the camp of the enemy that destroyed it. A few hapless old men sit and weep by the ashes of the temple precinct; a few women kept alive to sate the lust of the enemy. Who among us in this situation could bear to look on the sun's light any longer, even if he could himself live in safety? Who among us such an enemy of his fatherland, such a coward, such a lover of life, that he does not regret being alive to see all this? We should all have died rather than see that holy city sacked by enemy hands, that sacred temple so ruined and profaned. We cherished the noble hope of avenging the city. Since that hope has now left us, let us hurry to die honorably. Let us show mercy to ourselves, our wives, and our children, while it is still in our power to do so. For we and our children were fated to die; even the fortunate cannot escape death. But nature does not impose on men the necessity of bearing disgrace, slavery, and the sight of our wives and children shamefully treated; such things come to those who refuse to avoid them by seeking death. Trusting in our own courage, we revolted against the Romans. When offered, we refused the chance to save our lives. Who can doubt the fury we will meet if taken alive? Those young enough to stand it will endure prolonged suffering; those too old to bear it will break under such treatment. Are we to watch our wives raped and hear our children cry "Father" while our hands are tied? Let us use those hands, while they are yet free, to perform a noble deed. Let us die unenslaved; as free men with our children and wives, let us depart this life together. So much our laws command us, our wives and children beg of us. God requires us to seek death, the Romans want us to shirk it and fear lest a single one of us should evade capture in this way. Let us hurry to deprive them of their longed-for pleasure at our capture and leave them instead to wonder at the heroism of our deaths.

His audience cut off Eleazar's speech at this point, so overwhelmed were they by the desire to carry out the deed he proposed. Like madmen, they hastened to the act in hopes of anticipating their neighbors; they all believed it would be a proof of their bravery and resolve if they were not among the last to die. So fierce was their yearning to slay their wives, their children, and themselves. Nor did their resolve waver when they came to the deed. Instead, they held firm to the determination they had conceived while hearing Eleazar's speech. Reason, they trusted, advised them better than emotion or affection, in deciding their loved ones' fates. Even as they embraced their wives and held their children, weeping and prolonging those last kisses, at that same time, they carried out their plan as if with another's hands. The thought of what their families would endure at the enemy's hands solaced them for the necessary killing. In the event, not a single one failed to perform the bold deed; all followed through their plan. What poor prisoners of necessity, who judged it the least of evils to take the lives of their wives and children with their own hands! They could not bear the anguish at what they had had to do and felt they were cheating the slain by living even another moment. They heaped together the remaining supplies and set them alight. They then chose ten among them to execute the rest. Each lay by his family and gladly offered his neck to the unhappy executioners. The latter, having scrupulously performed their assigned task, then chose lots for one who would execute the other nine and finally kill himself. Such confidence did they have in their mutual commitment to duty. So the nine offered their throats to the sword, and the tenth, sole survivor, checked through the carnage to make sure none still needed his hand. Finding all dead, he set the palace afire and summoned the strength to drive the sword through his body and fall beside his family. These men died believing not a living soul would be left to fall into Roman hands. But two old women, one of them a kinswoman of Eleazar and both better educated and more intelligent than most women, escaped with five children by hiding in an underground water-cistern, while the slaughter went on. There were 960 victims in all, counting women and children. This tragedy was played out on the 15th of the month Xanthikos [2 May 73 C.E.].

The Romans meanwhile expected further fighting and at daybreak took up arms and approached along gangways spanning the space between siege platform and the summit. When they encountered no enemy but only a terrible solitude, fire, and silence, they could not fathom what had happened. They called out, as if giving a signal to shoot, expecting the enemy to emerge. The women in the cistern heard the shouting and emerged to inform the Romans what had occurred. One of them reported precisely Eleazar's speech and the subsequent actions. The Romans heard the tale with disbelief in such valor. They set about extinguishing the fires and made a passage into the palace. When they discovered the hordes of dead bodies, they did not exult as usual over the enemy. Instead, they marveled at the nobility of their determination and at the disdain for death shown by the many who had carried out the plan so unfalteringly.

Niese, B., ed. *Flavii Iosephi opera*. Vol. 6: *De bello Iudaico libri vii*. Berlin: Weidmann, 1895; rpt. 1955. Book 7, sections 275-326, 375-406. Translation by James P. Holoka.

THREE CHURCH FATHERS ON THE IMPORTANCE OF A CHRISTIAN UPBRINGING

► **An Archbishop**

Christianity triumphed in the fourth century C.E. over both the traditional pagan religions of Greece and Rome and over such philosophies of life as Stoicism and Epicureanism. Jesus, a teacher and miracle-worker in Roman Palestine, had taught a message of love of one's neighbor, repentance for one's sins, and the possibility of salvation for all. After his death in c. 30 C.E., his followers announced that Jesus had risen from the dead and was the long-awaited Messiah. They continued to spread his message and made converts through their dynamic preaching. Paul of Tarsus (3-67 C.E.) was a Jewish convert to Christianity. He carried the new faith to Greek-speaking non-Jews in three missionary journeys in Asia Minor, Greece, and Rome, where he founded Christian churches and kept in touch with his converts through letters. Some of Paul's epistles, along with the four canonical Gospels, form the New Testament. The organization of Christian scripture gave the new faith authority and a basis for spiritual guidance.

Christianity was persecuted sporadically till the reign of the Emperor Constantine (r. 308-337), during whose reign it was not only protected but promoted and approved. Under Emperor Theodosius (r. 379-395), it was proclaimed the only legal religion of the Roman Empire (391).

Christianity had a strong and persistent appeal for the following reasons: it required an absolute and unconditional allegiance to one single God and creed. It offered permanent spiritual values and a stable ethical system at a time when political and social order was disintegrating with the collapse of the Roman world. Further, it was open to all people, making no distinction between the lowest slave and the emperor himself; every soul was important and capable of salvation. Finally, Christianity satisfied the universal need to belong. Following the injunction to "Love thy neighbor," members of the Christian community shared rituals and ceremonies, a value system and manner of living. Persecution only strengthened this bond.

Distinguished early Christian thinkers and theologians, known as the Church Fathers, wrote extensively on the notion of a good Christian life. Interpreting scripture, they formulated and publicized a moral code, which especially encouraged the proper education of Christian children. The following selections are by Church Fathers. In the first, John Chrysostom (c. 354-407) gives advice on the rearing of male children to a life of Christian virtue. In the second, Jerome (c. 348-420), in a letter to a woman friend about her daughter, does the same for female children. In the third passage, the greatest of the Fathers, Augustine (354-430), in his *Confessions*, admits the many sins he committed as a young man and recalls the beginning of his conversion to Christianity and a better life. All three writers stress the vulnerability of young people to the temptations of the flesh.

QUESTIONS:

1) Do you think the advice given by John Chrysostom is practical in his world? in your own?
2) Do you see any subtle differences between John Chrysostom's advice and Jerome's?
3) What does Augustine seem to mean when he says "I was in love with the notion of love itself"?

JOHN CHRYSOSTOM

We must now discuss passion. In this matter, control and abuse both exhibit a double nature: the boy ought neither to prostitute himself nor to sleep around with girls. The doctors say this passion strikes most forcefully from age fifteen on. How are we to curb the monster? What brake can we apply? None but hell fire.

In the first place he must be kept from disgraceful sights and sounds. A free-born youth should not frequent the theater. If he yearns for it, indicate to him companions who avoid the place and spur him to compete with them in such avoidance: the appeal of competition is overpowering. We must always recognize this, but especially if the youth is competitive by temperament. The appeal to competitive instinct is more compelling than fear, rewards, or any other inducement.

We must not neglect other, beneficial enjoyments. Take him to see holy men; allow him his recreation, giving him gifts to compensate his spirit for the privations it must tolerate. Instead of sensuous visions, offer him enjoyable tales, the panorama of the landscape, the appreciation of architecture. Meet the temptation to watch theatrical displays with this advice: "My boy, not suitable for the free-born are performances by foul-mouthed naked women and suchlike. Pledge that you won't speak or listen to anything indecent, and you may leave. But there [in the theater] it is not at all possible to hear nothing offensive. Such goings-on are unsuited to your eyes." Kiss and hug the youth when advising thus, showing affection by our embrace. We should shape his character by such methods.

Furthermore, as I have warned, do not ever allow a girl to approach or serve him, or at any rate only an elderly woman. Your talks with him should concentrate on the kingdom of the Lord and on ancient examples--both pagan and Christian--of men renowned for their sobriety;

these models must ever be held up to him. Do not hesitate to adduce even a servant whose conduct is decorous, pointing out the paradox of a servant showing moderation while the free man debases himself by his actions.

Another cure for [immoderate passion] is to fast, at the minimum twice a week, Wednesdays and Fridays. He should also attend church.

The youth's father ought to take him to the theater when it closes in the evening and show him the patrons as they exit, belittling the elderly for being bigger fools than the young, and likewise the young for so indulging their lust. He should ask: "What have they gained from this but disgrace, reprimands, and damnation?" Self-control increases greatly through the avoidance of such sights and sounds.

Further, instruct the youth to make his prayers with diligently and penitently, for a boy is in fact capable of this.... In sum, imprint on the youth the mark of a devout man. If he tries not to swear, not to injure in return for injury, not to engage in slander and malice all this, together with fasting and prayer he will gain in self-control.

If he is to live his life in the secular world, choose a bride for him early, before he embarks on a military or public career. Educate his soul, then be concerned for his outward reputation. It is essential that both parties to a marriage should be virgins--it will strengthen the inner resolve of both the young man and his wife and ensure the integrity of their love. In addition, our gracious God will favor abundantly the marriage of those who join themselves in the way he commanded. The youth must keep this married love always foremost: his yearning for his wife will quash any yearning for other women.

Praise the bride for her looks, her proper bearing, and her other noble traits; then warn him: "She will spurn a marriage with you, if she learns that you are living a wanton life." This should bring it home to him that momentous issues are involved in his behavior. Warn him: "Your bride's family, her parents, servants, friends and relatives, all observe your actions carefully and will inform her about them." Restrict him with this fetter to guarantee his self-control. For this reason, you should betroth him at an early age, even if he cannot marry so soon, to give him incentive to demonstrate his moral probity, and to prevent any lapse into depravity.

JEROME

My task is ... to discuss with you how you ought to rear our little Paula, who was dedicated to Christ even before her birth .... The soul must be instructed to be a temple of the lord. It should learn to hear and to speak only what relates to the fear of God. It must be ignorant of profanity and his the songs of this world; the tongue at this age should be formed by sweet psalms. Keep lascivious boys away from her, and let even her handmaids keep clear of worldly acquaintances, lest they compound the evil they have learned by teaching it to her. An alphabet of wood or ivory should be made for her and called by their proper names. She should play with these often, so that learning may be a game .... When, with shaky hand she begins to handle the stylus, either guide her slender fingers by holding a hand over hers or have the letters carved on the border of her tablet, so that she may trace them without transgressing their outlines. Reward her for correct spelling with such small treats as children love. She should not learn in isolation, but with classmates whose accomplishments she may envy and whose accolades she may be spurred to surpass. She should not be scolded for being behind, but stimulated by the prospect of praise. She ought to rejoice in success and lament defeat. Above all, her studies must not be made tedious--a repulsion acquired in youth often outlives one's childhood. The very words she uses to cast her thoughts in sentences should not be chosen casually, but carefully premeditated; she should also know the names of the prophets, apostles, and the whole series of patriarchs as transmitted in Matthew and Luke ....

Choose as her teacher a man of suitable age, lifestyle, and learning. Even a learned man does not shrink from performing the same service for a female relative or noble maiden that Aristotle performed for Philip's son [Alexander the Great]

when he, like a school-teacher, instructed him in the elements of literature. Even seeming trivial things are not to be despised when they form the basis for greater things. A peasant and an educated man will differ even in the very pronunciation of the letters. Take care, therefore, that Paula should not acquire a foolish woman's way either of enunciating her words or of adorning herself in gold in purple: the former blemishes her speech, the latter her character. One should not be taught what will latter have to be unlearned....

Paula's governess should be a teetotaler, chaste, and not overly talkative; she should have a unpretentious woman attendant and a serious-minded male attendant.... She should be so lovable to her whole family that they rejoice that such a rose has bloomed in their midst....

He manner of dressing and bearing herself should reflect to One to whom she is dedicated. Take care that you neither pierce her ears nor make up that face consecrated to Christ with whitener or rouge. Place neither pearls nor gold on her neck, add no jewels to her hair, lest you herald for her the fires of Gehenna [Hell]. She ought to have other pearls, which she may exchange hereafter for the pearl of great price....

After Paula grows a little bigger and her wisdom, maturity, and favor increase before God and men, let her emulate her spouse [Christ] by accompanying her parents to the temple of her true Father and by not leaving the temple with them. Let them seek her on the road of the wide world among the crowd and the company of their relatives, but find her nowhere but in the shrine of the Holy Writ, quizzing the prophets and apostles regarding her heavenly wedding. She should emulate Mary whom Gabriel found alone in her room terrified at the sight of a stranger....

Paula should not dine in company, that is, at the table of her parents, lest she see some food she might long for.... Let her learn now not to drink wine .... Too strict a regimen, however, can imperil a child before she has reached her full strength. Till then, she may frequent the baths, drink a bit of wine for good digestion, and have a diet including meat, so that her feet do not fail before they begin the race.... Paula should be deaf to musical instruments: the pipes, the lyre, the cithara; she ought not even know of their very existence.

She should recite to you each day an allotment of Scriptures, a certain number in the original Greek, but then very soon Latin as well. The latter, our native tongue, if not formed to the mouth early enough is flawed by a foreign accentuation. You ought to be her model from her earliest childhood. She should see only exemplars of good behavior in you and her father. Be mindful that you are the parents of a virgin and can teach her better by deeds than by words.... She should not go forth in public without you, not even to churches or to basilicas of the martyrs. No young man, dandified and smooth, should come near her; she should not stray an inch from her mother at church services by day or night.... Let her also learn to work wool, to grasp the distaff, to hold the wool-basket in her lap, to turn the spindle and draw out the thread with her fingers. She should reject silk, Chinese fleeces, and gold brocade; she should have clothes to keep off the cold, not to expose the limbs they're supposed to conceal....

Some say that a virgin of Christ should not bathe in the company of eunuchs or married women, since the former retain the minds of males, and the latter when pregnant present an ugly sight with their swollen bellies. I myself disapprove of baths for a virgin altogether--she should blush and be unable to bear the sight of herself nude. She should not on the one hand stir her sleeping passions in the baths, when on the other she is subduing her body by vigils and fasts, seeking to stay the flame of lust and the spurs of feverish youth through cold abstinence.

AUGUSTINE

I wish to record the foul acts I committed and the fleshly corruptions of my soul, not because I love those deeds, but so that I may love you, my God. I do this out of love for you, recollecting my wickedness in bitterness, so that you may sweeten my life, not with a false sweetness, but happy and secure. I shall gather myself from the dissolution of vain endeavors that divided me from you. For I, as a young man, burned with infernal lusts and dared to run wild in numerous secretive love affairs. My own image--so foul and putrefying before your eyes--was pleasing to me who desired only to please other men....

What was there that pleased me but to love and to be loved? But I did not stay within the bounds of mental affection, the bright borders of friendship--the foul miasma of carnal urge emerged from the bubbling spring of adolescence and so overshadowed and beclouded my hea that I could not distinguish the serenity of affection from the darkness of lust. Both affection and lust raged in confusion within m and swept me in the weakness of youth over th cliffs of cupidity and submerged me in whirlpool of vices.

I burned wretchedly following the tide of foul impulses and leaving you [Lord] behind: violated all you laws and suffered you punishments; what mortal could have escape them? You were ever-present cruelly merciful a you spread bitter remorse over all my illic delights, forcing me to look for others untinge by pain. But you meant me to find no suc relief, except in you, Lord, who afflict us i order to heal, who kill us in order that we ma not die away from you....

When I was sixteen ... and living unoccupie in the home of my parents, the thornbushes o lust grew over my head and no one lifted a han to extricate me. My father one day saw m bathing and notice the signs of potent manhoo he rejoiced at the prospect of my producin grandchildren and he happily informed m mother. For he was intoxicated with th creations rather than--as he should have been-- with the Creator; the wine of earthly existenc perverts the will of humankind. But my mother' heart already held the foundations of your hol temple, while my father was still a mere novice She, in her piety, feared for me and was anxiou that I, being unbaptized, might be led astray b those who turn their backs on you....

[Later] I went to Carthage, where a cauldro of unholy loves raged about me. Though I trul loved no one, yet I was in love with the notion o love itself. I should have loved you [God], bu hated myself for not doing so. Instead, I soug other objects for my love .... Thus I fouled th friendship's stream with the muck of lust an polluted its waters with a hellish dark river o indecency....

The spectacles of the theater drew me, bein filled with images of my own miseries an fanning the flames of my desires. Why do w take pleasure in the sight of suffering an tragedy, though we would never want to endur the same things ourselves? Nonetheless, we actually wish to feel sorrow and in that sorrow is our pleasure--what a miserable form of insanity!...

In those days, I was living in sin with a woman, not a wife but a kept woman; I did so at the behest of my own excited passions. This experience taught me the distinction between proper marriage, formed for the purpose of producing children, and a mere lustful transaction, which resents the birth of offspring, though we cannot but love the children so produced....

[While I was teaching at Rome], the Prefect of the City received a petition from Milan for a teacher of literature and rhetoric, with an offer to cover travel expenses. I applied for the post, with supporting letters from my friends.... Eventually, the Prefect, Symmachus, having made a test of my competence, sent me to Milan.

In Milan, I met, Lord, Bishop Ambrose, a man to the world known for his goodness and a devoted servant to you. He, by his eloquence, diligently administered to your people the fat of your wheat, the joy of your olive oil, and the earnest intoxication of your wine.

I was (all unwitting) led to him by you, so that through him I might knowingly be led to you. This man of God received me from my wanderings with fatherly kindness and with episcopal concern. I soon began to love him, not at first because he was a teacher of the truth, but as one who had been so kind to me, something I hadn't expected to encounter within the Church....

I attended more to the manner than to the matter of what Ambrose said, since I had lost hope that a man could find the way to you; nonetheless, his meaning, which I strove to disregard, entered my mind together with the words that so impressed me.... I started to see the truth, though only slowly at first.... I refused to entrust the cure of my sick soul to the ministrations of philosophers, who neglected the name of Christ our Savior. I determined to remain a catechumen [convert under instruction before baptism] in the Catholic Church, something my parents had advised, at least until I could see the direction in life I ought to take.

Chrysostome, Jean. *Sur la vaine gloire et l'éducation des enfants*. Ed. Anne-Marie Malingrey. Paris: Éditions du Cerf, 1972. Pp. 178-190. Wright, F.A., ed. *Select Letters of St. Jerome*. Cambridge: Harvard Univ. Press, 1933. Pp. 342-350, 354-358, 360-364. Skutella, Martin, ed. *S. Aureli Augustini Confessionum libri tredecim*. Leipzig: Teubner, 1934. Book 2.1-3, 3.1-2, 4.2, 5.13-14. Translations by James P. Holoka.

READING 2.10

THE QUR'AN AND THE ISLAMIC WAY

► **Mosque Decoration**

Muslims believe the *Qur'an* (or *Koran*) is the holy book directly inspired by God and revealed to the Prophet Muhammad through the Archangel Gabriel. It teaches a strictly monotheistic faith and denounces idolatory. Although the *Qur'an* recognized Jews and Christians as children of God's revealed book, it nevertheless rejected Judaism as narrow and Christianity as corrupt. Therefore Muslims believe the *Qur'an* to be God's definitive revealed book, purged of errors, and Muhammad to be God's final prophet or the Seal of Prophets.

Written in poetic Arabic, the *Qur'an* is divided into 114 chapters, called *suras*, and arranged roughly in order of length. Except for sura one, a short prayer, sura two is the longest with 286 verses. Each succeeding sura is shorter, down to the final ones, each only a few verses long. Some suras combine revelations from different periods.

Muhammad began to receive revelations in Mecca when he was about forty years old. They dealt with faith, human and divine relations, and moral conduct. The revelations continued in Medina after Muhammad and his followers moved to that city in 622 C.E. Muhammad dictated his revelations to followers; they were compiled soon after his death in 632 C.E. Since the *Qur'an* interwove faith and morals, Muhammad treated the issues together in pronouncements that guided his community. Hence, early Islamic leaders made little distinction between the "religious" and the "legal."

Early Muslims organized the community into a disciplined group by quickly developing the *Shar'ia* or law that encompassed all aspects of life. It is first and foremost authority of the Shar'ia is the *Qur'an*. When further guidance is needed it relies on the Hadith (traditions of Muhammad), then it uses analogies through applying the *Qur'an* and traditions to similar situations, and finally on the consensus of the community as interpreted by the religious scholars. Thus the Islamic legal system is rigid and positive, emphasizing both religious and legal duties and demanding unquestioning obedience. It has been crucial in holding together believers from many disparate cultural traditions.

Parts of sura two dealing with social duties are quoted below.

QUESTIONS:

1) What rules did the Kor'an give for eating, drinking, and fasting?
2) What rules must Muslims follow regarding marriage and divorce?
3) What was the *Qur'an's* attitude regarding the borrowing of money?

Dietary Regulations

O you who believe, eat from the good things We provided for you, and be thankful to God, if it is Him you worship.

He only prohibits for you (the eating of) dead animals, blood, the flesh of swine, and that which is dedicated to other than God. However, if one is forced (to eat from these), without being deliberate, or malicious, then he incurs no guilt. Surely, God is Forgiver, most Merciful. (II, 172-173)

Fasting Prescribed

O you who believe, fasting is prescribed for you, as it was prescribed for those before you, that you may achieve salvation.

Specific days (are assigned for fasting). However, if any of you are ill or travelling, then an equal number of other days (shall be substituted). As for those who can fast with great difficulty, they may expiate by feeding one poor person (for each day of fasting). Whoever volunteers more good (by feeding more poor people), it would be better for him. But fasting is best for you, if you only knew.

The month of Ramadan is when the Qur'an was revealed for the guidance of mankind, and presenting clear guidelines and the state book. Therefore, whoever witnesses this month, shall fast therein; and whoever is ill or travelling shall fast an equal number of other days. God wants for you convenience, rather than difficulty, and to enable you to complete the asigned number of days, and to glorify God for guiding you, and to be appreciative. (II, 183-185)

Do Not Marry Pagans

You shall not marry pagan women unless they believe; a believing woman is far better than a pagan, even if you are fond of her. Nor shall you give your women in marriage to pagan men unless they believe; a believing man is far better than a pagan, even if you are fond of him. These lead towards the hellfire, while God leads towards paradise, in accordance with His will. He clarifies His revelations for the people, that they may remember. (II, 221)

Breaking the Engagement

You incur no guilt if you divorce the women before you touch them, and before setting the dowry for them. But in this case you shall compensate them in accordance with your means; the rich as he can afford, and the poor as he can afford; an equitable compensation. This is a duty upon the virtuous.

If you divorce them before you touch them, but after you have set the dowry for them, the compensation shall be half the dowry; unless they willingly forfeit the compensation, or you forfeit the whole dowry. It is more righteous that you forfeit. Do not abandon the amicable relations among you; God is Seer of everything you do. (II, 236-237)

Law of Divorce

Those who estrange their wives shall wait four months; if they reconcile thereafter, then God is Forgiver, most Merciful.

And if they decide to go through with the divorce, then God is Hearer, fully aware.

The divorced women shall wait a period of three menstruations (before remarriage). It is not permitted for them to conceal what God has created in their wombs, if they truly believe in God and the day of the hereafter. Their husbands shall have priority to remarry them (in case of pregnancy), if they wish to reconcile. The women are entitled to their rights, just as they have obligations, equitably. In this case (of pregnancy), the men's wishes shall prevail over the women's; God is Almighty, most wise.

Divorce may be retracted only twice; then either retain (the wife) amicably, or release (her) on good terms; and it is not permitted for you to take back anything you had given them....

If he divorces her (a third time), then he is not permitted to remarry her, unless she marries another man and he divorces her. If (the second husband) divorces her, then (she and the first husband) can remarry, if they believe they have fulfilled God's laws. These are God's laws; He clarifies them for people who know. (II, 226-230)

Marriage for Widows

Those of you who die and leave widows behind, their widows shall wait an interim of four months and ten days (to become eligible for marriage). Once they have fulfilled their interim, then you incur no guilt in letting them do whatever they wish with themselves, so long as they maintain righteousness; God is fully cognizant of everything you do.

You incur no guilt if you declare your engagement to the widows (during their interim) or by keeping it secret; God knows that you may be interested in them. But do not meet them secretly, unless you have something virtuous to say. You shall not consummate the marriage until the interim has been fulfilled, and know that God knows your innermost thoughts. Beware of Him, and know that God is Forgiver, Clement. (II, 234-235)

You Shall Leave A Will

It is prescribed for you that when death approaches the one of you, should he leave any wealth, he shall leave a will for the benefit of the parents and the relatives, equitably. This is a duty upon the righteous.

If anyone alters a will he has heard, the guilt thereof befalls those who do the altering. God is Hearer, fully aware.

However, if one senses from a testator obvious injustice or sinful partiality, and reconciles between them, then he incurs no guilt. God is Forgiver, Merciful. (II, 180-182)

Penalty for Murder

O you who believe, prescribed for you is equivalence as the (maximum) penalty for murder; the free person for the free person, the slave for the slave, and the female for the female. However, if one is pardoned by the victim's kin, the response should be graceful, and an equitable compensation should be paid. This is an alleviation from your Lord, and mercy; whoever transgresses after this, will suffer a painful retribution.

Equivalence shall be a life saving law for you, O you who possess understanding, that you may achieve salvation. (II, 178-179)

Intoxicants and Gambling Prohibited

They ask you about intoxicants and gambling; say, "In them is gross evil, as well as benefits for the people; but their evil outweighs their benefits." They ask you what to spend (for charity); say, "The excess." Thus does God clarify the revelation for you, that you may reflect upon this life and the hereafter. They ask you about the orphans; say "Caring for them is good; and whenever you interact with them, you shall treat them as your brethren." God knows which one is corrupting, and which one is reforming. Had God willed, He could have imposed harsher regulations upon you; God is Almighty, most Wise. (II, 219-220)

Usury Prohibited

Those who eat from usury stand only like one who is struck by the devil's touch. That is because they say that trade is the same as usury, though God permits trade and prohibits usury. Therefore, whoever heeds this admonition from his Lord, and abstains (from usury) he may keep his past earnings and his judgment rests with God. But whoever returns (to usury), these are the dwellers of the hellfire; they abide therein for ever.

God condemns usury and blesses charities. God does not love any guilty disbeliever. (II, 275-276)

Write Down Monetary Transactions

O you who believe, if you carry out a loan transaction for any period of time, you shall write it down. Let a scribe write for you equitably. No scribe shall refuse to write as God has taught him; he shall write while the debtor dictates; and beware of God his Lord; and never cheat.... You shall have two witnesses from among your men; if two men were not available, then one man and two women whom you accept as witnesses. Thus, if one woman deviates, the other would correct her...Do not neglect to write all the details, no matter how small or large the transaction is, including the time of repayment....(II, 282)

Khalifa, Rashad, ed. and trans. *The Glorious Qur'an: Standard Translation*. Tuscon, AZ: The Spirit of Truth, 1978. Vol. 1. Pp. 20-22, 27-28, 30, 36-37.

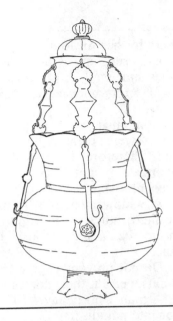

► **Mosque Lamp**

TRADITIONS OF MUHAMMAD

Muhammad (c. 570-632 C.E.) was born and raised at Mecca. He came from a distinguished family, but lost both parents at an early age. He worked with a camel caravan as young man, then married and settled down. At about age forty he began to receive revelations about a monotheistic religion called Islam. Called on to spread his teachings, he made both converts but even more enemies in his native Mecca. After his flight, called *hijira*, to Medina in 622 C.E., the Muslim community grew; at the time of his death ten years later all the Arabian peninsula had come under Muhammad's rule. Muhammad was both religious and political leader in Medina and was called on to judge and guide. He also acted to make the Medinans a model Muslim community. Followers recorded Muhammad's pronouncements.

Traditions or customs, called *sunna* in Arabic, played an important part in Arabian social life: every tribe prided itself on its traditions. Muslim traditions began to develop and became the "usage of the Community" under the Prophet Muhammad. These traditions of Muhammad were handed down through his Companions and later compiled as short narratives called the *hadith*, or statement. Next to the *Qur'an* (*Koran*) the *Hadith* is the most authoritative source of the *Shar'ai*, or law, that governs the life of Muslims.

There are altogether 2,762 hadiths divided into three categories, the sound, good, or weak, depending on the reliability and legitimacy of the chain of authority that told about each statement. The *Hadith* is constantly appealed to because it deals with numerous detailed circumstances of life and embodies the norms and standards of Muslims.

The *Hadith* also provides biographical details of the life of Muhammad. Since devout Muslims model their lives after the Prophet, the *Hadith* is important on this count as well. Both Sunni and Shi'i branches of Islam adhere to the *Hadith* but interpret the conduct of the community differently.

The following are from a standard compilation of the *Hadith* and show some of the wide range of subjects it deals with.

QUESTIONS:

1) What was Muhammad's attitude on work, making money, and charity?
2) How should women, slaves, and animals be treated?
3) How should governments behave and what makes a good ruler?

Of Charity

The liberal man is near the pleasure of God and is near Paradise, which he shall enter into, and is near the hearts of men as a friend, and he is distant from hell; but the niggard is far from God's pleasure and from paradise, and far from the hearts of men, and near the Fire; and verily a liberal uneducated man is more beloved by God than a niggardly worshipper.

A man's giving in alms one piece of silver in his lifetime is better for him than giving one hundred when about to die.

Think not that any good act is contemptible, though it be but your brother's coming to you with an open countenance and good humour.

Feed the hungry, visit the sick, and free the captive if he be unjustly bound.

Of Labour and Profit

The Prophet has cursed ten persons on account of wine: one, the first extractor of the juice of the grape for others; the second for himself; the third the drinker of it; the fourth the bearer of it; the fifth the person to whom it is brought; the sixth the waiter; the seventh the seller of it; the eighth the eater of its price; the ninth the buyer of it; the tenth that person who has purchased it for another.

Merchants shall be raised up liars on the Day of Resurrection, except he who abstains from that which is unlawful, and does not swear falsely, but speaks true in the price of his goods.

The taker of interest and the giver of it, and the writer of its papers and the witness to it, are equal in crime.

The holder of a monopoly is a sinner and offender.

A martyr shall be pardoned every fault but debt.

Give the labourer his wage before his perspiration be dry.

Of Women and Slaves

The world and all things in it are valuable, but the most valuable thing in the world is a virtuous woman.

A Muslim cannot obtain (after righteousness) anything better than a well-disposed, beautiful wife; such a wife as, when ordered by her husband to do anything, obeys; and if her husband look at her, is happy; and if her husband

swears by her to do a thing, she does it to make his oath true; and if he be absent from her, she wishes him well in her own person by guarding herself from unchastity, and takes care of his property.

Admonish your wife with kindness; for women were created out of a crooked rib of Adam, therefore if you wish to straighten it, you will break it; and if you let it alone, it will be always crooked.

A widow shall not be married until she be consulted; nor shall a virgin be married until her consent be asked, whose consent is by her silence.

Do not prevent your women from coming to the mosque; but their homes are better for them.

A man who behaves ill to his slave will not enter into paradise.

Forgive your servant seventy times a day.

Of Dumb Animals

Fear God in respect of animals: ride them when they are fit to be ridden, and get off when they are tired.

Verily there are rewards for our doing good to dumb animals, and giving them water to drink. An adulteress was forgiven who passed by a dog at a well; for the dog was holding out his tongue from thirst; which was near killing him; and the woman took off her boot, and tied it to the end of her garment, and drew water for the dog, and gave him to drink; and she was forgiven for that act.

Of Hospitality

Whosoever believes in God and the Day of Resurrection must respect his guest, and the time of being kind to him is one day and one night, and the period of entertaining him is three days, and after that, if he does it longer, he befits him more. It is not right for a guest to stay in the house of the host so long as to inconvenience him.

Of Government

Government is a trust from God, and verity government will be at the Day of Resurrection a cause of inquiry, unless he who has taken it be worthy of it and have acted justly and done good.

That is the best of men who dislikes power. Beware! you are all guardians; and you will be asked about your subjects: then the leader is the guardian of the subject, and he will be asked respecting the subject; and a man is a shepherd to his own family, and will be asked how they behaved, and his conduct to them; and a wife is guardian to her husband's house and children, and will be interrogated about them; and a slave is a shepherd to his master's property, and will be asked about it, whether he took good care of it or not.

There is no prince who oppresses the subject and dies, but God forbids Paradise to him.

There is no obedience to sinful commands, not to any other than what is lawful.

Of Vanities and Sundry Matters

Every painter is in Hell Fire; and God will appoint a person at the Day of Resurrection for every picture he shall have drawn, to punish him, and they will punish him in Hell. Then if you must make pictures, make them of trees and things without souls.

Whosoever shall tell a dream, not having dreamt, shall be put to the trouble at the Day of Resurrection of joining two barleycorns; and he can by no means do it: and he will be punished. And whosoever listens to others' conversation, who dislike to be heard by him, and avoid him, boiling lead will be poured into his ears at the Day of Resurrection. And whosoever draws a picture shall be punished by ordering him to breathe a spirit into it, and this he can never do, and so he will be punished as long as God wills.

Meekness and shame are two branches of faith, and vain talking and embellishing are two branches of hypocrisy.

It was asked, "O Messenger of God, what relation is most worthy of doing good to?" He said, "Your mother," this he repeated thrice; "and after her your father, and after him your other relations by propinquity."

God's pleasure is in a father's pleasure, and God's displeasure is a father's displeasure.

The best person near God is the best amongst his friends; and the best of neighbours near God is the best person in his own neighbourhood.

Lane-Poole, Stanley, ed. and trans. *The Speeches and Table-Talk of the Prophet Muhammad*. London: Macmillan, 1882. Pp. 152-153, 157-158, 160-168.

SECTION 3

EARLY STATES AND EMPIRES

By 1000 B.C.E. several great civilizations across Eurasia had completed their formative stages. They had formulated religions and philosophies that answered their needs, developed advanced technologies that allowed their economies to prosper, and devised mechanisms of government to give order to the lives of large and often diverse populations. The stage was set for the creation of large empires.

The readings in this section pertain to the Persian Empire and several other successful empires that followed later: Alexander the Great's Macedonian empire and its successor Hellenistic states that stretched from Egypt to the border of India, the Roman Empire, the Mauryan Empire in India, and the Chinese Empire under the Han and T'ang dynasties. All great and enduring empires shared some common characteristics: all were founded and stabilized by great rulers and maintained by capable bureaucracies and powerful armies; all were sustained by meaningful religions and philosophies; and all gained prosperity through trade, manufacturing, and agriculture. All eventually foundered and fell, but left lasting legacies to later generations, which looked back upon the earlier empires with pride and longing.

Classical Greece was exceptional among the array of ancient empires represented here. The Athenian empire that marked the zenith of classical Greek civilization was small in population and territory and of brief duration compared with the others. However, classical Greece's influence on humanity was not determined by its physical size. Its development of democratic institutions, and its manifold influence on the Hellenistic and Roman civilizations gave it an abiding importance and lasting influence among the civilizations of the world.

The readings in this section are varied. Some deal with the leading men and women who founded and shaped their empires, with their public and private lives, and their virtues and vices. Others pertain to the lives of ordinary men and women, how they made money, arranged marriages, and expressed their joys and sorrows. Still others paint pictures of manners and morals, customs and habits of peoples of all social classes. The selections are as diverse and panoramic in their range as the great empires and peoples they represent.

THE TRIUMPHS OF DARIUS, GREAT KING, KING OF KINGS

► **Cylinder-Seal Impression of Darius**

King Cyrus (559-530 B.C.E.), of the Achaemenid royal family, founded the Persian Empire by uniting the Indo-European-speaking tribes in the area of present-day Iran. In 550, Cyrus conquered the Medes, former masters of the Persians, and annexed their land. The Lydians and the Chaldeans fell next to Persian arms.

Cyrus's son, Cambyses (530-522), added Egypt to the empire. Cambyses, facing a major rebellion and perhaps suffering from mental illness, committed suicide in 522. After a period of bloody civil strife, a distant relative became King Darius I (522-486).

The dynamic and ambitious Darius eventually enlarged the Persian empire to the Indus River in the east, the Caucasus Mountains in the north, upper Egypt in the south, and even gained a small foothold in Europe in the west. But Darius's greatest achievement was his successful organization of ethnically, religiously, and linguistically diverse populations into a cohesive empire of over twenty provinces and several tributary kingdoms, garrisoned at strategic points by the Persian army. Darius allowed substantial autonomy in local governments and respected local religions, and ruled with relative leniency.

The Iranian nobility served as Darius's top military and civil officials, while provincial governors, called satraps, collected tribute, military provisions, and taxes, and recruited soldiers. Assisting Darius were intelligence officers, called the king's "Eyes and Ears," who made regular rounds of the provinces. The empire's abundant revenues paid for the administrative apparatus, an elaborate public works infrastructure, and a postal and transportation system of well maintained roads. Standardized weights and measures and a uniform gold and silver coinage expedited trade. Although internal uprisings, especially at times of transition in leadership, periodically disrupted the empire, the administrative apparatus Darius set up endured for 200 years till Alexander's conquest in 330 B.C.E.

The passage that follows is from an inscription Darius ordered carved around 520 B.C.E. in cuneiform in the three official languages of the empire--Persian, Elamite, and Akkadian, on a cliff-face three hundred feet above the site of the battle of Kundurush along the main road from Babylon to Ecbatana. It records Darius's accession to power and his military triumphs in quelling revolts of would-be usurpers after the death of Cambyses.

QUESTIONS:

1) Why does Darius mention Ahura Mazda so frequently in this inscription?

2) What does Darius appear to be trying to achieve with this inscription? That is, why did he have just these words carved just where they were?

3) What does Darius see as most important about the deeds recording in this inscription?

I am Darius, the great king, the king of kings, the king of Persia, the king of the provinces, the son of Hystaspes, the grandson of Arsames, the Achaemenian....

Says Darius the king--There are eight of my race who have been kings before me; I am the ninth; nine of us have been kings in succession.

Says Darius the king--By the grace of Ahura Mazda I am king; Ahura Mazda has granted me the empire.

Says Darius the king--These are the countries which have come to me; by the grace of Ahura Mazda I have become king of them: Persia, Susiana, Babylonia, Assyria, Arabia, Egypt, those which are of the sea, Saparda, Ionia, Media, Armenia, Cappadocia, Parthia, Zarangia, Aria, Chorasmia, Bactria, Sogdiana, Gandaria, the Sacae, Sattagydia, Arachotia, and Mecia; in all twenty-three provinces.

Says Darius the king--These are the provinces which have come to me; by the grace of Ahura Mazda they have become subject to me; they have brought tribute to me. That which has been said to them by me, both by night and by day, it has been done by them.

Says Darius the king--Within these countries, the man who was good, him have I right well cherished. Whoever was evil, him have I utterly rooted out. By the grace of Ahura Mazda, these are the countries by whom my laws have been observed....

Says Darius the king--Ahura Mazda granted me the empire. Ahura Mazda brought help to me, so that I gained the empire. By the grace of Ahura Mazda I hold this empire.

Says Darius the king--This is what was done by me after that I became king. A man named Cambyses, son of Cyrus, of our race, he was here king before me. Of that Cambyses there was a brother, Bardes was his name; of the same mother, and of the same father with Cambyses. Afterwards Cambyses slew that Bardes.... It was not known to the people that Bardes had been slain. Afterwards Cambyses proceeded to Egypt.... Then the state became wicked. Then the lie became abounding in the land, both in Persia, and in Media, and in the other provinces.

Says Darius the king--Afterwards there was a certain man, a Magian, named Gomates. He arose from Pissiachada, the mountain named Aracadres, from thence. On the 14th day of the month Vayakhna, then it was that he arose. He thus lied to the state, "I am Bardes, the son of Cyrus, the brother of Cambyses." Then the whole state became rebellious. From Cambyses it went over to him, both Persia, and Media, and the other provinces. He seized the empire. On the 9th day of the month Garmapada, then it was he so seized the empire. Afterwards Cambyses, unable to endure, died.

Says Darius the king--The empire of which Gomates, the Magian, dispossessed Cambyses, that empire from the olden time had been in our family. After Gomates the Magian had dispossessed Cambyses both of Persia and Media and the dependent provinces, he did according to his desire: he became king.

Says Darius the king--There was not a man, neither Persian, nor Media, nor any one of our family, who would dispossess that Gomates the Magian of the crown. The state feared him exceedingly. He slew many people who had known the old Bardes; for that reason he slew them. "Lest they should recognize me that I am not Bardes, the son of Cyrus." No one dared to say anything concerning Gomates the Magian, until I arrived. Then I prayed to Ahura Mazda; Ahura Mazda brought help to me. On the 10th day of the month Bagayadish, then it was, with my faithful men, I slew that Gomates the Magian, and those who were his chief followers. The fort named Sictachotes in the district of Media called Nisaea, there I slew him. I dispossessed him of the empire. By the grace of Ahura Mazda I became king: Ahura Mazda granted me the sceptre.

Says Darius the king--The empire which had been taken away from our family, that I recovered. I established it in its place. As it was before, so I made it. The temples which Gomates the Magian had destroyed, I rebuilt.

The sacred offices of the state, both the religious chants and the worship, I restored to the people, which Gomates the Magian had deprived them of. I established the state in its place, both Persia, and Media, and the other provinces. As it was before, so I restored what had been taken away. By the grace of Ahura Mazda I did this. I arranged so that I had established our family in its place. As it was before, so I arranged it, by the grace of Ahura Mazda, so that Gomates the Magian should not supersede our family....

Says Darius the king--Then I went to Babylon against that Nidintabelus, who was called Nabochodrossor. The people of Nidintabelus held the Tigris; there they were posted, and they had boats. There I approached with a detachment in rafts. I brought the enemy into difficulty. I carried the enemy's position. Ahura Mazda brought help to me. By the grace of Ahura Mazda I crossed the Tigris. There I slew many of the troops of Nidintabelus. On the 26th day of the month Atriyata, then it was we so fought.

Says Darius the king--Then I went to Babylon. When I arrived near Babylon, at the city named Zazana, on the Euphrates, there that Nidintabelus, who was called Nabochodrossor, came with his forces against me, to do battle. Then we fought a battle. Ahura Mazda brought help to me. By the grace of Ahura Mazda I slew many of the troops of that Nidintabelus--the enemy was driven into the water--the water destroyed them. On the 2nd day of the month Anamaka, then it was we so fought.

Says Darius the king--Then Nidintabelus with the horsemen that were faithful to him fled to Babylon. Then I went to Babylon. By the grace of Ahura Mazda I both took Babylon, and seized that Nidintabelus. Then I slew that Nidintabelus at Babylon.

Says Darius the king--While I was at Babylon, these are the countries which revolted against me: Persia, Susiana, Media, Assyria, Armenia, Parthia, Margiana, Sattagydia, Sacia....

Says Darius the king--[After his lieutenants had quelled many of the revolts] then I went out from Babylon. I proceeded to Media. When I reached ... a city ... named Kudrusia, there that Phraortes, who was called king of Media, came with an army against me, to do battle. Then we fought a battle. Ahura Mazda brought help to me; by the grace of Ahura Mazda, I entirely defeated the army of Phraortes. On the 26th day of the month Adukanish, then it was we thus fought the battle.

Says Darius the king--Then that Phraortes, with his faithful horsemen, fled from thence to a district of Media, called Rhages. Then I sent an army, by which Phraortes was taken and brought before me. I cut off both his nose, and his ears, and his tongue, and I put out his eyes. He was kept chained at my door; all the kingdom beheld him. Afterwards I crucified him at Ecbatana. And the men, who were his chief followers, I slew within the citadel at Ecbatana.

Says Darius the king--A man, named Sitrantachmes, a Sagartian, he rebelled against me. To the state thus he said, "I am king of Sagartia, of the race of Cyaxares." Then I sent forth an army of Persians and Medes. A man named Tachamaspates, a Mede, one of my subjects, him I made their leader. Thus I said to them, "Go forth, and smite that rebel state which does not acknowledge me." Then Tachamaspates set forth with his army. He fought a battle with Sitrantachmes. Ahura Mazda brought help to me; by the grace of Ahura Mazda, my troops defeated the rebel army, and took Sitrantachmes, and brought him before me. Then I cut off both his nose and his ears, and I put out his eyes. He was kept chained at my door. All the kingdom beheld him. Afterwards I crucified him at Arbela.

Says Darius the king--This is what was done by me in Media.

Says Darius the king--Parthia and Hyrcania revolted against me. They declared for Phraortes.... [My father] Hystaspes, with the troops under his orders, set forth. At a place called Hyspaostes, a town of Media, there he fought a battle. Ahura Mazda brought help to me; by the grace of Ahura Mazda, Hystaspes entirely defeated that rebel army. On the 22nd day of the month Viyakhna, then it was the battle was thus fought by them....

Says Darius the king--This is what I have done. By the grace of Ahura Mazda I have accomplished the whole. After that the kings rebelled against me, I fought nineteen battles. By the grace of Ahura Mazda I smote them, and took nine kings prisoners....

Says Darius the king--These are the provinces which rebelled. The god Ahura Mazda created lies that they should deceive the people. Afterwards the god Ahura Mazda gave the people into my hand. As I desired, so the god Ahura Mazda did.

Says Darius the king--Thou who mayest be king hereafter, keep thyself utterly from lies. The man who may be a liar, him destroy utterly. If thou shalt thus observe, my country shall remain in its integrity.

Says Darius the king--This is what I have done. By the grace of Ahura Mazda have I achieved the performance of the whole. Thou who mayest hereafter peruse this tablet, let that which has been done by me be a warning to thee, that thou lie not.

Says Darius the king--Ahura Mazda is my witness that I have truly, not falsely, made this record of my deeds throughout....

Says Darius the king--Thou who mayest hereafter behold this tablet, which I have engraved, and these figures, beware lest thou injure them. As long as thou livest, so long preserve them.

Says Darius the king--If thou shalt behold this tablet and these figures, and not injure them, and shalt preserve them as long as my seed endures, then may Ahura Mazda be thy friend, and may thy seed be numerous, and mayest thou live long; and whatever thou doest, may Ahura Mazda bless it for thee in after times.

Says Darius the king--If seeing this tablet, and these images, thou injurest them, and preservest them not as long as my seed endures, then may Ahura Mazda be thy enemy, and mayest thou have no offspring, and whatever thou doest, may Ahura Mazda curse it for thee.

Rawlinson, Henry, trans. "The Behistun Inscription of Darius" [1847]. Rpt. in *The Greek Historians*. Ed. Francis R.B. Godolphin. New York: Random House, 1942. Vol. 2. Pp. 623-628, 630-632.

► Persian Palace Guard

A GREEK ACCOUNT OF PERSIAN CUSTOMS

The Persians' artistic and intellectual attainments did not match their achievements in war and government. They produced little literature, inherited their science and mathematics from Babylonia and Egypt, and much of their art and architecture from Assyria, Babylonia, Greece, and Egypt.

The Persians, however, showed great originality in religion. The traditional Iranian religion was polytheistic; its chief officials were magi (priest-astrologers). In the early sixth century B.C.E., however, a reformer named Zoroaster taught a religion of two principal forces: one, representing goodness, light, and truth, was Ahura Mazda; the other was Ahriman, representing darkness and evil. Zoroastrianism was a strongly ethical religion. It taught that all men and women possessed free will and should avoid sin, abide by divine laws, and avoid sin.

The passage that follows is from the *History* by Herodotus (c. 484-c. 425 B.C.E.). It focuses chiefly on the conflicts between the Persian Empire and the Greek city-states between 499 and 479. Herodotus, of course, writes from the Greek point of view and manifests many of the Greek biases and stereotypes regarding the "barbarian" Persians. He was, however, fascinated by non-Greek cultures and value systems. Much of his work is devoted to stories he had heard from travelers to strange lands, or to his own observations made during his journeys outside Greece. Herodotus often shows an appreciation for the accomplishments of non-Greeks, something rare among usually chauvinistic Greek writers. While some of the details included in his discussion of Persian customs are suspect or erroneous (for example, regarding the ending of Persian personal names), the account does contain some accurate information. Herodotus's mastery as story-teller is evident.

QUESTIONS:

1) Given that Herodotus's narrative of Persian customs is that of an outside observer, what (if anything) strikes you as improbable or perhaps prejudiced in his account?

2) Does Herodotus appear to find anything admirable in Persian practices? Give specific examples.

3) On balance, does Herodotus seem to admire or despise the Persians? (Bear in mind that Greeks of his time were often xenophobic or bigoted in their attitudes toward "barbarians" [that is, non-Greeks].)

The customs which I know the Persians to observe are the following. They have no images of the gods, no temples nor altars, and consider the use of them a sign of folly. This comes, I think, from their not believing the gods to have the same nature with men, as the Greeks

129

imagine. Their wont, however, is to ascend the summits of the loftiest mountains, and there to offer sacrifice to Jupiter, which is the name they give to the whole circuit of the firmament. They likewise offer to the sun and moon, to the earth, to fire, to water, and to the winds. These are the only gods whose worship has come down to them from ancient times. At a later period they began the worship of Urania, which they borrowed from the Arabians and Assyrians. Mylitta is the name by which the Assyrians know this goddess, whom the Arabians call Alitta, and the Persians Mitra.

To these gods the Persians offer sacrifice in the following manner: they raise no altar, light no fire, pour no libations; there is no sound of the flute, no putting on of chaplets, no consecrated barley-cake; but the man who wishes to sacrifice brings his victim to a spot of ground which is pure from pollution, and there calls upon the name of the god to whom he intends to offer. It is usual to have the head-dress encircled with a wreath, most commonly of myrtle. The sacrificer is not allowed to pray for blessings on himself alone, but he prays for the welfare of the king, and of the whole Persian people, among whom he is of necessity included. He cuts the victim in pieces, and having boiled the flesh, he lays it out upon the tenderest herbage that he can find, trefoil especially. When all is ready, one of the Magi comes forward and chants a hymn, which they say recounts the origin of the gods. It is not lawful to offer sacrifice unless there is a Magus present. After waiting a short time the sacrificer carries the flesh of the victim away with him, and makes whatever use of it he may please.

Of all the days in the year, the one which they celebrate most is their birthday. It is customary to have the board furnished on that day with an ampler supply than common. The richer Persians cause an ox, a horse, a camel, and an ass to be baked whole and so served up to them: the poorer classes use instead the smaller kinds of cattle. They eat little solid food but abundance of dessert, which is set on table a few dishes at a time; this it is which makes them say that "the Greeks, when they eat, leave off hungry, having nothing worth mention served up to them after the meats; whereas, if they had more put before them, they would not stop

eating." They are very fond of wine, and drink it in large quantities. To vomit or obey natural calls in the presence of another, is forbidden among them. Such are their customs in these matters.

It is also their general practice to deliberate upon matters of weight when they are drunk; and then on the morrow, when they are sober, the decision to which they came the night before is put before them by the master of the house in which it was made; and if it is then approved of, they act upon it; if not, they set it aside. Sometimes, however, they are sober at their first deliberation, but in this case they always reconsider the matter under the influence of wine.

When they meet each other in the streets, you may know if the persons meeting are of equal rank by the following token; if they are, instead of speaking, they kiss each other on the lips. In the case where one is a little inferior to the other, the kiss is given on the cheek; where the difference of rank is great, the inferior prostrates himself upon the ground. Of nations, they honour most their nearest neighbours, whom they esteem next to themselves; those who live beyond these they honour in the second degree; and so with the remainder, the further they are removed, the less the esteem in which they hold them. The reason is, that they look upon themselves as very greatly superior in all respects to the rest of mankind, regarding others as approaching to excellence in proportion as they dwell nearer to them; whence it comes to pass that those who are the farthest off must be the most degraded of mankind. Under the dominion of the Medes, the several nations of the empire exercised authority over each other in this order. The Medes were lords over all, and governed the nations upon their borders, who in their turn governed the states beyond, who likewise bore rule over the nations which adjoined them. And this is the order which the Persians also follow in their distribution of honour; for that people, like the Medes, has a progressive scale of administration and government.

There is no nation which so readily adopts foreign customs as the Persians. Thus, they have taken the dress of the Medes, considering it superior to their own; and in war they wear the Egyptian breastplate. As soon as they hear of any luxury, they instantly make it their own: and hence, among other novelties, they have learnt [pederasty or "boy-love"] from the Greeks. Each of them has several wives, and a still larger number of concubines.

Next to prowess in arms, it is regarded as the greatest proof of manly excellence, to be the father of many sons. Every year the king sends rich gifts to the man who can show the largest number: for they hold that number is strength. Their sons are carefully instructed from their fifth to their twentieth year, in three things alone,--to ride, to draw the bow, and to speak the truth. Until their fifth year they are not allowed to come into the sight of their father, but pass their lives with the women. This is done that, if the child die young, the father may not be afflicted by its loss.

To my mind it is a wise rule, as also is the following--that the king shall not put any one to death for a single fault, and that none of the Persians shall visit a single fault in a slave with any extreme penalty; but in every case the services of the offender shall be set against his misdoings; and, if the latter be found to outweigh the former, the aggrieved party shall then proceed to punishment.

The Persians maintain that never yet did any one kill his own father or mother; but in all such cases they are quite sure that, if matters were sifted to the bottom, it would be found that the child was either a changeling [a child exchanged for another by stealth] or else the fruit of adultery; for it is not likely they say that the real father should perish by the hands of his child.

They hold it unlawful to talk of anything which it is unlawful to do. The most disgraceful thing in the world, they think, is to tell a lie; the next worst, to owe a debt: because, among other reasons, the debtor is obliged to tell lies. If a Persian has the leprosy he is not allowed to enter into a city, or to have any dealings with the other Persians; he must, they say, have sinned against the sun. Foreigners attacked by this disorder, are forced to leave the country: even white pigeons are often driven away, as guilty of the same offence. They never defile a river with the secretions of their bodies, nor even wash their hands in one; nor will they allow others to do so, as they have a great reverence for rivers. There is another peculiarity, which the Persians themselves have never noticed, but which has not escaped my observation. Their names, which are expressive of some bodily or mental excellence, all end with the same letter--the letter which is called San by the Dorians, and Sigma by the Ionians. Any one who examines will find that the Persian names, one and all without exception, end with this letter.

Thus much I can declare of the Persians with entire certainty, from my own actual knowledge. There is another custom which is spoken of with reserve, and not openly, concerning their dead. It is said that the body of a male Persian is never buried, until is has been torn either by a dog or a bird of prey. That the Magi have this custom is beyond a doubt, for they practise it without any concealment. The dead bodies are covered with wax, and then buried in the ground.

The Magi are a very peculiar race, different entirely from the Egyptian priests, and indeed from all other men whatsoever. The Egyptian priests make it a point of religion not to kill any live animals except those which they offer in sacrifice. The Magi, on the contrary, kill animals of all kinds with their own hands, excepting dogs and men. They even seem to take a delight in the employment, and kill, as readily as they do other animals, ants and snakes, and such like flying or creeping things. However, since this has always been their custom, let them keep to it.

Rawlinson, George, trans. *The Histories of Herodotus*. London 1858. Rpt. London: Dent, 1910. 1.131-140.

SOLON, POET AND LAWGIVER

▶ Athenian Coin

The world's first extended experiment in democracy took place in the ancient Greek polis (city-state) of Athens. In 594 B.C.E., Solon, a great statesman and lawgiver, was entrusted with special powers to revise the political, social, and economic structure of Athens. His work began the evolution from rule by an elite aristocratic clique toward a more egalitarian constitution; in short, Solon set Athens firmly on a course toward democracy. He successfully arbitrated a settlement between Athenian aristocrats and commoners and allowed for participation of many more citizens in the political process. In the first of the passages that follow, Plutarch outlines the reforms that Solon undertook and the kinds of opposition that confronted him.

Solon was justly proud of his achievements and sang of them in remarkable lyric poems; he is in fact the earliest Athenian man of letters known to us by name. The second passage is a poem in which Solon commemorates his solid accomplishments in a dangerous atmosphere of social and political instability and potential revolutionary violence.

Much like Abraham Lincoln in the American historical consciousness, Solon quickly became a stereotype of legendary sagacity. His stature as a sage is evident in the third passage, in which the historian Herodotus reports a famous conversation between the Athenian wise man and Croesus, the fabulously wealthy king of Lydia.

QUESTIONS:

1) Were the social and economic problems that existed in Athens prior Solon's reforms typical or atypical as compared to conditions in other cases of revolutionary unrest?

2) Solon claimed to have been fair to both the aristocrats and the common people in making his reforms. Do you agree with that claim?

3) What is the moral of Herodotus's story of Solon's conversation with Croesus?

Athens was in danger of violent revolution and tyranny appeared the only course by which to end civil dissension and stabilize the government. The mass of commoners were deeply in debt to the wealthy few aristocrats. Many worked land for the their wealthy creditors; because they handed over a sixth part of their yearly produce, they came to be known as Hektemoroi ["Sixth-Parters"]; others, having made their own persons over as loan collateral, had been sold into slavery both at home and abroad. There being no laws to prevent it, many sold their own children or were forced into exile by their creditors.

The majority of men, however, had more spirit and began to conspire to oppose these injustices and to back some popular leader. In particular, they aimed to free debt-slaves, reallocate land, and thoroughly revamp the constitution. The more astute of these men saw Solon as an ideal choice; since he was neither one of the extortionate rich nor one of the destitute poor, they called on him to arbitrate these class conflicts.... He was chosen archon [chief magistrate] ... with special powers of arbitration and legislation; the rich saw him as a man of substance, the poor saw him as a man of moral probity. His opinion that "equality engenders no discord" brought him favor with the whole electorate, both the rich and the poor; the former thought that by "equality" he meant quality and attainments, the latter that he meant by it simply the quantitative equality of the head-count. As a result, both sides encouraged Solon to capitalize on his special powers by seizing the powers of a tyrant. People unattached to either faction were also willing to see a single just and sage individual at the head of affairs, since they felt real change could be effected only very slowly and tediously through the usual legislative procedures. But Solon was unpersuaded, saying to his friends that tyranny, though well and good in itself, could never be relinquished....

His first official act was to cancel existing debts and forbid the practice of taking the person of the debtor as loan guarantee.... He also ... [brought] back from foreign lands some of those who had been sold for non-payment of debts.

At first, both factions were dissatisfied with these measures, the rich at being divested of their loan securities, the poor at Solon's failure to reallocate land or to dictate a strictly equal style of living on all citizens .... However, they soon realized the advantages of Solon's policies ... and granted him plenipotentiary powers to revise the constitution and code of law....

Solon first revamped the law code of Draco [Athenian lawgiver of 621 B.C.E.], which was extremely stringent and stipulated penalties disproportionate to offenses (with the exception of the homicide laws). Draco's code specified the death penalty for all manner of crimes .... Fruit and vegetable thieves were punished quite

the same as murderers and the sacrilegious. This was the reason for the ... witty observation that Draco's code had been written in blood, not ink.

Solon was also concerned both to leave the offices of state as the prerogative of the rich and to give the commoners an unprecedented share in the organs of government. To this end, he conducted a census according to citizens' property. The first class consisted of *Pentakosiomedimnoi* ["five-hundred-measure-men"], that is, all who commanded an annual income of 500 or more measures (wet or dry) of agricultural produce. Comprising the second class were the *Hippeis* [Knights], who were able to afford a horse (and to pay a "horse-tax" on it) or whose annual produce amounted to 300-500 measures. Comprising the third class were the *Zeugitai* ["yoke-of-oxen-men"], with annual income of 200-300 measures. The remainder of the citizenry were designated *Thetes* [landless]; though debarred from holding office, they were eligible to attend the *ecclesia* [assembly of citizens] and to serve on juries....

Solon made oil the only legally exportable farm product of Attica, requiring that violators of this law were to be cursed by the archon or made to pay 100 drachmas into the state treasury.... All his laws, which were to remain in effect for one hundred years, were written on *axones* [wooden tablets] that revolved on their rectangular frames....

After Solon had made these reforms ... people constantly wanted to query him and press him to explain his intent in proclaiming particular laws. He realized he could neither satisfy all these requests nor flatly refuse them altogether; he very much wanted to avoid controversies and evade the nitpicking and criticism of his compatriots.... For this reason, he claimed that business interests (he was a shipowner) would require him to be away from Athens for ten years; he then left the city in hopes that his fellow citizens would become habituated to his laws in the interval.

* * * * *

Did I stop then before I had accomplished my task in gathering back the common people? Great Olympian Mother Earth will swear before time's court that I took from her breast the mortgage-markers, freed her from bonds. I repatriated many sons of Athens--slaves (by law or not) or debt-exiles. Some had lost our Attic tongue so far from home. Others, fearfully cowed by masters here, I also freed. Fitting might to right, I worked the deed I'd promised, set straight laws alike for lords and lowly. Another man, less sage, less honest, could not have checked the mob. Had I favored one side over the other, our polis would have grieved many sons. Like the wily wolf amid a pack of hounds, I showed my strength toward all around.

* * * * *

After Solon left Athens, he visited the court of Egyptian Amasis and then went to see Croesus in Sardis. Croesus treated him hospitably at the royal palace and, after he had been there three or four days, bid his servants show Solon the magnitude and splendor of his royal possessions and treasures. After Solon had seen all this, Croesus said to him: "You legendary wisdom is well known to me, my Athenian friend, and I know too that you have traveled far and wide in your thirst for knowledge. I must ask you a question: "who, of all the men you have seen, is the happiest?"

Croesus of course put this question believing he himself was the happiest of men. Solon, however, choosing not to cajole the king but to tell the truth as he saw it, said "an Athenian named Tellus." Croesus, stunned by this reply, asked with some irritation what led him to give this answer.

"Two things," asserted Solon, "in the first place, he lived in a prospering polis where he survived to see his sons' children (and all these children still living); in addition, he had sufficient wealth and met an admirable death. Fighting side by side with his countrymen in conflict with neighboring Eleusis, he died a soldier's death after routing the enemy. The Athenians granted him the impressive tribute of a state funeral on very spot he fell in battle."

Solon had narrated the story of fortunate Tellus to point a moral for the king. Croesus nevertheless pressed on and asked who was the second happiest person Solon had seen (again expecting to take the prize himself).

Solon responded "two youths of Argos--Cleobis and Biton. They were comfortably well off and blessed with great physical gifts; evidence of the latter was their success in athletics, but particularly the glory they won in the following episode. The Argive festival of Hera was going on, and the youths' mother was to drive her ox-cart to the temple of the goddess. Since the oxen were late in returning from the fields and time was short, the woman's two sons yoked themselves to the cart and drew their mother to the temple nearly six miles distant. After this feat, witnessed by the assembled festival-goers, the two youths met an enviable death, a divine indication that death is to be preferred to life. The men were praising the youths and complimenting them on their strength, while the women were congratulating their mother on having borne such fine sons. Just then, the mother, euphoric at this public commendation of her sons' actions, besought Hera in her shrine before them to bestow on Cleobis and Biton the best godsend that man can receive in recognition of their mother's gratitude.

"After this prayer, the sacrificial rites and feasting were concluded, and the two youths went to sleep in the temple of the goddess. They never awoke again, having died there during the night. The Argives commemorated them with statues sent to Delphi."

Croesus was now properly irked at Solon for awarding the second prize for happiness to these two Argive youths. He growled "All well and good, my dear Athenian, but what about me? Is my happiness so despicable that you give preference to such common folk as you have spoken of?"

Solon answered, "My lord, the gods begrudge human prosperity and like to afflict us, and you are inquiring about human destiny here. Consider: in the course of a life, we must see and endure many things we could have wished away. If we grant seventy years as the limit of life, those years comprise … 26,250 days, and each day unlike the last in what it brings. You see, Croesus, what a unpredictable and risky thing life is. Though you are rich and rule many subjects, I cannot truthfully answer your question till I know the manner of your death. Great wealth is no better than moderate means unless a man's luck holds out to the end. Rich men have known bad luck and those with modest means have known good....

"If the man favored by wealth dies as he has lived, then you will have the man you seek--one who merits the label 'happy.' But do not grant that label till he is dead, for till then he is merely lucky and not truly happy....

"Whoever possesses the most of the good things I described before and retains them till he meets a peaceful death, that man, Croesus,

ought to be called happy. In all things, yo should look to the end, for the gods can let a ma taste happiness and then completely shatter him.'

Plutarch. *Solon*. Chaps. 13-18, 24-25. In Ziegler, K., ed *Plutarchi vitae parallelae*. Vol. 1.1. 4th ed. Leipzig Teubner, 1969. Solon. Poem 24. In Diehl, Ernestus, ed *Anthologia Lyrica Graeca*. Leipzig: Teubner, 1954. Pp 43-45. Legrand, Ph.-E., ed. *Hérodote: Histoires*. Vol. 1 Paris: Les Belles Lettres, 1932; rpt. 1970. 1.28-33 Translations by James P. Holoka.

READING 3.4

PERICLES AND ASPASIA: "FIRST COUPLE" OF CLASSICAL ATHENS

► **Musician and Hetaira**

Pericles (c. 495-429 B.C.E.) was the "complete man" of fifth-century Athens. He joined the democratic party as a young man and became the protégé of the democratic reformer Ephialtes. After Ephialtes' assassination in 461, Pericles soon became the leading democratic statesman in Athens.

Pericles was elected general (*strategos*) frequently between 457 and 443, and continuously thereafter till his death in 429. The Board of Ten Generals was the true executive branch of the Athenian government at this time, and Pericles' long service in office made him first among equals on the board and the most influential man in the government and in the society at large. Pericles used his influence to extend the democratic reforms begun by Solon, Cleisthenes, and Ephialtes.

By redirecting tribute monies that subject states were required to send to Athens, Pericles implemented full employment by promoting state-financed work on ships, dockyard facilities, temples, roads, fortifications, arsenals, granaries, etc. Under his leadership, Athens also became the cultural and artistic center of the Aegean world. Pericles was a friend of the arts. He served as financial backer/producer for a trilogy of plays including Aeschylus's *Persians*. He was a close personal friend of Anaxagoras the philosopher, Sophocles the dramatist, and Pheidias the sculptor-in-chief for the Parthenon construction. The Parthenon remains the most renowned symbol of Pericles' encouragement and support for the arts.

Pericles also had an unusual personal life: he had a long relationship with a notorious Milesian woman, Aspasia (c. 470-410), a *hetaira* ("female companion") or high-class prostitute. Aspasia became notorious as the "uncrowned queen" of Athens. She was a fashion-setter and shared Pericles' interests in the arts and philosophy. Their home became the meeting place of artists, writers, and politicians. Despite, or perhaps because of, her personal qualities, Aspasia was the butt of many risqué jokes and satiric attacks, often originating with political opponents of Pericles who feared to attack him directly because of his enormous prestige and popularity with the common people.

The passages that follow are from the *Life of Pericles* by Plutarch (c. 48-c. 124 C.E.) and from the *History of the Peloponnesian War* by Thucydides (c. 460-c. 400).

QUESTIONS:

1) Pericles is sometimes referred to as a "thinking man's" statesman. Why?
2) What made Aspasia such a unique figure in ancient Greek history?
3) What did Thucydides consider to be the most distinctive aspect of Pericles' character as a leader?

Pericles belonged to the tribe called Akamantis and the deme [precinct] called Kholargeus; his ancestry both, paternal and maternal, was among the noblest at Athens. His father, Xanthippos had served as general in the victory at Mycale. His mother, Agariste, was the niece of Cleisthenes, the very Cleisthenes who had ended tyranny at Athens by expelling the Peisistratids and setting up laws and a constitution well-suited to promoting both state security and cooperation among citizens. His mother bore Pericles after having dreamt that she had given birth to a lion. Pericles was physically well-proportioned, but his head was somewhat elongated. Hence artists generally show him helmeted in their portraits, not wishing to annoy him by showing the deformity. This is the source of the label "onion-head" [that comic poets have given him]....

Most say Pericles' music [lyre and poetry] teacher was Damon, though Aristotle says Pythocleides instructed him in the subject. This Damon was a master sophist who concealed his considerable talents under the guise of being a music teacher only. It was Damon who in fact readied Pericles for his political career much as a trainer prepares an athlete. But Damon could not hide behind his lyre altogether, and was ostracized for conspiracy and for favoring tyranny; the comic poets, too, took aim at him in the plays....

The Eleatic philosopher Zeno also tutored Pericles at this time; his subject, like that of Parmenides, was natural philosophy [physics]. He was skilled at cross-examination and could defeat his opponent by clever question-and-answer.... But it was Anaxagoras of Clazomenae who most influenced Pericles, giving him a lordly presence more powerful than the bluster of any mere rabble-rouser; under him, Pericles developed the natural talents of his personality to the fullest. People at the time used to call Anaxagoras "The Mind," perhaps because of the powers of intellect he showed in his research into natural phenomena; or it may have been because he opposed the notion of pure intelligence to those of chance and necessity as the ordering principle behind the cosmos, differentiating basic elements from the mishmash of matter.

Pericles revered Anaxagoras and steeped himself in his advanced speculations on natural and celestial phenomena. These studies engendered in Pericles a noble spirit and a speaking style that was always elevated above the crude and unconscionable foolery of mob orators. His face was correspondingly dignified (seldom distorted by laughter), his gestures serene, and his clothing attractively worn even in the course of his speeches. His voice was forceful yet well restrained. The whole effect of his comportment and speech on his audiences was profound.

Once, while on a pressing matter in the agora [business district], he let some rowdy fellow abuse and insult him all day long without making any retort at all. When he went home at evening, the ruffian followed him and continued bad mouthing him the whole time. As dark was falling and Pericles was going inside his house, he bid one of his house-slaves to take a torch and accompany the man back to his own home....

However, Pericles most pleased his fellow Athenians, most adorned their city, and most astounded their contemporaries by erecting temples and other public structures. These stand today as testimony that stories of the power and prosperity of old Greece are no mere falsehoods. Nonetheless, Pericles' enemies targeted this building program, more than any other policy of his, for abuse and misrepresentation. In the Assembly of citizens, they exclaimed "the people have lost face through the transferring of the funds contributed by the rest of Greece from Delos to Athens. Pericles has now given the lie to his own claim that these funds were moved out of fear of the barbarians [Persians] and in the interest of greater security. The Greeks have suffered an outrage and have clearly been treated tyrannically. They see themselves compelled to contribute toward the war against the Persians, while we adorn and gild our city like some pretentious woman dolled up in precious gems and statuary and temples costing a fortune."

Pericles, for his part, responded: "the people of Athens are not obligated to account for their use of the allies financial contributions, so long as we secure Greece against any threat of barbarian [Persian] attack. The allies supply neither horse nor man nor ship, only money-- money that belongs not to those who give it, but to those who receive it, so long as they met the conditions agreed on. It is only just that, having secured sufficient war materiel, the city should devote the surplus to completing projects that will bring itself glory and at the same time benefit its inhabitants. Thus there will be plenty of need and opportunity for the exercise of all the arts and crafts; every hand will be employed in work on these projects, as we become a city of full employment. Athens will thus both maintain and beautify itself from its own resources."

Of course, all those of military age and physically fit were always able to earn money through service on the campaigns Pericles sponsored. He also wanted the unskilled populace, which lacked military training, to share in the public largesse, but not by merely sitting idle. Thus he proposed for popular approval a whole host of huge public works enterprises and building plans. These all entailed the employment of many different arts and trades over extended periods; the intent here was to provide some share of the public wealth to those who stayed at home as well as to those who served in the fleet or the army or in garrisons abroad.

The materials required for these projects included stone, bronze, ivory, gold, ebony, and cypress wood; those who worked them included carpenters, sculptors, bronzesmiths, masons, dyers, goldsmiths, ivory-workers, painters, embroiderers, and engravers. Those who transported materials to the city included (by sea) merchants, sailors, and ship-masters, and (by land) wagon makers and drivers and animal handlers; also needed were rope-makers, weavers, leather-workers, road-workers, and miners. Each trade, like a general, had its army of soldiers working in obedience to command, as a tool conforms to the hand that wields it, or a body to the soul. In short, these great public projects ensured the widespread distribution of benefits to individuals of all age-groups and all abilities.

Thus the buildings took shape, impressive both in sheer magnitude and in elegance of design. Though the craftsmen all vied to outshine each other in their work, the most amazing aspect of it all was the speed with which the projects were implemented. Undertakings that would seem to require several generations to fulfill were in fact accomplished during the heyday of one man's political career. In contrast, the painter Zeuxis, overhearing another painter, Agatharkhos, boast how fast he could

work, commented: "My work takes long and lasts long." Certainly mere facility and speed of execution do not confer lasting quality or a beautiful precision; the time expended in painstaking composition repays us by endowing any work with a permanent vigor. For this reason, Pericles' works are striking: though were made in a brief span, they have endured forever. Every one of them was imbued with a venerable-seeming loveliness from birth, yet retains a vital freshness and energy to this day. There is a bloom of novelty securing them from the effects of time, as if some enduring spirit, an immortal élan animated them all....

After concluding a Thirty Years' Peace with the Lacedaemonians [Spartans], Pericles had a decree passed ordering an expedition against the island of Samos, on the grounds that the Samians had not ceased hostilities against Miletus when Athens instructed them to do so. It is generally thought that Pericles acted against Samos to gratify Aspasia, so this may be the time to inquire into the extraordinary art or charm this woman exerted on the most eminent statesmen, a charm that commanded the respect and reflections even of philosophers.

She was born to Axiokhos of Miletus. She emulated Thargelia, an Ionian woman of olden days, in directing her attentions only to men of power and prestige. Thargelia had combined extraordinary beauty, grace, and brains. She took many lovers and converted all to the Persian cause, in this way, since these were men of standing and influence, sowing the seeds of affinity with Persians in various Greek cities. So too, they say, Pericles was drawn to Aspasia chiefly by her unusual political acumen. Socrates himself used to visit her with some of his comrades; friends of his even brought their wives to hear her conversations, despite the fact that her profession was anything but respectable: she maintained an establishment for young prostitutes....

Pericles' attraction to Aspasia stemmed from passion. His wife was a kinswoman of his, formerly married to Hipponicus, to whom she bore a son, Callias "the Rich." To Pericles, she bore two sons, Xanthippos and Paralos. Later, when they found each other incompatible, Pericles handed her over to another man by her own consent. He himself then began [some five years later] to live with Aspasia, whom he loved most devotedly. Each day, on setting out for and returning from the marketplace, he greeted and kissed her.

Aspasia is alluded to in comedies as the new Omphale and Deianira [mistress and wife of the hero Herakles] and even as Hera. Cratinus calls her a whore in no uncertain terms: "To find him his Hera, the goddess of perversion spawned that tramp Aspasia." Pericles is thought to have had an illegitimate son [also named Pericles] by her.... They say she became so illustrious that Cyrus, who fought his brother [Artaxerxes] for the Persian throne, changed the name of his favorite concubine from Milto to Aspasia.

* * * * *

During the era of peace, while Pericles was in charge of affairs, Athens was well lead and secure; under his leadership, the city was at its acme. And when war broke out, he shrewdly gauged the power of Athens. He survived the opening of hostilities [of the Peloponnesian War, 431-404] by only two and a half years. His ability to foresee the course of wartime events was still more apparent after his death. He had predicted victory if only Athens would be patient and care for the fleet, forgo any attempt to expand the empire during wartime, and did

not jeopardize the security of the city itself. Those who came after him violated these recommendations, and in non-military matters too, allowed personal aspirations and personal gain to dictate policies harmful both to the Athenians and to their allies. When these policies did succeed, they profited individuals only; when they failed, they damaged the fighting capacity of the entire state. This was because Pericles, by his standing, his brains, and his honesty was able to restrain the populace while respecting its sovereignty. He led them rather than follow their lead. Since he never tried to aggrandize himself from base motives, he had no need to cajole the people; on the contrary his stature was such that he could upbraid and override them. When he saw their self-assurance leading them astray, he made them sensible of the perils involved. On the other hand, when they were unwarrantably downcast, he revived their confidence. While Athens was a democracy in name, power in fact lay in the hands of the first man.

Plutarch. *Pericles*. Chaps. 3-5, 12-13, 24. In Ziegler, K. ed. *Plutarchi vitae parallelae*. Vol. 1.2. 3rd ed. Leipzig: Teubner, 1964. Jones, H.S., and J.E.Powell, eds. *Thucydidis historiae*. Vol. 1. Oxford: Clarendon Press, 1942. 2.65.5-10. Translations by James P. Holoka.

THE ASSASSINATION OF KING PHILIP II OF MACEDON

Assassinations have sometimes changed the course of history. In the twentieth century, the assassinations of the Archduke Francis Ferdinand in 1914, John F. Kennedy in 1963, and Martin Luther King, Jr. in 1968 caused momentous changes. Similarly momentous in ancient Rome was the stabbing death of Julius Caesar on the Ides of March, in 44 B.C.E. But the assassination that had the greatest impact on the course of ancient history was that of Philip II (r. 359-336 B.C.E.), king of Macedon and father of Alexander the Great.

Had Philip's reign been shorter, it is highly unlikely that Alexander would have inherited a powerful, highly proficient military machine, supported by the resources of a newly reorganized and stabilized Macedonian kingdom. These were Philip's accomplishments. But had Philip lived longer-- and he was a vigorous man in his mid-forties when he died--it is unlikely that Alexander would have had the chance to alter world history by his conquests in western and south-central Asia, and in Egypt.

Philip's assassination came at precisely the right moment for his son. Two years earlier (338), Alexander had been entrusted with an important command at the battle of Chaeroneia and was popular with the troops. He had by this time had a first-rate physical and intellectual training and was ready to assume authority.

Lawyers, confronted by a suspicious death, often ask question *cui bono?*--"to whose benefit?" In Philip's case, obviously, it was to Alexander's. Father and son had their differences (see Plutarch in the first passage below), at the center of which was Alexander's forceful mother, Olympias, who had figured more prominently in her son's life than Philip had. When Philip took as his new wife (Macedonian kings often practiced polygamy) a high-born Macedonian woman named Cleopatra, his relations with Olympias naturally were strained and Alexander's position as likely heir to the throne was became insecure, since Olympias was not Macedonian by blood.

What if anything did Alexander's insecurity and Olympias's vindictiveness contribute to the plot to kill Philip? The account in our principal ancient source for the assassination, Diodorus Siculus (see second passage below), leaves the question open, just as Warren Commission Report left open questions about Lee Harvey Oswald's motivations and possible co-conspirators in President John F. Kennedy's assassination. Diodorus' story of homosexual jealousy turned violent is rather shaky. In his version of events, the assassin's real grievance was not primarily with Philip. But the killer (like Oswald) had no chance to explain himself, for he was immediately silenced by the spears of three men who were trusted friends of Alexander. For her part, Olympias openly glorified the memory of the assassin; Plutarch says that rumors of her complicity and Alexander's abounded: "Olympias was blamed for the murder, since she was thought to have spurred on [the assassin] Pausanias to take revenge. Others said that Pausanias met with Alexander to complain of the injury against him, whereupon Alexander quoted the lines from Euripides in which Medea threatens 'The father, the bride, and the groom all together'" [*Life of Alexander*, chap. 10]. As one modern historian, Peter Green, put it, "Circumstantial evidence does not ... amount to proof positive; but men have been hanged on weaker cumulative evidence than that assembled here. The motive was overwhelming, the opportunity ideal" [*Alexander the Great* (New York: Praeger, 1970), p. 68].

After ascending the throne, Alexander embarked on a remarkable career of conquest. His successes accelerated the spread of Greek culture in the eastern Mediterranean and ensured the persistence of Greek values and institutions in the Roman Empire and in subsequent eras of world history. Could Philip have done the same? An assassin's blade made that question academic.

QUESTIONS:

1) Do you believe Alexander was involved in the murder of Philip? What in the account by Diodorus points to his guilt (or innocence)?
2) Can we reconstruct a behind-the-scenes role for Olympias in the assassination of Philip?
3) Is the account of Pausanias's motivations convincing?

The marriages and love affairs of Philip not only led to conflicts in his household and among his womenfolk, but soon affected the state as a whole, when disputes arose between himself and his son Alexander. The envious and vengeful personality of Olympias fanned these flames, as she provoked Alexander to defy his father. Their differences came to a crisis with Philip's decision to marry Cleopatra, a very young woman with whom he had rashly fallen in love. At a banquet one night, Attalus, Cleopatra's uncle, being quite drunk, urged the Macedonians to pray the gods that the marriage of Philip and Cleopatra would produce a pure-blooded heir [i.e., Macedonian on both sides] to the throne. This infuriated Alexander, who shouted "You scoundrel, are you calling me a bastard?" He then flung his drink at Attalus. Philip rose to intervene, drawing his sword against his son. Luckily, he was so unbalanced by wine and anger that he stumbled and fell to the ground. At this, Alexander sneered and said "Here's the man who plans to travel from Europe to Asia, but he can't even make it from one couch to another without taking a header!" Following this drunken ruckus, Alexander left the capital, removing Olympias to Epirus and himself to Illyria.

* * * * *

In the archonship of Pythodorus [336 B.C.E.] ... Philip, having been appointed hegemon [commander-in-chief] by the Greek states, commenced the war with Persia by sending ahead into Asia [Minor] an advance expedition under the command of Attalus and Parmenio, with orders to liberate the Greek city-states there. Philip himself, anxious to have divine approval, consulted the Pythia [priestess at Delphi] to ask if he would defeat the Persian king. She responded as follows: "The bull is garlanded [for sacrifice]. All is ready and the sacrificer is at hand."

Though the response was equivocal, Philip took it as propitious to himself: that is, predicting the death of the Persian king. In fact, it foretold Philip's own death at a festival with solemn sacrifices; he, like the bull, would die wearing religious wreaths. But Philip rejoiced to think that he had the backing of the gods and trusted that Macedonian arms would subjugate Asia [Minor].

Philip now made plans for spectacular celebrations for the gods, in conjunction with the wedding of his and Olympias's daughter, Cleopatra, who was marrying Alexander, the king of Epirus (and brother of Olympias). Eager to have as many Greeks as possible participating in the sacred observances, he scheduled elaborate musical displays and feasts for his guests. He invited his own friends from all over Greece and urged his courtiers to do the same. He intended to impress the Greeks with his civility and to repay the honors bestowed on him as supreme commander by staging an appropriate social event.

Many people came to the festival at Aegae in Macedonia from all parts both for the games and for the marriage. Philip was awarded golden crowns not only by individuals but also by many major city-states, including Athens. When the herald announced the Athenian decoration, he closed by saying that the Athenians would surrender anyone plotting against Philip and seeking refuge at Athens. The words (later) seemed an omen from the gods that a conspiracy was in fact approaching. There were several other sayings at the time that seemed to foreshadow the king's demise....

The games were to begin the next day. The theater was already packed before dawn, and at sunrise the lavish procession began: it included dazzling images of the twelve Olympian gods meant to awe the spectators; and to the twelve was joined a thirteenth--that of Philip himself.

Philip appeared at the crowded theater attired in a white mantle. He bid his bodyguards to keep their distance, meaning to demonstrate his confidence in the adulation of the Greeks, which made armed guards unnecessary. Amidst the general applause and raves, the plot to assassinate unfolded itself. In the interest of clarity, I will examine the motives for it.

A Macedonian, Pausanias by name, from the Orestis district, had been a member of the king's bodyguard. Because of his attractiveness, Philip became his lover. When Philip then turned his attentions elsewhere (to another man named Pausanias), the first Pausanias mocked the second by saying he was androgynous and promiscuous. Cut to the quick by this slur, the second Pausanias secured his own death in a sensational way, after confiding in Attalus what he was intending to do. For, some days later, during a battle with Pleurias, an Illyrian king, Pausanias shielded Philip's body with his own, and died from fatal wounds so received.

The incident was widely reported. Attalus, a man of standing and influence in the court of Philip, thereupon invited the first Pausanias to dinner. Having gotten him drunk on undiluted wine, he then handed him over nearly unconscious to be raped by his mule-drivers. Pausanias, once sobered up, was deeply aggrieved by the assault on his person and denounced Attalus to the king. Philip, however, although outraged at the brutality of the deed, did not choose to bring Attalus to account because of their affiliation and because he had need of the man's services at the moment: Attalus was the [uncle] of Philip's new wife, Cleopatra, and, owing to his valor, had just been appointed general of the forward forces in Asia. Thus, Philip instead tried to quell Pausanias's justifiable rage over his injury by giving him gifts and elevating his position in the corps of his personal bodyguards.

Pausanias for his part kept his grudge and longed to exact vengeance not only from the man who had injured him, but also from the one who had declined to redress the injustice. His teacher, the sophist Hermocrates, unwittingly inspired him in his scheme. When Pausanias asked him how one could become most renowned, the sophist answered: "by slaying the man whose achievements were the greatest, for the assassin's fame would endure as long as the great man's." Pausanias took this opinion as applicable to his own situation. He immediately resolved to revenge himself during the distractions of the wedding festival. Having readied horses at the city gates, he went to the entrance of the theater carrying a concealed Celtic dagger. Philip on his arrival bid his companions to enter ahead of him and, with his bodyguard ordered to keep their distance, was by himself. Pausanias darted forward and stabbed the king through his ribs, killing him instantly. He then made a dash for the gates and his getaway horses. Meantime, the royal bodyguards sprang into action, some rushing to the fallen king, others pursuing the killer; these included Leonnatus, Perdiccas, and Attalus [not the uncle of Cleopatra]. Pausanias nearly made it to the waiting horses, but his shoe caught in a vine and he fell. As he was getting up, Perdiccas and the others overtook him and slew him with their javelins.

So perished Philip, the greatest European monarch of his era. The vast extent of his rule led him to claim a throne among the twelve great Olympian deities. He reigned twenty-four years, in that time rising from a man with little support for his claim to the throne to ruler of the greatest empire in Greece. The success of his career derived not so much from his military genius as from his facility and tact in diplomacy. They say that he prided himself more on his skills of strategy and diplomacy than on his battlefield courage, for his whole army shared the credit for success in combat, while he alone got the recognition for diplomatic victories.

Plutarch. *Life of Alexander*. Chap. 9. In Ziegler, K., ed. *Plutarchi vitae parallelae*. 4th ed. Vol. 2.2. Leipzig: Teubner, 1969. Diodorus Siculus. *The Library of History*. Book 16, sections 91-95. In Welles, C. Bradford, ed. *Diodorus of Sicily*. Vol. 8. Cambridge: Harvard Univ. Press, 1963. Translations by James P. Holoka.

► Papyrus Plant

LAW AND LIFE IN HELLENISTIC EGYPT

King Philip II of Macedon prepared the way and his son Alexander the Great conquered the largest empire the world had seen; it stretched from Greece to Egypt and across Asia to the Indus River Valley. When Alexander was lying on his deathbed in 322 B.C.E., he was asked to whom he wished to leave his empire. He answered, "To the strongest." During the next fifty years or so, his top generals fought to inherit his empire. Three kingdoms emerged: Macedon (including Greece); the Seleucid Empire in Asia; and the Ptolemaic kingdom of Egypt. Macedonians and Greeks formed the ruling class in all these states, known as Hellenistic kingdoms.

Compared with the old Greek city-states, the Hellenistic kingdoms were much larger in territory and ethnically more diverse. Each was administered by an elaborate bureaucracy headed by a remote, godlike king of Macedonian descent. Ordinary people had no political power and seldom participated in government. counted for much less politically than had their fifth-century ancestors and consequently felt little patriotic fervor.

The Hellenistic Age was one of relative peace, stability, and prosperity. Greek educators, artisans, craftsmen, merchants, and soldiers moved into recently conquered regions. Trade relations were secure and extensive, and Greek language and culture became widespread in West Asia and the eastern half of the Mediterranean region.

Manufacturing prospered and international trade boomed. The specialties of each region found markets throughout the Hellenistic world from India to the Strait of Gibraltar. Hellenistic governments fostered trade by maintaining good roads and harbor installations and by adopting standard monetary systems. Cities like Rhodes, Corinth, Ephesus, Pergamum, Antioch, and Alexandria flourished.

Egypt is an especially rich source of information about the Hellenistic world, because the arid climate has preserved thousands of papyrus documents. These materials give us a precious glimpse of an ancient society, both in its public, legal, and administrative aspects, and in the private sphere as well. The selections that follow shed light on legal conditions of marriage and divorce, criminal justice, sales agreements, and government business. The personal letters reveal details of daily life among citizens of Hellenistic Egypt.

QUESTIONS:

1) Does the marriage contract in the first selection seem fair and equitable to both parties?
2) Do the penalties prescribed in the sixth selection seem fair and equitable?
3) How would you handle the petitions in the seventh and eighth selections?

Marriage Contract (311 B.C.E.).

In the 7th year of the reign of Alexander son of Alexander, the 14th year of the satrapship [provincial governorship] of Ptolemy [Soter], in the month Dius. Marriage contract of Heraclides and Demetria. Heraclides takes as his lawful wife Demetria, Coan, both being freeborn, from her father Leptines, Coan, and her mother Philotis, bringing cloth and ornaments to the value of 1000 drachmae, and Heraclides shall supply to Demetria all that is proper for a freeborn wife, and we shall live together wherever it seems best to Leptines and Heraclides consulting in common. If Demetria is discovered doing any evil to the shame of her husband Heraclides, she shall be deprived of all that she brought, but Heraclides shall prove whatever he alleges against Demetria before three men whom they both accept. It shall not be lawful for Heraclides to bring home another wife in insult of Demetria nor to have children by another woman nor to do any evil against Demetria on any pretext. If Heraclides is discovered doing any of these things and Demetria proves it before three men whom they both accept, Heraclides shall give back to Demetria the dowry of 1000 drachmae which she brought and shall moreover forfeit 1000 drachmae of the silver coinage of Alexander. Demetria and those aiding Demetria to exact payment shall have the right of execution, as if derived from a legally decided action, upon the person of Heraclides and upon all the property of Heraclides both on land and on water. This contract shall be valid in every respect, wherever Heraclides may produce it against Demetria, or Demetria and those aiding Demetria to exact payment may produce it against Heraclides, as if the agreement had been made in that place. Heraclides and Demetria shall have the right to keep the contracts severally in their own custody and to produce them against each other. Witnesses: Cleon, Gelan; Anticrates, Temnian; Lysis, Temnian; Dionysius, Temnian; Aristomachus, Cyrenaean; Aristodicus, Coan.

Deed of Divorce (13 B.C.E.).

To Protarchus [an official in Alexandria] from Zois daughter of Heraclides, with her guardian her brother Irenaeus son of Heraclides, and from Antipater son of Zenon. Zois and Antipater agree that they have separated from each other severing the union which they had formed on the basis of an agreement made through the same tribunal in Hathur of the current 17th year of Caesar, and Zois acknowledges that she has received from Antipater by hand from his house the material which he received for dowry, clothes to the value of 120 drachmae and a pair of gold earrings. The agreement of marriage shall henceforth be null, and neither Zois nor other person acting for her shall take proceedings against Antipater for restitution of the dowry, nor shall either party take proceedings against the other about cohabitation or any other matter whatsoever up to the present day, and hereafter it shall be lawful both for Zois to marry another man and for Antipater to marry another woman without either of them being answerable. In addition to this agreement being valid, the one who transgresses it shall moreover be liable both to damages and to the prescribed fine. The 17th year of Caesar, Pharmouthi 2.

Sale of a House and Renunciation of Ownership (101 B.C.E.).

The 14th year of the reign of Ptolemy surnamed Alexander, god Philometor, the priests and priestesses and canephorus [a priestess] being those now in office, Coiach 2, at Pathyris, before Hermias agent of Paniscus, agoranomus [a government notary who drew up contracts]. Psenmenches son of Panechates, Persian of the Epigone, aged about 55 years, of medium height, fair-skinned, smooth-haired, bald in front, long-faced, straight-nosed, with a scar on the left cheek, limping on the right foot, with the concurrence of his son Harpaesis son of Psenmenches, Persian, aged about 30 years, of medium height, fair-skinned, rather curly-haired, long-faced, straight-nosed, without distinguishing mark, has sold the house belonging to him, built and furnished with vaults and doors, with the attached courtyard, situated in the northern part of Pathyris, its boundaries being, on the south the house of Nechoutes son of Panechates, on the north the house of Cephalon, on the east a street, on the west the house of Portis son of Petesouchus with a street between, or whatever the boundaries may be all round. Peteesis, son of Ones, Persian, aged about 40 years, of medium height, fair-skinned, rather curly-haired, with a scar on the forehead, has purchased it for 4 talents of copper. Negotiator and guarantor of all the terms of this deed of sale: Psenmenches the vendor, whom Peteesis the purchaser has accepted. Registered by me, Hermias agent of Paniscus.

Year 14, Choiach 2, at Pathyris, before Hermias agent of Paniscus, agoranomus.... Neither Psenmenches himself nor any of his assigns shall take proceedings against Peteesis or any of his assigns; and if anyone does so, the proceedings shall be invalid and in addition the aggressor shall straightway forfeit a penalty of 8 talents of copper and a fine, consecrated to the Crown, of 160 drachmae of coined silver, and he shall be none the less bound to conform to the above terms. This agreement shall be valid wherever produced. Registered by me, Hermias agent of Paniscus.

Sale of a Slave (259 B.C.E.).

In the 27th year of the reign of Ptolemy [Philadelphus] son of Ptolemy and of his son Ptolemy, the priest of Alexander and of the gods Adelphi [the deified king and queen Ptolemy II and Arsinoe] and the canephorus of Arsinoe Philadelphus being those in office in Alexandria, in the month Xandicus, at Birta [in present-day Jordan] in the land of Ammon. Nicanor son of Xenocles, Cnidian, in the service of Tobias, has sold to Zenon son of Agreophon, Caunian, in the service of Apollonius the diocetes [finance minister of Ptolemy II], a Babylonian girl named Sphragis, about seven years of age, for fifty drachmae. Guarantor ... son of Ananias, Persian, of the troop of Tobias, cleruch [soldier holding a grant of land]. Witnesses: ... judge; Polemon son of Straton, Macedonian, of the cavalrymen of Tobias, cleruch .... (Endorsed) Deed of sale of a girl.

Letter from Artemidorus to Zenon (252 B.C.E.).

Artemidorus [a physician on the staff of the finance minister] to Zenon greeting. If you are well, it would be excellent. I too am well and Apollonius is in good health and other things are satisfactory. As I write this, we have just arrived in Sidon after escorting the princess [Berenice] to the frontier [on her way to Syria to marry Antiochus II], and I expect that we shall soon be with you. Now you will do me a favour by taking care of your own health and writing to me if you want anything done that I can do for you. And kindly buy me, so that I may get them when I arrive, 3 metretae [c. 54 liters] of the best honey and 600 artabae [24000 liters] of barley for the animals, and pay the cost of them out of the produce of the sesame and croton [castor-oil, used for lamps], and also see to the house in Philadelphia in order that I may find it roofed when I arrive. Try also as best you can to keep watch on the oxen and the pigs and the geese and the rest of the stock there; I shall have a better supply of provisions if you do. Also see to it that the crops are harvested somehow, and if any outlay is required, do not hesitate to pay what is necessary. Goodbye. Year 33, intercalary Peritius 6. (Addressed) To Zenon. To Philadelphia. (Docketed) Year 33, Phamenoth 6. Artemidorus.

Penalties for Assault in Alexandrian Law (c. 250 B.C.E.).

Threatening with iron. If a freeman threatens a freeman with iron or copper or stone or ... or wood, he shall forfeit a hundred drachmae, if he is worsted in the suit. But if a male slave or a female slave does any of these things to a freeman or a freewoman, they shall receive not less than a hundred stripes, or else the master of the offender, if he is defeated in the suit, shall forfeit to the injured party twice the amount of the penalty which is prescribed for a freeman.

Injuries done in drunkenness. Whoever commits a personal injury in drunkenness. Whoever commits a personal injury in drunkenness by night or in a temple or in the market-place shall forfeit twice the amount of the prescribed penalty.

For a slave striking a freeman. If a male slave or a female slave strikes a freeman or a freewoman, they shall receive not less than a hundred stripes, or else the master, if he acknowledges the fact, shall pay on behalf of his slave twice the amount of the penalty which is prescribed for a freeman. But if he disputes it, the plaintiff shall indict him, claiming for one blow a hundred drachmae, and if the master is condemned, he shall forfeit three times that amount without assessment; and for a greater number of blows the plaintiff shall himself assess the injury when he brings the suit, and whatever assessment is fixed by the court, the master shall forfeit three times that amount.

Blows between freemen. If a freeman or a freewoman, making an unjust attack, strikes a freeman or a freewoman, they shall forfeit a hundred drachmae without assessment, if they are defeated in the suit. But if they strike more than one blow, the plaintiff in bringing the suit shall himself assess the damage caused by the blows, and whatever assessment is fixed by the court, the accused shall forfeit twice that amount. And if anyone strikes one of the magistrates while executing the administrative duties prescribed to the magistracy, he shall pay the penalties trebled, if he is defeated in the suit.

Outrage. If any person commits against another an outrage not provided for in the code, the injured party shall himself assess the damage in bringing his suit, but he shall further state specifically in what manner he claims to have been outraged and the date on which he was outraged. And the offender if condemned shall pay twice the amount of the assessment fixed by the court.

Petition of a Lentil-Cook (c. 250 B.C.E.).

To Philiscus [a financial administrator in Crocodilopolis] greeting from Harentotes, lentil-cook of Philadelphia. I give the product of 35 artabae a month [that is, of roasted lentils he had contracted to deliver to the government] and I do my best to pay the tax every month in order that you may have no complaint against me. Now the folk in the town are roasting pumpkins. For that reason then nobody buys lentils from me at the present time. I beg and beseech you then, if you think fit, to be allowed more time, just as has been done in Crocodilopolis, for paying the tax to the king. For in the morning they straightway sit down beside the lentils selling their pumpkins and give me no chance to sell my lentils.

Petition to the King (220 B.C.E.).

To King Ptolemy [Philopator] greeting from Philista daughter of Lysias resident in Tricomia. I am wronged by Petechon. For as I was bathing in the baths of the aforesaid village on Tubi 7 of Year 1, and had stepped out to soap myself, he being bathman to the women's rotunda and having brought in the jugs of hot water emptied one over me and scalded my belly and my left

thigh down to the knee, so that my life was in danger. On finding him I gave into the custody of Nechthosiris the chief policeman of the village in the presence of Simon the epistates [village-head]. I beg you, therefore, O king, if it please you, as a suppliant who has sought your protection, not to suffer me, who am a working woman, to be thus lawlessly treated, but to order Diophanes the strategus [district-governor] to write to Simon the epistates and Nechthosiris the policeman that they are to bring Petechon before him in order that Diophanes may inquire into the case, hoping that having sought the protection of you, O king, the common benefactor of all, I may obtain justice. Farewell. (Docketed) To Simon. Send the accused. Year 1, Gorpiaeus 28 Tubi 12.

(Endorsed) Year 1, Gorpiaeus 28 Tubi 12. Philista against Petechon, bathman, about having been scalded.

Notification of a Robbery (210 B.C.E.).

Year 12, Epeiph 10. Memorandum to Teos the royal scribe. Amosis, village scribe of Apollonias, to Teos greeting. I subjoin for your information a copy of the notification presented to me by Heracon the superintendent of the estate of Pitholaus [a commander of elephant-hunters]. Goodbye. (Year) 12, Epeiph 9.

Notification to Amosis, scribe of the village of Apollonias, from Heracon, superintendent of the estate of Pitholaus. On the ... of Epeiph Theophilus son of Dositheus, Philistion son of ..., and Timaeus son of Telouphis, all three Jews of the Epigone, raided the fruit-garden of the aforesaid Pitholaus, which is in the bounds of the aforesaid village, and stripped the grapes from ten vines; and when Horus the guard ran out against them, they maltreated him and struck him on any part of the body that offered: and they carried off a vine-dressers pruning-hook. The aforesaid robbers are living in Kerkeosiris. I estimate the grapes gathered as enough to make 6 metretae [c. 108 liters] of wine. (Endorsed) To the royal scribe. Year 12, Epeiph 10. Concerning a vineyard of Pitholaus stripped of its grapes.

Police Report (178 or 167 B.C.E.).

4th year, Hathur 6. To Osoroeris, royal scribe. On the 5th of the present month when patrolling the fields near the village I found an effusion of blood ..., and I learn from the villagers that Theodotus son of Dositheus, having set out in that direction, has not yet returned. I make this report.

Hunt, A.S., and C.C. Edgar, eds. and trans. *Select Papyri*. Cambridge: Harvard Univ. Press. Vol. 1 (1932): nos. 1, 6, 29, 31, 93 = pp. 3, 5, 23, 25, 87, 89, 97, 277, 279. Vol. 2 (1934): nos. 202, 266, 269, 334, 335 = pp. 7, 9, 229, 235, 237, 383, 385 (bis).

LETTERS OF PLINY THE YOUNGER: ROMAN LIFE AROUND 100 C.E.

In ancient Rome, a small, affluent upper class who derived their wealth from the labor of slaves and tenant farmers had the means to turn their attentions to political and cultural activities.

The upper class also had responsibilities to the societies they dominated. They were expected, and sometimes legally required, to contribute their talents and their financial resources to the service of the state. In ancient Rome in its heyday, the governing classes (more or less) often prided themselves on their charitable benefactions to less fortunate fellow citizens. The eventual decline of this public-spiritedness hastened the decline of the Roman Empire itself.

Pliny the Younger lived from about 60 to about 110 C.E., when the Imperial Rome was still at the pinnacle of its success. Like his scholarly uncle and namesake, Pliny the Elder, he had all the advantages of his social class: inherited wealth from large property holdings, a first-rate education, and rapid career advancement as a military officer and then as a lawyer and government official.

Fortunately, numerous letters by Pliny the Younger have survived; they give us valuable insights into the personal and professional life of an active and prominent Roman official. The letters touch on a wide variety of topics, such as the death of Pliny the Elder during the devastating eruption of Mt. Vesuvius in 79 C.E., advice regarding investment strategies, reports of odd natural phenomena (a tame dolphin), troubles with the Christian sect in the province of Bithynia (modern Turkey), and a ghost story. They also show his wife and sadness because they had no children. Pliny emerges from his letters as a genial, honorable man, careful to fulfill his personal and public duties. He was compassionate toward those less fortunate than himself (including slaves) and generous in using his own money for public purposes and private charity.

In the first letter included here, we see Pliny helping to arrange an advantageous marriage for personal friends and obviously enjoying the role of matchmaker and practical advisor. In the second letter, we hear of the fate of an abusive slave master. The third letter offers an early example of a "matching funds" charitable contribution to establish a school. The final letter provides insight into the intellectual pastimes and leisure activities, enjoyed by a Roman gentleman.

QUESTIONS:

1) What moral values are reflected in the letters of Pliny included here?
2) Does Pliny's attitude toward slaves seem enlightened or merely practical?
3) Why does Pliny arrange his educational benefactions to Comum in the way he does?

Greetings from Gaius Plinius to Junius Mauricus.

You request that I recommend a husband for your niece. This is as it should be, for you know the respect and affection I had for her father. He showed great concern for me in my youth and instilled in me a desire to merit the praises he bestowed on me. Nothing could give me more pleasure or honor than helping to choose the young man whose children will continue the family line of Rusticus Arulenus. I might have had to search a long time, except that Minicius Acilianus is made just to order. He loves me as an age mate but respects me as an elder (I am a little older than he). He is eager to be molded and instructed by me just as I was wanted to model myself on you and your brother. His home town is Brixia [Brescia] in a part of Italy that still retains the old-time humility, thrift, and simple country values. His father is Minicius Macrinus, a man content to be among the leaders of the Equestrian order [Knights]. The deified Vespasian chose to elevate him to the Praetorian rank, but he staunchly preferred an honorably quiet life to the ambitious quest for public recognition. His maternal grandmother is Serrana Procula. She is from Patavium [Padua], whose customs you know very well. She is a model of sobriety even among her fellow townspeople. Publius Acilius, his uncle on his father's side, is a serious-minded man, judicious and very responsible. In short, the character of the whole family is just what you would like to see in your own. Acilianus himself is energetic, industrious, and most respectful. Since he's already served honorably as quaestor, tribune, and praetor, you won't have to campaign for him. He has an honest face, robust and wholesome looking; his whole appearance has a natural comeliness and a certain senatorial air. These are not negligible things, I think, but rather a reward, as it were, owed to maidens for their chastity. I don't know whether I should add that his father is a man of considerable means. On the one hand, when I consider the character of those who are asking my advice, I think I should keep silent about money. On the other, when I contemplate the customs of our society and even the very laws of our state, which adjudge the income of men to be especially important, it seems something that shouldn't be passed over. And, of course, in considering the possibility of (perhaps numerous) offspring, financial resources must be one criterion in the choice of husband. You perhaps think my affection for the man has led me to exaggerate his qualities. I give you my word you will find all these things to surpass what I've reported. I am indeed keenly attached to the young man, as he deserves, but that attachment ensures that I would not be outlandish in my praise. Goodbye.

Greetings from Gaius Plinius to Acilius.

The atrocity that Larcius Macedo, a man of Praetorian standing, suffered at the hands of his own slaves really merits more than a mere letter. He was an overbearing and brutal master, who recalled too little--or perhaps too much--that his own father had once been a slave. He was in the baths at his villa at Formiae, when suddenly some of his slaves appeared on all sides. While one throttled him, others punched him in the face, chest, stomach, and even--shamefully-- his private parts. When they thought he was likely dead, they threw him onto the hot flooring of the heated bath, to see if he would move. Macedo, either because he actually felt nothing or was faking it, lay quite still and seemed really to be dead. The slaves then carried him out of the bathing room as if he'd been overcome by the heat. Some of his loyal slaves received him and his concubines ran to him shrieking and wailing. Roused by their cries and by the cool air, he indicated with his eyes and bodily movements that he was still alive (now that it was safe to do so). The culprits took to their heels. Most were captured and the remainder are being sought. Macedo was revived and barely kept alive for a few days; he then died but at least had the satisfaction of seeing his killers punished [i.e., executed]. And so you can appreciate what perils, insults, and abuses beset us, even if we are permissive and lenient masters. For slaves are led by their depravity and not by good reasoning when they murder their masters. But enough of this.

What else is new, you ask? Nothing much, or I would include it, for I've got the time (it's a holiday) and the papyrus to add more. I will insert one more thing that comes to mind in regard to Macedo. Once, when he was using a public bath at Rome, a remarkable and (in the event) prophetic thing took place. Macedo's attending slave tapped a Roman Knight with his hand to get him to make way. The man whirled and slapped not the slave but Macedo himself so hard he nearly fell down. And so baths were progressively unlucky places for him: he was first insulted and then killed in one! Goodbye.

Greetings from Gaius Plinius to Cornelius Tacitus.

I'm happy to hear you've arrived safe and sound at the city [Rome]. I always enjoy seeing you, but am especially eager to do so now. I'm going to spend just a bit more time at my Tusculan place to finish up a project I've got in hand at the moment. If I break off now when it's nearly done, I'm afraid I'll have trouble resuming work on it at all. Meantime, so as to be as timely as possible with my request to you, I send this letter in advance. Before making my appeal, however, I'll tell you a bit about what prompts me to make it. When I was visiting my home town [Comum] not long ago, a young man who is the son of one of my townsmen came to visit me. I asked "are you going to school?" He answered "yes." When I asked "where?" he said "Milan." I then asked "why not in Comum?" His father, who had come with the young man, now spoke up and said "we haven't any teachers." I asked "why?" and remarked "surely this is a matter of great concern for you fathers" (several happened to be present) "that your sons should be trained here. Where can they spend their youth more happily than here in their own town? And where can they be instilled with modest habits as inexpensively as in their own homes? Surely you could afford to hire teachers here if you were to pool the money you now spend on your sons' lodgings and travel and other costs of living away. Indeed I myself, though I have no children of my own yet, am willing to contribute half again what you see fit to allocate for this purpose. I do this from a sense of familial devotion to our nation. I'd even contribute the whole amount, but I fear that my donation might be misappropriated, which I know has been the case in other towns where teachers are engaged by the authorities. The cure for this problem is to leave the choice of instructors entirely to the parents, whose conscientiousness is guaranteed by their financial sacrifice. Though people are sometimes negligent in expending someone else's

resources, they'll be careful in using their own: only worthy men will get a salary that comes out of their pockets as well as mine. So let's agree together on this plan, and take heart from me: I'll be delighted to match funds--the higher the amount the better. There is nothing better you can do for your children, nothing more gratifying for our home town. Your sons will be educated here where they were born, in this way being raised to love their native soil and not to leave it. I hope you retain such brilliant teachers that neighboring towns look here for education: as now your children flock to distant places, may pupils soon flock here from those places."

I have thought it appropriate to explain this situation from its origins, so that you might better appreciate my gratitude to you should you undertake what I ask. I thus beseech you earnestly, as the matter requires, to identify, among the many learned men who are attracted to you by your genius, any teachers whom we might approach. It must be understood that I cannot make a binding agreement on my own. The parents themselves must be free to make the final selection; I contribute only my concern and my money. If anyone can be found who has confidence in his own abilities, let him apply, with the warning that he should count only on his recommendation and not mine. Goodbye.

Greetings from Gaius Plinius to Fuscus [Salinator].

You ask how I spend the summer days and my Tuscan villa. Well, I arise when I feel like it, generally in the first hour after dawn, sometimes before, rarely after. I keep the shades drawn, for the quiet and darkness help release me from distractions. My train of thought isn't diverted by visible things; my eyes can, so to say, focus on what the mind perceives. If I've got any project at hand, I mull it over even to the precise wording; I accomplish a lot or a little this way, depending on whether the material is difficult or easy to grasp and present. I then call my secretary and, letting the daylight in, dictate what I've formulated mentally.... After three or four hours (it varies), depending on the weather, I stroll out on the patio or in the covered portico, pondering the rest of my writing project and dictating as well. I go for a chariot ride, still meditating as I was when walking or lying down:

my powers of attention are restored by this change of position. Afterward, I nap a bit and then walk again. Next I read aloud a Greek or Latin speech with clarity and proper inflection. I do this not so much to exercise my voice as to build up an appetite, though both purposes are in fact served. I go for another stroll, get oiled, exercise, and bathe. If dining alone or with my wife and a few friends, I have a book read; after dinner, we hear a comedy or some music. Then I walk with members of my personal staff, some of whom are quite well educated. Thus the evening is drawn out in conversations on all sorts of topics. Thus even long summer days quickly pass by. Sometimes I vary the pattern of the activities I've mentioned. For example, if

I've stayed in bed longer or had a longer morning stroll than usual, after my nap and oral reading, I'll go out on horseback instead of in the chariot, to save time. Then too, friends from towns nearby sometimes visit and use part of my day, providing a welcome diversion when I'm a bit burnt out with work. I sometimes go hunting, but always bring my notebooks, so that I never come back empty-handed. Some time has to be devoted to my tenants, though not as much as they'd like. The countrified manner of their gripes contrasts pleasantly with my more literary and urbane pursuits. Goodbye.

Mynors, R.A.B., ed. *C. Plini Caecili Secundi*. Oxford: Clarendon Press, 1963. Letters 1.14, 3.14, 4.13, 9.36. Translations by James P. Holoka.

"MAY THE EARTH REST LIGHTLY": ROMAN GRAFFITI AND EPITAPHS

► Pompeian Graffiti

A major obstacle to forming an accurate picture of life in ancient Rome is the lack of primary sources concerning the lives of common people. The formal histories as well as the poetic forms of lyric, epic, and satire were composed largely by and for an educated elite. They generally focus on the lives and achievements of upper class Romans. By contrast, the thoughts and attitudes of the lower classes are seldom recorded. There are, however, a couple "sub-literary" forms of writing that partly fill this gap: graffiti and epitaphs.

Large numbers of graffiti have been preserved at the Roman sites of Pompeii and Herculaneum, two small south Italian towns buried during the eruption of Mt. Vesuvius on 24 August 79 C.E. The ancient Romans used the surface of walls, just as we do in modern times, for bulletin board, artists' canvas, advertising space, sports page, warning sign, and in general for airing a variety of opinions and feelings. Thus, we learn, for example, who supported whom for what political office, what goods or services were available in what locations, and who were successful and unsuccessful gladiators. There are also ads for all sorts of food. But perhaps most interesting are details of the personal lives of the ancient scribblers: the walls carry reports of sexual contacts or the desire for them and inform us generally about the likes and dislikes and the cracker-barrel philosophy of the writers. While many of the graffiti are vulgar or banal, collectively they provide a rare insight into the everyday existence of ordinary people, their humble pleasures and irritations, lust and greed, but also into the humor and joy their lightened life's burdens.

Tombstones, too, furnished a surface for recording thoughts, specifically final thoughts. Literally thousands of epitaphs have survived from various periods and places in the Roman world. Though the sentiments of the inscriptions are often cast in formulas ("may the earth rest lightly on you," etc., like our "Rest in Peace"), there are nevertheless many detailed remembrances of the incidents and accidents from of all sorts of lives. The concern of survivors properly to honor and to show their devotion to the dead family member is obvious in the mention of funeral expenditures, lavishness of tombs, etc. In addition to such material considerations, the last memorials show an overarching concern with family values. The epitaphs of deceased males carefully commemorate notable accomplishments, especially in civic or military service, but also in various private occupations, whereby they added to the dignity of the family name. This applies to all families, from aristocrats to freedmen.

The funeral inscriptions are especially valuable for the details they give about the lives of women and children. The domestic virtues of wives and mothers, their fidelity, fertility, and modest matronly behavior are frequently recorded. There are some genuinely touching testaments to the devotion of husbands and wives and at least one very frank assertion of joyous relief at the death of a spouse. The traits that Roman society admired and sought to inculcate in children, too, are often poignantly highlighted in their tomb inscriptions.

QUESTIONS:

1) What seems timeless about the Roman graffiti? What seems different from modern graffiti?

2) Given that the Roman epitaphs were mostly composed and inscribed on monuments paid for by surviving male relatives of the deceased, do the sentiments in them strike you as chauvinistic?

3) Would you describe the people who wrote the graffiti and epitaphs included here as more or less materialistic than people in your own society?

Graffiti.

I'm amazed, O wall, that you've not collapsed under the weight of so much written filth.

May Jupiter be ticked at whoever harms this.

Good luck to the Puteolians! Good things to all the Nucerians, but the hook to Pompeians and Petecusans.

Death, pulling your ear, says "live ... for I am coming."

Agilis, the surveyor.

Successor, the weaver.

Publius Cornelius Faventinus, the barber.

Phoebus, the ointment-maker.

Cresces, the architect.

Marcus Vecilius Verecundus, the clothes-maker.

[At a baker's] I made bread on April 29th.

The bathhouse of Marcus Crassus, with sea-water and fresh-water baths. The freedman Januarius, proprietor.

A bronze urn has disappeared from my tavern. Whoever returns it will get 65 sesterces reward. Whoever informs on the thief will get 20 sesterces, if we recover it.

Priscus the engraver wishes well to Campanius the jeweler.

Fuscus, you cocksucker!

Perarius, you're a thief!

No loiterers--scram!

Move on, sodomite.

Livia, to Alexander: "if you're well, I don't much care; if you're dead, I'm delighted."

Aemilius says "Hi" to his brother Fortunatus.

Pyrrhus to his colleague Gaius Heius: "I'm sad to hear you've died; and so, fond farewell!"

Cestila, queen of the Pompeians, sweetheart, farewell!

Farewell, Modestus, farewell. I wish you well wherever you are.

Samius Cornelius, go hang yourself!

Stronnius is an ignoramus.

Crescens is a public whore.

Felicity lives here.

Staphilus was here with Quieta.

This is a lucky place.

Urbanus was here on the 10th of December.

Apollinaris, the emperor Titus's doctor, took a good crap here.

Pacatus stayed here with his Pompeian relatives.

We live here; may the gods bless us!

Whoever doesn't invite me to dinner is a barbarian.

Whoever is in love, may he prosper. Whoever loves not, may he die. Whoever forbids love, may he die twice over!

No one is cool if he hasn't loved a woman.

Vibius Restitutus slept alone here and longed for his Urbana.

Marcus loves Spendusa.

Apelles Mus and his brother Dexter lovingly screwed a pair of girls here.

I beg you, lady Venus, to keep in mind what I just asked for.

If you haven't seen the Venus that Apelles painted, take a look at my girl--she's just as beautiful.

Now the anger is recent, now is the time to leave it. If the pain departs, believe me, love will return.

On February 22nd, ten pairs of the gladiators of Numisius Genialis will fight at Herculaneum.

There will be a venatio [hunting spectacle] here on August 28th and Felix will fight bears.

Alas, the bears might eat me up!

Rusticus Malius, 12 fights, 11 crowns.

Oceanus the freedman (13 victories) won; Aracinthus (4 victories) died.

Severus the freedman (13 victories) died; Albanus, freedman of Scarus (19 victories) won.

Thraex makes the girls sigh.

I pissed in the bed, I confess, I did wrong, my host. If you ask why--there wasn't any chamber pot.

All the goldsmiths support Gaius Cuspius Pansa for public works commissioner.

Trebius the barber for public works commissioner.

The mule-drivers support Gaius Julius Polybius for mayor.

Genialis supports Bruttius Balbus for mayor. He'll balance the budget.

I ask you to support Marcus Cerrinus Vatia for public works commissioner. All the late-night drunks back him. Signed, Florus and Frontus.

Epitaphs.

Gnaeus Cornelius Scipio Hispanus, son of Gnaeus, [was] praetor, curule aedile, quaestor, twice military tribune; member of the judiciary Board and of the Board for conducting sacrifices: By my behavior, I added to the excellence of my family name. I produced offspring and rivaled the deeds of my father. I revered my ancestors, so that they might rejoice that I was born to their line. My civic service has dignified my family line.

Stranger, stop and read this brief word. Here is the unattractive grave of an attractive woman, whose parents named her Claudia. She loved her husband wholeheartedly. She gave birth to two sons, one whom she leaves behind on earth, one whom she buried beneath it. She spoke with grace and a modest bearing. She kept house and worked her wool. I have spoken. Farewell.

Here rest forever the remains of Cupiennia Tertulla, the daughter of Lucius and last of her line.

Here lies a loyal, honorable, pure, and proper woman, Sempronia Moschis. Her husband gives thanks for her virtues.

[The tomb of] Posilla Senenia, daughter of Quartus and Quarta Senenia, freedwoman of Gaius. Rest a moment, stranger, and read what is written here: It was not granted a mother to enjoy her only daughter; I believe some god begrudged her life. Because that mother could not dress her living in finery, she has adorned her whom she loved with this memorial, as she deserved.

While I lived, I was Aurelia Philematium. I was pure, modest, shy of the mob, loyal to my husband. Like me a freedman, he was more even than a father to me; and now I've lost him. I was seven when he took me to his breast; now at forty I am overpowered by death. All times he prospered by my good services.

Albia Hargula, freedwoman of Albia, lived fifty-six years. She was a woman of purity and great fidelity. If the spirits below are wise, may her bones lying here rest well.

If you wish to add your sorrow to ours, come here and shed your tears. A sad parent has laid to rest his only daughter, Nymphe, whom he treasured with sweet love so long as the Fates permitted. Now, beloved of her kin, snatched from her home she lies buried; now her dear face and form are mere shadow and her bones mere ash.

Aulus Salvius Crispinus, son of Aulus, grandson of Aulus, fifty-six years old, is buried here. He was four times a member of the Board of Four at Ferentum. He was killed by a wall at lunch on his last day.

Here I lie, Lemiso. Only death has ended my labors.

Owned by Gaius Pagurius Gelos, freedman of Gaius. Stop, stranger, and inspect this grand tomb; it holds the bones of a little child. Here I lie buried in the springtime of my life. I did my duty and my wool-working with diligence. I grieve at Fortune so unjust and cruel. If you ask my name, it is "Salvia." Farewell, stranger, may your lot be happier.

Gaius Hostius Pamphilus, medical doctor and freedman of Gaius, purchased this monument for himself and for Nelpia Hymnis, freedwoman of Marcus, and for all their freedmen and freedwomen and their posterity. This is our eternal home, our farm, our garden, our monument. 13 feet wide by 24 deep.

Lucius Papius Pollio of the Teretine tribe, son of Lucius and member of the Board of Two, gave a feast of mead and cake to the colonists of Sinuessa and Caedex to honor his father Lucius Papius of the Falerine tribe, son of Lucius. He also gave gladiator contests and a meal to the colonists of Sinuessa and to the Papian clan. He erected a monument costing 12,000 sesterces in accordance with his father's testament and by the authorization of Lucius Novercinius Pollio, son of Lucius, of the Pupinian tribe.

Traveler, who walks so carefree and glances at my funeral gifts: if you wonder who the ash and embers once were, I was Helvia Prima before my sad end. My beloved husband was Scrateius Cadmus; we lived at one in heart and mind. Now I've been yielded forever to Dis [the god of the Underworld], through fatal fire and Stygian wave.

For my dearest wife, with whom I lived two years, six months, three days, and ten hours. On the day she died, I gave thanks before gods and men.

I was once famous among Pannonians, preeminent among thousands of strong Batavian men. With Hadrian watching, I swam across the mighty Danube in full armor. I once shot an arrow and split it with a second in midair. No Roman or barbarian ever beat me with the spear, no Parthian with the bow. This tombstone preserves the story of my feats. It will witness whether any hereafter may match my deeds. But I am still unique, the first to do such things as these.

Selections from *Corpus Inscriptionum Latinarum*. Also in Marx, Walter R. *Claimed by Vesuvius*. 2nd ed. Wellesley Hills, MA: Independent School Press, 1979. Translations by James P. Holoka.

► Asokan Bull Column Capital

READING 3.9

MAURYAN INDIA THROUGH THE EYES OF A GREEK AMBASSADOR

The conquest of northwestern India by Alexander the Great in 326 B.C.E. had epochal consequences. Although Greek rule over the Indus River valley lasted barely a decade, India was thereafter known to the Western world, and northwestern India as a result became a melting pot of Indian, Greek, and Persian cultures.

In the political vacuum left in northwest India in the wake of retreating Greek soldiers, a young Indian named Chandragupta Maurya, who may even have met Alexander, successfully forged an empire that encompassed the Indo-Gangetic valleys. He successfully battled Seleucus Nicator, a general who controlled most of the Asian regions of Alexander's empire, then signed a peace agreement that established the boundary between the Seleucid and Mauryan empires in present day Afghanistan.

King Seleucus appointed Megasthenes his ambassador to Chandragupta's court between approximately 306 and 298 B.C.E. Megasthenes lived in the Mauryan capital city Pataliputra and traveled widely through India. The materials he gathered on India became the basis for a book titled *Indica*. Although the original book was lost, many fragments survived in the quotations of ancient Greek and Roman authors such as Arrian and Strabo. The *Indica* is invaluable because it is the first authentic, essentially reliable, and connected account of India by a foreign observer, throwing light on life and conditions in ancient India. The following reading is taken from a collection of fragments of Megasthenes' writings.

QUESTIONS:

1) Describe Pataliputra and how it was governed.
2) What were the duties of the king in the Mauryan empire?
3) What were some of the customs that Indians lived by?

At the meeting of this river [Ganges] and another is situated Palibothra [Pataliputra, capital city of the Mauryan Empire], a city eighty stadia [one stade equalled about 200 meters] in length and fifteen in breadth. It is of the shape of a parallelogram, and is girded with a wooden wall, pierced with loopholes for the discharge of arrows. It has a ditch in front for defence and for receiving the sewage of the city. The people in whose country this city is situated is the most distinguished in all India, and is called the Prasii.

159

Of the great officers of state, some have charge of the market, others of the city, others of the soldiers. Some superintend the rivers, measure the land, as is done in Egypt, and inspect the sluices by which water is let out from the main canals into their branches, so that every one may have an equal supply of it. The same persons have charge also of the huntsmen, and are entrusted with the power of rewarding or punishing them according to their deserts. They collect the taxes, and superintend the occupations connected with land, as those of the woodcutters, the carpenters, and blacksmiths, and the miners. They construct roads, and at every ten stadia set up a pillar to show the by-roads and distances. Those who have charge of the city are divided into six bodies of five each. The members of the first look after everything relating to the industrial arts. Those of the second attend to the entertainment of foreigners. To these they assign lodgings, and they keep watch of their modes of life by means of those persons whom they give to them as assistants. They escort them on the way when they leave the country, or. in the event of their dying. forward their property to their relatives. They take care of them when they are sick, and if they die bury them. The third body consists of those who inquire when and how births and deaths occur, with view not only of levying a tax, but also in order that births and deaths among both high and low may not escape the cognizance of Government. The fourth class superintends trade and commerce. Its members have charge of weights and measures, and see that the products in their season are sold by public notice. No one is allowed to deal in more than one kind of commodity unless he pays a double tax. The fifth class supervises manufactured articles, which they sell by public notice. What is new is sold separately from what is old, and there is a fine for mixing the two together. The sixth and last class consists of those who collect the tenths of the prices of the articles sold. Fraud in the payment of this tax is punished with death.

Such are the functions which these bodies separately discharge. In their collective capacity they have charge both of their special departments, and also of matters affecting the general interest, as the keeping of public buildings in proper repair, the regulation of prices, the care of markets, harbours, and temples.

Next to the city magistrates there is a third governing body, which directs military affairs. This also consists of six divisions, with five members to each. One division is appointed to cooperate with the admiral of the fleet, another with the superintendent of the bullock-trains which are used for transporting engines of war, food for the soldiers, provender for the cattle, and other military requisites. They supply servants who beat the drum, and others who carry gongs; grooms also for the horses, and mechanists and their assistants. To the sound of the gong they send out foragers to bring in grass, and by a system of rewards and punishments ensure the work being done with despatch and safety. The third division has charge of the foot-soldiers, and fourth of the horses, the fifth of the war-chariots, and sixth of the elephants. There are royal stables for the horses and elephants, and also a royal magazine for the arms, because the soldier has to return his arms to the magazine, and his horse and his elephant to the stables. They use the elephant without bridles. The chariots are drawn on the march by oxen, but the horses are led along by halter, that their legs may not be galled and inflamed, nor their spirits damped by drawing chariots. In addition to the charioteer, there are two fighting men who sit up in the chariot beside him. The war-elephant carries four men--three who shoot arrows, and the driver....

A private person is not allowed to keep either a horse or an elephant. These animals are held to be the special property of the king, and persons are appointed to take care of them.

The manner of hunting an elephant is this. Round a bare patch of ground is dug a deep trench about five or six stadia in extent, and over this is thrown a very narrow bridge which gives access to the enclosure. Into this enclosure are introduced three or four of the best-trained female elephants. The men themselves lie in ambush in concealed huts. The wild elephants do not approach this trap in the daytime, but they enter it at night, going in one by one. When all have passed the entrance, the men secretly close it up; then, introducing the strongest of the tame fighting elephants, they fight it out with the wild ones, whom at the same time they enfeeble with hunger. When the latter are now overcome with fatigue, the boldest of the drivers dismount unobserved, and each man creeps under his own elephant, and from this position creeps under the belly of the wild elephant and ties his feet together. When this is done they incite the tame ones to beat those whose feet are tied till they fall to the ground. They then bind the wild ones and the tame ones together neck to neck with thongs of raw ox-hide. To prevent them shaking themselves in order to throw off those who attempt to mount them, they make cuts all round their neck and then put thongs of leather into the incisions, so that the pain obliges them to submit to their fetters and to remain quiet. From the number caught they reject such as are too old or too young to be serviceable, and the rest they lead away to the stables. Here they tie their feet one to another and fasten their necks to a firmly fixed pillar, and tame them by hunger. After this they restore their strength with green reeds and grass. They next teach them to be obedient, which they affect by soothing them some by coaxing words, and others by songs and the music of the drum. Few of them are found difficult to tame, for they are naturally so mild and gentle in their disposition that they approximate to rational creatures. Some of them take up their drivers when fallen in battle, and carry them off in safety from the field. Others, when their masters have sought refuge between their forelegs, have fought in their defence and saved their lives. If in a fit of anger they kill either the man who feeds or the man who trains them, they pine so much for their loss that they refuse to take food, and sometimes die of hunger....

The care of the king's person is entrusted to women, who also are bought from their parents. The guards and the rest of the soldiery attend outside the gates.... The sons succeed the father. The king may not sleep during the daytime, and by night he is obliged to change his couch from time to time, with a view to defeat plots against his life.

The king leaves his palace not only in time of war, but also for the purpose of judging causes. He then remains in court for the whole day, without allowing the business to be interrupted, even though the hour arrives when he must needs attend to his person,--that is, when

he is to be rubbed with cylinders of wood. He continues hearing cases while the friction, which is performed by four attendants, is still proceeding. Another purpose for which he leaves his palace is to offer sacrifice; a third is to go to the chase, for which he departs in Bacchanalian fashion. Crowds of women surround him, and outside of his circle spearmen are ranged. The road is marked off with ropes, and it is death, for man and woman alike, to pass within the ropes. Men with drums and gongs lead the procession. The king hunts in the enclosure and shoots arrows from a platform. At his side stand two or three armed women. If he hunts in the open grounds he shoots from the back of an elephant. Of the women, some are in chariots, some on horses, and some even on elephants, and they are equipped with weapons of every kind, as if they were going on a campaign....

[On customs] It is further said that the Indians do not rear monuments to the dead, but consider the virtues which men have displayed in life, and the songs in which their praises are celebrated sufficient to preserve their memory after death....

The Indians all live frugally, especially when in camp. They dislike a great undisciplined multitude, and consequently they observe good order. Theft is of very rare occurrence.... They live, nevertheless, happily enough, being simple in their manners and frugal. They never drink wine except at sacrifices. Their beverage is a liquor composed from rice instead of barley, and their food is principally a rice-pottage. The simplicity of their laws and their contracts is proved by the fact that they seldom go to law. They have no suits about pledges or deposits, nor do they require seals or witnesses, but make their deposits and confide in each other. Their houses and property they generally leave unguarded. Those things indicate that they possess good, sober sense....

Their favorite mode of exercising the body is by friction, applied in various ways, but especially by passing smooth ebony rollers over the skin.... In contrast to the general simplicity of their style, they love finery and ornament. Their robes are worked in gold, and ornamented with precious stones, and they wear also flowered garments made of the finest muslin. Attendants walking behind hold up umbrellas over them: for they have a high regard for beauty, and avail themselves of every device to improve their looks....

A person convicted of bearing false witness suffers mutilation of his extremities. He who maims any one not only suffers in return the loss of the same limb, but his hand also is cut off. If he causes an artisan to lose his hand or his eye, he is put to death....

McCrindle, J.W. *Ancient India*. London: Trubner, 1877. Pp. 66-73, 86-93.

READING 3.10

INDIA'S IDEAL EMPEROR

► **Asokan Lion Column Capital**

Emperor Asoka ruled India between approximately 269 and 232 B.C.E. He was the third ruler of the Mauryan dynasty, founded by his grandfather Chandragupta Maurya. The Mauryan Empire united most of the Indian subcontinent for the first time in history and Indian culture attained greatness under its first three rulers.

The empire Asoka inherited embraced all northern India and part of modern Afghanistan. The wars he waged during his first years expanded its boundary southward to all but the tip of the subcontinent. Deeply remorseful over the suffering brought by his conquest of Kalinga, a state in southeastern India, Asoka converted to Buddhism and renounced the use of force as an instrument of policy for himself and his successors. He had his conversion statement carved on a rock pillar as a public confession and manifesto. During the remainder of his reign Asoka ordered many laws, injunctions, and his personal pronouncements carved on stone pillars and rock surfaces throughout the empire, in the appropriate vernacular languages. He ordered local officials to read these inscriptions at public gatherings periodically so that ordinary people could learn of his goals and commands. The extant monuments provide rare and frank insights into the personality of a ruler who lived twenty-three centuries ago. They also give first hand information of the conditions in India during that period.

Buddhism thrived thanks to Asoka's patronage, although he honored all religions and holy men, and forced no one to convert. His own son and daughter traveled to Ceylon (present-day Sri Lanka) as Buddhist missionaries; they and others brought with them to Ceylon and other lands a great religion and also many of the high achievements of India's civilization.

Not much is known about Asoka's last years. Soon after his death, the Mauryan empire began to break down, ending by 185 B.C.E. However, the memory of the Mauryan dynasty continued to inspire people in India and elsewhere.

Indians of the twentieth century proudly recall this great era in their history and consider Asoka's aspirations still worthy of emulation. When India gained its independence from Britain in 1947, it adopted the lion capital that adorned the top of Asokan pillars as the national emblem [Asoka proclaimed the lion, guardian of Buddhist law, as his symbol]; the sacred wheel of Buddhist law that formed the pedestal for the lion is the central part of the national flag.

The following excerpts come from several of Asoka's inscribed pillars and rocks. They show what an exceptionally kind and humane person he was.

QUESTIONS:

1) Why was the war against the Kalingas a turning point in Asoka's reign?
2) How did Asoka extend his kindness to humans and animals?
3) How did Asoka promote religion and morality?

Eight years after his coronation King Devanampiya Piyadasi [of Gracious Mien, and Beloved of the Gods--titles Asoka used, henceforth ał eviated as King D.P.] conquered the Kanling In that (conquest) one hundred and fifty thousand people were deported (as prisoners), one hundred thousand were killed (or maimed) and many times that number died. Thereafter, with the conquest of the Kalinga, King D.P. (adopted) the practice of morality, love of morality and inculcation of morality. For there arose in King D.P. remorse for the conquest of Kalinga. For when an unsubdued country is conquered there occur such things as slaughter, death and deportation of people and these are regarded as very painful and serious by King D.P. Brahmans and ascetics live everywhere, as well as votaries of other sects and householders who practice such virtues as support of mother and father, service of elders, proper treatment of friends, relatives, acquaintances and kinsmen and slaves and servants and steadfastness in devotion to duties. They too suffer injury.... This plight of men is regarded as serious by King D.P. Outside of the territory of the Greeks there is no land where communities such as those of Brahmins and ascetics are not to be found. Nor is there any land where men do not have faith (religion) of one sect or another....

King D.P. considers the victory of morality as the greatest. And this victory has been accomplished by King D.P. up to all his frontiers, even to a distance of six hundred *yojanas* where the Greek King Antiochus rules,... everywhere people follow the instructions in morality by King D.P. And wherever the ambassadors of King D.P. have fared there, too, people hear of his moral acts, his teachings and instruction on morality, and they follow morality and will do so.

Whatever has been gained by this victory of morality, that has been pleasant. This happiness has been secured through victory of morality but even that is not as great of the King D.P. as the gain of the next world. For this purpose this rescript of morality has been written that my sons and great grandsons should cease to think of new conquests and in all the victories they may gain they should be content with forbearance and slight punishment. For them the true conquest should be that of morality; all their delight should

be delight in morality for benefit in this worl and the next.

At all times, whether I am eating, or in th women's apartments, or in the inner chambers, i the cattle-pen or riding, or in the garden everywhere reporters are posted so that they ma inform me of the people's business.... For regard the welfare of the people as my chie duty. The basis of that is exertion and prope dispatch of public business. There is no othe work more important for me than the welfare o all people. And why? For the discharge of m debt to the people, so that I may give happines to some here and win heaven hereafter....

[Asoka became a vegetarian and adopted strict life style, which he attempted to force or his subjects also. Thus] ... no animal may b slaughtered and offered in sacrifice. N convivial assembly too may be held. For Kin D.P. sees many a blemish in convivia assemblies. But there are some assemblie considered good by King D.P. Formerly in the kitchen of King D.P. every day hundreds o thousands of animals were slaughtered for curry But now since this rescript on morality has beer written only three animals are slaughtered fo curry; two peacocks and one deer, and that dee too not always. Even these three animals wil not be slaughtered hence....

[To ensure the carrying out of the mora decrees] I have appointed morality officers. They are engaged with votaries of all faiths, fo the firm establishment of morality, for it progress, for the happiness here and hereafter o those devoted to morality.... They are employed among the servants and masters, among Brahmins, the destitute and the aged.... They are engaged in helping those incarcerated, in preventing harassment and securing release o those who have large families or have been overwhelmed with calamity or are old. Here in Pataliputra [capital city of the Mauryan empire] or elsewhere they are employed in all towns, in all the harems of my brothers and establishments of my sisters and other kinsmen....

My [other] officers, too, whether of the highest, middling or low ranks, must follow my instructions and practice it so that they may encourage the weak or hesitant as much as they can. Similarly the high officers (mahamatras) of the frontiers must act. And this should be the norm of conduct that administration must confirm to morality, that legislation should be according to morality; this alone can make people happy according to morality and protect them according to the law of morality.

[Asoka proclaimed] Equality in judicial procedure and equality in penalties. And henceforth this is my rule that to those in prison, condemned to death, a grace of three days has been granted by me....

I have made inviolate these species (of animals and birds) to wit; parrots, starlings, arunas, Brahmany ducks, wild geese,... bats, queen ants, terrapins, boneless fish,... skate, turtles, squirrels, Borasing stags, Brahmany bulls, rhinoceros, white pigeons, common pigeons, all quadrupeds that are not in use or are not eaten. Similarly she-goats, ewes, and sows whether young or milch, are inviolable; also young ones within six months of age are not to be killed. Cocks must not be caponed. Husks with living things in them must not be burnt.

Forests must not be burnt just for mischief or to destroy living beings in them. Life must not be fed on life. On the three seasonal full moon days and on full moon days of the month of Tishya for three days in each instance, to wit, the fourteenth and fifteenth days of the first half of the month, as well as on fast days through the whole year, fish must not be killed or sold. During these days in the elephant-forest or fish-ponds no other species of animals must be destroyed....

[As for himself] ... since he was crowned ten years ago King D.P. went on a pilgrimage of (the place of) Enlightenment of the Lord [Buddha]. Therein his tour of piety comprised visits to Brahmins and ascetics, charity and visits to the Elders (of the Buddhist Order) and gift of gold and visit to the country folk, instruction in the law of morality and inquiries pertaining thereto. The pleasure thereof is, indeed, great, exceeding any other.

Gokhale, B.G. *Asoka Maurya*. New York: Twayne, 1966. Pp. 151-152, 154-155, 157-158, 165-167.

READING 3.11

BIOGRAPHIES OF MONEY-MAKERS IN ANCIENT CHINA

► Ssu-ma Ch'ien

Ssu-ma Ch'ien (c. 136-85 B.C.E.) came from a noted family in north China. Besides learning to manage his family's estates when a young man, he also traveled widely throughout China. An avid student, he reputedly read every book available at the time. He inherited his father's government position as Grand Astrologer, but offended the Emperor Wu of the Han dynasty when he gallantly defended a general who had been forced to surrender to the Hsiung-nu. He could not pay the required fine, nor would he commit suicide to avoid the punishment of castration. He devoted the remainder of his life to completing a multi-volume history of the world that his father had begun.

The more famous of a father-son team, Ssu-ma Ch'ien wrote the *Historical Records* (*Shih Chi*), a monumental and comprehensive history of the Chinese world up to his time. Its 130 chapters are divided into "Basic Annals" or records from earliest history, chronologies of princely houses and great families to his time, essays on important subjects such as rivers and canals, economic matters, geography, music, rituals, calendar, etc. The last seventy chapters are devoted to biographies of famous and interesting men and women, and accounts of foreign lands. The excerpt below is taken from a chapter in the biographical section.

The *Historical Records* has become the model for all later Chinese historians because of its elegant style and scholarly approach. Where possible, Ssu-ma Ch'ien quoted from reliable original sources with a minimum of commentary, thus setting a standard for historical scholarship in China that was probably not equalled anywhere in the world until recent times. The accounts of lives from "The Biographies of the Money-makers" are lively in their diversity. The fact that ordinary men and women were able to become rich through their hard work and ingenuity show the opportunities that the end of feudalism had brought.

QUESTIONS:

1) What sort of qualities made all the "money-makers" successful?
2) Could a woman become rich in Han China?
3) What sort of society allowed people to rise up on their own merits?

Wu-chih Lo raised domestic animals, and when he had a large number, he sold them and bought rare silks and other articles which he secretly sent as gifts to the king of the Jung barbarians. The king of the Jung repaid him ten times the original cost and sent him domestic animals until Wu-chih

167

Lo had so many herds of horses and cattle he could only estimate their number roughly by the valleyful. The First Emperor of the Ch'in ordered that Wu-chih Lo be granted the same honors as a feudal lord and allowed him to join the ministers in seasonal audiences at court.

There was also the case of a widow named Ch'ing of the region of Pa and Shu. Her ancestors got possession of some cinnabar caves and were able to monopolize the profits from them for several generations until they had acquired an inestimable amount of wealth. Ch'ing, although only a widow, was able to carry on the business and used her wealth to buy protection for herself so that others could not mistreat her or impose upon her. The First Emperor of the Ch'in, considering her a virtuous woman, treated her as a guest and built the Nu-huai-ch'ing Terrace in her honor.

Wu-chih Lo was a simple country man who looked after herds, while Ch'ing was only a widow far off in the provinces, and yet both were treated with as much respect as though they had been the lords of a state of ten thousand chariots, and their fame spread all over the world. Was this not because of their wealth?...

Now I should like to describe briefly the ways in which some of the worthy men of the present age, working within an area of a thousand miles, have managed to acquire wealth, so that later generations may see how they did it and select what may be of benefit to themselves.

The ancestors of the Cho family were natives of Chao who made a fortune by smelting iron. When the Ch'in armies overthrew the state of Chao, the family was ordered to move to another part of the empire for resettlement. Having been taken captive and plundered of all their wealth and servants, the husband and wife were left to make the move alone, pushing their belongings in a cart. All the other captives who were forced to move and who had a little wealth left vied with each other in bribing the officials to send them to some nearby locations, and they were therefore allowed to settle in Chia-meng. But Mr Cho said: "This region is narrow and barren. I have heard that at the foot of Mount Min there are fertile plains full of edible tubers so that one may live all his file without suffering from famine. The people there are clever at commerce and make their living by trade." He therefore asked

to be sent to a distant region, and was ordered to move to Lin-ch'iung. He was overjoyed, and when he got there and found a mountain which yielded iron ore, he began smelting ore and laying other plans to accumulate wealth until soon he dominated the trade among the people of Tien and Shu. He grew so rich that he owned a thousand young slaves, and the pleasures he indulged among his fields and lakes and on his bird and animal hunts were like those of a great lord....

Lu people are customarily cautious and miserly, but the Ping family of Ts'ao were particularly so. They started out by smelting iron and in time accumulated a fortune of a hundred million cash. All the members of the family, from the father and elder brothers down to the sons and grandsons, however, make a promise that they would

Never look down without picking up something useful

Never look up without grabbing something of value.

They traveled about to all the provinces and kingdoms, selling goods on credit, lending money and trading. It was because of their influence that so many people in Tsou and Lu abandoned scholarship and turned to the pursuit of profit....

The people of the old state of Chou have always been very close in money matters, but Shih Shih was an extreme example. With a couple of hundreds of cartloads of goods he traveled around to the various provinces and kingdoms peddling his wares; there was absolutely no place he did not go. The city of Lo-yang is situated right in the middle of the old states of Ch'i, Ch'in, Ch'u, and Chao, and even the poor people of the two study to become apprentices of the rich families, boasting to each other about how long they have been in trade and how they have several times passed their old homes but were too busy to go in the gate. By making use of men like this in his business, Shih Shih was finally able to accumulate a fortune of seventy million cash....

These, then, are examples of outstanding and unusually wealthy men. None of them enjoyed any titles or fiefs, or salaries from the government, nor did they play tricks with the law or commit any crimes to acquire their fortunes.

They simply guessed what course conditions were going to take and acted accordingly, kept a sharp eye out for the opportunities of the times, and so were able to capture a fat profit. They gained their wealth in the secondary occupations and held on to it by investing in agriculture; they seized hold of it in times of crisis and maintained it in times of stability. There was a special aptness in the way they adapted to the times, and therefore their stories are worth relating. In addition, there are many other men who exerted themselves at farming, animal raising, craft, lumbering, merchandising, and trade and seized the opportunities of the moment to make a fortune.... Thrift and hard work are without doubt the proper way to gain a livelihood. And yet it will be found that rich men have invariably employed some unusual scheme or method to get to the top....

All of these men got where they did because of their devotion and singleness of purpose.

From this we may see that there is no fixed road to wealth, and money has no permanent master. It finds its way to the man of ability like the spokes of a wheel converging upon the hub, and from the hands of the worthless it falls like shattered tiles. A family with a thousand catties of gold may stand side by side with the lord of a city; the man with a hundred million cash may enjoy the pleasures of a king. Rich men such as these deserve to be called the "untitled nobility," do they not?

Burton Watson, trans. *Records of the Historian: Chapters from the Shih Chi of Ssu-ma Ch'ien*. New York: Columbia Univ. Press, 1969. Pp. 340-341, 352-356.

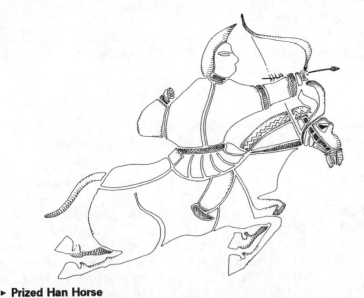

► **Prized Han Horse**

EMPIRE BUILDERS AND DIPLOMATIC PAWNS

Formidable geographic barriers and hostile northern nomads isolated early Chinese civilization from neighbors on the Eurasian continent. Preoccupied with great wars against one another, the feudal states of the late Chou dynasty had built walls along their northern frontier as barriers against nomad incursions. These walls had been linked into one Great Wall during the short lived Ch'in dynasty (221-206 B.C.E.), and, together with costly bribes to a formidable Turkic people called the Hsiung-nu, ensured peace during the early Han dynasty (202 B.C.E.-220 C.E.).

In 141 B.C.E., a boy of fifteen called Emperor Wu (the Martial) ascended the Han throne. He ruled until 87, the longest reign in China until the eighteenth century. Full of energy and ambition, he reversed the pacifist foreign policy of his predecessors and launched an era of discovery, conquest and expansion that made China a world power. Supported by a prosperous populace that would no longer stand for blackmail by the nomads, Emperor Wu launched a costly and desperate campaign that finally defeated them. But first he needed to find allies against the Hsiung-nu. In 138, a courtier named Chang Ch'ien set out westward to secure an alliance with the Ta Yueh-chih people, whom the Hsiung-nu had defeated in 165. Chang's quest lasted twelve years and took him to central Asia and northwestern India. Although he failed to persuade the Ta Yueh-chih to renew their fight with the Hsiung-nu, because they had meantime found a new home in the Indus river valley, his reports opened new horizons to the Chinese and fueled their desire to establish Han power in Central Asia. The Han decisively defeated the Hsiung-nu in 119, expelling them from their homeland. This cleared the way for Chinese contact with states in Central Asia.

Chang Ch'ien's second mission was directed at Wu-sun, another tribal state on China's northwestern border, whose friendship was crucial to Chinese penetration westward. Two Han princesses were given in marriage to rulers of the Wu-sun to cement the alliance. In compliance with Wu-sun custom that a new ruler married his father's wives except his own mother, as well as his brother's widows, each Han princess married in succession several Wu-sun rulers.

Later, Han Protector Generals were appointed to supervise the client states in Central Asia, and local rulers sent sons to the Han court at Changan to be educated in the Chinese manner and also to serve as hostages. Other Han princesses became wives of Central Asian kings. When necessary Han armies were despatched to Central Asia to protect Chinese princess. Thus, relations between the Han and Central Asian states were very complex.

Pan Ku's (32-92 C.E.) *The History of the Former Han Dynasty* chronicled these stirring events. He was the father of a great general, Pan Chao, whose successful campaigns expanded Chinese power to the Caspian Sea and of Pan Ch'ao, China's earliest famous female historian. The following selection

171

from Pan Ku's work details the exploits of Chang Ch'ien and the marriage of princess Hsi-chun to th
king of Wu-sun that cemented a alliance between the two countries.

QUESTIONS:

1) Who was Chang Ch'ien and what were some of his achievements?
2) Who were the Hsiung-nu and the Wu-sun and what was China's relationship with each?
3) What were princesses sometimes used for?

Chang Ch'ien was a man of Han-chung [commandary]. During the reign-period *Chien-yuan* [140-135 B.C.E.] he served as a gentleman. At the time deserters from the Hsiung-nu had said that they had defeated the king of the Yueh-chih and made a drinking vessel of his skull. The Yueh-chih had fled, but furious as they were with the Hsiung-nu, there was no party with whom they could attack them jointly. At it happened Han was wishing to start operations to eliminate the nomads; and, hearing of this report, wished to make contact [with the Yueh-chih] by means of envoys; their route would perforce have to pass through the Hsiung-nu.

A call was then made for persons able to undertake the mission. In his capacity as a gentleman [Chang] Ch'ien answered the call and was sent to the Yueh-chih.... He took the short route through the Hsiung-nu, who captured him and had him sent to the *Shan-yu*....

For ten years he [the *Shan-yu* or ruler of the Hsiung-nu--JH] detained [Chang] Ch'ien, giving him a wife by whom he had children. However [Chang] Ch'ien [constantly] retained the Han emblems of authority without loss. Living in the western part of the Hsiung-nu, he found an opportunity to escape with his followers in the direction of the Yueh-chih, and after speeding west for days numbered by the ten he reached Ta Yuan. Ta Yuan had heard of Han's abundant wealth and had wished to establish contact, but had not been able to do so. [The king of Ta Yuan] was delighted ... and sent off [Chang] Ch'ien, providing him with interpreters and guides. He reached K'ang-chu, who passed him on to the Ta Yueh-chih. The king of the Ta Yueh-chih had been killed by the nomads, and his wife had been established as king [sic]; having subjugated the Ta Hsia she reigned over it. The land was fertile, with few brigands, and [the Ta Yeuh-chih] had set their minds on [a life

of] peace and contentment. In addition, bein; themselves removed afar, they wished to kee] their distance from Han, and had no intention a all of taking revenge on the nomads. From th Yueh-chih, [Chang] Ch'ien reached Ta Hsia, bu in the end he was unable to rouse their interest o the Yueh-chih. After staying there for over year, he returned.... He was again captured b; the Hsiung-nu. After over a year's detentioi there the *Shan-yu* died and the state was throw: into confusion. In company with his nomad wif ... [Chang] Ch'ien escaped back to Han. H was appointed to be supreme counsellor of th palace....

[Chang] Ch'ien was a man of strong physique and of considerable generosity; he inspired the trust of others and the barbarian: loved him.... At the time when [Chang] Ch'ie: had started his journey, over a hundred men se out, but thirteen years later only two succeedec in returning. The states reached by [Chang: Ch'ien in person comprised Ta Yuan, Ta Yueh-chih, Ta Hsia and K'ang-chu, and those of whom he heard tell included five or six large states a their side. He told the Son of Heaven in full about the lay of the land and their resources....

The Son of Heaven frequently asked [Chang Ch'ien about the states such as Ta Hsia.... [Chang] Ch'ien took the opportunity to report as follows:

"When I was living among the Hsiung-nu] heard of Wu-sun; the king was entitled K'un-mo;... originally [Wu-sun] had lived with the Ta Yueh-chih between the Ch'i-lien [mountains] and Tun-huang; and they had been a small state. [Hsiung-nu and Wu-sun had quarreled, so....] If we could only make use of the present opportunity to send generous presents to Wu-sun, and induce [its people] to move east and live in their old lands; and if Han would send a princess to be the consort of [the king] and establish brotherly relations, the situation would be such that they would agree, and this would result in cutting off the right arm of the Hsiung-nu. Once a link has been forged with Wu-sun, the states such as Ta Hsia to its west could all be induced to come to court and become outer subjects of Han."

The Son of Heaven agreed with this [advice] and appointed [Chang] Ch'ien to be leader of the gentlemen of the palace, with a force of three hundred men; each man had two horses, and the cattle and sheep were counted by the ten thousand. He took gold, valuables, and silk which was worth an enormous amount.... As soon as he reached Wu-sun, [Chang] Ch'ien presented his gifts and a message [from the emperor].... The K'un-mo received [Chang] Ch'ien with ceremonial such as that [used for receiving] a *Shan-yu*. Greatly mortified, [Chang] Ch'ien said: "The Son of Heaven has sent some gifts, and unless the king makes obeisance, I shall return with them [to Han]." The K'un-mo stood up and made obeisance, and the other [parts of the ceremonial were continued] as formerly....

Having delivered the [imperial] presents, [Chang] Ch'ien gave [the K'un-mo] a message of guidance from the Han emperor, saying: "If the [people of] Wu-sun are able to move east and dwell in their former lands, then Han will send a princess to be [the K'un-mo's] wife, and a fraternal alliance will be formed; we will together stand against the Hsiung-nu who will not be hard to defeat."

Wu-sun thought that Han was remote, and had no informed idea of its size. Moreover [Wu-sun] was close to the Hsiung-nu, to whom it had been subject for a long period. None of the senior officials of Wu-sun wished to move. The k'un-mo was old; and, the state being divided, he was unable to exercise complete and single control. So he sent out envoys to escort [Chang] Ch'ien [back], and to take the opportunity to present the emperor with horses, numbered by the ten, and to reply [to his message] with apologies. The k'un-mo's envoys returned to their state after observing the large numbers of the Han people and the abundance of Han's wealth; and thereafter the state's appreciation of Han was considerably enhanced.

Hearing that Wu-sun was in contact with Han, the Hsiung-nu grew angry and wished to attack. Moreover, when the Han envoys to Wu-sun came to leave thence by the south, they made their way to Ta Yuan and the Yueh-chih continuously without interruption. Wu-sun now grew apprehensive, and sent envoys with presents of horses [to the emperor], in the hope of obtaining a princess in marriage and of forming a fraternal alliance. The Son of Heaven asked his attendant officials for their views. They advised that [the request of Wu-sun] should be granted, with the stipulation that only when the marriage gifts had been delivered to the court should a girl be sent. Wu-sun provided a marriage gift of 1000 horses; and during the *Yuan-feng* period [110-105 B.C.E.] Han sent Hsi-chun, daughter of [Liu] Chien, king of Chiang-tu, as a princess to wed [the K'un-mo]* The presents included imperial carriages, wearing apparel and equipment for imperial use. There was established for her an official staff, and a complement of several hundred eunuchs and serving attendants, and she was sent off with a very rich store of gifts. The K'ung-me of Wu-sun appointed her to be a Lady of the Right. The Hsiung-nu similarly sent a girl to be a wife for the K'un-mo, who appointed her to be a Lady of the Left.**

When the princess reached the state [of Wu-sun], she had buildings constructed for her residence. Once or twice a year she had a meeting with the K'un-mo, when a banquet was set out, and she presented the noblemen who attended the king with valuables and silk. The K'un-mo was old, and [he and the princess] had no verbal communication. In her deep sorrow the princess composed a song for herself, which ran:

> My family sent me off to be married on the
>   other side of heaven;
> They sent me a long way to a strange land,
>   to the king of Wu-sun.
> A doomed lodging is my dwelling place,
>   with walls made of felt;
> Meat is my food, with fermented mild as
>   the sauce.
> I live with constant thoughts of my home,
>   my heart is full of sorrow;
> I wish I were a golden swan, returning to
>   my home country.

When the Son of Heaven heard this, he felt pity for her, and every other year sent envoys carrying drapes, brocades and embroideries to supply her needs.

The K'uo-mo was old and wished to have his grandson the Ts'en-tsou married to the princess. However, she would not consent, and sent a written message to [the emperor] describing the state of affairs. The Son of Heaven replied "You should follow the customs of the state. I wish to make common cause with Wu-sun to destroy the Hsiung-nu." The Ts'en-tsou then took the princess as a wife; and when the K'un-mo died, the Ts'en-tsou was established in his place....

The Ts'en-tsou was married to the princess of Chiang-tu (i.e. Hsi-chun), and she bore one daughter named Shao-fu. At the death of the princess, Han for a second time appointed a princess to be wife of the Ts'en-tsou, in the person of Chieh-yu, granddaughter of Wu, king of Ch'u....***

In the time of Emperor Chao, the princess sent a written message [to the emperor] saying: "the Hsiung-nu have called out cavalry to work the land at Chu-shih; Chu-shih and the Hsiung-nu are forming a single unit to attack Wu-sun in concert; only the Son of Heaven is in a position to save Su-sun". Han was rearing horses for military [use]; and after taking counsel [the government] decided to attack the Hsiung-nu, but at that juncture Emperor Chao died.

As soon as Emperor Hsuan had acceded to the throne, the princess and the K'un-mi both sent envoys with letters saying: "The Hsiung-nu have time and again sent out large forces to penetrate and attack Wu-sun and have taken the lands of Chu-yen and Wu-shih, removing the inhabitants. They have sent envoys ordering Wu-sun to bring the princess with all speed, and they wish [Wu-sun] to sever relations with Han. The K'un-mi is willing to put half the state's best troops in the field; he will himself produce 50000

cavalry, men and horse, and will exert his strength to the utmost to attack the Hsiung-nu. It rests only with the Son of Heaven to send out a force so as to save the princess and the K'un-mi."

Han called out a large force which amounted to 150000 cavalry, with five generals setting out by separate routes at the same time.... Ch'ang Hui, a colonel, was sent with emblems of authority to act as protector of the forces of Wu-sun. The K'ou-mi took personal command of 50000 cavalry.... He took prisoner a paternal relative of the Shan-yu and his sister-in-law, noble women, famous kings, and 40000 men including the commandant of Li-wu, chiefs of the thousands and leaders of cavalry, in addition to over 700000 head of horse, cattle, sheep, asses and camels. The [men of] Wu-sun themselves took all their booty away, and on his return [Ch'ang] Hui was invested with the title of noble of Ch'ang-lo; [these events occurred] in the third year of [the reign-period] Pen-shih [71 B.C.E.].

---

*Princess Hsi-chun belonged to a cadet branch of the Han imperial family; her father was a king, a title reserved for sons of emperors. He had committed suicide in 121 B.C.E. when his plot to rebel against Emperor Wu had been discovered. His wife had been executed for practising witchcraft against the emperor. Princess Hsi-chun was therefore a dispensable member of the imperial family.

**The Hsiung-nu gave a higher place to the left than the right. Therefore the ruler of Wu-sun was in effect snubbing the Han.

***Again this princess was dispensable because her grandfather had been implicated in a rebellion against the emperor, and had committed suicide upon its failure. She was married to two Wu-sun rulers in succession. However princesses married to barbarian allies also held the Han hostage because the successor of Emperor Wu had to send a large force of 150,000 cavalry to defend her and her husband's country from Hsiung-nu attack.

Pan, Ku. China in Central Asia The Early Stage: 125 B.C.-A.D. 23. Ed. and trans. A.F.P. Hulsewe. Leiden: Brill, 1979. Pp. 145-152, 207-209, 213-214, 218.

▶ Shiva, God of Death and Fertility

INDIA'S GOLDEN AGE-- THE GUPTAS AND HARSHA

With the breakup of the Kushan empire in the second century C.E., northern India was once more fragmented into numerous petty states. In 320, Chandra Gupta, ruler of a small north Indian state, began conquests that eventually unified all northern India under the Gupta dynasty. His gifted successors brought peace and prosperity to much of India. Later ages have looked back to the Gupta dynasty as the classic golden age of India. Buddhism continued to flourish, while revitalized Hinduism took the form that would remain essentially unchanged to modern times.

By the late fifth century, the Guptas were in decline and India was once more in the throes of civil wars, while Hunnish invasions from the northwest added to the chaos. The Gupta dynasty ended in the mid sixth century. In 606, a petty ruler from the Jumna-Ganges valley called Harsha consolidated power in northern India and began a reign of forty-one years. He almost succeeded in restoring the glory days of the Guptas, but after his death north India once more fell into chaos.

During the prosperous centuries of the Guptas and Harsha, both Hindu and Buddhist art flourished. The numerous surviving examples of art, sculpture and architecture testify to the prosperity and sophistication of India during those centuries.

Traders, missionaries, pilgrims, and colonists brought Indian art and ideas to Central Asia, China, and Southeast Asia, where it was admired and copied. Thus art historians speak of an "international Gupta style" that prevailed until about the ninth century.

Indian and Central Asian missionaries introduced Buddhism to China beginning in the firth century C.E. But language barriers and problems of translation had hindered conversions and prompted Chinese Buddhist pilgrims to travel to India to study the original manuscripts. Fa Hsien was a sickly child when his devout parents sent him to live in a Buddhist monastery to bring him luck. He later became a monk. Fa Hsien was the first important Chinese pilgrim to go to India in search of Buddhist scriptures, setting out over land in 405 and returning by sea in 411. He devoted the remainder of his life to translating the religious manuscripts into Chinese, dying at age eighty-eight. Fa Hsien kept a travel journal, which recorded in glowing terms the peace and prosperity of Gupta India, the magnificent cities and efficient government.

Hsuan Tsang was the greatest Chinese pilgrim to visit India. Like Fa Hsien, he traveled to India by land via Central Asia and Afghanistan. He stayed for some time at Kanauj, capital of Harsha, and had numerous meetings with the King, who asked him many questions about China and its great emperor, T'ai-tsung of the T'ang dynasty. Hsuan Tsang returned to China after sixteen years, bringing many Buddhist texts and relics of the Buddha. Like Fa Hsien, Hsuan Tsang spent the remaining years of his long life translating Buddhist manuscripts into Chinese. At T'ai- tsung's request, he also wrote record of his travels.

The following are excerpts from the *Travels* of Fa Hsien and from Hsuan Tsang's *Records of th Western World.*

QUESTIONS:

1) Give examples of the prosperity Indians enjoyed under the Guptas and Harsha.
2) Give examples of the highly civilized habits and customs of Indians.
3) In what ways was Harsha a great ruler in war and peace?

All south from this is named the Middle Kingdom [central India]. In it the cold and heat are finely tempered, and there is neither hoarfrost nor snow. The people are numerous and happy; they have not to register their households, or attend to any magistrates and their rules; only those who cultivate the royal land have to pay (a portion of) the grain from it. If they want to go, they go; if they want to stay on, they stay. The king governs without decapitation or (other) corporal punishments. Criminals are simply fined, lightly or heavily, according to the circumstances (of each case). Even in cases of repeated attempts at wicked rebellion, they only have their right hands cut off. The king's body-guards and attendants all have salaries. Throughout the whole country the people do not kill any living creatures, nor drink intoxicating liquor, nor eat onions or garlic. The only exception is that of the Chandalas. That is the name for those who are (held to be) wicked men, and live apart from others. When they enter the gate of a city or a market-place, they strike a piece of wood to make themselves known, so that men know and avoid them, and do not come into contact with them. In that country they do not keep pigs and fowls, and do not sell live cattle; in the markets there are no butchers' shops and no dealers in intoxicating drink. In buying and selling commodities they use cowries. Only the Chandalas are fishermen and hunters, and sell flesh meat....

The cities and towns of this country are the greatest of all in the Middle Kingdom. The inhabitants are rich and prosperous, and vie with one another in the practice of benevolence and righteousness. Every year on the eighth day of the second month they celebrate a procession of images. They make a four-wheeled car, and on it erect a structure of five storeys by means o bamboos tied together. This is supported by king-post, with poles and lances slanting from it and is rather more than twenty cubits high having the shape of a tope [dome-shaped with cupola on top]. White and silk-like cloth of hai is wrapped all round it, which is then painted i various colours. They make figures of deva [deities], with gold, silver, and lapis lazul grandly blended and having silken streamers an canopies hung out over them. On the four side: are niches, with a Buddha seated in each, and Bodhisattva standing in attendance on him There may be twenty cars, all grand and imposing, but each one different from the others On the day mentioned, the monks and laity within the borders all come together; they have singers and skillful musicians; they pay thei devotions with flowers and incense. Th Brahmans come and invite the Buddhas to ente the city. These do so in order, and remain two nights in it. All through the night they keep lamps burning, have skillful music, and present offerings. This is the practice in all the othe kingdoms as well. The Heads of the Vaisya families in them establish in the cities houses fo dispensing charity and medicines. All the poor and destitute in the country, orphans, widowers, and childless men, maimed people and cripples, and all who are diseased, go to those houses, and are provided with every kind of help, and doctors examine their diseases. They get the food and medicines which their cases require, and are made to feel at ease; and when they are better, they go away of themselves.

* * * * *

When they sit or rest they all use mats; the royal family and the great personages and assistant officers use mats variously ornamented, but in size they are the same. The throne of the reigning sovereign is large and high, and much adorned with precious gems: it is called the Lion-throne. It is covered with extremely fine drapery; the footstool is adorned with gems. The nobility use beautifully painted and enriched seats, according to their taste.

Their clothing is not cut or fashioned; they mostly affect fresh-white garments; they esteem little those of mixed colour or ornamented. The men wind their garments round their middle, then gather them under the armpits, and let them fall down across the body, hanging to the right. The robes of women fall down to the ground; they completely cover their shoulders. They wear a little knot of hair on their crowns, and let the rest of their hair fall loose. Some of the men cut off their moustaches, and have other odd customs. On their heads the people wear caps (crowns), with flower-wreaths and jewelled necklets....

With respect to the divisions of families, there are four classifications. The first is called the Brahmans, men of pure conduct. They guard themselves in religion, live purely, and observe the most correct principles. The second is called Kshatriya, the royal caste. For ages they have been the governing class: they apply themselves to virtue (humanity) and kindness. The third is called Vaisya, the merchant class: they engage in commercial exchange, and they follow profit at home and abroad. The fourth is called the Sudra, the agricultural class: they labour in ploughing and tillage. In these four classes purity or impurity of caste assigns to every one his place. When they marry they rise or fall in position according to their new relationship. They do not allow promiscuous marriages between relations. A woman once married can never take another husband....

The Kshatriyas and the Brahmans are cleanly and wholesome in their dress, and they live in a homely and frugal way. The king of the country and the great ministers wear garments and ornaments different in their character. They use flowers for decorating their hair, with gem-decked caps; they ornament themselves with bracelets and necklaces.

There are rich merchants who deal exclusively in gold trinkets, and so on. They mostly go bare-footed; few wear sandals. They stain their teeth red or black; they bind up their hair and pierce their ears; they ornament their noses, and have large eyes. Such is their appearance.

They are very particular in their personal cleanliness, and allow no remissness in this particular. All wash themselves before eating; they never use that which has been left over (from a former meal); they do not pass the dishes. Wooden and stone vessels, when used, must be destroyed; vessels of gold, silver, copper, or iron after each meal must be rubbed and polished. After eating they cleanse their teeth with a willow stick, and wash their hands and mouth.

Until these ablutions are finished they do not touch one another. Every time they perform the functions of nature they wash their bodies and use perfumes of sandal-wood or tumeric.

When the king washes they strike the drums and sing hymns to the sound of musical instrument. Before offering their religious services and petitions, they wash and bathe themselves.

Every one who falls sick fasts for seven days. During this interval many recover, but if the sickness lasts they take medicine. The character of these medicines is different, and their names also. The doctors differ in their modes of examination and treatment.

When a person dies, those who attend the funeral raise lamentable cries and weep together. They rend their garments and loosen their hair; they strike their heads and beat their breasts. There are no regulations as to dress for mourning, or any fixed time for observing it.

There are three methods of paying the last tribute to the dead: (1) by cremation--wood being made into a pyre, the body is burnt; (2) by water--the body is thrown into deep flowing water and abandoned; (3) by desertion--the body is cast into some forest-wild, to be devoured by beasts....

In a house where there has been a death there is no eating allowed; but after the funeral they resume their usual (habits). There are no anniversaries (of the deaths) observed. Those who have attended a death they consider unclean; they all bathe outside the town and then enter their houses....

Among the products of the ground, rice and corn [cereal] are most plentiful. With respect to edible herbs and plants, we may name ginger and mustard, melons and pumpkins ... and others. Onions and garlic are little grown; and few persons eat them; if any one uses them for food, they are expelled beyond the walls of the town. The most usual food is milk, butter, cream, soft sugar, sugar-candy, the oil of the mustard-seed, and all sorts of cakes made of corn [cereal] are used as food. Fish, mutton, gazelle, and deer they eat generally fresh, sometimes salted; they are forbidden to eat the flesh of the ox, the ass, the elephant, the horse, the pig, the dog, the fox, the wolf, the lion, the monkey, and all the hairy kind. Those who eat them are despised and scorned, and are universally reprobated; they live outside the walls, and are seldom seen among men.

With respect to the different kinds of wine and liquors, there are various sorts. The juice of the grape and sugar-cane, these are used by the Kshatriyas as drink; the Vaisyas use strong fermented drinks; the Sramans and Brahmans drink a sort of syrup made from the grape or sugar-cane, but not of the nature of fermented wine....

Gold and silver, *teou-shih* (native copper), white jade, fire pearls, are the natural products of the country; there are besides these abundance of rare gems and various kinds of precious stones of different names, which are collected from the islands of the sea. These they exchange for other goods; and in fact they always barter in their commercial transactions, for they have no gold or silver coins, pearl shells, or little pearls....

[Upon ascending the throne Harsha] commanded his ministers saying, "The enemies of my brother are unpunished as yet, the neighbouring countries not brought to submission; while this is so my right hand shall never lift food to my mouth. Therefore do you, people and officers, unite with one heart and put out your strength." Accordingly they assembled all the soldiers of the kingdom, summoned the masters of arms.... They had a body of 5000 elephants, a body of 2000 cavalry, and 50,000 foot-soldiers. He went from east to west subduing all who were not obedient; the elephants were not unharnessed nor the soldiers unbelted (*unhelmeted*). After six years he had subdued the Five Indies. Having thus enlarged his territory, he increased his forces; he had 60,000 war elephants and 100,000 cavalry. After thirty years his arms reposed, and he governed everywhere in peace. He then practised to the utmost the rules of temperance, and sought to plant the tree of religious merit to such an extent that he forgot to sleep or to eat. He forbade the slaughter of any living thing or flesh as food throughout the Five Indies on pain of death without pardon. He built on the banks of the river Ganges several thousand *stupas*, each about 100 feet high; in all the highways of the towns and villages throughout India he erected hospices, provided with food and drink, and stationed there physicians, with medicines for travellers and poor persons round about, to be given without any stint. On all spots where there were holy traces (*of Buddha*) he raised *sangharamas* [shrines].

Once in five years he held the great assembly called *Moksha*. He emptied his treasuries to give all away in charity, only reserving the soldiers' arms, which were unfit to give as alms. Every year he assembled the Sramanas from all countries, and on the third and seventh days he bestowed on them in charity the four kinds of alms (viz., food, drink, medicine, clothing).... He ordered the priests to carry on discussions, and himself judged of their several arguments, whether they were weak or powerful. He rewarded the good and punished the wicked, degraded the evil and promoted the men of talent.... If it was necessary to transact state business, he employed couriers who continually went and returned. If there was any irregularity in the manners of the people of the cities, he went amongst them. Wherever he moved he dwelt in a ready-made building during his sojourn. During the excessive rains of the three months of the rainy season he would not travel thus. Constantly in his travelling-palace he would provide choice meats for men of all sorts of religion. The Buddhist priests would be perhaps a thousand; the Brahmans five hundred. He divided each day into three portions. During the first he occupied himself on matters of government; during the second he practised himself in religious devotion without interruption, so that the day was not sufficiently long.

Legge, James, ed. and trans. *A Record of Buddhist Kingdoms*. Rpt. New York: Paragon Book Reprint, 1965. Pp. 42-43, 79. Tsiang, Hiuen. *Si-Yu-Ki: Buddhist Records of the Western World*. Trans. Samuel Beal. London: Trubner, 1884; rpt. 1969. Pp. 75-77, 82, 86, 88-90, 213-215.

▶ **Phoenix--Symbol of the Chinese Empress**

READING 3.14

EMPRESS WU'S RUTHLESS QUEST FOR POWER

▶ **Phoenix--Symbol of the Chinese Empress**

Wu Tse-tien (622?-705 C.E.), the only Chinese woman who ruled in her own name, ranks as one of history's most famous and notorious rulers. The daughter of an officer, she became a junior concubine (secondary wife) of the great Emperor Tai-tsung of the T'ang dynasty when she was fourteen but bore him no children. When Tai-tsung died Lady Wu, like his other junior concubines, entered a Buddhist convent. Since the prospect of spending her remaining years in a convent was definitely not to her liking, she managed to leave the convent only a year later and reentered the palace as her step-son, the new emperor Kao-tsung's concubine.

Lady Wu's rise to power had begun. She reputedly killed her infant daughter to cause the downfall of the empress whom she then replaced. She later engineered the downfall and death of all who had or could opposed her ascent to power, including high officials, Kao-tsung's other consorts and their sons, and many other members of his family. She turned on her own sons when they became adults, deposing the two elder ones after each was installed crown prince, and then had them murdered; she ruled in all but in name as her husband's health deteriorated, and after his death, had her two remaining sons deposed in rapid succession, finally proclaiming herself "female-emperor." She later murdered several of her daughters-in-law and grand children. She also imposed a reign of terror against all loyalists to the T'ang dynasty, as she engineered to establish her own dynasty called the Chou.

These actions, her scandalous private life, and the incompetence of her nephews whom she declared as her heirs roused increasing opposition. Finally, at age eighty-three, she was deposed and a son she had imprisoned for most of his adult life became emperor of the resurrected T'ang empire. Empress Wu's ruthlessness and cruelty revolted moralists. Her debauchery scandalized her court and provided rich material for gossip. Her private life has thus obscured the great talents and skills which enabled her to hold power for almost half a century. Empress Wu thus must rank as one of history's most famous and notorious rulers.

Lin Yutang, the author of an eminently readable biography of Empress Wu, claimed to have written her story:

> not as fiction, but as a strictly historical biography, because the facts would be incredible if told as fiction. I have not included one character, or incident or dialogue which is not strictly based on Tang history.... I have chosen, however, to tell it from the point of view of her grandson, the Prince of Bin, to give it a sense of immediate experience. For it is characteristically a family feud of the two families, the princes of Tang (family name Li) on the one hand, and the Wus. the family of the empress, on the other. The prince, living from

the age of twelve to twenty-seven in strict confinement in the palace along with his Uncle Dan (later Emperor Ruitsung) and his children, played the passive role of the persecuted; he saw his own two brothers flogged to death and his aunts, the wives of Prince Dan, secretly murdered and other daughters-in-law of the empress persecuted to death. But he survived to see the end of the drama and the extinction of the Wus, and lived in peace and honour, after the restoration of the Tang House [Lin Yutang, *Lady Wu: A True Story*, p. x].

The following are excerpts from this famous biography of Lady Wu.

QUESTIONS:

1) Why did Empress Wu kill or imprison her sons and grandsons?
2) How did she try but fail to establish a new dynasty?
3) What arguments finally persuaded Empress Wu to restore her remaining son to power?

[In 672 Empress Wu had caused the death of her second son's wife. The woman's husband dared not protest but Wu's eldest son, the Crown Prince Hung, did.] Grandmother's fury was terrible to behold.... "Don't presume to tell me what to do!"

"I am not presuming," retorted Prince Hung. "On the other hand, I thought you would like your subjects to speak frankly and freely. I remember freedom of expression was one of your Twelve Points, so that wrongs might be righted, injustices redressed. I am just trying to be helpful...."

"You can withdraw!" said Lady Wu grimly, her voice settling back to a frightening coolness, her face tightened hard and flat, her eyes narrowed into slits.

Exactly eighteen days later, Prince Hung died of poison while visiting Hobigung in the company of his parents. Again, he "ate something wrong." Everybody grandmother disliked ate something wrong. One would have thought that even a lioness does not eat her young and that to suppose the mother as capable of poisoning her son was unreasonable. On the other hand, it would be wrong to measure grandmother by ordinary standards applicable to us common men.... The final score was as follows: of grandfather's eight sons, one died young, grandmother killed five, and the remaining two were imprisoned by her for over a dozen years, not counting the infant girl she strangled....

My father, Prince Shien, being the next in succession, was now crown prince, a rather unenviable position.... After waiting four or five

years, she saw father was getting on too successfully, too well. His reputation had been established. And he was already twenty-seven.... Here was a flaw in her grand plan. What about her own prospects when the king should die? [Prince Shien was framed on a trumped up sedition charge.]....

Father was deposed and imprisoned; the heir was changed. Prince Jer [Wu's third son] was next.

I was eight when the tragedy struck home. We had always lived in luxury and affluence and comfort. Father was Governor of Liangchow before he was made crown prince. I was seized with such fear as only children know. The next year father was banished to Chengtu (Szechuan), but we three children, being young, remained in the palace. There father languished, without communications with home, accepting his fate in silence.... We children never saw him again until the death of grandmother, when his remains were brought back to be buried with his ancestors....

[When Gaotsung died Empress Wu hesitated for six days before she consented to have her third son proclaimed new emperor. However he only lasted for fifty-four days before she deposed him on flimsy charges and then sent him to exile. Some days later Empress Wu] ... sent her nephew [Wu] Chengtse, to deliver a scroll appointing Dan [her fourth son, then twenty-three years old] as 'emperor' at his apartment. The 'emperor' was seen no more in public! For stranger still, for no reason or pretext whatsoever and without any effort at justification, the pawn-emperor was placed under detention at a back court and forbidden all communication with the ministers or the outside public...."

My father was then still living under detention at Chengtu. I was twelve then, having been away from my father for over three years. Grandmother had too much respect for father's ability and feared him more than the other remaining sons. He might be able to start a revolt, or serve as a rallying point of support for rebels to her regime. Lady Wu exercised forethought and took precautions. The murder of my father was necessary, and it was carried out with the same political skill. Three days after the arrest and forcible ejection of Prince jer from the throne, she sent a captain of palace guards to Chengtu. The mission was to "search his house and protect him from accidents." The court emissary first shut him up in a back room, then compelled father to hang himself....

To cover up the murder, grandmother ordered a public mourning ceremony with sacrifices to his spirit at the Shienfomen, at which she took part as the bereaved mother.... It was all a mistake on the part of the emissary Chiu (Shenji), it was said, and Chiu was dismissed to a lower post in the provinces.... However, hardly half a year had passed before Chiu was recalled and restored to his original post. The public then understood that he had carried out the empress dowager's orders and it had been no mistake at all.

Now began my period of confinement within the palace with my brothers. As orphans of a convicted and disgraced prince, already deprived of his ranks, we were shut up with Uncle Dan and his family. We were forbidden to put our foot outside the palace gate.... We learned to talk in whispers and felt like helpless children.... For fifteen long years I never saw the streets of Loyang. What we knew of court politics was learned indirectly by hearsay.... For our own protection, we kept to ourselves and consoled ourselves with the thought that our lot was no worse than occasional insults and floggings, at the hand of the Wu nephews....

[Empress Wu next orchestrated petitions for her own enthronement as ruler so that] ... unable and unwilling either to frustrate the hopes of the nation or disobey the will of God, modestly, on September the seventh [year?], she finally wrote

the word 'approve' on the document of the petition.

On September the ninth the decree was given. Henceforth the Tang Imperial Dynasty was abolished, and the new one was to be called Jou [Lin Yutang's own rendition, normally spelled Chou] ... Lady Wu appeared at the front tower of the palace and had the edict read and a general amnesty declared....

On September the twelfth, in accordance with a predetermined scale of promotion, she now assumed the audacious title 'Holy Spirit Emperor'.... It was an advance from 'Holy Mother Divine Sovereign' [a title she had assumed earlier]. At last her ambition was realized, She was a 'female emperor', not an empress only. The term 'Holy Spirit' constituted also an advance toward divinity. On the same day Prince Dan, whose royal surname Li had become a stigma, was graciously granted the surname of Wu.

On September the thirteenth the names of all princes of the Tang House were struck off the peerage list. The Wus ... were created princes ... and ... princesses .... The transition of dynasties was now completed.

[Many years later, in her old age empress] Wu found herself in a political dilemma.... How was a woman who wanted to found a dynasty, and yet not have her sons as heirs to do it .... Unfortunately, being a woman, she had married into the Lis, and her sons were Lis. The conferring of the surname "Wu" was necessarily superficial; Prince Jer and Dan, being Lis in blood, would feel like Lis. She had not wanted to see her son Prince Jer, now shut up and separated from her for fourteen years. She had not cared to send for him. She had Prince Dan at her apron-strings.... What was she to do with Dan?

Unfortunately, too, her father had only two grandsons, Changtse and Sanse, who were cousins. She tried her best to found a dynasty with them, but as she looked at them, her heart must have sunk within her. Changtse had tireless energy, but that was all. But he had no tact, no sense, no dignity.... Changtse and Sanse went about in their slick ingratiating way, haughty to some and obsequious to others--bullies and snobs at the same time, and invited only general hatred and contempt.... [Finally she confided her worries to a senior statesman who, although serving her, had remained stalwart in loyalty to the T'ang dynasty. Councillor Di replied]

"There is no question but that Your Majesty must make one of your sons the heir. Then your spirit tablet [erected after death to receive ancestor worship] will occupy a seat in the imperial ancestral temple, rightfully as the emperor's parent, and receive the sacrifices for ever and ever. But it would be unthinkable for an emperor to place his aunt's spirit tablet in the temple. It is unheard of, and against all rules.... What assurances have you that your nephews will always remember your kindness and not ignore you or turn against you?"

The argument went home. The rules and rituals about ancestor worship are sharply defined and rigorously prescribed, and Lady Wu knew it. She hated to think of herself as a starving soul, unprayed to and uncared for.... [Prince Jer was therefore recalled from exile and proclaimed crown prince.]

Uncle Dan had yielded to his brother's claim without any resentment. In the following year, [Earlier Empress Wu had Prince Bin's two brothers and several other grandchildren killed. Prince Bin was later reputed to have magic powers and able to predict rainfall. He explained it thus: "During my youth, when I was shut up inside the Eastern Palace, I used to receive flogging about three or four times a year at the hand of the Wus.... The scars healed, but the effect remains. When the weather changes I ache all over inside my bones, and when it is about to clear up, I feel well again. That's how. I have no magic."] and Uncle Dan's children ... were permitted to leave the palace and began our normal life of liberty. I was twenty-seven then.... I felt like a bird which had been let out of a golden cage. I should have been greatly excited at this new freedom to see the streets and the shops and the common people's houses once more. But I remember I wasn't. Something in me had died. It took me years before I shed the attitude of caution and silence and fear and began to live a normal life again.

[Empress Wu did not yield her power until age eighty-three, when she had become very ill, and then only under duress. Her third son Prince Jer was restored to the throne from which he had been expelled after only fifty-four days' reign. He treated her with honor during her remaining months, but proceeded to undo much of her life's work by destroying the house of Wu and restoring the T'ang empire, and the reputations of those she had ruined, in many cases posthumously.]

Lin, Yutang. *Lady Wu: A True Story*. London: Heinemann, 1957. Pp. 2, 3, 97-98, 100, 102. 105, 114-116, 178-179, 215, 218.

A JAPANESE MONK'S ACCOUNT OF LATE T'ANG CHINA

► Buddhist Monk

Ennin was a Japanese Buddhist monk. He went to China with an official Japanese embassy in 838 C.E., traveled extensively in search of Buddhist teachers and texts, and returned to Japan in 847. He was part of a great movement in history that spread the higher civilization of China to Southeast Asia, Korea, and Japan. Japan's enthusiastic embrace of Chinese culture between the sixth and ninth centuries was instrumental in its rapid advance; Ennin was a key player in this phase of East Asian history.

Ennin was a good tourist and keen observer. He filled a detailed dairy with accurate observations of the sights, sounds, and manners of the people he encountered. The diary supplements the official history of the time and breathes life into a long ago era. It is filled with vivid descriptions of Buddhist ceremonies and festivals. Ennin was also caught in the greatest government persecution of Buddhism in Chinese history (841-846). It was initiated by a pro-Taoist emperor, but had several deeply rooted causes. One was the revival of Confucian political ideals, coupled with resentment of Buddhism as a foreign religion. Another was the great wealth of the Buddhist institutions, their tax exempt estates and unproductive monks and nuns, all of which excited the envy of government bureaucrats at a time of financial hardship. The persecution, however, was aimed at the monasteries and clergy, not at lay Buddhists.

In the reading here, Ennin describes the Buddhist role in many ceremonies and celebrations, some laws that persecuted the Buddhist religious establishment, and anecdotes that shows public sympathy for the persecuted religion.

QUESTIONS:

1) Describe how the Buddhist clergy celebrated a festival.
2) Why did emperor proclaim laws to persecute the Buddhist clergy in 844? What happened to the Buddhist temples and the monks and nuns?
3) What was the public's attitude toward the persecution?

[On winter solstice day] Monks and laymen all offer congratulations. Those who are laymen pay their respects to the officials and congratulate them on the festival of the winter solstice....

Officials of high and low rank and the common people all offer one another congratulations when they meet. Clerics offer each other congratulations when they meet, uttering phrases about the winter solstice and making obeisances to one another. [Chinese monks greeted Ennin's party] ... with the words, "Today is the festival of the winter solstice. May you have a myriad of blessings; may the propagation of the lamp [of the Law] be without end; and may you return soon to your own land and long be National Teachers".... The monks exchanged felicitations, saying, "I humbly hope that you will long be in the world and will be in harmony with all creatures." The ordained and the novices in speaking to the Superior observed exactly the regulations of the written codes of conduct. The novices touched their right knees to the ground in front of the monks and spoke words of congratulations on the festival.... Laymen on entering the monastery also show the same courtesy.... All use congratulatory phrases on the season, conforming to the tastes of the man of former times....

In the evening [of New Year's Eve] they lighted lamps as offerings at the Buddha Hall and Scripture Storehouse of this Korean Cloister, but they did not light lamps elsewhere. They burned bamboo leaves and grass in the stoves in each of the cells, and smoke poured from their chimneys. At dusk, before midnight, after midnight, and before dawn they worshiped Buddha, and after midnight the novices and disciples went around to the various cells with congratulatory words on the new year, in the Chinese manner....

After midnight they struck the bells in the monastery, and the congregation of monks gathered in the dining hall to pay reverence to the Buddha. At the moment for worshiping the Buddha, the whole congregation descended from their benches and, spreading out their mats on the ground, worshiped the Buddha, after which they climbed back onto the benches. Then the Monastery Steward and Controller monks read out in front of the assembly the various account books for the year for the assembly to hear. Before dawn came, they dined on gruel in front of the lamps, after which they scattered to their rooms....

[New Year festivities continued for two weeks to the first full moon, which was celebrated with a great festival. In the capital] Hempseed cakes were given by the Emperor, and at the time for gruel [breakfast], the monastery served the hempseed cakes. All the lay households did likewise.

At night they burned lamps in the private homes along the streets to the east and west. It was not unlike New Year's Eve in Japan. In the monastery they burned lamps and offered them to the Buddha. They also paid reverence to the pictures of their teachers. Layman did likewise.

In the monasteries they erected a lamp tower in front of the Buddha Hall. Below the steps, in the courtyard, and along the sides of the galleries they burned oil. The lamp cups were quite beyond count. In the streets men and women did not fear the late hour, but entered the monastery and looked around, and in accordance with their lot cast coppers before the lamps which had been offered. After looking around, they went on to other monasteries and looked around and worshiped and cast their coppers.

The halls of the various monasteries and the various cloisters all vie with one another in the burning of lamps. Those who come always give coppers before departing.

On the fifteenth day of the seventh moon the various monasteries of the city made offerings. The monasteries made flowery candles, flowery cakes, artificial flowers, fruit trees, and the like, vying with one another in their rarities. Customarily they spread them all out as offerings in front of the Buddha halls, and [people of] the whole city go around to the monasteries and perform adoration. It is a most flourishing festival.

[The eighth day of the twelfth moon was a secular holiday in remembrance of the assassination of an emperor in 826.] Today was a national anniversary, and accordingly fifty strings of cash were given [by the Military Inspector who represented the emperor] to the K'ai-yuan-ssu [a monastery in Yangchow] to arrange a maigre [vegetarian] feast for five hundred monks. Early in the morning the monastic congregation gathered in this monastery and seated themselves in rows in the flanking buildings on the east, north, and west. At 8 A.M. the Minister of State and the General entered the monastery by the great gate ... [walking] in slowly side by side. Soldiers in ranks guarded them on all sides, and all the officials of the prefecture and of the regional commandery followed behind. They came as far as the foot of the steps in front of the lecture hall, and then the Minister of State and the General parted, the Minister of State going to the east side [of the courtyard], and the General going to the west and entering behind a curtain on the west side. They quickly changed their slippers, washed their hands, and came out again.... They took their seats and worshiped the Buddha.

After that, several tens of monks lined up in rows at both the east and west doors of the hall. Each one held artificial lotus flowers and green banners. A monk struck a stone triangle and chanted, "All be worshipful and reverence the three eternal treasures [Buddha, the Buddhist law, and the monastic community]." After that the Minister of State and the General arose and took censers, and the prefectural officials all followed after them, taking incense cups.... The monks who were carrying flowered banners preceded him, chanting in unison a two-line hymn in Sanskrit.... After all the monks had burned incense, they returned toward the hall by this route, chanting Sanskrit hymns without cease....

During this time, there was beautiful responsive chanting of Sanskrit hymns [by groups of monks] on the east and west. The leader of the chants, standing alone and motionless, struck a stone triangle, and the Sanskrit [chanting] stopped. They then again recited, "Honor the three eternal treasures." The Minister of State and the General sat down together in their original seats. When they burned incense, the incense burner in which their incense was placed stood side by side. A venerable monk ... read a prayer, after which the leader of the chants intoned hymns in behalf of the eight classes of demi-gods. The purport of the wording was to glorify the spirit of the [late] Emperor. At the end of each verse he recited, "Honor the three eternal treasures." The Minister of State and the officials rose to their feet together and did reverence to the Buddha, chanting three or four times. Then all [were free] to do as they wished.

The Minister of State and the others, taking the soldiers [with them], went into the great hall behind the [lecture] hall and dined. The congregation of five hundred monks dined in the galleries....

[Devout private individuals also sponsored religious feasts, one in the year 750 went as follows.] At noon they struck a bell, and the congregation of monks entered the hall. After the full monks, novices, laymen, children, and women had been seated in rows according to their rank, the Leader in Worship struck a mallet and chanted, "Let all be worshipful and pay reverence to the three eternal treasures; let all be widely reflective." Then two junior monks of the monastery, holding golden lotus flowers in their hands, struck gourd-[shaped] cymbals, and three or four men chanted together in Sanskrit. The patron burned incense, and everyone, regardless of whether he was a cleric or layman, man or woman, took his turn at burning incense. After that the Leader in Worship first read the text of offering by the patron and then offered praises [to the Buddha]. The ceremony concluded with the congregation chanting, "on behalf of the lasting prosperity of the holy reign [of the dynasty], we pay reverence to the three eternal treasures, on behalf of the manifold grandeur of today's patron, we pay reverence to the three eternal treasures; on behalf of the monks and our fathers and mothers and all sentient beings of the universe of the Law, we pay reverence to the three eternal treasures."

[The Leader in Worship then] struck a mallet and chanted, "Let the prayer for the presentation of food be said," and a monk in a raised seat said the prayer, after which they served the food. The noble and humble, the old and young, clerics and laymen, men and women, all were provided for equally.

After the congregation of monks had eaten the maigre feast, they purified themselves ritually with water, rinsing out their mouths. [After another prayer] the congregation dispersed at will....

* * * * *

[The imperial edict that began the persecution was issued in 842. It said in part:] ... all the monks and nuns of the empire who understand alchemy, the art of incantations, and the black arts, who have fled from the army, who have on their bodies the scars of flagellations and tattoo marks [for former offenses, who have been condemned to] various forms of labor, who have formerly committed sexual offenses or maintain wives, or who do not observe the Buddhist rules, should all be forced to return to lay life. If monks and nuns have money, grains, fields, or estates, these should be surrendered to the government. If they regret [the loss of] their wealth and wish to return to lay life [in order to retain it], in accordance with their wishes, they are to be forced to return to lay life and are to pay the "double tax" and perform the corvée....

As for the slaves they possess, monks may retain one male slave and nuns two female slaves. The others are to be returned and given over to the custody of their original families. Those who have no family should be sold by the government. Likewise, aside from their clothes and alms bowls, the wealth [of the monks and nuns] is to be stored up and its disposition is to await subsequent Imperial decree. If among the slaves retained by monks and nuns there are those who [are versed in] the military arts or understand medicine or the other arts, they may not be retained at all, nor may their heads be shaved in secret. If there are violations [of these orders], the Monastery Administrators and Supervisors are to record them and notify the government. The other property and money should all be turned over to the Commissioners of Good Works to be regulated by them.

[An edict in 844 was aimed at small monasteries and did the following:] Their scriptures and images were taken to the large monasteries, and their bells were sent to the Taoist monasteries. Those monks and nuns of the destroyed monasteries who were unrefined in their conduct or did not observe the rules, regardless of their age, were all forced to return to lay life, were sent back to their place of origin, and made to perform the local corvée. Those who were old and observed the rules were assigned to the great monasteries, but those who were young, even though they observed the rules, were all forced to return to lay life, going back to their places of origin.

[Emperor Wu-tsung, a Taoist enthusiast, gave articles confiscated from Buddhist monasteries to Taoist temples. At the All Souls Festival in 844 he invited people of the capital city to view his gifts at Taoist monasteries, but: the people cursed him, saying that since he had seized the offerings to the Buddhas and presented them to the spirits, who would be willing to look at them? The Emperor was surprised that the people did not come. [Desiring rain] the Commissioners of Good Works, an imperial command, notified the various Buddhist and Taoist monasteries to read scriptures and pray for rain. But, when in response it rained, the Taoist priests alone received rewards, and the Buddhist monks and nuns were left forlorn with nothing. The people of the city laughingly said that, when they pray for rain, they bother the Buddhist monks, but, when they make rewards, they only give them to the Taoist priests.

Reischauer, Edwin O. *Ennin's Travels in T'ang China*. New York: Ronald Press, 1955. Pp. 124-8, 131-133, 137-138, 238-239, 246, 254.

SECTION 4

THE ERA OF POLITICAL AND RELIGIOUS DISRUPTION AND CHANGE

Internal problems and external pressures caused all great and once successful empires to decline and fall. As a result of the contentions and disruptions that followed the fall of major empires, the successor states that eventually emerged always differed from their predecessors. This section is devoted to exploring the forces that disrupted the great empires, the people who effected the changes as well as those affected by them, and the gradual synthesis of new cultures from elements of the old.

Several readings deal with the lives and ferocious or unsavory habits of the feared barbarians, such as the Huns, Norsemen, and Bulgars. Others focus on the defenders against the attacking barbarians--the Byzantine warrior-emperor Basil II, and Mrs. Yueh Fei, the model wife of a revered Chinese general. Another describes the quest for a Shangri-la of personal tranquillity away from the strife of wars and invasions.

While wars, invasions, and group migrations of barbarians disrupted and destroyed, they also brought new ideas. Some of the readings below tell about the melting pot effect of people interacting in war and peace; others deal with patterns of life that emerged after the disruptions--they pertain to food and drink, beliefs and mores, schools and education. While some of the disorders were caused by wars between attacking barbarians and their more cultured victims, others were the result of wars between clashing cultures or proponents of different religions. The crusades mounted by Christian Europeans against Muslims in West Asia are prime examples of prolonged warfare between peoples of different faiths, with indelible consequences. Still other wars with lasting legacies were waged between rival nations, such as England and France, in which Joan of Arc became a victim.

This section thus portrays a rich mosaic of life and the clash of many cultures during times of hardship and dislocation as major empires disintegrated.

Buddhist Art along the Silk Road

MELTING POT OF INDIAN, GRECO-ROMAN, AND CHINESE CIVILIZATIONS

Beginning in the second century B.C.E. the Silk Road linked China with India, Central and Western Asia, and the Roman Empire and enabled goods to move from one end of the Eurasian continent to the other. Well over a thousand years before Marco Polo made his journey, merchants made the oasis towns of present-day western China, Central Asia, northwestern India, and Afghanistan melting pots of ancient cultures. Buddhism, Hinduism, Zoroastrianism, and other religions co-existed and flourished. In the fifteenth century, the overland routes were finally abandoned, casualties of climatic changes and of marauding armies that reduced the population and wrecked irrigation systems and because newly discovered sea-routes provided a cheaper way to transport freight. Desert sands covered ruined and deserted settlements. The remaining population was converted to Islam.

Until the end of the nineteenth century, even the memory of these cosmopolitan entrepôts was lost. Then intrepid European explorers and archaeologists retraced the steps of ancient merchants and pilgrims and revealed the riches of lost cultures. Sir Aurel Stein was one of the famous explorers who rediscovered many sites in northwestern India, Afghanistan, Central Asia, and western China. Archaeologist-explorers coined a name, Serindia, to describe that vast region, where a combination of Chinese (ancient Greeks called China "Seres," or land of silk) and Indian civilizations had thrived. Stein's account proves the civilization of Greece and Rome also contributed powerfully to the melting pot culture of ancient Serindia.

During a pioneering expedition in 1900-1901, amid ruins in the Taklamakan Desert in northwestern China, Stein found evidence of an ancient culture displaying Chinese, Indian, and classical influences. But he was not able to excavate them at the time.

During 1907-1908, he undertook a second great expedition that began in northwest India and proceeded into Afghanistan, Central Asia, and northwestern China. He traveled along dried ancient river beds and oases where once cosmopolitan settlements and international trade had thrived. At Niya and other sites in present Chinese Turkestan, Stein discovered writings in Sanskrit, Chinese, and a cursive form of Kharoshthi, previously found only in inscriptions and on coins in the northwestern part of the Indian subcontinent. They proved that in the centuries of disunity between the fall of the Mauryan empire in India and the post-Han era in China, international trade had persisted, and widespread cultural and artistic exchanges continued throughout the Eurasian continent.

This excerpt is from Sir Aurel Stein's account of his second expedition. His adventures, hardships, and exciting discoveries make wonderful reading for armchair travelers and archaeologists.

QUESTIONS:

1) What cultures were represented in the ancient melting pot discovered by Stein?
2) How had the desert sand preserved ancient artifacts?
3) How can we reconstruct the cultures along the Silk Road by the written records recovered?

On the morning of October 20th we left behind the last abode of the living, and also the present end of the Niya River. Five camels carried the first supply of water for my column, counting in all over fifty labourers. I was bent upon moving that day as far as possible ahead towards the ancient site to which my thoughts had turned so often since those happy days of labour in the winter of 1901....

The long shadows of the evening made the high swelling dunes to the north-west look doubly imposing. Yet I managed to drag my straggling column onwards for close on two miles before falling darkness compelled us to halt. From my detailed map of the site I knew that we were now close to some ruins which I had sighted on the last day of my previous stay.... While my tent was being pitched, I set out to find them, and soon set foot amidst their sand-buried timber. The distance and other difficulties overcome made me feel like a pilgrim who has reached his sacred goal after long months of wandering. At the ruin I had struck a large wooden bracket, decorated with carvings in Gandharan style, lay exposed on the surface. As I sat on it listening to the great silence around me, and thought of the life which seventeen hundred years ago had thronged this ground, now disputed only by the rival forces of drift sand and erosion, I enjoyed the happiest moments of rest I could wish for that evening....

[Next morning] Marching on over absolutely bare dunes for another two miles, I passed one after another of the ancient houses reported. They lay in a line along what must have been the extreme north-western extension of a canal once fed by the Niya River.... I selected a patch of open eroded ground near the northern end of the ruins, and lost no time in commencing my day's work at the farthest ruined structure we could trace.

It was a comparatively small dwelling covered only by three to four feet of sand.... As soon as the floor was being reached in the western end room Kharoshthi documents on wood began to crop out in numbers.... I had the satisfaction of seeing in each of the three living-rooms of the house specimen after specimen of this ancient record in Indian language and script emerge from where the last dweller, probably a petty official, about the middle of the third century A.D., had left behind his "waste paper." Rectangular tablets, of the official type, with closely fitting wooden covers serving as envelopes; double wedge-shaped tablets, as used ordinarily for short demi-official communications; oblong boards and labels of wood containing records and accounts of all kinds, were all represented among the remains of this first ruin....

I could not help feeling emotion, when I convinced myself on cleaning them from the fine sand adhering, that a number of the rectangular and wedge-shaped letter tablets still retained intact their original string fastenings, and a few even their seal impressions in clay. How delighted I was to discover on them representations of Eros and a figure probably meant for Hermes, left by the impact of classical intaglios! To be greeted once more at these desolate ruins in the desert by tangible links with the art of Greece and Rome seemed to efface all distance in time and space.

Equally familiar to me were the household implements which this ruin yielded. Remains of a wooden chair decorated with elaborate carvings in Graeco-Buddhist style, weaving instruments, a boot-last, a large eating tray, mouse-trap, etc....

But when I examined the ground underneath what appeared to have been an outhouse or stables about fifty feet square, I quickly realized that it was made up of the layers of a huge refuse heap. Previous experience supplied sufficient reason for digging into this unsavoury quarry; though the pungent smells which its contents emitted, even after seventeen centuries of burial, were doubly trying in the fresh eastern breeze, driving fine dust, dead microbes, and all into one's eyes, throat, and nose.

Our perseverance in cutting through layer upon layer of stable refuse was rewarded at last by striking, on a level fully seven feet below the surface, a small wooden enclosure about eight by six feet and over five feet high, which had probably served as a dustbin for some earlier habitation. In the midst of coarser refuse, mixed up with various grains, we found there curious sweepings of all sorts--rags of manifold fabrics in silk, wool, cotton, and felt; pieces of woollen pile carpet, embroidered leather and felt, plaited braids and cords, arrow-heads in bronze and iron, fragments of fine lacquer ware, broken implements in wood and horn. But more gratifying still was a find of over a dozen small label-like wooden slips inscribed with Chinese characters of exquisite penmanship....

Quite at the bottom of the enclosure there turned up a small heap of corn, still in sheaves and in perfect preservation, and close to it the mummified bodies of two mice which death had overtaken while nibbling at this store....

Karoshthi records on wood, whether letters, accounts, drafts, or memos, turned up in almost every one of these dwellings, besides architectural wood-carvings, household objects, and wooden implements illustrative of everyday life and domestic industries, such as weaving instruments and boot-lasts. Though nothing of intrinsic value had been left behind by the last dwellers of this modest Pompeii, there was sufficient evidence of the ease in which they had lived, in the number of individual rooms provided with fireplaces and comfortable sitting platforms. Remains of fenced gardens and of avenues of poplars or fruit trees could be traced almost invariably near the houses....

When at night I came to clear the clay sealings on the documents which I had carried away to my tent carefully wrapped up, I discovered that almost all remained as fresh as when first impressed, and that most of them were from intaglios of classical workmanship representing Pallas Promachos, Heracles with club and lion-skin, Zeus, and helmeted busts.

The fact that the majority of these tablets bore in the sunk sockets of their covers or envelopes the impressions of two, or in a few cases even three, seals strongly supported the assumption of their containing agreements or bonds executed before witnesses. Among the tablets with single seal impressions there were two showing the official title of the Chinese commander at Shan-shan or Lop-nor in Chinese lapidary characters....

In the light of my new finds it can still be asserted with confidence that the ruins belong to a widely scattered agricultural settlement which flourished in the third century A.D. and was abandoned when Chinese supremacy in the Tarim Basin came to an end towards the close of this century. The essential observation still holds good, that the administration of the tract was carried on in an Indian language and script. Their use lends support to the old local tradition recorded by Hsuan-tsang which tells of Khotan having received a large portion of its early population by immigration from Takshasila, the Taxila of the Greeks, in the extreme North-West of India. But since my subsequent explorations yielded proofs of Kharoshthi script and Prakrit language having been known as far east as the Lop-nor region, the question will claim attention hereafter whether their far-spread use was not partly due also to the powerful influence of that Indo-Scythian dominion which during the first centuries of our era seems for a time to have brought the Tarim Basin into direct political relations with Afghanistan and the distant Indian North-West.

Stein, M. Aurel. *Ruins of Desert Cathay: Personal Narrative of Explorations in Central Asia and Westernmost China.* London: Macmillan, 1912. Vol. 1. Pp. 269, 272-277, 283-284, 290-291.

T'AO YUAN-MING: A RECLUSE AND HIS SHANGRI-LA

▶ Idyllic Rural Life

At the fall of the Han dynasty in 220 C.E., China plunged into chaos which lasted until 589. In addition to civil wars among Chinese, north China was invaded and ruled by the reconsolidated nomadic tribes. In 311 and 316 the two imperial capitals of the Han dynasty, Loyang and Changan, were in turn captured and sacked by nomads called the Hsiung-nu. Most of the nomadic dynasties were short lived and failed to control all of north China; all subjected the Chinese to varying degrees of servitude. South China was ruled by Chinese dynasties which were similarly unstable and fragmented.

T'ao Ch'ien (also known as T'ao Yuan-ming, c.365-427) lived in this troubled period. He was born into a distinguished family that produced many officials, received a good education, and was appointed magistrate. However he resigned after only 83 days in office, proclaiming that he would not "bow and scrape for five pecks of rice a day." From then on he refused official service and lived humbly as a recluse in the countryside, playing music, cultivating a garden, and writing poems and essays that extolled rustic pleasures. This great and sometimes whimsical writer is admired for abandoning a corrupt world. In this respect T'ao resembles Henry Thoreau of nineteenth-century America, the Hermit of Walden Pond, who similarly lived a rustic life and made a simple living while pursuing his writings.

T'ao's "Peach Blossom Grove" describes a Shangri-la (an imaginary earthly paradise) where people who had escaped the turmoil of a previous era of wars had found happiness and lived a tranquil life. It is one of the most popular essays in Chinese literature and most educated Chinese memorized it by heart. Volumes have been written about this short essay; some assert that it is an allegory, others have tried to prove that the place it describes really existed in some specific location. Many painters have recreated the journey of the fisherman and the Peach Blossom Grove. The essay is popular perhaps because it reflects a common longing for Shangri-la that is especially strong in troubled times.

"The Biography of the Gentleman of the Five Willows" is an even shorter essay--only one hundred and seventy words long. While the author does not reveal who the subject is, most scholars agree that it is autobiographical. It is a succinct summary of T'ao's philosophy of life. He is admired for living his ideals of living simply and unostentatiously, for not being ashamed of poverty, and for enjoying good wine and company. These works by T'ao Yuan-ming follow.

QUESTIONS:

1) Why were the people of Peach Blossom Grove happy?
2) How did the Gentleman of the Five Willow Trees find happiness?

Peach Blossom Grove

During the reign of Tai-yuan [376-396 C.E.] of the Chin dynasty, there was a fisherman from a town called Wuling. One day he was fishing in his boat and sailed along a river forgetting the distance. All of a sudden he came upon a narrow stretch of the river. It was bordered by a grove of peach trees with no other kinds of trees in their midst. This grove stretched for several hundred paces. The air was fragrant with peach blossoms, whose falling petals swirled about in the air. The fisherman was amazed by what he saw. He continued on, hoping to find the end of the grove. Finally it ended at the head of the river, where a spring descended from a hill pierced by a narrow gorge. He saw a faint light through the gorge.

Tying up his boat the fisherman approached the gorge, which was at first so narrow that a person could barely pass through. After several scores of paces the gorge suddenly opened up to a wide plain dotted with hamlets among cultivated fields, beautiful ponds, mulberry and bamboo groves, etc., and linked by numerous paths. Men and women, dressed no differently from those in other parts of the country, were going about their businesses, old and young seemed happy. Dogs barked and cocks crowed.

They were very surprised to see the fisherman and asked where he came from. He answered all their questions. Then they asked him to come to their home, killed a chicken and prepared a meal in his welcome, which they served with wine. When others in the village heard about him they came to ask him questions too. They also told him the following story about themselves: "Our ancestors wished to escape from the turmoil during the rule of the Ch'in dynasty [221-206 B.C.E.], so they took their wives and children, and with their fellow villagers came to this place for refuge. We have since then been completely isolated from the outside world and no one has left." They then asked him what era it was now. They had never heard of the Han dynasty [202 B.C.E.-220 C.E.], let alone the Wei and the present dynasty called Chin. The fisherman told them about all these events to their great amazement.

In the following days many of the other families in the community invited him to their homes for food and drinks. After staying awhile the fisherman made ready to bid his hosts farewell. Before he left they all begged him saying: "Do not tell the outside world about us."

On departing the fisherman found his boat and retraced his steps, making careful notes of the landmarks along the way. When he arrived at the capital of the commandary he immediately went to see the magistrate and told him about his finding. The magistrate at once appointed his men to accompany the fisherman to find the location. They tried to retrace his route but could never find the place again.

Later an esteemed scholar, Liu Tzu-chi of Nanyang, heard about this tale. He too set off to try to rediscover the fisherman's find but to no avail. He later took ill and died. Since then no one has continued the quest.

Biography of the Gentleman of the Five Willow Trees

On one knows the gentleman's native place, nor does anyone know the details of his family or personal name. Because there are five willow trees growing near his little house, people began to call him the Gentleman of the Five Willow Trees. He is a man of few words and lives a quiet life, avoiding profit or glory. He loves learning, but eschews the abstruse. When he finds some work that he likes he becomes so absorbed that he forgets to eat.

He is fond of wine, but being poor, he cannot often afford to indulge. Knowing this his relatives and friends would sometimes invite him for drinks. He always drank to his full on those occasions, and did not stop until he was tipsy. Then he would leave and not regret having to go.

He lived in a meager house that barely sheltered him from the wind and the elements. He could only afford short robes of coarse cloth, and these were often patched. His larder was frequently empty. Yet he was at peace. He spent his time writing essays that expressed his ideals, intending them for his own enjoyment only. He was not bothered by the thought of gain or loss, and thus he wished to be until the end of his days. He was appraised thus:

Ch'ien Lou had said: "One should not grieve over poverty or lowliness, nor should one be concerned about riches or honors." Is this saying not appropriate to our subject? Drinking wine and writing poetry for his own enjoyment, such a man deserves to have lived in the time of Lord Wu-huai and Lord Ko-t'ien [legendary rulers of high antiquity].

T'ao Yuan-ming, T'ao. "Peach Blossom Grove" and "The Biography of the Gentleman of the Five Willows." Translations by Jiu-Hwa Lo Upshur.

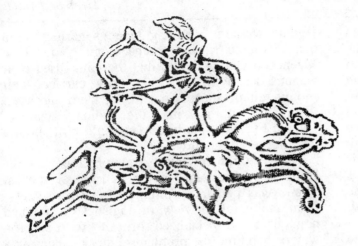

READING 4.3

"FIERCER THAN FEROCITY ITSELF": THE HUNS' ROLE IN HISTORY

▶ **Hun Horseman**

The image of the Huns that has come down through history is one of brutal, barbaric invaders who raped and pillaged with terrifying fury. This "bad press" came about because they had no written language and accounts of them come from their enemies and victims, including the Romans. While historical cliches nearly always contain some truth, modern archaeological finds have made possible a more well-rounded picture of the Huns.

The Huns were nomads of Turkish or Tatar origin, from the steppe region near the Caspian Sea. In the fourth and fifth centuries C.E., they made repeated attacks on the Roman empire. These invasions culminated in the career of Attila, the most famous of the feared Hunnic leaders. The wars that Rome fought with Attila brought both the eastern and western halves of the empire to the edge of collapse.

Archaeologists have been able to show that the Huns were themselves the product of a mobile melting pot, who absorbed a considerable variety of ethnic groups. In part because of their location in the central Eurasian plain, they both assimilated and transmitted the material characteristics of various cultures. Ironically, this most destructive of nomadic warrior groups also acted as a catalyst for cultural exchange throughout Eurasia.

At the peak of the Huns' power, Rome itself paid tribute to their king. Attila, their last great king, extended the Huns' conquests into Gaul (present-day France) and Italy. After his death, however, the Huns played only a very minor role in European history. As the Roman empire disintegrated, the Hunnish population dispersed, some joining with Roman armies, others merging with new groups of invaders along the northern and eastern frontiers.

The following passage describes the life and culture of the Huns, with particular emphasis on the light that archaeology has shed.

QUESTIONS:

1) In what ways have the Huns been victims of "bad press"? Is the bad press in fact justified?
2) What made the Huns such formidable warriors?
3) Can the Huns be compared to the ancient Phoenicians as regards their function as agents of cross-cultural contacts?

Into this vast domain of sedentary farmers and tiny scattered villages [in the Danube Basin] the Huns came riding, "like a tempest of snows from high mountains," says [the fourth-century Roman historian] Ammianus [Marcellinus]. These strangers personified horror: "Fiercer than ferocity itself," [the sixth-century Gothic historian] Jordanes wrote. They "flamed forth against the Goths," those spry riders on their rough horses. They were said to be descendants of outcast warlocks and unclean spirits of the wilderness; in a way there was a fleck of truth here. The Huns were mongrels....

The Huns came from somewhere in the steppes of central Asia and beyond, and in the course of their nomadic life through the centuries they had at least brushing contacts with many cultures.... To handle adequately the problem of the Huns, one would have to master [the] Chinese, Persian, Turkish, Greek, modern Hungarian, and Russian [languages]. Obscure records, needless to say, are in far-flung places. Archaeological finds, too, are impossibly scattered. Some progress has been made even so, and the literature now accumulating is no longer made up exclusively of contradictions and retractions. Archaeology is beginning to help sort out some of the strange assertions culled from Greek and Roman sources.

Ammianus may not have seen many Huns. From his account we derive a picture of a dirty rabble dressed in a patchwork of scruffy fur--"the skins of field mice," he says. They "eat the roots of wild plants and the half-raw flesh of any kind of animal whatever, which they put between their thighs and the backs of their horses and thus warm it a little." This presumably is the literary source of *boeuf tatar*. In actuality, the practice is supposed to have been a way of poulticing a horse's saddlesores.

[Some have] expressed the opinion that the Huns were wretchedly poor and that they were at such a low stage of development that they did not even possess those basic civilized skills spinning and weaving, though [this] point does not hold up too well, in view of the many spindle whorls that have been found. Spinning can be an ambulatory process. Women in the Middle East today wander along after their flocks, teasing out yarn from fleece that is wrapped around the wrist like a cuff. As for weaving, Ammianus refers to Hunnic women "weaving hideous garments" in their wagons, but [archaeologist] J. Otto Maenchen-Helfen denies that the Huns used their wagons as living space. They carried their roomy felt or sheepskin tents in them, he says. Ammianus "turned into the ordinary way of Hunnic life what his informants told him about a Hun horde on the move."

We should not think contemptuously of the Huns as rank savages living in filth and chaos. Theirs was perforce a highly organized society, from the point of view of logistics. Mounted nomadism is a specialized form of life, a specific way of handling the problem of stock raising in a region where the climate changes so drastically in a year that there must be two bases for grazing. Two fixed points of habitation are established, in other words, with regular movement between them according to the cycle of the seasons. In his discussion of Hunnic cauldrons Maenchen-Helfen refers to studies indicating that the nomads may have performed rites on watercourses in the spring, stored the vessels near the water when they went to summer pasture, and used them again in the fall. Transhumance [seasonal movement of herds to different grazing grounds] can entail the negotiation of tremendous distances not only with the herds under control but also with provision for the wants of the entire tribe during the trek. In the year 376 when reports about the Huns first began trickling through, they were supposedly largely dependent on their herds.

The very circumstance of the kind of life they led made it out of the question for the Huns ever to act as a huge, coherent army. The "horde" must not have counted many more than five thousand individuals. Such units, acting independently and not imbued with any particular feeling of kinship and solidarity, could easily turn out fighting on opposite sides. When Huns fell on the Ostrogoths led by ... Vithimiris, that was indeed the situation. Vithimiris had Hunnic mercenaries fighting for him on the Ostrogoth side.

When the Huns arrived on the frontiers of the [Roman] empire, they were an unknown quantity. Our modern chatter about little green men in flying saucers is not too different from the popular reaction in the fourth century to Huns mounted on wiry horses. The Huns were indubitably frightening, not only because of their Mongoloid features, their wild clothing, and their language that practically no one understood. Also frightening was their ability to dart around with lightening speed which must have multiplied their actual numbers in the minds of their alarmed adversaries. Their tactics involved a pretense of scattered flight, with quick reassembling and renewed attack. Then there were those deadly bows that they used. The Hunnic bow was a formidable weapon by anyone's standards. Only a skilled professional could make bows, taking months on end to produce just one. The bow was a composite construction, with a stave made of several carefully selected, cured, and worked materials such as wood, sinew, and horn. The Huns handled them with terrifying precision. We know from ancient art how fierce a backward "Parthian shot" could look.

If they shot arrows like Parthians and spoke a Turkish language and looked like Mongols, who were the Huns, and whence did they come? One clue is an extremely unattractive practice of theirs. They deliberately deformed the heads of their infants, the end result being anything but charming in the adult Hun. As [the fifth-century bishop and author of poems and letters] Sidonius Apollinaris describes them, "Their heads are great round masses rising to a narrow crown." The rest of Sidonius's statement is couched in his usual tortured Latin, but scholars agree on the meaning: the Hunnic nose was flattened "to make room for the helmets." In recent years statistical analysis has revealed that the earliest specimens of deformed skulls come from along the Talas River in the Tien Shan [in northwest China]; next in graves along the Volga; then in the Ukraine, the northern Caucasus, and the Crimea; then in Transcaucasia; and finally in central Europe. This pattern reflects the movements of the Huns.

Another indication is the characteristic Hunnic cauldron. This cast-bronze vessel is cylindrical, very deep, with rigid handle and often a kind of "mushroom" at the top. Its shape is such that it could be lashed onto a pack animal.... Such cauldrons make one think of early Chinese bronzes. Here again, as with the deformed skulls, there is a demonstrated progression from far east to west.

A small "many mountains" incense burner, of the late Chou or early Han period, is an enchanting piece of evidence that the Chinese were aware of the steppe nomads and that on the far side of the wastes they had their own notion of the strange environment in which the wanderers lived. Among the folds of tiny gold- and silver-inlaid mountain ranges toils a little trousered man with his oxcart--a rare illustration in the Orient of barbarian travel there. The combination of the burning of incense and an imagined barbarian world is instructive in itself, because incense was an import throughout China. There were two corridor routes for such trade across the steppe, encircling the Tien Shan region and splitting north and south around the Caspian Sea. The Huns must have come into contact with a number of cultural streams flowing to and fro across their pasturelands.

If it is true, as some scholars think, that part of the heritage of the Huns comes from the Hsiung-Nu nomads, whose enormous domain in the Mongolian steppes rivaled that of the Han Dynasty for centuries, they had a complex, sophisticated background. In the Baikal region, for instance, barrows [earthen or stone burial mounds] have been opened to reveal a wealth of embroidered felts, silks, and fur garments.

Sarmatian influences [from the Sarmatae, a nomadic people related to the Scythians] reached as far east as northern China and the Gobi, and something of this extraordinary culture must also have touched the Huns. The little pendant mirrors that the Huns carried are Sarmatian .... Even in the fastnesses of Siberia the Huns must have acted as go-betweens. They appeared in the Minusinsk Basin in the early centuries of the Christian Era. Along with their advent a new "hybrid" mirror appeared there, in what was an ancient mirror-manufacturing center....

Other ancient nomadic peoples moving westward out of Asia settled near trade routes, whence ideas and art motifs were carried back to the steppe. The amazing animal art of the Scythians spread in that way. Once again the Huns must have played a part in the interchange. Many influences from distant places crossed and recrossed the wastes. In the High Altai [a mountain range bordering present-day northwest China] are astounding frozen tombs that show the sophisticated use of complex materials from places as disparate as Siberia and Greece, China and Persia.

The Huns had their own distinctive ornaments probably made for them by goldsmiths from the Pontic region around the Black Sea. Golden plates, for example, that were fitted onto the rigid parts of a bow are characteristically Hunnic. Other, smaller bows have been found that are entirely covered with plates. It is surmised that these were symbols of a chieftain's authority or that they may have been made especially to be placed with the dead.

More utilitarian plates that are also typical of the Huns have been the subject of lively debate. They are flat, cut sometimes on a curve, sometimes triangular, and covered with a close repoussé "scale" pattern. The German word used to describe the scales is the same one that is applied to the tiny scales on a butterfly's wings, and indeed the effect is almost that delicate.... They were saddle ornaments, probably made especially for burial.... A Korean noble's grave from the same general period contained a saddle decorated with the scale pattern. Hunnic saddles were made of wood, not leather. When Attila thought that he might be defeated in the Battle of the Catalaunian Fields, he had saddles stacked to make a funeral pyre onto which he could leap.

In one famous instance the Hunnic scales appear on a Roman shield, shown on a diptych at Monza. The personage represented in that ivory was once thought to be Aëtius, the patrician who defeated Attila, but now he seems universally to be identified as Aëtius's predecessor, Stilicho. Either way a Hunnic design would have been appropriate. Aëtius was hostage to the Huns for years and was a friend of the Hunnic king Rua, while Stilicho had a loyal Hunnic bodyguard.

The Huns decked their women in beautiful jewelry. There are seven known "diadems," bandlike crowns made of gold sheet applied to bronze and profusely ornamented wit almandines [deep violet-red garnets Almandines come from India, by the way.

These diadems were worn over hoods c veils, and the women to whom they belonge went to their graves so dressed. Findspots fc these crowns extend from Kazakhstan t Hungary. There are also intricate paired piece of gem-covered clips, thought to have been wor at the temples, perhaps on a hood. They ar handsomely worked with filigrain. Again, this i the art of Pontic goldsmiths.

So here they come, those misshapen-heade people with their Chinese wagons and cauldrons their Indian gemstones and Korean saddl ornaments, their Pontic crowns and golden bows and their Sarmatian mirrors, riding horse branded with Turkish *tamgas* (propert marks)....

The first victims of their onslaught, in th year 374, were the Alans who lived in th Danube Basin. Next were the Ostrogoths, wh fell after having tried to make a stand. Ol Ermanaric died, of wounds, chagrin, or suicide who is to say?--and his wobbly [Ostrogothic domain disintegrated into vassalage.

The changes that the conquest wrought wer more drastic for the Huns than for the conquerec peoples, whom they could now exploit. Thi must have been the first time that the Huns hac continuous access to the products of agricultura settlements, as opposed to what they could snatc in sporadic raids. The new arrangemen gradually altered their living patterns. By Attila's time [reign 434-453] ..., they were living in wooden houses built for them by Gothic carpenters and wearing linen.

Randers-Pehrson, Justine Davis. *Barbarians and Romans. The Birth Struggle of Europe, A.D. 400-700.* Norman Univ. of Oklahoma Press, 1983. Pp. 40-47.

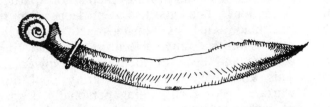

BASIL II, BYZANTINE EMPEROR AND "SLAYER OF BULGARS"

While the western Roman Empire collapsed in the fifth century C.E., the eastern part survived for another eleven hundred years until 1453. The Eastern Roman Empire is also known as the Byzantine Empire, from the Greek city of, Byzantium, where the Emperor Constantine established a new capital city, Constantinople, in 330.

The Byzantine Empire experienced two periods of great prosperity. The first was early, during the reign of Justinian I (r. 527-565) and his wife, Theodora, who tried to revive the former glory of the Roman Empire and to reclaim territories in the west lost to Germanic peoples. This effort was only briefly successful. To the east, the empire was increasingly threatened and hard pressed by the Sassanian Empire in Persia and, from the seventh century, by the Arab Muslims.

The second period of prosperity for the Byzantine Empire was during the Macedonian dynasty (867-1042). At the height of their power, the Macedonian emperors reconquered lost territories in Bulgaria, northern Mesopotamia, and Syria. The greatest Macedonian emperor was Basil II (r. 976-1025). An able general, he was best known for crushing a rebellion in Bulgaria, earning the nickname Bulgaroctonos ("slayer of Bulgars") in the process. He also extended Byzantine control into Armenia and Georgia, till then independent principalities.

There was a revival of intellectual activity during the Macedonian dynasty. Ancient manuscripts were copied and preserved, learned books were written and encyclopedias were compiled in classical Greek. Michael Constantine Psellus, a scholar and statesman prominent at the court of Constantine IX (r. 1042-1055), wrote the *Chronographia*, which includes a wealth of fascinating first-hand observations of the lives of several emperors. The following is his account of Emperor Basil II.

QUESTIONS:

1) What sort of political shrewdness does Psellus ascribe to Basil II?
2) Does Psellus seem to present an unbiased portrait of Basil II?
3) Can we identify stereotypically "tyrannical" behaviors in Basil II as he is portrayed by Psellus?

Basil, after expelling the barbarians from the empire, proceeded to dominate his own people, and dominate is indeed the right word.... After humbling the noble families and levelling them with the rest of society, he began to engage in power politics with great shrewdness. For his closest ministers, he chose men who possessed neither keen minds, nor noble blood, nor great learning. To these he committed the imperial rescripts and state secrets. However, his responses to inquiries and petitions were nearly always the same, couched in blunt, forthright language (Basil avoided ornate phraseology in both spoken and written communications). In fact, he would simply give impromptu dictation to his secretaries, just as the words came to mind, with no pointless attempts at subtlety.

Basil made his own life easier by his practice of puncturing the arrogance or envy of his subjects. He also kept a close watch over the contents of the treasury, accumulating a large reserve through stringent frugality and new accessions of funds. As a result, the imperial treasury eventually grew to a total of 200,000 talents. The full extent of his acquisitions beggars description. He collected up all the treasures of the barbarian peoples along the empire's borders--the Iberians [in present-day Georgia], Arabians, Celts, and Scyths--and stored them in his own coffers. Besides this, he hoarded up in his treasure-house vast sums exacted from defeated rebellious subjects. Eventually, the vaulted halls of the treasury proved too small and he took to constructing underground chambers to hold much of his riches, in the Egyptian manner. Basil personally had little joy of all this wealth; indeed, even the most gorgeous items--pearls and colorful gem-stones--adorned no crowns or pectorals, but lay hidden away in these repositories beneath the earth. When he did show himself before officials in procession or in audience, he wore a garment of dark, not brilliant, purple, with a few gems to signal his status. Since he spent most of his reign with the military along the frontiers forestalling barbarian incursions, he withdrew little from the treasury and increased its contents many fold.

In campaigning against the barbarians, Basil shunned the practice of other emperors, who normally set out in mid-spring and ended the expedition at the end of the summer; instead, he returned only after accomplishing his mission. To the cold of winter and the heat of summer alike, he was quite insensible. He conditioned himself against thirst and, indeed, kept tightly reined all his appetites and human needs--the man had iron self-control. He was extremely well-informed about the details of military life. He did not stop at a general understanding of the army's talent, the relations of the various elements within the whole, and the diverse combinations and arrangements of particular formations. His expertise went deeper than that: he made it his business to know the responsibilities and functions of the junior officers and even of men of still lower rank. This knowledge served the army well during warfare. For Basil, being personally cognizant of each man's temperament and combat duties, knew how to assign tasks appropriate to each rank and to each individual's make-up and background.

Furthermore, Basil was a shrewd tactician, partly through study, partly through his own ingenuity in the actual situations of battle. He undertook to guide the course of battle and to array his troops according to his own battle plans, but he avoided exposing himself directly to the chances of actual combat, to evade capture should the tide of battle turn suddenly. For this reason, he generally kept the main body of his troops stationary, building war-machinery and skirmishing from a distance, leaving the rapid maneuvering to his light-armed forces. Having engaged the enemy, he methodically set up a regular system of liaison among the various contingents of the army. The whole system was like a tower, with close communications from headquarters to cavalry detachments to light infantrymen to the units of heavy infantrymen. As soon as all was in readiness, he gave orders that the soldiers should proceed in fixed ranks, with no breaking of those ranks under any circumstances. Those who broke this order, even if they did so courageously to engage the enemy at the forefront, could expect no rewards for their acts of fortitude. Rather, Basil would have them summarily discharged and treated like common criminals. For, in his view, it was the rigid coherence and solidity of the army that ensured victories and made the Romans so unconquerable. The men used to complain openly about the punctilious inspections Basil always made before battle, but the emperor opposed his common sense to their disdain. He would hear their gripes and then observe with a smile that, but for his precautions, their battles might go on indefinitely.

Basil had a double temperament, adaptable both to the emergencies of war time and the tranquillity of peace time. But in fact, he was more a tyrant in war and an emperor in peace. He normally controlled his anger, like smoldering embers beneath the ash. If his battlefield orders were disobeyed, however, then, once he was back in the palace, he let his anger flame forth. The culprit sometimes felt the terrible force of his vengeance. He typically held fast to his own view, but did on occasion change his mind. He also had a practice of determining what individuals were really the prime movers of a crime, letting off those who were merely instruments. Most transgressors were forgiven, because Basil felt some compassion for them or took some interest in their plight. He seldom changed a decision once made, though he was very cautious in reaching it. As a result, his estimate of his friends was unalterable, unless he was forced by evidence to relinquish it. On the other side of the coin, once he had shown anger toward someone, he was very slow to temper his resentment. His opinions of men were, in his own mind, of the order of inspired and irreversible judgments.

To turn from his character to his personal appearance: the latter was well-suited to the inborn dignity of the man. His eyes were light blue and brilliant, his eyebrows were arched and expressive of self-regard rather than beetling or morose or forming one straight line, like a woman's. The eyes themselves glowed with a manly vigor, being neither sunken (a sign of deceitfulness and wiliness) nor protuberant (a sign of flightiness). His countenance was well-rounded and his neck strong and not too long. His chest appeared neither thrust outward, nor merely hanging from his shoulders, nor sunken and restrictive. It was, in short, just right, as was the rest of his well-proportioned frame.

He was a bit below normal in height, though he held himself well and seemed well-shaped in his physique. On foot, he presented a figure like that of many others, but on horseback he was magnificent: rider and horse both seemed the work of the sculptor of some great equestrian statue. When he charged to the attack, he bore himself firmly and upright, whether going uphill or down. When checking his horse, reining in, he used to rise up as if winged; he was perfectly smooth in mounting or dismounting.

As he grew older, the hair beneath his chin fell out, but that of his cheeks grew more profusely, so that he would entwine the two sides to give him the look of a full beard. He had a habit of rolling his beard between his fingers, particularly when angry, or especially attentive, or lost in thought. He also liked to stand with hands on hips, arms akimbo. He was not an impressive orator, his speech being clipped and choppy; he spoke more the language of a farmer than of a learned man. His laugh was vociferous and shook his body.

Basil lived and reigned a very long time, more indeed than any other sovereign. From birth to his twentieth year, he shared imperial authority with his father and Phokas Nikophoros, and then with the latter's successor, John Tzimiskes. He was, of course, in a subordinate position during this period of his life, but then for the next fifty-two years he was supreme ruler. He died, therefore, in the seventy-second year of his life [15 December 1025].

Psellus, Michael. *Chronographie, ou histoire d'un siècle de Byzance (976-1077)*. Ed. and [French] trans. Emile Renauld. Paris: Les Belles Lettres, 1926. Book 1.30-37. English translation by James P. Holoka.

LIFE AND DEATH AMONG NORTHMEN ALONG THE VOLGA RIVER IN 922

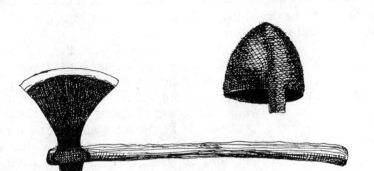

▶ Battle-ax and Helmet

While eastern Slavs began to settle in present-day European Russia in the sixth century, little is known of their history or society. The traditional date for the beginning of the Russian state is 862 C.E., when the Scandinavian chief called Rurik (or Ryurik) became ruler of the city of Novgorod. Between 800 and 1000, people called Vikings or Norsemen from Scandinavia began to raid, trade, and settle across much of Europe. The Russian Chronicles called them Varangians or Rus, from which the name Rossiya or Russia derives. During the ninth century, these enterprising merchants and adventurers crossed the Baltic Sea and followed the courses of the Dnepr and the Volga rivers south to the Black and Caspian Seas. They founded two important states centered on Novgorod and Kiev. The House of Rurik ruled present-day Ukraine from Kiev for several centuries. The rulers of Kiev were converted to Eastern Christianity in the tenth century by missionaries from the Byzantine Empire. As a result, Byzantine civilization exerted a strong influence on Russian culture.

The Kievan state dominated western Russia until its destruction by the Mongols in 1240. Russia subsequently endured three centuries of Mongol overlordship, after which it came under Moscow's leadership.

The passage that follows is an account of the manners and mores of the Northmen or Russians who had settled on the banks of Volga River. The reporter is Ahmed ibn Fadlan, who observed them while traveling to Bulgaria as ambassador of the Abbasid caliph Al-Muktadir (r. 908-932) in 922. Though the refined sensibilities of this Muslim envoy were offended by what he saw among the coarse Northmen, he nonetheless took care to record in accurate detail the customs he observed, including an interesting account of the suttee-like sacrifice of a woman at the funeral of a prominent man.

QUESTIONS:

1) What does Ahmed ibn Fadlan find most objectionable about the Northmen he describes?

2) Is the human sacrifice carried out during the funeral of the Norse nobleman utterly unique or are there parallels from other cultures and times?

3) Does the system of justice among the Northmen seem primitive? reasonable? both? neither?

I saw how the Northmen had arrived with their wares, and pitched their camp beside the Volga. Never did I see people so gigantic; they are tall as palm trees, and florid and ruddy of complexion.... Every one carries an axe, a dagger, and a sword, and without these weapons they are never seen. Their swords are broad, with wavy lines, and of Frankish make. From the tip of the finger-nails to the neck, each man of them is tattooed with pictures of trees, living beings, and other things. The women carry, fastened to their breast, a little case of iron, copper, silver, or gold, according to the wealth and resources of their husbands. Fastened to this case they wear a ring, and upon that a dagger, all attached to their breast. About their necks they wear gold and silver chains.... Their most highly prized ornaments consist of small green shells, of one of the varieties which are found in [the bottom of] ships. They make great efforts to obtain these, paying as much as a dirham [an Arabic monetary unit] for such a shell, and stringing them as a necklace for their wives.

They are the filthiest race that God ever created. They do not wipe themselves after going to stool, nor wash themselves after a nocturnal pollution, any more than if they were wild asses.

They come from their own country, anchor their ships in the Volga, which is a great river, and build large wooden houses on its banks. In every such house there live ten or twenty, more or fewer. Each man has a couch, where he sits with the beautiful girls he has for sale. Here he is as likely as not to enjoy one of them while a friend looks on. At times several of them will be thus engaged at the same moment, each in full view of the others. Now and again a merchant will resort to a house to purchase a girl, and find her master thus embracing her, and not giving over until he has fully had his will.

Every morning a girl comes and brings a tub of water, and places it before her master. In this he proceeds to wash his face and hands, and then his hair, combing it out over the vessel. Thereupon he blows his nose, and spits into the tub, and, leaving no dirt behind, conveys it all into this water. When he has finished, the girl carries the tub to the man next him, who does the same. Thus she continues carrying the tub from one to another, till each of those who are in the house has blown his nose and spit into the tub, and washed his face and hair....

If one of their number falls sick, they set up a tent at a distance, in which they place him, leaving bread and water at hand. Thereafter, they never approach nor speak to him, nor visit him the whole time, especially if he is a poor person or a slave. If he recovers and rises from his sick bed, he returns to his own. If he dies, they cremate him; but if he is a slave they leave him as he is, till at length he becomes the food of dogs and birds of prey.

If they catch a thief or a robber, they lead him to a thick and lofty tree, fasten a strong rope round him, string him up, and let him hang until he drops to pieces by the action of the wind and rain.

I was told that the least of what they do for their chiefs when they die, is to consume them with fire. When I was finally informed of the death of one of their magnates, I sought to witness what befell. First they laid him in his grave--over which a roof was erected--for the space of ten days, until they had completed the cutting and sewing of his clothes.... At the death of a rich man, they bring together his goods, and divide them into three parts. The first of these is for his family; the second is expended for the garments they make; and with the third they purchase strong drink, against the day when the girl resigns herself to death, and is burned with her master. To the use of wine they abandon themselves in mad fashion, drinking it day and night; and not seldom does one die with the cup in his hand.

When one of their chiefs dies, his family asks his girls and pages: "Which of you will die with him?" Then one of them answers, "I." From the time that he [a page] utters this word, he is no longer free: should he wish to draw back, he is not permitted. For the most part, however, it is the girls that offer themselves. So, when the man of whom I spoke had died, they asked his girls, "Who will die with him?" One of them answered, "I." She was then committed to two girls, who were to keep watch over her, accompany her wherever she went, and even, on occasion, wash her feet. The people now began to occupy themselves with the dead man--to cut out the clothes for him, and to prepare whatever else was needful. During the whole of this period, the girl gave herself over to drinking and singing, and was cheerful and gay.

When the day was now come that the dead man and the girl were to be committed to the flames, I went to the river in which his ship lay, but found that it had already been drawn ashore…. The dead man, meanwhile, lay at a distance in his grave, from which they had not yet removed him. Next they brought a couch, placed it in the ship, and covered it with Greek cloth of gold, wadded and quilted, with pillows of the same material. There came an old crone, whom they call the angel of death, and spread the articles mentioned on the couch. It was she who attended to the sewing of the garments, and to all the equipment; it was she, also, who was to slay the girl. I saw her; she was dark …, thick-set, with a lowering countenance.

When they came to the grave, they removed the earth from the wooden roof, set the latter aside, and drew out the dead man in the loose wrapper in which he had died. Then I saw that he had turned quite black, by reason of the coldness of that country. Near him in the grave they had placed strong drink, fruits, and a lute; and these they now took out. Except for his color, the dead man had not changed. They now clothed him in drawers, leggings, boots, and a *kurtak* [loose shirt] and *chaftan* [long, belted tunic] of cloth of gold, with golden buttons, placing on his head a cap made of cloth of gold, trimmed with sable. Then they carried him into a tent placed in the ship, seated him on the wadded and quilted covering, supported him with the pillows, and, bringing strong drink, fruits, and basil, placed them all beside him. Then they brought a dog, which they cut in two, and threw into the ship; laid all his weapons beside him; and led up two horses, which they chased until they were dripping with sweat, whereupon they cut them in pieces with their swords, and threw the flesh into the ship. Two oxen were then brought forward, cut into pieces, and flung into the ship. Finally they brought a cock and a hen, killed them, and threw them in also.

The girl who had devoted herself to death meanwhile walked to and fro, entering one after another of the tents which they had there. The occupant of each tent lay with her, saying, "Tell your master, 'I [the man] did this only for love of you.'"

When it was now Friday afternoon, they led the girl to an object which they had constructed, and which looked like the framework of a door. She then placed her feet on the extended hands of the men, was raised up above the framework, and uttered something in her language, whereupon they let her down. They again raised her, and she did as at first. Once more they let her down, and then lifted her a third time, while she did as at the previous times. They then handed her a hen, whose head she cut off and threw away; but the hen itself they cast into the ship. I inquired of the interpreter what it was that she had done. He replied: "The first time she said," 'Lo, there is my master, who is sitting in Paradise. Paradise is so beautiful, so green. With him are his men and boys. He calls me, so bring me to him.'" Then they led her away to the ship.

Here she took off her two bracelets, and gave them to the old woman who was called the angel of death, and who was to murder her. She also drew off her two anklets, and passed them to the two serving-maids, who were the daughters of the so-called angel of death. Then they lifted her into the ship, but did not yet admit her to the tent. Now men came up with shields and staves, and handed her a cup of strong drink. This she took, sang over it, and emptied it. "With this," so the interpreter told me, "she is taking leave of those who are dear to her." Then another cup was handed her, which she also took, and began a lengthy song. The crone admonished her to drain the cup without lingering, and to enter the tent where her master lay. By this time, as it seemed to me, the girl had become dazed; she made as though she would enter the tent, and had brought her head forward between the tent and the ship, when the hag seized her by the head, and dragged her in. At this moment the men began to beat upon their shields with the staves, in order to drown the noise of her outcries, which might have terrified the other girls, and deterred them from seeking death with their masters in the future. Then six men followed into the tent, and each and every one had carnal companionship with her. Then they laid her down by her master's side, while two of the men seized her by the feet, two by the hands. The old woman known as the angel of death now knotted a rope around her neck, and handed the ends to two of the men to pull. Then with a broad-bladed dagger she smote her between the ribs, and drew the blade forth, while the two men strangled her with the rope till she died.

The next of kin to the dead man now drew near, and, taking a piece of wood, lighted it, and walked backwards toward the ship, holding the stick in one hand, with the other placed upon his buttocks (he being naked), until the wood which had been piled under the ship was ignited. Then the others came up with staves and firewood, each one carrying a stick already lighted at the upper end, and threw it all on the pyre. The pile was soon aflame, then the ship, finally the tent, the man, and the girl, and everything else in the ship. A terrible storm began to blow up, and thus intensified the flames, and gave wings to the blaze.

At my side stood one of the Northmen, and I heard him talking with the interpreter, who stood near him. I asked the interpreter what the Northmen had said, and received this answer: "'You Arabs,' he said, 'must be a stupid set! You take him who is to you the most revered and beloved of men, and cast him into the ground, to be devoured by creeping things and worms. We, on the other hand, burn him in a twinkling, so that he instantly, without a moment's delay, enters into Paradise.' At this he burst out into uncontrollable laughter, and then continued: 'It is the love of the Master [God] that causes the wind to blow and snatch him away in an instant.'" And, in very truth, before an hour had passed, ship, wood, and girl had, with the man, turned to ashes.

Thereupon they heaped over the place where the ship had stood something like a rounded hill, and, erecting on the center of it a large birchen post, wrote on it the name of the deceased, along with that of the king of the Northmen. Having done this, they left the spot.

Cook, Albert Stanburrough. "Ibn Fadlan's Account of Scandinavian Merchants on the Volga in 922." *Journal of English and Germanic Philology* 22 (1923) 56-63.

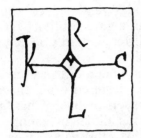

A REPORT CARD FROM CHARLEMAGNE

Monogram of Charlemagne (Karolus)

Charlemagne or Charles the Great was the most famous ruler of the European Middle Ages. He enlarged his kingdom to include present-day France, northern Italy, and parts of central Europe. He reigned both as king of the Franks (768-814 C.E.) and, after his coronation in Rome by Pope Leo III, as Roman Emperor (800-814). He was a devout Christian and often forcibly converted peoples he conquered to Catholic Christianity. He fostered reforms in various Christian institutions and monastic life, and promoted adherence to Christian doctrine.

Charlemagne had the greatest respect for education. Under his guidance and patronage, the royal palace at Aix-la-Chapelle (present-day Aachen, in Germany) became a flourishing center of learning during the "Carolingian Renaissance." He welcomed scholars from all over Europe, notably the famous English priest and savant, Alcuin, whom Charlemagne placed in charge of the palace school. The emperor also encouraged and made available resources for the copying and preservation of manuscripts and advocated the study of Latin as the language of learning.

Charlemagne was an amazingly versatile man: on the one hand a Germanic warrior-king, on the other an accomplished linguist and Latin scholar. While he admired literature and honored men of letters, he never learned to write, though he tried diligently.

The first of the following passages is by Einhard (c. 770-840), who attended the palace school at Aachen as a youth and later served as Charlemagne's adviser for more than twenty years. His lively and entertaining biography of Charlemagne is modeled on the Roman biographer Suetonius's life of Augustus. The second passage is from an anecdotal work written some years after Charlemagne's death by Notker the Stammerer (c. 840-912), a monk at the Benedictine monastery of St. Gall. The selections describe some of Charlemagne's personal habits and idiosyncrasies and his deep concern with the education of the young.

QUESTIONS:

1) The Roman author Juvenal once wrote that the ideal for a human being was to attain "a sound mind in a sound body." According to the selection from Einhard, did Charlemagne approach that ideal?

2) What sort of personality emerges from the anecdotes recounted by Notker?

3) How did Charlemagne's Christian faith manifest itself in his conduct of affairs and his policies?

He [Charlemagne] was a big, sturdy man of imposing stature, but not disproportionately so-- for it is said his height measured seven times the length of his foot. His head was rounded on top, his eyes very large and lively, his nose a bit larger than the norm, his hair a handsome gray-white, his face happy and jovial. Whether sitting or standing, he gave the appearance of great authority and dignity. Though his neck was thick and short and he had a bit of a paunch, still the seemly look of the rest of his body concealed these. He had a strong gait, and his whole bearing was stalwart; he spoke distinctly but softly for a man of his size. He had excellent health, except that he suffered frequently from fever during the last four years of his life and near the end of his life was lame in one foot. Even then he behaved to suit himself rather follow the orders of doctors, whom he despised because they advised him to forego the roast dishes he was used to in favor of boiled fare.

He was an avid horseman and hunter. This was typical of his people, you can scarcely find another nation on earth which can equal the Franks in these pursuits. He enjoyed natural hot baths and often exercised by swimming, at which he was so adept that none could match him. It was on account of this that he built a palace at Aachen and lived there continuously in the latter years of his life till his death. He used to invite not only his sons to the bath but also various worthies and friends, and sometimes even a whole crowd of aides and bodyguards, so that often a hundred or more men were bathing at once.

He wore traditional Frankish clothing: linen undershirt and shorts, a tunic trimmed with a silk edging, and stockings. He wrapped his legs and wore shoes on his feet. In winter, he protected his chest and shoulders with a jacket made from otter or ermine pelts. He was clad in a blue cloak and always had strapped on a sword, whose haft and belt were of gold or silver. He sometimes sported a bejeweled sword, but only on festive occasions or to impress foreign envoys. He disliked non-Frankish clothing, however attractive it might appear, and would never deign to wear them. He made exceptions to this preference when asked by Pope Hadrian, and again by his successor Pope Leo, to don a long tunic, chlamys [Greek cloak], and Roman style shoes. On festival days, he would go forth in gold cloth, gem-studded shoes, and a cloak secured with a golden brooch. On all other days his dress differed hardly at all from that of the common folk.

He was moderate in eating and especially in drinking; he despised drunkenness in anyone, let alone in himself or one of his family. He could not be so fastidious in eating, and he used to complain that abstinence was harmful to his constitution. He gave banquets very rarely, normally only on feast days, but then to a large number of invited guests. His dinner each day was in four courses, not counting the roasts his hunters would bring in on spits, and which he enjoyed eating more than anything else. During his meal he would listen to music or a recitation. Histories and the deeds of the ancients were favorites. He also liked the works of Saint Augustine, particularly his *City of God*. He was so sparing in his drinking of wine or other beverages that he would seldom drink more than three times in the course of dinner.

In the summer, after lunch, he would take some fruit and a drink and then take off his clothes and shoes--just as he did in the evening-- and nap for two or three hours. He slept so lightly in the evening that he would awaken and get up three or four times a night.

In the morning, while donning shoes and clothing, he would admit not only his friends, but also, if the Count of the Palace indicated there was a dispute that could not be adjudicated without his ruling, he would bid the disputants be brought in as if he were sitting in a tribunal; he would then hear the case and render a judgment. At the same time he would proceed with whatever official business was pressing on that day and issue orders to his ministers.

As a speaker, he had a fluent and rich eloquence and could express perspicuously whatever he wished. He was not content with his native tongue alone, but took pains to learn foreign languages also. Indeed, he was so adept in Latin that he was accustomed to speak it just as well as his native tongue. Greek he could understand better than speak. He was so proficient a speaker that he sometimes seemed long-winded.

He cultivated the liberal arts very assiduously, admiring those learned in them, and distinguishing them with high honors. He studied grammar with the elderly Peter, deacon of Pisa. All other subjects he studied with Albinus, surnamed Alcuin, also a deacon, a man of the Saxon race in Britain and the most learned of all scholars. With him, Charlemagne devoted much time and energy to the study of rhetoric, dialectic, and particularly astronomy. He learned mathematics and painstakingly drew the course of the stars with wonderful attention to detail. He tried also to write and used to keep tablets and notebooks around him in bed under his pillows, so he could devote his spare time to practicing the formation of letters. But he had begun too late in life and made little progress.

The Emperor practiced the Christian religion, in which he had been raised from infancy, very piously and with much devotion. Because of this zeal, he had built at Aachen a most magnificent basilica adorned with gold and silver and with lamps, lattices, and doors of solid bronze. When he could not get columns and marble for the construction anywhere else, he ordered them to be transported from Rome and Ravenna. So long as his health allowed, he diligently went to church mornings, evenings, and late night hours, as well as for Mass. He took care that all ceremonies should be conducted with the greatest respect, often warning the custodians not to allow anything improper or unclean to be brought into or left in the church. He procured for the church sacred vessels of gold and silver and priestly vestments in such quantity that at holy services even those who attended as doormen (surely the lowest ranking church officials) had no need to serve in their ordinary clothes. He carefully revised the practices of ecclesiastical reading and singing. Though he was himself very proficient in both these activities, he did not read publicly and sang (in a low voice) only along with the congregation.

Charlemagne was quite active in supporting the poor and in the voluntary charity that the Greeks call *eleemosyne* [alms]. He did these charitable acts not only in his own country and realm; he also sent money overseas to Syria, Egypt, and Africa, to Jerusalem, Alexandria, and Carthage, showing compassion for poor Christians wherever he might learn they were. For this reason, too, he cultivated the friendship of kings across the seas, so that some comfort and relief might come to needy Christians under their rule.

* * * * *

When Charlemagne began his sole rule of the western regions of the world, learning had nearly fallen into oblivion in his whole realm and the worship of the true God also was not very enthusiastic. It so happened that just then two Scots from Ireland arrived with some British merchants on the shores of Gaul. These men were unsurpassed in their knowledge of both sacred and profane letters. These men, though they had no actual wares to sell, used to exclaim to the crowds of market goers: "If anyone wants wisdom, let him come to us and get it, for we have it on sale...." Charlemagne, always avid for wisdom, ordered them to be brought to him as quickly as possible. He asked if it was true, as word had it, that they truly possessed wisdom. They responded "Yes we do and we are prepared, in the Lord's name, to impart it to those worthily seeking it." When he inquired what price they asked, they answered "We ask no price, Oh king, save only a suitable place and intelligent minds to teach, together with the food and clothing needed to accomplish our mission." Delighted with this response, Charlemagne kept the two with him for some time. Later, when he had to set out on a military expedition, he set up one of the two, Clement by name, in Gaul. He entrusted to him a goodly number of boys from the nobility and from the middle and lower classes as well. He ordered that food and whatever accommodations were necessary for study should be made available to them....

When, much later, the victorious Charlemagne returned to Gaul, he ordered the boys he had entrusted to Clement to come to him with their compositions in prose and verse. The middle and lower class boys brought works unexpectedly replete with the signs of learning; the noble boys, however, turned in work flawed with all manner of absurdities. Then the very wise Charlemagne, mimicking the court of the eternal Judge, separated to the right those who had done good work and addressed them as follows: "Thank you, my sons, for so carefully fulfilling my command and taking the opportunity of pursuing what was useful to you. Now then carry your studies to completion and I will grant you episcopal seats and splendid monasteries; you will always win honor in my eyes." Then, turning his face to those on his left with great sternness and with a glance that burned into their consciences, he contemptuously thundered rather than spoke these terrifying words to them: "You nobles, sons of the eminent, you pampered pretty boys, confident in your birthrights and possessions, caring not a straw for my command or your own glory, you have neglected your literary studies and indulged in games of luxurious idleness and inane pastimes." In sending them away, he raised his venerable head and invincible right hand to the heavens and thundered thus against them: "By the heavenly King, I disdain your noble birth and good looks. Let others admire you for these. Know this for a certainty: unless you immediately begin to make good your former delinquency by conscientious study, you will never gain anything worth having from Charlemagne."

Jaffé, Philipp, ed. *Einharti Vita Caroli Magni*. Chaps. 22-27. *Monachus Sangallensis De Carolo Magno*. Chaps. 1-3. In *Bibliotheca Rerum Germanicarum*. Vol. 4: *Monumenta Carolina*. Berlin 1867. Pp. 529-533, 631-633. Translations by James P. Holoka.

WE ARE WHAT WE EAT: FOOD AND DRINK IN THE TIME OF CHARLEMAGNE

Food and drink are a constant in the texture of everyday existence. They not only sustain life, they can materially enhance it by providing a pleasurable experience. The quality of life--both biologically and aesthetically--is immediately linked to the quality of one's diet.

One of the special attractions of travel to foreign lands is the chance to encounter and enjoy food that differs from our own familiar fare. It can be similarly enjoyable and useful for students of history, in their intellectual travels to other times, and especially to remote periods, to consider the foods available in those times. In a very basic sense, this can furnish a more vivid notion of what it would have been like to live in other eras of history.

The following account of food and drink in the Carolingian era (c. 800 C.E.) describes a diet that had remained fairly constant in Europe from the days of the Roman Empire. For the lower orders of society, it was a simple, largely vegetarian diet; for the aristocrats, the menu was much more varied and palatable. Perhaps most striking for the modern reader, however, is what is missing: Europeans, Africans, and Asians before the voyages of discovery in the western hemisphere, beginning with Columbus in 1492, lacked such (to us) nearly indispensable items as potatoes, tomatoes, corn (maize), chocolate, tobacco, coffee, cola drinks.

The need to secure sufficient, and preferably plentiful, supplies of food has always preoccupied individuals and societies. The natural demand for nourishment has motivated great historical upheavals of mass migration and warfare. In the following passage, we see leading politicians and churchmen--including even the Emperor Charlemagne--carefully attending to the provision of both staples like meat, poultry, and cheese as well as less essential products like honey. For every human being, the difference between starvation or mere subsistence and the joyful satisfaction of an appetite has always depended directly on the make-up of one's diet.

QUESTIONS:

1) Does anything about the typical monk's diet seem surprising?
2) Do religious scruples about over-indulgence play a part in the monks' diet?
3) What was the place of alcoholic beverages in the time of Charlemagne?

To Each His Menu

The peasant picked vegetables from the patches near his house--peas, vetches, and beans. In addition, he combed the underbrush, marsh, and river for supplements to his diet.

Monks, in obedience to the Benedictine rule, got one meal in winter and two in summer: a *collatio* at noon and the *cena* in the evening. The monastic rule prescribed a daily pound of bread, a hemin of wine (between a quarter and half a liter), or double that amount of beer. It forbade the monks to eat fruit or lettuce between meals. Each meal included three dishes (*pulmentaria*) of dairy products and vegetables. At Reichenau, sick monks could request *warmosium*, a dish apparently made of cream and leeks. Feasts, held in the great monasteries on holy days or royal anniversaries, consisted of a special meal called the *refectio*. Poultry, such as stuffed chickens and geese, and cakes were distributed. This scandalized the Breton ascetics, who ate only barley bread--and that mixed with ashes, bowls of gruel, and vegetables, denying themselves even fish and shellfish. On Saturday and Sunday, they accepted a little cheese thinned with water. At Guéret, Saint Pardoux refused all poultry, preferring to eat the mushrooms the peasants brought him. Walafrid Strabo recommended a more moderate frugality: "some salt, bread, leeks, fish, and wine; that is our menu. I would not spare even a glance for the splendid tables of kings."

Princes and aristocrats could not forgo meat, particularly roasted meat. Charlemagne took an aversion to his doctors because they advised him to give up his accustomed roast meat in favor of boiled meat. Spicy dishes were particularly appreciated at the tables of the great: "This table covered with pimentoed meat is a far cry from the insipidity of boiled food and softly pressed curds of milk," wrote Theodulf in a description of a meal at Aix-la-Chapelle.

Main Ingredients

Though Carolingian menus have not survived, we can study the principal ingredients of the diet of the time.

Bread, particularly white bread, was the dietary base of the most privileged classes as well as monks and canons. At Corbie, 450 loaves were baked every day, and the oven at Saint-Gall was reputed to have a capacity of nearly 1000 loaves. While white bread was kept at Saint Denis for monks and guests, the servants had to be content with rye bread. In the same monastery, some flour was kept back to make what the text calls *pulempta*, or polenta (porridge). Finally a gruel made of barley or oats was used by many peasants as a substitute for bread.

Meat was brought in from the hunt. When Gerald of Aurillac's cook lamented that he had no meat, a deer happily came to fall at his feet. That enabled him to prepare "a delicate repast worthy of his lord." In addition, the flesh of cattle, sheep, and even goats was consumed. Pork occupied a special position of its own. At Corbie, an entire chapter of Adalhard's *Institutiones* was devoted to pork. He figured that 600 pigs a year would be consumed in the refectory, with 50 reserved to the abbot. Monastic cellarers and royal intendants [managers] had pork smoked or salted to ensure provisions of meat through the winter. While such parts as tripe had to be consumed swiftly, salted pork (*baccones*) hung in the *lardarium* of Corbie waiting for several months to be eaten.

When they wanted to be sparing, Carolingians ate fish. Charlemagne advised his intendants that "when the fish in our ponds are sold, new fish should be put in their place, so that there may always be fish." In the palace, fish dishes were prepared for service with condiments. It was considered good manners to eat them without turning them over. The cellarer at Reichenau supplied the fishermen with nets, indicating which fish were in season in the Rhine, and paid them with a cup of wine for their catch. Though many texts mention fish and fisheries, few are informative about the varieties of fish. The Abbot of Saint-Denis was supplied with fat fish in Cotentin and flat fish in Ponthieu; conger eels were caught in the Rance; 200 eels, a much sought-after food, had to be delivered to the Abbot of Saint-Germain-des-Prés each year.

When there was a feast, eggs, geese, moorhens, and chickens flowed into the kitchens of the great lay and ecclesiastical aristocrats. Charlemagne protected himself against a possible shortage of fowl by ordering that his great estates should maintain a stock of at least 100 hens and

30 geese, while the smaller farms should have 50 hens and 12 geese. It has been estimated that in the year 893 the Abbey of Prüm controlled 2000 farms with a production of roughly 20,000 eggs a year.

Dairy products were more difficult to procure unless they were preserved in the form of butter and cheese. A bishop who was entertaining Charlemagne substituted cheese for the fish which he lacked. He was astounded when the Emperor removed the crust, which the clergymen considered the best part, before eating it. While thanking his host, Charles asked him to send two carts of the cheese to Aix each year. Monks consumed large quantities of cheese. The tenants of Saint-Germain-des-Prés furnished them with 160 *pensae* of cheese. If, as we suppose, a *pensa* was roughly 75 pounds, that would represent 12,000 pounds. The estates of Boulogne and Therouanne sent 21 *pensae* to Saint-Wandrille. Ten sheepfolds were designated to produce cheese at Corbie. When entertained by the Bishop of Utrecht, Alcuin said he had been given an excellent meal of honey, gruel, and butter, for, he said, the Frisians have neither oil nor wine. Fat and lard were generally replaced by butter during days of abstinence and Lent.

Turning to a discussion of vegetables, we find two categories. The term legumes (*legumina*) referred to the vegetables which grew in the fields: beans, lentils, peas, green beans, chick peas, and other types of edible herbs. Roots (*olera*) grew in the kitchen gardens: leeks, garlic, onions, carrots, etc. The capitulary [collection of ordinances] *De villis* and the plan of Saint-Gall include exhaustive lists of garden stocks. The bishop's gardens provided vegetables for the canons' table, the most common being beans and leeks. The tenants of Saint-Denis had to supply the abbey daily with "crushed herbs for the preparation of legumes."

Everyone appreciated fruits. Complaints were common against the schoolboys who devastated the orchards. The redactor of the capitulary *De villis* lingered over the names of certain types of apples: sweet apples and sour apples; apples for immediate eating and those for keeping. Intendants planned for the provision of fruits over as long a period as possible. At Bobbio, there was a *custos pomorum* [fruits custodian] in charge of fruit storage. Charlemagne advised the possessors of vineyards to hang grapes from hoops in order to preserve them.

Let us end this glance at Carolingian alimentation with a reminder of the importance of honey and spices. Not only was honey used to sweeten food, but it was the base for many drinks: hydromel (mead), honeyed wine, and mixtures of honey and beer. On the royal domains, there was a special supervisor for the honey harvest. Certain estates specialized in its production. Saint-Wandrille designated 8 estates for regular deliveries of honey. Einhard wrote his intendant to complain that the honey harvest had fallen below the yield he had expected.

Carolingian cuisine depended heavily on spices and condiments. Pepper, cummin, cloves, and cinnamon were purchased from merchants in touch with the Orient. A text of uncertain date mentions the monks of Corbie going to buy 100 kilos of spices in the shops of Cambrai. Cinnamon, galanga, cloves, mastic, and pepper reached the market at Mainz. A ninth-century manuscript from Echternach provides a recipe for *garum*, a fish-based condiment which had been well known in antiquity. It begins:

> Mix fish, salt, and anise; stir daily, mixing in some herbs--mint, Greek fennel, laurel, sage, etc. Take the whole from the fire when half-cooked, strain, and preserve in well-sealed vases.

Drink

> "Hey, boy! rinse my glass, pour the wine, get out the best! In the name of Almighty Christ, toast me with a cup of what they bring you, friend!"

This poetic fragment from a ninth-century manuscript is no simple echo of the Bacchic poems of antiquity but mirrors the daily reality of wine. Every class of society drank heavily, even to excess. Abbots and bishops set the example: "At Angers, they say, an abbot lives, and the first man's name he bears. They say he wished, all by himself, to equal all the Angevins [natives of Anjou, a region in western France] in drink. Eia! Eia! Eia! Glory, eia, glory to Bacchus."

These verse by some *écolâtre* or schoolboy correspond to the observations of Theodulf of

Orleans: "A bishop who keeps his gullet full of wine should not be permitted to forbid it to others. He ought not to preach sobriety who is drunk himself." We know that, without going to such excess, Alcuin did not distrust beer and wine, for he tells us that he used them to clear his throat before teaching or singing. While staying in England, he sent several butts [casks] to his monks of Saint-Martin, praying one of his pupils to drink in the place of one who was living so sad a life, far from his habitual sources of merriment. One of them, nicknamed the "cuckoo," followed his advice only too well and earned the reproaches of Arn of Salzburg. Alcuin wrote to him: "Unhappy me, if Bacchus drowns my cuckoo in his flood!" Taverns were intrinsic to rural and urban life. Even the curate was no stranger to the village tavern. They were found in market places, places of pilgrimage, on royal domains, episcopal and abbatial estates. Drinking contests were common: "Does drunken bravado encourage you to attempt to out-drink your friends? If so, thirty days fast," admonishes a penitential. "I have lost all hope in life and my soul is sorely troubled, for I have no wine," wrote a scholar on his way to the market to exchange his grammar book for a couple of drinks. "But no one would buy it or even look at it." Perhaps the poem was a joke, but it echoed a daily preoccupation. Similarly, a parody of the Salic Law in "popular" Latin levied fantastic fines on those who drank too much. Bilingual conversation manuals, whether Latin-Greek or Latin-Germanic, always began with "Give me a drink."

Moralists warned against the maladies provoked by drunken excesses. Civil and religious law condemned the intoxication of priests, laymen, soldiers, and penalized those who participated in religious or secular associations devoted to drinking bouts (*potationes*). But people still drank, at every hour of the day, on every occasion, to celebrate the closing of a bargain or the feast of a saint.

But what did they drink? Wine for a certainty. We have already seen the care lavished by bishops and abbots on their vintages and their anxiety to cart or ship in a supply if the harvest fell short. During the Norman invasions, fleeing monks often attempted to bring their casks but rarely succeeded in the effort. In 845,

returning to their monastery, the monks of Saint-Germain gave thanks to God and their patron because the Normans had not touched their wine and the supply would last until the next harvest. They needed wine for the Sacrifice of the Mass, but it was also served at the monks' and canons' meals, and better wine was kept in reserve for passing guests. The Council of Aix in 818 attempted to limit each canon to a fixed quantity of wine.

Some considered it a penance to have to content themselves with beer if wine was lacking. Installed at Liège, Sedulius Scotus could never accustom himself to the regional beer and begged his bishop to send him some bottles of wine. He wrote in praise of a certain Robert, who had 1000 barrels of wine of the highest quality in his caves, and the abbot thanked him by sending him 300 bottles of Moselle. In the northern and eastern regions of the Carolingian world, however, beer was a popular drink. It was made in part from cereals reduced to malt in the maltery (*malatura* or *camba*), boiled down, and mixed with hops by specialized craftsmen. The regulations of the Abbeys of Saint-Denis, Saint-Trond, Corbie, and others gave instructions for the furnishing of breweries and the brewing of beer, which they called *cervisia*. The guest house on the plan of Saint-Gall had its own brewery. Beer like wine could not be kept very long. The amount to be consumed had to be produced on order.

There are scattered references to other fermented drinks. Lupus of Ferrières recommended cider (*pomaticum*) to his correspondents, made either from wild apples or pears. Mulberry wine, hydromel, or some other beverage made partly from honey was also available.

Many people simply drank water. Fearing a shortage of pears and an equally severe shortage of beer because of a bad grain harvest, Lupus of Ferrières wrote: "Consequently, let us make use of a healthy, natural drink which will sometimes be of benefit to both body and soul--if it is drawn not from a muddy cistern but from a clear well or the current of a transparent brook."

Carolingian bishops and abbots display much concern for the provision of drinking water. Until Aldric built his aqueduct, water from the Sarthe was being sold at a penny a hogshead [63 gallons]. The abbot of Saint-Denis was preoccupied with the constant care of the Crou River which passed through the monastery. The best solution was to control the water from a spring and bring it to the cloister or kitchen fountains through conduits. But that was not always possible. The monks of Laon complained that they had nothing with which to quench their thirst but non-potable water: "Bacchus is not there to soothe throats desiccated by summer, and now we must fill our bellies with unhealthy water...."

Without a doubt, this was an age obsessed with wine.

Riché, Pierre. *Daily Life in the World of Charlemagne*. Trans. Jo Ann McNamara. Philadelphia: Univ. of Pennsylvania Press, 1978. Pp. 171-177.

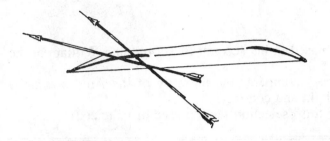

WILLIAM THE CONQUEROR AND THE BATTLE OF HASTINGS

The Battle of Hastings was a momentous event in England's history. It brought about the Norman Conquest over Anglo-Saxon England. After the fall of the Roman Empire, Britain had been invaded and settled by Germanic peoples known as Angles and Saxons. By the eleventh century, the Anglo-Saxons had evolved a remarkably stable political system, with strong royal authority supported by a vital and vigorous nobility. Anglo-Saxon kings commanded the army and were advised by a council of nobles, clergy, and officials. England was divided into regions called shires, each with a royal administrative officer called a sheriff, who collected taxes and mustered local contingents for the royal army.

When King Edward the Confessor (r. 1042-1065) died, his successor, Harold II was challenged by Edward's cousin, William, Duke of Normandy, who ruled a region in northern France inhabited by descendants of Viking immigrants. With the approval of Pope Alexander II (r. 1061-1073), William invaded England and won a decisive victory at the battle of Hastings in southern England on 14 October 1066. Harold was killed in action. The victor became King William I, better known as the Conqueror (r. 1066-1087). William consolidated his position by introducing Norman political principles and feudal practices to England. He replaced many Anglo-Saxon nobles with his Norman followers, giving them English fiefs. In return, they provided him with mounted knights and fulfilled various other obligations. Norman lords built castles, established baronial courts, and ruled the land in the king's name.

William kept one-fifth of the conquered territory as royal lands. He also ordered a thorough survey of the land and its wealth, registered in the *Domesday Book*, which detailed the feudal landholdings and provided a basis for calculating tax levies and other financial assessments. William further bolstered royal power by claiming sole right of minting money, collecting land taxes, and judging major criminal cases, such as homicide, robbery, and disputes between barons. He controlled the English church by placing loyal and experienced Norman churchmen in key English bishoprics.

A permanent major result of the Norman conquest was the enrichment of the English language by the Norman French elements. The richness of modern English derives from this cross-fertilization of languages.

The following description of the Battle of Hastings is from a verse chronicle of the Norman conquest by an Anglo-Norman poet, Wace of Jersey (c. 1100-c. 1174). The second selection, comparing and contrasting the character of Anglo-Saxons and Normans, is from the *Chronicle of the English Kings* by a twelfth-century historian, William of Malmesbury. The third, a brief sketch of

William the Conqueror's personality and aspects of his reign, is from the *Anglo-Saxon Chronicles*, the first significant prose work in English literature.

QUESTIONS:

1) In the first selection, does the author seem unbiased in his account of Harold and William at the battle of Hastings?

2) In the second selection, William of Malmesbury compares the morality of the Angles and the Normans. What aspects of each society does he highlight and contrast?

3) Does the biographical sketch of William in the third selection seem biased or balanced?

From nine o'clock in the morning, when the combat began, till three o'clock came, the battle was up and down, this way and that, and no one knew who would conquer and win the land. Both sides stood so firm and fought so well, that no one could guess which would prevail. The Norman archers with their bows shot thickly upon the English; but they covered themselves with their shields, so that the arrows could not reach their bodies, nor do any mischief, how true soever was their aim, or however well they shot. Then the Normans determined to shoot their arrows upward into the air, so that they might fall on their enemies' heads, and strike their faces.... And the arrows in falling struck their heads and faces, and put out the eyes of many; and all feared to open their eyes, or leave their faces unguarded.

The arrows now flew thicker than rain before the wind .... Then it was that an arrow, that had been thus shot upwards, struck Harold above his right eye, and put it out. In his agony he drew the arrow and threw it away, breaking it with his hands: and the pain to his head was so great, that he leaned upon his shield. So the English were wont to say, and still say to the French, that the arrow was well shot which was so sent up against their king; and that the archer won them great glory, who thus put out Harold's eye....

Duke William pressed close upon the English with his lance; striving hard to reach the standard with the great troop he led; and seeking earnestly for Harold, on whose account the whole war was. The Normans follow their lord, and press around him; they ply their blows upon the English; and these defend themselves stoutly, striving hard with their enemies, returning blow for blow....

Where the throng of the battle was greatest, the men of Kent and of Essex fought wondrously well, and made the Normans again retreat, but without doing them much injury. And when the duke saw his men fall back, and the English triumphing over them, his spirit rose high, and he seized his shield ... and his lance, which a vassal handed to him, and took his post ....

Then those who kept close guard by him, and rode where he rode, being about a thousand armed men, came and rushed with closed ranks upon the English; and with the weight of their good horses, and the blows the knights gave, broke the press of the enemy, and scattered the crowd before them, the good duke leading them on in front. Many pursued and many fled; many were the Englishmen who fell around, and were trampled under the horses, crawling upon the earth, and not able to rise. Many of the richest and noblest men fell in that rout, but still the English rallied in places; smote down those whom they reached, and maintained the combat the best they could; beating down the men and killing the horses. One Englishman watched the duke, and plotted to kill him; he would have struck him with his lance, but he could not, for the duke struck him first, and felled him to the earth....

And now the Normans had pressed on so far, that at last they reached the standard. There Harold had remained, defending himself to the utmost; but he was sorely wounded in his eye by the arrow, and suffered grievous pain from the blow. An armed man came in the throng of the battle, and struck him on ... his helmet, and beat him to the ground; and as he sought to recover himself, a knight beat him down again, striking him on the thick of his thigh, down to the bone....

The standard was beaten down ... and Harold and the best of his friends were slain; but there was so much eagerness, and throng of so many around, seeking to kill him, that I know not who it was that slew him.

The English were in great trouble at having lost their king, and at the duke's having conquered and beat down the standard; but they still fought on, and defended themselves long, and in fact till the day drew to a close. Then it clearly appeared to all that the standard was lost, and the news spread throughout the army that Harold, for certain, was dead; and all saw that there was no longer any hope, so they left the field, and those fled who could....

The English who escaped from the field did not stop till they reached London, for they were in great fear, and cried out that the Normans followed close after them. The press was great to cross the bridge, and the river beneath it was deep; so that the bridge broke under the throng, and many fell into the water.

William fought well; many an assault did he lead, many a blow did he give, and many receive, and many fell dead under his hand. Two horses were killed under him, and he took a third when necessary, so that he fell not to the ground, and lost not a drop of blood. But whatever any one did, and whoever lived or died, this is certain that William conquered, and that many of the English fled from the field, and many died on the spot. Then he returned thanks to God, and in his pride ordered his gonfanon [standard] to be brought and set up on high, where the English standard had stood; and that was the signal of his having conquered, and beaten down the standard. And he ordered his tent to be raised upon the spot among the dead, and had his meat brought hither, and his supper prepared there.

* * * * *

This was a fatal day to England, a melancholy havoc of our dear country, through its change of masters. For it had long since adopted the manners of the Angles, which had been very various according to the times: for in the first years of their arrival, they were barbarians in their look and manners, warlike in their usages, heathens in their rites; but, after embracing the faith of Christ, by degrees, and in process of time, from the peace they enjoyed, regarding arms only in a secondary light, they gave their whole attention to religion.... Nevertheless, in process of time, the desire after literature and religion had decayed, for several years before the arrival of the Normans. The clergy, contented with a very slight degree of learning, could scarcely stammer out the words of the sacraments; and a person who understood grammar was an object of wonder and astonishment. The monks mocked the rule of their order by fine vestments, and the use of every kind of food. The nobility, given up to luxury and wantonness, went not to church in the morning after the manner of Christians, but merely in a careless manner, heard matins and masses from a hurrying priest in their chambers.... The commonalty, left unprotected, became a prey to the most powerful, who amassed fortunes, by either seizing on their property, or by selling their persons into foreign countries; although it be an innate quality of this people, to be more inclined to revelling than to the accumulation of wealth.... Drinking in parties was a universal practice, in which occupation they passed entire nights as well as days. They consumed their whole substance in mean and despicable houses; unlike the Normans and French, who, in noble and splendid mansions, lived with frugality. The vices attendant on drunkenness, which enervate the human mind, followed; hence it arose that engaging William, more with rashness and precipitate fury than military skill, they doomed themselves and their country to slavery, by one, and that an easy, victory. "For nothing is less effective than rashness; and what begins with violence, quickly ceases, or is repelled."

In fine, the English at that time wore short garments reaching to the mid-knee; they had their hair cropped; their beards shaven; their arms laden with golden bracelets; their skin adorned with punctured designs. They were accustomed to eat till they became surfeited, and to drink till they were sick. These latter qualities they imparted to their conquerors; as to the rest they adopted their manners. I would not, however, have these bad propensities universally ascribed to the English. I know that many of the clergy, at that day, trod the path of sanctity by a blameless life; I know that many of the laity, of all ranks and conditions, in this nation, were well-pleasing to God. Be injustice far from this account; the accusation does not involve the whole indiscriminately. "But, as in peace, the mercy of God often cherishes the bad and the good together; so, equally, does his severity sometimes include them both in captivity."

Moreover, the Normans, that I may speak of them also, were at that time, and are even now, proudly apparelled, delicate in their food, but not excessive. They are a race inured to war, and can hardly live without it; fierce in rushing against the enemy; and where strength fails of success, ready to use stratagem, or to corrupt by bribery. As I have related, they live in large edifices with economy; envy their equals, wish to excel their superiors; and plunder their subjects, though they defend them from others; they are faithful to their lords, though a slight offence renders them perfidious. They weigh treachery by its chance of success, and change their sentiments with money. They are, however, the kindest of nations, and they esteem strangers worthy of equal honour with themselves. They also intermarry with their vassals. They revived, by their arrival, the observances of religion, which were everywhere grown lifeless in England. You might see churches rise in every village, and monasteries in the towns and cities, built after a style unknown before; you might behold the country flourishing with renovated rites; so that each wealthy man accounted that day lost to him, which he had neglected to signalize by some magnificent action....

* * * * *

Rueful deeds he did, and ruefully he suffered. Wherefore ruefully? He fell sick and became grievously ill. What can I say? The sharpness of death, that spareth neither rich nor poor, seized upon him. He died in Normandy, the day after the nativity of St. Mary, and he was buried in Caen, at St. Stephen's monastery, which he had built and had richly endowed. Oh, how false, how unstable, is the good of this world! He, who had been a powerful king and the lord of many territories, possessed not then, of all his lands, more than seven feet of ground; and he, who was erewhile adorned with gold and with gems, lay then covered with mould. He left three sons: Robert, the eldest, was earl of Normandy after him; the second, named

William, wore the crown of England after his father's death; and his third son was Henry, to whom he bequeathed immense treasures.

If any would know what manner of man king William was, the glory that he obtained, and of how many lands he was lord; then will we describe him as we have known him, we, who have looked upon him, and who once lived in his court. This king William, of whom we are speaking, was a very wise and a great man, and more honoured and more powerful than any of his predecessors. He was mild to those good men who loved God, but severe beyond measure towards those who withstood his will. He founded a noble monastery on the spot where God permitted him to conquer England, and he established monks in it, and he made it very rich. In his days the great monastery at Canterbury was built, and many others also throughout England; moreover this land was filled with monks who lived after the rule of St. Benedict; and such was the state of religion in his days that all that would, might observe that which was prescribed by their respective orders. King William was also held in much reverence: he wore his crown three times every year when he was in England: at Easter he wore it at Winchester, at Pentecost at Westminster, and at Christmas at Gloucester. And at these times, all the men of England were with him, archbishops, bishops, abbots, and earls, thanes [men granted land by the king in return for military service], and knights. So also was he a very stern and a wrathful man, so that none durst do anything against his will, and he kept in prison those earls who acted against his pleasure. He removed bishops from their sees, and abbots from their offices, and he imprisoned thanes, and at length he spared not his own brother Odo. This Odo was a very powerful bishop in Normandy, his see was that of Bayeux, and he was foremost to serve the king. He had an earldom in England, and when William was in Normandy he was the first man in this country, and him did he cast into prison. Amongst other things the good order that William established is not to be forgotten; it was such that any man, who was himself aught, might travel over the kingdom with a bosom-full of gold unmolested; and no man durst kill another, however great the injury he might have received from him. He reigned over England and being sharp-sighted to his own interest, he surveyed the kingdom so thoroughly that there was no a single hide of land throughout the whole, of which he knew not the possessor, and how much it was worth, and this he afterwards entered in his register. The land of the Britons was under his sway, and he built castles therein; moreover he had full dominion over the Isle of Man (Anglesey): Scotland also was subject to him from his great strength; the land of Normandy was his inheritance, and he possessed the earldom of Maine; and had he lived two years longer he would have subdued Ireland by his prowess, and that without a battle. Truly there was much trouble in these times, and very great distress; he caused castles to be built, and oppressed the poor. The king was also of great sternness, and he took from his subjects many marks of gold and many hundred pounds of silver, and this, either with or without right, and with little need. He was given to avarice, and greedily loved gain. He made large forests for the deer, and enacted laws therewith, so that whoever killed a hart [buck] or a hind [doe] should be blinded. As he forbade killing the deer, so also the boars; and he loved the tall stags as if he were their father. He also appointed concerning the hares, that they should go free. The rich complained and the poor murmured, but he was so sturdy that he recked nought of them; they must will all that the king willed, if they would live; or would keep their lands; or would hold their possessions; or would be maintained in their rights.

Master Wace, His Chronicle of the Norman Conquest from the Roman de Rou. Trans. E. Taylor. London 1837. Pp. 197-198, 249-256. William of Malmesbury. *Gesta Regum Anglorum*. Trans. J.A. Giles. London 1847. Pp. 278-280. *The Anglo-Saxon Chronicle*. Trans. J.A. Giles. London 1847. Pp. 460-463.

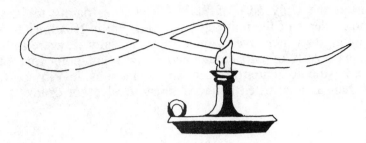

UNIVERSITY LIFE IN THIRTEENTH-CENTURY PARIS

An important aspect of intellectual life in the European late Middle Ages was appearance of the university. Before 1000, education was conducted mostly in monastery and cathedral schools. During the eleventh and twelfth centuries, the expansion of royal and church bureaucracies coupled with growing commercial activity created a demand for educated men to perform various clerical and administrative tasks.

Schools extended their offerings to an intensified study of seven liberal arts (grammar, logic, rhetoric, arithmetic, geometry, astronomy, and music) in order to meet the increased demand for educated men. During the late twelfth century, cathedral and municipal schools evolved into universities, where masters and students could explore ideas and pursue truths that had no immediate practical or vocational application; fueling their curiosity was a growing acquaintance with classical Greek knowledge, transmitted and spread by Muslim and Jewish scholars. Lacking legal status and the protection of citizenship privileges, students often suffered from the hostility of townspeople and church authorities. Therefore, scholars organized themselves, like artisans, into corporations, known as universities from the Latin *universitas* meaning "guild."

Though many universities began by emphasizing one area of learning, most became gathering places of many scholars who studied and provided instruction in the liberal arts, theology, law, and medicine. Students obtained master's degrees and a license to teach after completing a six- to eight-year program of study. Bachelor's programs of four to five years' duration developed later, but holders of that degree could not teach.

Universities were organized as self-governing bodies, but varied in their make-up. The University of Paris stressed liberal arts and attracted younger students; as a corporation of masters, it became a model for north European universities. The University of Bologna began as a center of higher studies for older professionals seeking further training; as a corporation dominated by students, it became the model for southern European universities.

Originally, European universities did not have buildings and campuses. Classes met in rented rooms or masters' homes. Scholars sometimes lived together in rented houses, which evolved into residential colleges. Because relations between the university community and adjoining towns were often strained and periodically violent, sometimes students and masters left hostile towns and established their universities in friendlier surroundings. Later, wealthy patrons--including monarchs, nobles, the church, and municipalities--endowed colleges and universities with buildings and funds to pay for housing, feeding, and instructing students.

The passages that follow contain statutes of the University of Paris. The first, dating to 1200, records a grant of privileges to the masters and students of the university by King Philip II Augustus (r. 1165-1223), occasioned by a "terrible crime owing to which five of the clergy and laity ... were killed by certain malefactors." The second stipulates details of curriculum and other regulations for both masters and students. A concluding piece is a hostile contemporary account by Jacobus de Vitriaco (c. 1170-1240) of student life at Paris; students then as now often behaved boisterously, got drunk, and fought among themselves.

QUESTIONS:

1) What problems seem to underlie the stipulations about student security in the first selection?
2) Do the regulations in the second selection appear reasonable or overly harsh?
3) What are the chief grievances of the author of the third selection? Do they strike you as justified, bigoted, neither?

Concerning the safety of the students at Paris in the future, by the advice of our subjects we have ordained as follows: we will cause all the citizens of Paris to swear that if any one sees an injury done to any student by any layman, he will testify truthfully to this, nor will any one withdraw in order not to see [the act]. And if it shall happen that any one strikes a student, except in self-defense, especially if he strikes the student with a weapon, a club or a stone, all laymen who see [the act] shall in good faith seize the malefactor or malefactors and deliver them to our judge; nor shall they withdraw in order not to see the act .... Also, whether the malefactor is seized in open crime or not, we will make a legal and full examination through clerks or laymen or certain lawful persons; and our count and our judges shall do the same. And if by a full examination we or our judges are able to learn that he who is accused, is guilty of the crime, then we or our judges shall immediately inflict a penalty, according to the quality and nature of the crime; notwithstanding the fact that the criminal may deny the deed and say that he is ready to defend himself in single combat, or to purge himself by the ordeal of water.

Also, neither our provost nor our judges shall lay hands on a student for any offence whatever; nor shall they place him in our prison, unless such a crime has been committed by the student, that he ought to be arrested. And in that case, our judge shall arrest him on the spot, without striking him at all, unless he resists, and shall hand him over to the ecclesiastical judge, who ought to guard him in order to satisfy us and the one suffering the injury. And if a serious crime has been committed, our judge shall go or shall send to see what is done with the student. If, indeed, the student does not resist arrest and yet suffers any injury, we will exact satisfaction for it, according to the aforesaid examination and the aforesaid oath. Also our judges shall not lay hands on the chattels of students at Paris for any crime whatever. But if it shall seem that these ought to be sequestrated, they shall be sequestrated and guarded after sequestration by the ecclesiastical judge, in order that whatever is judged legal by the church, may be done with the chattels. But if students are arrested by our count at such an hour that the ecclesiastical judge can not be found and be present at once, our provost shall cause the culprits to be guarded in some student's house without any ill-treatment, as is said above, until they are delivered to the ecclesiastical judge....

In order, moreover, that these [decrees] may be kept more carefully and may be established forever by a fixed law, we have decided that our present provost and the people of Paris shall affirm by an oath, in the presence of the scholars, that they will carry out in good faith all the above-mentioned. And always in the future, whosoever receives from us the office of provost in Paris, among the other initiatory acts of his office, namely, on the first or second Sunday, in one of the churches of Paris,--after he has been summoned for the purpose,--shall affirm by an oath, publicly in the presence of the scholars, that he will keep in good faith all the above-mentioned. And that these decrees may be valid forever, we have ordered this document to be confirmed by the authority of our seal and by the characters of the royal name, signed below.

Done near Betisi in the 1200th year of the Incarnation of our Lord, in the 21st year of our reign, those being present in our palace whose names are signed below....

* * * * *

R[obert de Courçon], servant of the cross of Christ, by the divine mercy cardinal priest with the title of St. Stephen in Monte Celio and legate of the apostolic seat, to all the masters and scholars at Paris--eternal safety in the Lord.

Let all know, that having been especially commanded by the lord pope to devote our energy effectively to the betterment of the condition of the students at Paris, and wishing by the advice of good men to provide for the tranquility of the students in the future, we have ordered and prescribed the following rules:

No one is to lecture at Paris in arts before he is twenty years old. He is to listen in arts at least six years, before he begins to lecture. He is to promise that he will lecture for at least two years, unless he is prevented by some good reason, which he ought to prove either in public or before the examiners. He must not be smirched by any infamy. When he is ready to lecture, each one is to be examined according to the form contained in the letter of lord ... bishop of Paris (in which is contained the peace established between the chancellor and the students by the judges appointed by the lord pope, approved and confirmed namely by the bishop and deacon of Troyes and by ... the bishop, and ... the chancellor of Paris)....

In the inceptions and meetings of the masters and in the confutations or arguments of the boys or youths there are to be no festivities. But they may call in some friends or associates, but only a few. We also advise that donations of garments and other things be made, as is customary or even to a greater extent, and especially to the poor. No master lecturing in arts is to wear anything except a cope [a long cloak or mantle], round and black and reaching to the heels--at least, when it is new. But he may well wear a pallium [monk's garment]. He is not to wear under the round cope embroidered shoes and never any with long bands.

If any one of the students in arts or theology dies, half of the masters of arts are to go to the funeral, and the other half to the next funeral. They are not to withdraw until the burial is completed, unless they have some good reason. If any master of arts or theology dies, all the masters are to be present at the vigils, each one is to read the psalter or have it read. Each one is to remain in the church, where the vigils are celebrated, until midnight or later, unless prevented by some good reason. On the day when the master is buried, no one is to lecture or dispute....

Each master is to have jurisdiction over his scholars. No one is to receive either schools or a house without the consent of the occupant, if he is able to obtain it. No one is to receive a license from the chancellor or anyone else through a gift of money, or furnishing a pledge or making an agreement. Also, the masters and students can make among themselves or with others agreements and regulations, confirmed by a pledge, penalty or oath, about the following matters: namely, if a student is killed, mutilated or receives some outrageous injury and if justice is not done; for taxing the rent of Hospitia; concerning the dress, burial, lectures and disputations; in such manner, however, that the university is not scattered nor destroyed on this account.

We decide concerning the theologians, that no one shall lecture at Paris before he is thirty-five years old, and not unless he has studied at least eight years, and has heard the books faithfully and in the schools. He is to listen in theology for five years, before he reads his own lectures in public. No one of them is to lecture before the third hour on the days when the masters lecture. No one is to be received at Paris for the important lectures or sermons unless he is of approved character and learning. There is to be no student at Paris who does not have a regular master.

In order moreover that these may be inviolably observed, all who presume contumaciously to violate these our statutes, unless they take care, within fifteen days of the date of the transgression, to correct their presumption in the presence of the university of masters and scholars, or in the presence of some appointed by the university, by the authority of the legation with which we are entrusted, we bind with the bond of excommunication.

Done in the year of grace 1215, in the month of August.

* * * * *

Almost all the students at Paris, foreigners and natives, did absolutely nothing except learn or hear something new. Some studied merely to acquire knowledge, which is curiosity; others to acquire fame, which is vanity; others still for the sake of gain, which is cupidity and the vice of simony [buying or selling of church offices, privileges, etc.]. Very few studied for their own edification, or that of others. They wrangled and disputed not merely about the various sects or about some discussions; but the differences between the countries also caused dissensions, hatreds and virulent animosities among them, and they impudently uttered all kinds of affronts and insults against one another.

They affirmed that the English were drunkards and had tails; the sons of France proud, effeminate and carefully adorned like women. They said that the Germans were furious and obscene at their feasts; the Normans, vain and boastful; the Poitevins, traitors and always adventurers. The Burgundians they considered vulgar and stupid. The Bretons were reputed to be fickle and changeable, and were often reproached for the death of [King] Arthur. The Lombards were called avaricious, vicious and cowardly; the Romans, seditious, turbulent and slanderous; the Sicilians, tyrannical and cruel; the inhabitants of Brabant, men of blood, incendiaries, brigands and ravishers; the Flemish, fickle, prodigal, gluttonous, yielding as butter, and slothful. After such insults from words they often came to blows.

I will not speak of those logicians before whose eyes flitted constantly "the lice of Egypt," that is to say, all the sophistical subtleties, so that no one could comprehend their eloquent discourses in which, as says Isaiah, "there is no wisdom." As to the doctors of theology, "seated in Moses' seat," they were swollen with learning but their charity was not edifying. Teaching and not practicing, they have "become as sounding brass or a tinkling cymbal," or like a canal of stone, always dry, which ought to carry water to "the bed of spices." They not only hated one another, but by their flatteries they enticed away the students of others; each one seeking his own glory, but caring not a whit about the welfare of souls.

Having listened intently to these words of the Apostle, "If a man desire the office of a bishop, he desireth a good work," they kept multiplying the prebends [clergymen's stipends], and seeking after the offices; and yet they sought the work decidedly less than the preëminence, and they desired above all to have "the uppermost rooms at feasts and the chief seats in the synagogue, and greetings in the market." Although the Apostle James said, "My brethren, be not many masters," they on the contrary were in such haste to become masters, that most of them were not able to have any students except by entreaties and payments. Now it is safer to listen than to teach, and a humble listener is better than an ignorant and presumptuous doctor. In short, the Lord had reserved for himself among them all only a few honorable and timorous men who had not stood "in the way of sinners," nor sat down with the others in the envenomed seat.

Chartularium Universitatis Parisiensis. Sects. 1.1, 1.20. Jacobus de Vitriaco. *Historia occidentalis*. Chap. 2.7. Trans. D.C. Munro. *The Medieval Student*. Rev. ed. Philadelphia 1899. Pp. 5-7, 12-15, 19-21.

READING 4.10

MRS. YUEH FEI--A MODEL WIFE

► **Early Chinese Flame-Thrower**

Yueh Fei (1103-1141) was the outstanding general of the Sung dynasty (960-1279). He is one of the most revered figures in Chinese history because of the loyalty and patriotism that his widowed mother instilled in him from childhood. Yueh had the misfortune to live under weak, pacifist rulers who distrusted military men, especially successful ones.

In 1127, nomads called the Chin overran northern China and took captive the Sung Emperor Hui-tsung, who had preferred spending his time with fellow painters (he was an accomplished artist) to strengthening the defenses of the country. Remaining members of the government fled across the Yangtze River to southern China and installed a Sung prince as emperor at a new capital, Hangchow. Thus ended the Northern Sung (960-1127) and began the Southern Sung (1127-1279) dynasty.

With the regular army a shambles, General Yueh raised and trained an irregular force and fought his way northward, winning victory after victory. Recovery of northern China seemed a distinct possibility. Despite widespread public support for Yueh, the emperor and Chief Councilor Ch'in Kuei (1090-1155) favored peace, and recalled Yueh lest his military successes sabotage the peace negotiations. Yueh was imprisoned and murdered in jail in 1141 to appease the Chin, his death a secret condition for peace. His eldest son, a promising young officer, was executed on specious charges.

In 1142, the Southern Sung and the Chin signed a peace treaty in which the Sung ceded the entire Yellow River drainage area, acknowledged vassalage, and paid an annual tribute to the Chin. In dying a martyr's death, Yueh earned respect as a great patriot; his tomb in Hangchow remains a shrine and destination for pilgrims. Conversely, Ch'in Kuei and the other appeasers are reviled figures in Chinese history. His statue, and that of his influential wife, kneel in front of Yueh's tomb in perpetual penance.

While both Yueh and his mother are deservedly famous in Chinese history and folklore, the following account shows his wife equally worthy of honor.

QUESTIONS:

1) How did Mrs. Yueh help her husband with his work?
2) Why was Mrs. Yueh regarded as a model wife in her domestic life?
3) How did Mrs. Yueh carry on her husband's legacy after his death?

All Chinese know and admire Yeuh Fei's mother because she instilled in her son a deep sense of loyalty and service to the Sung dynasty and to China. Much less is known about his wife, Li Hsiao-o, who was also a remarkable woman.

Yueh Fei and his wife came from the same village called Kang, located thirty-five *li* (a li is 1/3 of a mile) from T'angyin county in Honan province. They were married in 1118 when he was sixteen and she was eighteen. Between 1119 and 1139, she bore five sons and two daughters. They raised their children frugally and strictly: they wore plain clothes, were forbidden alcohol, had to study hard, did physical exercise, and cultivated a vegetable garden in their spare time. Whatever the family had they shared with his subordinates and the soldiers under his command.

Yueh Fei is credited with being a model filial son to his mother, but it is less well known that his wife was equally devoted to his mother, caring for her during his absences. When he went on campaigns, Mrs Yueh also took sole responsibility for the discipline and education of their children. Yueh Fei had such respect and affection for his wife that he rejected out of hand suggestions that he take concubines into their household.

The couple was widely respected for their loyalty and fidelity to each other.

Mrs. Yueh also helped her husband take care of the families of the officers and men under his command. When General Yueh was away on campaigns, Mrs. Yueh would visit the wives and families of the men of his army, bringing them money and gifts, and giving them encouragement. She wept and mourned with the bereaved families at news that their loved ones had died in battle, helped take care of the orphaned children, and even helped arrange their marriages. She also visited the sick and wounded soldiers and helped care for them and prepare their medicines. By these actions she contributed to the high morale of the soldiers who fought under her husband.

The family faced calamity when General Yueh was falsely accused, imprisoned, and murdered in jail. At the same time, their eldest son Yun, who had followed his father into battle since age twelve and who had repeatedly distinguished himself in war, was executed on trumped up charges. In grief their younger daughter, then only thirteen, committed suicide, drowning herself in a well. Determined to keep the remaining children together, Mrs. Yueh Fei kept her grief to herself. She gathered the little family property that the government had not confiscated, mainly a library of several thousand books, her husband's sword, a jade belt [an honor conferred by the emperor], and a mere nine thousand strings of cash, and began the journey of exile under military guard that would take the family first to Kwangnan [in modern Kwangtung] and later to Fukien [unhealthy, tropical frontier areas where convicted criminals and political prisoners served their time]. To compound the family tragedy, Yun's widow committed suicide during the journey when her jailer separated the young mother from her infant son. Proclaiming that her husband could not be left without descendants, Mrs. Yueh also assumed responsibility for raising her orphaned grandson.

For twenty years they lived in exile, under military surveillance, reporting to the local authorities every month. When General Yueh was finally exonerated, he and Yun were both restored to their ranks. Yueh Fei was given the posthumous rank of Imperial Tutor and title of the Prince of O. His four surviving sons and the grandson were rewarded with some of the honors due to their father and also given titles. When Mrs. Yueh was awarded the title of Duchess of Chu, the government issued a proclamation that extolled her many virtues during her husband's lifetime and lauded her for continuing his legacy after his death. She was given a public funeral when she died.

Facts about Mrs. Yueh's life has been culled from many sources. Although overshadowed by her famous husband and mother-in-law, she was nevertheless a remarkable woman with a strong character and unbending principles. She was dignified and self-reliant, diligent and frugal, and she endured hardship and adversity. She set an example of a devoted wife who was her husband's helpmate at home and at work. She was a pioneer in caring for the families of servicemen; her concern and devotion to them raised the morale of the men in her husband's units, contributing to his successful career as a great general.

An, Li. "Yueh wu-mu fu-jen Li Hsiao-o nu-shih shih chi." In Lo, Lien-t'ien, ed. *Sung shih nien-chiu ch'i*. Vol. 13. Taipei: Kuo-li p'ien-i kuan Chung-hua ts'ung shu p'ien shen wei-yuan hui, 1981. Pp. 473-479. Edited and translated by Jiu-Hwa Lo Upshur.

TEA DURING THE SUNG DYNASTY

The tea plant (*thea sinensis*) is indigenous to China. The Chinese were the first to drink tea, a beverage brewed from dried and processed tea leaves. The spread of tea drinking among all classes undoubtedly contributed to more healthy Chinese, first because tea often replaced alcoholic beverages, and second because boiling water for tea killed harmful bacteria.

From China tea drinking spread to the nomads of inner Asia, Japan, Korea, and Southeast Asia. Centuries later it spread to Russia where it is called *cha*, from the northern Chinese pronunciation of the word. When Europeans sailed to the southern Chinese coast in the sixteenth century, they brought tea, *the* in the Fukien dialect of southern China, back to western Europe. Tea drinking, from Chinese porcelain cups (hence the synonymy of "china" and "porcelain") spread throughout Europe. In England tea supplanted gin as the national drink in the early eighteenth century. Beginning in the nineteenth century, tea plants were shipped to India and Ceylon where conditions allowed their cultivation. The plant has subsequently spread to other parts of Asia and to Africa, ceasing to be a Chinese monopoly.

Much folklore is associated with tea in China and elsewhere. The reading below describes its popularization in China between the tenth and thirteenth centuries, during the Sung dynasty.

QUESTIONS:

1) What are the good properties attributed to tea drinking?
2) What social roles did tea drinking play during the Sung dynasty?
3) Why was tea important in China's international trade and foreign relations?

The *Book of History* is the earliest document in which the word *cha* (tea) is found. Although there are other words for tea, *cha* became the most commonly used. Both the origin of the word and the early use of tea is lost in legends, but by the Western Han [202 B.C.E.-9 C.E.] tea had become a common drink for peoples of Szechuan and Yunnan [in southwestern China] where the plant is native.

According to the *Canon of Tea* [by Lu Yu, eighth century] it is "a cure for ulcers, eases urinating problems and heat stress, prevents dozing off, and helps the digestion." Other works cite its uses for curing hangovers, headaches and other aches and pains, for raising energy and focusing concentration, as an aid to thinking and in dieting, and for many other purposes; no bad effects are associated with tea drinking.

The many varieties of the tea plant range from the dwarf of only a foot high to others that grow to several tens of feet tall. Soil and growing conditions, the species of the plant, the tenderness of the leaves at the time of picking, and the method of curing determine the quality and variety of the tea. The tea plant needs a warm moist climate and grows best on slopes that get the morning sun. Tea leaves can be harvested throughout the growing season. The Yangtze River basin and lands to the south possess climatic conditions most suitable for tea growing, which is why the custom of tea drinking originated in southern China and spread northward. The Yellow River valley is unsuited to tea cultivation.

Because southern China was generally undeveloped during the Han dynasty, tea did not become widespread nationally during that era. During the Three Kingdoms period [220-263 C.E.] tea became fashionable as a substitute for alcoholic drinks in entertaining guests in the southern state Wu.

The enduring achievements of the short-lived Sui dynasty [581-618] were the reunification of China and the digging of the Grand Canal that linked the Yangtze River basin with the Yellow River valley. The succeeding T'ang dynasty [618-906] reaped the benefit of the monumental engineering project. The Grand Canal was a boon to north-south trade and contributed to the economic development of southern China. Tea was among the goods shipped from south to north via this waterway. An eighth-century work said: "Tea shops have opened in cities all the way to the capital [Changan]. They stock many varieties of tea from the Yangtze and Huai River regions that arrive by cart and boat. Peoples of all classes have also taken to drinking tea in tea shops." The most popular tea shops were located at scenic spots, many also offered music and entertainers. Lu Yu added: "From the palace to country dwellings, for Chinese and barbarians, tea is drunk at home, at parties and in religious rituals. Merchants have made fortunes in trading tea." Buddhist monks and Taoist priests drank tea as an aid in meditation. Tea's popularity continued unabated through the Sung dynasty [960-1279].

Many developments during the T'ang and Sung dynasties would define the Chinese culture to the present, the popularization of tea was one of them. Many books were written on tea. Lu Yu's *Canon of Tea* was followed by others. Records cite eleven other books written on tea during the T'ang dynasty and eighteen written during the Sung. Many have perished, only the titles survived.

The refined Sung court required top grade of tea for its own use and as gifts. Tea especially prepared for the court was called tribute tea. Among Northern Sung rulers none presided over a more refined and effete court than Hui-tsung [r 1101-1125]. Tea appreciation and drinking reached great height under Hui-tsung, who personally supervised the compiling of an encyclopedic work on tea. His court required annually approximately 47,100 catties [30 tons] of tribute tea, of fifty-one different varieties. Tribute tea was produced under government supervision; cultivating and transporting it frequently resulted in hardships for the producers.

Besides keeping a portion for use at court, Sung rulers routinely gave gifts of tribute tea to officials, officers and men of the army, imperial relatives, and priests and monks, and in addition made special tea presentations as rewards for meritorious service. Palace ante-rooms and government offices routinely provided tea, and at palace meetings high officials could order many varieties of tea.

Tea played a major role in changing social customs among the elite during the T'ang and Sung dynasties, and from the upper class, they filtered down to the rest of society. Prior to the T'ang, alcoholic drinks were the mainstay of parties and entertaining. Guests were routinely served drinks upon arrival at the host's house, and were often served soups before departure to offset the effects of inebriation. Tea replaced alcohol as the common social drink. Because it was believed that tea enhanced the poetic muse and good conversation, it became the favored beverage at literary and other learned gatherings. Rich and cultivated men competed with one another over the quality of tea they served, the refined way it was served, and the costly and beautiful utensils used in serving tea. Many ingenious craftsmen and clever merchants earned handsome sums for producing and finding unique tea sets and tea implements for rich patrons. One account, perhaps exaggerated, states that a tea set had cost one thousand ounces of gold.

Tea also contributed to new trends in prosperous urban life, because ordinary citizens began to enjoy tea and the social life associated with it. By the Sung dynasty all cities had tea shops and tea houses; the latter became social gathering places. Many Sung era tea house names have survived, for example: Mother Wang's Tea House, Skeleton Chu's Tea House, and Kuo the Number Four Son's Tea House. Some tea houses also provided entertainment and prostitutes for patrons. Market places even had mobile tea carts from which passers by could buy cups of tea dipped from large jars.

Tea merchants and shippers organized into associations or guilds which provided warehouses, carts and vessels, hostels, and meeting places for their members, and also loaned them money. Tea merchants' guilds were located at major cities or transportation junctions. In many cities tea merchants were concentrated on the same street.

Tea also played an important role in Sino-barbarian relations, because China's nomadic neighbors also took to drinking tea, which they had to obtain from China. Tea sold to the nomads fetched extremely high profits, leading to the sayings: "One catty [1 1/4 lb.] of tea is worth an ounce on gold" and "A load of tea is worth a top stallion." Thus there was no problem recruiting merchants willing to participate in selling tea to the nomads. Beginning with the T'ang dynasty, China exported large quantities of tea in ordinary trade, as part of diplomatic exchanges, and as a barter item for horses. Between 960 and 1098, Sung emperors gave presents of tea to the nomads on twenty-eight occasions. In addition, trade centers were established between the Northern Sung and the Liao and the Hsi Hsia and later between the Southern Sung and the Chin. Although China exported other goods such as medicines, ivories and rhinoceros horns, tea was the main merchandise and the most profitable one. Because of the high profit margin and the importance of trade as an adjunct of defense and foreign policies, both parties controlled the cross-border trade and attempted to interdict illegal private transactions.

Because the Chin controlled all northern China where the nomads were a minority, most Chin subjects were Han Chinese; thus the demand for tea by the Chin was particularly great. The Southern Sung established government monopolies in all items traded with the Chin and strictly forbad private trade across the border both by land and sea routes. Because of the lure of profits, however, smuggling persisted.

Among imports, China desired above all horses bred by the nomads; because it lacked good pasturelands for horse breeding, native horses tended to be small and puny. Whereas the powerful T'ang was able to control the horses' source, the Sung often had difficulty buying horses because their enemies the Liao and Chin refused to sell the valuable animals.

Thus from the beginning of the dynasty the Sung had to seek long and hard to buy horses from other nomadic peoples to the northwest of the Liao and Chin, initially with copper money. Since copper coins could easily be melted down, alloyed with other metals and converted into weapons, the Sung forbad the export of cash in exchange for horses after 983. Instead it encouraged the exchange of textiles and other products, but especially tea, for horses. The Southern Sung government had even greater trouble obtaining horses than its predecessor since it was almost entirely cut off from the nomads of the northwest by the Chin. It therefore sought to develop a horses for tea barter with tribal neighbors in the southwest, but the horses these nomads bred were inferior compared with those indigenous to the northwest. Lack of good horses contributed to the Southern Sung's difficulties in defense and its final downfall.

Tea also played an increasingly important role in the fiscal and financial policies of the T'ang and Sung governments. In 780, financial difficulties resulting from the suppression of a major rebellion forced the T'ang government to enact a 10 percent tax on four hitherto untaxed items, namely, tea, lacquer, bamboo, and lumber. T'ang records show that the tax on tea immediately added only 400,000 strings of cash [1000 coins per string] to the treasury annually. Once the precedent had been set, a tea tax was regularly imposed during the late T'ang to finance the relief of natural disasters and in alleviating fiscal emergencies. A tea tax became a regular item in the fiscal policy of the Sung. It realized increasing amounts of revenue, reaching an annual maximum of 5,600,000 strings of cash in 1004.

Thus tea was an important item in both the foreign relations and the economic policy of the Sung dynasty. Many complex laws and regulations pertaining to the taxing of tea at all stages of production and merchandising were enacted in the Sung codes, entailing many levels of bureaucratic supervision and control. As nomadic aggressions intensified, the Sung sought protection behind defense lines manned by its huge infantry army. Always in need of funds to pay soldiers' salaries, it taxed production of and trade in, among other things, tea.

In summary, while tea originated in the mists of antiquity, its popularization began in the T'ang. But it was during the Sung dynasty that tea became a universal drink, not only among Chinese but also among the nomads beyond China's borders. In replacing alcohol as the national drink, it contributed to more healthful living. Since so much that is associated with China and the Chinese way of life is defined by tea drinking, and because so many of the customs accompanying tea drinking were established during the Sung dynasty, this era must be considered a crucial one in the evolution of Chinese culture.

Chu, chung-sheng. "Wu kuo yin cha cheng feng chih yuan yin chi ch'i tui T'ang Sung she hui yu kuan fu chih yin hsiang." In Sung shih tsu tan hui, ed. *Sung shih nien chiu chi.* Vol. 14. Taipei: Kuo-li p'ien-i kuan Chung-hua ts'ung shu p'ien shen wei-yuan hui, 1983. Edited and translated by Jiu-Hwa Lo Upshur.

LETTERS HOME BY TWO FRENCH OFFICERS IN THE FIRST CRUSADE

► **Crusader Knight and Fallen Muslim**

Christians demonstrated their religious ardor by making pilgrimages to the Holy Land, which was captured by Arabs in 638 C.E. Until the eleventh century, Christian pilgrims went largely unmolested by Muslim rulers in the region. Several changes in the late eleventh century led to the launching of European Christian military expeditions to conquer the Holy Land. One was the rise of a new Muslim group, the Seljuk Turks, who gained control of much of Asia Minor and the eastern Mediterranean by defeating the forces of other Muslims and of the Byzantine Empire. In 1092, the death of the Seljuk ruler Malik Shah (r. 1072-1092) and of the empire's architect and chief minister, Nizam al-Mulk (1018-1092) left the Seljuks leaderless and threw the empire into civil war.

Monastic reforms in Western Europe and the resurgence of religious fervor during the eleventh century motivated many Christians to go on pilgrimage to the Holy Land. They often returned with horror stories of mistreatment by the Seljuk Turks. Capitalizing on tales of Muslim atrocities and answering an appeal by the Byzantine emperor, Pope Urban II (r. 1088-1099) made a rousing speech in 1095 for a crusade to recapture the Holy Land from the Muslims. The Pope also promised to forgiveness the sins of all who fought against the Muslims. There was enthusiastic response to the Pope's call as high and low flocked to join armies.

The four armies of Western fighters that departed for Constantinople in 1096 enjoyed astonishing success. Allying with the Byzantine Emperor Alexius, they seized strongholds and defeated Seljuk armies in Anatolia. They then conquered the cities of Edessa and Antioch in Syria and finally entered Jerusalem in 1099, crying "God wills it!" The Crusaders then established European style feudal states in the region, ruled by French noblemen. The most important was the Kingdom of Jerusalem. After building strong forts to guard their gains and leaving garrisons to hold them, the main body of Crusaders returned to Europe.

Although the first crusade was a success, the crusaders confronted several persistent problems in Palestine and never received enough additional manpower to consolidate their position. They were forced to trade and make treaties with their Muslim neighbors. The Crusaders' interest also conflicted with those of the Byzantine empire. Starting in the 1140s, Islamic resistance was revitalized, culminating in the Seljuk annihilation of the Byzantine army in 1176 and the reestablishment of Turkish control of Anatolia. In the 1180s, the dynamic Muslim leader Saladin, decisively defeated the crusaders recaptured most of the crusader territories except for a few seaports.

Although subsequent crusades regained control of some lost holdings, European crusading zeal eventually waned. The Muslim capture of Acre in 1291 marked the end of the Latin presence in the Holy Land.

The following letters are written by Frankish commanders during the First Crusade. They repo[rt] on some of the spectacular early successes of the campaign. The first, to the archbishop of Reims, [is] by Anselme of Ribemont, count of Ostrevant and Valenciennes, who was killed in battle in April 109[9]. The second is written by Count Stephen to his wife. He too was later slain in battle (1102).

QUESTIONS:

1) What biases can be detected in these letters?
2) What do the motivations of the French forces seem to be on this expedition?
3) How does Christianity figure in the attitudes of the letter-writers?

Anselme of Ribemont to Manasses II, Archbishop of Reims. Before Antioch, about 10 February 1098:

To his reverend lord M., by God's grace archbishop of Reims, A. of Ribemont, his vassal and humble servant--greeting.

Inasmuch as you are our lord and as the kingdom of France is especially dependent upon your care, we tell to you, our father, the events which have happened to us and the condition of the army of the Lord....

After the army had reached Nicomedia, which is situated at the entrance to the land of the Turks, we all, lords and vassals, cleansed by confession, fortified ourselves by partaking of the body and blood of our Lord, and proceeding thence beset Nicaea on ... [6 May]. After we had for some days besieged the city with many machines and various engines of war, the craft of the Turks, as often before, deceived us greatly. For on the very day on which they had promised that they would surrender, Soliman and all the Turks, collected from neighboring and distant regions, suddenly fell upon us and attempted to capture our camp. However the count of St. Gilles with the remaining Franks, made an attack upon them an killed an innumerable multitude. All the others fled in confusion. Our men, moreover, returning in victory and bearing many heads fixed upon pikes and spears, furnished a joyful spectacle for the people of God. This was on ... [16 May].

Beset moreover and routed in attacks by night and day, they surrendered unwillingly on ... [19 June]. Then the Christians entering the walls with their crosses and imperial standards, reconciled the city to God, and both within the city and outside the gates cried out in Greek and Latin, "Glory to Thee, O God." Having accomplished this, the princes of the army me[t] the emperor who had come to offer them hi[s] thanks, and having received from him gifts [of] inestimable value, some withdrew with kind[ly] feelings, others with different emotions.

We moved our camp from Nicaea on ... [2? June] and proceeded on our journey for thre[e] days. On the fourth day the Turks, havin[g] collected their forces from all sides, agai[n] attacked the smaller portion of our army, kille[d] many of our men and drove all the remainde[r] back to their camps. Bohemond, count of th[e] Romans, count Stephen, and the count o[f] Flanders commanded this section. When thes[e] were thus terrified by fear, the standards of th[e] larger army appeared. Hugh the Great and th[e] duke of Lorraine were riding at the head, th[e] count of St. Gilles and the venerable bishop o[f] Puy followed. For they had heard of the battl[e] and were hastening to our aid. The number o[f] Turks was estimated at 260,000. All of our arm[y] attacked them, killed many and routed the rest[.] On that day I returned from the emperor, t[o] whom the princes had sent me on publi[c] business.

After that day our princes remained togethe[r] and were not separated from one another[.] Therefore, in traversing the countries of Romani[a] and Armenia we found no obstacle, except tha[t] after passing Iconium, we, who formed th[e] advance guard, saw few Turks. After routing these, on ... [21 October], we laid siege t[o] Antioch, and now we captured the neighborin[g] places, the cities of Tarsus and Laodicea an[d] many others, by force. On a certain day[,] moreover, before we besieged the city, at th[e] "Iron Bridge" we routed the Turks, who had se[t] out to devastate the surrounding country, and w[e] rescued many Christians. Moreover, we led back the horses and camels with very great booty.

While we were besieging the city, the Turks from the nearest redoubt daily killed those entering and leaving the army. The princes of our army seeing this, killed 400 of the Turks who were lying in wait, drove others into a certain river and led back some as captives. You may be assured that we are now besieging Antioch with all diligence, and hope soon to capture it. The city is supplied to an incredible extent with grain, wine, oil and all kinds of food.

I ask, moreover, that you and all whom this letter reaches pray for us and for our departed brethren....

Again and again I beseech you, readers of this letter, to pray for us, and you, my lord archbishop, to order this to be done by your bishops. And know for certain that we have captured for the Lord 200 cities and fortresses. May our mother, the western church, rejoice that she has begotten such men, who are acquiring for her so glorious a name and who are so wonderfully aiding the eastern church. And in order that you may believe this, know that you have sent to me a tapestry by Raymond "de Castello."

Farewell.

* * * * *

Stephen, Count of Blois and Chartres, to his wife, Adele. Before Antioch, 29 March 1098:

Count Stephen to Adele, his sweetest and most amiable wife, to his dear children, and to all his vassals of all ranks--his greeting and blessing.

You may be very sure, dearest, that the messenger whom I sent to give you pleasure, left me before Antioch safe and unharmed, and through God's grace in the greatest prosperity. And already at that time, together with all the chosen army of Christ, endowed with great valor by Him, we had been continuously advancing for twenty-three weeks toward the home of our Lord Jesus. You may know for certain, my beloved, that of gold, silver and many other kind of riches I now have twice as much as your love assigned to me when I left you. For all our princes with the common consent of the whole army, against my own wishes, have made me up to the present

time the leader, chief and director of their whole expedition.

You have certainly heard that after the capture of the city of Nicaea we fought a great battle with the perfidious Turks and by God's aid conquered them. Next we conquered for the Lord all Romania and afterwards Cappadocia [both in northern Anatolia]. And we learned that there was a certain Turkish prince Assam, dwelling in Cappadocia; thither we directed our course. All his castles were conquered by force and [we] compelled him to flee to a certain very strong castle situated on a high rock. We also gave the land of that Assam to one of our chiefs and in order that he might conquer ... Assam, we left there with him many soldiers of Christ. Thence, continually following the wicked Turks, we drove them through the midst of Armenia, as far as the great river Euphrates. Having left all their baggage and beasts of burden on the bank, they fled across the river into Arabia.

The bolder of the Turkish soldiers, indeed, entering Syria, hastened by forced marches night and day, in order to be able to enter the royal city of Antioch before our approach. The whole army of God learning this gave due praise and thanks to the omnipotent Lord. Hastening with great joy to ... Antioch, we besieged it and very often had many conflicts there with the Turks; and seven times with the citizens of Antioch and with innumerable troops coming to its aid, whom we rushed to meet, we fought with the fiercest courage, under the leadership of Christ. And in all these seven battles, by the aid of the Lord God, we conquered and most assuredly killed an innumerable host of them. In those battles, indeed, and in very many attacks made upon the city, many of our brethren and followers were killed and their souls were borne to the joys of paradise.

We found the city of Antioch very extensive, fortified with incredible strength and almost impregnable. In addition, more than 5,000 bold Turkish soldiers had entered the city, not counting the Saracens, Publicans, Arabs, Turcopolitans, Syrians, Armenians and other different races of whom an infinite multitude had gathered together there. In fighting against these enemies of God and of our own we have, by God's grace, endured many sufferings and innumerable evils up to the present time. Many also have already exhausted all their resources in this very holy passion. Very many of our Franks, indeed, would have met a temporal death from starvation, if the clemency of God and our money had not succoured them. Before ... Antioch indeed, throughout the whole winter we suffered for our Lord Christ from excessive cold and enormous torrents of rain. What some say about the impossibility of bearing the heat of the sun throughout Syria is untrue, for the winter there is very similar to our winter in the west.

When truly Caspian [Bagi Seian], the emir of Antioch--that is, prince and lord--perceived that he was hard pressed by us, he sent his son Sensodolo [Chems Eddaulah] by name, to the prince who holds Jerusalem, and to the prince of Calep, Rodoam [Rodoanus], and to Docap [Deccacus Ibn Toutousch], prince of Damascus. He also sent into Arabia to Bolianuth and to Carathania to Hamelnuth. These five emirs with 12,000 picked Turkish horsemen suddenly came to the aid of the inhabitants of Antioch. We, indeed, ignorant of all this, had sent many of our soldiers away to the cities and fortresses. For there are one hundred and sixty-five cities and fortresses throughout Syria which are in our power. But a little before they reached the city, we attacked them at three leagues' distance with 700 soldiers, on a certain plain near the "Iron Bridge." God, however, fought for us, His faithful, against them. For on that day, fighting in the strength that God gives, we conquered them and killed an innumerable multitude--God continually fighting for us--and we also carried back to the army more than two hundred of their heads, in order that the people might rejoice on that account. The emperor of Babylon also sent Saracen messengers to our army with letters and through these he established peace and concord with us.

I love to tell you, dearest, what happened to us during Lent. Our princes had caused a fortress to be built before a certain gate which was between our camp and the sea. For the Turks daily issuing from this gate, killed some of our men on their way to the sea. The city of Antioch is about five leagues' distance from the sea. For this reason they sent the excellent Bohemond and Raymond, count of St. Gilles, to the sea with only sixty horsemen, in order that they might bring mariners to aid in this work.

When, however, they were returning to us with those mariners, the Turks collected an army, fell suddenly upon our two leaders and forced them to a perilous flight. In that unexpected flight we lost more than 500 of our foot-solders--to the glory of God. Of our horsemen, however, we lost only two, for certain.

On that same day truly, in order to receive our brethren with joy, and ignorant of their misfortunes, we went out to meet them. When, however, we approached the above-mentioned gate of the city, a mob of horsemen and foot-soldiers from Antioch, elated by the victory which they had won, rushed upon us in the same manner. Seeing these, our leaders sent to the camp of the Christians to order all to be ready to follow us into battle. In the meantime our men gathered together and the scattered leaders, namely Bohemond and Raymond, with the remainder of their army came up and narrated the great misfortune which they had suffered.

Our men, full of fury at these most evil tidings, prepared to die for Christ and, deeply grieved for their brethren, rushed upon the sacrilegious Turks. They, enemies of God and of us, hastily fled before us and attempted to enter their city. But by God's grace the affair turned out very differently: for, when they wanted to cross a bridge built over the great river Moscholum [Orontes], we followed them as closely as possible, killed many before they reached the bridge, forced many into the river, all of whom were killed, and we also slew many upon the bridge and very many at the narrow entrance to the gate. I am telling you the truth, my beloved, and you may be very certain that in this battle we killed thirty emirs, that is princes, and three hundred other Turkish nobles, not counting the remaining Turks and pagans. Indeed, the number of Turks and Saracens killed is reckoned at 1,230, but of ours we did not lose a single man.

While on the following day (Easter) my chaplain Alexander was writing this letter in great haste, a party of our men lying in wait for the Turks, fought a successful battle with them and killed sixty horsemen, whose heads they brought to the army.

These which I write to you, are only a few things, dearest, of the many which we have done, and because I am not able to tell you, dearest, what is in my mind, I charge you to do right, to carefully watch over your land, to do your duty as you ought to your children and your vassals. You will certainly see me just as soon as I can possibly return to you.

Farewell.

Riant, Paul E.D. *Inventaire critique des lettres historiques des croisades*. Paris 1880. No. 97. Achery, Luc d'. *Spicilegium sive collectio veterum aliquot scriptorum qui in Galliae bibliothecis delituerant*. Vol. 3. Paris 1723. Pp. 430 ff. Trans. D.C. Munro. *Letters of the Crusaders Written from the Holy Land*. Philadelphia 1894. Pp. 2-8.

READING 4.13

SALADIN'S VICTORY AT HITTIN AND THE FALL OF JERUSALEM

► Saladin

Western European Christians undertook a total of seven military expeditions known as Crusades, between 1095 and 1270, to recover the "Holy Land" from Muslim control. They enjoyed initial successes and established a number of Christian-controlled states along the eastern shores of the Mediterranean. One of these was the holy city of Jerusalem, whose Arab defenders were massacred after the fall of the city on 15 July 1099. This loss was an especially grievous one for Muslims, since Jerusalem's Dome of the Rock and al-Aqsa mosques make it, after Mecca and Medina, the third holiest city in the Islamic world.

Beginning in 1169, under the leadership of the great sultan and commander Salah al-Din Yusuf (1138-1193), known to the West as "Saladin," the Muslims began an offensive against the crusader states. On 4 July 1187, Saladin's forces won a decisive victory at Hittin in Galilee; three months later, Jerusalem surrendered.

The story of the Crusades has often been told from the European perspective. The word "Crusade" derives from the Latin word for "cross," the emblem of the Christian armies; Arab writers refer to conflicts as the "Frankish wars" or "Frankish invasions." The passage that follows presents the Arab or Muslim viewpoint; it is taken from a recent "true-life novel" of the Crusades assembled from a variety of contemporary Arab histories and chronicles. It describes the Muslim victory at Hittin and the recapture of Jerusalem from the "Franj" (the Arabic term for Franks).

QUESTIONS:

1) How does this account of a famous battle during the Crusades differ from those told from the European perspective?

2) What do Saladin's motives seem to have been in taking Jerusalem, according to this reconstruction?

3) How are Christians depicted in this reading?

Everything was ready for the battle. The army of Saladin was deployed in a fertile plain covered with fruit trees. Behind it was the fresh water of Lake Tiberias, fed by the Jordan River, while further on, toward the north-east, the majestic outline of the Golan Heights could be seen. Near the Muslim camp was a hill with two peaks, called "the horns of Hittin," after the village perched on its slopes.

On 3 July [1187] the Frankish army, about twelve thousand strong, began to move. In normal times, it did not take long to travel from Saffuriya to Tiberias: it was four hours' march at most, but in summer this stretch of Palestinian land was arid. There were no sources of water and no wells, and the river-beds were dry. Nevertheless, as they left Saffuriya in the early morning, the Franj were confident that by afternoon they would be able to slake their thirst at the lakeside. Saladin, however, had laid his trap carefully. Throughout the day his cavalry harassed the enemy, attacking from behind, from in front, and then on both flanks, pouring clouds of arrows down upon them relentlessly. Some losses were inflicted on the Occidentals in this way, but more important, they were forced to slow their advance.

Shortly before nightfall, the Franj reached a promontory from which they could overlook the entire area. Just below them lay the small village of Hittin, a few earth-colored houses, while the waters of Lake Tiberias glimmered at the bottom of the valley. Between the Franj and the lake, in the verdant plain stretching along the river bank, was the army of Saladin. If they were to drink, they would need the sultan's permission.

Saladin smiled. He knew that the Frank were exhausted, dying of thirst, that they had neither the strength nor the time to cut themselves a passage to the lake before dark, and that they would therefore have to spend the night without a drop to drink. Would they really be able to fight in these conditions? That night, Saladin divided his time between prayers and meetings with his general staff. At the same time, he ordered several of his emirs to slip behind the enemy in order to cut off any possible retreat, while making sure that all his men were in position and understood their orders.

The next day, 4 July 1187, at first light of dawn, the Franj, now surrounded and crazy with thirst, desperately tried to move down the hill to reach the lake. Their foot-soldiers, more sorely tested than the knights by the previous day's exhausting march, rushed ahead blindly, bearing their battleaxes and maces like a burden. Wave upon wave of them were crushed as they encountered a solid wall of swords and lances. The survivors were pressed back up the hill in disarray, where they intermingled with the knights, now certain of their own defeat. No line of defence could be held. Yet they continued to fight with the courage born of despair. At the head of a handful of close collaborators Raymond tried to cut a pathway through the Muslim lines. Saladin's lieutenants recognized him and allowed him to escape. He rode all the way back to Tripoli.

After the count's departure, the Franj were on the point of capitulating, Ibn al-Athir writes. The Muslims had set fire to the dry grass, and the wind was blowing the smoke into the eyes of the knights. Assailed by thirst, flames, and smoke, by the summer heat and the fires of combat, the Franj were unable to go on. But they believed that they could avoid death only by confronting it. They launched attacks so violent that the Muslims were about to give way. Nevertheless, with each assault the Franj suffered heavy losses and their numbers diminished. The Muslims gained possession of the True Cross. For the Franj, this was the heaviest of losses, for it was on this cross, they claim, that the Messiah, peace be upon him, was crucified.

According to Islam, Christ was crucified only in appearance, for God loved the son of Mary too much to allow such an odious torture to be inflicted upon him.

In spite of this loss, the last of the Franj survivors, nearly a hundred and fifty of their best knights, continued to fight bravely, digging in on the high ground above the village of Hittin, where they pitched their tents and organized resistance. But the Muslims pressed them from all sides, and finally only the king's tent remained standing. What happened next was recounted by the son of Saladin himself, al-Malik al-Afdal, who was seventeen at the time.

I was at my father's side during the battle of Hittin, the first I had ever seen. When the king of the Franj found himself on the hill, he and his men launched a fierce attack that drove our own troops back to the place where my father was standing. I looked at him. He was saddened; he frowned and pulled nervously at his beard. Then he advanced, shouting "Satan must not win!" The Muslims again assaulted the hill. When I saw the Franj retreat under the pressure of our troops, I screamed with joy, "We have won!" But the Franj attacked again with all their might, and once again our troops found themselves grouped around my father. Now he urged them into the attack once more, and they forced the enemy to retreat up the hill. Again I screamed "We have beaten them!" But my father turned to me and said, "Silence! We will have crushed them only when that tent on the hill has fallen!" Before he had time to finish his sentence, the king's tent collapsed. The sultan then dismounted, bowed down and thanked God, weeping for joy....

Even before that memorable day had ended, Saladin assembled his chief emirs and congratulated them on their victory, which, he said, had restored the honour so long scorned by the invaders. The Franj, he believed, no longer had an army, and it was necessary to seize upon this opportunity without delay to recover all the lands unjustly occupied. The next day, a Sunday, he therefore attacked the Tiberias citadel, where the wife of Raymond, knowing that further resistance would have been futile, surrendered. Saladin, of course, allowed the defenders to leave unmolested, with all their property.

The following Tuesday the victorious army marched on the port of Acre, which capitulated without resistance. The city had acquired considerable economic importance during these past years, for trade with the west was channelled through it. The sultan tried to convince the many Italian merchants to remain, promising that they would enjoy all the necessary protection. But they preferred to depart for the neighboring port of Tyre. Although he regretted their decision, the sultan did not try to stop them. He even allowed them to take away all their riches and offered them an escort to protect them from brigands.

Saladin saw no point in his roaming the countryside at the head of such a powerful army, so he ordered his emirs to reduce the various strongholds of the Franj in Palestine. The Frankish settlements of Galilee and Samaria surrendered one after the other, sometimes in a few hours, sometimes over several days....

On 4 September Ascalon capitulated, followed by Gaza, which was held by the Templars. At the same time, Saladin dispatched several of his army's emirs to the environs of Jerusalem, where they seized a number of positions, including Bethlehem. The sultan now had but one desire: to crown his victorious campaign, and his career, with the reconquest of the holy city.

Would he be able to duplicate the feat of the caliph Umar, and enter this venerated city without destruction or bloodshed? He sent a message to the inhabitants of Jerusalem inviting them to hold talks on the future of the city. A delegation of notables came to meet him in Ascalon. The victor's proposal was reasonable: the city would be handed over to him without combat; those inhabitants who desired to leave could do so, taking their property with them; the Christian places of worship would be respected; in the future, those who wished to visit the city as pilgrims would not be molested. But to the sultan's great surprise, the Franj responded as arrogantly as they had during the time of their ascendancy. Deliver Jerusalem, the town where Jesus had died? Out of the question! The city was theirs and they would defend it come what may.

Swearing that he would now take Jerusalem only by the sword, Saladin ordered his troops, dispersed in the four corners of Syria, to assemble around the holy city. All the emirs came at the run. What Muslim would not wish to be able to say to his creator on Judgement Day: I fought for Jerusalem. Or better still: I died a martyr for Jerusalem. An astrologer had once predicted that Saladin would lose an eye if he entered the holy city, to which Saladin had replied: "To take it I am ready to lose both eyes!"

Inside the besieged city, the defence was under the command of Balian of Ibelin, the ruler of Ramlah, a lord, according to Ibn al-Athir, who held a rank among the Franj more or less equal to that of king. He had managed to escape from Hittin shortly before the defeat of his troops, and had taken refuge in Tyre. During the summer he had asked Saladin for permission to go and fetch his wife from Jerusalem, promising that he would not bear arms and that he should spend only a single night in the holy city. Once there, however, they begged him to stay, for no one else had sufficient authority to direct the resistance. Balian, who was a man of honour, felt that he could not agree to defend Jerusalem and its people without betraying his agreement with the sultan. He therefore turned to Saladin himself to ask what he should do. The magnanimous sultan released him from his commitment. If duty required that he remain in the holy city and bear arms, so be it! And since Balian was now too busy organizing the defence of Jerusalem to look after his wife, the sultan supplied an escort to lead her back to Tyre!...

As it happened, the resistance of the Franj was courageous but short-lived, and conducted with few illusions. The encirclement of Jerusalem began on 20 September. Six days later Saladin, who had established his camp on the Mount of Olives, asked his troops to intensify their pressure in preparation for the final assault. On 29 September sappers managed to open a breach in the northern part of the wall, very close to the place where the Occidentals had achieved their own breach back in 1099. When he saw that there was no longer any point in continuing the fight, Balian asked for safe conduct and presented himself before the sultan.

Saladin was intractable. Had he not offered the inhabitants the best possible terms on which to capitulate well before the battle? Now was not the time for negotiations, for he had sworn to take the city by the sword, just as the Franj had done. He could be released from his oath only if Jerusalem threw open its gates and surrendered to him completely and unconditionally.

Balian insisted on obtaining a promise from Saladin to spare his life, Ibn al-Athir reports, but Salah al-Din would promise nothing. Balian tried to soften his heart, but in vain. He then addressed him in these terms: "O sultan, be aware that this city holds a mass of people so great that God alone knows their number. They now hesitate to continue the fight, because they hope that you will spare their lives as you have spared so many others, because they love life and hate death. But if we see that death is inevitable, then, by God, we will kill our own women and children and burn all that we possess. We will not leave you a single dinar of booty, not a single dirham, not a single man or woman to lead into captivity. Then we shall destroy the sacred rock, al-Aqsa mosque, and many other sites; we will kill the five thousand Muslim prisoners we now hold, and will exterminate the mounts and all the beasts. In the end, we will come outside the city, and we will fight against you as one fights for one's life. Not one of us will die without having killed several of you!"

Although he was not impressed by the threats, Saladin was moved by his men's fervour. In order not to appear to soften too easily, he turned to his advisers and asked them if he could not be released from his pledge to take the city by the sword--simply in order to avoid the destruction of the holy places of Islam. Their response was affirmative, but since they were aware of their master's incorrigible generosity, they insisted that he obtain financial compensation from the Franj before he allowed them to leave, for the long campaign had emptied the state treasury. The infidels, the advisers explained, were virtual prisoners. To purchase their freedom, each should pay a ransom: ten dinars for each man, five for a woman, and one for a child. Balian accepted the principle, but he pleaded for the poor, who, he said, would be unable to pay such a sum. Could not seven thousand of them be released in exchange for thirty thousand dinars? Once again, the request was granted, despite furious protests from the treasurers. Satisfied, Balian ordered his men to lay down their arms.

So it was that on Friday 2 October 1187, or 27 Rajab 583 by the Muslim calendar, the very day on which Muslims celebrate the prophet's nocturnal journey to Jerusalem, Saladin solemnly entered the holy city. His emirs and soldiers had strict orders: no Christian, whether Frankish or Oriental, was to be touched. And indeed, there was neither massacre nor plunder. Some fanatics demanded that the Church of the Holy Sepulchre be destroyed in retaliation for the excesses committed by the Franj, but Saladin silenced them. On the contrary, he strengthened the guard at the Christian places of worship and announced that the Franj themselves would be allowed to come on pilgrimage whenever they liked. The Frankish cross attached to the Dome of the Rock mosque was removed, of course. And al-Aqsa mosque, which had been turned into a church, became a Muslim place of worship again, after its walls had been sprinkled with rose water....

Saladin had conquered Jerusalem not to amass gold, and still less to seek vengeance. His prime objective, as he himself explained, was to do his duty before his God and his faith. His victory was to have liberated the holy city from the yoke of the invaders--without a bloodbath, destruction, or hatred. His reward was to be able to bow down and pray in places where no Muslim would have been able to pray had it not been for him. On Friday 9 October, a week after the victory, an official ceremony was organized in al-Aqsa mosque. Many religious leaders competed for the honour of delivering the sermon on this memorable occasion. In the end, it was the qadi [judge] of Damascus Muhi al-Din Ibn al-Zaki, the successor of Abu Sa'ad al-Harawi, who was designated by the sultan to mount the pulpit, garbed in a superb black robe. Although his voice was clear and powerful, a slight tremor betrayed his emotion as he spoke: "Glory to God who has bestowed this victory upon Islam and who has returned this city to the fold after a century of perdition! Honour to this army, which He has chosen to complete the reconquest! And may salvation be upon you, Salah al-Din Yusuf, son of Ayyub, you who have restored the spurned dignity of this nation!"

Mallouf, Amin. *The Crusades through Arab Eyes*. Trans. Jon Rothschild. New York: Schocken, 1985. Pp. 190-200.

JOAN OF ARC, "SENT BY THE HEAVENLY LORD TO FIGHT THE ENGLISH"

▶ **Contemporary Drawing of Joan of Arc**

Joan of Arc (1412-1431) is a patron saint of France. Her inspired leadership at a critical juncture of the Hundred Years' War turned the tide in favor of France against England.

Joan was born to a peasant family in the village of Domrémy. Her mystical visions led her to the court of the Dauphin (French crown prince). She claimed that God had called on her to lead the French army against the English. The Dauphin had Joan examined by a panel of church officials and, with their approval, entrusted an army to her command. She turned the tide from defeat to victory for the French forces and lifted the siege of Orléans. As a result, Joan occupied a place of honor at the subsequent coronation of the Dauphin as King Charles VII of France.

The remainder of Joan's brief career was brief and pathetic. She was captured by Burgundians, who were allies of the English, at Compiègne, not far from Paris. The Burgundians sold her to the English, who empaneled an ecclesiastical kangaroo court. Joan was tried and convicted of heresy and sorcery, for her defiance of the authority of the Roman Catholic church and for claiming that God had spoken to her through Saints Catherine and Margaret. On 30 May 1431, she was burned at the stake in the square at Rouen.

Twenty-five years later, her case was reopened at the urging of Charles VII, her family, and friends. The report concluded that the trial had been invalid. In 1456, Pope Calixtus III completely exonerated Joan on the grounds that the original trial and verdict had been corrupt and full of legal errors. The legend of Joan the Maid gained momentum from that time on. She was beatified in 1894 and canonized in 1920 as Saint Joan by Pope Benedict XV.

The passage that follows is from testimony given at Joan of Arc's retrial in 1456. The character witness here is Jean II, Duke of Alençon, a cousin of Charles VII. He recalls his impressions of her in their days of campaigning together.

QUESTIONS:

1) What were some of the wonders that made Joan seem to be chosen by God for her task?
2) What was Joan's principal accomplishment as a an actual historical figure?
3) Why is Joan a distinctively French national hero?

When Joan arrived at Chinon [to see the Dauphin, the future King Charles VII], I was at Saint-Florent. On a day when I was going quail-hunting, a messenger came to say that a young girl had come to the King; she claimed to have been sent by God to fight the English and to lift the siege they were maintaining at Orléans. For this reason, I departed next day for Chinon, where I found the King conversing with Joan. When I approached them, she asked who I was. "My cousin, the Duke of Alençon," answered the King. "You have come at a good time," she told me, "for the more the blood of the King of France is gathered together, the better it will be." Next day, she went to the King's Mass; when she saw the King, she bowed deeply. After the Mass, the King conducted Joan into his private chamber together with myself and the Lord de la Trémouille, dismissing everyone else. Joan then made several requests of the King, among others that he should make a gift of his kingdom to the Heavenly King, because the Heavenly King would then do for him what he had done for his predecessors-restore to him all his rightful prerogatives. Many other things that I do not recall were discussed right up till dinner time. After dining, the King went for a walk, and before his eyes, Joan made a charge, with a spear in hand. Having seen her handle the spear so well in doing this, I presented her with the gift of a horse.

Following all this, the King had her examined by churchmen. He chose the bishop of Chartres, the King's own confessor, the bishops of Senlis, Mende, and Poitiers, Master Pierre of Versailles, then bishop of Meaux, Master Jourdain Morin, and many others whose names escape me. In my presence, they interrogated her, asking her why she had come and who had told her to come to the King. She responded that she had come on behalf of the Heavenly King. She said she heard voices and a counsel advising her what she ought to do, but I do not recall whether she revealed what these voices said.

One day at dinner, she said to me that the scholars had examined her carefully, but that she knew more and was capable of more than she had told them. When he had received the report of the examiners, the King wanted her sent to Poitiers to submit to another examination. I did not take part in this; I only know that it was afterwards reported that the examiners at Poitiers were of the opinion that there was nothing contrary to the faith to be found in her and that the King, in view of the extreme necessity, could avail himself of her services. At this news, the King sent me to the Queen of Sicily to prepare a

convoy of provisions for the army he was intending to lead to Orléans. With the queen, I found Lord Ambroise de Loré and a Lord Louis, whose full name I forget, in the process of preparing the convoy. But there was a lack of funds, and so I returned to the King to secure them. I let him know that the provisions had been bought and that it remained only to procure the funds with which to pay the army. The King then sent envoys with the necessary sums, so that provisions and soldiers were both paid for and it remained only to relieve and regain the besieged city of Orléans.

Joan was sent along with the army. The King had had arms made for her. The King's army then departed with Joan. Of what happened en route and afterwards at Orléans I know only by hearsay, since I was not present myself. But I did go a little later and viewed the siege works that the English had built around the city. I was able to assess the strength of these works; I believe that the taking of these works-- especially the Fort des Tournelles at the foot of the bridge and the Fort des Augustins--truly amounted to a miracle for the French. Had I been in command of either of these forts with even a few men, I would have dared to defy a whole army for six or seven days--it could not have taken the fort. I have heard from officers and soldiers who were present that they considered everything that occurred there a miracle, wrought not by human hand, but by a supernatural force. Lord Ambroise de Loré, formerly governor of Paris, has asserted this to me on several occasions.

I had not seen Joan between the time she left the King and the lifting of the siege of Orléans. After the siege, we assembled 600 spearmen, with which we determined to march on Jargeau, which the English were still occupying. At nightfall of the day we set out, we encamped in a wood. The next morning, we were joined by another army corps under the command of the Lord Bastard of Orléans, Lord Florent d'Illiers, and many other officers. When we had joined together, we numbered some 1200 spearmen. There ensued a discussion among the captains: some thought we should make an attack, others opposed this, in view of the great strength of the English and their superior numbers. Joan, seeing them so divided, said "Do not fear their numbers or hesitate to attack. God will guide your endeavor. Were I not certain that God is leading us, I would prefer to be a shepherd rather than expose myself to such great dangers!" At these words, we marched on Jargeau, intending to seize the suburbs that day and to spend the night there. But, at the news of our approach, the English came out to meet us and at first repulsed us. At this moment, Joan, seizing the standard, went on the attack. She urged us to take heart and be brave. We fought so well that we were able to lodge in the suburbs that night. I truly believe that God himself was guiding us, for that night we posted no actual guards, and if the English had made a raid, we would have been in the gravest peril. The next morning, we prepared the artillery and put the bombardment machines in place. We next held consultations over several days regarding what had to be done in order to take the city. While these deliberations were taking place, it was reported to us that La Hire was conferring with the English Lord of Suffolk. I and the other officers were upset with La Hire and sent for him. When we had resolved to attack, heralds went round the army crying "To the attack!" Joan cried out to me "To the fore, gentle Duke, to the attack!" I observed to her that we were going too hastily in making our attack so quickly. She said, "have no fear, the time is right when it pleases God; it is necessary to do as he wills; act and God will act!" Moments later, she said, "Gentle Duke, can you be afraid? Don't you know I have promised your wife to return you safe and sound?" And, in fact, when I had left my wife to go with Joan at the head of the army, my wife had told her that she feared terribly for me. I had been taken prisoner before and had been ransomed at such a great cost that she would have liked to beg me to stay with her. To this, Joan had responded, "Madame, have no fear, I will return him to you safe and sound, and even in better condition than he now is."

During our attack on Jargeau, I happened to be standing next to Joan, when she said to me "retire from the place where you are now or that machine [artillery in Jargeau] will kill you!" I did as she said and a little later that same machine did in fact kill the Lord de Lude on the very spot I had left. This event made a deep impression on me and I was amazed at what Joan

was able to forecast. Joan then went on the attack, and I followed her. When our men were on the point of overrunning the place, the Count of Suffolk had his crier shout that he wanted to speak with me. He could not be heard and the attack continued. Joan was mounting a ladder with her standard in her hand; the standard was struck and she herself was hit on the head by a stone that smashed against the helmet she was wearing that day. She was thrown to the ground. But she immediately got back up, shouting "Friends, friends, up, up--our Lord has damned the English! They are ours! Be of good spirit!" At that very moment, the town was taken and the English withdrew toward the bridges, with our men in pursuit, killing more than 1100 of them in the process.

With the town now taken, Joan and the whole army proceeded to Orléans, and from Orléans to Meung on the Loire, where the English were .... Under the walls of Meung, I spent the night in a church with a very few soldiers and was in great peril. The day after taking Meung, we went to Beaugency and in the vicinity of this city we assembled a portion of the army, with which we attacked the English in Beaugency. Following our attack, the English abandoned the town to withdrew to a camp, which we kept under surveillance during the night, for fear they would make a retreat. While we were there news reached us that the constable was coming to rejoin us with an army corps. Joan, the other officers, and myself were disturbed by this news and wanted to withdraw, for we were under orders from the King not to receive the lord constable. I told Joan that if the constable insisted on coming I was going to withdraw.

The next day, before the arrival of the constable, we were informed that the English were marching on us in force, under the command of Talbot. We immediately called the men to arms! Knowing that I wished to withdraw because of the constable's arrival, Joan told me not to do it, saying that we had to help each other. The English broke camp and I granted them safe conduct, since I was the King's lieutenant and at that time commander of the army under that title. We were expecting them to retire, when a member of La Hire's company came to tell us that they [the English] were advancing on us and that we would shortly be face to face with 1000 enemy soldiers. Joan asked what this envoy had announced and when she learned what it was she said to the lord constable, "Ah, good constable, you have not come at my wish, but since you are here, welcome!" Many of the men were afraid and saying that it would be a good thing if we could secure the arrival of cavalry before the battle. "In God's name," said Joan, "they must be fought; even if they were suspended from clouds, we would take them, because God has sent them to us so that we might punish them." She assured us of her confidence in victory. "The gentle King," she said, "shall have today his greatest victory. My counsel says that they are completely ours." The English were beaten in the event and Talbot taken captive, amidst prodigious slaughter.

Then the army returned to Patay, where Talbot was brought before me and the constable, in the presence of Joan. I told Talbot that in the morning I had not expected things to turn out as they had. "The fortunes of war," he said. Then we returned to the King. He determined to go to Rheims for his coronation and consecration.

Several times, in my presence, Joan said to the King that she would last only a year and that it behooved them to use it well. Her mission, she said, consisted in four things: to beat the English, to cause the King to be crowned and consecrated at Rheims, to deliver the duke of Orléans from English hands, and to cause the siege of Orléans to be lifted.

This was a young woman of complete chastity; she had the greatest contempt for the sort of women who follow armies. I saw her one day at St. Denis, returning from the King's consecration, take sword in hand and chase such a woman so hard that she broke her sword. She would become furious when she heard profanity. I myself was the object of her reproaches when I would occasionally use profanity in her hearing, so that I also had need to restrain my tongue.

Sometimes, on campaign, I slept on the same bed of straw with her, myself and other soldiers. I watched as she removed her armor and glimpsed her breasts, which were very lovely. Still, I never felt an improper desire for her. She was a true Christian and an honorable woman. She received the Eucharist often and wept profusely at the sight of the body of Christ. Apart from the conduct of war, she was a very simple young woman. But in military matters, the bearing of arms, the gathering of the army, the choice of vantage for attack, the targeting of artillery, in these things she was highly proficient. Everyone marveled that she could act with such sagacity and foresight, like a twenty- or thirty-year veteran officer. She was especially admirable in her use of artillery.

O'Reilly, E., ed. *Les deux procés de condamnation, les enquêtes et la sentence de réhabilitation de Jeanne d'Arc.* Paris: Henri Plon, 1868. Vol. 1. Pp. 206-214. Translation by James P. Holoka.

WITCH TRIALS IN SEVENTEENTH-CENTURY GERMANY

▶ Witches at Work

Practitioners of witchcraft claim to use supernatural forces in service to the Devil. The practice is based on a belief that Satan or devils and demons exist and work with witches (both male and female) toward their nefarious goals. In return for their allegiance to Satan, witches receive special powers enabling them to affect human beings and other living things, as well as weather and other natural phenomena.

Witches are supposed to have special knowledge of poison and potions of all kinds, as well as of voodoo-like black magic. They are also thought to fly or become invisible or change into animal forms, to foresee the future, and to energize inanimate objects, including corpses. Since the Middle Ages, most witches were believed to be women organized into covens, usually with a male leader. They allegedly assembled in secret and performed elaborate ceremonies and revels, most notably the annual celebration of Halloween.

The Christian church was extremely hostile towards witches and witchcraft. Pope Innocent VIII (1432-1492) issued a bull [pronouncement] denouncing the practice in 1484, and authorized inquisitors to investigate and judge cases of witchcraft. This heightened the witch-hunting hysteria throughout Europe. Both the practice and persecution of witchcraft were brought by Europeans to colonial settlements in the western hemisphere. The witchcraft mania at Salem Village in Massachusetts in 1692 is a famous example.

The first passage below is a letter from Johannes Junius, the burgomaster or chief magistrate of the town of Bamberg, to his daughter, describing his interrogation and trial on charges of witchcraft. He was convicted and burned at the stake. The second is from an anonymous work decrying the methods employed in prosecuting cases of witchcraft. The author was Friedrich von Spee, a Jesuit priest who served as confessor for convicted "witches."

QUESTIONS:

1) According to the first selection, what method do the witch-hunters use to identify their victims?
2) Is the second selection a compelling exposé of the methods of witch-hunters?
3) What could secure a person against charges of witchcraft?

Many hundred thousand good-nights, dearly beloved daughter Veronica. Innocent have I come into prison, innocent have I been tortured, innocent must I die. For whoever comes into the prison must become a witch or be tortured until he invents something out of his head and--God pity him--bethinks him of something. I will tell you how it has gone with me. When I was the first time put to the torture, Dr. Braun, Dr. Kötzendörffer, and two strange doctors were there. Then Br. Braun asks me, "Kinsman, how came you here?" I answer, "Through falsehood, through misfortune." "Hear, you," he says, "you are a witch; will you confess it voluntarily? If not, we'll bring in witnesses and the executioner for you." I said "I am no witch, I have a pure conscience in the matter; if there are a thousand witnesses, I am not anxious, but I'll gladly hear the witnesses." Now the chancellor's son was set before me ... and afterward Hoppfen Elss. She had seen me dance on Haupts-moor.... I answered: "I have never renounced God and will never do it--God graciously keep me from it. I'll rather bear whatever I must." And then came also--God in highest Heaven have mercy--the executioner, and put the thumb-screws on me, both hands bound together, so that the blood ran out at the nails and everywhere, so that for four weeks I could not use my hands, as you can see from the writing.... Thereafter they first stripped me, bound my hands behind me, and drew me up in the torture. Then I thought heaven and earth were at an end; eight times did they draw me up and let me fall again, so that I suffered terrible agony....

And this happened on Friday, June 30 [1628], and with God's help I had to bear the torture.... When at last the executioner led me back into the prison, he said to me: "Sir, I beg you, for God's sake confess something, whether it be true or not. Invent something, for you cannot endure the torture you will be put to; and, even if you bear it all, yet you will not escape, not even if you were an earl, but one torture will follow after another until you say you are a witch. Not before that," he said, "will they let you go, as you may see by all their trials, for one is just like another."...

And so I begged, since I was in wretched plight, to be given one day for thought and a priest. The priest was refused me, but the time for thought was given. Now, my dear child, see in what hazard I stood and still stand. I must say that I am a witch, though I am not,--must now renounce God, though I have never done it

before. Day and night I was deeply troubled, but at last there came to me a new idea. I would not be anxious, but, since I had been given no priest with whom I could take counsel, I would myself think of something and say it. It were surely better that I just say it with mouth and words, even though I had not really done it; and afterwards I would confess it to the priest, and let those answer for it who compel me to do it.... And so I made my confession ... in order to escape the great anguish and bitter torture, which it was impossible for me longer to bear....

Then I had to tell what people I had seen [at the witch-sabbath]. I said that I had not recognized them. "You old rascal, I must set the executioner at you. Say--was not the Chancellor there?" So I said yes. "Who besides?" I had not recognized anybody. So he said: "Take one street after another; begin at the market, go out on one street and back on the next." I had to name several persons there. Then came the long street. I knew nobody. Had to name eight persons there. Then the Zinkenwert--one person more. Then over the upper bridge to the Georgthor, on both sides. Knew nobody again. Did I know anybody in the castle--whoever it might be, I should speak without fear. And thus continuously they asked me on all the streets, though I could not and would not say more. So they gave me to the executioner, told him to strip me, shave me all over, and put me to the torture. "The rascal knows one on the market-place, is with him daily, and yet won't name him." By that they meant Dietmeyer: so I had to name him too.

Then I had to tell what crimes I had committed. I said nothing.... "Draw the rascal up!" So I said that I was to kill my children, but I had killed a horse instead. It did not help. I had also taken a sacred [communion] wafer, and had desecrated it. When I had said this, they left me in peace.

Now, dear child, here you have all my confession, for which I must die. And they are sheer lies and made-up things, so help me God. For all this I was forced to say through fear of the torture which was threatened beyond what I had already endured. For they never leave off with the torture till one confesses something; be he never so good, he must be a witch. Nobody escapes, though he were an earl....

Dear child, keep this letter secret so that people do not find it, else I shall be tortured most piteously and the jailers will be beheaded. So strictly is it forbidden.... Dear child, pay this man a dollar.... I have taken several days to write this: my hands are both lame. I am in a sad plight....

Good night, for your father Johannes Junius will never see you more. July 24, 1628.

[The following added marginally:]

Dear child, six have confessed against me at once: the Chancellor, his son, Neudecker, Zaner, Hoffmaisters Ursel, and Hoppfen Els--all false, through compulsion, as they have all told me, and begged my forgiveness in God's name before they were executed.... They know nothing but good of me. They were forced to say it, just as I myself was....

* * * * *

What, now, is the outline and method of the trials against witches to-day in general use?--a thing worthy of Germany's consideration.

I answer:...

Incredible among us Germans and especially (I blush to say it) among Catholics are the popular superstition, envy, calumnies, back-bitings, insinuations, and the like, which, being neither punished by the magistrates nor refuted by the pulpit, first stir up suspicion of witchcraft. All the divine judgments which God has threatened in Holy Writ are now ascribed to witches. No longer do God or nature do aught, but witches everything.

Hence it comes that all at once everybody is clamoring that the magistrates proceed against the witches--those witches whom only their own clamor has made seem so many.

Princes, therefore, bid their judges and counselors to begin proceedings against the witches....

If now some utterance of a demoniac or some malign and idle rumor then current (for proof of the scandal is never asked) points especially to some poor and helpless Gaia [Jane Doe], she is the first to suffer.

And yet, lest it appear that she is indicted on the basis of rumor alone, without other proofs, as the phrase goes, lo a certain presumption is at once obtained against her by posing the following dilemma: Either Gaia has led a bad and improper life, or she has led a good proper one. If a bad one, then, say they, the proof is cogent against her; for from malice to malice the presumption is strong. If, however, she has led a good one, this also is none the less a proof; for thus, they say, are witches wont to cloak themselves and try to seem especially proper....

If, too, there are any who have borne her ill will, these, having now a fine opportunity to do her harm, bring against her such charges as it may please them to devise; and on every side there is a clamor that the evidence is heavy against her.

And so, as soon as possible, she is hurried to the torture, if indeed she be not subjected to it on the very day of her arrest, as often happens.

For in these trials there is granted to nobody an advocate or any means of fair defense, for the cry is that the crime is an expected one, and whoever ventures to defend the prisoner is brought into suspicion of the crime--as are all those who dare to utter a protest in these cases and to urge the judges to caution; for they are forthwith dubbed patrons of the witches. Thus all mouths are closed and all pens blunted, lest they speak or write....

Before she is tortured ... she is led aside by the executioner, and, lest she may by magical means have fortified herself against pain, she is searched, her whole body being shaved, ... although up to this time nothing of the sort was ever found....

Then, when Gaia has thus been searched and shaved, she is tortured that she may confess the truth, that is to say, that she may simply declare herself guilty: for whatever else she may say will not be the truth and cannot be.

She is, however, tortured with the torture of the first degree, i.e., the less severe. This is to be understood thus: that, although in itself it is exceedingly severe, yet, compared with others to follow, it is lighter. Wherefore, if she confesses, they say and noise it abroad that she has confessed without torture.

Now, what prince or other dignitary who hears this can doubt that she is most certainly guilty who thus voluntarily without torture confesses her guilt?

Without any scruples, therefore, after this confession she is executed. Yet she would have been executed, nevertheless, even though she had not confessed; for, when once a beginning has been made with the torture, the die is already cast--she cannot escape, she must die....

If she does not confess, the torture is repeated--twice, thrice, four times: anything one pleases is permissible, for ... there is no limit of duration or severity or repetition of the tortures. As to this, think the judges, no sin is possible which can be brought up before the tribunal of conscience.

If now Gaia, no matter how many times tortured, has not yet broken silence--if she contorts her features under the pain, if she loses consciousness, or the like, then they cry that she is laughing or has bewitched herself into taciturnity, and hence deserves to be burned alive, as lately has been done to some who though several times tortured would not confess.

And then they say--even clergymen and confessors--that she died obstinate and impenitent, that she would not be converted or desert her paramour [the Devil], but kept rather her faith with him.

If, however, it chances that under so many tortures one dies, they say that her neck has been broken by the Devil.... Wherefore justly, forsooth, the corpse is dragged out by the executioner and buried under the gallows. But if, on the other hand, Gaia does not die and some exceptionally scrupulous judge hesitates to torture her further without fresh proofs or to burn her without a confession, she is kept in prison and more harshly fettered, and there lies for perhaps an entire year to rot until she is subdued....

In the meantime ... there are not wanting to her industrious judges clever devices by which they not only find new proofs against Gaia, but by which moreover they so convict her to her face ... that by the advice of some university faculty she is then at last pronounced to deserve burning alive....

Some, however, to leave no stone unturned, order Gaia to be exorcised and transferred to a new place, and then to be tortured again, in the hope that by this exorcism and change of place the bewitchment of taciturnity may perhaps be broken. But, if not even this succeeds, then at last they commit her alive to the flames. Now, in Heaven's name, I would like to know, since both she who confesses and she who does not perish alike, what way of escape is there for any,

however innocent? O unhappy Gaia, why has thou rashly hoped? why hast thou not, at first entering prison, declared thyself guilty? why, O foolish woman and mad, wilt thou die so many times when thou mightest die but once? Follow my counsel, and before all pain declare thyself guilty and die. Thou wilt not escape; for this were a disgrace to the zeal of Germany.

If, now, any under stress of pain has falsely declared herself guilty, her wretched plight beggars description. For not only is there in general no door for her escape, but she is also compelled to accuse others, of whom she knows no ill, and whose names are not seldom suggested to her by her examiners or by the executioner, or of whom she has heard as suspected or accused or already once arrested and released. These in their turn are forced to accuse others, and these still others, and so it goes on: who can help seeing that it must go on without end?

Wherefore the judges themselves are obliged at last either to break off the trials and so condemn their own work or else to burn their own folk, aye themselves and everybody: for on all soon or late false accusations fall, and, if only followed by the torture, all are proved guilty.

And so at last those are brought into question who at the outset most loudly clamored for the constant feeding of the flames; for they rashly failed to see that their turn, too, must inevitably come--and by a just verdict of Heaven, since with their pestilent tongues they created us so many witches and sent so many innocent to the flames.

But now gradually many of the wiser and more learned begin to take notice of it, and, as if aroused from deep sleep, to open their eyes and slowly and cautiously to bestir themselves....

From all which there follows this corollary, worthy to be noted in red ink: that, if only the trials be steadily pushed on with, there is nobody in our day, of whatsoever sex, fortune, rank, or dignity, who is safe, if he have but an enemy and slanderer to bring him into suspicion of witchcraft....

Leitschuh, Friedrich. *Beiträge zur Geschichte des Hexenwesens in Franken.* Bamberg 1883. Spee, Friedrich von. *Cautio criminalis.* Rinteln 1631. Pp. 378-392. In G. Burr, trans. *The Witch Persecutions.* Philadelphia 1907. Pp. 26-28, 30-35.

SECTION 5

NEW CENTERS OF CIVILIZATION

By the late first millennium, new centers of political power and culture were emerging, some from the ruins of ancient civilizations, others in primitive regions. To varying degrees, all were amalgamations of the old and new, the imported and the indigenous. West Asia was an example of an old land with a new culture, the result of the rise of a new religion--Islam. Ancient Egypt and the Fertile Crescent, the first regions to be incorporated into the new Islamic empire, became the center of the Golden Age of Islam. Early great Muslim caliphs built vibrant new cities from ancient ruins, while their enlightened rule fostered the flowering of cultures. Islam and Arab culture expanded to northwest and sub-Saharan Africa, and to the already Christianized Ethiopia.

New centers of civilization emerged in Southeast Asia and parts of East Asia during the first millennium as a result of the expanding influence of two ancient cultures--India and China. Chinese and Indians brought literacy, religions, philosophies, advanced sciences and technologies, art and architecture, which local peoples adopted and adapted to their indigenous ways in unique combinations. The Buddhist monument of Borobodur in Java with its stone-engraved artwork illustrates Buddhism from India as it was practiced by the Javanese. A Chinese traveler's account vividly portrays Khmer life as a blend of local elements with Indian and Chinese imports. Japan's evolving culture mixed native myths with Chinese political and philosophical values, eventually forming a uniquely Japanese culture of courtly ladies and valiant warriors.

A similar transformation was meantime taking place in the Western Hemisphere. In Mexico, the Aztec culture rose on the foundations of earlier peoples, as did the Inka culture in South America.

Thus new centers of civilization emerged around the world, enriched by borrowings and adaptations from older civilizations. The readings in this section offer examples of the reintegration of old traditions of life and the advent of new civilizations. They illustrate a never ending process of cultural change.

► Arab Coin

READING 5.1

CALIPH OMAR THE GREAT

The office of Caliph of Islam (vice-regent of the Prophet) was created when Muhammad died in 632 C.E. Abu Bakr, one of Muhammad's earliest converts and a close companion, was chosen first caliph by acclamation of the community. Abu Bakr consolidated Muslim rule over the Arabian peninsula and began its expansion beyond, engaging its first major enemy, the Byzantine Empire; but he died before the campaign had born fruit. Before his death in 634, Abu Bakr nominated Omar, another companion of Muhammad, as his successor; his choice was confirmed by the community and Omar reigned as caliph between 334 and 344 C.E.

Immediately after assuming office, Omar launched the army in simultaneous and many-pronged attacks against both the Byzantine and Persian Empires. By 642, Jerusalem and the entire eastern shore of the Mediterranean, Iraq and Mesopotamia, Persia and Egypt had all fallen to Muslim arms. These astonishing victories are attributable to Omar's good military organization and leadership, the religious zeal of Muslim soldiers, and internal weaknesses in both the Byzantine and Persian empires. After his victories, Omar shrewdly ordered a fair distribution of much loot to his supporters. As a result, the Muslim army had no difficulty attracting recruits. Omar's caliphate is also distinguished for the compiling of the Qur'an, the beginning of the codification of Muslim laws, the setting up of an educational system, and the establishment of a stable government for the growing empire.

This reading is from a biography of Omar, and concentrates on his achievement in two key areas: the compiling of a register of the population of the Arabian peninsula and the organization of Arab manpower into active and reserve military units. This militarization of the Arabs made possible the rapid expansion of the Islamic empire. The other is Omar's founding of cities in newly conquered lands and settlement of Arab tribes therein. This policy both consolidated the expanding Islamic empire and made much of the Middle East and north Africa ethnically Arab. Thus Omar's foresight brought success to his caliphate and continued growth to Islam.

QUESTIONS:

1) How did Omar organize the Arabs into a military force?
2) How did Omar provide for the army and how did he use it?
3) What great cities did Omar build? Describe some of them.

In 15 A.H [637 C.E. The Muslim calendar began in 622 C.E. when Muhammad and his followers fled from Mecca to Medina, and is called in Latin Annus Hijra or A.H.].... Omar decided to organize the army into a separate department.   The most noteworthy of his proposals in this connection was to turn the whole man-power of the country into an army. Omar proposed to turn into practical reality the principle that every Muslim is a soldier of the army of Islam.   But it was not practicable to apply the principle to the whole of Arabia all at once.   So he made the beginning with the Quraish and the Ansar [tribes].... The keeping of genealogies was a hereditary science among the Arabs.... Omar commissioned [three most distinguished genealogists] to prepare a register of the whole of Quraish and the Ansar, giving the name and parentage of each person.... The register was prepared accordingly and salaries were fixed per annum [according to each man's participation in important battles].... Stipends were also fixed for the wives and children of those whose names were entered in the register....

The men so registered were all liable to military service, but were divided into two categories, namely, (1) those who were on active service, i.e., formed the regular standing army, and (2) those who lived at their homes, but were liable to be called to the colours in time of need....

For the purpose of army administration he established a few big military centres ... at Madinah, Kufah, Basrah, Musal, Fustat in Egypt, Damascus, Urdan and Palestine. Though Omar's conquests extended to Baluchistan, the provinces that constituted what may be called "home countries" were only Iraq, Egypt, Jazirah and Syria, and military centres were established in these four provinces only....

The following arrangements were made for the army at these centres:

1. Barracks were built for the residence of troops....

2. Big stables containing four thousand horses, fully equipped and ready for service at short notice, were kept at every military centre with a view to having thirty-two thousand horses available for any emergency.... Much care was given to the maintenance and training of these horses. The charge of those at Madinah Omar had kept in his own hands. Pasture lands were reserved at four stages from the capital, and the Caliph appointed his own slave named Hani for its care and maintenance.   The horses were branded on the hams with the words ... "Army for the service of God."...

3. All records pertaining to the army were kept at military centres.

4. Food and stores of the commissariat were kept at these centres and therefrom sent to other places.

In addition to these great centres, Omar built numerous cantonments at big towns and other suitable points and spread the Arab race throughout the conquered lands.   It was a common practice of Omar to post permanently a number of troops at every new town that was conquered.... But even after peace had been established, no big city or district remained without its quota of troops....

Recruitment of the army, which began with the Muhajirin and Ansar, was gradually expanded to cover almost the whole of Arabia. All the tribes which had their habitats between Madinah and Asfan, two stages beyond Makkah, were one by one brought on the army register. Similarly, the Arab tribes of Bahrain, which is one of the farthest tracts of Arabia ... is put on the army register. All the Arabs who had settled at Kufah, Basrah, Musal, Fustat, Jazirah and other towns were also registered. All this innumerable host had their stipends and salaries fixed according to their ranks. Though their entire strength is not given in works of history, there seems reason to believe that their numbers must have mounted to between eight and ten lakhs [one lakh is 100,000] of well-equipped soldiers....

It was by virtue of this organization that the Arabs were able to maintain their power and prestige in the world for a long time, and the flood of conquests continued to flow. As the system began to fall into disrepair, the Arab power also began to decline.... That was indeed the day when the empire passed out of the hands of the Arabs for good....

In the earlier days of the administration, the military department was not completely separated from other departments, and people who received salaries for purposes other than service in the army were also put on the army pay roll.... Time came when this confusion was also removed. In the earlier days the fixation of the salary of a person depended also upon his knowledge of the Holy Qur'an. But as it had no direct connection with the army as such, Omar relegated knowledge of the Qur'an to the education department and removed the distinction from the pay roll of the army. Accordingly, he wrote ... "Pay no salaries for the knowledge of the Holy Qur'an."

Thereafter he turned his attention to increasing the salaries of the army. As the Caliph desired to keep the army entirely free from trade, agriculture or other occupations, it was necessary that all the needs of the soldiers should be provided for. For this purpose necessary increases were made in their salaries.... Children [of soldiers] used to have their stipends from the date they were weaned. Omar ordered that thenceforth the stipends should be paid from the dates of their birth....

The cities founded in the time of Omar, the needs that led to their foundation and the peculiarities in their construction, each forms a page in the history of Islam. Of these cities Basrah and Kufah for long remained witnesses of the glory of Islam. It was here that the science of Arabic Syntax was founded, and the two cities remained centres of the study of this part of Arabic literature. The Hanafi Law, which is accepted far and wide in the Islamic world, had its origins at Kufah....

Basrah. Omar, for security against sea raids from Persia and India, appointed 'Utba b. Ghazwan in 14 A.H. to build a city near the port of Aballah where ships from India and Persia plying in the Persian Gulf used to anchor. The site and aspect of the proposed town were determined by Omar himself. 'Utba went with eight hundred men and came to Kharibah where Basrah now stands. The site was empty desert at the time. The land was gravely [sic]; water and pasturelands were available, and the whole tract suited the Arab temperament. 'Utab laid the foundations of the town, divided the areas into quarters for tribal units.... 'Asim b. Dalf was given the task of assigning the quarters to the various tribes....

The Tigris flows at a distance of about ten miles from Basrah. A canal was brought from the river to the town by the command of Omar.... The population of Basrah increased by

leaps and bounds until in the reign of Ziad b. Abi Sufyan the people whose names were on the army register alone numbered eighty thousand, while their children and grand-children numbered one hundred and twenty thousand souls....

The foundations of Arabic learning were laid here. The first Arabic dictionary ever written was compiled in this city.... The study of Arabic prosody and the development of music also began at Basrah. Saibwiyah, the first writer on Syntax, received his education here, and Hasan Basri, one of the leading Imams of Islam, was born on the soil of Basrah.

Kufah. [After conquering northern Iraq Omar ordered the selection of a site] which should have the characteristics of both sea and land. [A place was chosen where] the soil was sandy and gravely, and for this reason the place was named Kufah. Before Islam, the dynasty of Nu'man b. Mundhir, who ruled over Iraq, had their capital here.... The aspect of the land was pleasant, and the site was only two miles from the Euphrates....

The city was founded in 17 A.H. and, as Omar had expressly commanded, houses sufficient to lodge forty thousand persons were built. Arab tribes were allotted separate quarters ....

Omar had also given clear instructions with regard to the plan of the city as well as its construction. Accordingly the principal streets were forty cubits wide, those of second class thirty cubits.... The Jami Masjid [mosque] was built on a raised square platform and was so big that forty thousand persons could pray in it at one time.... In front of the mosque was built a vast pavilion, two hundred cubits long, which was supported on pillars of marble that were procured from the palaces of the ancient emperors of Iran.... At a distance of two hundred cubits from the mosque was built the government house which comprised the public treasury as well. A public guest house was also added, in which travellers were lodged....

In Omar's own lifetime the city came to attain such greatness and splendour that the Caliph called it the head of Islam. It had indeed become a centre of Arab power. The population continued to expand in later times, but retained its original Arab character by the fact that most of the new settlers were Arabs....

The place of Kufah in the history of learning is distinguished by the fact that the science of Syntax took its birth here.... The foundations of the Hanafi Law were also laid here. It was in Kufah that Imam Abu Hanifah founded the society for the development of *Fiqh*.

Fustat [modern Cairo]. When 'Amr b. al-'As conquered Alexandria [Egypt], most of its Greek population evacuated the city. Finding their houses vacant, 'Amr b. al'-As thought of making it his capital and wrote to the Caliph for permission. Omar had apprehensions about communications and did not like the idea of having a river intervening between himself and a provincial capital. At the time of founding the cities of Basrah and Kufah, too, he had instructed his officers to choose sites so that no river should intervene between Madinah [capital of the caliphate] and these cities. As Alexandria was on the other side of the Nile, the Caliph did not approve of the provincial capital being located in that city.

'Amr b. al-'As left Alexandria for Qasr-ul-Shama where he found his tent which he had left behind before his attack on Alexandria still standing. He put up in the same tent and laid up the foundations of a new city at the same place. As before, separate quarters were built for various tribal units.... As the founding of the city had started with a tent, it received the name of Fustat, which in Arabic means a tent. The town was founded in 21 A.H.

Fustat made rapid progress and became the centre of Egypt in place of Alexandria. In the reign of Mu'aviyah, those of its Arab inhabitants whose names were on the army register totalled forty thousand.... The city remained the capital of the rulers of Egypt and a centre of culture and advancement for a long time. Bashari who made a world tour in the fourth century of Hijra writes of this city in his *Geography*: "This city is the eclipser of Baghdad, the treasure-house of the West and the pride of Islam. In no mosque in the whole Muslim world are held as many learned gatherings as here, nor is any city visited by as many ships."

Numani, Shamsul 'Ulama 'Allama Shibli. *Omar the Great (The Second Caliph of Islam)*. Trans. Muhammad Saleem. Rpt. Lahore, Pakistan 1962. Vol. 2. Pp. 92-100, 104-106, 108-111, 114-115, 118-119.

READING 5.2

BAGHDAD DURING THE GOLDEN AGE OF ISLAM AND OF THE ARABIAN NIGHTS

► Tomb of Timurlane

Medina in western Arabia was the first capital of the Muslim empire from 622 C.E. to the assassination of the fourth caliph Ali in 661. The Ummayad caliphate that followed derived its power from Syria and therefore chose Damascus as its capital. The next dynasty of caliphs, the Abbasids, drew its support from Persia and nearby lands, and made their capital at Baghdad, on the Tigris River near ancient Babylon and Ctesiphon (capital of the Hellenistic Seleucid empire).

Baghdad of the Abbasids was protected by a mighty rectangular wall 125 feet thick at the base and pierced by four iron gates so heavy that each took a company of soldiers to operate. A moat and an inner wall surrounded the Caliph's palaces, residences of his relatives, and government offices. A gilded gateway called the Golden Gate commanded the approach to the caliph's quarters. His palace covered over one-eighth of a square mile; it had two domed audience halls. The taller one, 130 feet high and covered by green tiles, could be seen from every quarter of the city.

Paved roads separated quarters between the walls, where mosques, public baths, warehouses, bazaars, and residential quarters were located. The main streets measured 85 feet wide. Canals from the nearby Euphrates River provided drinking water for the people and for the numerous gardens of the rich. Although Muslim Arabs and Persians formed the bulk of the city's residents, its fame and wealth attracted people from many lands. Baghdad also had a considerable Jewish and Christian community and became the seat of the patriarch of Nestorian Christians (a branch of the Eastern church founded by Nestorius in the fifth century).

Baghdad reached its peak under Caliph Haroun Al-Raschid (r. 786-809 C.E.) whose reign is looked back upon as the Golden Age. Haroun (Aaron to Jews and Christians) earned the title Al-Raschid which means "the upright" in English, because although his father, then caliph, designated him heir, he graciously ceded the throne to his older half-brother upon their father's death. Haroun was a successful soldier in wars against the Byzantine empire, and capably presided over a rich empire. Ambassadors from China to Charlemagne's empire visited his court. Einhard reports in his biography of Charlemagne that Haroun gave the Frankish king elephants and a bronze water clock that marked the time by means of little figures of knights emerging from doors. His favorite wife, Zubaida, set shoe fashion by ornamenting her shoes with jewels.

Haroun Al-Raschid is the prince of the *Arabian Nights* or *Thousand and One Nights*, written around the middle of the tenth century. This is a collection of popular Arab stories reputedly told over one thousand and one nights by Sharazad to her woman-hating husband, who was also a king. He avenged himself of an unfaithful wife by killing all his later wives after only one night. Sharazad's nightly stories so entranced her husband that he postponed killing her after each night in order to hear more. By the time she finished her stories, one thousand and one nights later, she had borne him three sons and he had forgotten his grievance against women. One of these stories is quoted below. The telling of this story lasted from the eighteenth through the twenty-fourth nights. Although fictional, it gives some feel for life in Baghdad during the Golden Age of Islam.

QUESTIONS:

1) Is there a moral to this story, if so what is it?

The Story of the Three Apples

One night ... the Khaleefeh [or caliph] Haroon Er-Rasheed said to Jaafar, his Wezeer [or vizier, a high government officer], "We will go down to-night into the city, and inquire respecting the affairs of those who are at present in authority, and him against whom any one shall complain we will displace." Jaafar replied, "I hear and obey": and when the Khaleefeh had gone forth with him and Mesroor, and they had passed through several of the market-streets, they proceeded along a lane, and saw there an old man, with a net and basket upon his head, and a staff in his hand, walking at his leisure, and reciting verses [in which he lamented his bad luck]....

Then approaching the man, he said to him, "O sheykh, what is your occupation?" "Oh my master," answered the old man, "I am a fisherman, and have a family to maintain, and I went forth from my house at noon, and have remained until now, but God has allotted me nothing wherewith to obtain food for my household; therefore I have hated myself and wished for death." "Will you," said the Khaleefeh, "return with us to the river, and station yourself on the bank of the Tigris, and cast your net for my luck? If you will do so I will purchase from you whatever comes up for a hundred pieces of gold." The fisherman rejoiced when he heard these words ... [and] went again to the river, and cast his net, and, having waited till it sank, drew the cords, and dragged back the net, and there came up in it a chest, locked and heavy. When the Khaleefeh saw it, he felt its weight, and found it to be heavy; and he gave a hundred pieces of gold to the fisherman, who went away, while Mesroor, assisted by Jaafar, took up the chest ... [and] broke it open, and they found in it a basket of palm-leaves sewed up with red worsted; and they cut the threads, and

saw within it a piece of carpet, and, lifting up this, they ... discovered under it a damsel like molten silver, killed, and cut in pieces.

When the Khaleefeh beheld this, tears ran down his cheeks, and, looking towards Jaafer, he exclaimed, "O dog of Wezeers, shall people be murdered in my time, and be thrown into the river, and become burdens upon my responsibility? By Allah, I must retaliate for this damsel upon him who killed her, and put him to death!" Then said he to Jaafar ... "if you do not bring to me him who killed this woman ... I will crucify you at the gate of my palace, together with forty of your kinsmen!"... "Grant me," said Jaafar, "a delay of three days." "I grant you the delay," replied the Khaleefeh. Jaafer then went forth from his presence ... saying within himself "How shall I discover him who killed this damsel, that I may take him before the Khaleefeh?.... I know not what to do."... For three days he remained in his house, and on the fourth day the Khaleefeh sent to summon him, and, when he had presented himself before him said to him, "Where is the murderer of this damsel?" "Oh Prince of the Faithful," answered Jaafar, "am I acquainted with things hidden from the senses, that I should know who is her murderer?" The Khaleefeh, incensed at this answer, gave orders to crucify him at the gate of his palace, and commanded a crier to proclaim through the streets of Baghdad, "Whosoever desires to amuse himself by seeing the crucifixion of Jaafar El-Barmekee, the Wezeer of the Khaleefeh, and the crucifixion of his kinsmen, at the gate of the Khaleefeh's palace, let him come forth and amuse himself." So the people came forth from every quarter to see the crucifixion of Jaafar and his kinsmen.... The Khaleefeh then gave orders to set up the crosses, and they did so, and placed the Wezeer and his kinsmen beneath, to crucify them and were awaiting the Khaleefeh's permission....

But while they were thus waiting, a handsome and neatly-dressed young man came forth quickly through the crowd, and said ... "It was I who killed the woman whom you found in the chest: kill me therefore for her".... [Then] an old sheykh pressed hastily through the crowd ... and said, "O Wezeer, believe not the words of this young man, for no one killed the damsel but myself; therefore retaliate her death upon me."...

On witnessing this scene, the Wezeer was astonished; and he took the young man and the sheykh to the Khaleefeh, and said, "O Prince of the Faithful, the murderer of the damsel has come." "Where is he?" said the Khaleefeh.... [Both confessed to the killing.] The young man then said, "By Him who raised the heavens and spread out the earth, it was I who killed her," and described what the Khaleefeh had found. The Khaleefeh therefore was convinced that the young man ... had killed the damsel; and he was astonished, and said, "What was the cause of your killing this damsel unjustly, and of your confessing the murder without being beaten".... The young man answered as follows:

"Know, O Prince of the Faithful, that this damsel was my wife, and the daughter of my uncle: this sheykh was her father, and is my uncle. I married her when she was a virgin, and God blessed me with three male children by her, and she loved me and served me, and I saw in her no evil. At the commencement of this month she was attacked by a severe illness, and I brought to her the physicians, who attended her until her health returned to her; and I desired them to send her to the bath; but she said to me, 'I want something before I enter the bath.... I have a longing for an apple....' So I went out immediately into the city, and searched for the apple, and would have bought it had its price been a piece of gold: but I could not find one.... [On the next day I] went about to all the gardens, one after another; yet I found none in them.... [I asked a gardener] and he said to me, 'Oh my son, this is a rare thing, and not to be found here, nor anywhere except in the garden of the Prince of the Faithful at El-Basrah, and preserved there for the Khaleefeh.' I returned therefore to my wife, and my love for her so constrained me that I prepared myself and journeyed fifteen

days, by night and day, in going and returning, and brought her three apples which I purchased of the gardener at El-Basrah for three pieces of gold; and going in, I handed them to her; but she was not pleased by them and left them by her side. She was then suffering from a violent fever, and she continued ill during a period of ten days.

"After this she recovered her health, and I went out and repaired to my shop, and sat there to sell and buy; and while I was thus occupied, at mid-day there passed by me a black slave, having in his hand an apple, with which he was playing: so I said to him 'Where did you get this apple?'... Upon which he laughed, and answered, 'I got it from my sweetheart: I had been absent, and came, and found her ill, and she had three apples; and she said to me, 'My unsuspecting husband journeyed to El-Basrah for them, and bought them for three pieces of gold,' and I took this apple from her.' When I heard the words of the slave ... the world became black before my face, and I shut up my shop, and returned to my house, deprived of my reason by excessive rage. I found not the third apple, and said to her, 'Where is the apple?' She answered, 'I know not where it is gone.' I was convinced thus that the slave had spoken the truth, and I arose, and took a knife, and throwing myself upon her bosom, plunged the knife into her: I then cut off her head and limbs, and put them in the basket in haste ... then I put the basket in the chest, and, having locked this conveyed it on my mule, and threw it with my own hands into the Tigris."

"And now," continued the young man, "I conjure by Allah, O Prince of the Faithful, to hasten my death in retaliation for her murder, as I dread, otherwise, her appeal for vengeance upon me on the day of resurrection: for when I had thrown her into the Tigris without the knowledge of anyone, I returned to my house, and found my eldest boy crying.... So I said to him, 'What makes you cry?' and he answered, 'I took one of the apples that my mother had, and went down with it into the street to play with my brothers, and a tall black slave snatched it from me ... he took it from me and beat me, and went away with it; and I am afraid that my mother may beat me on account of the apple.' When I heard my son's story, I discovered that the slave had forged a lie against the daughter of my uncle, and found that she had been killed unjustly; and as I was weeping bitterly for what I had done, this sheykh, my uncle and her father, came to me, and I informed him of the event; and he seated himself by me, and wept. We wept until midnight, and continued our mourning for her five days.... By the honour of your ancestors, therefore, hasten my death, to retaliate her murder upon me."

The Khaleefeh wondered at the young man's story, and said, "By Allah, I will not put to death any but the wicked slave; for the young man is excusable." Then looking towards Jaafar, he said to him, "Bring before me this wicked slave who has been the cause of the catastrophe; or, if you bring him not, you shall be put to death in his stead." So the Wezeer departed weeping, and saying ... "I have no stratagem to employ in this affair: but He who delivered me in the first case may deliver me in the second. By Allah, I will not go out from my house for three days.... So he remained in his house three days, and on the fourth day he caused the Kadee [judge] to be brought, and made his testamentary arrangements; and as he was bidding farewell to his children, and weeping, lo, the messenger of the Khaleefeh came and said to him, "The Prince of the Faithful is in a most violent rage, and has sent me to you, and he has sworn that this day shall not pass until you are put to death if you do not bring to him the slave."

On hearing this Jaafar wept, and his children wept with him; and when he had bidden them all farewell except his youngest daughter, he approached her for the same purpose. He loved her more than all his other children;

and he pressed her to his bosom, and wept at the thought of his separation from her; but in doing this, he felt something round in her pocket, and said to her, "What is in your pocket?" She answered, "O my father, it is an apple; our slave Reylan brought it, and I have had it four days: he would not give it me until he had received from me two pieces of gold." At this mention of the slave and the apple, Jaafar rejoiced, and exclaimed, "O ready Dispeller of trouble!" and immediately he ordered that the slave should be brought before him. He was therefore brought in, and he said to him, "From where came this apple?" "O my master," he answered, "I went out five days ago, and, entering one of the by-streets of the city, I saw some children playing, and one of them had this apple; and I snatched it from him, and beat him; and he cried, and said, 'That belongs to my mother, and she is sick: she wanted my father to bring her an apple, and he made a journey to El-Basrah, and brought it back for her three apples which he bought for three pieces of gold; and I took this to play with it'- then he cried again; but, paying no regard to him, I took it away and brought it hither; and my little mistress bought it of me for two pieces of gold." When he heard this story, Jaafar was filled with wonder at discovering that this distressing event, and the murder of the damsel had been occasioned by his slave; and he took the slave and went with him to the Khaleefeh, who ordered that the story should be committed to writing, and published.

Lane, Edward William, trans. *The Thousand and One Nights*. Vol. 1. London 1889. Pp. 222-229.

LEO AFRICANUS

▶ Arab Camel Rider

Travel writing is a genre of literature that gives special pleasure because of the allure of distant places and foreign peoples. For those unable to make the journeys themselves, the memoirs of travelers have delighted by satisfying their curiosity about the world. For the historian, the accounts of travelers often provide valuable information. Such is the case with the famous Spanish-Arab traveler and scholar, al-Hasan Ibn Muhammad al-Wazzan al-Zaiyati, better known in the West as "Leo Africanus."

Leo was born around 1485 in Granada, in Muslim Spain, and received an excellent education. As a young man, he traveled extensively in Muslim Africa, on commercial and diplomatic business. While returning from a mission to Egypt in 1517, he was abducted by pirates and (as a kind of exotic specimen) eventually came into the service of Pope Leo X. The pope, recognizing Leo's talents, released him from bondage and even granted him a pension. He also converted him to Catholicism, bestowing on him his own Christian names--Johannes and Leo.

While in Italy, Leo learned Latin and Italian and wrote in Italian a very influential work, titled *Descrittione dell'Africa (Description of Africa)*. This book was published in 1550 and translated into Latin, the universal language of learning, six years later. Leo eventually returned to his beloved Africa, re-embraced Islam, and died in Tunis sometime after 1554.

Leo Africanus' description of Africa is devoted chiefly to the Muslim regions of north Africa. However, he devotes an extremely interesting chapter called "The Land of the Blacks" to west African kingdoms, including Ghana, Mali, and Songhai. His account became the basis of European knowledge of this region for centuries to come. While modern scholars can detect errors in some of Leo's names and dates, his account of "Black Africa" remains fascinating and instructive reading.

QUESTIONS:

1) Does Leo seem to be overly judgmental in his account of "Black Africa"?
2) Which of the kingdoms described by Leo seems to be the most advanced in its culture?
3) What, for Leo, are the most typical aspects of the African kingdoms he visited?

The Land of Blacks:

The ancient geographers ... have written nothing about the Land of Blacks, except for El Guechet and Gana. From their time, in effect nothing has been known about other lands inhabited by Blacks. But they have been explored after the year 380 of the hegira [990 C.E.], because at that time the Lumtuna and the entire population of Libya became Muslims thanks to the propaganda of a preacher who, furthermore, lead the Lumtuna to the conquest of all of Berber lands.

At this time, the Black Lands began to be visited and became familiar.

These lands are all inhabited by people who live like animals, without kings, lords, states, governments, customs. They scarcely know how to sow grain. They are clothed in sheep skins. No one possesses a wife that belongs to him in particular. By day, they graze livestock and work the land. At night, they collect in groups of ten or twelve males and females in each hut; each sleeps with whoever pleases him most, reclining and sleeping on sheep skins.

They do not fight one another, and no one sets foot outside his own country. Some of them worship the sun and prostrate themselves as soon as they see it rising on the horizon. Others, like the Gualata people, revere fire. Still others, finally, are Christians in the manner of [Coptic] Egyptians; this is so among the people of the region of Gaogao. Joseph, the king and founder of Marrakech, and the five peoples of Libya conquered the Blacks and taught them Islamic law and the knowledge essential to guide them in life. Many among them became Muslims. It was at this time that merchants from Berber lands began to go to this country to trade various commodities, with the result that they learned the languages.

The five peoples of Libya divided this land into fifteen parts and each of the people of Libya had three parts. It is true that the present king of Timbuktu, Askia Muhammad, is of the black race. He had been named captain general by Sunni Ali, king of Timbuktu and Gao, of Libyan origin.

After the death of Sunni Ali [1493], Askia Muhammad revolted against the king's children and killed them. Then he freed all the black peoples from the leaders of the Libyan tribes, in the process defeating many kingdoms in six years. When he had made his country peaceful and tranquil, he conceived a desire to make the pilgrimage to Mecca. On this pilgrimage, he spent all his treasure and incurred debts of 50,000 ducats.

These fifteen kingdoms known to us extend the whole length of the two rivers of Niger and their tributaries. They are located between two immense deserts, one that begins at Numidia and ends in these countries, the other, to the south, that goes right up to the Ocean. There are very many regions there, for the most part unknown to us. This is true both because of the distance and difficulty of the journey, and because of the diversity of languages and beliefs, which keep them from having relations with the lands we do know of and keep us from having relations with them. There are some contacts, however, with the Blacks who live on the shore of the Ocean.

Kingdom of Gualata:

This kingdom is small and mediocre in comparison with other Black kingdoms. Its inhabited areas consist only of three large villages and of some huts scattered among palm groves. These villages are 300 miles south of Nun, 500 miles almost due north of Timbuktu and about 100 miles from the Ocean.

When the Libyan peoples were dominating the region, they had established there the seat of royal government and, consequently, many merchants from Berber lands were in the habit of visiting there. But from the period of Sunni Ali, who was a great man, the merchants have gradually abandoned Gualata and have gone to Timbuktu and Gao, so that the lord of Gualata has been poor and powerless.

The people of the country speak a language called Songhai. The people are extremely black complexioned and poor, but they are very good-natured, especially with foreigners. The lord who governs them pays tribute to the king of Timbuktu, because the latter once came into the country with his army. The lord of Gualata immediately took flight and went into the desert, where his relatives found him. The king of Timbuktu saw that he could not hold the country as he would like because the lord, helped by his relatives from the desert, would cause him problems. He therefore made an accord with him, requiring the payment of a stipulated tribute. The lord returned to Gualata, and the king to Timbuktu.

The style of life and customs of the people of Gualata are the same as those of their desert neighbors. Only a little grain is grown in the country: some millet and another kind of round white grain like the chickpea, which is not known in Europe. There is precious little meat. Women and men both have the practice of keeping their faces covered. All laws are unknown in the region: there are neither judges nor juries. These peoples live in great misery.

Kingdom of Ghana:

This kingdom ... is the next one encountered after Gualata, but only after crossing about 500 miles of desert. Gualata is to the north, Timbuktu to the east, and Mali to the south. It extends the length of the Niger, about 250 miles, and lies partly along the Ocean, where the Niger debouches into the sea.

Barley, rice, cattle, fish, and cotton are very plentiful. The inhabitants of the country make a good profit by trading cotton cloth with Berber merchants. The latter sell in return European fabrics, copper, brass, and arms such as daggers. The Blacks use unminted gold for money. They also use pieces of iron for smaller purchases, for example, of milk, bread, and honey; these pieces weigh a pound, a half pound, or a quarter pound. Fruit trees do not grow in the region, and there is no fruit save for dates imported from Gualata or Numidia.

There is neither town nor castle. Only one large village is inhabited by the lord, the priests, the doctors, the merchants, and the nobility. All the houses are made like huts, rough clay constructions, with straw roofs. The people are very well dressed: they wear a large cotton shawl--either black or blue--that covers even their heads, though priests and doctors wear white. The town forms a sort of island three months a year (July through September) when the Niger has a flood stage like the Nile's. This is the time when merchants come from Timbuktu. They carry their merchandise in small, narrow boats made from hollowed out tree trunks. They make the whole journey by water, mooring their boats on the bank each evening and sleeping on land.

A family of Libyan origin once governed this kingdom; its lord became a tribute-paying subject of Sunni Ali. When Askia Muhammad deposed and succeeded Sunni Ali, he interned the lord of Ghana at Gao until his death. Thereafter, a lieutenant of Askia Muhammad governed the kingdom.

Kingdom of Mali:

Mali lies along the length of a branch of the Niger over a distance of perhaps 300 miles. It borders on Ghana to the north and on the desert and some arid mountains to the south. Its western frontier is jungle reaching to the Ocean and to the east it borders on the territory of Gao. There is a very large village, of 6000 dwellings, in this country; it is called Mali, from which comes the name of the whole realm. The king and his court reside there. The land abounds in grains, meat, and cotton. There are in the village many craftsmen and merchants, both native and foreign; the latter have particular prestige with the king. The natives are quite prosperous owing to their extensive trade with Ghana and Timbuktu. There are many temples and priests and professors who teach in them (there are no colleges). They are the most civilized, intelligent, and respected of all the Blacks. They were practically the first [Blacks] to rally to Islam. At the time of their conversion, they were ruled by the greatest of the Libyan princes, the uncle of Joseph, the king of Marrakech. Power remained in the hands of his descendants till the time of Askia Muhammad, who placed such heavy burdens of tribute on the last lord that he could not even feed his own family.

Timbuktu:

Timbuktu is a modern name. It refers to a town that king Mense Suleiman built in the year 610 of the hegira [1213-1214 C.E.] around 12 miles from a branch of the Niger. The houses of Timbuktu are huts made of stakes and clay, with straw roofs. In the center of the town is a temple built of stones faced with a lime mortar. An architect from Betica, a native of Al Mana, erected it; he also constructed a large royal palace. There are many shops of craftsmen, merchants, and especially cotton weavers. European textiles--brought by Berber merchants-- also arrive at Timbuktu.

The women of the town retain the custom of veiling their faces, except for the slaves who sell all manner of food. The inhabitants are very wealthy, especially foreigners who have settled in the country. The present king has even given two of his daughters in marriage to a pair of brothers, whose mercantile activities have made them rich. There are many fresh-water wells in Timbuktu and when the Niger is in flood, canals also convey water to the town. Grain and cattle are extremely abundant and the consumption of milk and butter is substantial. There is a lack of salt, however, which has to be brought from Tegaza, some 500 miles away. I myself have witnessed times when salt in the village was priced at 80 ducats. The king possesses a large treasure in money and gold ingots, each weighing 300 pounds.

The royal court is elaborate and impressive. When the king visits another town with his court, he rides a camel and his horses are lead by hand by armed escorts. If it is necessary to fight, the escorts tether the camels and the soldiers mount the horses. Whenever anyone speaks to the king, he kneels before him and takes dirt and sprinkles his head and shoulders. This is a way of showing respect; it is required only of ambassadors or others who have not spoken with the king previously. The king has 3000 cavalry and unlimited infantry armed with bows made of wild "fennel"; they shoot poisoned arrows. The king makes war only on neighboring enemies and those who refuse to pay him tribute. When he is victorious, he sells at Timbuktu those taken in battle (even to the children).

The only horses native to the country are a small breed that merchants or courtiers use in making their rounds of the town. Good horses come from Berber lands. They arrive by caravan and, ten or twelve days later, are led before the king. He chooses what he pleases and pays a fair price.

The king is the declared enemy of the Jews. He wishes none to live in the town; if he hears that a Berber merchant has had dealings with them, he confiscates his goods. Timbuktu has many judges, doctors, and priests, all appointed by the king. The king greatly respects literature and purchases many manuscripts which come from Berber lands. The sale of these is more profitable than that of all other merchandise.

Instead of coined money, they use pieces of pure gold and, for small purchases, of cowries, that is seashells brought from Persia valued at four hundred per ducat. One Roman ounce of gold is the equivalent of six and two-thirds of their ducats.

The people of Timbuktu are lively and playful by nature. They stroll through town during the night, between 10:00 PM and 1:00 AM, playing musical instruments and dancing.

The townsmen have many slaves, both male and female, at their service.

The town is quite vulnerable to fire. When I was on my second visit there, half the town burned in the space of five hours. The wind was strong and the inhabitants of the other half of the town began to move their belongs out of fear that it too would burn.

There are no gardens or orchards around Timbuktu.

Town of Cabra:

Cabra is a large town that has the look of an unwalled village. It is twelve miles from Timbuktu on the Niger, where merchandise headed for Ghana and Mali is embarked. Houses and people are like those of places already mentioned. One finds Blacks of various tribes there, because it is the port where they come from diverse regions in their canoes.

The king of Timbuktu has sent a lieutenant there to furnish the people royal audiences and to spare them the trouble of a twelve-mile journey. At the time I found myself in Cabra, this lieutenant was a relative of the king named Askia Muhammad and surnamed Pargama. He was an extremely black-complexioned man, invaluable because of his intelligence and scrupulous honesty.

The town is afflicted by frequent outbreaks of disease, resulting from the quality of the food they eat there: a mixture of fish, milk, butter, and meat. Nearly half the foodstuffs to be found at Timbuktu derive from Cabra.

Gao and Its Kingdom:

Gao is a very large town like Cabra, also unwalled. It lies about 200 miles southeast of Timbuktu. Its houses are humble for the most part, though some, where the king and his court reside, are very impressive. It is inhabited by wealthy merchants who constantly canvas the region with their wares. Vast numbers of Blacks go there bringing huge amounts of gold to purchase items imported from Berber lands and Europe. They never find enough to spend all their gold on, and often return with half or two thirds of it unspent. The town is well policed compared to Timbuktu. Bread and meat are plentiful, but one can find neither wine nor fruit.

Actually, melons, cucumbers, and excellent pumpkins abound; rice also is available in immense quantities. Fresh-water wells are numerous. There is a place where, on market days, an infinite number of slaves--both male and female--are sold. A young girl of around fifteen years goes for six ducats; a young man for about the same. Small children and the elderly sell for about half that price. The king possesses a special palace reserved for an enormous number of women, concubines, and slaves and eunuchs assigned to guard these women. He also has an important guard consisting of cavalry and infantrymen armed with bows. Between the city gate and the entrance to the king's palace, there is a large court surrounded by a wall. On each side of the court is a gallery set aside for royal audiences. Although the king manages all his own affairs, he is assisted by many secretaries, counselors, captains, and supervisors.

The revenues of the kingdom are substantial, but expenses are still greater. For example, a horse that sells for ten ducats in Europe costs forty or fifty here. Very mediocre European cloth brings four ducats a measure, while fine fabrics ... fetch fifteen ducats, and fine Venetian fabric dyed scarlet, purple, or turquoise costs thirty. The worst sort of European sword worth a third of a ducat costs four ducats or at least three. The same applies for spurs and bridles.... Medicines are also very dear, and a tenth of a measure of salt goes for one ducat.

The remainder of the kingdom consists of market-towns and villages where farmers and shepherds live. In winter, they dress in sheep skins; in summer, they go naked and shoeless. They do, however, conceal their private parts with a small piece of cloth and they sometimes protect the soles of their feet with sandals made of camel hide.

The people are absolutely uneducated. It is difficult to find within a hundred miles anyone who can read and write. But their king treats them as they deserve, since it is only right if he leaves them a subsistence, in light of the burden of the taxes he makes them pay.

Leo Africanus. *Descrittione dell'Africa*. Rome 1550. Part 7, passim. Translation by James P. Holoka.

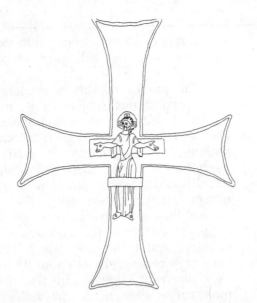

THE QUEST FOR PRESTER JOHN OF ETHIOPIA

▶ **Coptic Cross**

Ethiopia, located in east Africa, is difficult to reach because of harsh climate and mountainous terrain. It was home to an ancient civilization that had many connections with Egypt and reputedly with the Hebrews. Ethiopians are dark skinned; their ancient language, called Ethiopic or Geez, belongs to the Semitic family and is still used in religious ceremonies. During the early centuries of the Christian era, many Ethiopians converted to Christianity. Many Ethiopians, like Egyptians, were Coptic Christians, who believe in a single divine nature in the person of Christ. A bishop, always an Egyptian monk appointed by the Coptic Patriarch of Alexandria, headed the Ethiopian church. A small Ethiopian community in Jerusalem helped pilgrims from its homeland; there were sporadic contacts between the Ethiopians and the Mediterranean world throughout the Middle Ages.

European medieval lore mentioned a Prester John, a legendary Christian priest and king associated with either the Far East or Ethiopia. Europeans wanted to locate Prester John to form an alliance with him against the forces of Islam. As the Portuguese explored the coast of Africa in the fifteenth century, they tried to find a way inland to Ethiopia.

In 1517, Dom Roderigo led an expedition from Portugal to find Prester John. This first European embassy to reach Ethiopia returned to Europe six years later. The land of Prester John was neither fabulously rich nor ruled by a mighty monarch of medieval legend. In 1540, Father Francisco Alvares, a member of Roderigo's embassy published an account of the mission and his travels in Ethiopia. It is the earliest extant eyewitness account of Ethiopia, written just before it was devastated by Muslim Somali and pagan Galla invaders. The book gives many interesting details, including the religious practices of the Ethiopians. Alavares' description of the locust plague is reminiscent of Biblical accounts; such devastating insect plagues cause starvation in Ethiopia and other parts of Africa even today.

QUESTIONS:

1) What was the religion of most Ethiopians and by what means did the people of Ethiopia make a living?
2) How did Ethiopian priests and nuns live and behave?
3) What great natural enemy afflicted Ethiopia periodically?

All [the monasteries] are situated on the greatest and highest cliffs, or the deepest they can find. This one of St Michael is situated on a very steep rock at the foot of another very high rock, where no one can ascend.... They are very great rocks. The land around these rocks is all covered with very great forest, mostly wild olive trees with tall plants between them, in which there is much basil. The trees which are not wild olive trees are not trees known to us; all are without fruit. In the narrow valleys which belong to this monastery there are orange trees, lemon trees, citron trees, pear trees, and fig trees of all kinds, both of Portugal and India, peach trees, cabbages, coriander, cress, worm-wood, myrtle, and other sweet-smelling and medicinal herbs.... The monastery house looks quite like a church building, constructed like ours. It has around it a circuit like a cloister, covered above in the same way as the body of the monastery. It has three entrances, like ours, one principal one, and two side ones. The roof of the church and of its cloisters is of coarse straw which lasts a man's life: the body of the church is built with aisles very well constructed, and their arches are very well closed; all appear to be vaulted.... In all churches and monasteries they ring for matins two hours before dawn. They say the prayers by heart and without light, except in the lamps or chandeliers.... They burn butter in these chandeliers, for they have not got oil. They pray or chant very loud, without art in singing and they do not recite verses, but all sing straight on. Their prayers are psalms, and on feast days besides psalms they recite prose, according as the feast is so is the prose. They always stand in the churches....

In the monastery of St Michael, where we were staying, we said mass each day, not in the monastery, but in the circuit which is like a cloister. In this country they do not say more than one mass in each church or monastery. The monks came to our mass with great devotion, as they showed; and they supplied a thurible [metal container for burning incense] and incense, because we had not brought any with us, and they do not think mass is properly said without incense; and they said that they approved of all, except that we had only one priest to say mass; because among them not less than three, five, or seven stand at the altar to say mass. They were

also surprised at out coming into the church with our shoes on, and still more at our spitting in it....

The monks of this monastery, and of the other monasteries subject to it, might do good works by planting trees and vines and making gardens and orchards by their labour; and they do nothing. The country is ready to produce everything, as is seen from that which is uncultivated: they do not plant or grow anything except millet and bee-hives. When it is night, neither they nor anybody else go out from their houses from fear of the wild beasts that are in the country, and those who watch the millet have very high resting places upon the trees, in which they sleep at night. In the district of this monastery there are, in the valleys between the mountains, very large herds of cows kept by Arab Moors [actually local Muslims], and there go with each herd forty or fifty Moors, with their wives and children; and their captain is a Christian, because the cows that they keep belong to Christian gentlemen of the country of the Barnagais.... The revenues of this monastery are very large; those which I saw and heard of are, chiefly, this mountain in which the monastery is situated, of an extent of ten leagues, in which they sow much millet, barley, rye, and all these pay dues to the monastery, and they are also paid on the herds. On the skirts of this mountain there are many large villages, most of them belonging to the monastery, and at a distance one or two days' journey endless places belong to the monastery....

I saw people married, and was at a marriage which was not in a church, and it was done in this way. On the open space before some houses they placed a *catre* [platform?], and seated upon it the bridegroom and the bride, and there came thither three priests, and they began a chant with Alleluia, and then continued the chant, the three priests walking three times round the *catre* on which the couple were seated. Then they cut a lock of hair from the head of the bridegroom and another from the head of the bride. They wetted those locks with mead, and placed the hair of the bridegroom on the head of the bride, and that of the bride on the head of the bridegroom, on the place from which they had cut them, and then sprinkled them with holy water: after that they kept their festivities and wedding feast....

I saw the Abima Marcos, whom they call Pope [abima is the title of the head of the Ethiopian church], give blessings in the church, that is to say, before the main door; the bride and the bridegroom were also seated on a catre, and the Abima walked round them with incense and cross, and laid his hands on their heads, telling them to observe that which God had commanded in the Gospel.... There they remained until mass had been said, and he gave them the communion, and bestowed on them the blessing.... When they make these marriages they enter into contracts, as for instance: If you leave me or I you, whichever causes the separation shall pay such and such a penalty. And they fix the penalty according to the persons, so much gold or silver, or so many mules, or cloth, or cows, or goats, or so many measures of corn. And if either of them separate, that one immediately seeks a cause of separation for such and such reasons, so that few incur the penalty, and so they separate when they please, both the husbands and the wives. If there are any that observe the marriage rule, they are the priests, who never can separate....

The priests are married to one wife, and they observe the law of matrimony better than the laity: they live in their houses with their wives and children. If their wife should die they do not marry again; neither can the wife, but she may become a nun or remain a widow as she pleases. If a priest sleeps with another woman whilst his wife is alive he does not enter the church any more, nor does he enjoy its property, and remains a layman. And this I know from having seen a priest accused before the Patriarch of having slept with a woman, and I saw that the priest confessed the offence, and the Patriarch commanded him not to carry a cross in his hand, not to enter a church, nor to enjoy the liberties of the church, and to become a layman. If any priests after becoming widowers marry, they remain laymen.... The sons of the priests are mostly priests, because in this country there are no schools, or lecture-halls, nor masters to teach, and the clergy teach what little they know to their sons: and so they make them priests without more legitimization, neither does it seem to me that they require it, since they are legitimate sons. All are ordained by the Abima Marcos, for in all the kingdoms of Ethiopia there is no other Bishop or person who ordains....

Circumcision is done by anybody without any ceremony, only they say that so they find it written in the books, that God commanded circumcision. And let not the reader of this be amazed--they also circumcise the females as well as the males, which was not in the Old Law. Baptism they do in this way: they baptize males at forty days, and females at sixty days after their births, and if they die before they go without baptism.... They perform this baptism in the church, with water which they keep in a vase, and which they bless, and they put oil on the forehead and on the breasts and shoulder-blades....

There is a great fair ... in all the places which are chief towns of districts, every week. The fairs consist of bartering one thing for another, as for instance, an ass for a cow.... With bread they buy cloth, and with cloth they buy mules and cows, and whatever they want, for salt, incense, pepper, myrrh, camphor, and other small articles. They buy fowls and capons, and whatever they need or want to buy is all to be found at these fairs in exchange for other things, for there is no current money. The principal merchants at these fairs are priests, monks, and nuns. The monks are decent in their habits, which are full, and reach to the ground. Some wear yellow habits of coarse cotton stuff, others habits of tanned goat skins like wide breeches, also yellow. The nuns also wear the same habits; they monks wear, besides, capes of the fashion of Dominican friars, of the same yellow skins or cloth; they wear hats, and the nuns wear neither capes nor hats, but only the habit, and are shaven with a razor; and they wear a leather strap wound or fastened round the head. When they are old women they wear skull-caps round their heads over their tonsures. These nuns are not cloistered, nor do they live together in convents, but in villages, and in the monasteries of the monks, as they belong to those houses and that order. The order is all one, and the nuns give obedience where they receive their habits.... There is a great multitude of nuns, as well as of monks; they say that some of them are very holy women, and others are not so. The priests show very little difference from the laity in their dress, because all wear a good cloth wrapped round, like smart men, and the difference is that they carry a cross in their hand,

and are shaven, and the laity wear matted hair. The priests also have this, that they do not cut their beards, and the laity shave under the chin....

The way of living in this town of Barua and the neighbouring towns is this. There are ten, twelve, or fifteen houses, in one walled and closed yard, served by one gate: in this yard they shut up their domestic cows which they use for their milk and butter, and also the smaller animals, mules and asses. They keep the gate well fastened, and a great fire, and watchmen who sleep there, from fear of the animals that roam about the towns all night: and if they did not keep this watch nothing alive would remain which they would not devour. The people who go to sow millet in the mountains of Bisam belong to this country and the neighbouring towns. The reason why they go and do it is this. Here there are very numerous grain crops of every kind and nature that can be mentioned, as I have already said; and because it is near to the sea, by which go all the provisions for Arabia, Mequa, Zebide, Juda, and Toro, and other parts; and they carry the provisions to the sea to sell them....

In these parts and in all the dominions of the Prester John there is a very great plague of locusts which destroy the fresh crops on a very big scale. Their multitude, which covers the earth and fills the air, is not to be believed; they darken the light of the sun. I say again that it is not to be believed by any one who has not seen them. They are not general in all the kingdoms every year, for if they were so, the country would be a desert in the consequence of the destruction they cause.... Wherever they come the earth is left as though it had been set on fire. These locusts are like large grasshoppers, and have yellow wings; when they are on the way it is known a day before, not because the people see them, but because they see the sun yellow, and the earth yellow, that is the shadow which they cast over it.... I will relate what I saw on three occasions. The first was in the town of Barua; we had then been three years in this country ... while we were there, we saw this sign: the sun became yellow, and the shadow on the earth too, and the people were dismayed. Next day it was a thing not to be believed, for they spread over a width of eight leagues, according to what we learned later....

Another time we saw locusts in another country called Abrigima.... We travelled five days through country entirely depopulated, and through millet stalks as thick as canes for propping vines; it cannot be told how they were all cut and bitten, as if bitten by asses, all done by the locusts. The wheat, barley and *tafo*, as though they had never been sown there, the trees without any leaves, and the tender twigs all eaten, there was no trace of grass of any sort, and if we had not been prepared with mules laden with barley and provisions for ourselves, we and the mules would have perished from hunger.... The people were going away from this country, and we found the roads full of men, women, and children, on foot, and some in their arms, with their little bundles on their heads, removing to a country where they might find provisions.

Alvares, Francisco. *The Prester John of the Indies: A True Relation of the Lands of the Prester John, Being the Narrative of the Portuguese Embassy to Ethiopia in 1520.* Trans. Lord Stanley of Alderley [1881]. Rev. and ed. G.F. Beckingham and G.W.B. Huntingford. Cambridge: Cambridge Univ. Press [for the Hakluyt Society], 1961. Vol. 1. Pp. 74-77, 85, 93, 106-107, 109-110, 117-120, 125-127, 132-133, 136-137.

► **Khmer Dancing Maidens**

KHMER LIFE THROUGH THE EYES OF A CHINESE TRAVELER

Ancient Cambodia, called Khmer, is known from its monuments, temples, statues, and stone reliefs as well as from written records, both native and foreign. Khmer civilization learned writing from India, and used Sanskrit in religious and literary works. Both Sanskrit and Old Khmer, derived from a south Indian language, were used in recording laws and government documents. The only extant Khmer written remains are stone inscriptions. Foreign written sources, primarily Chinese, provide additional information. The earliest mention of the Khmer kingdom occurs seventh century Chinese annals. They document regular tributes offered by the Khmer kingdom which the Chinese called Ch'en-la.

In 1195, the Mongol rulers of China sent an embassy to demand greater subservience from the Khmer kings. The embassy spent a year in Cambodia. Chou Ta-kuan was among the delegation. He wrote a lively and uniquely informative little book titled *Notes on the Customs of Ch'en-la* recording his observations of the sights, sounds, manners, and morals of twelfth century Khmer peoples. It corroborates the surviving monuments of the capital city, Angkor, including many of the friezes portraying contemporary Khmer life. It shows a unique culture that derived its higher religion and many other cultural characteristics from India, and that relied heavily on trade with and owed some philosophical teachings to China. Although Chou takes a Chinese perspective, he was nevertheless a keen and perceptive observer of ancient Cambodia as the following sample illustrates.

QUESTIONS:

1) What three religions predominated in the Khmer state?
2) Describe the appearance, clothing, and customs of the people.
3) How is trading done and what items are desired in trade?

The Capital

The city wall is twenty *li* [about a third of a mile] in circumference and is pierced by five gates, each with two portals. Except for the eastern wall which has two gates, each of the other three walls has one. A huge moat protects the city wall, spanned by massive bridges. Fifty-four stone carved warrior deities stand guard on either side of each bridge, looking huge and fierce. All five gates are similar. The parapets of the bridges are of solid stone, carved in the shape of nine-headed serpents. Each of the fifty-four warrior deities is shown grasping the serpents with his hands, so as not to let them escape. There are five massive stone Buddha heads atop each of the city gates: four are facing the four cardinal directions, the [fifth] central one is decorated in gold. Stone carved elephants stand guard on either side of the gates.

The city wall is twenty feet tall and made of stone, so well fitted together that grass cannot grow in the crevasses. There are no crenellations. Sago palm trees are growing on top of the battlements at irregular intervals. On the inside of the wall there is a sloping earthen rampart over a hundred feet wide, pierced by gates that are open during day hours and closed at night, and watched by guards. Dogs are forbidden to enter the gates as are convicted criminals.

The city is shaped as a square, and has a stone tower at each corner. A golden tower rises at the center of the city [symbolically the center of the kingdom] surrounded by more than twenty lesser stone towers and several hundred stone chambers. On the eastern side is a golden bridge guarded by two golden lions, one on each side. Eight golden Buddhas are placed below the stone chambers. About a *li* north of the golden tower there is a bronze tower, even taller than the former, and flanked by ten odd stone chambers, a truly amazing sight. About another *li* further north is the king's residence. Another golden tower rises from the midst of his quarters. These are the monuments that cause merchants from afar to speak of Ch'en-la as a magnificently rich land....

The Three Religions

There are three religious groups here, the *pan-ch'i* [pandits or Brahmins] or learned men, the Buddhist monks or *ch'u-ku*, and the Taoists or *pa-ss'u*.

I do not know about the inherited creed of the *pan-ch'i*, and because there are no schools where they are educated, I do not know what they studied. But I see that they dress like ordinary people, except for a white thread that they wear throughout their lives around their neck, which designates them as men of learning. Some among them rise to high places.

The *ch'u-ku* shave their head and wear saffron colored garb that leave their right shoulders bare; they tie a strip of saffron colored cloth around the waist and go bare footed. Their tile roofed temples have a central statue that

appears like Sakyamuni that they call Po-lai, which is made of clay and decorated in colors. There are no other statues in the central hall. The Buddha statues in the pagodas appear different and are caste in bronze. There are no bells, drums, cymbals, or banners. The monks eat meat and fish, but do not drink liquor. Meat and fish are also made as offering to the Buddhas. The monks eat one meal a day, prepared at the homes of the donors because there are no kitchens in the temples. Their numerous canons are written in black on palm-leafs neatly bound together. They do not use writing brush or ink and I do not know how they write....

The *pa-ss'u*, dress like ordinary people, except for a headdress made of red or white cloth in the manner of Mongol women....They also live in monasteries, which are smaller than those of the Buddhists because Taoists are not as prosperous as the Buddhists. There are no statues in Taoist monasteries: they worship only a stone, like the stone in Chinese Temples of the Earth. I do not know the origin of their teaching....

The People

The local customs are those of other southern barbarians. The people are coarse, ugly and dark....But because the ladies in the palaces and homes of the nobles are not exposed to the sun they are as fair as white jade. Generally both men and women wear only a cloth tied at the waist, exposing their upper torso. They also go bare-footed. This is so even for the wives of the king. The king has five wives, one in the center palace and one in a palace for each of the four directions. I have heard that he has in addition three to five thousand concubines and waiting women, divided according to rank, who are seldom allowed to leave the palaces. Each time I was admitted to an audience with the king in the palace, he was always accompanied by his chief consort, the two of them seated inside a golden enclosure in the main hall, attended by the palace ladies who stood below the enclosure along the corridor in rows according to rank....When a beautiful girl is born to any family, the parents vie to have her selected for service in the palace....

Ordinary women wear their hair in a knot and do not wear ornament in the hair. But they wear gold bangles on their arms and gold rings on their fingers, as do ladies of the palace. Men and women alike anoint their bodies with scents made from sandalwood, musk and other essences.

All families worship the Buddha.

Every day in the markets groups of ten or more boy prostitutes can be seen roaming around, looking for Chinese customers, and soliciting them for presents. Such a shameful, disgusting custom!

Justice

Even minor altercations among the people are brought before the courts. There is no flogging, fines being exacted as penalty. People are not beheaded or strangled even for major offenses, but are buried alive in a pit outside the western gate of the city. For lesser crimes an offender can have his hands or feet amputated, or his nose cut off. There are no penalties for adultery or gambling....If an object is missing and the suspected thief refuses to own up, there is a curious procedure. A pot of oil is heated to boiling. The suspect is ordered to plunge his hand into the oil. If he stole the item, his hand will be blistered, if not, it will not be injured....

Slavery

Savages are bought as slaves. Wealthy families can have over a hundred slaves, less well off have ten to twenty, poor families have none. Although there are different kinds of savages, they all come from the mountains. They are commonly called the Chuang....It is the worst insult in quarreling to call someone a Chuang....A young and healthy slave costs a hundred pieces of cloth, old and weak ones cost thirty to forty pieces.

Savages

There are two categories of savages. The first kind can understand the language of the country. They are the ones sold as slaves. The other kind resist civilization and cannot understand the language of the people [Khmer]. These have no houses and wander about the mountains, carrying clay jars on their heads. They kill beasts with bows and arrows and lances, make fire with flint, cook their kill and eat communally, then resume their wandering. They are fierce by nature and their poisons are very dangerous. They commit murder amongst themselves. Those who live near to civilization practise some agriculture and cultivate cotton. They weave a coarse cotton cloth with strange patterns.

Clothing

From the king down every man's and woman's hair is knotted. Everyone wears a cloth around the waist, adding a larger piece on top when leaving to go out. There are many grades of cloth. The king's is worth three to four ounces of gold; it is extremely fine in quality, beautiful and opulent. Although some cloths are woven locally, others are imported from Siam and Champa, while those imported from India are counted as best because of their fine design and delicate quality. Only the king can wear fabrics with an all over woven pattern. He also wears a golden diadem on his head, much like the ones worn by Buddhist guardian deities. When the king does not wear his diadem his hair is dressed with garlands of fragrant flowers such as jasmine. He wears about three pounds of pearls around his neck. He wears gold bracelets, anklets, and rings around his arms, legs and fingers, all set with gemstones called cats-eyes. He goes bare-footed, the palms of his hands and feet are dyed red with henna. On outings he carries a gold sword in his hand. Among the people, only women may dye the palms of their hands and feet with henna, men may not. Only great officials and royal relatives may wear cloths with all-over woven patterns, ordinary officials may wear cloths with two groups of patterns, also womenfolk among the people. However newly arrived men from China are not charged with breaking the law when they wear clothes with two groups of patterns, because they do not know the rules.

Trade

In this country most trading is done by women; that is why as soon as a Chinese man arrives in the country he marries a local woman, to help him in business. Everyday the market opens at six and continues until noon. Trading is not conducted in shops, but by displaying the goods on a mat spread on the ground. Each merchant has an allotted space. I have heard that officials collect fees for ground rental. Small transactions are carried out by bartering in rice, other grains, and Chinese goods, larger ones are done using textiles as medium; gold and silver are exchanged only in major transactions. The local people are simple by nature. They are very respectful towards Chinese, addressing them as Buddha, and they bow low and prostrate themselves on the ground upon encountering them. However in recent times many natives have been swindling and taking advantage of Chinese visitors.

Desirability of Chinese goods

I do not think gold and silver are found in this country, and that is why they desire above all gold and silver from China. Next in demand are light weight and heavy weight textiles, after that tin-wares from Chenchou, lacquered dishes from Wenchou, celadon glazed ceramics from Chuanchou, and mercury, vermilion, paper, sulphur, saltpeter, sandalwood, angelica-root, musk, linen, yellow grass cloth, umbrellas, iron pots, copper trays, fresh-water pearls, tung oil, bamboo nets, baskets, wooden combs and needles. They also want mats from Mingchou. But above all they want to buy pulse and wheat, but export of these items is forbidden.

Immigration

Chinese sailors who come to the country like the local custom of going without clothes. They also like the facts that food is easily accessible, women are easily available, houses are easily run, furniture is easily obtainable, and trading is easily profitable. As a result many sailors desert to live here permanently.

Chou, Ta-kuan. *Ch'en-la feng-tu chi* [Notes of the Customs of Ch'en-la]. Pp. 4, 6-8, 11-12, 14, 18, 24. Translation by Jiu-Hwa Lo Upshur.

READING 5.6

THE BOROBODUR RELIEFS: LIFE IN JAVA IN 800 C.E.

▸ **Javanese Puppet**

Indian traders, religious teachers, and settlers began sailing to Southeast Asia around two thousand years ago. They brought to the region Hinduism and Buddhism, the arts and sciences, and other elements of Indian civilization. Indian influence reached its apogee during the Gupta period (c.320-535 C.E.). Many cultural historians refer to Southeast Asia as greater India or Indianized Southeast Asia. Java and Sumatra in Indonesia were heavily influenced by India, as many structures on the islands attest.

The greatest example of Buddhist art in Southeast Asia, and the largest Buddhist monument in the world is the Great Stupa of Borobodur (or Barabudur), built around 800 C.E. on Java. When Islam became the dominant religion several centuries later, this monument was abandoned and became overgrown by the jungle, until the eighteenth century. It has since been carefully restored and studied by Dutch archaeologists.

Borobodur was intended to be a microcosm of the Mahayana Buddhist universe. It was built with the locally abundant lava stone and is square in shape, with each side measures 136 yards long. It is oriented to the four cardinal points of the compass. The edifice is covered with more than ten miles of relief sculpture that recreate the Buddhist cosmology. The pilgrim to Borobodur follows a path symbolizing his own spiritual progress. The scenes on the bottom layer teach the doctrine of karma by showing the cycles of birth and rebirth of trapped souls. The second level portrays jataka stories of Gautama Buddha's previous incarnations; the third level shows episodes of the Buddha's life and his enlightenment; the top level, the crowning stupa, represents union with the Cosmic Buddha.

Besides its religious and artistic significance, Borobodur is a treasure house of information on life in ninth-century Java, doubly important in the absence of surviving contemporary written materials on daily life. In Indian Gupta artistic styles adapted to Java, we find detailed scenes of the activities of men, women, and children of various social classes. Many occupations appear, as do buildings, foods, animals, and modes of travel. The rich panorama on the friezes proves that a picture is indeed worth a thousand words.

Below are descriptions of some of the friezes recorded during a comprehensive examination of the site by specialists who restored Borobodur between 1907 and 1911. They bring to life the manners and mores of Javanese who lived over a thousand years ago.

QUESTIONS:

1) How did clothing and ornaments distinguish men and women of different social classes?
2) What occupations are pictured in the stone friezes?
3) The food scenes engraved in stone resemble modern Indonesian eating habits. What are they?

The figures displayed before us on the reliefs of Barabudur belong to all classes of society, from ... the king who is ruler of the world, to the most simple dweller of the desa. No wonder then, if we begin with the dress, we find it in all possible variety.

The most primitive sort of costume used by the lower class particularly in country districts, appears specially in the reliefs on the buried base which represents mostly scenes of humble life. This dress is nothing more than a loin-cloth.... The hair dressing of these people is also very plain. The hair is brushed back smoothly and then sometimes hangs down loose, but generally it is twisted into a knot at the back of the head....

The first sign of a better class is a polished necklace and a pair of earrings with a plain flower ornament. The hair too is dressed differently with a thick band, probably a wreath, round it and the hair if not hanging loose, is twisted up into a small knot that hangs in the neck under the wreath....

Very gradually we rise from these people of the lowest class ... by a little more ornament, and more costly outfits, till at last we reach the kings and their attendants.... Still worn with the short loin-cloth, the necklaces begin to be handsomer; they are made of beads or show a widening on the breast evidently of gold or silver work. At the same time the headdress gets more elaborate.... The next step is a diadem, not loose on the hair but forming the border to a cap which covers the hair and that begins to have a pointed shape; here we already have a simple kind of tiara, low in form but already showing resemblance to the lofty pointed tiaras of kings and royal persons....

After the earrings and necklaces, we get rings on the wrists, ankles and upper arms, especially the latter become elaborately ornamented with wide, always triangular plates of metal. The girdle, at the same time as the headdress, is more richly adorned and the caste-cord [worn by upper caste Hindu men] appears;

with the women the so-called woman's girdle, a double band going over both shoulders and under both arms and fastened with a handsome clasp on the breast....

Children are dressed in various ways. Sometimes they wear nothing at all, at least those of the lower classes; they are carried in the *slendang* [a long scarf, sometimes tied into a sling for carrying purposes] which is still in use. Infant princes on the other hand often wear miniature royal dress....

Weapons on the whole seem to have been little worn; they certainly do not belong to the ordinary kinds of dress and only very seldom do we see any person engaged in peaceful conversation who is armed ... but of course the soldiers, palace guards etc. are always armed.... Armed guards and soldiers are to be found on nearly all reliefs in the retinue of kings and persons of importance on their journeys and at the doors of the palace etc., but the weapons are always the same: straight swords, large oval shields, bow and arrows and the flat curved swords.... The pictures of fighting are few and must be cautiously treated.... [Some] represent battles between celestial armies, but the same weapons are used as above-mentioned....

Eating and drinking takes up a very small place, less perhaps than we might expect though it is hardly a subject for edifying tales. A few times we see food being prepared.... [In one scene] a cauldron is fixed on to a trivet over a wood fire, which a man is blowing up with a blowpipe; another sits next to him cleaning fish to be cooked in the pot.... [In another scene] fish and tortoises are being boiled by two evildoers, who will soon receive the same treatment themselves in the infernal regions.

The meal itself we find ten times, the bill of fare appears to be always the same, the well-known "rijsttafel" [modern day Indonesian banquet]. There is always a large ball of rice in the middle with small dishes of various viands all round it.... Sometimes fish are served on top of the ball of rice. Drink is not always given.... On very rare occasions we are shown a drinking-party with its attendant dissoluteness....

Next we come to the various trades and occupations represented. Agriculture, to begin with, only appears in a few scenes. Two of these show us ploughing. The plough is drawn by a pair of bulls, the yoke resting on the shoulder in front of the hump, with a collar round each beast's neck. The plough itself is the ordinary primitive square shape, by which one side scrapes along the ground and forces the ploughshare into the earth; the other side sticks up with the top bent over to the back and guided by the hand of the ploughman who walks behind and directs it with his left hand.... [In another scene] a couple of men are keeping guard under a grain-shed next to a field of maize that is ravaged by rats.

As for craftsmanship the most remarkable scene is the bridgebuilding [on one frieze where a] ... bridge is being laid over a swiftly-flowing river, and is apparently made of bamboo.... It is three-cornered in shape; bamboo poles, fixed into the ground on both banks on the stream and bound firmly together at the top, from the two sides and hold the base that is the actual bridge....

Another example of work that can be clearly understood is the potter's on [one frieze].... On one side we see the jars already made, on the other side the potter is at work, using a flat stick to get a good shape. Bearers with carrying-poles are bringing large round balls, it may be clay or gourds with water. Women and children are looking on....

A real merchant or trader is certainly to be seen [on another frieze]. In the first scene he is not actually shopkeeping but just handing over the profits to his mother, but the jars standing near to her may of course contain some of his wares. [Another scene] however certainly represents a shop.... As far as the damaged state of the relief allows, we may take it to be the goldsmith's. The purchaser seated opposite to the merchant, is holding a pair of scales, on one scale there is a ring and in the other there seems to be a bag of money....

The men we see carrying various things in a yoke may often be street-vendors, but sometimes they are on other errands, as for instance a man

... taking home the corn that fell from heaven in a miraculous shower ... [or] the one who is carrying away the fish caught in the tunnel-traps....

There were of course literary men and artists in the society here depicted, so some of the scenes show [for example ... where teaching is going on ... [or] where books appear.... The books correspond to the well-known kropak shape; they open into loose leaves held in the hand, and when closed are bound round in the usual way with bands.... Sometimes a rosette can be seen, probably an ornament on the cover. When necessary, books are laid on stands or trays or may be ... on a small three-legged table.... Hunting and fishing, however much forbidden by the Buddhist creed and included in the crimes punishable by hell, as we see by the reliefs on the buried base, were naturally common enough in the not altogether Buddhist Java; we need not be surprised to find scenes of this kind often enough on Barabudur, where several of the jatakas [tales of the Buddha's past incarnations] are stories of the chase. In contrast to these there are a few instances where animals that have been caught are set free again....

Fishing is done in various ways ... [one being by] tunnel-traps ... the same as what we use nowadays, with a wide opening, then narrowing to the end.... The second way seems to be with a scoop; the man stands ready with a round wooden scoop open at the end which he manages with his left hand, holding in his right a rope that runs through two holes in the sides of the scoop close to the open end; the way of fishing is evidently to steer the scoop with the left hand so that it comes under the fish and then pull the rope up suddenly so that it cannot get away....

Hunting of the simplest kind can be seen on the reliefs of the buried base; smoking out rats, bird-killing, with club and blow-pipe of small birds; of larger birds with bow and arrow.... Monkeys are hunted with bow and arrow as well as with blow-pipe.... There is often a whole hunting party depicted entering the forest ... after deer and wild boars.... With a royal hunting-party we may of course find an armed escort sometimes, but bow and arrows are never missing, they are evidently the weapons of the chase. The king himself is often seen on horse-back, the animals he hunts are either deer and wild boar....

The animal of state and ceremony is of course the elephant. Horses and elephants are seen together in a royal procession, or standing in readiness in the retinue of distinguished persons; the mahout [elephant keeper] ... often sitting on its neck....

Palanquins are also used for travelling.... The most primitive kind of palanquin ... is no more than a piece of cloth fastened to two poles and borne on the shoulders of four men, the person carried sitting only on the cloth hanging between the two poles....

The carriages drawn by horses are all four-wheeled and with only one exception there are a pair of horses (having collars with bells as well as saddles); the wheels have always eight spokes....

We now come to the conveyance by water, the ships.... The simplest vessel, the *djukung*, is nothing more than a hollowed-out tree trunk.... The outrigger ship can [also be seen].... This type with its high stem and stern resembles the *kura-kura* of the Moluccas that are mentioned in the earliest descriptions of European travellers....

Krom, N.J. *Barabudur: Archaeological Description*. The Hague: M. Nijhoff, 1927. Rpt. New York: AMS Press, 1986. Vol. 2. Pp. 196-200, 208-210, 215-216, 227-235.

EARLY JAPAN: MYTH AND HISTORY

▶ Haniwa—Clay Figurines of Pre-Historic Japan

The Japanese are a predominantly Mongoloid people whose ancestors migrated to the islands from northeast Asia and Korea from prehistoric times through circa 1000 C.E. Chinese histories from the third century on have recorded traders' account of the Japanese as a law-abiding people living under strictly ordered social ranks in small states with both male and female rulers.

Beginning in the sixth century Japanese leaders began systematic borrowing from the much more advanced Chinese culture. There were two reasons for this. First was the rise of the Yamato clan, which had unified Japan. To rule effectively, it needed to borrow the more advanced Chinese institutions and practices. The second was the founding of the mighty Sui empire in sixth-century China, followed by the T'ang in the seventh century; their power and riches offered impressive models for Japan to emulate.

Tradition said that the first Chinese Buddhist monks arrived in Japan in 552 C.E. Although some Japanese nobles resisted the foreign religion, most were impressed by Buddhist ceremonies and teachings. Thus Buddhism transmitted many aspects of Chinese culture to the Japanese. In 587, the powerful pro-Buddhist Soga clan placed its candidate, Suiko, on the throne as empress. However, she gave actual power to her nephew, crown prince Shotoku Taishi (r. 596-622), who ruled as regent.

Prince Shotoku is called the Great Civilizer because of he started an ambitious program to learn from China that continued for two centuries. It changed the Japanese from a primitive, preliterate people to a sophisticated and highly cultured one. A devout Buddhist, Shotoku proclaimed Buddhism Japan's official religion; but he turned to Confucianism for models in government and social organization. He established official contact with the Chinese government and sent three embassies to China, each accompanied by many students. Up to mid-ninth century, a continuous flow of Japanese officials and students went to China, some staying to study for up to ten years. Chinese and Koreans were also welcomes in Japan. This massive, and entirely voluntary transfer of culture and technology was unprecedented.

In adopting the Chinese written language, the Japanese also learned to respect history. Early Japanese myths and history were set down in the *Kojiki* (*Record of Ancient Matters*), completed in 712, and the *Nihongi* or *History of Japan*, completed in 720. Both chronicles began with the creation myths that became Shintoism. To enhance the prestige of the ruling house, they established the tradition of a divinely descended monarchy of the Yamato clan. Both chronicles are, however, essentially correct for events after the fifth century. The first reading below retells the Japanese creation myth and links the ruling house with Amaterasu, sun goddess and patroness of Japan, who gave her grandson the treasures that are still the Japanese imperial regalia. The second reading deals with the life and accomplishments of Prince Shotoku.

QUESTIONS:

1) Who was Amaterasu and how did she become the founding ancestress of Japan?
2) How were the Korean kingdoms responsible for the transmission of Buddhism to Japan?
3) Who was Prince Shotoku and why was he important to Japan?

Then Amaterasu ... commanded the heir apparent [her son] ... saying: "Now it is reported that the pacification of the Central Land of the Reed Plain has been finished. Therefore descend and rule it, as you have been entrusted with it."

Then the heir apparent ... replied saying: "As I was preparing to descend, a child was born; his name is Ninigi.... This child should descend."

Whereupon ... they imposed the command upon Ninigi: "Toyo-asi-para-no-midu-po-no-kuni [The Land of the Plentiful Reed Plains and of the Fresh Rice-ears, that is, Kyushu Island] has been entrusted to you as the land you are to rule. In accordance with this command, descend from the heavens!"...

Hereupon, she [Amaterasu] imparted [unto him] the myriad Maga-tama beads and the mirror ... as well as the sword ... and said: "This mirror--have [it with you] as my spirit, and worship it just as you would worship in my very presence...."

* * * * *

1st year [of emperor Tachibana no Toyohi's reign], Spring, 1st month, 1st day. The Imperial Princess Anahobe no Hashibito was appointed Empress Consort. She bore four sons. The first was called the Imperial Prince Mumayado [also called Mimito Shotoku, or as some have it Toyoto-mimi, Great King of the Law, or again Master King of the Law]....

Summer, 4th month, 10th day [593]. The Imperial Prince Shotoku was appointed Prince Imperial.   He had general control of the Government, and was entrusted with all the details of administration.... He was able to speak as soon as he was born, and was so wise when he grew up that he could attend to the suits of ten men at once and decide them all without error. He knew beforehand what was going to happen.

Moreover he learnt the Inner Doctrine [Buddhism] from a Koryo [a Korean state] priest named Hye-cha, and studied the Outer Classics [Chinese Classics] with a doctor named Hak-ka. In both these branches of study he became thoroughly proficient....

2nd year, spring, 2nd month, 1st day [594]. The Empress instructed Prince Shotoku ... to promote the prosperity of the Three Precious Things [of Buddhism, namely the Buddha, the Dharma or sacred law, and the Sangha or community of monks]. At this time, all the Omi and Muraji [clan chieftains and titled lords] vied each with one another in erecting Buddhist shrines for the benefit of their Lords and parents. These were called Temples....

5th month, 10th day [594]. A priest of Koryo, named Hye-cha, migrated to Japan, and was taken as teacher by the Prince Imperial. In the same year a Pekche [another Korean state] priest, named Hye-chhong arrived. These two priests preached the Buddhist religion widely, and were together the mainstay of the Three Precious Things....

Winter, 10th month [602]. A Pekche priest named Kwal-leuk arrived and presented by way of tribute books of Calendar-making, of Astronomy, and of Geography, and also books of the art of invisibility and of magic. At this time three or four pupils were selected, and made to study under Kwal-leuk.... They all studied so far as to perfect themselves in these arts....

11th year [603] ... 12th month, 5th day. Cap-ranks were first instituted [a Chinese custom that used caps of different shapes and materials to denote official ranks] ... --in all twelve grades.

Each was made of sarcenet of a special colour. They were gathered up on the crown in the shape of a bag, and had a border attached. Only on the first day of the year were hair flowers worn.

12th year [604], Spring, 1st month, 1st day. Cap-ranks were for the first time granted to the various Ministers, there being a distinction for each.

12th year ... Summer, 4th month, 3rd day [604] The Prince Imperial in person prepared for the first time laws. There were seventeen clauses as follows:-

I. Harmony is to be valued, and an avoidance of wanton opposition to be honored....

II. Sincerely reverence the three treasures. The three treasures, viz. Buddha, the Law and the Priesthood, are the final refuge of the four generated beings, and are the supreme objects of faith in all countries....

III. When you receive the Imperial commands, fail not scrupulously to obey them. The lord is Heaven, the vassal is Earth. Heaven overspreads, and Earth upbears. When this is so, the four seasons follow their due course, and the powers of Nature obtain their efficacy. If the Earth attempted to overspread, Heaven would simply fall in ruin. Therefore it is that when the lord speaks, the vassal listens; when the superior acts, the inferior yields compliance. Consequently when you receive the Imperial commands, fail not to carry them out scrupulously. Let there be a want of care in this matter, and ruin is the natural consequence.

IV. The Ministers and functionaries should make decorous behaviour their leading principle, for the leading principle of the government of the people consists in decorous behaviour....

VIII. Let the Ministers and functionaries attend the Court early in the morning, and retire late. The business of the State does not admit of remissness, and the whole day is hardly enough for its accomplishment....

IX. Good faith is the foundation of right. In everything let there be good faith.... If the lord and the vassal observe good faith one with another, what is there which cannot be accomplished? If the lord and the vassal do not observe good faith towards one another, everything without exception ends in failure....

XII. Let not the provincial authorities or the Kuni no Miyakko [local officers] levy exactions on the people. In a country there are not two lords; the people have not two masters. The sovereign is the master of the people of the whole country. The officials to whom he gives charge are all his vassals. How can they, as well as the Government, presume to levy taxes on the people?

XIII. Let all persons entrusted with office attend equally to their functions....

XIV. Ye ministers and functionaries! Be not envious. For if we envy others, they in turn will envy us. The evils of envy know no limit....

XVI. Let the people be employed (in forced labour) at seasonable times. This is an ancient and excellent rule. Let them be employed, therefore, in the winter months, when they are at leisure. But from Spring to Autumn, when they are engaged in agriculture or with the mulberry trees, the people should not be so employed. For if they do not attend to agriculture, what will they have to eat? if they do not attend to the mulberry trees, what will they do for clothing?...

Autumn, 7th month [606]. The Empress requested the Prince Imperial to lecture on the Sho-man-gio {Buddhist scripture}. He completed his explanation of it in three days.

16th year, Summer, 4th month...An envoy from Great Thang [China] named P'ei Shih-ch'ing, with a suite of twelve persons, arrived at Tsukushi in company with Imoko no Omi. Wonari, Naniha no Kishi, was sent to bring the guests of Great Thang, Pe'ei Shih-ch'ing and the others, and a new official residence was erected for them over the Koryo official residence at Naniha.

6th month, 15th day. The guests anchored in the harbour of Naniha. Thirty gaily decked boats were sent to meet them at Yeguchi (river mouth) and they were lodged in the new official residence....

Autumn, 8th month, 3rd day. The Thang guests entered the capital. On this day seventy-five caparisoned horses were sent to meet the Thang guests on the Tsubaki no ichi highway, where Hirafu, Nukada be no Muraji, delivered a message of welcome to them.

12th day. The Thang guests were summoned to Court, and caused to state the object of their mission....

Now the presents from the land of Great Thang were placed in the courtyard. Then the chief envoy, P'ei Shih-ch'ing, bearing in his own hands the letter (of credence), made obeisance twice, and declared the purport of his mission. He then stood up.

The letter was as follows:-"The Emperor greets the Sovereign of Wa [both Chinese and Koreans called Japan Wa]. Your envoy, the provincial governor ... and his suite have arrived, and have given us full information.

We have reverently received the precious command (of Heaven), rule over the universe. It is Our desire to diffuse abroad Our civilizing influences, so as to cover all living things, and Our sentiment of loving nurture knows no distinction of distance.

Now We learn that Your Majesty, dwelling separately beyond the sea, bestows the blessings of peace on your subjects, that there is tranquility within your borders, and that the manners and customs are mild.

With the most profound loyalty, you have sent Us tribute from afar, and We are delighted at this admirable token of your sincerity.

Our health is as usual, notwithstanding the increasing warmth of the weather.

Therefore We have sent P'ei Shih-ch'ing, Official Entertainer of the Department charged with the Ceremonial for the reception of Foreign Ambassadors, and his suite, to notify to you the preceding. We also transmit to you the products of which a list is given separately....

16th day. The Thang guests were entertained at Court....

11th day. the Thang guest, P'ei Shih-ch'ing, took his departure.... Now the Emperor addressed the Thang Emperor in the following terms:-

"The Emperor of the East respectfully addresses the Emperor of the West. Your Envoy, Pe'ei Shih-ch'ing, Official Entertainer of the Department of foreign receptions, and his suite, having arrived here, my long-harboured cares were dissolved. The last month of autumn is somewhat chilly. How is Your Majesty? We trust well. We are in our usual health. We now send the Dairai, So In-ko, the Dairai Wonari, and others to you. This is respectfully presented, but informal."

At this time there were sent to the Land of Thang the students ... in all eight persons.

In this year many persons from Silla came to settle in Japan....

18th year [610], Spring, 3rd month. The King of Koryo sent tribute of Buddhist priests named Tam-chhi and Pop-chong. Tam-chhi knew the five (Chinese) classics. He was moreover skilled in preparing painters' colours, paper, and ink. He also made mills. This was apparently the first time that mills were made....

26th year [618], Autumn, 8th month, 1st day. Koryo sent envoys with tribute of local productions, and reported that Yang-Ti of the Sui dynasty had invaded that country with a force of 300,000 men, but had, on the contrary, been beaten by them. They therefore sent a present of two captives, named Chen-kung and P'u-t'ung, with such things as flutes, cross-bows, and catapults--ten in all. They also sent one camel, bred in their country....

29th year [621], Spring, 2nd month, 5th day. In the middle of the night the Imperial Prince ... died in the Palace of Ikaruga. At this time all the Princes and Omi, as well as the people of the Empire, the old, as if they had lost a dear child, had no taste for salt and vinegar in their mouths, the young, as if they had lost a beloved parent, filled the ways with the sound of their lamenting. The farmer ceased from his plough, and the pounding woman laid down her pestle. They all said:-"The sun and moon have lost their brightness; heaven and earth have crumbled to ruin: henceforward, in whom shall we put our trust?"

Aston, W.G., trans. *Nihongi Chronicles of Japan from the Earliest Times to A.D. 697*. Rpt. London: Allen and Unwin, 1956. Pp. 107, 122-123, 126-129, 131-132, 135-140, 146, 148. Philippi, Donald L., ed. and trans. *Kojiki*. Tokyo: Univ. of Tokyo Press, 1969. Pp. 137-140.

A JAPANESE NOBLE LADY'S OBSERVATIONS

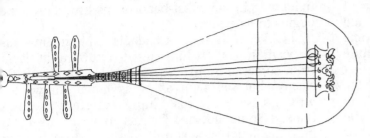

► Japanese Lute

Sei Shonagon was born in 966 or 967 C.E., the daughter of a high-ranking official related to the imperial clan. Many of her forebears had been provincial governors, distinguished scholars, court poets, and historians. In 991, Shonagon became lady-in-waiting to the young empress Sadako and lived in the palace till 1001. Her jottings and diary during those years were compiled in the *Pillow Book*, a sampling of which is reproduced here.

Like other fashionable court ladies she kept a journal, but Shonagon's work is so well written and entertaining that it was widely read in court circles in manuscript copies. It was first printed in 1666. The *Pillow Book* documents tenth-century court life in Heian (capital of Japan since 794, now known as Kyoto). It is one of the finest examples of native Japanese literature written in *kana*, a syllabary script adapted from Chinese. While male aristocrats learned to write in formal Chinese, aristocratic women wrote in the simplified kana script, using Japanese grammar and syntax. Thus all early purely Japanese literature was written by women, who described aristocratic life from their point of view. Since morals were lax and etiquette extraordinarily important, much of the book deals with clandestine love affairs and the correct behavior of lovers. Religious observances were mere formalities. While male courtiers of the Heian era occupied themselves with elegant and frivolous pursuits and neglected government, power slipped away to provincial warriors became the true rules of Japan in the ensuing feudal age.

QUESTIONS:

1) What would you say is the main preoccupation of ladies in Shonagon's world?
2) What role did Buddhism play in the court circles?
3) How did aristocratic ladies and gentlemen spend their time in Japan around 1000 C.E.?

Of the gentlewomen's apartments attached to the Empress's own quarters, those along the Narrow Gallery are the most agreeable. When the wooden blinds at the top are rolled up, the wind blows in very hard, and it is cool even in summer. In winter, indeed, snow and hail often come along with the wind; but even so I find it very agreeable. As the rooms have very little depth and boys, even when so near to the Imperial apartments, do not always mind their manners, we generally ensconce ourselves behind screens, where the quiet is delightful, for there is none of the loud talk and laughter that disturb one in other quarters of the palace.

I like the feeling that one must always be on the alert. And if this is true during the day, how much more so at night, when one must be prepared for something to happen at any moment. All night long one hears the noise of footsteps in the corridor outside. Every now and then the sound will cease in front of some particular door, and there will be a gentle tapping, just with one finger; but one knows that the lady inside will have instantly recognized the knock. Sometimes, this soft tapping lasts a long while; the lady is no doubt pretending to be asleep. But at last comes the rustle of a dress or the sound of someone cautiously turning on her couch, and one knows that she has taken pity on him.

In summer she can hear every movement of his fan, as he stands chafing outside; while in winter, stealthily though it be done, he will hear the sound of someone gently stirring the ashes in the brazier, and will at once begin knocking more resolutely, or even asking out loud for admittance, And while he does so one can hear him squeezing up closer and closer against the door....

If someone with whom one is having an affair keeps on mentioning some woman whom he knew in the past, however long ago it is since they separated, one is always irritated.

It is very tiresome when a lover who is leaving one at dawn says that he must look for a fan or pocket-book that he left somewhere about the room last night. As it is still too dark to see anything, he goes fumbling about all over the place, knocking into everything and muttering to himself, "How very odd!" When at last he finds the pocket-book he crams it into his dress with a great rustling of the pages; or begins flapping it about, so that when he finally takes his departure, instead of experiencing the feelings of regret proper to such an occasion, one merely feels irritated at his clumsiness....

It is important that a lover should know how to make his departure. To begin with, he ought not to be too ready to get up, but should require a little coaxing....Then he should raise the shutters, and both lovers should go out together at the double-doors, while he tells her how much he dreads the day that is before him and longs for the approach of night. Then after he has slipped away, she can stand gazing after him, with charming recollections of those last moments. Indeed, the success of a lover depends greatly on his method of departure. If he springs to his feet with a jerk and at once begins fussing round,

tightening in the waist-band of his breeches...one begins to hate him.

I like to think of a bachelor--an adventurous disposition has left him single--returning at dawn from some amorous excursion. He looks a trifle sleepy; but, as soon as he is home, draws his writing-case towards him, carefully grinds himself some ink and begins to write his next-morning letter--not simply dashing off whatever comes into his head, but spreading himself to the task and taking trouble to write the characters beautifully. He should be clad in an azalea-yellow or vermilion cloak worn over a white robe. Glancing from time to time at the dewdrops that still cling to the thin white fabric of his dress, he finishes his letter, but instead of giving it to one of the ladies who are in attendance upon him at the moment, he gets up and, choosing from among his page-boys one who seems to him exactly appropriate to such a mission, calls the lad to him, and whispering something in his ear puts the letter in his hand; then gazing after him as he disappears into the distance. While waiting for the answer he will perhaps quietly murmur to himself this or that passage from the *Sutras* [Buddhist scriptures]. Presently he is told that his washing-water and porridge are ready, and goes into the back room, where, seated at the reading-table, he glances at some Chinese poems, now and then reciting out loud some passage that strikes his fancy. When he has washed and got into his Court cloak, which he wears as a dressing-gown...he takes the 6th chapter of the Lotus Scripture and reads it silently. Precisely at the most solemn moment of his reading--the place being not far away--the messenger returns, and by his posture it is evident that he expects an instant reply. With an amusing if blasphemous rapidity the lover transfers his attention from the book he is reading to the business of framing his answer....

ANNOYING THINGS

When one sends a poem or a *kayeshi* ("return-poem") to someone and, after it has gone, thinks of some small alteration--perhaps only a couple of letters--that would have improved it.

When one is doing a piece of needlework in a hurry, and thinking it is finished unthreads the needle, only to discover that the knot at the beginning has slipped and the whole thing come undone. It is also very annoying to find that one has sewn back to front....

It is particularly annoying if a letter goes astray and gets delivered to someone to whom one would never have dreamt of showing it. If the messenger would simply say straight out that he has made a mistake, one could put up with it. But he always begins arguing and trying to prove that he only did as he was told. It is this that is so trying, and if there was not always someone looking on, I am sure I should rush at him and strike him....

A lady is out of humour about some trifle, and leaving her lover's side goes and establishes herself on another couch. He creeps over to her and tries to bring her back, but she is still cross, and he, feeling that this time she has really gone too far, says: "As you please," and returns to the big bed, where he ensconces himself comfortably and goes to sleep. It is a very cold night and the lady, having only an unlined wrap to cover herself with, soon begins to suffer. She thinks of getting up; but everyone else in the house is asleep and she does not know what to do or where to go. If she must needs have this quarrel, it would have been better, she thinks, to start it a little earlier in the evening. Then she begins to hear strange noises both in the women's quarters and outside. She becomes frightened and softly creeps towards her lover, plucks at the bedclothes, and raises them. But he vexingly pretends to be fast asleep; or merely says: "I advise you to go on sulking a little longer."

Small children and babies ought to be fat. So ought provincial governors, or one suspects them of being bad-tempered. As regards appearance, it is most essential of all that the boys who feed the carriage-oxen should be presentable. If one's other servants are not fit to be seen, they can be stowed away behind the carriage. But outriders or the like, who are bound to catch the eye, make a painful impression if they are not perfectly trim. However, if it is too obvious that one's men servants have been lumped together behind the carriage in order to escape notice, this in itself looks very bad.

It is a mistake to choose slim, elegant youths on purpose that they may look well as footmen, and then let them wear trousers that are grimy at the ends and hunting-cloaks or the like that have

seen too much wear. The best that can be hoped is that people will think they are walking beside your carriage by chance and have nothing to do with you.

But it is a great convenience that all one's servants should be handsome. Then if they should happen to tear their clothes or make themselves in any way shabby or untidy, it is more likely to be overlooked....

VERY TIRESOME THINGS

When a poem of one's own, that one has allowed someone else to use as his, is singled out for praise.

Someone who is going a long journey wants introductions to people in the various places through which he will pass, and asks you for a letter. You write a really nice letter of recommendation for him to present to one of your friends who lives at some place through which he will pass. But your friend is cross at being bothered and ignores the letter. To be thus shown up as having no influence is very humiliating.

MISCELLANEOUS

There is nothing in the whole world so painful as feeling that one is not liked. It always seems to me that people who hate me must be suffering from some strange form of lunacy. However, it is bound to happen, whether at Court or in one's own home, that some people like one and some don't; which I find very distressing. Even for a child of the servant-class (and much more for one of good-breeding) it is very painful, after having always been petted at home, to find itself the object of a disapproving stare. If a girl in question has anything to recommend her, one thinks it quite reasonable that she should have been made a fuss of. But if she is without attractions of any kind, she knows that everybody is saying, "Fancy anyone making a pet of a creature like that! Really, parents are very odd!" Yes, at home or at Court the one thing that matters is to be liked by everyone, from their Majesties downward!

ON PLEASANT THINGS

In the fifth month I love driving out to some mountain village. The pools that lie across the road look like patches of green grass; but while the carriage slowly pushes its way right through them, one sees that there is only a scum of some strange, thin weed, with clear, bright water underneath. Though it is quite shallow, great spurts fly up as our horsemen gallop across, making a lovely sight. Then, where the road runs between hedges, a leafy bough will sometimes dart in at the carriage window; but however quickly one snatches at it, one is always too late.

Sometimes a spray of *yomogi* will get caught in the wheel, and for a moment, as the wheel brings it level, a delicious scent hovers at our window.

I love to cross a river in very bright moonlight and see the trampled water fly up in chips of crystal under the oxen's feet....

CONCERNING RELIGION

A Recitant [of the Scriptures] ought to be good-looking. It is only if it is a pleasure to keep one's eyes on him at all times that there is any chance of religious feeling being aroused. Otherwise one begins looking at something else and soon one's attention wanders from what he is reading; in which case ugliness becomes an actual cause of sin....

The time has come for me to stop putting down ideas of this kind. Now that I am getting to be a good age, and so on, it frightens me to discover that I ever wrote such blasphemous stuff. I remember that whenever any priest was reported to be of particular piety I would rush off immediately to the house where he was giving his readings. If this was the state of mind in which I arrived, I see now that I should have done better to stay away.

Waley, Arthur, trans. *The Pillow Book of Sei Shonagon.* London: Allen and Unwin, 1929. Pp. 85-86, 88, 90-91, 93-94, 114-115, 117-121, 126-128.

READING 5.9

THE SAMURAI IDEAL IN PRACTICE

▶ Samurai in Armor

By 1000 C.E. the centralized bureaucratic government Japan borrowed from China had broken down. Because hereditary ranks and aristocratic privilege remained strong in Japan, the provincial warrior aristocracy reemerged to govern the countryside under a system similar to medieval feudalism in Europe.

Although the emperor remained sovereign in theory, and retained ritual responsibilities, he held no political power. Real power belonged to the *shogun* or generalissimo (commander-in-chief) of fief-holding lords called *daimyo* or "great names." The daimyo in turn were helped by a much larger class of *bushi* (warrior) or *samurai* (retainer), together about five percent of the population. Although sharp economic and social distinctions separated the great lords from their samurai retainers, the latter were distinguished from ordinary people by dress style, family names, rules of conduct, and the exclusive right to bear two swords. The aristocrats were supported by hereditary serfs who lived in villages.

Over the centuries, there evolved a code of ethics called *bushido*, or "the way of the warrior," an idealized combination of Confucian moral teachings and feudal ethics. It emphasized absolute loyalty to superiors, simplicity, frugality, and self-sacrifice for lord and cause. It also inculcated a disregard for pain and death that had roots in Zen Buddhism.

Not all samurai lived up to the code, especially in the century-long era of strife and civil wars before the establishment of the Tokugawa shogunate in 1603. Indeed treachery was selfish ambition often characterized behavior of the feudal lords. Honor for bushido nevertheless survived. Torii Mototada (1539-1600) exemplified the samurai ideal. A daimyo himself, and also vassal of Shogun Tokugawa Ieyasu, he volunteered to defend a castle although all knew it was a hopeless task. He did so to stall the enemy while his lord won crucial victories elsewhere. He held out for ten days against impossible odds, and committed *seppuku* or suicide by disembowelment (a samurai ritual) when all around him had fallen. The following letter is his moving last testament, addressed to his eldest son a few days before the final battle. It shows the moral heights a man can attain in service to his cause and lord.

The second excerpt is by Kumazawa Banzan (1619-1691). Born into a poor samurai family, he rose to become chief minister of a major daimyo. His writings and economic reforms made him famous. Kumazawa lived by the code of the samurai and maintained a strict physical regime; he also became a famous Confucian scholar, setting a trend among samurai.

Having unified Japan, the Tokugawa shoguns and the daimyo turned their attention to administration. They had their retainers educated and trained to become good bureaucrats. Neo-Confucian ideals developed by Chu Hsi in twelfth century China became the standard in Japan also.

Kamazawa, however, espoused the rival school of Wang Yang-ming, another scholar and contemporary of Chu Hsi in interpreting Confucianism.

QUESTIONS:

1) Why did Mototada resolve to die defending the castle? What ideals did he live by?
2) How should Mototada's eldest son treat his younger brothers and toward his lord?
3) How should a good samurai discipline his body and mind?

For myself, I am resolved to make a stand within the castle and to die a quick death. It would not take much trouble to break through a part of their [the besiegers'] numbers and escape, no matter how many tens of thousands of horsemen approached for the attack or by how many columns we were surrounded. But that is not the true meaning of being a warrior, and it would be difficult to account as loyalty. Rather, I will stand off the forces of the entire country here, and, without even one-hundredth of the men necessary to do so, will throw up a defense and die a resplendent death. By doing so I will show that to abandon a castle that should be defended, or to value one's life so much as to avoid danger and to show the enemy one's weakness is not within the family traditions of my master Ieyasu. Thus I will have taken the initiative in causing Lord Ieyasu's other retainers to be resolved, and in advancing righteousness to the warriors of the entire country. It is not the Way of the Warrior to be shamed and avoid death even under circumstances that are not particularly important. It goes without saying that to sacrifice one's life for the sake of his master is an unchanging principle. As this is a matter that I have thought over beforehand, I think that circumstances such that I am meeting now must be envied by people of understanding.

You, Tadamasa, should understand the following well. Our ancestors have been personal vassals of the Matsudaira [former surname of the Tokugawa family] for generations. My late father, the Governor of Iga, served Lord Kiyoyasu [Tokugawa Ieyasu's grandfather], and later worked loyally for his son, Hirotada. My older brother, Genshichiro, manifested his absolute loyalty and was cut down in battle at Watari. When the present Lord Ieyasu was a child and sent to Suruga, the Governor of Iga accompanied him as a guardian.

Later, at the age of 19, Ieyasu returned to Okazaki, and the Governor of Iga served him with unsurpassed loyalty, living more than 80 years with unswerving steadfastness. Lord Ieyasu, for his part, regarded the Governor as a matchless vassal. When I was 13 and Lord Ieyasu seven, I came before his presence for the first time, and the blessings I have received since must not be forgotten for all the generations to come.

Because Lord Ieyasu is well aware of my loyalty, he has left me here in charge of the important area of Kamigata as Deputy of Fushimi Castle while he advances toward the East, and for a warrior there is nothing that could surpass this good fortune. That I should be able to go ahead of all the other warriors of this country and lay down my life for the sake of my master's benevolence is an honor to my family and has been my most fervent desire for many years.

After I am slain, you must lovingly care for all your younger brothers, beginning with Hisagoro, in my stead. Your younger brothers must earnestly look to you as they would to their father, and must never disobey you. As they grow up, they should one by one present themselves to the Lord Ieyasu, make efforts with their own various talents, do whatever they are commanded, be on friendly terms with one another, and remain forever grateful to their ancestors, by whose blessings our clan was established and its descendants succored. They must be determined to stand with Lord Ieyasu's clan in both its ascent and decline, in times of peace and in times of war; and either waking or sleeping they must never forget that they will serve his clan, and his clan alone. To be avaricious for land or to forget old debts because of some passing dissatisfaction, or to even temporarily entertain treacherous thoughts is not the Way of Man. Even if all the other provinces of Japan were to unite against our lord, our descendants should not set foot inside another fief to the end of time. Simply, in no matter what circumstances, unify with the heart of one family--of elder and younger brothers--exert yourselves in the cause of loyalty, mutually help and be helped by one another, preserve your righteousness and strive in bravery, and be of a mind never to stain the reputation of a clan that has not remained hidden from the world, but has gained fame in military valor for generations, especially since the days of the Governor of Iga. At any rate, if you will take it into your mind to be sincere in throwing away your life for your master, you will not have the slightest fear or trembling even with the advent of innumerable impending calamities.

I am now 62 years of age. Of the number of times that I have barely escaped death since the time I was in Mikawa I have no idea. Yet, not once have I acted in a cowardly way. Man's life and death, fortune and calamity are in the fate of the times, and thus one should not search out after what he likes. What is essential is to listen to the words of the older retainers, to put to use men of skill and understanding, to not commit acts of adolescent self-will, and to receive the remonstrances of your retainers. The entire country will soon be in the hands of your master, Lord Ieyasu. If this is so, the men who served him will no doubt hope to became daimyo by his appointment. You should know that if such feelings arise, they are inevitably the beginning of the end of one's fortunes in the Way of the Warrior. Being affected by the avarice for office and rank, or wanting to become a daimyo and being eager for such things ... will not one then begin to value his life? And how can a man commit acts of martial valor if he values his life? A man who has been born into the house of a warrior and yet places no loyalty in his heart and thinks only of the fortune of his position will be flattering on the surface and construct schemes in his heart, will forsake righteousness and not reflect on his shame, and will stain the warrior's name of his household to later generations. This is truly regrettable. It is not necessary to say such a thing, but you should raise the name of your ancestors in this world yet a second time. Moreover, as I have already spoken to you about the management of our clan's affairs, there is no

need to speak of that again. You have already seen and heard of what has been regulated from the past.

Be first of all prudent in your conduct and have correct manners, develop harmony between master and retainers, and have compassion on those beneath you. Be correct in the degree of rewards and punishments, and let there be no partiality in your degree of intimacy with your retainers. The foundation of man's duty as a man is in "truth." Beyond this, there is nothing to be said.

* * * * *

When I was about sixteen I had a tendency toward corpulence. I had noticed a lack of agility in other fleshy persons and thought that a heavy man would not make a first class *samurai*. So I tried every device to keep myself agile and lean. I slept with my girdle drawn tight and stopped eating rice. I took no wine and abstained from sexual intercourse for the next ten years. While on duty at Yedo there were no hills and fields at hand where I could hunt and climb, so I exercised with spear and sword. When I was on the night watch in my master's residence at Yedo, I kept a wooden sword and a pair of straw sandals in my bamboo hamper with which I used to put myself through military drill alone in the dark court after every one was asleep. I also practiced running about over the roofs of the out buildings far removed from the sleeping rooms. This I did so as to be able to handle myself nimbly if a fire should break out. There were very few who noticed me at these exercises and they were reported to have said that I was probably possessed by a hobgoblin (*Tengu*.) This was before I was twenty years old and in my zeal I overdid a little....

When I had grown to manhood I was eager to study, but I had neither natural talent nor proper culture. For unfortunately when I was young and plastic I knew not that there was anything worth doing besides military drill. I spent my energy upon useless matters. After I fell ill in my twenty-first year I learned for the first time to read the "Four Books." The commentaries helped me to understand the text. In July of my twenty-third year I went to Ogawa and saw Mr. Nakae and asked him many questions.... After that my father went to Yedo to seek for a position and, as my mother and sisters were left alone in a lonely castle at Kirihara in East Omi, it was impossible for me to go to Kyoto or to Toju at Ogawa in West Omi. So I cared for my mother and studied by myself for five years. I served no master. We were very poor and lived upon the meal commonly taken by the Omi peasants. I had no tea, wine, soup, fish nor relish except the poorest kind of bean sauce. To keep myself warm I had only a paper coat and cotton clothes. But I was so absorbed in my books that I forgot the creative enjoyments of past days.

Wilson, William Scott, trans. *Ideals of the Samurai: Writings of Japanese Warriors*. Burbank, CA: Ohara Publications, 1982. Pp. 120-124. Fisher, Galen M. "Kumazawa Banzan, His Life and Ideas." *The Transactions of the Asiatic Society of Japan* 16 (May 1938) 230-231, 234.

▶ **Spanish Drawing of Inca Ceremony**

MANCO CAPAC, THE FIRST INCA

When the first Spaniards arrived in South America in 1532, they met the powerful Empire of the Incas. (Inca in the Quechua language means "king" or "prince," but the Spanish applied the name to all the Quechuan-speaking people of the Andes.) The Inca empire was centered on a capital city at Cuzco, near Lake Titicaca in Peru. It reached it greatest size during the reign of Huayna Capac (1493-1525), extending 2500 miles from north to south and 500 from east to west, with a population of between twelve and fifteen million inhabitants.

Because the Incas were engaged in civil strife in the early sixteenth century, they became easy prey for Francisco Pizarro and his small force of about 180 men, who had the tremendous advantage of firearms. Pizarro captured and executed King Atahualpa. Inca history ended in 1572, when a revolt led by Tupac Amaru, last in the royal line, was quelled.

The Incas lacked a writing system and relied exclusively on oral tradition. Fortunately, some of this oral history was set down by Garcilaso de la Vega (c. 1540-1616), the son of a Spanish father and a Peruvian mother. After moving from Cuzco to Spain in 1560, he wrote a lengthy history titled *Royal Commentaries of the Incas*, published between 1609 and 1617. Though his account contains much legend and romance, it is based on the living oral tradition of the Inca people. The passage that follows recounts the story of Manco Capac, the Incas' founding father. While many of the colorful details of the first Inca are fictional, the customs and institutions whose mythical origins are depicted were authentic.

QUESTIONS:

1) Garcilaso speaks of "idolatrous customs ... festivals and superstitions"; why does he use such tendentious terminology?

2) Does Garcilaso's portrait of Manco Capac seem even-handed or prejudiced?

3) Does the Incas' use of insignia and distinguishing dress, etc. seem like or unlike the practices of other cultures?

I was brought up amongst these [Inca] Indians and held intercourse with them until I was twenty years of age. During that time I acquired a knowledge of all the matters on which we are about to treat; ... and if I had written it all down, this history would be more copious. Besides what the Indians told me, I had the opportunity of seeing with my own eyes, a great many of their idolatrous customs, their festivals and superstitions, which were still celebrated even until I was twelve or thirteen years of age. I was born eight years after the Spaniards conquered my country, and ... I was brought up in it until my twentieth year, so that I myself saw many things that were practised by the Indians....

"The first settlement that was made in this valley," continued my uncle the Inca, "was on the hill called Huanacauti, to the south of this city. It was here that the sceptre of gold buried itself in the ground with great ease, and it was never seen more. Then our Inca [Manco Capac] said to his wife and sister:--"Our Father the Sun orders that we settle in this valley to fulfil his wishes. It is therefore right, O queen and sister, that each of us should gather these people together, to instruct them and to do the good which has been ordered by our Father the Sun." Our first rulers set out from the hill of Huanacauti, in different directions, to call the people together, and as this is the first place we know of which they pressed with their feet, we have built a temple there ... to worship our Father the Sun, in memory of this act of benevolence which He performed for the world....

"When our princes saw the large multitude of people that had arrived, they ordered that some should occupy themselves in procuring supplies for the rest, that hunger might not force them to scatter themselves over the mountains again, while the rest worked at building houses according to a plan made by the Inca. In this manner he began to settle this our imperial city, dividing it into two parts, called Hanan Cuzco, which ... means Upper Cuzco, and Hurin Cuzco, which is Lower Cuzco....

"At the same time that the city was being peopled, our Inca taught the Indians those occupations which appertain to a man, such as breaking up and cultivating the ground, and sowing corn and other seeds, which he pointed out as fit for food and useful. He also taught them to make ploughs and other necessary instruments, he showed them the way to lead channels from the brooks which flow through the valley of Cuzco; and even instructed them how to prepare the sandals which we now wear. On the other hand, the Queen employed the Indian women in such work as is suitable to them, such

as to sew and weave cotton and wool, to make clothes for themselves, their husbands, and children, and to perform other household duties. In fine, our princes taught their first vassals everything that is needful in life, the Inca making himself king and master of the men, and the Coya being queen and mistress of the women.... In a few years, so great a multitude was assembled that, after the first six or seven years, the Inca had a body of armed and disciplined men to defend him against any invader, and even to subject by force all who were not willing to submit of their own accord. He taught them to make offensive arms, such as bows and arrows, lances, clubs, and others, which are still used...."

After founding Cuzco in the two divisions which we have described before, [the Inca Manco Capac] ordered many other towns to be built.... These villages, which numbered more than a hundred, were at first small, the largest not having more than a hundred houses, and the smallest about twenty-five or thirty. Afterwards, owing to the favours and privileges granted to them by Manco Capac ... they increased very much, and many of them reached a population of a thousand inhabitants, the smaller ones having from 300 to 400. Long afterwards the great tyrant Atahualpa destroyed many of these towns. In our own times, not more than twenty years ago, these towns, which were founded by the Inca Manco Capac, and almost all the others in Peru, were moved from the original sites to other very different situations; because a Viceroy ... ordered all to be converted into a smaller number of larger towns, uniting five or six into one, and seven or eight into another. Whence resulted much inconvenience, which, being hateful, I will refrain from describing.

The Inca Manco Capac, in establishing his people in villages, while he taught them to cultivate the land, to build houses, construct channels for irrigation, and to do all other things necessary for human life; also instructed them in the ways of polite and brotherly companionship, in conformity with reason and the law of nature, persuading them, with much earnestness, to preserve perpetual peace and concord between themselves, and not to entertain anger or passionate feelings toward each other, but to do one another as they would others should do to them, not laying down one law for themselves and another for their neighbours. He particularly enjoined them to respect the wives and daughters of others; because they were formerly more vicious in respect to women, than in any other thing whatever. He imposed the penalty of death on adulterers, homicides, and thieves. He ordered no man to have more than one wife, and that marriages should take place between relations, so as to prevent confusion in families, also that marriages should take place at the age of twenty years and upwards, that the married couples might be able to rule their households, and work their estates. He directed the tame flocks [of llamas], which wandered over the country without a master, to be collected, so that all people might be clothed with their wool, by reason of the industry and skill which had been taught to the women by the Queen Mama Occllo Huaco. They were also taught to make the shoes which are now used, called *usata* [sandals made of llama hides]. A Curaca, which is the same as a Cacique in the language of Cuba and San Domingo, and means lord of vassals, was appointed over every nation that was subjugated. The Curacas were chosen from among those who had done the most in conquering the Indians, for their merit, as being most affable, gentle, and pious, and most zealous for the public good. They were constituted lords over the others, that they might instruct them as a father does his children, and the Indians were ordered to obey them, as sons obey their parents.

He ordered that the harvests gathered by each village, should be preserved in common, so that each might be supplied with what it required, until arrangements could be made for giving an allotment of land to each Indian. Together with these precepts and laws, he taught the Indians the worship of his idolatrous religion. The Incas selected a spot for building a temple where they might sacrifice to the Sun, persuading the people that it was the principal God whom they should worship, and to whom they should give thanks for the natural benefits which he conferred on them by his light and heat....

In the above affairs, and in other similar occupations, the Inca Manco Capac was occupied during many years, conferring benefits on his people; and, having experienced their fidelity and love, and the respect and adoration with which

they treated him, he desired to favour them still farther by ennobling them with titles, and badges such as he wore on his own head, and this was after he had persuaded them that he was the child of the Sun. The Inca Manco Capac, and afterwards his descendants, in imitation of him, were shorn, and only wore a tress of hair one finger in width. They were shaven with stone razors, scraping the hair off, and only leaving the above-mentioned tress. They used knives of stone, because they had not invented scissors, shaving themselves with great trouble, as any one may imagine. When they afterwards experienced the facility and ease afforded by the use of scissors, one of the Incas said to an old schoolfellow of mine:--"If the Spaniards, your fathers, had done nothing more than bring us scissors, looking-glasses, and combs, we would have given all the gold and silver there is in our land, for them." Besides having their heads shaved, they bored their ears, just as women's are usually bored for ear-rings; except that they increased the size of the hole artificially ... to a wonderful greatness, such as would be incredible to those who have not seen it, for it would seem impossible that so small a quantity of flesh as there is under the ear, could be so stretched as to be able to surround a hole of the size and shape of the mouth of a pitcher. The ornaments they put in the holes were like stoppers, and if the lobes were broken the flesh would hang down ... half a finger in thickness. The Spaniards called the Indians *Orejones* (large-eared men) because they had this custom.

The Incas wore, as a head-dress, a fringe which they called *llautu*. It was of many colours, about a finger in width, and a little less in thickness. They twisted this fringe three or four times round the head, and let it hang after the manner of a garland.

These three fashions, the *llautu*, the shaving, and the boring of the ears were the principal ones that were introduced by the Inca Manco Capac.... The first privilege that the Inca granted to his vassals was to order them to imitate him in wearing a fringe; only it was not to be of many colours like the one worn by the Inca, but of one colour only, and that colour was black.

After some time another fashion was granted to the people, and they were ordered to go shaven, but in a fashion different one from another, and all from the Inca, that there might be no confusion in the distinctions between nations and provinces, and that they might not have too near a resemblance to the Inca. Thus one tribe was ordered to wear the tail plait like a cap for the ears; that is, with the forehead and temples bare, and the plaits reaching down so as to cover the ears on either side. Others were ordered to cut the tail plait so as only to reach half way down the ears, and others still shorter. But none were allowed to wear the hair so short as that of the Inca. It is also to be observed that all these Indians, and especially the Incas, took care not to let the hair grow, but always kept it at a certain length, that it might not appear after one fashion on one day, and after another on another. Thus regulated as to the fashion and differences of the head-dress, each nation kept to its own, which was decreed and ordained by the hand of the Inca.

After several months and years had elapsed, the Inca granted his people another privilege, more important than those already mentioned, which was that of boring their ears. This privilege, however, was limited with reference to the size of the hole, which was not to be so much as half that of the Inca, and each tribe and province wore a different stopper in the ear hole....

Besides the signs which were intended to prevent confusion between one tribe and another, the Inca ordered other differences in the fashions of his vassals, which they said were intended to show the degree of favour and trust in which they were held, according as they resembled the badges of the Inca. But he did not like one vassal more than another from any caprice, but in conformity with reason and justice. Those who most readily followed his precepts, and who had worked most in the subjugation of other Indians, were allowed to imitate the Inca more closely in their badges, and received more favours than the others. He gave them to understand that all he did with regard to them was by an order and revelation of his father the Sun. And the Indians, believing this, were well satisfied with every thing that was ordered by the Inca, and with any manner in which he might treat them; for, besides believing that his orders were revelations of the Sun, they saw, by experience, the benefits that were derived from obedience to them.

Vega, Ynca Garcilasso de la Vega. *First Part of the Royal Commentaries of the Incas* [1609].   Ed. and trans. Clements R. Markham. Vol. 1. London: Hakluyt Society, 1869. Pp. 76-77, 65-69, 79-87.

THE GRAND LIFE OF MONTEZUMA, LAST LORD OF THE AZTECS

▶ Aztec Deity

The Aztec empire was the most successful of all the Mesoamerican civilizations. Its rise to power from several marshy islands in Lake Texcoco (in present-day Mexico) in the mid-fourteenth-century was dramatic. By 1500, The Aztec domain stretched from the Pacific Ocean to the Gulf of Mexico, with a great capital city at Tenochtitlán (Mexico City). The Aztecs had a highly developed culture with a rich oral literature, an elaborate calendrical system (inherited in part from the Maya), and an advanced technological knowledge, especially in architecture, hydraulic engineering, and metallurgy.

Some thirty million people in Mesoamerica lived under Aztec domination. The Aztecs prospered economically by exploiting the agricultural potential of the Basin of Mexico. They also extracted tribute from subject peoples in conquered territories in the form of food, luxury goods, and human victims for the sacrificial rites of their bloody religion. A prime impetus to warfare was the desire to obtain human victims; indeed, the Aztec king Montezuma that he had sacrificed as many as 40,000 persons on the occasion of his accession to the throne in 1502.

The passage that follows was written by Bernal Díaz del Castillo, a veteran of many campaigns during the Spanish conquest of Mexico by Hernán Cortés (1484-1547). He wrote his history of the conquest in 1568. It records the author's impressions of the Aztec ruler Montezuma (Moctezuma) and the last days of the great king's life in Tenochtitlán, a city of some 250,000 inhabitants. Díaz admiringly portrays the remarkable material sophistication of Aztec culture and its arts and crafts; he also deplores the barbaric and sanguinary practices of Aztec religion. Aztec exactions from conquered populations, especially the tribute in human beings for sacrificial victims led many to aid Cortés and the Spanish against their Aztec masters.

QUESTIONS:

1) Do the biases of Bernal Díaz, as a member of western European society, show through in his account of Montezuma?

2) What does Bernal Díaz seem to find surprising about Aztec social and religious customs?

3) Are there any obvious exaggerations, misinterpretations, or misunderstandings in Bernal Díaz's account of Aztec customs?

The great Montezuma was at this time aged about forty years, of good stature, well proportioned, and thin: his complexion was much fairer than that of the Indians; he wore his hair short, just covering his ears, with very little beard, well arranged, thin, and black. His face was rather long, with a pleasant countenance, and good eyes; gravity and good humour were blended together when he spoke. He was very delicate and clean in his person, bathing himself every evening. He had a number of mistresses, of the first families, and two princesses his lawful wives: when he visited them, it was with such secrecy, that none could know it except his own servants. He was clear of all suspicion of unnatural vices. The clothes which he wore one day, he did not put on for four days after. He had two hundred of his nobility as a guard, in apartments adjoining his own. Of these, certain persons only, could speak to him, and when they went to wait upon him they took off their rich mantles, and put on others of less ornament, but clean. They entered his apartment barefooted, their eyes fixed on the ground, and making three inclinations of the body as they approached him. In addressing the king they said, "Lord, my lord, great lord." When they had finished he dismissed them with a few words, and they retired, with their faces towards him, and their eyes fixed upon the ground. I also observed, that when great men came from a distance about business, they entered his palace barefooted, and in a plain habit; and also, that they did not enter the gate directly, but took a circuit in going towards it.

His cooks had upwards of thirty different ways of dressing meats, and they had earthen vessels so contrived as to keep them always hot. For the table of Montezuma himself, above three hundred dishes were dressed, and for his guards, above a thousand. Before dinner, Montezuma would sometimes go out and inspect the preparations, and his officers would point out to him which were the best, and explained of what birds and flesh they were composed; and of those he would eat. But this was more for amusement than any thing else. It is said that at times the flesh of young children was dressed for him; but the ordinary meats were, domestic fowls, pheasants, geese, partridges, quails, venison, Indian hogs, pigeons, hares, and rabbits, with many other animals and birds peculiar to the country. This is certain; that after Cortés had spoken to him relative to the dressing [of] human flesh, it was not practised in his palace. At his meals, in the cold weather, a number of torches of the bark of a wood which makes no smoke and has an aromatic smell, were lighted, and that they should not throw too much heat, screens, ornamented with gold, and painted with figures of idols, were placed before them. Montezuma was seated on a low throne, or chair, at a table proportioned to the height of his seat. The table was covered with white cloths and napkins, and four beautiful women presented him with water for his hands, in vessels which they call Xicales [gourds], with other vessels under them like plates, to catch the water; they also presented him with towels. Then, two other women brought small cakes of bread, and when the king began to eat, a large screen of wood, gilt, was placed before him, so that people should not during that time see him. The women having retired to a little distance, four ancient lords stood by the throne, to whom Montezuma from time to time spoke or addressed questions, and as a mark of particular favor, gave to each of them a plate of that which he was eating. I was told that these old lords, who were his near relations, were also counsellors and judges. The plates which Montezuma presented to them, they received with high respect, eating what was in them without taking their eyes off the ground. He was served on earthenware of Cholula, red and black. While the king was at table, no one of his guards, or in the vicinity of his apartment, dared for their lives make any noise. Fruit of all the kinds that the country produced was laid before him; he [ate] very little, but from time to time, a liquor prepared from cocoa, and of a stimulative, or corroborative, quality, as we were told, was presented to him in golden cups. We could not at that time see if he drank it or not, but I observed a number of jars, above fifty, brought in, filled with foaming chocolate, of which he took some, which the women presented to him. At different intervals during the time of dinner, there entered certain Indians, hump-backed, very deformed, and ugly, who played tricks of buffoonery, and others who they said were jesters. There was also a company of singers and dancers, who afforded Montezuma much entertainment. To these he ordered the vases of chocolate to be distributed. The four female attendants then took away the cloths, and again with much respect presented him with water to wash his hands, during which time Montezuma conversed with the four old noblemen formerly mentioned, after which they took their leave with many ceremonies. One thing I forgot, and no wonder, to mention in its place, and that is, that during the time Montezuma was at dinner, two very beautiful women were busily employed making small cakes with eggs and other things mixed therein. These were delicately white, and when made they presented them to him on plates covered with napkins. Also another kind of bread was brought to him in long loaves, and plates of cakes resembling wafers. After he had dined, they presented to him three little canes highly ornamented, containing liquid amber, mixed with an herb they call tobacco; and when he had sufficiently viewed and heard the singers, dancers, and buffoons, he took a little of the smoke of one of these canes, and then laid himself down to sleep; and thus his principal meal concluded. After this was over, all his guards and domestics sat down to dinner, and as near a I could judge, above a thousand plates of those eatables that I have mentioned were laid before them, with vessels of foaming chocolate, and fruit in an immense quantity. For his women and various inferior servants, his establishment was of a prodigious expence; and we were astonished, amidst such a profusion, at the vast regularity that prevailed. His major domo was at this time a prince named Tapiea; he kept the accounts of Montezuma's rents, in books which occupied an entire house. Montezuma had two buildings filled with every kind of arms, richly ornamented with gold and jewels, such as shields large and small, clubs like two-handed swords, and lances much larger than ours, with blades six feet in length, so strong that if they fix in a shield they do not break, and sharp enough to use as razors. There was also an immense quantity of bows and arrows, and darts, together with slings, and shield which roll up into a small compass, and in action are let fall and thereby cover the whole body. He had also much defensive armour of quilted cotton ornamented with feathers in different devices, and casques [helmets] for the head, made of wood and bone, with plumes of feathers, and many other articles too tedious to mention.

In this palace was a most magnificent aviary, which contained every description of birds that continent afforded, namely, royal eagles, and a smaller species, with many other birds, down to the smallest parroquets, of beautiful colours. It was here that the ornaments of green feathers were fabricated. The feathers were taken from birds which are of the size of our pyes [magpies] in Spain, and which they call here Quetzales, and other birds, whose plumage is of five different colours, green, red, white, yellow, and blue. The name of this species of bird I do not know. Here was also an immensity of parrots, and certain geese of fine plumage, and a species which resembled geese. All these bred here, and were stripped of their feathers every year at the proper season. Here was a large pond of clear running water, where were a number of great birds, entirely red, with very long legs; there are some like them in the Island of Cuba, which they call Ipiris. There was also a species which lives entirely in the water.

We likewise saw another great building, which was a temple, and which contained those which were called the valiant or fighting gods, and here were many kinds of furious beasts, tygers, and lions of two species, one of which resembles a wolf, called here Adive. Also foxes, and other smaller animals, but all carnivorous. Most of these were bred in the place, being fed with game, fowls, dogs, and as I have heard the bodies of Indians who were sacrificed, the manner of which as I have been informed is this. They open the body of the victim while living, with large knives of stone; they take out his heart, and blood, which they offer to their gods, and then they cut off the limbs, and the head, upon which they feast, giving the body to be devoured by the wild beasts, and the skulls they hang up in their temples. In this accursed place were many vipers, and poisonous serpents which have in their tails some[thing] that sounds like castanets; these are the most dangerous of all, and were kept in vessels filled with feathers, where they reared their young, and were fed with the flesh of human beings, and dogs; and I have been assured, that after our expulsion from Mexico, all these animals lived for many days upon the bodies of our comrades who were killed on that occasion. These beasts and horrid reptiles were retained to keep company with their infernal gods, and when these animals yelled and hissed, the palace seemed like hell itself.

The place where the artists principally resided was named Escapuzalco, and was at the distance of about a league from the city. Here were the shops and manufactories of all their gold and silver smiths, whose works in these metals, and in jewellery, when they were brought to Spain, surprised our ablest artists. Their painters we may also judge of by what we now see, for there are three Indians in Mexico, who are named, Marcos de Aquino, Juan de la Cruz, and Crespillo, who, if they had lived with Apelles in ancient times, or were compared with Michael Angelo or Berruguete in modern times, would not be held inferior to them. Their fine manufactures of cotton and feathers, were principally brought from the province of Costitlan.

Díaz del Castillo, Bernal. *The True History of the Conquest of Mexico*. Trans. Maurice Keatinge. London 1800. Pp. 138-142.

SECTION 6

GREAT LAND EMPIRES

The readings in this section describe the great land empires that arose across Asia and Europe beginning in the early second millennium and lasting into the early modern era. The first was also the largest of any empire the world had seen: the Mongol Empire was founded by Genghis Khan, one of the world's most terrifying conquerors, and enlarged by his sons and grandsons. Several readings offer views of the Mongol empire from different perspectives, through the eyes of proud Mongol chroniclers, through those of terrified Russian monks in a city besieged by Mongol armies, and through the awestruck eyes of the Venetian traveler Marco Polo who served Genghis Khan's grandson Kubilai Khan, who described China under Mongol rule. Timurlane was descended from Genghis Khan, and his ruthless conquest formed the final chapter of several centuries of Mongol ravages.

Although not nearly as extensive as the Mongol realm, several great and enduring empires arose out of the ashes of Mongol imperialism. They ranged from the Mamluk dynasty of Turkic slaves who ruled Egypt to the Ottoman Turks who finally extinguished the Byzantine Empire and built an empire that embraced West Asia, southern Russia and the Balkan Peninsula in Europe, and all North Africa. They included also the Moghul Empire in India and the Ming Empire in China. The accounts selected here range from autobiographical tales of wars and conquest to accounts of life in the empires as recorded by visiting ambassadors and private travelers to a recounting of the naval expeditions of China's greatest admiral around Asia and East Africa.

The Russian chronicle of Mongol barbarity and oppression explain Russian fear of the "Yellow Peril" even in the twentieth century; Marco Polo's tales of the fabulous East inspired later European voyages of explorations; the horrific impression that Timurlane's army made across northern India led Indians to call all later central Asian conquerors Mongols (or Moghuls). Similarly Serbian nationalism originated in the crucible of the Ottoman conquest and dominion of their country for six hundred years, while Hindu resistance to Muslim conquerors was epitomized in the desperate but ineffective sacrifice of the Rajputs. In a somewhat different vein, China's Ming emperor sent grand naval expeditions to show the flag across the Asian continent to signify China's expulsion of the hated Mongols and recovery of national pride. These readings are thus instructive in their own right and for their depiction of the lasting effects of historical events on peoples and nations.

► Chingis Khan

CHINGIS KHAN
AND HIS SON

Since earliest times various nomadic groups have lived and wandered in Mongolia, a landlocked region between present-day China and Russia. The Mongols, who claimed descent from the feared Hsiung-nu of a thousand years earlier, became an identifiable people in the early 1100s. They were organized into clans; related clans formed tribes. Tribal chieftains were elected by clan nobles for their military prowess, and retained power by success in war. War captives became slaves, which motivated the strong to go to war. Mongols learned to ride as others learned to walk; they and their horses were equally renowned for their stamina and toughness. In war all men were soldiers.

Like other nomads in the region, Mongols practiced unlimited polygyny [one husband, many wives], a man's power and status being defined by the number of his wives. The first wife, however, enjoyed unique privileges--her sons had first claim to succeed their father, and she could act as regent for sons.

Temujin (1155-1227) was born in a time of conflict both among Mongol tribes and against neighboring Turkish peoples. Tribes feuded and fought for grazing land, animals, and women. Temujin was a great military genius. Inured in youth to hardship caused by his father's early death, he capitalized on prevailing conditions and trends in his rise to power. For example, when a sharp drop in temperatures in the region reduced the grass available for the nomads' animals, the Mongols sought access to outside resources through raids and war. Conflicts with non Mongols fostered a growing sense of ethnic identity and unity. Initially relying on family and friends, Temujin organized a disciplined army with an effective command structure and intelligence network. He ruthlessly used massacres and enslavement to terrorize victims into submission. On the other hand, he liberally rewarded his supporters for loyalty and success.

In 1206, after subduing all other tribal groups in Mongolia, Temujin was acclaimed Chingis (or Genghis) Khan ("universal ruler"). In his remaining twenty-one years, Chingis led his Mongols to conquer all north and northwest China, Afghanistan, Persia, and Central Asia. He also paved the way for his sons and grandsons to expand the Mongol realm across much of Eurasia till it became the biggest land empire in history.

The Secret History of the Mongols was written in the thirteenth century in the newly invented Mongolian script by compilers from oral traditions. Although the original Mongolian texts have perished, a later Chinese translation called *Yuan Ch'ao Pi Shih* (*The Secret History of the Mongols*) provides the basis for all modern translations.

The Secret History of the Mongols begins with the mythical origins of the Mongols, continues with Temujin's family and early struggles, his election as Chingis Khan, his military organization, and his campaigns in north China against the Chin Empire (Cathay, in present-day northwest China), and the Middle East. Its final section deals Chingis's death, the election of his third son Ogotai as successor in 1228/9, Ogotai's campaign in the Middle East and eastern Europe, and an assessment of his reign.

This selection is from *The Secret History of the Mongols*. It deals with Temujin's election as Chingis Khan, his campaigns, and the election of his successor.

QUESTIONS:

1) What did Temuchin's supporters promise when they elected him Chingis Khan? What does the promise reflect of their values?

2) Show an example of an effective Mongol military tactic.

3) How did Chingis Khan arrange his succession and how did his followers ratify it?

Altan, Khuchar, and Sacha Beki conferred with each other there [at Temujin's camp at Kingurcha Stream], and then said to Temujin:

"We want you to be khan. Temujin, if you'll be our khan we'll search through the spoils for the beautiful women and virgins, for the great palace tents, for the young virgins and loveliest women, for the finest geldings and mares. We'll gather all these and bring them to you. When we go off to hunt for wild game we'll go out first to drive them together for you to kill. We'll drive the wild animals of the steppe together so that their bellies are touching. We'll drive the wild game of the mountains together so that they stand leg to leg. If we disobey your command during battle take away our possessions, our children, and wives. Leave us behind in the dust, cutting off our heads where we stand and letting them fall to the ground. If we disobey your counsel in peacetime take away our tents and our goods, our wives, and our children. Leave us behind when you move, abandoned in the desert without a protector."

Having given their word, having taken this oath, they proclaimed Temujin khan of the Mongol and gave him the name Chingis Khan....

And so in the Year of the Tiger, having set in order the lives of all the people whose tents are protected by the skirts of felt, the Mongol clans assembled at the head of the Onan. They raised a white standard of nine tails and proclaimed Chingis Khan the Great Khan....

After this in the Year of the Sheep Chingis Khan set out to fight the people of Cathay [the Chin Empire in north China]. First he took the city of Fu-chou then marching through the Wild Fox Pass he took Hsuan-te-fu. From here he

sent out an army under Jebe's command to take the fortress at the Chu-yung Kuan. When Jebe arrived he saw the Chu-yung Kuan was well defended, so he said:

"I'll trick them and make them come out in the open. I'll pretend to retreat and when they come out I'll attack them."

So Jebe retreated and the Cathayan army cried:

"Let's go after them!"

They poured out of their fortifications until the valleys and mountainsides were full of their soldiers. Jebe retreated to Sondi-i-wu Ridge and there he turned his army around to attack as the enemy rushed towards him in waves. The Cathayan army was beaten and close behind Jebe's forces Chingis Khan commanding the great Middle Army attacked as well, forcing the Cathayan army to retreat, killing the finest and most courageous soldiers of Cathay, the Jurchin and Khara Khitan fighters, slaughtering them along the sides of Chu-yung Kuan so that their bodies lay piled up like rotting trees. Jebe charged on through the gates of Chu-yung Kuan, capturing all the forts in the pass, and Chingis Khan led his army through to pitch camp at Lung-hu-tai. He sent an army to attack the capital at Chung-tu and sent others out to take all the cities and towns nearby. He sent Jebe off with an army to attack the city of Tung-ching. When Jebe arrived at the walls of the city, he attacked, but he saw that it couldn't be taken this way. So he hastily abandoned his encampment outside Tung-ching, leaving a great deal behind just outside the city walls, and retreated to a place six days march from the city. This caused the people of Tung-ching to drop their defenses and open their gates to loot the camp our army had left. Then Jebe turned his army around, and having each of his men take a spare horse, they rode back across the six days march in one night, surprising the enemy outside their walls and taking the city of Tung-ching. After he'd taken the city Jebe rejoined Chingis Khan....

[The king of Chin or Cathay decided to surrender as a result of his defeats.] He sent a message offering tribute to Chingis Khan and gave him one of his daughters as a wife. The gates of Chung-tu [capital of the Chin empire] were opened and they set out great quantities of gold, silver, satins, and other goods, letting the men of the Mongol army divide it themselves depending on how many beasts each had to carry the load....

During the same campaign Chingis Khan went off to fight the Tanghut. When he arrived at their cities the Tanghut leader, Burkhan Khan said to him:

"I'll surrender to you and be like your right hand, giving all my strength to you."

He gave Chingis Khan one of his daughters, Chakha, as a wife....

[Subsequently the Tanghut king attempted to reassert his independence, was badly defeated, and again offered to surrender.] He brought out images of the Buddha made from gold. Then followed bowls and vessels made of silver and gold, nine and nine, young boys and young maidens, nine and nine, fine geldings and fine camels, nine and nine, and every other thing in his realm, each arranged according to its color and form, nine and nine.

Chingis Khan ordered Burkhan to present himself outside the closed door of his tent. Burkhan was told to wait there three days, and on the third day Chingis Khan decided what to do....

Chingis Khan said:

"See that he is executed."...

Chingis Khan took everything from the Tanghut people.... He ordered that the men and women of their cities be killed, their children and grandchildren, saying:

"As long as I can eat food and still say, 'Make everyone who live in their cities vanish,' kill them all and destroy their homes. As long as I am still alive keep up the slaughter."

This is because the Tanghut people made a promise they didn't keep. Chingis Khan had gone to war with the Tanghut people a second time. He had destroyed them, and coming back to Mongolia, in the Year of the Pig, Chingis Khan ascended to Heaven. After he had ascended [his wife] Yesui Khatum was given most of the Tanghut people who remained....

In the Year of the Rat a Great Assembly was called. All the people of the Right Wing led by [his second son] Chagadai and [his grandson] Jochi's son Batu came. All the people of the Left Wing arrived, led by Prince Odchigin and Khasar's sons, Yegu and Yesunge [Chingis's sons by his secondary wives]. The people of the Middle Wing were led by [Chingis's fourth son] Tolui, and with him were all the royal daughters and their husbands. This huge assembly met at Kodegu Aral on the Keluren River, and according to the wishes of Chingis Khan they raised up Ogodei [Chingis's third son] as the Great Khan. Chagadai raised up his younger brother as the Khan and both Elder Brother Chagadai and Tolui delivered the nightguard, the archers, and the eight thousand dayguards to Ogodei, the same men who had guarded the golden life of their father Chingis Khan, along with his private slaves and the ten thousand men who had served him. They also gave him command of all the people of the Middle Wing.

Once Ogodei Khan had allowed himself to be named Khan...he took the advice of Elder Brother Chagadai and sent Okhotur and Mungetu to relieve Chormakhan, who was still at war with the Caliphate Sultan of Baghdad, a war his father Chingis Khan had left unfinished. Subetei the Brave had already crossed the Volga and Ural rivers into the lands of the Kanghli, Kipchakh, Russian, Magyar, and Bulghar peoples. He had gone to war against the city of Kiev and had run into great resistance there. So Ogodei sent off an army to relieve him, led by Jochi's eldest son Batu.... "

Kahn, Paul. *The Secret History of the Mongols: The Origins of Chingis Khan*. [Based on *Yuan Ch'ao Pi Shih*. Trans. Francis W. Cleaves.] San Francisco: North Point Press, 1984. Pp. 48-49, 125, 160-162, 180-182.

MONGOLS SEEN THROUGH RUSSIAN EYES

► **Mongol Horseman**

Between Temuchin's election as Genghis Khan or Universal Ruler in 1206 and Timurlane's death while marching towards China in 1405, Mongol hordes terrified and terrorized much of Asia and Europe. Genghis and his descendants conquered and plundered Korea, China, Persia, Central Asia, the Middle East, Russia to the Baltic and Caspian seas and Caucasus mountains, and Europe to the gates of Vienna and Adriatic Sea. With their unmatched cavalry and uncanny ability to master new military techniques, they dominated the largest empire the world had seen. They ruled conquered lands ruthlessly as an occupation force until, divided and weakened, they were overthrown by their resurgent victims. Mongol conquests altered the course of history in most of the lands of their victims, generally for the worse.

Genghis Khan's armies first invaded southern Russia in 1224 and plundered the Grand Duchy of Kiev. After his death the sons of his oldest son received southern Russia as their patrimony. Mongols who settled in southern Russia were called the Golden Horde. To consolidate and extend the Golden Horde's territory, Genghis's sons and grandsons later extended their conquests through northern Russia, taking Moscow and other cities, then proceeding to Poland and Hungary. Mongol rule was short-lived in the rest of Europe, but during the next two centuries most of Russia submitted to Mongol overlordship, paying heavy tribute, which was often collected by force. Mongol domination also isolated Russia from Europe and European political and cultural developments.

Novgorod was a Russian principality: its capital was about a hundred miles southeast of St. Petersburg. It was a prosperous trading city in the Middle Ages, comparable to Florence and Bruges, and enjoyed great wealth. It was unique in Russia because its citizens had republican freedoms and elected their princes. Located in the northern frontier of Russia, Novgorod was moreover a bastion of Russian culture, which it upheld in numerous battles against neighboring Swedes, Germans, and Lithuanians.

Novgorod was also unique because it escaped Mongol conquest. At the time of the Mongol invasion Novgorod was ruled by Prince Alexander (1218-1263), who received the surname Nevsky for his epochal defeat of the Swedes on the Neva River near present-day city St. Petersburg. His feats made him a hero to Russians, and a saint of the Russian Orthodox church. Although cold, wet weather and swampy terrain compelled the Mongols to lift their siege of Novgorod, Alexander Nevsky submitted to the Mongols so that his city could be spared the devastation inflicted on other Russian cities. Thus he obeyed the "Tartar Tsar," paid the tribute Mongols assessed (even protecting the hated Mongol assessors against harm from Novgorod's outraged citizens), and rendered personal homage (in 1247) at Sarai, capital of the Golden Horde. Novgorod and the rest of Russia were liberated from Mongol rule at the end of the fourteenth century.

The Chronicles of Novgorod, 1016-1471, written by anonymous monks, record events that affected the principality. The selection that follows deals with the Mongol invasions and rule, in Novgorod and Russia generally. Russians, like many other Christians, believed the Mongols, or Tartars, had been sent by God to punish them for their sins.

QUESTIONS:

1) How did the Mongol invaders appear to the Russian chroniclers?
2) What did the Mongols do to instill fear among Russians?
3) By what means and at what price did Prince Alexander save Novgorod from Mongol rule?

[In 1224] unknown tribes came, whom no one exactly knows, who they are, nor whence they came out, nor what their language is, nor what race they are, nor what their faith is; but they call them Tartars.... God alone knows who they are and whence they came out.... For we have heard that they have captured many countries, slaughtered a quantity of the godless Yas, Obez, Kasog and Polovets people and wrought much evil to the Russian Land.... And the cursed Polovets people, the survivors of those who were killed, escaped [to Russia] ... and brought many gifts: horses and camels, buffaloes and girls; and they gave gifts [of these] to the Russian *Knyazes* [princes], saying thus: "Our land they have taken away to-day; and yours will be taken to-morrow."....

[The Russians decided to give help. One of their princes] Mstislav having forded the Dnieper went across with 1,000 men, against the Tartar outposts, and defeated them and the remainder of them fled ... to the Polovets *kurgan* [fort].... And the Tartars turned back from the river Dnieper, and we know not whence they came, nor where they hid themselves again; God knows whence he fetched them against us for our sins....

[In 1236] the godless Tartars having come, they captured all the Bolgar Land [Bulgaria on the Volga, the present-day Kazan, etc.] and took their great city, and they slew all, both wives and children....

[In 1238] foreigners called Tartars came in countless numbers, like locusts, into the land of Ryazan, and on first coming they halted at the river Nukhla, and took it, and halted in camp there. And thence they sent their emissaries to the Knyazes of Ryasan, a sorceress and two men with her, demanding from them one-tenth of

everything: of men and Knyazes and horses--of everything one tenth. And the Knyazes of Ryazan, Gyurgi, Ingvor's brother, Oleg, Roman Ingorevich, and those of Murom and Pronsk, without letting them into their towns, went out to meet them to Voronszh. And the Knyazes said to them: "Only when none of us remain then all will be yours." And then they let them go to Yuri in Volodimir, and then they let the Tartars at Voronazh go back to the Nukhla. And the Knyazes of Ryazan sent to Yuri of Volodimir asking for help, or himself to come. But Yuri neither went himself nor listened to the request of the Knyazes of Ryasan, but himself wished to make war separately. But it was too late to oppose the wrath of God.... And then the pagan foreigners surrounded Ryazan and fenced it in with a stockade. And Knyaz Yuri of Ryazan, shut himself in the town with his people, but Knyaz Roman Ingorovich began to fight against them with his own men ... and the Tartars surrounded them at Kolomno, and they fought hard and drove them to the ramparts. And there they killed Roman ... and many fell here with the Knyaz.... And the men of Moscow ran away having seen nothing. And the Tartars took the town on December 21, and they had advanced against it on the 16th of the same month. They likewise killed the Knyaz and Knyaginya, and men, women, and children, monks, nuns and priests, some by fire, some by the sword, and violated nuns, priests' wives, good women and girls in the presence of their mothers and sisters.... And who, brethren, would not lament over this, among those of us left alive when they suffered this bitter and violent death? And we, indeed, having seen it, were terrified and wept with sighing day and night over our sins....

But let us return to what lies before us. The pagan and godless Tartars, then, having taken Ryazan, went to Volodimir.... And it was in the morning Knyaz Vsevolod ... saw that the town must be taken, and entered the Church of the Holy Mother of God and were all shorn into the monastic order.... And when the lawless ones had already come near and set up battering rams, and took the town and fired it on Friday ... Knyaz and Knyaginya ... seeing that the town was on fire and that the people were already perishing, some by fire and others by the sword, took refuge in the Sacristy. The pagans breaking down the doors, piled up wood and set fire to the sacred church; and slew all, thus they perished.... And the accursed ones having come then took Moscow, Pereyaslavl, Yurek, Dmitrov, Volok, and Tver; there they also killed the son of Yaroslav. And then the lawless ones came and invested Torzhok on the festival of the first Sunday in Lent. They fenced it all round with a fence as they had taken other towns, and here the accursed ones fought with battering rams for two weeks. And the people in the towns were exhausted and from Novgorod there was no help for them; but already every man began to be in perplexity and terror. And so the pagans took the town, and slew all from the male sex even to the female, all the priests and the monks, and all stripped and reviled gave up their souls to the Lord in a bitter and wretched death.... And the accursed and godless ones then pushed on from Torzhok by the road of Seregeri up to Ignati's cross, cutting down everyone like grass, to within 100 versts [about 60 miles] of Novgorod. God, however, and the great and sacred apostolic cathedral Church of St. Sophia, and St Kyuril, and the prayers of the holy and orthodox Vladyka, of the faithful Knyazes, and of the very reverend monks of the hierarchical Veche, protected Novgorod....

[In 1245] There was an invasion of pagan Tartars into the Russian Land; and these [Mikhail and Fedor, Russian princes] shut themselves in the towns. And envoys came from *Tsar* Baty [Batu Khan, a grandson of Genghis, and leader of the Golden Horde] to Mikhail, who then held Kiev; and he seeing their words of deceit, ordered them to be killed and himself fled with his family to Hungary; and some fled to distant parts; and others hid in caves and forests, and

few of them stayed behind; and these after some time settled in the towns; and they [Tartars] counted their number and began to levy tribute upon them. And Knyas Mikhail having heard this, he brought back the people who had fled on all sides to strange lands, and they came to their own land. And the Tartars began to summon them with insistence to go to Baty, saying to them: "It is not meet for you to live in the land of the Khan and of Baty without doing homage to them." And many having gone bowed. And Baty had this custom of the Khan's: If any one came to do obeisance, he would not order him to be brought before him, but wizards used to be ordered to bring them through fire and make them bow to a bush and to fire; and whatever anyone brought with him for the Tsar, the wizards used to take some of everything and throw it into the fire, and then they used to let them go before the Tsar with their gifts. And many Knyazes and their Boyars [nobles] passed through the fire, and bowed to the bush, their idols, for the glory of this world....

[When ordered to perform the ritual] Mikhail and Fedor answered as with one mouth: "We will not bow, and will not listen to you, for the sake of the glory of this world," and began to sing "Thy martyrs, O Lord, did not deny Thee, nor did they turn away from Thy commandments, but rather suffered for Thy sake, O Christ, and endured many tortures and received perfect crowns in heaven," and so forth. And the executioners having arrived, and having jumped off their horses, they seized Mikhail, they stretched him out and holding his arms, began to strike him with their hands over the heart, and threw him prone on the ground and struck him with their heels ... [then] cut off the head of the holy ... Mikhail, and hurled it away.... [When Fedor also refused] they began to torture Fedor as before they had Mikhail, and then they cut off his honoured head too....

[In 1257] Evil news came from Russia, that the Tartars desired the tamga [a customs tax] and tithe on Novgorod; and the people were agitated the whole year....

The same winter Tartar envoys came with Alexander, and ... began to ask the tithe and *tamga* and the men of Novgorod did not agree to this, and gave presents to the Tsar, and let the envoys go with peace....

[In 1259] The same winter the accursed raw-eating Tartars, Berkai and Kasachik, came with their wives, and many others, and there was a great tumult in Novgorod, and they did much evil in the province, taking contribution for the accursed Tartars. And the accursed ones began to fear death; they said to Alexander: "Give us guards, lest they kill us." And the Knyaz ordered the son of the Posadnik and all the sons of the Boyars to protect them by night. The Tartars said: "Give us your numbers for tribute or we will run away [and return in greater strength]." And the common people would not give their numbers for tribute but said: "Let us die honourably for St. Sophia and for the angelic houses." Then the people were divided: who was good stood by St. Sophia and by the True Faith; and they made opposition; the greater men bade the lesser be counted for tribute. And the accursed ones wanted to escape, driven by the Holy Spirit, and they devised an evil counsel how to strike at the town at the other side, and the others at this side by the lake, and Christ's power evidently forbade them and they durst not. And becoming frightened they began to crowd to one point to St. Sophia, saying: "Let us lay our heads by St Sophia." And it was on the morrow, the Knyaz rode down from the *Gorodishche* and the accursed Tartars with him, and by the counsel of the evil they numbered themselves for tribute; for the Boyars thought it would be easy for themselves, but fall hard on the lesser men. And the accursed ones began to ride through the streets, writing down the Christian houses; because for our sins God has brought wild beasts out of the desert to eat the flesh of the strong, and to drink the blood of the Boyars. And having numbered them for tribute and taken it, the accursed ones went away, and Knyaz Alexander followed them, having set his son Dmitri on the throne....

[In 1325] Knyaz Alexander Mikhailovich came back from the Horde and with him came Tartar collectors, and there was much hardship in the Low Country [Novgorod]....

The same winter [1327] a very great force of Tartars came, and they took Tver and Kashin and the Novi-torg district, and to put it simply, laid waste all the Russian Land, God and St. Sophia preserved Novgorod alone, and Knyaz Alexander fled to Pleskov, and his brothers Kostyantin and Vasili to Ladoga. And the Tartars sent envoys to Novgorod, and the men of Novgorod gave them 2,000 in silver, and they sent their own envoys with them, with numerous presents....

And then, too, the Tartars killed Knyas Ivan of Ryazan.

Michell, Robert and Nevil Forbes, trans. *The Chronicle of Novgorod, 1016-1471*. Vol. 25. London 1914. Pp. 64-66, 81-84, 88, 91, 96-97, 123, 125.

► Marco Polo

READING 6.3

MARCO POLO'S AWESTRUCK DESCRIPTION OF MONGOL RULE

Marco Polo's *Travels* describe his journey from Europe to Asia and his stay in China between 1274 and 1290. Dictated to Polo's cell-mate in prison in Genoa in 1298, his book soon appeared in many languages.

Marco Polo described Yuan dynasty China under his host and patron, Kubilai Khan, the last great Mongol conqueror. Because Kubilai Khan distrusted Chinese, and few Mongols had the training or liking for administration, he appointed non-Chinese to important positions in his government. He trusted them because they were entirely dependent on him, had no roots in the country where they governed. Marco Polo was one of the Khan's appointees and ruled a large city in southern China, though he never learned Chinese. Thus his book described China from the Mongol's point of view. The many wonders he described so amazed contemporary Europeans that for centuries the book was ridiculed as fanciful. Tradition has it that up to his last days in 1324, his friends begged him to confess to having lied about his experiences. The phrase "its a Marco Polo" meant a tall tale.

Even during Kubilai Khan's rule and while the last conquests were still fresh in memory, the legendary prowess of the Mongol warriors was becoming a thing of the past. Incredibly successful in war, they settled down to enjoy fabulous wealth and power, soon degenerating to useless drones. In the first excerpt, Polo describes the hardy life and the military organization that made the intrepid Mongol warrior a world conquerors. Next he describes the riches and splendor of Kubilai's life, imitated in lesser degrees by his followers. Finally he describes with awe such things as coal for fuel, paper money, and porcelain or chinaware utensils, which had long been common in China but seemed fantastic to Europeans.

QUESTIONS:

1) What Mongol military organization and practices made them invincible?
2) What pursuits of Kubilai Khan suggested his nomadic origins?
3) What practices in Kubilai Khan's China amazed Marco Polo?

Their arms are bows, iron maces, and in some instances, spears; but the first is the weapon at which they are the most expert, being accustomed, from children, to employ it in their sports. They wear defensive armour made from buffalo and hides of other beasts, dried by the fire, and thus rendered extremely hard and strong. They are brave in battle, almost to desperation, setting little value upon their lives, and exposing themselves without hesitation to all manner of danger. Their disposition is cruel.

They are capable of supporting every kind of privation, and when there is a necessity for it, can live for a month on the milk of their mares, and upon such wild animals as they may chance to catch. Their horses are fed upon grass alone, and do not require barley or other grain. The men are trained to remain on horseback during two days and two nights, without dismounting; sleeping in that situation whilst their horses graze. No people on earth can surpass them in fortitude under difficulties, nor show greater patience under wants of every kind. They are most obedient to their chiefs, and are maintained at small expense. From these qualities, so essential to the formation of soldiers, it is, that they are fitted to subdue the world, as in fact they have done in regard to a considerable portion of it.

When one of the great Tartar chiefs proceeds on an expedition, he puts himself at the head of an army of an hundred thousand horse, and organizes them in the following manner. He appoints an officer to the command of every ten men, and others to command an hundred, a thousand, and ten thousand men, respectively. Thus ten of the officers commanding ten men take their orders from him who commands a hundred; of these, each ten, from him who commands a thousand; and each ten of these latter, from him who commands ten thousand.

By this arrangement each officer has only to attend to the management of ten men or ten bodies of men....When the army proceeds on service, a body of two hundred men is sent two days' march in advance, and parties are stationed upon each flank and in the rear, in order to prevent its being attacked by surprise.

When the service is distant they carry but little with them, and that, chiefly what is requisite for their encampment, and utensils for cooking. They subsist for the most part upon milk, as has been said. They are provided with small tents made of felt, under which they shelter themselves against rain. Should circumstances

render it necessary, in the execution of a duty that requires despatch, they can march for ten days without lighting a fire or taking a meal. During this time they subsist upon the blood drawn from their horses, each man opening a vein, and drinking from his won cattle.

They make provision also of milk, thickened and dried to the state of a paste....Upon going on service they carry with them about ten pounds for each man, and of this, half a pound is put, every morning, into a leathern bottle, with as much water as is thought necessary. By their motion in riding the contents are violently shaken, and a thin porridge is produced, upon which they make their dinner.

When these Tartars come to engage in battle, they never mix with the enemy, but keep hovering about him, discharging their arrows first from one side and then from the other, occasionally pretending to fly, and during their flight shooting arrows backwards at their pursuers, killing men and horses, as if they were combating face to face. In this sort of warfare the adversary imagines he has gained a victory, when in fact he has lost the battle; for the Tartars, observing the mischief they have done him, wheel about, and renewing the fight overpower his remaining troops, and make them prisoners in spite of their utmost exertions. Their horses are so well broken-in to quick changes of movement, that upon the signal given, they instantly turn in any direction; and by these rapid manoeuvres many victories have been obtained.

All that has been here related is spoken of the original manner of the Tartar chiefs; but at the present day they are much degenerated. Those who dwell in Cathay, forsaking their own laws, have adopted the customs of the people who worship idols, and those who inhabit the eastern provinces have adopted the manners of the Saracens [Muslims].

* * * * *

In this [capital city, Shangtu, Kubilai Khan caused a palace to be erected, of marble and other handsome stones, admirable as well for the elegance of its design as for the skill displayed in its execution. The halls and chambers are all gilt, and very handsome. It presents one front towards the interior of the city, and the other towards the wall; and from each extremity of the building runs another wall to such an extent as to enclose sixteen miles in circuit of the adjoining plain, to which is no access but through the palace. Within the bounds of this royal Park there are rich and beautiful meadows, watered by many rivulets, where a variety of animals of the deer and goat kind are pastured, to serve as food for the hawks and other birds employed in the chase, whose pens are also in the grounds. The number of these birds is upwards of two hundred, without counting the hawks; and the Great Khan goes in person, once every week, to inspect them. Frequently, when he rides about this enclosed forest, he has one or more small leopards carried on horseback, behind their keepers; and when he pleases to give direction for their being slipped, they instantly seize a stag, goat, or fallow deer, which he gives to his hawks, and in this manner he amuses himself.

In the centre of these grounds, where there is a beautiful grove of trees, he has built a Royal Pavilion, supported upon a colonnade of handsome pillars, gilt and varnished. Round each pillar a dragon, likewise gilt, entwines its tail, whilst its head sustains the projection of the roof, and its talons or claws are extended to the right and left....The building is supported on every side like a tent by more than two hundred very strong silken cords, and otherwise, from the lightness of the materials, it would be liable to oversetting by the force of high winds. The whole is constructed with so much ingenuity of contrivance that all the parts may be taken apart, removed, and again set up, at his Majesty's pleasure....

It is to be understood that the Khan keeps up a stud of about ten thousand horses and mares, which are white as snow. Of the milk of these mares no person can presume to drink who is not of the family descended from Chinghis Khan....

So great, indeed, is the respect shown to these horses that, even when they are at pasture in the royal meadow or forest, no one dares to place himself before them, or otherwise to check their movements. The astrologers whom he entertains in his service, and who are deeply versed in the art of magic have pronounced it to be his duty, annually, on the twenty-eighth day of the moon in August, to scatter in the wind the milk taken from these mares, as an honour to all the spirits and idols whom they adore.

* * * * *

In this city of Kanbalu is the mint of the Great Khan, who may truly be said to possess the secret of the alchemists, as he has the art of producing money by the following process.

He causes the bark to be stripped from those mulberry-trees the leaves of which are used for feeding silk-worms, and takes from it that thin inner rind which lies between the coarser bark and the wood of the tree. This being steeped, and afterwards pounded in a mortar, until reduced to a pulp, is made into paper, resembling, in substance, that which is manufactured from cotton, but quite black. When ready for use, he has it cut into pieces of money of different sizes, nearly square, but somewhat longer than they are wide. Of these, the smallest pass for half a tournois; the next size for a Venetian silver groat; others for two, five, and ten groats; others for one, two, three and as far as ten bezants of gold. The coinage of this paper money is authenticated with as much form and ceremony as if it were actually of pure gold or silver; for to each note an number of officers, specially appointed, not only subscribe their names, but affix their seals also. When this has been regularly done by the whole of them, the principal officer, appointed by his Majesty, having dipped into vermilion the royal seal committed to his custody, stamps with it the piece of paper, so that the form of the seal tinged with the vermilion remains impressed upon it. In this way it receives full authenticity as current money, and the act of counterfeiting it is punished as a capital offence.

When thus coined in large quantities, this paper currency is circulated in every part of the Great Khan's dominions; nor dares any person, at the peril of his life, refuse to accept it in payment. All his subjects receive it without hesitation, because, wherever their business may call them, they can dispose of it again in the purchase of merchandise they may require; such as pearls, jewels, gold, or silver. With it, in short, every article may be procured....

When any person happens to be possessed of paper money which from long use has become damaged, they carry it to the mint, where, upon the payment of only three per cent, they receive fresh notes in exchange. Should any be desirous of procuring gold or silver for the purpose of manufacture, such as of drinking-cups, girdles, or other articles wrought of these metals, they in like manner apply to the mint, and for their paper obtain the bullion thy require.

All his Majesty's armies are paid with this currency, which is to them of the same value as if it were gold or silver. Upon these grounds, it may certainly be affirmed that the Great Khan has more extensive command of treasure than any other sovereign in the universe....

Throughout this province [Cathay] there is found a sort of black stone, which they dig out of the mountains, where it runs in veins. When lighted, it burns like charcoal, and retains the fire much better than wood; insomuch that it may be preserved during the night, and in the morning be found still burning. These stones do not flame, excepting a little when first lighted, but during their ignition give out a considerable heat.

It is true there is no scarcity of wood in the country, but the multitude of inhabitants is so immense, and their stoves and baths, which they are continually heating, so numerous, that the quantity could not supply the demand. There is no person who does not frequent a warm bath at least three times in the week, and during the winter daily, if it is in their power. Every man of rank or wealth has one in his house for his own use; and the stock of wood must soon prove inadequate to such consumption; whereas these stones may be had in the greatest abundance, and at a cheap rate....

The noble and handsome city of Zai-tun [from which the English word "satin" derives], which has a port on the seacoast celebrated for the resort of shipping, [is] loaded with merchandise, that is afterwards distributed through every part of the province of Manji. The quantity of pepper imported there is so considerable, that what is carried to Alexandria, to supply the demand of the western parts of the world, is trifling in comparison, perhaps not more than the hundredth part. It is indeed impossible to convey an idea of the number of merchants and the accumulation of goods in this place, which is held to be one of the largest ports of the world. The Great Khan derives a vast revenue from this place, as every merchant is obliged to pay ten per cent upon the amount of his investment....

Many persons arrive in this city from the interior parts of India for the purpose of having their persons ornamented by puncturing with needles in the manner before described, as it is celebrated for the number of its artists skilled in that practice.

The river that flows by the port of Zai-tun is large and rapid....At the place where it separates from the principal channel stands the city of Tin-gui. Of this place there is nothing further to be observed, than that cups or bowls and dishes of porcelainware are there manufactured. The process was explained to be as follows. They collect a certain kind of earth, as it were, from a mine, and laying it in a great heap, suffer it to be exposed to the wind, the rain, and the sun, for thirty or forty years, during which time it is never disturbed. By this it becomes refined and fit for being wrought into the vessels above mentioned. Such colours as may be thought proper are then laid on, and the ware is afterwards baked in ovens or furnaces. Those persons, therefore, who cause the earth to be dug, collect for their children and grandchildren. Great quantities of manufacture are sold in the city, and for a Venetian groat you may purchase eight porcelain cups.

Konroff, Manuel, ed. *The Travels of Marco Polo*. [Based on Marsden's Translation.] New York: H. Liveright, 1926. Pp. 93-95, 105-107, 159-161, 171-172, 254-256.

TIMURLANE, THE LAST MONGOL CONQUEROR

► Timurlane

Timur the Lame or Timurlane was the last great, terrifying Mongol conqueror. His rule and that of his successors were a continuation both politically and culturally of the Mongols of the Chagatai Khanate. All Turkic and Mongol peoples who competed for power in central and western Asia in the fourteenth century were Muslims. But Timur's conquests wrought so much terror and destruction to all his victims that Christians and Muslims alike called him the Scourge of God.

Timur, who claimed descent from Genghis Khan, was born in 1336, the son of a petty chief in central Asia, when the Chagatai khanate was breaking up. Ascending the throne of a minor state based in Samarkand in 1369, he took advantage of the fragmented political conditions in western and central Asia and northern India to conquer huge territories. His first victims were the Persians in the time of the last weak rulers of the il-khanate. Massacring those who resisted him by the tens of thousands, he gained a reputation as fearsome as that of Genghis Khan. After mastering the Persian world, he extended his conquests to Mesopotamia, Armenia, and Anatolia. Next his troops subjugated the Golden Horde in southern Russia. His forces went as far north as Moscow, which they held for a year.

In 1398 Timur invaded India. He ordered 100,000 male captives slaughtered after taking Delhi, and enslaved most of the remaining population of the city. After staying for fifteen days Timur moved on, leaving behind such desolation that according to one account, "for two months not a bird moved a wing in Delhi." He was planning to attack China when he died in 1405, at age seventy.

Whereas Genghis Khan and his successors superimposed their rule over subjugated areas, Timur devastated and then retreated from many of his conquered lands, leaving them in political chaos. Since he left no capable successors, Timur's empire fell apart soon after his death. However, Timur did enrich his capital Samarkand with loot from every conquered land. He also settled captured artisans there to build and decorate his palaces, mosques and other public buildings. These monuments consequently show many cultural influences.

The reading below is from the *Decline and Fall of Byzantium to the Ottoman Turks* by Doukas, a famous historians of the late Byzantine Empire. His work chronicled the rise of the Ottoman Turks and also their set back at the hands of Timur, who soundly defeated and captured Sultan Bayazid in 1402. Timur's forces controlled Anatolia, Asia Minor, and Mesopotamia until his death in 1405. The excerpt shows something of Timur's ability both as a military commander and as a savagely brutal destroyer of defeated peoples.

QUESTIONS:

1) Describe some of Timur's actions that gave him the name the Scourge of God.
2) How did Timur defeat the Ottoman sultan?

3) Give some examples of Timur's military genius.

With the coming of Spring [1402], lo, Temir-khan went from Persia to the regions of the Don and gathered the Tauro-Scythians and Zykhians and Abasgians. He demolished the fortresses of the Bosporos and then crossed to the region of Armenia. He passed through Cappadocia with a large army, conscripting many Armenians, until he came to the region of Galatia, by which time he had as large an army as did Xerxes of old.

With all his Thracian and Eastern troops and newly conscripted forces assembled, and with the Serb Stefan, Lazar's son, and a host of lancers, Bayazid set out to meet Temir....

That evening, the Scythian [Timur] issued orders throughout the whole camp that all were to be ready in the morning, mounted and fully armed. Rising at early dawn, he deployed all his commanders. He placed his eldest son commander over the right wing and his grandson (for Temir was more than sixty years old) over the left. Temir took up his position in the rear. He addressed his troops as follows:

"O my assembled troops and invincible army, adamantine in nature, and stalwart wall, and of an indomitable breed. You have heard of the heroic exploits performed from the beginning by our fathers, not only in the East but also in Europe and Libya and, in a word, throughout the world. You know full well the expedition undertaken by Xerxes and Artaxerxes against the Greeks--the Greeks, I say--those heroic men and demigods. Compared to them these half-Greek and half-Turkish barbarians are like the locust to lions. It is not to give you courage that I recall these feats for the prey is already in our hands. Let not this bugbear escape from our hands. Capture it whole and uninjured so that we may take it back to Persia where we will exhibit it to our children and teach it not to demand that we abjure our wives. Now I wish this great field which lies before us to be surrounded. Let the right wing be led forward in a circling maneuver and also the left wing. Encircle the whole

plain and let the enemy be enclosed in the middle like the center of the polar axis...."

At sunrise Bayazid deployed his legions. Sounding the call to battle, he stood there waiting for the initial charge of the Scythians. The Scythians, on the other hand, carried out their orders without sound or clamor or noise of any kind, working like indefatigable ants. Bayazid began to jabber and to curse his nobles. He berated the commanders and flogged them for not deploying themselves properly for battle. One commander fighting under Aydin's standard, hearing that his lord Aydin had joined his brother, abandoned his position, and taking up the standard, defected to the enemy with five hundred heavily armed troops. The forces of Saruchan did the same. The troops of Menteshe and Germiyan, when they saw their rulers shouting and signaling, also deserted and went over to their adversaries. Bayazid, like the jackdaw, was gradually shorn of his feathers. The Scythian troops enfolded him until the circle was finally closed....

When Bayazid [who had been captured] was conducted to the door of the tent, Temir's followers raised their voices acclaiming Temir-khan, and along with the acclamation they referred to Bayazid, saying, "Lo, the leader of the Turks has come to you a captive."...Glancing up and beholding the guards with Bayazid standing in the middle like a criminal, he inquired, "Is this he who a short while ago insisted on our divorcing our wives unless we opposed him in battle?" Bayazid answered, "I am the one, but it is not fitting that you should despise those who have fallen. Since you are also a ruler, you must know that it is your duty to defend the borders of your dominion."... After Bayazid had entered the tents which Temir had provided, Temir issued orders for a trench to be dug around the tents. One thousand heavily armed Persian troops were to keep watch in a ring around the tents. Outside the trench five thousand lightly armed household troops were to stand guard in rotation day and night.... [After a failed attempt to rescue Bayazid led by his son] a careful watch was set over Bayazid. During the night he was bound by iron collars and manacles while during the day many soldiers kept watch over him.

Temir remained eight days in that field where the battle had taken place. During that time the Persian army was dispersed from Galatia to Phrygia, Bithynia, Paphlagonia, Asia Minor, Caria, Lycia, and Pamphylia, so that it seemed that the entire army of Temir, as well as Temir himself, was in every province and city. In those eight days the army spread out and inundated everything. Temir took many captives and, seizing the riches of Ankara, burned and destroyed all those who resisted him....

Departing from Kutahiya, Temir came to Prusa, wreaking destruction, taking captives, and seizing every treasure whose existence was revealed through torture and diverse punishments. He burned, lynched, buried men alive, and inflicted every conceivable kind of torment. Opening up the coffers, he emptied out the gold and silver treasures which had been won from the Romans; precious stones and pearls were counted by the bushels like grains of wheat. In Prusa he also found Bayazid's wives and concubines.... He took captive the youths and maidens. He chastised and punished everyone, both Turks and Romans, by burning them alive or leaving them to die in prison from starvation in order to amass gold and silver....

Temir pitched his tents before the fortress of the Knights Hospitalers, rebuilt in the days of Umer, and demanded its surrender. The Knights Hospitalers, however, refused because there were many men and women ... from other cities as well who had taken refuge in the fortress. They were confident that the fortress would not fall to anyone. Bayazid had annually attacked the fortress and had, moreover, set a secure watch over the exits in order to compel its surrender because of famine, but he achieved nothing by warfare. Temir conceived the idea of blockading the mouth of the harbor. He issued orders in the evening that at daybreak every soldier was to pick up one stone and cast it into the mouth of the harbor, and it was done. When the defenders of the fortress saw this, they lost heart.... Temir's troops had transformed the sea into dry land by the first hour of the morning....

The Scythians succeeded in crossing the mouth of the harbor, and appeared before the moat. The Knights Hospitalers fought bravely from the battlements, and their arrows cut down the Scythians who fell into the moat like locusts swallowed up by swallows. Their corpses filled up the moat, but the Scythians multiplied like the heads of Hydra. When the moat, therefore, became full of bodies, the remaining Scythians, countless numbers of them, crossed the moat by treading on the corpses. They set up scaling ladders and some ascended to the top while others took the descent to Hades. The living had no concern for the dead whether he was father or son. There was only one objective in everyone's mind: Who should be the first to reach the top and raise the standard on the tower? Climbing up on all sides, they pursued the Friars who fled inside to save themselves. The triremes [boats] were drawn up to the citadel, and the Knights Hospitalers boarded in utter confusion and disorder, taking with them the *baiulus* and the remaining members of their order.... The Scythians then took possession of the acropolis, and, herding the captives into one place (for together, with wives and children, there were more than a thousand), led them before Temir, who commanded that all should be beheaded by the sword. He erected a tower by laying rows of stones and heads in alternating sequence. Where there was a stone, on one level, a head was placed above it on the next level, and where there was a head, a stone was set above it, and all the faces looked outwards. It was indeed a strange sight to behold and an inhuman contrivance!...

The troops moved from city to city, leaving each in such a state of desolation that not even the bark of a dog nor the cackle of a hen nor the cry of a child was any longer heard. Like the fisherman who casts his net and pulls it to land, bringing from the sea whatever his catch might be, large fish or small, even the paltriest little fish and tiny crab, so did they plunder all of Asia before riding away.

From Mylasa they went to Kaptiane of upper Phrygia and perpetrated the same crimes. From Laodicia they moved to Phrygia Salutaria which the Turks call Qara Hisar in their tongue. It was here that after much suffering Yildirin Bayazid died. It is rumored that he took his own life by poison. Temir, however, wanted to take him alive to Persia to show the Persians what sort of beast he had captured: first, to exhibit him as a spectacle and to parade him about, and then after he had suffered much torment, to take his life....

After he had spent a full year outside Persia, Temir returned as conqueror and trophy-bearer, bringing back more spoils and booty than any Persian tyrant who had preceded him.

Doukas. *Decline and Fall of Byzantium to the Ottoman Turks* [Historia-Byzantina]. Ed. and trans. Harry J. Magoulias. Detroit: Wayne State Univ. Press, 1975. Pp. 90, 92-93, 95-96, 99-100.

► Egyptian Lusterware of Mamluk Era

MAMLUK RULE IN EGYPT

"Mamluk" in Arabic means slave and applies mainly to ex-slave soldiers of Turkish origin. Beginning as the former slave professional soldiers of early Muslim caliphates, Mamluks had become masters in the thirteenth century upon the collapse of the Ayyubid dynasty, founded by Salah ed-Din (victor against Christian forces during the Third Crusade). Mamluk sultans ruled Egypt and Syria between 1250 and 1517. They successfully resisted Mongol attempts to conquer Egypt.

Although the institution of recruiting slave soldiers in Muslim empires was a cohesive and long lived one, it however was often full of strife, and Mamluk rule in Egypt was anything but stable. The average reign of a Mamluk sultan was six years; there were often bloody power struggles. Mamluks controlled the local inhabitants and excluded them from power through a feudal land tenure system, and scorned local ways. Even though Ottoman conquest ended the Mamluk dynasty in 1517, Mamluks continued to rule Egypt until early nineteenth century as vassals of the Ottoman dynasty.

This reading, by a leading expert on the subject, explains the unique features of the Mamluk recruitment system and governing institution.

QUESTIONS:

1) Who were the Mamluks, how were they recruited, trained and maintained as a military elite?
2) What was the relationship between the Mamluks and the Arabs?
3) How did the Mamluks rule Egypt and perpetuate themselves?

The *mamluk* military-slave institution is, generally speaking, an exclusively Muslim phenomenon. In any case, it has no parallel worthy of the name outside the Muslim world.

The basic reason for the adoption of the *mamluk* system is to be sought in the very character of Islam and in its achievements: the Muslim religion had set itself from the outset the target of islamizing the whole world, with force of arms as the main instrument for attaining that objective.... The swift expansion of Islam in the early years of its existence, on the one hand, and the adherence of the Muslims to their basic idea of conquest, on the other, created immediately a very wide gap between the growing need of suitable military manpower and the quite limited human resources available in the Arabian peninsula. At a somewhat later stage the need for non-Arab manpower was accentuated by the inevitable decline of the military qualities of the Arabs, in general, and of those of the Arab tribesmen in particular, as a result of their constant contact with a higher civilization and its luxuries, [and] the waning of their religious fervour....

The beginnings of the Mamluk institution are shrouded in obscurity. What is certain, however, is that there are clear indications to its existence already under the Umayyads ... in the eighties of the seventh century.... The turning point [came] in the first half of the ninth century. Henceforward Mamluk regiments, constituting the core of the Muslim rulers' armies, spread quickly over most of the important military centers of Islam, where they stayed for many generations. The only interpretation for this astounding success is the superiority and relative reliability of the Mamluk system on the one hand, and the far better military qualities of the human material from which the Mamluk recruits had been selected on the other....

The appearance of the Mamluks in such a great force did not bring about the elimination of the other kinds of armies.... It did reduce them, however, to a much lower status. This created tensions between the Mamluks and those armies. In addition, there were splits and strife inside Mamluk aristocracy, based mainly on the allegiance to different patrons.... It was a system with its grave defects.... Yet any other Muslim army would have had most of its defects with little of its great merits....

One basic trait of [this] Muslim military aristocracy is that, throughout its history ... it is of a specifically urban character....

The Muslim warriors who settled in the towns, in the old ones or in the new ones which they themselves built, used to establish their own separate quarters. Arabs of a certain tribe lived separately from those of a different one, and woe betide a tribesman who chanced to enter an 'alien' quarter! Moreover, the Arabs lived apart from the non-Arab citizens, the aim being to fortify the Arab military power by retaining the tribal organization. Although this urban concentration of the tribes helped to achieve this end and facilitated their employment in battle, at the same time it deepened and sharpened the ancient inter-tribal conflicts and provoked new ones on a scale unknown in the Arabian Peninsula.... But, even without inter-tribal enmity, there is no doubt that the Arabs would have been displaced within a short interval of time; for a nomad body which erupts into an area of civilization inevitably loses its original

character, and its military strength decays sooner or later....

The fate that befell the Arab nomads was bound also to overtake other nomads who invaded the Muslim world while retaining their tribal organization, such as the Turks and the Mongols. The only way in which nomad vitality could be preserved in an area of civilization, and particularly as part of an urban society, was that provided by the mamluk system. In no other civilization did this system reach such a peak of perfection and endurance, or encompass as many splendid achievements as it did in the Muslim world. The essence of it was this. Young children from nomad tribes were brought as slaves from the non-Muslim areas into the Muslim world; they were converted to Islam, given a fanatical orthodox education and trained in the finest methods of combat. On the completion of their Muslim education and military training they were set free. Thus there grew up a soldier of nomad origin with an excellent military training and a strong Muslim conscience, faithful to the masters who had bought him and then set him free, and to his companions in slavery and manumission. The descendants of these soldiers were not allowed to join the military aristocracy to which their fathers belonged, since they had been born free and had grown up in an area of civilization and were Muslim by birth. The Mamluk aristocracy was, therefore, a one-generation nobility only, all its members having been born in the steppe and being Muslims of the first generation. To assure continuity of this aristocracy, it was necessary constantly to bring in new nomad children from the non-Muslim areas. In theory it was possible to safeguard both the nomad vitality and the Muslim freshness *ad infinitum*. In practice, things did not work out like that, primarily because of the conflict which arose between the theory behind the system and human nature itself.... Nonetheless, no other Muslim military aristocracy succeeded in surviving for so long--a thousand years at least--and with so much power as the Mamluk aristocracy wielded, in all its ramifications. Without the Mamluk military and social system, there is no doubt that the destiny of Islam would have been very different from what it actually was.

The Mamluk system was based on a clear racial preference, since the Mamluks were not taken from just any nomad or non-Muslim area, but chiefly from the area stretching from Central Asia to the Balkans and the Adriatic Sea, which constitutes a large part of what is usually called the European-Asiatic or Eurasian steppe. For this, there were three main reasons: (a) The Eurasian steppe was a huge reservoir of nomad man-power, second to none in the world and far larger than the corresponding resources of the Arabian peninsula. (b) The majority of the steppe-peoples had superior military qualities, to a degree found hardly anywhere else. (c) The areas of civilization where Islam established itself, there was a very marked preference for the fair-skinned races of the North over the darker ones of the South; this no doubt originated in the pre-Islamic period, but Islam did not bring about its supersession. These three elements were the cause that no other group--either within the Muslim world, or in the areas beyond it whence slaves were brought--could effectively challenge the Mamluks or counterbalance them.

The Mamluk military aristocracy acquired a thoroughly exclusive character at a very early state. It was entirely closed to those who did not fulfil the conditions enumerated, and its members looked down on those who did not belong to it....

The military aristocracy of Cairo during the Mamluk Sultanate, which lasted from 1250 to 1517 ... included Egypt and Syria in its territory.... Few military aristocracies in Islamic history were as bound to the capital and as closely identified with it, in almost total disregard of the other towns, as were the Mamluks in relation to Cairo during the years 1250-1517. The physical structure of the Nile country, which creates almost ideal conditions for a centralized system of government, enabled the vast majority of Mamluks stationed in Egypt to live in the capital.... The fact that there were no important inland towns in Egypt except Cairo and the growing inclination of the holders of feudal fiefs to be absentee landlords--combined to strengthen and hasten the process of concentration of military society in the capital.... The history of the Mamluk military aristocracy, was, therefore, first and foremost, the history of the aristocracy within the narrow confines of Cairo....

During the epidemics which afflicted Egypt again and again, the Mamluks, as foreigners, were stricken more severely than the natives, and the Mamluks of the reigning Sultan suffered more fatalities than those of his predecessors, who had lived in Egypt for a longer period. Entire barracks were emptied during the epidemics, yet the Mamluks did not leave Cairo even once. They would not abandon the capital even during the Black Death in 1348/9, for to have done so would have meant relinquishing their power to an opponent Mamluk faction besides losing their feudal estates and other kinds of property which changed hands frequently during an epidemic when the owners died....

Throughout the long period of their rule, there was no challenge whatsoever to the social and military predominance of the Mamluks....

The exclusive character of the Mamluk military aristocracy was expressed in several ways, chiefly these:

1. The first names of the Mamluks were Turkish; Mamluks of races other than Turkish were also given Turkish names. This was the immediate distinguishing mark of the military aristocracy, and whoever did not belong to it was not permitted to be called by a Turkish first name. This embargo was particularly strict for the urban population throughout the Mamluk Sultanate, and especially so for that of the capital.... Still more important, even the sons of Mamluks were, with rare exceptions, given not Turkish but Arab-Muslim names. This facilitated their exclusion from the Mamluk aristocracy, the one-generation nobility, on the one hand, and their integration with the local urban population on the other. The sons of the Mamluks, who were called *Awlad al-nas*, and of whom the vast majority lived in Cairo, belonged to a military unit, or class, of free people ... [and] formed a kind of intermediate link between the Mamluk aristocracy and the civil population of the capital, and their sons were already completely assimilated to that population. One may infer the crucial importance of Turkish names in the Mamluk Sultanate from the following episode. The Sultan Jaqmaq (1438-1453), who was very pious, wanted to alter his name to Muhammad, but changed his mind and decided to be called by

the two names Jaqmaq and Muhammad, because he feared that the rulers who were neighbours of the Mamluk Sultanate might think that he was not a Mamluk, and be tempted to covet his throne....
2. the Mamluks spoke a Turkish dialect. They did not want the local population to understand or speak it. The few local officials who learned Turkish, and were used by the Mamluks as interpreters, enjoyed a special status; the Mamluks usually despised the Arab language; many among them did not know it, and those who studied it knew it only superficially....
3. The Mamluks usually married either slave-girls of their own provenance, or married the daughters of other Mamluks.... It follows, therefore, that most descendents of Mamluks were of pure Mamluk blood, yet they were excluded from the upper class because they were not themselves born in the countries of origin of the Mamluks and had not been slaves.
4. Only Mamluks were allowed to purchase Mamluk slaves. The rest of the population, with few exceptions, could own only negro slaves.
5. The dress of the Mamluk aristocracy was very different from that of the rest of the inhabitants.
6. Only Mamluks, again with rare exceptions, were allowed to ride horses,
7. Although the Mamluks were successfully educated to Muslim orthodoxy, law cases in which both parties were Mamluk were often judged not according to the laws of the Muslim *Shari'a* but according to the laws of the Mongol *Yasa* [code created by Genghis Khan]....

The population of Cairo never seriously troubled the Mamluks, and even less did it ever become a threat to them as did the population of Baghdad at certain stages. Sporadic outbursts of unrest caused by the harshness of Mamluk domination, outbursts seldom accompanied by violence, were extinguished almost before they started....

That the Mamluk aristocracy formed a one-generation nobility of Islamized unbelievers had far-reaching repercussions on the social and religio-cultural character of Cairo as well as on its physical character. The Mamluks, under whom the city reached its zenith of greatness and wealth, erected religious and public buildings in it on a scale unknown till then. Their monuments there, especially the religious ones, are even today one of Cairo's outstanding features. In point of fact many sons of Mamluks became men of religion and letters, and a large part of the history of the Mamluk Sultanate was written by Mamluk descendants.... [This is because] the Mamluks are concerned for the fate of their descendants because they cannot introduce them into the upper class, they try to assure their future in the following ways: They build many mosques, *madrasahs*, *zawiyas* [religious schools] and the like and assign to them *waqfs* [charities endowed with religious funds] with high incomes. They appoint their sons as administrators or superintendents of the *waqfs* or else guarantee them part of the *waqf* income by other means.... For this reason, the *waqfs* have become very numerous and the incomes and profits from them enormous.... People have travelled from Iraq and the Maghreb [North Africa] to Egypt seeking knowledge. There has been a great demand for religious sciences and these have been very much cultivated there....

But the expansion of endowments could not go on for ever; it was, after all, detrimental to the vital interests of the military aristocracy, whose own revenues it reduced. As long as the Mamluk sultanate flourished and prospered, as long as the expansion of the *waqfs* property was in its early stages, the rival interests did not clash sharply. The economic decline of Egypt, however, which was hastened by the special structure of Mamluk society, was, sooner or later, bound to bring about a confrontation....

The peculiar fabric of Mamluk society gave rise to a paradoxical situation. Whilst a Mamluk, as an individual, had every interest in promoting the well-being of his descendants, the interests of the Mamluk aristocracy, as a body, were exactly the reverse. The contrast was particularly marked between the young and aspiring Mamluks, who wished to secure their income, and the sons of veteran Mamluks, whose power and influence were contracting.

Cairo, in this way, was the scene of an extraordinary phenomenon. The principle of a one-generation nobility, on which every Mamluk aristocracy rested, worked in two contrary directions: in the beginning it encouraged the study of religion and the foundation of religious institutions, while at a later stage its responsibility for the enfeeblement of both was pronounced.

Ayalon, David. "Aspects of the Mamluk Phenomenon" and "Preliminary Remarks on the Mamluk Military Institution in Islam." In *The Mamluk Military Society: Collected Studies*. London: Variorum Reprints, 1979. Pp. 44, 205-207. Ayalon, David. "The Muslim City and the Mamluk Military Aristocracy." *Studies on the Mamluks of Egypt (1250-1517)*. London: Variorum Reprints, 1977. Pp. 311-314, 319-325, 327-328.

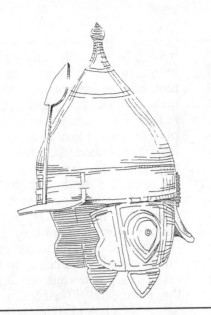

A SERBIAN ACCOUNT OF OTTOMAN CONQUESTS

▶ Ottoman Helmet

Just as Mamluks (Islamized former slave soldiers) played a key role in early Arab conquests, the Ottoman Turks' elite fighting force, the Janissary Corps, similarly played a crucial role in their Empire's rise to power. At its height the Ottoman Empire ruled Hungary and the Balkan peninsula, Anatolia, the Middle East, and all north Africa to the Atlantic.

Memoirs play an important part in reconstructing history. *The Memoirs of a Janissary* by Konstantin Mihailovic is a crucial first hand document of the Ottoman Empire's conquests. This unique fifteenth-century account of a Slav's experiences among the Ottomans is invaluable to understanding Balkan, especially Serbian, and Turkish history.

Konstantin Mihailovic was a Serb, born in an obscure village near Belgrade in the 1430s. Nothing is known about his parents. He and his two brothers were captured by the Turks; their attempted escape failed, they were tortured, and "taken across the sea." Probably he himself did not become a Janissary, because he was too old to go through the lengthy training and education that Janissaries received. He did, however, have some function in the Janissary corps.

Konstantin Mihailovic took part sieges at Constantinople in 1453, as part of a Serbian contingent, and at Belgrade. He also served in campaigns in Bosnia and against Vlad Drakul (Dracula) in Wallachia. Stationed with a Janissary garrison in the fortress of Zvejac in Bosnia, he was freed by Hungarian troops who captured Zvejac in 1463. Nothing is known of his life thereafter, but he did leave an important memoir that recorded some previous encounters between Ottomans and Slavs. The following details of his experiences with the Turks explain the Ottoman recruitment and training of the Janissary corps, the critical role of the Janissaries in war and in Ottoman power struggles, and Ottoman battle strategy.

QUESTIONS:

1) Who were the Janissaries, how were they recruited and trained, and what were they used for?
2) How did the Ottomans destroy the Serbian nation?
3) By what effective military strategy did the Ottomans capture Constantinople?

Whenever the Turks invade foreign lands and capture their people an imperial scribe follows immediately behind them, and whatever boys there are, he takes them all into the janissaries and gives five gold pieces for each one and sends them across the sea. There are about two thousand of these boys. If, however, the number of them from enemy peoples does not suffice, then he takes from the Christians in every village in his land who have boys, having established what is the most every village can give so that the quota will always be full. And the boys whom he takes in his own land are called *cilik*. Each one of them can leave his property to whom ever he wants after his death. And those whom he takes among the enemies are called *pendik*. These latter after their deaths can leave nothing; rather, it goes to the emperor, except that if someone comports himself well and is so deserving that he be freed, he may leave it to whomever he wants. And on the boys who are across the sea the emperor spends nothing; rather, those to whom they are entrusted must maintain them and send them where he orders. Then they take those who are suited for it on ships and there they study and train to skirmish in battle. There the emperor already provides for them and gives them a wage. From there he chooses for his own court those who are trained and then raises their wages. The younger must serve the older, and those who come of age and attain manhood he assigns to the fortress so that they will look after them, as mentioned earlier.

And at the court there are about four thousand Janissaries, and among them there is the following organization. They have over them a senior hetman called an *aga*, a great lord. He receives ten gold pieces a day, and his steward, one gold piece a day. To each centurion they give a gold piece every two days, and to their stewards, a gold piece every four days. And all their sons who grow out of boyhood have a wage from the emperor.... And no Janissary nor any decurion of theirs dare ride a horse, save the hetman himself and the steward. And among them it is so arranged that some are archers who shoot bows, some are gunners who shoot mortars, others muskets, and still others, crossbows. And every day they must appear with their weapons before their hetmans. And he gives each one a gold piece per year for a bow, and in addition a tunic, a shirt, and large trousers made, as is their fashion, of three ells of cloth, and a shirt of eight ells. And this I myself distributed to them for two years from the imperial court....

The Turkish emperor storms and captures cities and also fortresses at great expense in order not to remain there long with the army. First having battered the city or fortress walls until it seems sufficient to him, and seeing that it is the moment to launch a general assault, he then orders it to be cried throughout the army first that horses and camels and all kinds of stock be brought from pastures to the army; and when that is accomplished, he then orders it to be cried throughout the army second specifying the day of the assault. And they prefer to set the day of Friday. And they crying this, they name the rewards in this fashion: to the one who carries a banner upon the wall they promise a voivodeship [governorship]; and to the one who goes out after him the rank of *subasa*; to the third, the rank of *czeribassa*; and thus to others, money, naming the sum; and in addition, distributing various garments. And whatever is mentioned then, without fail all of this if fulfilled and carried out whether the city is taken or not taken.

Then they cry in the evening throughout the army that lighted tallow candles be raised profusely above the clouds. And that night and early in the morning the next day they prepare themselves for the assault, right up to evening.

And then they go toward the city from all sides silently, slowly approaching the fosse, carrying before them barricades woven of branches and also strongly-built ladders so that they can climb up and down both sides of the ladder. The Janissaries then in this fashion go to the place where the wall is breached, and having approached the breached place, they wait until day begins to appear. Then first the gunners fire from all the cannon and when they have fired off the cannon, the Janissaries quickly scale the walls, for at this moment the Christians are retreating before the cannon, and when they see that the Janissaries are on the walls, having turned about suddenly, they begin to fight bravely on both sides. And here the Janissaries, urging one another on, climb up. And in addition the shot from bows come very thick, for they continually bring and replenish their shot, and besides [there is] a great tumult from drums and human outcry....

Turkish or heathen expansion is like the sea, which never increases or decreases, and it is such nature: it never has peace but always rolls. If it falls calm in one region, in another it crashes against the shores.... The Turks are also of such a nature as the sea: they never have peace, but always carry on a struggle from year to year from some lands to others. If they make a truce somewhere, it is better for them, and in other regions they perpetrate evils; they take people into bondage, and whoever cannot walk they kill. And this happens many times every year: they round up and bring several thousand good Christians amongst the heathens.... Having forgotten their good Christian faith they accept and extol the heathen faith. And such heathenized Christians are much worse than true-born heathens. This then adds to the expansion of the Turks....

And thus the heathens expand, as was said of the above-mentioned sea. And this you can know yourselves, that the Turks capture people and not livestock. Who can then prevent them? Having taken [captives] they swiftly ride them away with them, and before the Christians are ready they are already where they ought to be. And the more men you maintain, wanting to prevent this, the greater the expense and torment you will bear ... [even] if you defeat them sometime on a foray they will do just the same damage as before....

The Serbian kingdom after King Uros, became a principality. They chose for themselves as ruler Prince Lazar ... some were for Prince Lazar and others were against him.... And whenever there is no unity, it cannot be good for anything in this world; as faith without deed is dead. Emperor Morat, having heard that Prince Lazar was the successor of his ruler in the Sherpa kingdom; having assembled an army, Emperor Morat marched to the Sherpa land, to the Plain of Kosovo. And Prince Lazar, without delaying, also having assembled an army, marched to the Plain of Kosovo and took up a position opposite the Emperor on the other side, at Smagovo beside a stream called the Laba.

And it was on Wednesday; on St Vitus' Day [1389] a pitched battle began, and lasted until Friday. The nobles who favored Prince Lazar fought alongside him bravely, loyally and truly; but the others, looking through their fingers, watched. And through such disloyalty and envy and the discord of evil and disloyal men this battle was lost....

Here they had brought Prince Lazar and Voivode Krajmir before Emperor Baiazit. Morat

his father and also his brother both lay on biers. And Emperor Baiazit said to Prince Lazar: "Now you see lying on biers my father and brother; how did you dare try this and oppose my father?" Prince Lazar was silent, and Voivode Krajmir said, "Dear Prince, answer the Emperor. A head is not like a willow stump that it will grow a second time." And Prince Lazar said, "Emperor, it is an even greater wonder that your father dared attack the Sherpa kingdom." And he said, "Emperor Baiazit, had I known earlier what I now see with my eyes, you would lie on a third bier. But perhaps the Lord God has deigned to have it so for our transgressions. May God's will be done this day." And with that the Emperor ordered that Prince Lazar be decapitated. And Krajmir, having asked permission of the Emperor, kneeling, held the skirt of his tunic under the head of Prince Lazar so that it would not fall to the earth; and when the head had fallen into the skirt, then Voivode Krajmir, having placed his head next to the head of Prince Lazar, said, "I have sworn to the Lord God, 'Where Prince Lazar's, there mine also.'" Both heads fell to the ground. And a Janissary brought the head of Milos Obilic and threw it before the Emperor together with those two heads, saying "Emperor, here now are the three heads of your fiercest enemies."

Later the Serbs or Raskans who were with Emperor Baiazit asked for the body of Prince Lazar and carried it to a monastery called Ravanica and there he was buried and was elevated to sainthood....

[Before the final attack on Constantinople, while a truce existed between the two sides, Emperor Mahomet] encamped on the seashore beside the Arm of St. George five Italian miles above Constantinople. He ordered his master craftsmen to take measurements, wanting to build a good fortress here; and he immediately began to carry stones himself.... And he did not move anywhere from that spot for two whole years until that fortress was finished....

At that time the Turkish emperor did not have any ships with him on the sea, and he ordered thirty-five fine ships to be made in the forest four Italian miles from the seashore. And some who knew about those ships considered it to be madness on the part of the Emperor....

And so the Turkish emperor sent to the Despot [his Sherpa vassal] asking that he dispatch fifteen hundred horses according to the earlier agreement.... The Despot dispatched a certain voivode ... and sent with him the fifteen hundred horses--for the Despot did not know his intentions.

Having finished the fortress the Emperor without giving any warning to his own men or to foreigners, and without denouncing the truce, released raiders toward Constantinople, in order to murder and beat whomever they might come upon anywhere right up to the very walls.... The Emperor, having arrived with all his might, surrounded Constantinople....

And when we had been there a week, then the Emperor wondrously and at great expense made preparations for those same ships, so that the whole army and the city looked on, and thus: The army, having made a trench up and down hill, having lined it with planks and having greased it heavily with tallow (and besides, fine runners were attached to each ship); having raised specially [prepared] sails on high, as if upon water they went, with banners, with the beating of drums and the firing of cannon, all thirty ships, one after the other. And at that moment the battle was stopped because of the great wonder: ships which were drawn on dry land by footsoldiers and buffaloes, right down to the sea. The Greeks, seeing the ships prepared thus, wanted to prevent them from reaching the sea, but they could do nothing about that. And so Constantinople was besieged by land and sea....

And the heathens lay eight weeks outside the city, firing great siege cannons so that they smashed the wall for a half furlong.... Therefore, in that place where the wall had been breached, the Emperor's Janissaries, by storming, killed the Greek officer to whom it had been entrusted. And when the leader was lost, then the others, being frightened, had to yield; and the Janissaries, having been reinforced, running along the walls, killed them. And all the Emperor's forces was turned upon the city, and there killed them in the streets, in houses, in churches.

And the Greek emperor had in readiness in the city one thousand infantry. Not being able so quickly to reach the place where the walls were breached because the Turks had greatly reinforced themselves, he fought with them bravely, holding back the heathens until he too was overpowered, and he was killed there on that spot. Having severed his already lifeless head, a Janissary brought it and cast it before the Emperor, saying, "Fortunate Lord, there you have the head of your cruelest enemy."... Thus was Constantinople conquered through ignoble falsehood and their heathen truce....

And there is among the Turks the following custom: when two brothers are left after an emperor and carry on a struggle between them, the one who first takes refuge at the court of the Janissaries will gain the imperial throne. And therefore, since one of the standing treasures is five Italian miles above Constantinople at that fortress which is called Geniassar--in our language "New Castle"--whichever of these brothers comes wanting to have some of the treasure, they will not give anything to anyone, for the fortress is securely enclosed and guarded in all things as if against enemies, and they will give them the following answer if one of them should come: "Fortunate Lord, as long as the two of you are carrying on a struggle, nothing will be given to anyone." But when one already sits securely on the throne without hindrance of the other, then the man to whom the fortress is entrusted, having taken the keys, will bring them to the emperor, submitting the fortress and all the treasures. The emperor, having rewarded him, entrusts the keys to him again so that he can administer as before as it was of old.

First it must be known that the Turkish emperor holds securely all the fortresses in all his lands, having garrisoned them with his Janissaries or protégés, not giving a single fortress to any lord; and moreover the emperor holds any fortified city and the fortress within it, having garrisoned it with his own men. And those Janissaries who are in a fortress the emperor himself supplies so that if they are besieged they will have the necessities. They have no wine or *kvas* in the fortress. But at other times [i.e. unless besieged] each must live on his wages. Wages are paid them by the imperial court every quarter year in full and without fail, and it also gives them clothing once a year.... And you must live on that and not touch the emperor's provisions unless besieged. And you yourselves must stand the night watch diligently and two guards must always be at the gate. The gate must always be closed except for the small gate....

And thus are the emperor's fortresses supplied, and also all of heathendom even to the lowliest: be he rich or poor, each looks to the emperor's hands, and the emperor further provides for each and every one according to his distinction and merit. And so no one has an inheritance, nothing from his estate that he could make a living on....

Mihailovic, Konstantin. *Memoirs of a Janissary*. Trans. Benjamin Stolz. Ed. Svat Soucek. Ann Arbor: Univ. of Michigan, 1975. Pp. 47-49, 89-93, 149-153, 157-159, 185-187, 191-193.

► Roxelana, Suleiman's Favorite Wife

THE OTTOMAN EMPIRE AT ITS HEIGHT

The Ottoman Empire reached its zenith under Sultan Suleiman the Magnificent (r. 1520-1566), one of the greatest monarchs of history. Suleiman's wars added Hungary, parts of the Balkan peninsula and north Africa, Rhodes, and Crete to an already huge empire that stretched from Baghdad to the Atlantic, and from Mecca almost to the walls of Vienna. Suleiman was an able diplomat, conscientious administrator, and a chivalrous foe. Although a devout Muslim, he was tolerant of other religions. Commerce flourished and culture prospered under his able and enlightened rule.

Unfortunately the Ottoman dynasty had no firm tradition of primogeniture in succession. Thus intrigues between members of the imperial family complicated court politics. Favorite wives often influenced the succession, and the ascent of a new sultan to the throne was frequently followed by the killing or blinding of his half-brothers. Suleiman's favorite wife reputedly induced him to kill his able son by another wife, and appoint her unworthy son his successor. This was Selim II, nicknamed "The Sot." The long decline of the Ottoman Empire began with this reign.

Ogier Ghiselin de Busbecq (1522-1592) was born in present-day Belgium, then part of the Holy Roman Empire. After receiving an excellent classical education he entered government service. In 1554 he was appointed Imperial Ambassador to the Ottoman Empire. His predecessor, who had been flung into prison when hostilities broke out between the Holy Roman and Ottoman Empires, languished for two years and died soon after being freed. De Busbecq's diplomacy helped to maintain peace between the two empires. A keen collector, in 1562 he brought back to Vienna precious manuscripts, rare ancient coins and specimens of two flowers, the lilac and tulip, previously unknown in Europe. In the letters to a friend and colleague quoted below, de Besbecq gives a unique insight into the Ottoman Empire at its height, about the life of a diplomat and the succession struggle between Suleiman and one of his sons.

QUESTIONS:

1) What were Suleiman's strong points as ruler?
2) How did the Ottoman rulers pick their successors, with what resulting problems?
3) What rules and practices made the Ottoman army strong and effective?

You will probably wish me to describe the impression which Soleiman made upon me. He is beginning to feel the weight of years, but his dignity of demeanour and his general physical appearance are worthy of the ruler of so vast an empire. He has always been frugal and temperate, and was so even in his youth, when he might have erred without incurring blame in the eyes of the Turks. Even in his earlier years he did not indulge in wine or in those unnatural vices to which the Turks are often addicted. Even his bitterest critics can find nothing more serious to allege against him than his undue submission to his wife and its result in his somewhat precipitate action in putting Mustapha [his son by another wife] to death, which is generally imputed to her employment of love-potions and incantations....He is a strict guardian of his religion and its ceremonies, being not less desirous of upholding his faith than of extending his dominions. For his age--he has almost reached his sixtieth year--he enjoys quite good health, though his bad complexion may be due to some hidden malady; and indeed it is generally believed that he has an incurable ulcer or gangrene of his leg. This defect of complexion he remedies by painting his face with a coating of red powder, when he wishes departing ambassadors to take with them a strong impression of his good health; for he fancies that it contributes to inspire greater fear in foreign potentates if they think that he is well and strong....

Soleiman had had a son by a concubine, who, if I mistake not, came from the Crimea. His name was Mustapha, and he was then in the prime of life and enjoyed a high repute as a soldier. Soleiman, however, had several other children by Roxolana, to whom he was so much attached that he gave her the position of a legal wife....

Mustapha, on account of his remarkable natural gifts and the suitability of his age, was marked out by the affection of the soldiers and the wishes of the people as the certain successor of his father, who was already verging on old age. His stepmother, on the other hand, was doing her best to secure the throne for her own children, and was eager to counteract Mustapha's merits and his rights as the eldest son by asserting her authority as a wife....

The position of the sons of the Turkish Sultan is a most unhappy one; for as soon as one of them succeeds his father, the rest are inevitably doomed to die. The Turks tolerate no rival to the throne....Whether Mustapha was afraid of this fate or Roxolana wished to save her own children by sacrificing him, it is certain that the action of the one or the other of them suggested to Soleiman the advisability of slaying his son....[On campaign, he summoned Mustapha to his camp.]

On the arrival of Mustapha in camp there was considerable excitement among the soldiers. He was introduced into his father's tent, where everything appeared peaceful; there were no soldiers, no body-servants or attendants, and nothing to inspire any fear of treachery. However, several mutes (a class of servants highly valued by the Turks), strong, sturdy men, were there--his destined murderers. As soon as he entered the inner tent, they made a determined attack upon him and did their best to throw a noose round him. Being a man of powerful build, he defended himself stoutly and fought not only for his life but for the throne; for there was no doubt that, if he could escape and throw himself among the Janissaries, they would be so moved with indignation and with pity for their favourite, that they would not only protect him but also proclaim him as Sultan. Soleiman, fearing this, and being only separated by the linen tent-hangings from the scene upon which there was a delay in the execution of his plan, thrust his head out of the part of the tent in which he was and directed fierce and threatening glances upon the mutes, and by menacing gestures sternly rebuked their hesitation. Thereupon the mutes in their alarm, redoubling their efforts, hurled the unhappy Mustapha to the ground and, throwing the bowstring round his neck, strangled him. Then, laying his corpse on a rug, they exposed it in front of the tent, so that the Janissaries might look upon the man whom they had wished to make their Sultan....

I do not generally [leave my house] unless I have dispatches from the Emperor for presentation to the Sultan, or instructions to protest against the ravages and malpractices of the Turkish garrison. These occasions occur only twice or three times a year. If I wished from time to time to take a ride through the city with my custodian, permission would probably not be refused; but I do not wish to put myself under an obligation, and I prefer that they should imagine that I think nothing of my close confinement. Indeed what pleasure could it give me to parade before the eyes of the Turks, who would rail at me or even hurl insults at me?...

The Turks are prone to suspicion and have conceived an idea that the ambassadors of Christian princes bring different sets of instructions, which they produce in turn to suit the circumstances and the needs of the moment, trying at first, if possible, to come to an agreement on the most favourable terms, and then, if they are unsuccessful, gradually agreeing to more onerous conditions. For this reason the Turks think it necessary to intimidate them, threatening them with war or else treating them practically as prisoners and annoying them in every possible way, so that their sufferings may make them produce sooner the instructions which they have been ordered to reserve till the last possible moment....

When it became known that Soleiman was on the point of crossing over into Asia and the day of his journey was fixed, I announced to my cavasse that I wished to witness the Sultan's departure, and bade him come early that morning and open the gates for me, as he took the keys away with him each evening....

A window was allotted to me at the back of the house, looking out upon the street by which the Sultan was to leave the city. I was delighted with the view of the departure of this splendid army. The Ghourebas and Ouloufedjis rode in pairs, the Silihdars and Spahis in single file. These are the names given to the household cavalry, each forming a separate body and having its own quarters. Their total number is said to be about 6,000 men. There was also a vast number of the household slaves of the Sultan himself and of the Pashas and the other high officials.

The Turkish horseman presents a very elegant spectacle, mounted on a horse of Cappadocian or Syrian or some other good breed, with trappings and horsecloths of silver spangled with gold and precious stones. He is resplendent in raiment of cloth of gold and silver, or else of silk or satin, or at any rate of the finest scarlet, or violet, or dark green cloth. At either side is a fine sheath, one to hold the bow, the other full of bright-coloured arrows, both of wonderful Babylonian workmanship, as also is the ornamental shield which is attached to the left arm and which is only suited to ward off arrows and the blows dealt by a club or sword. His

right hand is encumbered by a light spear, usually painted green, unless he prefers to keep that hand free; and he is girt with a scimitar studded with gems, while a steel club hangs from his horsecloth or saddle....

After the cavalry had passed, there followed a long column of Janissaries, scarcely any of whom carried any other arms except their muskets. Almost all wore uniforms of the same shape and colour, so that you could recognize them as the slaves or household of the same master....Behind them followed their captains and colonels, each with their distinguishing marks of rank. Last came their commander-in-chief, riding by himself....Next came the Sultan's own chargers, remarkable for their fine appearance and trappings, led by grooms. The Sultan himself was mounted on a splendid horse. His expression was severe and frowning, and he was obviously in an angry mood....

A few days later I was myself summoned to cross the sea. The Turks thought it advisable in their own interests that I should put in an appearance in their camp and be courteously treated as the representative of a friendly sovereign. An abode was, therefore, assigned to me in a village near the camp, and I was very comfortably lodged. The Turks were in tents in the plains hard by. Here I lived for three months and had a good opportunity of visiting their camp and acquainting myself pretty well with their system of discipline....Putting on a dress of the kind usually worn by Christians in that district, I used to wander about everywhere, unrecognized, with one or two companions. The first thing that I noticed was that the soldiers of each unit were strictly confined to their own quarters. Any one who knows the conditions which obtain in our own camps will find difficulty in believing it, but the fact remains that everywhere there was complete silence and tranquility, and an entire absence of quarrelling or act of violence of any kind, and not even any shouting or merrymaking due to high spirits or drunkenness. Moreover, there was the utmost cleanliness, no dungheaps or rubbish, nothing to offend the eyes or nose, everything of this kind being buried by the Turks or else removed from sight. The men themselves dig a pit in the ground with their mattocks and bury all excrement, and so keep the whole camp scrupulously clean. Moreover, you never see any drinking or revelry or any kind of gambling, which is such a serious vice amongst our soldiers, and so the Turks know nothing of the losses caused by cards and dice....

When I asked what [their] rations consisted, a Janissary was pointed out to me who was seated there devouring off an earthenware or wooden trencher of mixture of turnip, onion, garlic, parsnip, and cucumber, seasoned with salt and vinegar, though it would perhaps be truer to say that it was hunger that was his chief sauce, for he could not have enjoyed his meal more if it had consisted of pheasants and partridges. They drink nothing but water, the common beverage of all living creatures; and their frugal diet suits their health as well as it suits their purse....

Thus all is quiet, and silence reigns in their camp, especially at the season of their Lent, if I may so call it. Such is the powerful effect of their military discipline and the severe traditions handed down from their forefathers. There is no crime and no offense which the Turks leave unpunished. Their penalties are deprivation of office and rank, confiscation of property, flogging, and death. Flogging is the most frequent punishment, and from this not even the Janissaries are exempt, although they are not liable to the extreme penalty. Their lighter offences are punished by flogging, their more serious crimes by dismissal from the army or removal to another unit, a punishment which they regard as more serious than death itself, which is indeed the usual result of this sentence; for being deprived of the badges of their corps, they are banished to distant garrisons on the farthest frontiers, where they live in contempt and ignominy; or if the crime is so atrocious that a more impressive example must be made of the offender, an excuse is found for making away with him in the place of his exile. Such a man, however, dies not as a Janissary but as an ordinary soldier.

Busbecq, Ogier Ghislain de. *The Turkish Letters of Ogier Ghiselin de Busbecq, Imperial Ambassador at Constantinople, 1554-1562.* Trans. Edward S. Forster. Oxford: Clarendon Press, 1927. Pp. 28-32, 65-66, 132, 141-143, 146-147, 149-151, 155.

► **Persian Miniature Painting**

LIFE IN SAFAVID PERSIA

The Safavid Empire in Persia was founded by Shah Ismail in 1500 and reached its zenith under the iron hand of an able autocrat named Shah Abbas the Great, 1587-1629. The capital city Isfahan was noted for its architecture under the early Safavids. It was also known for its luxuries, culture, and learning. Many of the great mosques and palaces from that golden era still survive.

Early Safavid rulers encouraged economic development, searched for new markets, and welcomed foreign merchants. Thus a northern trade flourished with Russia, while in the south Bandar Abbas on the Persian Gulf became a thriving port for trade with Europe. English trade was conducted through the English East India Company, which had by the late seventeenth century captured the strategically important port of Hormuz from Portugal and supplanted the Portuguese as the dominant European traders. Persian silk fabrics and finely knotted carpets became famous throughout Europe. Renaissance paintings often showed Persian rugs and carpets as either floor or table coverings in their depictions of domestic scenes.

John Fryer, an Englishman connected with the English East India Company, traveled through India and Persia between 1672 and 1681. An experienced traveler with a keenly observant eye, he wrote lengthy letters to report on his travels and to help the company identify and develop its interests in the region. The excerpts below report on some of the recreational pursuits of Persians, their clothing and manners. Fryer describes only men's clothing, and mainly male entertainments, because of Islam's strict segregation of the sexes and seclusion of women.

QUESTIONS:

1) Why was Isphahan considered one of the most beautiful cities in the world?
2) Why did rich Persians hide their wealth?
3) What was a lavish Persian party like and how does it differ from ours?

The air is very rare at Isphahan, and the wind drying. The city has no need of walls, where so many marble mountains stand as a guard, or bulwark of defence. It has indeed a tower, but it is a mud one, rather serving as an armory, than to be relied on as a place of strength. The circumference of the body of the city I guess may measure seven miles....

The magnificently-arched bazaars, which form the Noble Square to the Palace, the several public inns, which are so many seraglios, the stately rows of sycamores, which the world cannot parallel, the glorious summer-houses, the pleasant gardens, the stupendous bridges, sumptuous temples, the religious convents, the College for the professors of Astronomy, are so many lasting pyramids and monuments of his [Shah Abbas'] fame; though many of them begin to sink in their own ruin, for want of timely repair....

The public bazaars are kept in better repair than less-frequented buildings.... Few cities in the world surpass it [Isphahan] for wealth, and none come near it for those stately buildings, which for that reason are kept entire, while others made of lime and slate, belonging to private persons, hardly last their founders lives, for want of timely care.

For the citizens rather choose to dwell in a tottering house, than appear lavish in costly building or apparel, for fear their governors should suspect they have too much riches, when they are sure never to be at rest till they have dived into the bottom of their treasuries ... whereby the Emperor's treasure grows exuberantly great. Which is the cause the citizens so often lay up their talents in napkins [keep under wraps], since it is a crime to expose their wealth by specious or luxurious shows....

In all their bazaars which are locked up in the dead of the night, there are watches to prevent thieves, at the common expense of every shopkeeper....

Their *Balneas* [bath houses] ... are the most sumptuous, which are in all their cities, always hot; and it is lawful for every one of both sexes, on stated times of the day to bath for a small price. The proprietor of each house gives notice to all comers by blowing a horn, when the houses are ready to attend to them ... each trying to outshine the other; insomuch that no time either of day or night passes, but you shall hear perpetual noise of horns to invite you to them. For no sooner is the fire kindled under them, but they let every one know by those loud instruments....

Their coffee-houses, where they sell *coho*, [are] better than any among us, which being boiled, has a black oil or cream swimming at top, and when it has not, they refuse to drink it. Hither repair all those that are covetous of news, as well as barterers of goods; where not only fame and common rumour is promulgated, but poetry too, for some of that tribe are always present to rehearse their poems, and disperse their fables to the company....

They are modelled after the nature of our theatres, that every one may sit around, and suck choice tobacco out of long Malabar canes ... fastened to crystal bottles [filled] with fragrant and delightful flowers into the water. Upon every attempt to draw tobacco, the water bubbles, and makes them dance in various figures, which both qualifies the heat of the smoke, and creates together a pretty sight.

All night here are abundance of lamps lighted, and let down in glasses from the concave part of the roof, by wires or ropes, hanging in a circle....

But the set dress of the Persian [city gentleman] is after this manner: His head being shaved, a large turban is placed upon his crown, of diverse colours, either silk or cotton, the figure of an over-grown cabbage, with a great broad leaf a top, which is wrought of gold or silver, and spread to make a show. His beard is cut neatly. and the whiskers kept in cases, and encouraged from one ear to the other, in fashion of an half-moon on the upper lip, with only a decent peak on the under.... Next, upon his body is a shirt, which he covers with a vest, tied double on his breast, and strait to his body as far as the waist, from whence it hangs in pleats to his ankles, sometimes quilted, sometimes not. His loins are girt with Phrigian girdles or rich sashes, above which his belt carries a falched sword or scimitar. From his hips long close breeches of linen come down to his hose, of London sackcloth of any colour, which are cut loose, not respecting the shape of the leg. Over all a loose coat of the same, without sleeves, lined with furs, or sables, or else silk, the outside either scarlet, or the finest wool of Europe, or cloth of silver or gold of their own manufacture. His shoes [are] of the best shagreen [granular surfaced] leather, mostly green, with narrow toes, high narrow heels, shod with neat iron half-moons, without shoe-ties or quarters to pull up about their heels, being the readier to slip off and on as occasion requires. Instead of gloves they tincture not only their hands, but feet, with a dark red colour ... They dye their hair yellow, or of a sandy red....

Those that breed cattle and wandering shepherds ... have no stated habitation; but where they find the best pasture they pitch their tents, together with their wives, children, and families, with all their troops, in the fattest valleys, living abroad far from great towns, like the wild Arabs, whose chief, or Father of the Tribe, is owned by them, and no other, he giving account to the Emperor for the number of their flocks, and the annual increase. For they are morose and untamed, and are apt enough to worry any who fall unadvisedly among them. Their dogs, with which they guard the folds, are like wolves, as fierce and stronger than their wolves are here....

These go clad in coarse cloths underneath, above which felts, kneaded into the form of a coat, and are covered with hats of the same, but their hats are grey, bound about with a linen cloth either of white, green or blue. Their coats are of what colour they please, but mostly blue; their hats are high-crowned, and brim slit before and behind, which if it be cold, they pull down and bind with their cloth; if the sun offend their eyes, they draw it over their faces, or cock up when it is shady. When they rest, their upper garment is put on with sleeves, armed with an undressed sheep's-skin against the injury of the weather. Their shirt next their skin is rugged enough; over it a plain jerkin is tied with a hard linen girdle of the same woof with the shirt. About the calves of their legs they bind rowlers [like modern puttie] for want of stockings, and their shoes are soled with wood, and the upper part wrought over with packthread.

The *Dervishes* professing poverty, assume this garb here ... being without beasts of burden, without wallets full of provisions, which the others seize by force, without attendance, without other ensigns or weapons more than a staff and horn, travelling without company, or indeed any safe-pass; and if they fix up their standard, it is among the tombs, none giving them harbour, or encouraging this sort of madness, as well as for the natural antipathy to beggary, as for that under this cloak many intrigues and ill designs have been carried on....

[At parties or banquets of important people] Alighting they are introduced [into] the guest-chamber, all bestrewed with flowers and sweet herbs, besides perfumed with odoriferous gums, or the aloes wood alone, or other resiny matters made into candles, and in massive silver fuming-pots very costly and delicate. Leaving their slippers where they begin to tread on carpets, they take their seats on *susannes*, a rich tapestry of needle-work that borders the carpets, behind which are placed huge velvet bolsters, before them spitting pots to void their spittle in when they smoke tobacco, or eat *pawn*. These rooms are large and airy, and open folding windows on every side, where being placed they bring their *coloons*; after which they welcome you by a flood of rose-water, or other compound water poured on your head and beard. Then they bring in, in voiders [baskets or trays], china plates of fruit, as pistachios, walnuts, almonds, hazelnuts, grapes, prunes, prunellos, apricots dried, and sweetmeats wet and dry of all sorts, amidst whereof they fill out coffee, tea, and hot rose-water, and all the while have mimicks, stage-players, and dancers to divert, between whose interludes is mixed the custom, as ancient as Nebuchadnezzar, of certain wise men repeating verses in their praise, or reading monuments of antiquity, which continues till victuals are brought in, and the cloth spread on the carpets, everyone keeping their places. First water being brought in great silver basins and ewers to wash, the courses are ushered in with loud music, and the table being filled, the servitors are placed so as to furnish every one with plates of several varieties, which they place before each, and give them long wheaten cakes, both for napkins, trencher, and bread, and sometimes thin pancakes made of rice; though boiled rice serves usually for bread, which they mix with their soups and pottage.

The usual drink is *sherbet*, made of water, juice of lemons and ambergreece, which they drink out of long thin wooden spoons, wherewith they ladle it out of their bowls.

The most admired dainty, wherewith they stuff themselves is *pullow* [a rice dish], whereof they will fill themselves up to the throat and receive no hurt, it being so well prepared for the stomach. After they have eaten well, and the cloth is removed, they wash again....

When they have tired themselves of feasting (which is not suddenly) as they depart, they return thanks, by inviting every one in course to an entertainment of the like nature, where they strive to outdo each other. Thus extravagantly luxurious and immoderately profuse are they in their great feasts, stately dining-rooms, magnificent gardens, and water-courses, exceeding the Roman voluptuousness.

Fryer, John. *A New Account of East India and Persia, Being Nine Years' Travels, 1672-1681.* Ed. William Crooke. Vol. 3. London: Hakluyt Society, 1911. Pp. 19, 21, 23, 25, 32, 34-35, 121-125, 135-138.

CODE OF THE RAJPUTS

► Dancing Rajput Prince and Princess

Rajputs means "sons of kings" and *Rajasthan*, the land of the Rajputs, means "land of kings." Situated in north central India, Rajasthan sat astride the ancient invasion route to the subcontinent. During the era of disunity after the fall of the Gupta dynasty and the rule of Harsha, there rose in Rajasthan numerous states such as Chitor, Amber, and Mewar, headed by aristocratic Rajput clans that warred among themselves and defended India heroically against Muslim invaders from the northwest. These proud warrior clans claimed descent from the sun and moon and cited ancient Hindu texts, the *Puranas*, to prove their exalted genealogy. In fact their ancestors were ancient indigenous peoples, and early invading Scythians and Huns who were assimilated into the Hindu culture and given the status of kshatriyas or warriors. A Rajput rite, the *johar*, or mass immolation of women and children at the imminent fall of a fortress while the men rush to death in a last charge, came from outside of India.

The feudal civilization of Rajasthan was built according to strict code that emphasized war, loyalty, bravery, blood feuds, and honor. Rajput men disdained manual labor and farming. They hunted when not at war, but also patronized poetry, painting, and the arts. Their code of chivalry demanded defense of women, but Rajput women were no mere passive objects; they led armies into battle, mothers ruled on behalf of young sons, and rather than suffer dishonor, they died by leaping into flaming pyres. Many also committed suicide or *suttee* [it literally means a virtuous woman, one who immolates herself on her husband's funeral pyre] upon hearing news of their husbands' death in battle.

Glorifying war as the highest art of life, the Rajputs cultivated a military spirit that enabled them to resist formidable Muslim invaders. Tragically, incessant internal wars and feuds undermined their own cause.

Rajput warriors resembled the knights of medieval Europe and the samurai of feudal Japan. As in medieval Europe, bards composed heroic songs that celebrated the deeds of Rajput lords and ladies. The most famous example is the *Annals of Rajasthan*, which is comparable to the tales of King Arthur, or the *Song of Roland* which glorified Charlemagne's knights. Like the medieval European tales, the *Annals of Rajasthan* embroidered facts with much fiction.

Colonel James Tod spent seventeen years in Rajasthan when he served the British East India Company. He became an enthusiastic student of Indian history, ethnology and antiquities, collecting the materials for a ground breaking work titled *Annals and Antiquities of Rajasthan*, which he wrote after his retirement in England, and published between 1829 and 1832. Weaving together stories of the many Rajput clans, he depicted the deeds of a heroic people and their awful fate. The following selections show the Rajputs decimating each others' forces, and the fatal consequences for India, their heroic defense of Chitor against Muslim invaders, and how the last doomed Rajput men and women died.

QUESTIONS:

1) Who were the invaders the Rajputs were defending against, with what success?
2) What was expected of Rajput women?

Samarsi, prince of Chitor [13th century], had married the sister of Prithiraj, and their personal characters, as well as this tie, bound them to each other throughout all these commotions [wars between Indian rulers], until the last fatal battle on the Ghaggar. From these feuds Hindustan never was free.... From time immemorial such has been the political state of India, as represented by their own epics, or in Arabian or Persian histories: thus always the prey of foreigners, and destined to remain so....

[Samarsi was called on to defend Delhi by his brother-in-law.] The bard gives a good description of the preparation for his departure from Chitor, which he was destined never to see again. The charge of the city was entrusted to a favourite and younger son, Karna: which disgusted the elder brother, who went to the Deccan to Bidar.... Another son, either on this occasion or on the subsequent fall of Chitor, fled to the mountains of Nepal.... His arrival at Delhi is hailed with songs of joy as a day of deliverance. Prithiraj and his court advance seven miles to meet him....

In the planning of the campaign Samsarsi is consulted, and his opinions are recorded. The bard represents him as the Ulysses of the host: brave, cool, and skilful in the fight; prudent, wise, and eloquent in council; pious and decorous on all occasions; beloved by his own chiefs, and reverenced by the vassals of the Chauban.... His tent is the principal resort of the leaders after the march or in the intervals of battle, who were delighted by his eloquence or instructed by his knowledge....

On the last of three days' desperate fighting Samarsi was slain, together with his son Kalyan, and thirteen thousand of his household troops and most renowned chieftains. His beloved Pirtha, on hearing the fatal issue, her husband slain, her brother captive, the heroes of Delhi and Chitor "asleep on the banks of the Ghaggar, in the wave of the steel," joined her lord through the flame, or waited the advance of the Tatar king, when Delhi was carried by storm, and the last stay of

the Chaubans, Prince Rainsi, met death in the assault. The capture of Delhi and its monarch, the death of his ally of Chitor, with the bravest and best of their troops, speedily ensured the further and final success of the Tatar [Muslims from Afghanistan] arms.... Scenes of devastation, plunder, and massacre commenced, which lasted through ages; during which nearly all that was sacred in religion or celebrated in art was destroyed by these ruthless and barbarous invaders. The noble Rajput, with a spirit of constancy and enduring courage, seized every opportunity to turn upon his oppressor. By his perseverance and valour he wore out entire dynasties of foes, alternately yielding 'to his fate,' or restricting the circle of conquest. Every road in Rajasthan was moistened with torrents of blood of the spoiled and the spoiler. But all was of no avail; fresh supplies were ever pouring in, and dynasty succeeded dynasty, heir to the same remorseless feeling which sanctified murder, legalized spoilation, and deified destruction. In these conflicts entire tribes were swept away whose names are the only memento of their former existence and celebrity.

What nation on earth would have maintained the semblance of civilization, the spirit or the customs of their forefathers, during so many centuries of overwhelming depression but one of such singular character as the Rajputs? Though ardent and reckless, he can, when required, subside into forbearance and apparent apathy, and reserve himself for the opportunity of revenge. Rajasthan exhibits the sole example in the history of mankind of a people withstanding every outrage barbarity can inflict, or human nature sustain, from a foe whose religion commands annihilation, and bent to the earth, yet rising buoyant from the pressure, and making calamity a whetstone to courage.... [Some states surrendered or made humiliating peace] Mewar alone, the sacred bulwark of religion, never compromised her honour for her safety, and still survives her ancient limits; and since the brave Samsarsi gave up his life, the blood of her princes has flowed in copious streams for the maintenance of this honour, religion, and independence.

Samarsi had several sons; but Karna was his heir, and during his minority his mother, Kuramdevi, a princess of Patan, nobly maintained what his father left. She headed her Rajputs and gave battle in person to Kutbu-d-din, near Amber, when the viceroy was defeated and wounded. Many Rajas, and eleven chiefs of inferior dignity with the title of Rawat, followed the mother of their prince.

[A later siege of Chitor] is described with great animation in [an epic] the Khuman Raesa. Badal was but a stripling of twelve, but the Rajput expects wonders from this early age. He escaped, though wounded, and a dialogue ensues between him and his uncle's wife, who desires him to relate how her lord conducted himself ere she joins him. The stripling replies: "He was the reaper of the harvest of battle; I followed his steps as the humble gleaner of his sword. On the gory bed of honour he spread a carpet of the slain; a barbarian prince his pillow, he laid him down, and sleeps surrounded by the foe." Again she said: "Tell me, Badal, how did my love behave?" "Oh! mother, how further describe his deeds when he left no foe to dread or admire him?" She smiled farewell to the boy, and adding, "My lord will chide my delay," sprung into the flame.

Alau-d-din, having recruited his strength, returned to his object, Chitor.... They had not yet recovered the loss of so many valiant men who had sacrificed themselves for their prince's safety.... [After a prolonged defense and when all hope had gone] the Rana [prince], calling his chiefs around him, said, "Now I devote myself for Chitor."

But another awful sacrifice was to precede this act of self-devotion in that horrible rite, the *Johar*, where the females are immolated to preserve them from pollution or captivity. The funeral pyre was lighted within the "great subterranean retreat," in chambers impervious to the light of day, and the defenders of Chitor beheld in procession the queens, their own wives and daughters, to the number of several thousands. The fair Padmini [a beautiful princess, the surrender of whose person was one of the invading Tatar ruler's demand] closed the throng, which was augmented by whatever of female beauty or youth could be tainted by Tatar lust. They were conveyed to the cavern, and the opening closed upon them, leaving them to find security from dishonour in the devouring element.

A contest now arose between the Rana and his surviving son; but the father prevailed, and Ajaisi, in obedience to his commands, with a small band passed through the enemy lines, and reached Kelwara in safety. The Rana, satisfied that his line was not extinct, now prepared to follow his brave sons; and calling around him his devoted clans, for whom life had no longer any charms, they threw open the portals and descended to the plains, and with a reckless despair carried death, or met it, in the crowded ranks of Ala. The Tatar conqueror took possession of an inanimate capital, strewed with brave defenders, the smoke yet issuing from the recesses where lay consumed the once fair object of his desire; and since this devoted day the cavern has been sacred: no eye has penetrated its gloom, and superstition has placed as its guardian a huge serpent, whose 'venomous breath' extinguishes the light which might guide intruders to 'the place of sacrifice.'

Thus fell, in A.D. 1303, this celebrated capital, in the round of conquest of Alau-d-din, one of the most vigorous and warlike sovereigns who have occupied the throne of India.

Tod, James. *Annals and Antiquities of Rajasthan, or the Central and Western Rajput States of India*. Vol. 1. London: Oxford Univ. Press, 1920. Pp. 297-298, 302-304, 309-312.

► Moghul Relief

BABUR, FOUNDER OF THE MOGHUL EMPIRE

Babur (1483-1530), was a descendant of Timurlane. At age twelve and after his father died, he became king of a petty and unstable Turkish state called Ferghana in Central Asia. Driven out of his ancestral land, he conquered Afghanistan. In 1524 he set out for India with twelve thousand followers. Two years later at the battle of Panipat Babur's forces routed the much larger army of the Muslim Sultan of Delhi, whose dynasty had originally come from Afghanistan. Agra and other north Indian cities followed.

While many of his followers only coveted the rich booty of northern India, Babur dreamed of building a lasting empire there. In his remaining years, he laid the foundations of the Moghul Empire that later included most of the subcontinent, and established twin capitals at Delhi and Agra. Under the Moghuls, India enjoyed unity not seen since the Guptas and Harsha. This dynasty ruled India in fact until the eighteenth century, and in name until 1857.

Babur was also a builder and patron of the arts, traits shared by many of his successors, who left a rich cultural legacy throughout India. Europeans who visited the court of the Moghuls were dazzled by its splendor; they called the emperors Great Moghuls, adding the word "Mogul" or great magnate, to the English language.

Babur wrote an autobiography called *Babur-nama* (Memoirs of Babur) in his native language, Turki; much of it is in diary form, recounting his battles and plans, dealings with friends and foes, and much more. He freely admitted his love for alcoholic drinks, and described his efforts to stop drinking to obey the dictates of Islam. In the following excerpts from the *Babur-nama*, a remarkable man and his career comes alive in the author's own words.

QUESTIONS:

1) By what means did Babur inspire and retain the loyalty of his followers?
2) What were the attractions of India for Babur, and what repelled him?
3) What was Babur's personal vice and how did he combat it?

[In 1526, Babur's army was about to fight the crucial Battle of Panipat which was the key to gaining entrance to the Ganges valley.] People estimate the army opposing us at 100,000 men; Ibrahim's elephants and those of his amirs were said to be about 1000. In his hands was the treasure of two forebears. In Hindustan, when work such as this has to be done, it is customary to pay out money to hired retainers....If it had occurred to Ibrahim to do this, he might have had another *lak* [100,000] or two of troops. God brought it right! Ibrahim could neither content his braves, nor share out his treasures. How should he content his braves when he was ruled by avarice and had a craving insatiable to pile coin on coin? He was an unproved brave; he provided nothing for his military operations, he perfected nothing, neither stand, nor move, nor fight....

When the incitement to battle had come, the Sun was spear-high; till mid-day fighting had been in full force; noon passes, the foe was crushed in defeat, our friends rejoicing and gay. By God's mercy and kindness, this difficult affair was made easy for us! In one half-day, that armed mass was laid upon the earth. Five or six thousand men were killed in one place close to Ibrahim. Our estimate of the other dead, lying all over the field, was 15 to 16,000, but it came to be known, later in Agra from the statements of Hindustani, that 40 or 50,000 may have died in that battle.

The foe defeated, pursuit and unhorsing of fugitives began. Our men brought in amirs of all ranks and the chiefs they captured; *mahouts* [elephant keepers] made offering of herd after herd of elephants.

Ibrahim was thought to have fled; therefore while pursuing the enemy, we told [several officers]...to lead swift pursuit to Agra and try to take him. We passed through his camp, looked into his own enclosure and quarters, and dismounted on the bank of standing water.

It was the Afternoon Prayer when Khalifa's younger brother-in-law Tahir Tibri who had found Ibrahim's body in a heap of dead, brought in his head....

In Sultan Ibrahim's defeat [his vassal] the Raja of Gualiar Bihramajit the Hindu had gone to hell [Babur's way of describing what happened to Hindus when they died].

Bikramajit's children and family were in Agra at the time of Ibrahim's defeat. When Himayun [Babur's son and heir] reached Agra, they must have been planning to flee, but his postings of men (to watch the roads) prevented this and guard was kept over them. Himayun himself did not let them go. They made him a voluntary offering of a mass of jewels and valuables amongst which was the famous diamond [later known as the Kohinor Diamond, now part of Great Britain's Crown Jewels] which 'Alau'u'd-din must have brought. Its reputation is that every appraiser has estimated its value at two and half days' food for the whole world....Himayun offered it to me when I arrived at Agra; I just gave it him back....

[Babur distributed loot to reward his followers after the famous victory.] On Saturday the 29th of Rajab the examination and distribution of the treasure were begun. To Himayun were given 70 laks from the Treasury, and other and above this, a treasure house was bestowed on him just as it was, without ascertaining and writing down its contents. To some begs [lords] 10 laks were given, 8, 7, or 6 to others. Suitable money-gifts were bestowed from the Treasury on the whole army, to every tribe there was, Afghan, Hazara, 'Arab, Biluch etc. to each according to its position. Every trader and student, indeed every man who had come with the army, took ample portion and share of bounteous gifts and largess. To those not with the army went a mass of treasure in gift and largess...to the whole various train of relations and younger children went masses of red and white (gold and silver), of plenishing, jewels and slaves....

[Little wonder then] On our first coming to Agra, there was remarkable dislike and hostility between its people and mine, the peasantry and soldiers running away in fear of our men....

It was the hot-season when we came to Agra. All the inhabitants had run away in terror. Neither grain for ourselves nor corn for our horses was to be had. The villages, out of hostility and hatred to us had taken to thieving and highway-robbery; there was no moving on the roads. There had been no chance since the treasure was distributed to send men in strength into the parganas and elsewhere. Moreover the year was a very hot one; violent pestilential winds struck people down in heaps together; masses began to die off.

On these accounts the greater part of the begs and best braves became unwilling to stay in Hindustan, indeed set their faces for leaving it....

When I knew of this unsteadiness amongst (my) people, I summoned all the begs and took counsel. Said I. "There is no supremacy and grip on the world without means and resources; without lands and retainers sovereignty and command are impossible. By the labours of several years, by encountering hardships, by long travel, by flinging myself and the army into battle, and by deadly slaughter, we, through God's grace, beat these masses of enemies in order that we might take their broad lands. And now what force compels us, what necessity has arisen that we should, without cause, abandon countries taken at such risk of life? Was it for us to remain in Kabul, the sport of harsh poverty? Henceforth, let no well-wisher of mine speak of such things! But let not those turn back from going who, weak in strong persistence, have set their faces to depart!" By these words, which recalled just and reasonable views to their minds, I made them, willy-nilly, quit their fears.

As Khwaja Kalan had no heart to stay in Hindustan, matters were settled in this way:--As he had many retainers, he was to convoy the gifts, and, as there were few men in Kabul and Ghazni, was to keep these places guarded and victualled. I bestowed on him Ghazni, Girdiz and the Sultan Mas'udi Hazara, gave also the Hindustan *pargana* of G'huram, worth 3 or 4 *laks* [as fiefs]....

Loathing Hindustan, Khwaja Kalan, when on his way, had the following couplet inscribed on the wall of his residence in Delhi:--

If safe and sound I cross the Sind
Blacken my face ere I wish for Hind!

It was ill-mannered in him to compose and write up this partly-jesting verse while I still stayed in Hind. If his departure caused me one vexation, such a jest doubled it. I composed the following off-hand verse, wrote it down and sent it to him:--

Give a hundred thanks, Babur, that the generous Pardoner
Has given thee Sind and Hind and many a kingdom.
If thou have not the strength for their heats,
If thou say, "Let me see the cold side,"
Ghazni is there.

[Although many fierce campaigns remained to be fought, the Battle of Paniput had secured northern India for Babur. Much of the remainder of his memoirs describe India and his building plans for his new capital.]

Pleasant things of Hindustan are that it is a large country and has masses of gold and silver. Its air in the Rains is very fine. Sometimes it rains 10, 15 or 20 times a day; torrents pour down all at once and rivers flow where no water had been. While it rains and through the Rains, the air is remarkably fine, not to be surpassed for healthiness and charm. The fault is that the air becomes very soft and damp. A bow of those (Transoxanian) countries after going through the Rains in Hindustan, may not be drawn even; it is ruined. Not only the bow, everything is affected, armour, book, cloth, and utensils all; a house even does not last long. Not only in the Rains but also in the cold and the hot seasons, the airs are excellent; at these times, however, the north-west wind constantly gets up laden with dust and earth....

Another good thing in Hindustan is that it has unnumbered and endless workmen of every kind. There is a fixed caste for every sort of work and for every thing, which has done that work or that thing from father to son till now....

One of the great defects of Hindustan being its lack of running-waters, it kept coming to my mind that waters should be made to flow by means of wheels erected wherever I might settle down, also that grounds should be laid out in an orderly and symmetrical way. With this object in view, we crossed the Jun-water to look at garden-grounds a few days after entering Agra. Those grounds were so bad and unattractive that we traversed them with a hundred disgusts and repulsions. So ugly and displeasing were they, that the idea of making a Char-bagh in them passed from my mind, but needs must! as there was no other land near Agra, that same ground was taken in hand a few days later.

The beginning was made with the large well from which water comes for the Hot-bath, and also with the piece of ground where the tamarind-trees and the octagonal tank now are. After that came the large tank with its enclosure; after that the tank and *talar* [open-fronted audience hall] in front of the outer residence; after that the private-house with its garden and various dwellings; after that the Hot-bath. Then in that charmless and disorderly Hind, plots of garden were seen laid out with order and symmetry, with suitable borders and parterres [flower beds] in every corner, and in every border rose and narcissus in perfect arrangement.

Three things oppressed us in Hindustan, its heat, its violent winds, its dust. Against all

three the Bath is a protection, for in it, what is known of dust and wind? and in the heats it is so chilly that one is almost cold....
[Although Sunni Muslims, Babur and his followers were also hearty drinkers. Babur tells of his efforts to forswear drinking.]

On Monday the 23rd of the first Humada [1527], when I went out riding, I reflected, as I rode, that the wish to cease from sin had been always in my mind, and that my forbidden acts had set lasting stain upon my heart. Said I. "Oh! my soul!"

"How long wilt thou draw savour from sin?

Repentance is not without savour, taste it!"....

The fragments of the gold and silver [drinking] vessels were shared out to deserving persons and to darwishes [Muslim holy men]. The first to agree in renouncing wine was 'Asas; he had already agreed also about leaving his beard untrimmed. That night and the next day some 300 begs and persons of the household, soldiers and not soldiers, renounced wine. What wine we had with us was poured on the ground; what Baba Dost had brought was ordered salted to make vinegar. At the place where the wine was poured upon the ground, a well was ordered to be dug, built up with stone and having an almshouse beside it....

And I made public the resolution to abstain from wine, which had been hidden in the treasury of my breast. The victorious servants, in accordance with the illustrious order, dashed upon the earth of contempt and destruction the flagons and the cups, and the other utensils in gold and silver, which in their number and their brilliance were like the stars of the firmament. They dashed them in pieces, as, God willing! soon will be dashed the gods of the idolaters,-- and they distributed the fragments among the poor and needy. By the blessing of this acceptable repentance, many of the courtiers, by virtue of the saying that men follow the religion of their kings, embraced abstinence at the same assemblage, and entirely renounced the use of wine, and up till now crowds of our subjects hourly attain this auspicious happiness. I hope that in accordance with the saying "He who incites to good deeds has the same reward as he who does them" the benefit of this action will react on the royal fortune and increase it day by day by victories.

After carrying out this design an universal decree was issued that in the imperial dominions- -May God protect them from every danger and calamity--no-one shall partake of strong drink, or engage in its manufacture, nor sell it, nor buy it or possess it, nor convey it or fetch it....

Beveridge, Annette S., trans. *Babur-nama (Memoirs of Babur)*. Vols. 1, 2. New Delhi: Oriental Books Reprint Corp., 1979. Pp. 470, 474-475, 477, 519-520, 522-523, 524-526, 531-532, 551-552, 554-555.

► **Indian View of European**

A FRENCHMAN'S ACCOUNT OF MOGHUL INDIA

François Bernier (1620-1688) was a French medical doctor who traveled widely through India between 1659 and 1668. He was a keen observer and recorded the sights and sounds of India in lengthy letters to friends and patrons in France. After his return, he published his collected letters as *Travels in the Mogol Empire A.D. 1656-1668*. Because his audience was primarily French Bernier frequently compared India with France.

Bernier arrived in India soon after the Moghul Emperor Aurengzeb's successful revolt against his father, whom he deposed and imprisoned. After more than one hundred years, the Moghul empire was past its prime. Corruption in government was rampant, offices were sold to highest bidders. The ever more opulent life style of the court and nobility, which was mostly Muslim, ground down the majority of Indians, who were Hindu. Unlike some of his predecessors, who were relatively tolerant of other religions, Aurengzeb fanatically persecuted Hinduism. The empire entered a tailspin of decline after Aurengzeb's death.

In samples reproduced below Bernier describes Moghul court life, some corrupt and oppressive government practices, Hindu and Muslim social practices, specially regarding women, and in general the sounds and smells of bustling city life in seventeenth-century Delhi.

QUESTIONS:

1) How did seventeenth-century Delhi compare with contemporary Paris?
2) Why did the emperor need so much money to run his government and household, with what results for the people?
3) Describe a practice that Bernier found strange and cruel.

Delhi, then, is an entirely new city, situated in a flat country, on the banks of the Gemna [Jumna], a river which may be compared to the Loire, and built on one bank only in such a manner that it terminates in this place very much in the form of a crescent, having but one bridge of boats to cross to the country. Excepting the side where it is defended by the river, the city is encompassed by walls of brick....

The citadel, which contains the Mahalle or Seraglio, and the other royal apartments of which I shall have occasion to speak hereafter, is round, or rather semicircular. It commands a prospect of the river, from which it is separated by a sandy space of considerable length and width.

On these sands are exhibited the combats of elephants, and there the corps ... pass in review before the Sovereign, who witnesses the spectacle from the windows of the palace....

Here [in the royal square] too is held a bazaar or market for an endless variety of things; which like the Pont-neuf at Paris, is the rendez-vous for all sorts of mountebanks and jugglers. Hither, likewise, the astrologers resort, both Mahometan and Gentile [Hindu]. These wise doctors remain seated in the sun, on a dusty piece of carpet, handling some old mathematical instruments, and having open before them a large book which represents the signs of the zodiac. In this way they attract the attention of the passengers, and impose upon the people, by whom they are considered as so many infallible oracles.... Silly women, wrapping themselves in a white cloth from head to foot, flock to the astrologers, whisper to them all the transactions of their lives, and disclose every secret with no more reserve than is practised by a scrupulous penitent in the presence of her confessor....

The most ridiculous of these pretenders to divination was a half-caste Portuguese, a fugitive from Goa. This fellow sat on his carpet as gravely as the rest, and had many customers notwithstanding he could neither read nor write. His only instrument was an old mariner's compass, and his books of astrology a couple of old Romish prayer-books in the Portuguese language, the pictures of which he pointed out as the signs of the European zodiac....

The two principal streets of the city, already mentioned as leading into the square, may be five-and-twenty or thirty ordinary paces in width. They run in a straight line nearly as far as the eye can reach.... In regard to houses the two streets are exactly alike. As in our Place Royale, there are arcades on both sides; with this difference, however, that they are only brick, and that the top serves for a terrace and has no additional building. They also differ from the Place Royale in not having an uninterrupted opening from one to the other, but are generally separated by partitions, in the spaces between which are open shops, where, during the day, artisans work, bankers sit for the despatch of their business, and merchants exhibit their wares. Within the arch is a small door, opening into a warehouse, in which these wares are deposited for the night.

The houses of the merchants are built over these warehouses, at the back of the arcades: they look handsome enough from the street, and appear tolerably commodious within; they are airy, at a distance from the dust, and communicate with the terrace-roofs over the shops, on which the inhabitants sleep at night; the houses, however, are not continued the whole length of the streets. A few, and only a few, other parts of the city have good houses raised on terraces, the buildings over the shops being often too low to be seen from the street. The rich merchants have their dwellings elsewhere, to which they retire after the hours of business.

The interior of a good house has the whole floor covered with a cotton mattress four inches in thickness, over which a fine white cloth is spread during the summer, and a silk carpet in the winter. At the most conspicuous side of the chamber are one or two mattresses, with fine coverings quilted in the form of flowers and ornamented with delicate silk embroidery, interspersed with gold and silver. These are intended for the master of the house, or any person of quality who may happen to call. Each mattress has a large cushion of brocade to lean upon, and there are other cushions placed round the room, covered with brocade, velvet, or flowered satin, for the rest of the company. Five or six feet from the floor, the sides of the room are full of niches, cut in a variety of shapes, tasteful and well proportioned, in which are seen porcelain vases and flower-pots. The ceiling is gilt and painted, but without pictures of man or beast, such representations being forbidden by the religion of the country.

This is a pretty fair description of a fine house in these parts, and as there are many in Delhi possessing all the properties above mentioned, I think it may be safely asserted, without disparagement to the towns in our quarters of the globe, that the capital of Hindoustan is not destitute of handsome buildings, although they bear no resemblance to those in Europe.

That which so much contributes to the beauty of European towns, the brilliant appearance of the shops, is wanting in Delhi. For though this city be the seat of a powerful and magnificent court, where an infinite quantity of the richest commodities is necessarily collected, yet there are no streets like ours of *S.* Denis, which has not perhaps its equal in any part of Asia. Here the costly merchandise is generally kept in warehouses, and the shops are seldom decked with rich or showy articles. For one that makes a display of beautiful and fine cloths, silk, and other stuffs striped with gold and silver, turbans embroidered with gold, and brocades, there are at least five-and-twenty where nothing is seen but pots of oil or butter, piles of baskets filled with rice, barley, chick-peas, wheat, and an endless variety of other grain and pulse....

There is, indeed, a fruit market that makes some show. It contains many shops which during the summer are well supplied with dry fruit from Persia, Balk, Bokara, and Samarkand [places in Central Asia]; such as almonds, pistachios, and walnuts, raisins, prunes, and apricots; and in winter with excellent fresh grapes, black and white, brought from the same countries, wrapped in cotton; pears and apples of three or four sorts, and those admirable melons which last the whole winter. These fruits are, however, very dear; a single melon selling for a crown and half....

There are many confectioners' shops in the town, but the sweetmeats are badly made, and full of dust and flies.

Bakers also are numerous, but the ovens are unlike our own, and very defective. The bread, therefore, is neither well made nor properly baked....

In the bazaars there are shops where meat is sold roasted and dressed in a variety of ways. But there is no trusting to their dishes, composed, for aught I know, of the flesh of camels, horses, or perhaps oxen which have died of disease. Indeed no food can be considered wholesome which is not dressed at home.

Meat is sold in every part of the city; but instead of goats' flesh that of mutton is often palmed upon the buyer....

The people of this neighbourhood are indifferent fishermen; yet good fish may sometimes be bought, particularly two sorts, called sing-ala and rau. The former resembles our pike; the latter our carp. When the weather is cold, the people will not fish at all if they can avoid it; for they have a much greater dread of cold then Europeans have of heat....

You may judge from what I have said, whether a lover of good cheer ought to quit Paris for the sake of visiting Delhi. Unquestionably the great are in the enjoyment of everything; but it is by dint of the numbers in their service, by dint of the korrah [whip?] and by dint of money. In Delhi there is no middle state. A man must either be of the highest rank or live miserably....

The heat is so intense in Hindustan, that no one, not even the King, wears stockings; the only cover for the feet being ... slippers, while the head is protected by a small turban, of the finest and most delicate materials. The other garments are proportionally light. During the summer season, it is scarcely possible to keep a hand on the wall of an apartment, or the head on a pillow. For more than six successive months, everybody lies in the open air without covering--the common people in the streets, the merchants and persons of condition sometimes in their courts or gardens, and sometimes on their terraces, which are first carefully watered....

But I have not enumerated all the expenses incurred by the Great Mogol. He keeps in Delhi and Agra from two to three thousand fine horses, always at hand in case of emergency: eight or nine hundred elephants, and a large number of baggage horses, mules, and porters, intended to carry the numerous and capacious tents, with their fittings, his wives and women, furniture, kitchen apparatus ... and all the other articles necessary for the camp, which the Mogol has always about him, as in his capital, things which are not considered necessary in our kingdoms in Europe.

Add to this, if you will, the enormous expenses of the Seraglio [ladies' quarters], where the consumption of fine cloths of gold, and brocades, silks, embroideries, pearls, musk, amber and sweet essenses, is greater than can be conceived.

Thus, although the Great Mogol be in the receipt of an immense revenue, his expenditure being much in the same proportion, he cannot possess the vast surplus of wealth that most people seem to imagine. I admit that his income exceeds probably the joint revenues of the Grand Seignior and the King of Persia; but if I were to call him a wealthy monarch, it would be in the sense that a treasurer is to be considered wealthy who pays with one hand the large sums which he receives with the other....

The country is ruined by the necessity of defraying the enormous charges required to maintain the splendour of a numerous court, and to pay a large army maintained for the purpose of keeping the people in subjection. No adequate idea can be conveyed of the sufferings of that people. The cudgel and the whip compel them to incessant labour for the benefit of others; and driven to despair by every kind of cruel treatment, their revolt or their flight is only prevented by the presence of a military force.

The misery of this ill-fated country is increased by the practice which prevails too much at all times, but especially on the breaking out of an important war, of selling the different governments for immense sums in hard cash. Hence it naturally becomes the principal object of the individual thus appointed Governor, to obtain repayment of the purchase-money, which he borrowed as he could at a ruinous rate of interest.... The Governor must also enforce the payment of the regular tribute to the King; and although he was originally a wretched slave, involved in debt, and without the smallest patrimony, he yet becomes a great and opulent lord.

Thus do ruin and desolation overspread the land. The provincial governors, as before observed, are so many petty tyrants, possessing a boundless authority; and as there is no one to whom the oppressed subject may appeal, he cannot hope for redress, let his injuries be ever so grievous or ever so frequently repeated.

[Religious law kept Muslim women in seclusion. When Bernier was called into the Seraglio or women's quarters to treat an ill court lady.] ... a Kashmir shawl covered my head, hanging like a large scarf down to my feet, and an eunuch led me by the hand, as if I had been a blind man....

The Princesses and great ladies of the Seraglio have also different modes of travelling. Some prefer *tchaudoules*, which are borne on men's shoulders.... They are gilt and painted and covered with magnificent silk nets of many colours, enriched with embroidery, fringes, and beautiful tassels. Others travel in a stately and close *paleky*, with gilt and covered, over which are also expanded similar silk nets. Some again

use capacious litters, suspended between two powerful camels, or between two small elephants....

Close to the Princess are the chief eunuchs, richly adorned and finely mounted, each with a wand of office in his hand, and surrounding her elephant, a troop of female servants.... Besides these attendants are several eunuchs on horseback, accompanied by a multitude of *Pagys*, or lackeys on foot, with large canes, who advance a great way before the Princess, both to the right and to the left, for the purpose of clearing the road and driving before them every intruder....

Truly it is with difficulty that these ladies can be approached, and they are almost inaccessible to the sight of man. Woe to the unlucky cavalier, however exalted in rank, who, meeting the procession, is found too near. Nothing can exceed the insolence of the tribes of eunuchs and footmen which he has to encounter, and they eagerly avail themselves of any such opportunity to beat a man in the most unmerciful manner. I shall not easily forget being once surprised in a similar situation, and how narrowly I escaped the cruel treatment that many cavaliers have experienced: but determined not to suffer myself to be beaten and perhaps maimed without a struggle, I drew my sword, and having fortunately a strong and spirited horse, I was enabled to open a passage, sword in hand, through a host of assailants, and to dash across the rapid stream....

Many persons whom I then consulted on the subject [of *suttee* or widow immolation] would fain have persuaded me that an excess of affection was the cause why these women burn themselves with their deceased husbands; but I soon found that this abominable practice is the effect of early and deeply rooted prejudices. Every girl is taught by her mother that it is virtuous and laudable in a wife to mingle her ashes with those of her husband, and that no woman of honour will refuse compliance with the established custom. These opinions men have always inculcated as an easy mode of keeping wives in subjection, of securing their attention in times of sickness, and of deterring them from administering poison to their husbands....

She [a woman about to commit suttee] was of middle age, and by no means uncomely. I do not expect, with my limited powers of expression, to convey a full idea of the brutish boldness, or ferocious gaiety depicted on this woman's countenance; of her undaunted step; of the freedom from all perturbation with which she conversed, and permitted herself to be washed; of the look of confidence, or rather of insensibility which she cast upon us; of her easy air, free from dejection; of her lofty carriage, void of embarrassment, when she was examining her little cabin, composed of dry and thick millet straw, with an intermixture of dry wood; when she entered into that cabin, sat down upon the funeral pile, placed her deceased husband's head in her lap, took up a torch, and with her own hand lighted the fire within, while I know not how many *Brahmens* were busily engaged in kindling it without....

It is true, however, that I have known some of these unhappy widows shrink at the sight of the piled wood; so as to leave no doubt on my mind that they would willingly have recanted, if recantation had been permitted by the merciless *Brahmens*; but those demons excite or astound the affrighted victims, and even thrust them into the fire. I was present when a poor young woman, who had fallen back five or six paces from the pit, was thus driven forward; and I saw another of these wretched beings struggling to leave the funeral pile when the fire increased around her person, but she was prevented from escaping by the long poles of the diabolical executioners.

Bernier, François. *Travels in the Mogul Empire*. Trans. Irving Brock. Rev. Archibald Constable. New Delhi: S. Chand and Co., 1891; 2nd ed. 1968. Pp. xxiii, 221-222, 230-231, 240-245, 247-252, 267, 310-311, 313, 371-374.

READING 6.12

CHINA'S BRIEF MARITIME HEGEMONY

▶ **15th-Century Chinese Ship**

China dominated the seas from the western Pacific to the coast of East Africa during the first half of the fifteenth century, thanks to the efforts of the eunuch courtier-diplomat, admiral Cheng Ho. This remarkable episode in Chinese history is the topic of this reading.

In 1368, the army of Chu Yuan-chang (1368-1398) defeated the Mongols and established the Ming ("brilliant") dynasty (1368-1644). Because his eldest son the crown prince had died earlier, Chu Yuan-chang (Emperor Hung-wu) was succeeded by his teenage grandson, Hui-ti, in 1398. Prince Yen, the young emperor's ambitious uncle, revolted after the boy's accession, and in a civil war captured the capital city Nanking in 1402. He became Emperor Yung-lo (r. 1402-1425). Hui-ti, however, disappeared in the confusion. Yung-lo moved the capital city from Nanking of bad memory, to Peking, where his power base lay. His rule was successful: he subdued the nomads of inner Asia, and restored economic prosperity. Yung-lo, however, remained uneasy because he could not find his fugitive nephew in China. Had Hui-ti fled abroad?

In 1405, Yung-lo ordered a large naval expedition to head for the "Western Oceans" with a eunuch soldier-diplomat, Cheng Ho, as its commander. Yung-lo's ostensible goal was to proclaim the resurgence of Chinese power under the Ming dynasty and to cow the rulers of Southeast and South Asia into enrolling as vassals of the Ming. This display of force in local political disputes had the desired effect, and at least twenty states in South and Southeast Asia enrolled as Chinese tributary states. Cheng also brought with him Chinese luxury products, notably silks and porcelain, and made gifts of them to local rulers and held trade fairs. The result was increased Chinese trade throughout Asia, and even to East Africa. Cheng also had a secret mission: to obtain information about Hui-ti, but he found no trace of him. Hui-ti, who had become a Buddhist monk, was in fact found in China in 1441. Yung-lo had long since died and his great-grandson, then emperor, allowed the aged ex-emperor to end his days in monastic peace.

Cheng Ho headed seven naval expeditions, and brought great diplomatic prestige, increased trade, and geographic knowledge to China. However, China established no overseas naval bases and planted no colonies although many Chinese from coastal provinces settled in Southeast Asia.

Since Cheng was a eunuch and not a civil servant, the civil service opposed his expensive and seemingly impractical exploits, which ended with his death. A later emperor failed to equip a new expedition because the bureaucrats claimed that Cheng's charts were lost. Subsequent rulers lost interest and China never led the way in maritime matters again.

QUESTIONS:

1) What personal qualities did Cheng Ho possess that made him a successful commander?
2) What benefits did China derive from Cheng Ho's voyages?
3) What are the names of some of the modern countries visited by Cheng Ho's fleet?

[Cheng Ho] lived approximately from 1371 to 1435.... Different versions have been given by various scholars of his life. The one which is generally accepted [says the following:] ... At the beginning of the Ming dynasty, a number of generals who fought on the frontiers were in charge of selecting eunuchs for the Imperial Court. In 1381, Yunnan was pacified and Cheng Ho was one of the selected children who at that time must have been less than ten years old....

From other sources, we learn that he was born in a Mohammedan family by the name of Ma, at K'unyang in Yunnan.... His life [after he became a eunuch] may be divided into two stages. Before the age of thirty-five he had built a home in Peking but spent most of his time in army service. His long years of military life had made him courageous, adaptable and resolute. This had much to do later with his organizing technique, command ability and adaptability. The remaining thirty years of his life were almost entirely spent on the sea.

On January 1, 1404 ... he was [appointed] Superintendent of Eunuch Affairs and given the name of Cheng by the Emperor [Chinese emperors bestowed their own or other surnames as rewards to meritorious servants and government officials]. Shortly after he was appointed commander of the great [naval] expedition. Meanwhile local governments in some coastal regions were ordered to construct ocean vessels. By July, 1405, 1180 ships were built.

The largest ocean vessel was about 500 feet in length and 211.5 feet broad. The first expedition consisted of 27,000 men and 62 large vessels each of which carried about four or five hundred people, valuable gifts of silks, embroideries, and curiosities, as well as all the necessary provisions....

The fleet set sail from Liuchia Ho on the Yangtze estuary [on a southward course. After passing] ... through the Malacca Straits it entered ... the Indian Ocean. Its object was to reach the country of Kuli, the present Calicut on the Malabar Coast of India, which was then the focal point of all sea routes in the Indian Ocean, and held the key position between many states in Southern Asia and the Near East.... For some years Kuli had maintained very amicable relations with China. On account of its frequent delivery of tribute to the Ming Court, Cheng Ho was authorized to entitle the chief, Sami, king of Kuli. Cheng Ho handed Sami the imperial gifts and Sami in return gave a great celebration for their visit....

Two years later, the expedition sailed homeward. As the fleet passed by Chiu Kang ... present Palembang [on Sumatra in Indonesia], it encountered the fleet of a powerful [Chinese] pirate named Ch'en Tsu-i who had for years been a threat to the voyagers passing the Malacca Strait.... After a major sea battle, Ch'en's fleet was badly defeated. More than five thousand of his crew were killed, ten of his vessels were burned, seven others damaged and Ch'en ... was captured alive. The victory undoubtedly gave great prestige to the ... Ming dynasty in Southern Asia.

On their way back the whole expedition visited Java [where a civil war was raging. Cheng intervened on behalf of the rightful ruler and] ... raised the heir of the East King to regain his kingdom. In the summer of 1407, Cheng Ho returned to Peking and reported to the Emperor....

When winter [1407] came, Cheng Ho was against sent overseas. Two events were the outcome of his second voyage. First, Peking received tribute from the king of Po-ni or Borneo ... [who] with all his family and loads of tribute came to visit China.... Second, an international exhibition was conducted by Cheng Ho in Ceylon ... [where] he displayed the best Chinese products such as gold and silver candlesticks, embroideries and articles used in Buddhist ceremonies.... In 1911, an old stone ... [monument commemorating] this exhibition was discovered on [Ceylon] inscribed in Chinese, Tamil, and Persian....

[In 1409] Cheng Ho made his third voyage ... with the same number of crew but only forty-eight vessels.... More countries were visited [than during the previous voyages] and their rulers received gifts from the Imperial court of China. It ... was the first time a Chinese expedition succeeded in making an extended voyage to the Persian Gulf, the Red Sea and the east coast of Africa.... [While in Ceylon Cheng Ho fought] the second large battle in his overseas expeditions.... With a force of about 2,000 men [Cheng] cracked the blockade [imposed by the king of Ceylon], joined his main force, and pressed on with an all-out attack on the capital. The king was captured alive. Cheng Ho [then] set the king free ... and selected another [prince] from the royal house to replace him.... The increase in [China's] prestige from this battle was beyond measure....

Six years later, for the fourth time, Cheng Ho set out again. This time he took with him a number of interpreters ... and sailed along the same route as before ... in forty vessels.... Their mission on this voyage was to acquire information. Many books from the Near Eastern countries were translated [into Chinese as a result]. The climatic conditions and surface features of these countries were described in great detail, together with their important products....

In 1416, in return for the enormous quantities of tribute paid to the Ming court by nineteen countries, Cheng Ho was again sent out, to deliver gifts [on behalf of the Chinese emperor]. He ... brought home a variety of strange animals from different places ... [including] lions, panthers, "Western horses," giraffes, and ostriches....

In the spring of 1421, Cheng Ho was ordered to convoy a number of foreign envoys from sixteen countries [back to their homes], and for the sixth time he set sail, heading toward the Near East. The sixteen countries [included] Hormuz, Aden,.. Mogadishu, Calicut, Cochin, Ceylon, Maldive Islands, Sumatra, Malacca, etc. ....

His last voyage was begun in July, 1430.... They spent three years abroad. Everything was recorded in great detail and in chronological order. Dates of departure and anchorage and the distances from one place to another were measured by time....

It is still hard to ascertain the number of states the great voyager officially visited.... [However it is clear that Cheng went to places] which had never been visited by any Chinese before, such as the Flores group, southern Sumatra, Sembilon, Andaman Islands, Maldive Islands, Hormuz, La-sha, Juwar, Mogadishu, Brawa, Jubaland etc. .... What deserves special mention are the two voyages to East Africa ... [because before this] there is no indication that the Chinese had ever reached the shores of East Africa.... [As a result] not only were the geographical features of these countries brought to light, but many myths of the African coast told by the Arabs were converted into real knowledge.

The great extent of treeless country in present Somaliland was impressive to the Chinese. Of the interior of Mogadishu, Fei Hsin [a member of the expedition] wrote, "The land is composed of chains of hills and extensive waste. As far as the eye can reach, one fails to grasp anything but the yellow dust and barren rocks. The soil is poor and the crops sparse. It may not rain for a number of years. People make very deep wells and draw up the water in sheep-skin bags by means of cog-wheels.

[The quarter century of Cheng's voyages] was indeed the most fascinating era in China's history of ocean navigation.... Cheng Ho's expeditions succeeded in making a thorough survey of every possible sea route to nearly all insular countries in southern Asia, the Arab countries in the Near East and around the whole Indian Ocean.... What seems [especially] important are that the major sea lanes they used have been little altered by modern maritime navigation.... By reading some of the legends on the nautical charts, we find that the navigators of this period counted very little on the location of the stars in seeking their sailing directions but depended upon very delicate compasses and instruments. By looking at the stars they simply checked their general direction and thus the cartographers could ascertain the approximate location of each place they visited. As to the size of the vessels, we are surprised to see that it represented the greatest achievement in ocean craft previous to the Industrial Revolution. The last voyage was composed of 27,750 men but with only forty ships. Each ship carried about 700 men, not counting the load of tribute and presents and necessary provisions....

No name should be written greater in the history of Chinese overseas exploration than that of Cheng Ho. The scale of his operations indeed has not only dwarfed all those of his predecessors in China but also set a record scarcely matched by any in world history prior to the Industrial Revolution.... It is true that Cheng Ho missed a great share of fame and glory because he did not sail around Africa as Vasco da Gama did seventy-six years later. But it would be false to assume that he was unable to do so.... Why [is it that] Cheng Ho did not take advantage of his great task force and sail around Africa?.... [Because, in contrast to hostility between European Christians and Muslim Arabs] there was no religious conflict nor any economic rivalry between the Chinese and the Arabs [who lived to the west of China and who dominated the trade routes to Europe].... For the Chinese,

there was no pressing need to find a long winding route around Africa while they could carry on their trade directly through the Indian Ocean and the Persian Gulf to the Mediterranean shore. In 1487, Bartholomew Dias sailed around the Cape of Good Hope to the mouth of the Great Fish River. From 1492 to 1498, Christopher Columbus made four voyages across the Atlantic to the West Indies. In 1497, Vasco da Gama succeeded in sailing around the Dark Continent and hit Calicut or Kuli as ... [the Chinese] called it. Following this was the circum-navigation of Ferdinand Magellan.... What made da Gama, Columbus, and Magellan more widely known than this great Chinese explorer is largely that the former three had the great good fortune to have many successors who carried on their task. In contrast to this is China's fading maritime interest where not a single "Cheng Ho" emerged as successor to the great Eunuch Admiral.

Chang, Kuei-sheng. *Chinese Great Explorers: Their Effect upon Chinese Geographic Knowledge prior to 1600.* Diss. Michigan 1955. Pp. 299-309, 315-316, 318-319, 324, 328-329.

ACKNOWLEDGMENTS

A full source citation follows each of the readings included in this book. We thank the following for their permission to use previously published material in the readings indicated:

1.1: Sterling Lord Literistic, Inc. **1.2**: The University of Chicago Press. **1.4**, **1.6**: University of California Press. **1.6**: Cambridge University Press. **1.8**, **2.6**: Princeton University Press. **1.13**: Yale University Press. **1.13**: University of Washington Press. **1.15**: Stanford University Press. **1.16**: American Heritage Magazine, a Division of Forbes Inc. **2.4**: Indological Publishers and Booksellers. **2.6**: Columbia University Press. **3.6**, **7.2**, **7.7**: Harvard University Press **3.10**: Twayne Publishers, Inc. **3.14**: William Heinemann, Ltd. **3.15**: The Ronald Press Co. **4.3**: University of Oklahoma Press. **4.5**: Journal of English and Germanic Philology. **4.7**: University of Pennsylvania Press **4.13**: Al Saqi Books. **6.3**: Liveright Publishing Corp. **6.6**: Wayne State University Press. **9.11**: Zed Books, Ltd. **9.18**: Madison Books, Lanham, MD. **10.3**: Little, Brown and Co. **10.7**: HarperCollins. **10.8**: The Brookings Institution. **10.10**: The Putnam Publishing Group. **10.11**: Macmillan Publishing Co. **10.12**: Penguin Books. **11.3**: John F. Blair, Publisher, Winston-Salem, NC. **11.12**: William Morrow and Co., Inc. **11.13**: National Archives and Records Administration. **11.14**: University Press of Mississippi. **11.15**: Servant Publishers.

We have made every reasonable effort to identify and acknowledge the copyright owners of materials excerpted in this work. We will be grateful to anyone who can provide additional information about copyright holders and will gladly make whatever further acknowledgments might be necessary.